THE CERTIFIED QUALITY ENGINEER HANDBOOK

Third Edition

Also available from ASQ Quality Press:

The Certified Six Sigma Black Belt Handbook, Second Edition
T. M. Kubiak and Donald W. Benbow

The Certified Quality Inspector Handbook
H. Fred Walker, Ahmad K. Elshennawy, Bhisham C. Gupta, and Mary
McShane Vaughn

The Certified Reliability Engineer Handbook
Donald W. Benbow and Hugh W. Broome

The Certified Software Quality Engineer Handbook
Linda Westfall, editor

The Metrology Handbook
Jay Bucher, editor

The Certified Six Sigma Green Belt Handbook
Roderick A. Munro, Matthew J. Maio, Mohamed B. Nawaz, Govindarajan Ramu,
and Daniel J. Zrymiak

The Quality Calibration Handbook: Developing and Managing a Calibration Program
Jay L. Bucher

Design of Experiments with MINITAB
Paul Mathews

The Certified Manager of Quality/Organizational Excellence Handbook, Third Edition
Russell T. Westcott, editor

The Certified Quality Technician Handbook
Donald W. Benbow, Ahmad K. Elshennawy, and H. Fred Walker

The Weibull Analysis Handbook, Second Edition
Bryan Dodson

Statistical Engineering: An Algorithm for Reducing Variation in Manufacturing Processes
Stefan H. Steiner and R. Jock MacKay

Lean Kaizen: A Simplified Approach to Process Improvements
George Alukal and Anthony Manos

To request a complimentary catalog of ASQ Quality Press publications,
call 800-248-1946, or visit our Web site at http://www.asq.org/quality-press.

THE CERTIFIED QUALITY ENGINEER HANDBOOK

Third Edition

Connie M. Borror, Editor

ASQ Quality Press
Milwaukee, Wisconsin

American Society for Quality, Quality Press, Milwaukee 53203
© 2009 by ASQ
All rights reserved. Published 2008
Printed in the United States of America
14 13 12 11 10 09 08   5 4 3 2 1

Library of Congress Cataloging-in-Publication Data

The certified quality engineer handbook / Connie M. Borror, editor.—3rd ed.
   p. cm.
  Includes bibliographical references and index.
  ISBN 978-0-87389-745-7 (hard cover : alk. paper)
  1. Production management—Quality control. 2. Reliability (Engineering).
 I. Borror, Connie M.

  TS156.C423 2008
  658.4'013—dc22   2008040494

ISBN: 978-0-87389-745-7

Publisher: William A. Tony
Acquisitions Editor: Matt T. Meinholz
Project Editor: Paul O'Mara
Production Administrator: Randall Benson

ASQ Mission: The American Society for Quality advances individual, organizational, and community excellence worldwide through learning, quality improvement, and knowledge exchange.

Attention Bookstores, Wholesalers, Schools and Corporations: ASQ Quality Press books, videotapes, audiotapes, and software are available at quantity discounts with bulk purchases for business, educational, or instructional use. For information, please contact ASQ Quality Press at 800-248-1946, or write to ASQ Quality Press, P.O. Box 3005, Milwaukee, WI 53201-3005.

To place orders or to request a free copy of the ASQ Quality Press Publications Catalog, including ASQ membership information, call 800-248-1946. Visit our Web site at www.asq.org or http://www.asq.org/quality-press.

Printed in the United States of America

 Printed on acid-free paper

Quality Press
600 N. Plankinton Avenue
Milwaukee, Wisconsin 53203
Call toll free 800-248-1946
Fax 414-272-1734
www.asq.org
http://www.asq.org/quality-press
http://standardsgroup.asq.org
E-mail: authors@asq.org

Table of Contents

CD-ROM Contents

The following files are provided on the CD-ROM accompanying this book.

Certified Quality Engineer Certification *(simulated exam)*
File name: CQE-SimulatedExam.pdf
Eighty questions distributed by topic approximately proportional to those in the CQE Body of Knowledge.

Sample Exam Questions
File name: CQE-SampleExam.pdf
A set of questions from the Body of Knowledge.

Acceptance Sampling Tables
File name: SamplingTables.pdf
Selected tables from ANSI/ASQ Z1.4 and Z1.9.

Audio Presentations
Folder name: Audio Presentations
Presentations of some statistical methods are narrated by the editor.

List of Figures and Tables

Part V

Preface to the Third Edition

The third edition of *The Certified Engineering Handbook* was written to provide the quality professional with an updated resource that follows the CQE Body of Knowledge. Today it is not uncommon for the quality engineer to be involved in quality improvement activities in healthcare, finance, education, software applications, and other nonmanufacturing sectors. In response, numerous new examples and illustrations that cover applications in some of these areas are included in this edition.

Key features of the third edition include:

- New and updated references

- Extensive revision of the statistical methods complete with numerous updated examples and illustrations

- Over 75 new glossary entries

Much of the material in Parts I and II of the second edition has been retained in this edition, with updated references. However, the reader will find an extensive revision of the statistical methods presented throughout the book. Part V and Part VI have been significantly revised with new discussion, definitions, and examples illustrating each of the statistical techniques as they appear in the Body of Knowledge. Portions of Part IV have also been rewritten to reflect advances in methods and applications in quality improvement activities such as conducting gage repeatability and reproducibility studies.

The goal in writing the third edition was to provide a handbook that could be used in preparation for the CQE Exam or as a reference text for professional development. When a complete description or discussion of a topic is beyond the scope of the handbook, useful references have been included for further reading. It is our hope that the reader will find the new examples, explanations, and references useful.

It is important to recognize that a handbook of this magnitude could not be completed without the dedication of many people. I would like to thank the previous editors, Roger W. Berger, Donald W. Benbow, Ahmad K. Elshennawy, and H. Fred Walker, for their contributions and organization of the material in the first and second editions. In addition, gratitude goes to the authors who contributed to the first edition of the text. They wrote many of the chapters in the first edition, portions of which were included in the second edition. The oversight and production of the third edition was professionally and carefully carried out by Paul O'Mara, Matthew Meinholz, William Tony, and Randy Benson at ASQ, and Leayn and Paul Tabili at New Paradigm Graphics, Inc.

Lastly, I would like to thank Dr. G. Geoffrey Vining and Dr. Douglas C. Montgomery for their efforts in seeing the third edition come to fruition, their careful editing of the new material, and recommendations for presentation of material. They rightfully could have been coeditors of this edition.

Connie M. Borror
Editor

Preface to the Second Edition

In revising *The Certified Quality Engineering Handbook* our primary goal has been to reflect the changes in the Body of Knowledge for the Certified Quality Engineer that was published by the American Society for Quality early in 2006. We recognize new developments in the quality engineering profession such as:

Greater emphasis on communications

New problem-solving tools

More widespread application of Six Sigma and lean enterprise concepts

Revisions to the ISO 9000 standards

A need for more examples of how tools are applied to quality problems

As Dr. Gregory Watson said in his preface to the first edition, the American Society for Quality has been developing a more strategic perspective of the quality profession and has investigated the implications that current trends across business sectors will have on our profession. The role of quality engineers has continued to shift toward being mentors and trainers for others in using the tools and concepts of quality. Mastering these tools and passing the certification exam are essential steps along the path of becoming recognized as professional quality engineers.

The revised edition provides you with both a textbook and a reference book that is completely aligned with the 2006 ASQ Body of Knowledge.

The Editors

Preface to the First Edition

QUALITY ENGINEERING—AN ENDURING PROFESSION

Perspective on the Origins of Quality Engineering

Quality engineering was one of the disciplines that drove the American Society for Quality (ASQ, formerly known as ASQC) into its existence at the close of the Second World War. ASQ was founded to preserve and expand the expertise acquired in the war. Many improvements in production, statistical application, inspection, and management became standard practice thanks to the ASQ pioneers.

From its inception, ASQ emphasized both technical and educational aspects of the quality profession. The first certification program we developed was for quality engineering, and the body of knowledge (BoK) was prepared by a team of educators and practitioners. It was supported by the ASQ General Technical Council and soon became recognized as the core of the emerging science of quality. By creating the CQE and its body of knowledge, ASQ stabilized the meaning of "quality engineer" and also created an operational definition of quality engineering. Over the years this credential has come to mean that the person who possesses it has achieved an objective standard of performance that indicates the ability to perform those tasks required of a quality engineer.

Challenge for Future Quality Engineers

Over the past 10 years, the American Society for Quality has been developing a more strategic perspective of the quality profession and has investigated the implications that current trends across business sectors will have on our profession. In 1995 and again in 1999, ASQ took out crystal balls to "study the future" and determine what actions to take in supporting the quality movement and its cadre of professionals.

Several trends have been observed in these studies: some are disturbing and others serve as a beacon to warn us to take corrective action in navigating our course into the future. One major implication already observed in many companies is the transference of advanced quality tools from their almost exclusive use by quality professionals into application by frontline managers and their specially trained problem solvers. This trend will challenge quality engineering professionals in two major ways.

First, while we observe that quality tools are being disseminated to the masses, this cascade may or may not involve quality professionals. This wider application of advanced statistical methods and quality tools requires quality professionals to accept new roles as technical mentors to the managers of our organizations. This challenge requires each of us to develop a new approach to leadership and to be the catalyst that aids in the dissemination of these methods by finding ways to encourage the proper use and application of these tools.

Second, with more and more managers knowing the same tools that we use, we cannot afford to be amateurs in the use and application of advanced quality methods. In order to earn the right to serve as the technical advisors to this next generation of more enlightened managers, all quality professionals must not only seek training in the more advanced technical methods but also must become the masters of these tools and be perceived as such by senior managers.

Call to Continuous Learning and Personal Excellence

Rather than giving up on the viability of our profession, this challenge is a call for an even higher commitment to professional performance. In the quality profession, our tradition has been to use independent certifications as evidence of personal mastery of a particular body of knowledge.

The achievement of certification as a quality engineer through the ASQ CQE examination is a distinction of professional achievement that represents personal mastery of the basic quality tools and analytical methods. The certified quality engineer is exposed to increased professional opportunity, promotion potential, and salary increases. Most CQEs go on to further develop skills as quality trainers, facilitators, business managers, auditors, applied statisticians, and technical specialists. For all of these career potentials the CQE certification serves as a mark of professionalism that proclaims a readiness to meet new levels of professional challenge and extend knowledge into more complex and difficult areas to master.

Significance and Meaning of Certification

There is an old story of a young man who served as an apprentice, passed the tests and skill demonstrations as a journeyman, and was ready to be named an independent tradesman. He went to his master craftsman and told him that he was ready to go out and establish his own practice. The master said he had one more test to pass. The young man replied: "I am ready." The master asked him to describe the true meaning of his professional credential. The young man immediately replied: "It means the end of my journey, a well-deserved reward for all of my hard work." The master said that he did not have the right perspective. After a month the young man returned saying that he was ready to answer the question. Again the master asked him the true meaning of his professional credential. This time the young man replied: "It is a symbol of distinction and a sign of high achievement." Again the master was dissatisfied, and said, "Return to me next month when you understand the full meaning!" In humility, the young man returned after a third month. The master again asked his question and the young man replied: "This credential only represents the beginning. It is the start of a never-ending journey of work, discipline, and a ceaseless commitment to continuous learning." The master said: "Now you are ready to work on your own!"

Studying for Self-Improvement

As markets become more and more competitive, companies will need to enhance their agility in order to provide a flexible response to changing customer demands. This trend will require more customer intimacy as companies seek to understand the value proposition required by the market and define what customer requirements will deliver the most value to the market that they choose to serve. Quality professionals will be asked to develop real-time quality monitoring systems and data collection and analysis methods that provide corrective feedback to minimize waste, reduce defects, and improve cost-effectiveness of inventory and capital equipment. Quality professionals also will be asked to build systems for monitoring customer behavior, and to use the information in defining better product designs. Quality will become more and more fundamental in the management of routine business operations. Preparation for this emerging trend will call for personal dedication to developing oneself as not only a competent technician, but also as a local leader capable of influencing others to achieve quality performance results in a wide variety of applications.

Enhancing professional competence is the starting point to prepare yourself to be a force in this field. The certified quality engineer credential is a big step in the right direction toward personal development and assuring the continued viability of your set of professional skills.

This handbook will guide you through the recently updated body of knowledge and provide you with an exceptionally relevant textbook in your preparation for taking the CQE examination.

Gregory H. Watson
Past President, American Society for Quality (2000–2001)
Fellow, American Society for Quality
Certified Quality Engineer, American Society for Quality

How to Use This Book

Quality engineering is recognized as a core technical discipline in a variety of different industries and functions. The effective quality engineer must understand numerous concepts and techniques. To foster and recognize such achievement, the American Society for Quality Control (as it was then called) created a Certified Quality Engineer (CQE) program in 1967 and has updated it frequently since then. This handbook and the certification program are both offered by ASQ as ways to maintain and stimulate the profession of quality engineering.

This book has two main uses: as a *learning* tool and as a *reference* tool. The editors have kept these two different uses in mind as we assembled the various parts of the book.

LEARNING TOOL

When you are in the learning mode, you first need to see the big picture and then fill in details. You seek continuity, rationale, and examples. Following the ASQ-prescribed body of knowledge (BoK), we have organized the subject into six broad categories:

1. Management and Leadership

2. The Quality System

3. Product and Process Design

4. Product and Process Control

5. Continuous Improvement

6. Quantitative Methods and Tools

Each of these sections has an introduction and summary to give a broad picture of how the details fit together. There are 82 elements in the CQE BoK, and each element is highlighted at the beginning of the pertinent section. Keep in mind that the book was not written as a study guide to pass the certification exam, but as a comprehensive guide to the field of quality engineering. Therefore, most of the sections include material that goes well beyond the CQE exam requirements. If you are using this book to study for the exam you must carefully examine the wording of the BoK to see which topics are of most immediate concern.

Some of the more technical material must be studied intensely and repetitively before it is fully grasped. Examples are often essential to complete the learning process, and we have therefore provided many. We also recognize that often your thirst for knowledge cannot be satisfied by the contents of just this one book, so we have listed many sources of additional information.

REFERENCE TOOL

When you are in the reference-using mode, your thought process is quite different. You want information and you want it quick. Often a single fact, procedure, or definition is required. Regardless of the kind of information you seek, the best starting point is the index. The editors and production staff have greatly extended the index of this second edition, and we recommend you use it regularly to look things up.

Several other features serve your reference needs. Immediately following the main text are the necessary statistical tables, all of which are cited in the text. Once familiar with a given statistical tool, you can often use the appropriate table without consulting the chapter. Statistical tables are listed both in the Table of Contents (front matter) and immediately preceding Appendix A (back matter).

All figures and tables in the chapters are listed in the front matter, immediately following the Table of Contents. Consulting these lists may lead you to a key answer in certain cases.

An extensive glossary provides another reference tool. These definitions come from a variety of sources, including the fourth edition of the Quality Press's *Glossary and Tables for Statistical Quality Control*.

The editors believe that you will find this book a valuable learning and reference tool. But you are the final judge of our success, so we welcome your comments and suggestions. Please e-mail, phone, or mail using the contact information located on the back cover and copyright page.

Acknowledgments

We would like to acknowledgment the following authors and contributors to the previous editions of this book:

Martha Atkins

Dennis Arter

Andy Barnett

Dale H. Besterfield

Forrest W. Breyfogle III

Elsayed A. Elsayed

Hugh Jordan Harrington

Bradley Jones

William Kolarik

Kreg Kukor

Becki Meadows

Roderick A. Munro

Duke Okes

Jack B. ReVelle

Denise Robitaille

David Shores

Galal Wehaba

Russ Wescott

Chris White

In addition, we are grateful to Tae-Yeon Cho, Busaba Laungrungrong, Eric M. Monroe, and Dr. Rong Pan for their review of the examples and calculations, and also to John A. Bringer Jr., for his assistance on some technical material.

Part I

Management and Leadership

The two main themes of Part I are a broad perspective on the quality profession and the human element in quality. Areas such as strategic planning and leadership may require additional training and years of experience before full competency is achieved. In the same vein, developing communication skills and removing barriers to quality improvement could be callings of a lifetime. After a careful study of this chapter, you will have a clear idea of the elements upon which the profession of quality engineering is based.

Chapter 1

A. Quality Philosophies and Foundations

Explain how modern quality has evolved from quality control through statistical process control (SPC) to total quality management and leadership principles (including Deming's 14 points), and how quality has helped form various continuous improvement tools including lean, Six Sigma, theory of constraints, and so on. (Remember)

Body of Knowledge I.A

HISTORY OF QUALITY

The quality profession has a long history, which has greatly accelerated over the last 80 years. Joseph M. Juran (1988) has traced the practice of the quality profession back to the ancient Egyptians and the building of the pyramids. For centuries, quality was intrinsically associated with craftsmanship, and each craftsman controlled all aspects of the final product of his craft. This changed dramatically with the Industrial Revolution.

Modern quality practices originated in two stages: mass inspection in the early 1900s and the control chart around 1930. Mass inspection became commonplace as a result of Frederick Taylor's *Scientific Management*. Workers stopped checking the quality of their work and instead passed it on to specially trained inspectors. Although inspection is a vital element of quality, Walter Shewhart's invention of the process control chart really initiated the quality profession. Awareness of worker motivation and attitudes as contributors to quality became prevalent in the early 1930s as a result of Elton Mayo's Hawthorne studies for Western Electric.

The next big push for quality emerged during World War II when suddenly peoples' lives could be destroyed by poor-quality products. At the same time hundreds of American companies were called upon to manufacture goods to the most exacting requirements. Many quality control techniques, such as

2

acceptance sampling and process control charts, which were merely encouraged before the war, became mandatory as part of the defense effort. Two of the leading practitioners of the quality profession—W. Edwards Deming and Joseph M. Juran—established their professional credentials during this time. Both later went to Japan to teach the defeated nation statistical and management tools. In the 1970s it became apparent that the Japanese had learned their lessons well: Americans, the former masters, made repeated trips to the Japanese, the former students, to explore Japanese successes and to bring home proven Japanese methods.

The American Society for Quality Control, now known as the American Society for Quality (ASQ), was born soon after World War II when Martin Brumbaugh saw that great benefits would be attained if he could unify various local quality control societies into one national organization. As he struggled with this task, he recognized the superb skills of George Edwards, who was then head of inspection engineering at Bell Telephone Laboratories. Edwards became the first president of the society and helped establish policies that guide its operation to this day.

The first three awards the society created to recognize these three pioneers of quality were the Brumbaugh Award, the Shewhart Medal, and the Edwards Medal. In time, the society created numerous other awards, each honoring a specific hero of the profession and recognizing outstanding achievement in a particular area of the profession.

Walter A. Shewhart

The industrial age was approaching its second century when a young engineer named Walter A. Shewhart altered the course of industrial history by bringing together the disciplines of statistics, engineering, and economics. He referred to his greatest achievement, the invention of the process control chart, as "the formulation of a scientific basis for securing economic control." The Shewhart control chart is now sometimes referred to as a process behavior chart.

Shewhart wanted statistical theory to serve the needs of industry. He exhibited the restlessness of one looking for a better way. A man of science who patiently developed his and others' ideas, he was an astute observer of the world of science and technology. While the literature of the day discussed the stochastic nature of both biological and technical systems, and spoke of the possibility of applying statistical methodology to these systems, Shewhart actually showed how it was to be done. In that respect, the field of quality control can claim a genuine pioneer in Shewhart. His book *Economic Control of Quality of Manufactured Product*, published in 1931, is regarded as a complete and thorough exposition of the basic principles of quality control.

Called upon frequently as a consultant, Shewhart served the War Department, the United Nations, the government of India, and others. He was active with the National Research Council and the International Statistical Institute. He was a fellow of numerous societies and in 1947 became the first honorary member of the American Society for Quality. Many consider the Shewhart Medal, given for outstanding technical contributions to the quality profession, to be by far the most prestigious award the American Society for Quality offers.

W. Edwards Deming and Joseph M. Juran

The impact of the Bell Telephone System on the quality profession is almost beyond belief. Shewhart, Edwards, Juran, and Deming all worked for and learned from the Bell System in one way or another. Edwards and Shewhart retired as Bell System employees. Both Juran and Deming went on from the Bell System to become world-famous consultants and authors.

Deming became the best-known quality expert in the United States. He delivered his message on quality not only throughout the United States but also around the world. In recognition of his valuable contribution to Japan's post-war recovery, the Union of Japanese Scientists and Engineers established an annual award for quality achievement called the Deming Prize.

Deming (1982) emphasized that the keys to quality are in management's hands—85 percent of quality problems are due to the system and only 15 percent are due to employees. The heart of his quality strategy is the use of statistical quality control to identify special causes (erratic, unpredictable) and common causes (systemic) of variation. Statistical tools provide a common language for employees throughout a company and permit quality control efforts to be widely diffused. Each employee assumes considerable responsibility for the quality of his or her own work. Those in traditional quality control functions are then able to take more proactive roles in the quality improvement effort.

Deming introduced statistical quality control to the Japanese in the early 1950s when Japan was recovering from World War II and trying to overcome a reputation for shoddy workmanship. Deming's guidance was instrumental in transforming "made in Japan" from a liability to an asset. Deming asserted that there was no point in exhorting employees to produce higher-quality work because the changes needed to improve quality were almost always outside of the workers' control, such as having the right tools, training, and materials. Instead, management had to accept responsibility for quality. Based on his experience, Deming developed a 14-point set of requirements called *Deming's 14 points*, shown in Figure 1.1. He also described *seven deadly diseases* of the workplace, including emphasis on short-term profits, use of personnel performance evaluations, which he labeled "management by fear," and mobility of management (that is, management as a profession independent of the product/service or commitment to the organization).

Juran, like Deming, built his quality reputation in America and then took his expertise to Japan in the 1950s. The two complemented each other well in Japan, as Deming showed the use of statistical tools and Juran taught the techniques of managing for quality. Juran originated the concept of "the vital few" and the "useful (originally 'trivial') many," which he labeled the Pareto principle, now enshrined in the well-known Pareto diagram. An economist, Vilfredo Pareto, had noticed the phenomenon but it was Juran who applied it to quality improvement.

Juran recognized that to improve quality requires a completely different approach from what is needed to *maintain* existing quality. He demonstrated this idea in his book *Managerial Breakthrough*, first published in 1964, and later condensed his ideas into the Juran trilogy:

1. Quality *control*: monitoring techniques to correct sporadic problems (analogous to special causes)

2. Quality *improvement*: a breakthrough sequence to solve chronic problems (analogous to common causes)

3. Quality *planning*: an annual quality program to institutionalize managerial control and review

Juran served the quality profession well when in 1951 he created the monumental *Juran's Quality Handbook,* now in its fifth edition. Juran's contributions are extensive and varied. He defined quality as "fitness for use by the customer." He emphasized

1. Create consistency of purpose toward improvement of products and services, with a plan to become competitive and to stay in business. Decide to whom top management is responsible.

2. Adopt the new philosophy. We are in a new economic age. We can no longer live with commonly accepted levels of delays, mistakes, defective materials, and defective workmanship.

3. Cease dependence on mass inspection. Require instead statistical evidence that quality is built-in to eliminate need for inspection. Purchasing managers have a new job and must learn it.

4. End the practice of awarding business on the basis of price tag. Instead, depend on meaningful measures of quality, along with price. Eliminate suppliers who cannot qualify with statistical evidence of quality.

5. Find problems. It is management's job to work continually on the system (design, incoming materials, composition of material, maintenance, improvement of machines, training, supervision, retraining).

6. Institute modern methods of training on the job.

7. Institute modern methods of supervision of production workers. The responsibility of foremen must be changed from sheer numbers to quality. Improvement of quality will automatically improve productivity. Management must prepare to take immediate actions on reports from foremen concerning barriers such as inherited defects, machines not maintained, poor tools, fuzzy operation definitions.

8. Drive out fear, so that everyone may work effectively for the company.

9. Break down barriers between departments. People in research, design, sales, and production must work as a team, to foresee problems of production that may be encountered with various materials and specifications.

10. Eliminate numerical goals, posters, and slogans for the workforce, asking for new levels of productivity without providing methods.

11. Eliminate work standards that prescribe numerical quotas.

12. Remove barriers that stand between the hourly worker and his right to pride of workmanship.

13. Institute a vigorous program of education and retraining.

14. Create a structure in top management that will push every day on the above 13 points.

Figure 1.1 Deming's 14 points.

the need for top managers to become personally involved in order for a quality effort to be successful and for middle and lower-level managers to learn the language and thinking of top management—money, for example—in order to secure their involvement. Juran's *universal process for quality improvement* requires studying symptoms, diagnosing causes, and applying remedies. He repeatedly emphasized that major improvement could be achieved only on a project-by-project basis. The basis for selecting projects was return on investment, now a major component of Six Sigma.

Modern Developments

In the six decades since World War II ended, great quality leaders have emerged. Besides those mentioned previously, the following individuals have become famous for their contributions. Philip Crosby popularized the concept of *zero defects* and established the Crosby Quality College. Kaoru Ishikawa, who helped sponsor Deming's seminars in Japan, created *quality circles* and invented the cause-and-effect diagram, also called the Ishikawa diagram. Armand Feigenbaum coined the phrase *total quality control* and tirelessly preached its fundamentals around the world. Genichi Taguchi, a Japanese engineer, developed a unique system for designing industrial experiments. Eliyahu Goldratt created an improvement system built around the phrase *theory of constraints*. Other notable contributors to the profession include George Box, Eugene Grant, Jack Lancaster, Frank Gryna, Richard Freund, and Dorian Shainan.

Kaizen, a Japanese word that translates roughly into English as improvement, means that workers perform consistent, gradual improvements as they do their regular jobs. The goals of kaizen include the elimination of waste (defined as activities that add cost but do not add value), just-in-time delivery, production load leveling of amount and types, standardized work, paced moving lines, right-sized equipment, and others. Its application is not limited to quality, but quality professionals have effectively applied it. When done correctly it humanizes the workplace, eliminates hard work (both mental and physical), and teaches people how to use the scientific method and to detect waste. Some companies have created a spin-off called *kaizen blitz*. This is a carefully orchestrated intensive activity designed to produce a significant improvement quickly.

Theory of constraints (TOC) has become a popular catchphrase for a system improvement program. It is based on the principle that one—and often more than one—specific factor or element *constrains*, or prevents, the system from reaching a more desirable state of existence. Goldratt had an insight: managing a complex system or organization can be made both simpler and more effective by providing managers with a few specific areas on which to focus, maximizing performance in the areas of key constraints, or *elevating* the constraints, making them less constraining. This leads to a view of the company where the constraint guides all strategic decisions. Goldratt's clients and students have claimed numerous major successes in applying his concepts. He co-authored *The Goal*, the first famous business novel that informed and entertained many thousands of managers and engineers as it showed the path to success by applying his concepts. TOC, sometimes referred to as *constraint management,* is being actively developed by a loosely coupled community of practitioners around the world.

Lean philosophy is exemplified by its terse name: get the job done as simply as possible. It was originally called lean manufacturing but has migrated into many different service industries. A good example of lean philosophy is *just-in-time* (JIT), where a process is managed so that parts arrive just prior to their actual insertion into the assembly. Another is the famed 5S system, which teaches the benefits of keeping the workplace clean, avoiding waste, and so on. A final example of lean is *visual management,* which means to post as much information as possible about processes' requirements, progress, successes, and failures in prominent places where people can see it at a glance, without having to open a notebook or rely on word-of-mouth transmittal.

Six Sigma is the final quality philosophy mentioned in this section, but this is not the final time it will be mentioned. Six Sigma has combined and exploited the strengths of the other approaches to the extent that it now dominates all the others. There are journals, conferences, study groups, and consulting firms devoted solely to Six Sigma. Six Sigma combines effective communications, organization of effort, financial accountability, and strong techniques to enable organizations to make sustained improvements over a period of time. Improvements such as cost reduction, quality improvement, cycle time reduction, improved morale, greater profits, and so forth, are all attainable through Six Sigma, but these improvements require a great deal of dedicated work, dedication to the process, and continuous training and learning. See Chapter 29 for more about Six Sigma.

WHAT IS QUALITY?

Quality means different things to different people and in different situations. This list gives some of the informal definitions of quality:

- Quality is not a program; it is an approach to business.

- Quality is a collection of powerful tools and concepts that are proven to work.

- Quality is defined by customers through their satisfaction.

- Quality includes continual improvement and breakthrough events.

- Quality tools and techniques are applicable in every aspect of business.

- Quality is aimed at perfection; anything less is an improvement opportunity.

- Quality increases customer satisfaction, reduces cycle time and costs, and eliminates errors and rework.

- Quality is not just for businesses. It works in nonprofit organizations such as schools, healthcare and social services, and government agencies.

Table 1.1   Comparing the impact quality can have.

99.74% Good = 3 Sigma	99.9998% Good = 6 Sigma
20,000 lost articles of mail per hour	Seven articles lost per hour
Unsafe drinking water for almost 15 minutes each day	One unsafe minute every seven months
5000 incorrect surgical operations per week	1.7 incorrect operations per week
Two short or long landings at most major airports each day	One short or long landing every five years
200,000 wrong drug prescriptions each year	68 wrong prescriptions per year
No electricity for almost seven hours each month	One hour without electricity every 34 years

Results—performance and financial—are the natural consequence of effective quality management. Table 1.1 compares the consequences and impact of quality management at two different quality levels, three sigma and six sigma.

Formal Definitions of Quality

The above definitions show that quality is difficult to define, and no one definition can be all-inclusive. The word *quality* is highly nuanced, and allows many interpretations. For example, a popular online dictionary defines quality as "an inherent or distinguishing characteristic" (http://dictionary.reference.com/search?q=quality); this definition is only the first of ten distinctively different definitions from the same authority. The reader quickly comes to realize that most of the definitions are quite specialized and not really pertinent to the practice of quality engineering. It gets worse: the quality page on Dictionary.com lists specialized meanings from several other authorities, each with a little different twist. One of these meanings, from the ISO 8402 standard, is simultaneously more comprehensive, more explicit, and more authoritative:

> *Quality: the totality of features and characteristics of a product or service that bear on its ability to satisfy stated or implied needs. Not to be mistaken for "degree of excellence" or "fitness for use" which meet only part of the definition. (ISO 8402)*

This definition is really quite interesting, first because it is published by ISO, an international standards organization, and second because it specifically rebuts the definition that Joseph Juran used throughout his career, "quality = fitness for use." In contrast, Philip Crosby used the definition, "quality = conformance to specifications," which is also narrower than ISO 8402.

So here you have four quite different definitions and each can be successfully defended as the best in the right situation. There probably never will be an ultimate definition of this all-important word, as the definition is constantly evolving.

The views of eight well-known quality experts appear in the July 2001 issue of *Quality Progress*. Although these experts differ on details and nuances, some common themes appear in all their different quality philosophies:

1. Quality improvement is a never-ending process.

2. Top management commitment, knowledge, and active participation are critical.

3. Management is responsible for articulating a company philosophy, goals, measurable objectives, and a change strategy.

4. All employees in the organization need to be active participants.

5. A common language and set of procedures are important to communicate and support the quality effort.

6. A process must be established to identify the most critical problems, determine their causes, and find solutions.

7. Changes in company culture, roles, and responsibilities may be required.

Chapter 2

B. The Quality Management System

The quality management system (QMS) will be viewed in three parts: strategic planning, deployment of the strategy, and the information system for monitoring, analyzing, and improving the deployment. The difference between strategic planning and deployment of the strategy can be understood this way:

- Strategic planning means deciding what to do.

- Deployment means using the best methods to carry out the strategic plan.

1. STRATEGIC PLANNING

> Identify and define top management's responsibility for the QMS, including establishing policies and objectives, setting organization-wide goals, and supporting quality initiatives. (Apply)
>
> **Body of Knowledge I.B.1**

Strategic planning usually begins with an analysis phase. The strengths and weaknesses of the organization are assessed and forecasts are generated to predict how market opportunities and competitive threats will change during the time period covered by the study. This analysis is sometimes called a SWOT (the acronym for strengths, weaknesses, opportunities, and threats) study. Ideally, strategic planning for quality will address each aspect of the SWOT analysis.

The strengths of the organization can be leveraged to create or sustain competitive advantage. The weaknesses of the organization should be addressed through appropriate measures such as training initiatives to develop strategic skills or process improvement efforts. The opportunities available to the organization can be identified through various marketing research techniques. Key outputs of the marketing research may include estimates of the size and growth rate of the market and clearly articulated customer expectations, desires, and perceptions. This information should drive new product development efforts.

Finally, the business environment should be assessed, with particular emphasis on potential threats to the success of the organization. Threats can come from direct competitors offering similar products, indirect competitors offering substitute products or services (butter versus margarine), suppliers of critical proprietary components, and even from distributors who can influence the purchase decisions of the final customers.

After the SWOT analysis is complete, the organization can develop strategic quality plans. As the strategy is being formulated, management should evaluate whether the plans will ensure the success of the organization. To discern the effectiveness of strategic quality plans, management should employ a series of sequentially ordered effectiveness tests, shown in Figure 2.1 and discussed following in more detail.

1. The strategy should address all four elements of the SWOT analysis. Leverage the organization's strengths; remedy the weaknesses. Exploit the opportunities in the market; minimize the potential impact of external threats. It also may be prudent to prepare contingency plans that can be implemented quickly in response to threatening competitor actions. It is crucial for this stage of the planning process to be data-driven. The analysis should be comprehensive, including product quality, finance, purchasing, human resources, marketing and sales, delivery, customer service, and the internal processes that drive these activities. The notion that quality improvement is limited to the factory floor is obsolete. When management begins to apply quality disciplines and statistical methods to assess advertising campaigns and HR initiatives, the transformation is under way. The organization is poised to establish strategic quality plans.

Strategic Planning Effectiveness Tests

1. Does the plan adequately address *strengths, weaknesses, opportunities*, and *threats* (SWOT)?

2. Will the plan result in a *significant competitive advantage* in the marketplace?

3. Is this advantage *sustainable?*

4. Does the *vision statement inspire a sense of mission and purpose* among employees?

5. Are the goals and objectives *SMART* (specific, measurable, achievable, realistic, and time-based)?

6. Are the goals and objectives *aligned* throughout the organization?

7. Have *adequate resources been allocated* to achieve the plan?

8. Are organizational *structures, systems, and processes appropriate* to execute the plan?

9. Is a *review/reporting system* in place to monitor the execution of the plan?

10. Does the strategic planning team *include representatives from all key stakeholders?*

Figure 2.1   Ten effectiveness tests for strategic quality plans.

2. A strategic plan is useful only insofar as it creates a significant competitive advantage in the marketplace. Incremental improvements in quality may not be sufficient to ensure success. Furthermore, the advantage must be recognized and valued by the customer. Engineering and manufacturing can create superior products but that may not help the organization succeed if the customers do not know about the products. Other activities must be involved in the strategic planning process. For example, marketing is responsible for raising customer awareness of product enhancements and influencing purchase decisions through advertising or promotions. Keep in mind that the current strengths of an organization may only generate passing interest among customers. For example, a product may have best-in-class durability but customers may be more interested in appearance, availability, or ease of use. In such cases, consider strategic initiatives that will strengthen the organization's ability to maximize customer satisfaction throughout the purchase and ownership experience. Such market research tools as conjoint analysis and the Kano quality model can measure how product or service features influence customer purchase behavior. Companies that use market research to help select targets for creating a competitive advantage are more likely to thrive in the marketplace.

3. Is the competitive advantage sustainable? Can your competitors quickly and easily imitate your strategy? Will they respond with counteroffensives that weaken your position? Will your competitors' strategic efforts pay off a year from now and undermine your leadership in the market? Some consultants recommend avoiding cost reduction as a primary strategy because price is one of the easiest things to imitate in the market. Both you and your competitors will lose if a price war erupts. Anyone can reduce costs by using cheaper components or reducing staff in service or support activities. The risk of this approach is that customers may perceive deteriorating quality, damaging the organization's reputation and resulting in lost sales. Insisting on a strategy that will deliver outstanding quality through continuous improvement is much more likely to generate a sustainable competitive advantage. The growing popularity of the Six Sigma movement and its impressive success stories demonstrate that it is possible to embark on a major, strategic quality improvement initiative and reap substantial benefits on the bottom line.

4. Does the vision inspire and motivate your employees? The vision should be customer-focused and provide a clear, succinct view of the desired future state of the organization. A major strategic effort will require dedication and commitment. Resources may be stretched to achieve the vision. If the vision is too difficult to achieve, employees may become discouraged and give up. If the vision is too easy to achieve, your competitors may implement something better, and you will be playing catch-up.

5. Goals and objectives are established to direct the efforts of the organization and measure whether the vision is being achieved. The goals and objectives should be SMART, that is, they should be:

Specific. State what is expected in precise terms.

Measurable. Demonstrate progress through quantitative rather than qualitative or subjective measures.

Achievable. The goal can be achieved with available resources if appropriate actions are taken.

Realistic. A reasonable, sensible person would accept the goal after considering the degree of difficulty and the probability of success.

Time-based. Deadlines serve a useful purpose. Studies have shown that companies who are first to market with new innovations frequently enjoy a significant, sustainable advantage over their competitors.

6. Goals and objectives must be in harmony with each other. As goals are cascaded through an organization and broken down into manageable tasks to be performed by various departments or individuals, unity of purpose and alignment of priorities must be maintained to avoid conflicts.

7. Are resources (staffing, equipment, financing, and so on) adequate to achieve the plan? Can the additional workload be absorbed? Are the skill levels of the employees sufficient? Has the time line been reviewed by affected participants to ensure that there are no scheduling conflicts? Project management techniques such as critical path method (CPM) may be helpful. CPM (see Figure 2.2) will identify the critical paths in the program and provide documentation as to when the resources will be required.

8. Are organizational structures, systems, and processes suitable for executing the plan? Is a departmental reorganization necessary to streamline the flow of work and facilitate concurrent activities? Is an R&D effort necessary to upgrade designs or manufacturing equipment capability?

9. Is a review and reporting system in place to periodically assess progress? These reviews should be conducted by management at a high enough level within

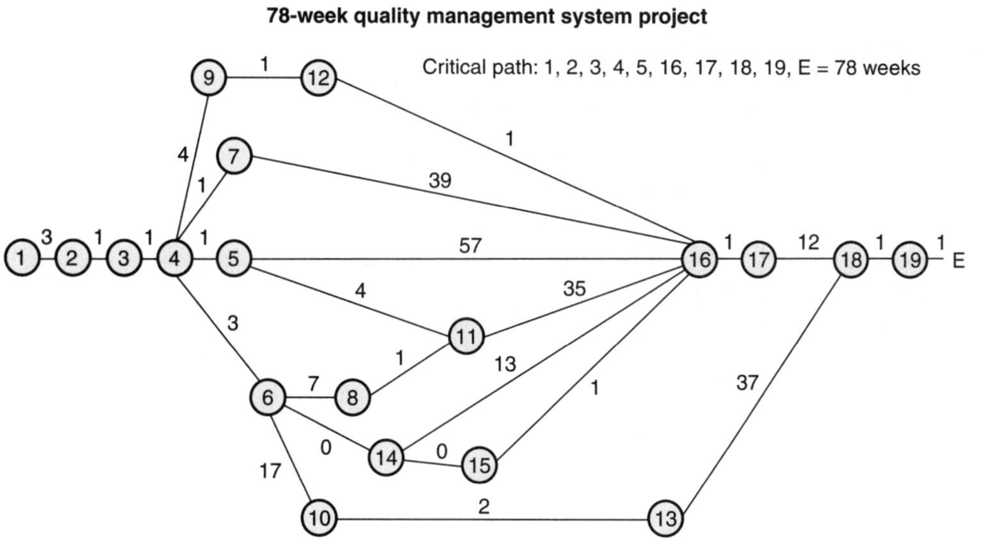

Figure 2.2 Critical path method (CPM) chart.

the organization to marshal additional resources as needed when the program is in danger of falling behind schedule. Key program milestones should have clearly defined expectations to ensure consistency and excellence in the execution of the activities. Checklists are a simple yet effective means of communicating the expectations.

10. Does the strategic planning team include the participation of experienced professionals from all affected work groups? Does the team fully understand the strategy, and have they bought into it? The benefits of a cross-functional planning effort cannot be overemphasized. Consider an analogy to the product development process: manufacturing personnel contribute expert advice during the early stages of product design and thereby avoid costly, time-consuming delays and redesigns. Ford Motor Company's advanced quality planning process lists the use of a cross-functional team as the number one expectation for executing many of the quality disciplines within a product development effort.

The importance of establishing the right strategy is critical to the success of an organization. Countless years of sincere toil have been wasted implementing poorly developed strategies. Excellent execution will not assure success unless the plan also is excellent. Juran argues that a structured planning process results in products that perform better and have a shorter development cycle from concept to customer (Juran and Godfrey 1999).

Management must explore strategic quality initiatives that go beyond mere incremental improvement. Drive the philosophy of continuous improvement throughout the organization and create a culture of innovation. Look beyond the factory floor for breakthroughs in all systems, such as research and development (R&D), product development, marketing, human resources, and purchasing. Strive for quality initiatives that add value for the customer and establish a sustainable competitive advantage.

2. DEPLOYMENT TECHNIQUES

> Define, describe, and use various deployment tools in support of the QMS: benchmarking, stakeholder identification and analysis, performance measurement tools, and project management tools such as PERT charts, Gantt charts, critical path method (CPM), resource allocation, and so on. (Apply)
>
> **Body of Knowledge I.B.2**

Quality improvement does not just happen. It must be planned, supported, and monitored just as any other process. Planning requires ways to identify the specific initiatives to be taken on, while support and monitoring require methods for tracking and communicating progress.

Policy Deployment

Policies provide direction to guide and determine present and future decisions. They indicate the principles to be followed or what is to be done but not specifically how it is to occur. For example, a quality policy should summarize the organization's view on the meaning and importance of quality as it relates to competitiveness, customers, suppliers, employees, and continual improvement.

To ensure consistency and understanding throughout the organization, policies need to be integrated with the strategic plan, then deployed through appropriate initiatives and performance checks. Projects must be justified and scheduled. Performance must be measured and reported. An organization's policies should be actionable. Some situations may call for temporary adaptation of the policy to meet unanticipated needs. A documented and deployed quality policy provides:

- A written guide to managerial action, lending stability to the organization

- Consideration of quality problems and their ramifications

- A basis for auditing practices against policy

Deployed policies cascade throughout the organization, directly impacting each functional area and indirectly affecting events, activities, and outcomes depending on those functions. If policies do not have this effect, they are not fulfilling their purpose. Each function and person impacted by the organization's policy must align their objectives and procedures to support the policy.

Goals and Objectives

Simply establishing goals is not enough. Goals must be supported by measurable objectives that are in turn supported by action plans that delineate how the objectives are to be achieved, by when, and by whom. There must be measurable objectives in order to know what the projected results should be and as the means for measuring attainment of those objectives. Similarly, action plans provide more specific information about attaining objectives. An example of the hierarchical relationships between strategy, a goal, objectives, and action plans follows:

Organization strategy: Continually build and retain a loyal customer base.

Organizational goal: Deliver all products to all customers 100 percent on time.

Organizational objective: Given current capacity, improve delivery dates of all future customer orders from 35 percent to 75 percent on-time delivery by February 2010 and to 100 percent by August 2010.

Functional objectives: The quality department will assign a quality engineer to convene a cross-functional process improvement team by November 1, 2009. The team will utilize lean manufacturing techniques to reduce cycle time and will continue its efforts until the production process has achieved 100 percent on-time delivery performance.

Action plans: Detailed plans state how, when, and by whom the objective will be achieved. Action plans may resemble mini project plans or may be more complex project planning documents as needs dictate. In either case, action plans influence planning and scheduling.

Benchmarking

Benchmarking is a process by which organizations evaluate their performance in comparison to their competition or to best practices found internally or in outside organizations. It was pioneered by Xerox in the late 1970s in response to growing pressure in the photocopy industry. Benchmarking is now recognized as an important input to strategic planning. It can be applied to any business process or function, such as optimizing inventory levels or improving service delivery.

Benchmarking can help an organization identify new ideas and methods to improve operational effectiveness. It can help break through institutional barriers and resistance to change because some other organization has already demonstrated that the new methods are more effective. Once these best practices are identified, the organization can develop plans to adopt them in their own organization. In this way, benchmarking can become an integral part of the continuous improvement process.

Internal benchmarking is used to compare performance between plants or divisions. Competitive benchmarking is used to assess performance relative to direct competitors within an industry. Internal and competitive benchmarks are useful in identifying gaps in performance. For example, automotive manufacturers use customer surveys to compare quality and customer satisfaction. Poor performance must be addressed to ensure survival in the marketplace. However, competitive benchmarking may not identify the best practices needed to close the gap in performance. Furthermore, although benchmarking internally or among competitors may identify incremental improvement opportunities, it is not likely to identify breakthroughs leading to world-class performance.

Collaborative benchmarking requires cooperation between two or more organizations. Each organization freely shares information about their best practices in exchange for information about other best practices from a partner. Suppose, for example, Wal-Mart wishes to team with Dell Corporation. Wal-Mart offers to share information on forecasting consumer demand, and Dell reciprocates by sharing insights on how they minimize order-to-delivery times. With collaborative benchmarking, the key is to identify the very best performer. Use trade associations, publications, financial analysis, market research, or other tools to find the leader.

External benchmarking may identify the best opportunities, but it requires a significant investment of time and effort. It may be useful to employ internal benchmarking first because it will generate quicker results. Internal successes should receive recognition. This will convince skeptics that the process works. The benchmarking team also will gain valuable experience and be better prepared for pursuing external benchmarking partners. A typical benchmarking project will include:

- *Planning.* Identify what is to be benchmarked. Establish the objectives for the study. If the scope is too narrow, the benefits will be limited. If the scope is too broad, the task may become unmanageable and the probability of successfully implementing the best practices will diminish. Select the team members and search for target organizations to benchmark.

- *Data collection.* Develop a mutually acceptable protocol with the partner, including a code of conduct, confidentiality agreements, and performance measures to be analyzed. Data sharing may include information about procedures, standards, software, training, and other supporting systems. The key is to gain enough understanding and direction to replicate the best practice within your organization.

- *Analysis.* Assess the data for accuracy and credibility. Determine current performance levels and identify gaps. Explore the feasibility of implementing the best practice. Some practices are not readily transferable—is adaptation necessary? Forecast the expected improvement.

- *Implementation.* Obtain the support of key stakeholders. Use project management techniques or action plans to initiate the change. Monitor performance. Document activities and communicate progress.

Benchmarking is not a precise discipline, and common pitfalls include lack of commitment, insufficient planning, comparing processes that are not sufficiently similar to generate useful insights, and measuring processes that have little potential for significant gains. A well-executed benchmarking project will help both in deploying strategic plans and suggesting modifications to future strategic plans. But real leadership means not just catching up with industry leaders, but surpassing them. Benchmarking can never accomplish that.

Stakeholder Identification and Analysis

Congruence between policy and results is evaluated through audits that periodically check for conformance. The stakeholders need to be clearly identified and their differing needs must be met. If adaptation of a policy must occur, it must remain within the original intent if the policy is to remain credible to the stakeholders. Frequent feedback from all stakeholders helps to quickly identify and correct any disparity. Performance measures, discussed below, must take into account the differing needs and perceptions of each stakeholder group. Stakeholders include the following:

- *Stockholders, the owners of the company.* Their role is often passive and their needs are primarily of a financial nature. They expect the company to maintain its credibility in the financial markets and hope for growth in earnings and share price.

- *The executive group, including the board of directors and the top tier of managers.* They must acknowledge and serve the other stakeholders. Conversely, the health of any organization is critically dependent on their decision making and deployment.

- *Employees other than top management.* This critical group of stakeholders has little direct impact on policy but all other groups depend on them to carry out the policy efficiently and promptly. The quality of any organization's end product depends on how well the employees are recruited, trained, and supervised.

- *Suppliers and customers.* These two groups are concerned with external inputs and outputs. Suppliers must adhere to contractual requirements and therefore can insist on fair and prompt payment for their goods and services. Customers are paramount stakeholders, for if customers do not want the organization's products, it will eventually cease to exist. Two later chapters deal with customer relations and supplier management.

- *The community at large.* Communities, neighbors, environmental regulators, law enforcement agencies, chambers of commerce, legislatures, and similar bodies often are indirect stakeholders. Individually their impact is relatively slight but if a major issue arises, the concerns of a community can have an overwhelming influence. This stakeholder group is especially critical when plants are being planned for opening or closing. The community often is concerned about treatment of minorities, public service (or the absence thereof), and environmental abuses.

Performance Measurement Tools

The strategic plan is a vision with broad goals and objectives for the organization to achieve. Management at all levels is charged with implementing the strategic plan. Metrics must be developed to monitor activities and track progress toward achieving the goals and objectives. But before discussing numbers and types of metrics, it is important to emphasize that the metrics should reflect the strategic vision. Some authors use the word *linkage* to describe the connection between strategic goals and performance metrics. We are on the right path if people two or three levels down from top management in the organization can articulate how their activities support a strategic objective.

Once the strategic plan is finalized, management must *cascade* the goals and objectives down through the organization and identify specific tasks with time lines, methods, and responsibilities. This is not a trivial task. Considerable care should be taken to select appropriate measures. Stakeholders and subject matter experts within the organization should be involved in the selection process. Team participation is more likely to result in performance measures that are aligned with strategic objectives. Participation also fosters ownership of the metrics. Some managers go a step further and link the objectives to annual employee performance evaluation programs or to bonus programs.

For a clear example of how to cascade performance measures, we can look to the field of reliability engineering. When designing a system, we establish reliability targets for the system as a whole. When designing the components of the system, we must establish more stringent reliability targets for each component so that the system as a whole continues to meet the overall performance target. This process, called *reliability allocation,* is a highly technical process that should be performed by someone with expertise in reliability. Unfortunately, management science has not progressed to the same level of discipline as the reliability field. Nevertheless, the basic concepts still apply. When cascading a high-level objective down to operations, we must allocate tasks and apportion the targets to ensure that the organization as a whole will meet the objectives. For more details on reliability concepts see Chapter 20.

Guidelines for Performance Measures

- Measures should be linked to strategic objectives.

- Measures should be rigorous, objective, quantifiable, and standardized.

- Measures should be achievable, realistic, and time-based.

- Measures should be assigned to appropriate personnel who are held accountable and who are empowered with some level of control to influence outcomes.

- Focus on the *vital few*. Many authors suggest using no more than two dozen measures. Use your judgment. Avoid using too many metrics, which may dilute the results.

- Automate data collection and calculations if possible. Spend more time making decisions than generating reports.

- Select measures that are resistant to perverse behavior.

Most of these guidelines are self-evident but the last bullet warrants explanation. Suppose an organization faces stiff competition in a commodity market. Cost reduction is a key strategic initiative. When the objective is cascaded to plant operations, the maintenance department decides to support the objective by postponing costly equipment overhauls. This "perverse" behavior may help in the short run but could cause a catastrophe in the future. How can this be avoided? One solution is to use combined metrics. For example, we could create a maintenance productivity metric:

$$\text{Maintenance productivity} = \frac{\Delta^R \text{MTTF}}{\Delta^R \text{Maintenance budget} * \Delta^R \text{MTTR}}$$

In this metric, bigger is better. The symbol Δ^R is applied to each variable and refers to the ratio of the variable in period t divided by the variable in period $t–1$. This little math trick results in a dimensionless equation that is "normalized" to a value of 1.0 when there is no change in the variable from one period to the next. If the productivity value is greater than 1, performance is improving; if less than 1, performance is deteriorating. Since maintenance spending is in the denominator, less spending is encouraged because it will increase the productivity metric. But we can also increase the productivity metric by increasing the equipment mean time to failure (MTTF) or by decreasing the mean time to repair (MTTR) (for more details see Chapter 20). If the maintenance department starts scrimping on the budget, breakdowns will probably occur more frequently and repair times may increase. Declining performance will offset the benefit of reduced spending in the metric. Thus this combined metric encourages appropriate behavior.

The point of this example is not to advocate specifically for a maintenance productivity metric but to suggest that a little creativity can overcome inherent weaknesses in traditional performance measures.

Balanced Scorecard

Robert Kaplan and David Norton introduced the balanced scorecard in 1992. Refer to the list of stakeholders above. Kaplan and Norton argued that most strategic plans were unbalanced because one stakeholder group—the stockholders—was overemphasized. They proposed a "balanced" scorecard with four perspectives:

1. Financial fundamentals

2. Business processes

3. Customer

4. Learning and growth

Financial measures include traditional indicators such as cash flow, sales, and return on investment. Business processes include manufacturing measures such as yield and rework. It can also include support activities such as order processing. Customer measures may include trends in customer satisfaction or average wait times on telephone hot lines. The learning and growth perspective recognizes the human element in an organization and looks at softer measures such as participation in employee suggestion programs and training.

The balanced scorecard provides a framework to translate the strategic plan into specific tasks that can be managed by frontline employees. In a typical scorecard, the objective is listed along with associated measures, targets for performance, and initiatives that will drive the organization to achieve the objective.

Dashboard

A dashboard provides a visual, at-a-glance display of key business indicators (see Figure 2.3). Dashboards provide a compact view of the current organizational state. Dashboards may include trend charts, bar charts, and green/yellow/red lights to indicate performance relative to target. Some dashboards include "drill down" features so that managers can dig into lower-level data. Digital dashboards must be customized for various activities throughout the organization. High-level dashboards are appropriate for executives, but frontline employees need to access low-level data appropriate for their sphere of influence.

The elements in a dashboard should be linked to the strategic objectives. Sales are targeted to grow at 3.75 percent per year. To avoid revealing confidential information, the dashboard shows only deviation to target. Sales below target are negative. In Figure 2.3, although sales in the recent past have fallen short of the goal, the trend is favorable. Inventory turns (annual sales divided by current inventory)

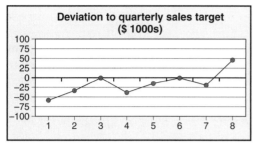

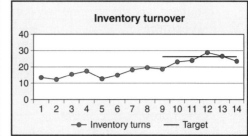

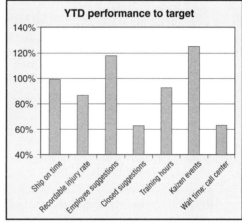

Figure 2.3   XYZ corporation dashboard.

Part I.B.2

have met or exceeded the target in two of the past three quarters. The milestone review for new product development shows two tasks behind schedule. The year-to-date (YTD) performance to target chart includes several elements that were selected in the balanced scorecard process. Calculating the ratio between actual performance and the target allows us to combine various metrics on a single chart with a common scale. In this example, management should be concerned that employee suggestions are not being closed promptly and customer calls are still not being processed fast enough through the call center.

Remember that *what* you measure will determine to a great extent the activities of your organization. Therefore, carefully select the metrics for your dashboards, scorecards, and other performance measurement tools.

More information on performance measures such as process capability indices is presented in Chapter 38.

Planning and Scheduling

Follow the old adage: plan your work, work your plan. Work planning requires a clear understanding of the overall goal and the objectives—also referred to as outcomes—to be achieved (the "what"). The planning process must also take into account how the initiative relates to other projects (for example, sharing of resources), and therefore often requires input from or participation by multiple stakeholders.

Figure 2.4 shows an action plan format that can be used to document the plan, while Figure 2.5 shows a format for an implementation schedule. A Gantt chart may be added to show the timing of each step in the schedule.

Periodic work review meetings are held to provide:

- A prescheduled meeting between the project leader and the manager to discuss progress of the project

- A summary of performance (presuming day-to-day feedback was given), evaluation of progress, determination of actions to correct/improve performance, and renegotiation of such activities as may be necessary

- A meeting where both parties come prepared with documentation relative to the work objectives

- An effective time for the manager to reinforce work done well, assuming the work climate is conducive to frank, open, two-way discussion and problem solving

The specific time to review progress is a matter of preference. Different objectives or projects may be reviewed at different time intervals depending on complexity, time span of work, competency level of performer, criticality of work outcomes, disruptions in due dates, resource shortages, and so on. As a rule of thumb, work reviews should be scheduled at least once a month for objectives spanning more than a three-month period. It is never appropriate to wait until just before the planned achievement date to review progress on work objectives.

Project Management

Quality engineers often become involved in project activity—either as a project team member or as a project leader. A number of proven techniques and tools are available to assist in cost-effective project management. The first is proper project selection.

Project Justification and Prioritization Tools. Projects must be prioritized to select those having the most merit. Projects should be evaluated for their fit to overall business needs, financial payoff, and potential risks. Exceptions will be made for legal mandates and customer demands. Only projects that are optional should be prioritized.

Major projects involve risk of loss. Risk assessment involves identifying potential problems that could occur, their impact, and what, if any, actions should be taken to offset them, such as taking countermeasures, purchasing risk insurance, or developing contingency plans. For complex projects, it may be prudent to apply a formal risk assessment tool such as a *failure mode and effects analysis* (FMEA) or simulation. (See Chapter 20 for more details on FMEA.)

If the benefits of a project are uncertain and multiple outcomes are possible, then a decision tree can help to estimate the expected value of gain or loss. A decision tree lists the potential outcomes and assigns a probability to each branch. The

Action plan

Objective/plan title:	Plan no.: _____
Description	Date initiated: _____
	Date needed: _____
	Approval: _____
	Team (L): _____
	Team (M): _____
	Team (M): _____
	Team (M): _____
	Team (M): _____

Major outcomes desired/required:

Scope (Where will the solution/implementation be applied? What limitations exist?):

By what criteria/measures will completion and success of project be measured?

Assumptions made that may impact project (resources, circumstances outside the project):

Describe the overall approach to be taken:

When should the project be started in order to meet the date needed/wanted?:

Estimate the resources required (time and money):

Outline the tentative *major* steps to be taken, a projected *start* and *complete date* for each step, and the *person to be responsible* for each step. (Use the back of this sheet to sketch your time line.)

Figure 2.4   Action plan format example.

© 2000 R. T. Westcott & Associates (Reprinted with permission of R. T. Westcott & Associates)

Action plan implementation schedule

Step no.	Activity/event description	Depends on step	Start date	Finish date	Person responsible

Figure 2.5   Action plan implementation schedule example.
© 2000 R. T. Westcott & Associates (Reprinted with permission of R. T. Westcott & Associates)

financial payout for each outcome is shown at the end of the branch. A few simple rules apply to the creation of a decision tree:

- At each branch point, the probabilities must sum to 1.0.

- The expected value for each branch is calculated by multiplying all the probabilities along the branch by the financial payout.

- Add the expected payout for all the outcomes within a decision branch.

- Choose the decision with the highest payout.

Additional Project Justification Tools. There are many other financial methods for justifying projects. Three very common methods of justifying projects are:

- *Payback period.* The number of years it will take to recover the investment from net cash flows.

- *Net present value (NPV).* Taking into account the time value of money, NPV involves finding the present value of each cash flow (yearly) discounted at the cost of capital percentage used by the organization, summing the discounted cash flows, and determining if the project is a candidate for approval based on how positive the NPV is.

- *Internal rate of return (IRR).* A discount rate that causes the NPV to equal zero. If the IRR is greater than the minimum required by the organization for typical capital investments, the project is a candidate for acceptance.

EXAMPLE 2.1: DECISION TREE EXAMPLE

A quality engineer is considering several options to fix a problem with a production machine. The machine is starting to wear out, so it has excessive variation and approximately one percent of production must be scrapped. He can replace the machine with a prototype machine. There is an 80 percent chance the new machine will eliminate the variability problem and it will probably increase capacity by two percent. The second choice is to overhaul the machine, with a 60 percent chance of improving the yield. The third choice is to perform selected repairs. This choice has the lowest initial investment but also is least likely to solve the variability problem. This problem is summarized in the decision tree below. The probabilities associated with the choices are shown in brackets.

	Reduce variation?	Increase capacity?	Financial payout
Choice			
	Yes [0.8]	Yes [0.85]	$150,000
		No [0.15]	$ 50,000
New machine		Yes [0.85]	$100,000
$110,000	No [0.2]		
		No [0.15]	$0
	Yes [0.6]		$ 50,000
Overhaul			
$ 35,000	No [0.4]		$0
	Yes [0.3]		$ 50,000
Selective repair			
$ 15,000	No [0.7]		$0

Currently, the variation problem generates scrap worth $50,000 per year. A two percent increase in capacity would be worth an additional $100,000 profit per year. Therefore, the financial payout changes depending on whether the scrap is eliminated and the capacity is increased.

The expected value for a decision is given by the equation:

$$EV = \Sigma x\, p(x)$$

where x is the financial payout, and $p(x)$ is the associated probability of the outcome. We sum all the values within the decision branch. Therefore, the expected value of the new machine is:

EV = (0.8)(0.85)$150,000 + (0.8)(0.15)$50,000 + (0.2)(0.85)$100,000 + (0.2)(0.15)$0
EV = $125,000

Note that the expected value of the new machine is less than the maximum payout because there is a chance the new machine will not work perfectly. We can calculate the expected value for the other options using the same approach.

Continued

Continued

For the overhaul: EV = (0.6)$50,000 + (0.4)$0 = $30,000
For the repairs: EV = (0.3)$50,000 + (0.7)$0 = $15,000

Finally, we must subtract the initial investment from the expected value to get the *net* return.

New machine = $125,000 – $110,000 = $15,000
Overhaul machine = $ 30,000 – $ 35,000 = ($ 5,000)
Selective repairs = $ 15,000 – $ 15,000 = $ 0

In the first year, we will make money on the new machine, we will break even using repairs, but we will lose money if we select the overhaul. (Note: when evaluating projects, you should always consider the savings in future years, not just the first year.) At the end of the first year, we will gain experience with the option that we implemented. We can update the probability assumptions and repeat the decision tree exercise in subsequent years.

The payback period is widely used because it is so easy to calculate and simple to understand. In the decision tree example above, the payback period for installing a new machine was less than one year, which implies a very high return on the investment. But a major weakness of payback is that it does not give any insight into the magnitude of future savings, that is, savings after the initial investment has been recovered.

Internal rate of return (IRR) rectifies this deficiency, as does net present value (NPV). Both give more accurate information, provided that suitable estimates of future cash flows can be obtained. The major difference between the two methods is that IRR generates an interest rate that balances all future cash flows against the present outlay, while NPV generates a dollar amount of present and future cash flows. With both calculation methods, bigger is better. Many companies have an internal hurdle rate, such as an IRR greater than 10 percent or 20 percent, that projects must achieve to be considered. The company probably could not consistently earn such a high return on stocks or bonds, yet they require projects to clear this hurdle. One reason for this conservatism is the difficulty of getting accurate estimates of future cash flows.

A final cautionary word about project estimating: sometimes things do not work out as planned. Assumptions may be misleading, probabilities may be optimistic, and factors beyond your control may come into play. If you enter the calculations in a spreadsheet, it is easy to make adjustments and perform a sensitivity analysis. For example, how much would the NPV change if the probability of success decreased by 10 percent? This is sensitivity analysis. For more details and examples see Park (2007).

EXAMPLE 2.2: NPV EXAMPLE

The NPV method converts all future cash flows to today's dollars at a specified interest rate. It is easy to calculate using a spreadsheet. From the decision tree example above, we enter the initial investment and the expected values of the payouts for year 1, year 2, and so on. In year 3, the warranty expires and we start performing repairs. After year 5, the machine is starting to wear out, and by year 7, we are ready to overhaul or replace the machine. Note: the NPV example shown here can be understood without reference to the decision tree above.

	A	B	C	D
		Cash flow New machine	Cash flow	
1	Year		Overhaul	Comments
2		0.10	0.10	Interest rate
3	0	($110,000)	($35,000)	Initial investment
4	1	$125,000	$30,000	First year, expected value
5	2	$125,000	$30,000	Second year
6	3	$110,000	$15,000	Offset savings, paying for repairs
7	4	$110,000	$15,000	$15,000 in repairs
8	5	$105,000	$10,000	Machine is starting to wear out
9	6	$ 98,000	$8,500	Variability increasing, yield decreasing
10	7	$ 62,000	$2,400	Time to replace machine?

To calculate the NPV for the new machine using Excel software, and with the data entered in the spreadsheet as shown in the table above, click in an empty cell and type:

=NPV(B2,B3:B10)

The first cell reference inside the parentheses points to the interest rate. The interest rate should be the prevailing rate for raising cash in capital markets (that is, a bank loan). Ten percent is typical. Enter this as a decimal in the spreadsheet. The second cell reference refers to a range and shows where all the cash flows are, including the initial investment. The NPV function assumes that the initial investment is made at year 0 and the first payout is at the end of year 1. Column A is shown for reader comprehension, but it is not needed by Excel. The results are surprising:

NPV, New machine = $379,136
NPV, Overhaul = $ 46,200

The net return for the new machine option in the first year was $15,000. But when you consider the life of the investment, the return is enormous. The overhaul option loses money in the first year but proves to generate positive cash flows in subsequent years. The selective repair option has zero NPV—it is a basic maintenance strategy.

Table 2.1 A typical project planning sequence.

S#	Tool/Technique	Comment
01	Statement	This is where the kernel of an idea or the basic concept visualized is translated into a clear statement of the problem, deficiency, or opportunity to be realized. Careful definition at this point helps later to clarify the scope of the project.
02	Project justification	Risk analyses and assessment (payback period, NPV, IRR, ROI, ROA, and benefits/cost). Go/no-go decision made.
03	Drafts of mission statement, project scope, and project objectives	These documents clarify the overall direction of the project and what it is to accomplish, the breadth and depth of the project, and the measurable objectives by which progress and completion are to be measured.
04	Stakeholder requirements	Stakeholders would consist of two groups: (1) those with a direct commitment to the project team, for example, a process manager who provides a skilled person to serve on a process improvement team working to reduce machine downtime and (2) those without involvement but who can influence project results, for example, the purchasing department that selects the vendor for a new machine. A macro-level process map may be used to identify areas from which potential team members should be selected.
05	Project team formation	Team members should be selected based on the need to represent a stakeholder group and/or specific skill sets required. Stakeholder groups not represented on the project team should have opportunities to provide input. Some members may be required on an as-needed basis only. Whenever possible, the interests, values, and personality profiles of individuals nominated should be considered. The Myers-Briggs Type Indicator (www.myersbriggs.org) can be a useful tool for building a team with complementary interpersonal skills and interests.
06	Finalized mission statement, project scope, project objectives, and project charter	Team members refine the original drafts. A benchmarking study may be appropriate to better define target outcomes.
07	Contractual requirements and deliverables	All requirements and outputs of the project are identified, defined, and documented.
08	Work breakdown structure (WBS)	Project work is further defined by breaking the work down into a hierarchy of work categories (families of like work clusters) down to the task level. Boxes on a WBS may be annotated with "person/work unit responsible," "resources required," "cost estimates," various other cross-references, and so on.

Continued

Table 2.1   A typical project planning sequence. *(Continued)*

S#	Tool/Technique	Comment
09	Gantt chart	Major project steps or task clusters are listed vertically on a time line chart with each item's estimated start-to-finish time depicted as a bar across the chosen time intervals (weeks, months, quarters). As the project progresses, the same chart may be used to plot the actual time expended next to the estimated time. Major milestones are shown as points along the time bar.
10	Time-dependent task diagram (AND, CPM, PERT charts)	Depending on the size, complexity, and duration of the project, it may be necessary to plot the time dependencies of each task to each other task. An activity network diagram (AND) depicts the interrelationships of each task, or task cluster, in the project. A critical path method (CPM) chart adds the dimension of normal (most likely) time to complete tasks and allows for computing the critical path (longest time line) through the project. A program evaluation and review technique (PERT) chart adds two additional time estimates for each task (optimistic, pessimistic), allowing further "what if" planning. Typically AND is used for shorter-term, simpler projects, CPM is used where there is data available for reasonably accurate time estimates, and PERT is most often used for projects for which there may be no prior precedent.
11	Resource requirements matrix (RRM)	An RRM delineates the various types of resources needed (for example, personnel, facilities, equipment, materials, consultants, and so on), quantity, when needed, and cost.
12	Linear responsibility matrix (LRM)	An LRM, for larger projects, defines the interfaces: who has what responsibility for what tasks, and to what degree (for example, primary, secondary, resource only, need to know).
13	Project budget	A detailed, itemized budget is prepared based on the time and cost estimate prepared by the team.
14	Measurements	The quantifiable measurements by which project progress and determination that project objectives have been achieved are defined. The progress monitoring process, methods for analyzing data gathered, reporting protocols, and checkpoints for initiating corrective action are determined and documented.
15	Approved project plan	Final approval of the project and authorization for implementation is given.

Project Planning and Estimation. Success of a project is significantly impacted by effectiveness of project planning. A typical project-planning sequence for a larger project is outlined in Table 2.1. Examples of some planning documents are provided in the following figures:

- Figure 2.6 is a three-level work breakdown structure (WBS) under development. A WBS allows determination of the many activities that must occur during the project. The numbering scheme in Figure 2.6 may seem unduly complex at first. But the consistent use of multiple decimal points allows nesting of levels and facilitates changes to dynamic projects.

- Figure 2.7 is a Gantt, or milestone, chart for an ISO 9001 implementation showing the major implementation phases and their relative timing. The Gantt chart is one of the earliest planning tools, dating back to the early years of the 20th century. Solid bars indicate activities that require an elapsed period of time, while triangles denote events that occur at specific points in time. The figure is fairly primitive; computerized Gantt charts can involve multiple layers and interactions of activities.

```
1.0    ISO 9001 Quality management system implementation project
1.1    Quality system documentation
       1.1.1   Quality policy and objectives
       1.1.2   Quality system manual (QSM)
       1.1.3   Quality system procedures (QSP)
       1.1.4   Quality system work instructions (WI)
1.2    Training
       1.2.1   ISO 9001 briefing
       1.2.2   Steering committee meetings
       1.2.3   Management representative training
       1.2.4   Internal auditor training
       1.2.5   Audit behavior training
       1.2.6   Statistical process control training
1.3    Quality system implementation
       1.3.1   Calibration system
       1.3.2   QSPs and WIs
       1.3.3   Supplier qualification process
       1.3.4   Document control system
       1.3.5   Auditing schedule
       1.3.6   Customer information system
       1.3.7   Corrective/preventive action process
1.4    Controls
       1.4.1   Document control
               1.4.1.1   QSM, QSP, WI
               1.4.1.2   Forms
               1.4.1.3   External documents
       1.4.2   Audits
               1.4.2.1   Internal audits
               1.4.2.2   Preassessment
               1.4.2.3   Certification assessment
               1.4.2.4   Surveillance audits
       1.4.3   Corrective/preventive actions
       1.4.4   Supplier evaluations
       1.4.5   Management reviews
```

Figure 2.6   Work breakdown structure (partial).

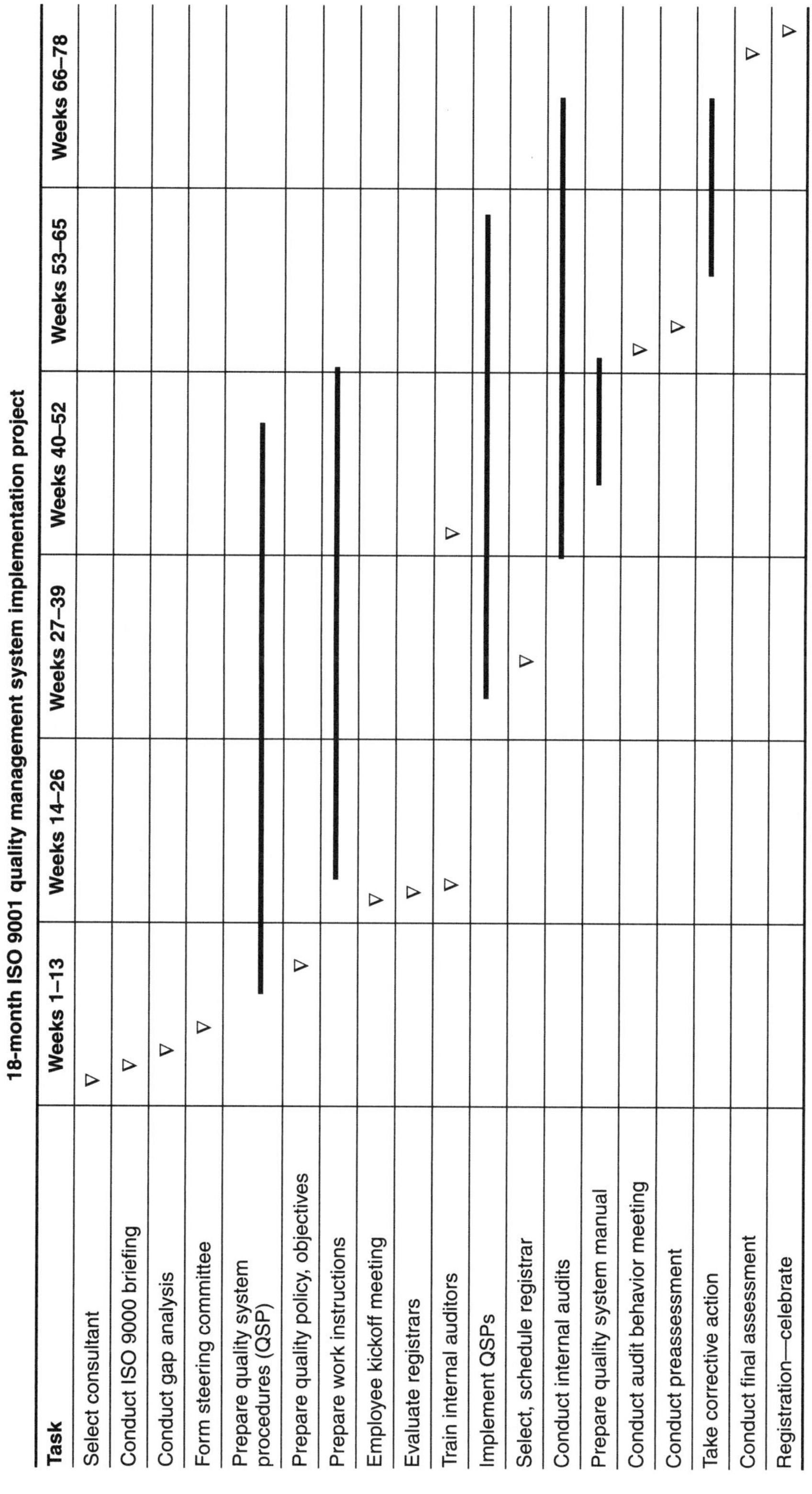

18-month ISO 9001 quality management system implementation project

Task	Weeks 1–13	Weeks 14–26	Weeks 27–39	Weeks 40–52	Weeks 53–65	Weeks 66–78
Select consultant	▷					
Conduct ISO 9000 briefing	▷					
Conduct gap analysis	▷					
Form steering committee	▷					
Prepare quality system procedures (QSP)	▬▬▬▬▬▬▬▬▬▬▬▬					
Prepare quality policy, objectives	▷					
Prepare work instructions		▬▬▬▬▬▬▬▬▬▬▬▬				
Employee kickoff meeting		▷				
Evaluate registrars		▷				
Train internal auditors		▷		▷		
Implement QSPs			▬▬▬▬▬▬▬▬▬▬▬▬			
Select, schedule registrar			▷			
Conduct internal audits				▬▬▬▬▬▬▬▬▬▬▬▬		
Prepare quality system manual				▬▬		
Conduct audit behavior meeting					▷	
Conduct preassessment					▷	
Take corrective action					▬▬▬▬▬▬▬	
Conduct final assessment						▷
Registration—celebrate						▷

Figure 2.7 Gantt chart example.

- Figure 2.2 depicts a critical path method (CPM) chart showing every activity in the project and how its start depends on the completion of other activities. The sequence that takes the longest total time constitutes the critical path and determines the minimum time to completion of the project.

Resource requirements matrices (RRM) are essentially spreadsheets laying out the requirements over time against the activities in the project. RRMs may be compiled for facilities, equipment, materials, contract/consulting services, personnel, and so on.

The project budget details the anticipated expenditures over time for each category of expense. Depending on the size of the project, budgets may be prepared for successive levels of the project (usually paralleling the WBS hierarchy).

Understanding the project lifecycle can also help in estimating the resources required. The five stages of a project are: (1) concept, (2) planning, (3) design, (4) implementation, and (5) evaluation and closeout.

Monitoring and Measuring Project Activity and Results. Critical project performance measures include timeliness, budget variance, and resource usage. Project measurements must then be determined and a system for tracking, monitoring, and reporting progress is established.

In medium to large projects, milestones (critical checkpoints) are established in the planning stage and the project monitored against these milestones. The critical path method (CPM) is discussed elsewhere in this chapter and illustrated in Figure 2.2. A CPM can be built into the quality information system for projects of any size. Thorough periodic project reviews are conducted, including assessment of schedules against the critical path, expenditures against budgets, resource utilization against plans, implementation results achieved, a possible reevaluation of risks, and any major issues impacting project continuance. Based on these reviews, the project may be continued as planned, modified, put on hold, or canceled. A similar review is conducted to evaluate the results when the project is completed.

Project Documentation. A project is not finished until the paperwork is completed. Documenting the project all along will make it easier to complete the paperwork that closes the project. If the team has not documented every aspect of the project, begin to document as soon as you can in order to capture details such as the following while they are still available:

- Assumptions, risks, and rationale for selecting the project

- Decisions made to initiate project and approvals

- Detailed plans for design and implementation

- Design and/or implementation changes

- Major obstacles encountered and how they were resolved

- Details of implementation (for example, measurements established)

- Progress reports and resulting decisions

- Final evaluation of project results

- Results of post-project audits

All documentation is valuable in planning and estimating new projects and in avoiding previous mistakes. Likewise, the documented knowledge base is a tool for training those new to project management.

3. QUALITY INFORMATION SYSTEM

> Identify and define the basic elements of a QIS, including who will contribute data, the kind of data to be managed, who will have access to the data, the level of flexibility for future information needs, data analysis, etc. (Remember)
>
> **Body of Knowledge I.B.3**

A *quality information system* (QIS) is a collection of data, rules, and equipment that creates information about quality in a systematic way. A QIS will collect, store, analyze, and manage quality-related data from customers, suppliers, and internal processes. It will generate information in the form of printed reports, screen displays, and signals sent to mechanical devices. Depending on the degree of automation, it may give answers to questions posed by humans, or it may have built-in action rules. Above all, if it is well done it will enhance profit and productivity.

Concept and Objectives

The first requirement in studying quality information systems is to understand what, exactly, a "system" is. The word is used in many different contexts. For example, this book discusses management systems, information systems, strategic planning systems, and quality systems, just for starters. From other sources you can learn about transportation systems, manufacturing systems, educational systems, social systems, gambling systems, and planetary systems (for example, the solar system). The essence of a system is this: it ties a number of components together that act in common with each other. Systems that quality engineers are interested in are dynamic and goal-oriented. They have inputs, outputs, operating rules (procedures or transformational processes), data storage, and boundaries. They are designed by people to achieve specified goals.

The term "system" does not imply "computer," but in today's computer-intensive world the term "information system" generally evokes computerized information systems. There are large-scale, well-run manual information systems, and there are computerized systems that are recognized as abominations. The manual systems often have evolved over a long period of time through informal cooperation. Computerized information systems are explicitly designed, and usually by cross-functional teams.

A quality information system is both a quality system and an information system. It is naïve to speak of "the" quality information system, because an effective organization will have numerous quality systems, which may be manual, computerized, or hybrid (with both manual and computer elements). A well designed information system allows information generated at one level or in one part of the organization to be used for many different purposes.

Uses of Quality Information Systems

Information systems may be used to:

- Initiate action (for example, generating a shop order from a customer's order)

- Control a process (for example, controlling the operation of a laser cutting machine within given specification limits)

- Monitor a process (for example, real-time production machine interface with control charting)

- Record critical data (for example, measurement tool calibration)

- Create and deploy operating procedures (for example, an ISO 9001–based quality management system)

- Manage a knowledge base (for example, capturing, storing, and retrieving needed knowledge)

- Schedule resource usage (for example, personnel assignments)

- Archive data (for example, customer order fulfillment)

The importance of information systems becomes apparent when looking at their impact on various aspects of quality management. Both process management and problem solving require accurate and timely information. Contrast the following two cases: One information system might be hard-wired into manufacturing and testing equipment, with monitors displaying real-time information complete with alarms and action signals; it could have options for graphic display of statistical and trend analysis for quick intervention. Another system in the same plant could tie executives, project teams, and off-site employees together through an intranet; organizational objectives and milestones appropriate for each level and function could be displayed as both text and graphics, along with actual performance and gaps. These two QISs are quite different.

Good information systems are critical to cross-functional collaboration, since distributed information access is required in order for groups and employees to make quicker and better decisions. For example, some projects can be carried out largely through computerized discussions and transmission of documents. Often this enables highly skilled team members to participate regardless of their physical location and can also reduce the amount of time required for the project.

The modern quality engineer must be competent in the selection, application, and use of hardware and software technology appropriate to the tasks and responsibilities assigned. Consideration should be given not only to the functionality of the system for the task, but also issues such as required user skills, compatibility with other systems, and information security. Furthermore, if the quality system is of any magnitude, the quality engineer must understand project management techniques and must be a good team member.

PLC and SCADA Systems

The widespread use of microcomputers and programmable logic controllers (PLCs) has transformed the factory floor. There is a growing trend toward distributed measurement and control, where PLCs have built-in programs and logic to control machines and processes. Fewer and fewer technicians are turning dials or opening and closing valves to control processes. These tasks are now controlled by PLCs. But many PLCs do not have a human interface such as a monitor or keyboard. The PLCs are widely distributed throughout the plant, so manual data collection is time-consuming and cumbersome. Furthermore, PLC language is not user-friendly. This situation has given rise to large-scale supervisory control and data acquisition (SCADA) systems. The SCADA system interfaces with all of the PLCs through a network. The SCADA system periodically polls the PLC memory registers to collect data. The system includes a human interface, usually in a central location such as a control room, to monitor the processes, generate alarms, and allow the operator to intervene or override as necessary. The SCADA system typically includes real-time trend charts and graphic displays of the current status of the equipment. The system also provides for data storage in a database program, which provides rapid retrieval of data for subsequent analysis and reporting.

What is the role of a quality engineer in the creation of a large-scale SCADA system? The information system should be viewed as no different from a manufacturing system. The QE should be involved from the earliest planning stages to ensure that user and system requirements are thoroughly documented. It may be appropriate and beneficial to apply some of the advanced quality planning disciplines discussed in Chapter 17, even though the "product" is a software system. For example, customer requirements should be fully understood, even if the "customer" is an hourly employee who will use the system to monitor and adjust the process. The quality engineer should participate in creating the user requirements—after all, the quality engineer is typically considered the local expert in data analysis and reporting. What reports are needed? How should the data be displayed and summarized?

Information System Strategy and Tactics

Although there are many ways to design information systems, it is a truism that the larger they get the more fraught with risk of failure they become. So the quality engineer can render a real service to the employer by studying strategy and tactics of systems development.

	What	Who	Where
Hardware	List of physical components of the system	Individuals who use it, individuals who manage it	Physical location
Software	List of programs, applications, and utilities	Individuals who use it, individuals who manage it	What hardware it resides on and where that hardware is located
Networking	Diagram of how hardware and software components are connected	Individuals who use it, who manage it, and the company from whom service is obtained	Where the nodes are located, where the wires and other transport media are located
Data	Bits of information stored in the system	Individuals who own it, individuals who manage it	Where the information resides

Figure 2.8   Information systems strategy matrix.

The need for a strategy was emphasized by Pearlson and Saunders (2004) who produced an information systems strategy matrix, as shown in Figure 2.8.

In this matrix, four different categories are displayed: hardware, software, networking, and data. Other categorizations could be made. This is just a small example of the kinds of analysis required. Another tool to consider is the V-model.

The V Model

The V model starts on the left side at the top of the V (see Figure 2.9), with high-level user requirements, and cascades down through functional specifications and detailed design requirements. On the right side of the V, test protocols are developed, executed, and documented to verify that the design specifications have been met. The QE should be involved in this process to ensure quality and data integrity during the execution of the project.

Tasks that seem trivial, such as naming conventions, can have a huge impact down the road. Large real-time control systems may have hundreds of PLCs and thousands of sensors. Imagine the complexity of creating a downtime report for the packaging area of the plant. Every machine and sensor in the area must be included in the database query. A good naming convention will allow a group of variables to be captured with a single query statement that includes a "wild card." If a naming standard is not used or is poorly executed, then the user has no choice but to individually specify each sensor and PLC when the database query is created.

Similar care and consideration should be given when creating the test protocols. How much data should be collected? How often will the samples be collected? If the sampling duration is too short, or the elapsed time between samples is too long, then it may not be possible to detect variation that is directly caused by the PLC control system. Is there a difference between the process target and the actual steady-state process average? What about including process upsets in the test protocol? Does the controller overshoot the target during initial recovery?

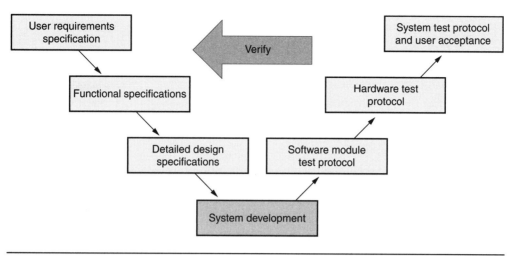

Figure 2.9   The V model for software development.

Further ideas to improve the success of system development projects are reported by Long and Gryna (1999), who drew the following conclusions:

- Carefully define the scope of the QIS and what it is expected to accomplish. From the very beginning emphasize operational benefits, not technical specifications. It may be wise to develop a pilot project that can be used to show what really does work and what does not. Getting some benefits in a short period of time builds confidence, not only in the system itself but in the competence of the system developers.

- Be sure that the goal of the QIS supports the goal of the business. (This point was discussed earlier in this chapter when we discussed strategic planning.) Once the goal is set, use well-proven project management techniques.

- Get advance agreement on who will do what and when. Get buy-in to clearly understood milestones. Do not simply delegate the project to the information technology (IT) folks but keep quality engineers and managers fully engaged in the development.

- Concentrate on user expectations and how they are being realized. Focus attention on the overall performance of the system rather than specific metrics. Ongoing discussion and comparison between the users and the developers is an important key to success.

- Publish regular progress reports and keep the language in user terms. A common trap in large-scale information systems projects is to get bogged down in technical metrics and jargon; the user may cross their fingers and hope for the best without really understanding what is going on. A corollary of this is to be sure that the end user has the technical competency to understand what is being said. Reports cannot be watered down simply to avoid confusing the uneducated.

Repeatedly stress the anticipated benefits that were specified at the outset and do not abandon original goals under pressure. The exception is if it becomes clearly evident that the original specifications *can not* be met. Then the top-level sponsors must be fully briefed and must participate in the revised benefit statement. This should be viewed as a last resort and is in a sense a salvage operation.

Productivity improvement is perhaps the most frequently cited justification to invest in an information system. The investment can be considerable because the infrastructure requires hardware, networks, sensors, customized software, and information systems support personnel. Estimating the payback can be a challenge. The payback estimates may include optimistic forecasts and tenuous assumptions. Some people focus on the human benefits such as automating periodic reports. Relief from mundane tasks will free up personnel to pursue other important tasks. But much larger gains usually can be achieved by using the information system to improve production processes. A well-designed information system can identify opportunities that probably would be missed by even the most conscientious and determined analyst using a manual or paper-based data system. At many facilities, a one percent gain in production yield is a realistic assumption and will generate a much larger return than a few hours saved per month generating manual reports.

Example of an Internally Developed QIS

To illustrate the tremendous value of a quality information system, consider this case study. A highly automated packaging plant in Texas started production in 2001. Equipment breakdowns plagued the facility for the first year of production. Downtime was so excessive that the plant was operating below the break-even point. Management decided to make a major investment in a new information system. Over the course of the next year, nearly every machine in the facility was linked through a network to a database. Sensors were added to monitor key production processes. Automatic feedback systems were installed and gradually tuned to achieve stability in the most complex processes. Customized reports were created to distill vast amounts of data into usable information. The reports summarized and prioritized the current status so that management could quickly allocate resources where they were most needed. One such report is shown in Figure 2.10. The report executes automatically at the end of each production shift. It analyzes data from nearly 700 machines, identifies the top three concerns in each functional area, and prints a one-page summary.

The quality department and the maintenance department worked together to develop the format. The general manager participated in establishing the equipment performance standards needed to support the balanced scorecard objectives. If performance does not meet the objectives, then the report highlights the total with a large, bold font. Management and maintenance employees can quickly identify concerns and focus their process improvement efforts accordingly.

The team designing this system took several months and gave a great deal of thought to balancing the automatic collection and processing of data with the human interpretation of information. It would have been easier to design a

Equipment Exception Report
7/2/06 3:00 PM to 7/2/06 10:00 PM

Concern		Number of faults	Concern		Number of faults
Critical / misc machine alarms		4	**Annealing oven faults**		1
No. 2 compressor, low oil pressure		3	Shop 1, zone 5, high temperature		1
No. 2 compressor, oil temperature		1			

Cooling hood jams		23	Coating sprayer alarms		260
	Prior shift	This shift			
Shop 1:	14	19	Shop 1:	No spray alarm	157
Shop 3:	7	2	Shop 3:	No spray alarm	89
Shop 2:	3	2	Shop 2:	No spray alarm	14

Inspection conveyor jams		34	Discharge conveyor jams		11
Shop 3, loop A	Check detector	23	Shop 2, loop A	Check detector	6
Shop 2, loop C	Leak test	4	Shop 3, loop A	Leak test	2
Shop 3, loop A	Leak test	3	Shop 3, loop A	Scanner	1

Carton forming faults		12	Carton packer faults		18
CF 2	Case not at madrel	11	Shop 1, north packer	Missing jars	13
CF 2	In flight jam	1	Shop 1, north packer	Elevator jam	2
			Shop 2, west packer	No glue	1

Downtime summary (minutes)		285	Throughput % of budget		0
Shop 3	Total downtime	146		Shop 3	94.6%
Shop 1	Total downtime	83		Shop 2	98.1%
Shop 2	Total downtime	56		Shop 1	98.4%

Figure 2.10   Current status report example.

completely closed-loop control system but this would have precluded human intervention and thoughtful study of what the processes were saying. But at the same time, the data on which the daily and weekly reports were based was massive and it was essential that it be condensed and summarized before being presented to humans.

The plant achieved a dramatic improvement in throughput in less than six months after implementing this QIS. The report shown in Figure 2.10 (and others like it) helped drive a transformation in quality and productivity. By the end of the second year, the plant achieved best-in-class quality and their profit margin was over 10 percent, exceeding the original performance target.

Example of a Web-Based QIS

Cequent Performance Products, a small manufacturing company in Tekonsha, Michigan, supplies parts to the automotive industry. In 2002 this company decided to use information systems development to automate their quality recording, analysis, and reporting. They also sought ISO 9000:2000 registration (see Chapter 12). Cequent did not want to develop their own software, so they contracted with IQS, a quality information systems vendor in Cleveland, Ohio, to provide the software on demand through the Internet. Cequent partnered with suppliers of automated test equipment (ATE) to feed process parameters, process data, and test data directly into the IQS software, which eliminated duplicate inspections. Inspectors began use roving laptop computers with wireless I/O and power supplied by car batteries on small carts. The system integrated several different small stand-alone quality systems and manufacturing resource planning (MRP) systems into one integrated factorywide system.

Most of the system development was done through interactive online messaging. Using the vendor's experience with ISO 9000 processes, Cequent was able to achieve registration within about nine months of their initial commitment to seek it. And because they followed carefully planned system development procedures, their actual operations were simplified and enhanced as a result.

Summary

The two examples above are but a small sample of the tremendous number and variety of QISs now being implemented. There are so many new developments. Bar codes, voice entry, optical character recognition, local area and wide area networks, are among the host of new technologies available for cost-effective automation of quality systems. Knowledge management, audiovisual presentations, individual learning programs, decision support systems, computerized conferencing, systems modeling, automated online reference services—the list goes on and on. The foresighted quality engineer will study computerized information systems techniques and possibilities with great zeal. This is an area that will continue to revolutionize all aspects of life, both organizational and personal.

Chapter 3

C. ASQ Code of Ethics for Professional Conduct

> Determine appropriate behavior in situations requiring ethical decisions. (Evaluate)
>
> **Body of Knowledge I.C**

All professions are bound by specific codes of ethics, and one mark of any profession is publishing and upholding standards of conduct. The American Society for Quality has adopted the following code of ethics:

Code of Ethics

Fundamental Principles

ASQ requires its members and certification holders to conduct themselves ethically by:

I. Being honest and impartial in serving the public, their employers, customers, and clients

II. Striving to increase the competence and prestige of the quality profession, and

III. Using their knowledge and skill for the enhancement of human welfare

Members and certification holders are required to observe the tenets set forth below:

Relations with the Public

Article 1—Hold paramount the safety, health, and welfare of the public in the performance of their professional duties.

Relations with Employers and Clients

Article 2—Perform services only in their areas of competence.

Article 3—Continue their professional development throughout their careers and provide opportunities for the professional and ethical development of others.

Article 4—Act in a professional manner in dealings with ASQ staff and each employer, customer, or client.

Article 5—Act as faithful agents or trustees and avoid conflict of interest and the appearance of conflicts of interest.

Continued

Continued

Relations with Peers

Article 6—Build their professional reputation on the merit of their services and not compete unfairly with others.

Article 7—Assure that credit for the work of others is given to those to whom it is due.

ASQ's code of ethics will help you decide how to treat your subordinates, peers, and managers, but numerous laws, as well as company policies, are applicable. Knowledge of same may be mandatory. For example, if you are interviewing someone for a position, the law requires you to follow certain rules for asking questions. Likewise, your company may have internal rules for dealing with peers, subordinates, and suppliers.

Quality engineers must be aware of legal issues, such as equal employment opportunity (EEO) laws and other guidelines. Another example of how the legal system impinges on quality engineers is the Sarbanes-Oxley legislation. Because of several instances of large-scale corporate fraud at the turn of the last century, the U.S. Congress passed this law, sometimes called *Sarbox*, which mandates a number of stringent requirements for corporate financial reporting that can be understood as quality assurance techniques applied to the corporate financial system. Sarbox actually enhances the role of quality engineering because it carries the same concept from the quality arena to the financial arena.

Whether your work is governed by EEO, Sarbox, or other relevant statutes, the point to remember is that your personal behavior must at all times be such that no embarrassment will come to the supplier, your employer (subordinates, peers, or management), the customer, or yourself. You must be polite and diplomatic and show respect to all persons. In the final analysis, you must be honest with yourself that you have acted fairly and legally, and that you have a good feeling in your gut about the things you have been involved with, including resolving ethical dilemmas.

ETHICAL DILEMMAS

Ethical dilemmas arise every day in the application of technology and its effects on human and nonhuman processes and the advancement or decline of society. Technology can harm people by inducing stress, triggering injuries, and demoralizing them. Conversely, technology can stimulate personal development and organizational growth. How technology is applied and the consequences of the application often call for ethical decisions. Some have equated the definition of quality and ethics with "do the right thing."

A case in point is the ongoing need for guidelines governing ethical behavior in the application of computers, e-commerce, e-business, and other new technologies. Some of the issues demanding critical attention are:

1. Misusing employers' computers for personal gain or pleasure

2. Destroying others' property (for example, injecting a virus, wiping out files, and so on)

3. Using or condoning the use of computers for fraudulent activities

4. Violating individual and company rights to privacy and confidentiality

5. Omitting safeguards that protect users

6. Infringing on copyrights and trademarks

7. Failing to maintain a sufficient level of accuracy and completeness implied when data is collected and stored in computer databases

8. Failing to make critical information known to appropriate decision makers in time to prevent a negative outcome

9. Failing to capture, manage, and make available critical knowledge to those who need it

10. Failing to upgrade computer technology

11. Managing retrieval of data files from old or different software programs/versions

12. Dealing with global employees, businesses, and markets

13. Dealing with legal requirements (including safety and environmental regulations) of different governmental groups across geographic boundaries

14. Ensuring the usage quality of the new technology itself, and ensuring that people are trained to use the new technology

Another area of concern to the engineer is the Occupational Safety and Health Administration (OSHA). Both federal-level agencies and state-level agencies monitor organizations to ensure compliance with the respective rules and regulations. Some of the more common sets of rules and regulations are:

OSHA, Labor	(*Randall's Practical Guide to ISO 9000* provides a more comprehensive list)
29 CFR 1910.95	Occupational Noise Exposure (Ear Protection)
29 CFR 1910.120	Hazardous Waste Operations and Emergency Response
29 CFR 1910.132	Personnel Protective Equipment
29 CFR 1910.133	Eye and Face Protection
29 CFR 1910.147	The Control of Hazardous Energy (Lockout/Tagout)
29 CFR 1910.1200	Hazard Communication

Engineers also are finding themselves involved with issues usually handled by management, such as interviewing potential new employees for the organization. Without the proper training, engineers could be putting themselves and their employers at great risk for lawsuits by asking inappropriate questions. Some items that the interviewers must be aware of include:

- Ask only job-related questions

- Do not ask about age, race, national origin, marital status, or religion

- Focus on the competencies and skills for the job in question

- Avoid any small talk that is not related to the job

In conclusion, the ASQ code of ethics emphasizes that we are professionals and must act accordingly. Federal law and employer rules create additional requirements for compliance. You must understand all of the above, and more as it is presented to you.

Chapter 4

D. Leadership Principles and Techniques

> Describe and apply various principles and techniques for developing and organizing teams and leading quality initiatives. (Analyze)
>
> **Body of Knowledge I.D**

Leadership is an essential part of any quality initiative. The leader's role is to establish and communicate a vision and to provide the tools, knowledge, and motivation necessary for those individuals or teams who will collaborate to bring the vision to life. This can apply to an entire organization as well as each specific department or work group. For example, the leader of the quality engineering function is responsible for helping shape the policies for the quality technologies that will be deployed throughout the organization and for ensuring that department personnel are sufficiently qualified to support the use of the technologies.

A leader may or may not hold an officially designated position. Often someone in a work group will emerge as a leader because of their knowledge, skills, experience, and/or abilities. Further, teams often include facilitators, another leadership role. The facilitator's purpose is to provide support to the team's effort, while at the same time allowing the team to maintain ownership of its decisions.

A good leader always tries to understand where the other person is coming from, what makes them act the way they do—in other words, what motivates them. Good leaders recognize and apply Maslow's hierarchy of needs. This is the assertion that people are driven by their needs and wants and that all human needs can be roughly placed in a hierarchy. Higher-level needs are not really relevant until lower-level needs are satisfied, but once a need is met, it no longer motivates behavior. The five levels are (1) physiological (hunger, thirst, sleep), (2) safety and security (protection from the elements and predators), (3) socialization, (4) ego, and (5) self-actualization. Many people never get their ego needs fully satisfied, so do not experience self-actualization needs, but all the great thinkers and leaders of the ages are in fact self-actualized. When trying to lead recalcitrant followers, it often helps to think about what need-level they are working on.

Leadership of the quality engineering function involves defining and carrying out projects that support the organization's strategic plan, as well as providing the resources for and overseeing day-to-day quality engineering activities. While some of these activities may be performed by an individual, in today's complex environment more are conducted in a team setting. Examples would include working with an advanced quality planning team to analyze repeatability and reproducibility (R&R) of a new measurement system or working with a software engineer to implement a new automated statistical process control (SPC) online package.

DEVELOPING, BUILDING, AND ORGANIZING TEAMS

Since around 1980, quality concepts and team concepts have moved in tandem through the economy. Teamwork is now vital in government, space exploration, healthcare, education, and most profit-oriented businesses. The autocratic leader of one or two generations ago would be utterly perplexed by how much control has now shifted to the team level.

The Need for Teams

The drive for excellence includes better deployment of people at all levels. Workers at all levels now expect to have some say in designing and implementing change, and only through change can quality improve. Managing an organization through teams has become recognized as a core component of business.

There are many types and purposes of teams, each requiring different structures, skills, resources, and support. Leaders of an organization must therefore be clear about what they are trying to accomplish and ensure that the appropriate team processes are utilized for their situation.

A team-based environment might be initiated as part of the strategic plan or as a response to a specific problem encountered by the organization. Regardless of the reason, there should be a process for planning and carrying out the team-based initiative. This process is often done through a steering committee that focuses on driving business improvement. A member of management called the sponsor also typically is identified and takes responsibility for initiating and guiding a team. The sponsor usually is the individual with ownership of the process or area where the team's actions are focused.

Types of Teams

Although each organization may utilize different names, three major types of teams are widely used:

• *Process improvement team.* These are temporary teams whose missions are to develop a new process or improve an existing process. These teams are often cross-functional, consisting of representatives from multiple departments involved in the process under study. The management sponsor typically selects the team leader and will negotiate with other area managers to identify other team members appropriate for the project mission. Figure 4.1 shows how teams should be integrated within the organizational hierarchy.

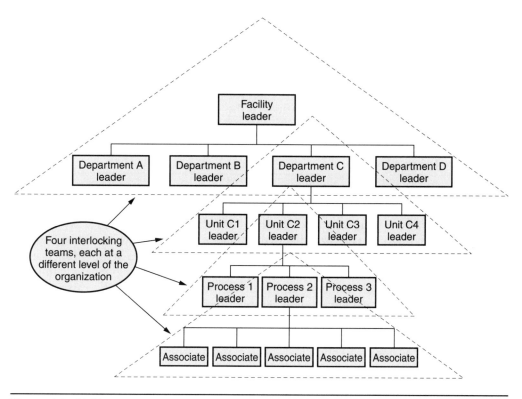

Figure 4.1   Linking team structure.

• *Work group.* These teams consist of the personnel who work in a particular department or process area. Their mission is the ongoing monitoring and improvement of process performance and they typically meet on a regular basis (for example, weekly) to review indicators and identify any actions required. The work group leader usually is the individual with supervisory responsibility for the process area. The team also may initiate a process improvement team, especially when the improvement requires interfacing with other departments who are suppliers or customers of the work group. Organizations committed to applying work group–based improvement from top to bottom can use an interlocking team structure that includes all members of the organization.

• *Self-directed work team (SDWT).* A self-directed work team is a group of individuals who have much broader and deeper day-to-day responsibility for management and improvement of their process area. SDWT members are highly trained in subjects such as quality, safety, maintenance, and scheduling, and in some cases also carry out human resource functions. These teams are highly empowered to make their own decisions, although of course there are still limits, such as spending authority.

Whether and to what extent an organization utilizes teams usually is dependent on factors such as the rate of change in their industry, the culture of the organization, the predominant management style, employee educational levels, and where the company's product or service is in the maturity cycle.

Some teams are less formally structured, such as an ad hoc group organized to address a customer complaint or a virtual team that wants to compare the process used for design reviews by several different facilities. Regardless, many of the following considerations will influence the success of the team and the satisfaction of its members.

Selecting Team Members

The primary determination of who will participate in a team effort is whether the person is involved in the process to be improved. However, when selecting team members other issues also often are considered. For example, a process improvement team might not be very effective if all team members have the same personal style (for example, as measured by a personality evaluation instrument such as the Myers-Briggs Type Indicator/MBTI, see www.myersbriggs.org). Some teams also intentionally include someone from outside the process area who can provide a more objective, or different, view. Supplier or customer personnel also often are invited to participate when their input is deemed especially valuable.

Selection of team members for organizational management and improvement is vital just as it is for a sports team. The many different activities to be carried out call for certain roles and responsibilities, which then require a certain set of skills and/or mind-set. For example, a team needs to analyze process data, minimize disruptive conflict, monitor meeting time effectiveness, and maintain records of activities. Specific roles, timekeeper and scribe, are usually defined for individuals who will carry out the latter two of these responsibilities.

Support Mechanisms Required for Team Success

Team-based improvement requires more than creating teams—it requires providing them with adequate support to ensure success. Examples of support include:

• *Equipment.* Teams need meeting space, equipment (such as tables and chairs and flipcharts), and access to computer hardware and software (for writing up meeting minutes, analyzing process data, preparing presentation materials).

• *Training.* Unless an organization is extremely lucky, most employees who become involved in teams will not have all of the necessary skills. Such skills may include how to plan and effectively manage meetings, how to analyze processes and data, and how to make group decisions based on consensus. The organization must therefore determine the specific skills required and the current skill levels of employees, and provide opportunities to close the gap.

• *Management sponsor.* The sponsor role is a vital leadership function that goes beyond simply launching a team. It also includes staying in contact with the team leader to ensure sufficient progress and resolving any conflicting issues with other parts of the organization. The sponsor typically has authority to cross organizational boundaries that team members would need to negotiate and can therefore resolve some types of issues quicker. The sponsor also is ultimately responsible for effective implementation of the team's recommendations.

• *Systems change.* Setting up a new team in an organization that is not adequately designed for this way of working is a prescription for failure. An organization is a system, meaning that if one part is changed, other parts will be affected. If the primary management style is autocratic and people are rewarded for competition versus cooperation, teams are unlikely to be an effective mechanism. Before beginning the team process, leadership must consider what other changes will be necessary to align the various parts of the organization. How team success will be recognized and rewarded is an especially vital component.

Team Development

Each new team is a new mini-organization. The team will therefore progress— and often regress—through the traditional stages of group development that are described briefly here:

• *Stage 1: forming.* When teams first begin to meet, each member brings his/ her individual identity and the perspective of their own environment (for example, functional process area). Even for members who have participated in other teams, each team is a unique experience and individuals often approach it cautiously, uncertain of how they will perform in the new situation. During the forming stage, a team usually clarifies its mission, specifies roles that need to be carried out and who is to perform them, and defines rules of acceptable behavior, often called norms.

• *Stage 2: storming.* During this phase, team members finally realize the size of the task before them. They still think primarily as individuals and often attempt to shape decisions to their own advantage rather than considering the impact on other team members. Arguments, testing the leader's authority, and attempts to change the team's mission are typical behaviors.

• *Stage 3: norming.* In this phase, the individuals begin to shift their focus from personal concerns to that of helping the team meet the challenge at hand. Interpersonal conflicts and the tug of external loyalties have less of an impact as team members realize their interdependence. They are more willing to discuss differences of opinion in order to understand them and how they might impact team success.

• *Stage 4: performing.* At this stage, the team has matured to the point where it is working as a smooth cohesive unit. Team members have a good understanding of each other's strengths and weaknesses and how they support the mission and are now able to work through group conflict. There is a greater appreciation of the importance of the team's processes and members are more satisfied with being a member of the team. During this phase, the team typically makes significant progress toward achieving its goals.

Although these stages indicate a logical sequence that occurs over time, actual progress by a particular team will vary greatly. For example, a team that has progressed to stage 3 or 4 may fall back to stage 1 or 2 if they find that some previous assumptions about one another are not true or if team membership changes as a result of a job transfer. Some teams may not progress beyond the earlier stages due to a short project duration or if they are unable to successfully resolve group dynamics issues.

Team development can be enhanced by making sure that team members have a basic understanding of how to: (1) interact in positive ways, (2) deal with difficult people or situations, (3) contribute to accomplishing the team's goals, and (4) give or receive constructive feedback. A facilitator can help ensure that the team is aware of its progress by commenting during meetings but special interventions are also sometimes useful. Examples include simulations or outdoor adventures that allow the group members to become more familiar with each other's styles, strengths, and weaknesses, and to become more effective at working with and through their differences.

LEADING QUALITY INITIATIVES

A quality engineer is frequently called on to lead particular quality initiatives. Such projects might involve improving an existing product or service, working to resolve supplier performance issues, addressing product field performance failures, implementing new measurement technology, or obtaining ISO 9001 quality system registration.

Following are some recommendations for leadership of such initiatives. Most are appropriate whether or not the project is a team-based initiative, because, by definition, most initiatives will influence others in the organization (and/or the supply chain), and the roles of others should therefore be taken into account throughout the project.

- Ensure that the project mission is clear, including expected results, timing, limitations, and reporting structure and methods. Obtain supporting data used to indicate the value of the project and determine how the project is related to the bigger picture (for example, strategic plan, other projects, and/or day-to-day operations).

- Determine who the other players in the project will be and make contact with them individually. Learn of their interest in and commitment to the project.

- Define the technical process and the time schedule to be used to carry out the initiative. For example, a problem-solving project might use a seven-step problem-solving process, while a Six Sigma project might use the DMAIC process (see Chapter 29.)

- Execute the project according to the process defined in the previous step, involving others as appropriate and keeping management informed.

- Evaluate outcomes of the project against the original mission. Ensure that all people involved receive appropriate recognition for their contributions.

Most of these steps are basic to effective project management. However, a significant portion of the impact of such initiatives also will be related to the quality of leadership demonstrated throughout the project. Following are some useful guidelines:

- Ensure that all involved understand the mission, the goals, and the project objectives and how the team fits with the bigger picture.

- Understand that all people—and organizations—involved will have their own priorities, perspectives, and skills. Learn what they are, recognize the validity of the differences, and find ways to integrate them effectively.

- Be aware of your own strengths and weaknesses and how they can affect project success. Find ways to learn from and utilize the skills of others to compensate. Also, provide as many opportunities as possible for other project personnel to utilize their full capability and to develop new skills.

- Communicate, communicate, communicate. People tend to fill gaps in their understanding with their own bias or fears, so keep the gaps to a minimum.

- Be a role model by emphasizing and demonstrating the importance of high-quality work.

Additionally, a quality engineer will frequently be called on for technical advice regarding particular methods for process analysis, such as conducting a process failure mode and effects analysis (see Chapter 17). Although they may not be in a leadership role, they must still understand these principles.

Chapter 5

E. Facilitation Principles and Techniques

Define and describe the facilitator's role and responsibilities on a team. Define and apply various tools used with teams, including brainstorming, nominal group technique, conflict resolution, force-field analysis, etc. (Analyze)

Body of Knowledge I.E

FACILITATOR ROLES AND RESPONSIBILITIES IN THE TEAM ENVIRONMENT

Concurrent with the development of teams was the emergence of the facilitator as a key organizational player. Teams and facilitators go together like love and marriage, horse and carriage. Whereas the old fashioned "boss" would simply *tell* workers what was to be done, the facilitator must understand the objectives, needs of, and constraints on the team.

Purposes of Facilitation

In an ideal world there would be no need for facilitators. Everyone would have the skills necessary for their roles and would work effectively with everyone else. However, it is not an ideal world, since all of us are continually learning. The role of facilitator is therefore a valuable one since it allows special additional skills to be readily available to the team.

A facilitator's primary mission is to ensure that a team is successful, but this must be done in a way that ensures that the team, not the facilitator, is responsible for the outcome. A really successful facilitator is one that is continually working him/herself out of the role through helping the team develop higher and higher levels of competency.

The facilitator is termed a marginal role, since facilitators are not actually members of the team with which they are working. However, facilitators usually are present at most or all of the team's meetings and their role is to provide support that helps the team work better. Simple examples of this support include notifying the team that they have veered off the meeting agenda, have jumped to a conclusion without any supporting data, or are not allowing all team members to voice their opinions.

Different Facilitator Roles

Facilitators usually take one of two major roles with a team. One is that of meeting manager, whereby the facilitator is actually guiding the team through the agenda and flipcharting discussions that occur. The other is that of an observer, where the facilitator sits quietly to the side and simply comments when it seems necessary or useful to further team progress. The observer role also provides the opportunity to gain information that can be used to coach the team leader in team process skills.

An important distinction, though, is that facilitators do not discuss content issues, only process issues. For example, if a team were trying to reduce the amount of time patients spend in the waiting room of a healthcare clinic, the facilitator would not interject comments such as, "Should we change the patient scheduling process?" since it is relative to technical content of the subject matter. However, at the appropriate time the facilitator might ask, "What are some additional ways that the time could be reduced?" since it only involves ensuring that the team has taken a broad view of potential opportunities.

It is not necessary that facilitators be someone from outside the team. The team leader or a specific team member who has sufficient skills and experience may also take on the role of facilitator. In this case, the facilitator is allowed to contribute content, because the person is in fact a bona fide member of the team. The ultimate objective, of course, is for all teams to be fully capable of working without the need for anyone in a designated facilitation role. Each member simply pays attention to both content and process issues and ensures that the team works effectively.

What a Facilitator Pays Attention To

Because a facilitator tries to help the team be more effective, there is a wide range of issues to consider. Here is a list of just a few of the items that facilitators must pay attention to:

- *Meeting agenda.* Is there an agenda for each meeting, and does the team follow it?

- *Communication.* Do team members listen to and discuss each other's opinions, or does each simply state his or her own? Are discussions on a positive note or does negativity sap people's energy? Does everyone have the opportunity to speak, does the team leader appear to give more attention to some, or do some individuals dominate?

- *Technical process model.* Has the team engaged in procedural conflict— negotiating the where, when, how, and why issues, such as defining the steps they are going to use to carry out the project (for example, a seven-step problem-solving model, if appropriate), or are they simply wandering around with no defined direction?

- *Conflict.* Is there interpersonal or procedural conflict between group members that prevents them from working together effectively? Is all conflict being suppressed, which causes ideas to be withheld? Is substantive conflict—deferring consensus when discussing ideas to get to the best ideas—encouraged?

- *Decision making.* Does the team make decisions based on data, or do they jump to conclusions? Is consensus used when the decision is one that requires everyone's commitment?

- *Follow-up.* Does the group identify action items, then ensure that they are carried out?

Skills Required of a Facilitator

An effective facilitator must have a broad range of capabilities. Three of the most important are:

- *Meeting management skills.* A facilitator should know how to run meetings in a manner that effectively uses the time available. In many ways, meetings are like mini-projects, with a mission (purpose of the meeting), technical process (meeting agenda), and boundaries (meeting duration). In addition, since meetings consist primarily of discussion, the ability to communicate effectively is vital.

- *People skills.* Since each person brings his/her own background, skills, and priorities to meetings, the ability to understand and work with different perspectives is critical for a facilitator. An understanding of psychology (both individual and social) and methods for change (for example, from the field of organization development) are therefore valuable.

- *Technical process analysis skills.* Improvement of processes involves analysis of processes. An understanding of the seven basic QC tools, the seven management tools, statistical process control, and design of experiments gives a facilitator a wide range of tools that can be introduced at an appropriate time. (These tools are all discussed in Parts V and VI.) Perhaps the most important knowledge for facilitators is also the most difficult to obtain: understanding themselves. It is difficult to understand others if you do not understand yourself, because you may make interpretations using filters of which you are unaware. An effective facilitator must be able to sort out the difference between whether a particular intervention is being done because of the needs of the team or the needs of the facilitator. If the latter, it's being done for the wrong reason.

Ways of Intervening

When facilitators believe that the team should change the way they are working, they can select from several different ways of bringing the need to change to the attention of the team. The particular method the facilitator chooses often will depend on a combination of the facilitator's personal style, level of comfort with the team, and how the team has responded to previous interventions. Following are some of the different ways to intervene:

- *Tell them.* The easiest way is simply to tell the team either what they are doing wrong or what they need to do differently. For minor issues this is a quick and probably safe intervention but may cause more resistance with some teams since it can be interpreted as being a bit authoritative.

- *State observations.* A slightly more discreet way of intervening is for the facilitator to simply state what he/she is seeing that the team may want to do differently. This puts the information in front of the team, allowing them to decide whether or not to pay attention to it.

- *Have them explore.* Another choice is to ask the team to think about what they are doing at the moment (and perhaps frame the context of the issue, for example, whether it is relative to communications or agenda issues). Although this method takes more time, it causes the team to take more ownership of the intervention, meaning that learning is more likely to be internalized.

Perhaps it is clear from some of the above discussion but it is worth emphasizing again: it is vital for the team to have ownership of decisions that are made regarding content and, when possible, also of team process decisions. A facilitator who gets glory from making such decisions for the team simply reduces the likelihood of the team learning from and being committed to the team process.

There are, however, situations when facilitators have a higher level of involvement than has been presented here. For example, with kaizen blitz teams, which typically last three to five days, acceleration of the improvement process comes about partially due to reducing concerns over how decisions are made. The facilitator in such projects usually has much more authority to specify the direction the team will take.

IDEA PROCESSING AND DECISION MAKING

Most people are familiar with brainstorming as a means of generating many ideas in a short period of time to identify solutions to problems. Groups and teams can use both structured and unstructured brainstorming methods.

For unstructured brainstorming, a topic is agreed on and written in front of the group. The leader/facilitator then asks for ideas to be randomly called out and all are recorded without any discussion. When the flow of ideas stops, the list is reviewed and discussed, which may result in the elimination or combination of some.

A structured approach involves a round-robin process whereby each person in the group is asked to state one idea. If a person has none, he/she passes and the next person is asked, and so on. When everyone has passed on a round the brainstorming is complete. A similar process can be used by posting several sheets of paper around the room with a topic or problem at the top of each. Each team member goes to one sheet and writes down ideas that come to mind, then the members rotate repeatedly until all have contributed to each sheet. Another alternative is to simply circulate sheets of paper among the group.

Another method of brainstorming, called *Crawford slip,* is especially useful when the team is working on a particularly sensitive topic or when the team does not yet have a high level of trust. All the team members are asked to record their

Part I.E

ideas on pieces of paper that are then given to a trusted individual (for example, facilitator) who compiles all the items into a single list (for example, on a flip-chart). The anonymous nature of this method helps people feel freer to include their ideas, and the team often finds that several members had the same idea, which begins to build cohesiveness.

Nominal Group Technique

Nominal group technique is one way of processing lists of brainstormed items. It involves using the following steps to reduce a large list to a shorter one:

1. Ask each participant to rank the items in numeric order (for example, 1 is best to 8 is worst in a list of eight items).

2. Record the ranks of all participants beside each item.

3. Total the rankings for each item. Those with the lowest totals are the preferred options.

Figure 5.1 shows an example applied by a group of course participants who were trying to decide where to go for lunch. Of the four choices, Marlow's received the lowest total (therefore the highest priority) and was then the group's first choice.

Multivoting. Another way to narrow down a list of items is to have the group select from the list only those that they prefer. The number they are to select is usually approximately one-half of the total number. After all participants have made their selection, the facilitator asks how many participants voted for each option, and records this. The Pareto principle will usually work, with some of the options getting very few votes; they are then dropped from the list. The voting process is then repeated until the desired number of items remains. Figure 5.2 shows multivoting on a larger version of the lunch selection problem. Five people are voting, and in the third round of voting Grunge Café finally emerges as the winner by a 4:1 margin.

Resolving Conflict

Most people identify conflict as a problem to be solved, as something that is inevitable—and undesirable—in teams and only comes about when two or more people have ideas that appear to be totally different and where it is perceived that

Restaurant	Individuals and rankings					
	Tom	**Joe**	**Mary**	**Sue**	**Terry**	**Total**
Marlow's	1	2	3	1	2	9
Grunge Café	3	1	1	2	3	10
Stew & Brew	2	4	2	4	4	16
Fancaé	4	3	4	3	1	15

Figure 5.1   Nominal group technique ranking table.

Restaurant	First vote (select 4)	Second vote (select 3)	Third vote (select 1)
~~Pizzas R Us~~	~~2~~		
~~Marlow's~~	~~4~~	~~3~~	
~~Alice's Restaurant~~	~~1~~		
Grunge Café	5	5	4
~~Mom's Diner~~	~~0~~		
~~Stew & Brew~~	~~3~~	~~2~~	
~~Fancaé~~	~~5~~	~~5~~	~~1~~

Figure 5.2   Multivoting.

a choice must be made between them. In reality, however, two kinds of conflict—*substantive* conflict and *procedural* conflict—can actually enhance teamwork. A third kind, *affective* or *interpersonal* conflict, results when team members "allow personal feelings to negatively affect group interaction" (Burnett 2005), such as when hidden biases surface, normally inconsequential behaviors become irritants, or past slights or unresolved issues spill over into team interaction. Dealing directly with affective conflict means that a facilitator or other team member either reminds the team of its common goal or puts the grievances on the table in as neutral a fashion as possible to defuse the situation or negotiate a compromise that will allow the team to function.

Negotiation is a key to resolving procedural conflict, especially when a team is first convened, at key points in reaching an objective or goal, and at the beginnings of project meetings. As the name suggests, procedural conflict has to do with how the group runs, and requires participants to be very clear, to write down and maintain group memory documents that keep track of where and when the team will meet, who will take on certain roles (such as team leader, recorder, time manager, devil's advocate), what procedures and tools the team will use (such as consensus versus voting, flipcharts versus an intranet), and the anticipated time line for meeting the team's objectives. All of these issues are important and some may need to be renegotiated on an ongoing basis to keep the group running smoothly.

By engaging in substantive conflict, teams actively work at avoiding hasty consensus (such as jumping on the first idea instead of waiting for possibly better alternatives or making a decision before everyone has had a chance to give input). Teams can use three strategies to defer consensus:

- *Elaborate key ideas* by adding details, examples, or explanations. Remember that one good idea can spark several other good ideas, which means the team has more choices.

- *Consider alternatives* by adding to an idea or exploring an idea that has not been previously considered. One team member might add details to help another explain a suggestion or might restate the idea so that everyone understands.

- *Voice disagreements* to strengthen the product or process. Remember that disagreeing does not mean you do not like someone; in fact, disagreeing about ideas can mean that you are sufficiently engaged to notice strengths and weaknesses (Gillette et al. 1993).

The following guidelines incorporate each of the three kinds of conflict:

- Encourage people to exchange ideas freely before coming to a decision

- Treat the discussion as a problem to be solved instead of an attack on a person

- Take the time to attend to housekeeping issues such as regular breaks, room temperature, and sufficient supplies of necessary items (paper, pens, tissues)

- Consider—and keep records of—the benefits and drawbacks of each option

- Keep the team's goals and objectives—the team's common interests— on the front burner, especially when tempers run high

One difficulty is getting everyone on the team to really understand both what the others are saying and why it is important to them. When everyone understands and is willing to share their values and the assumptions underlying their positions, asking team members to restate in their own words what has been said helps ensure true understanding.

Time also is an ally for conflict resolution. If the issue is over a decision that can be delayed, the time between subsequent discussions may allow the players to not only cool off, but also to think over both their own positions and those of other team members. When all is said and done, many of the skills related to conflict are also communication skills.

Chapter 6

F. Communication Skills

> Describe and distinguish between various communication methods for delivering information and messages in a variety of situations across all levels of the organization. (Analyze)
>
> Body of Knowledge I.F

Every communication interaction is unique in terms of purpose, context, mode of communication, and people involved. Therefore, within this section the terms *audience, reader, listener,* and *customer* are used interchangeably as are the terms *speaker* and *writer.*

THE NEED FOR COMMUNICATION SKILLS

Communication skills are essential for success whether measured by promotion or by higher-quality processes and products. Only the rarest job does not require excellent communication skills. In the quality field, effective communication is essential in order for everyone to understand and have a sense of ownership of the common vision. Every employee must be aware of objectives and necessary actions that are required for successful quality initiatives within the organization. Common goals are a unifying factor in virtually all successful teams. The complex communication skills required to accomplish complex goals and objectives require comprehensive understanding of communication theory and practice.

Communication is a key to leadership. Leaders must establish a vision, communicate that vision to those in the organization, and provide the tools and knowledge necessary to accomplish the vision. So good leaders understand and employ efficient and effective communication in order to achieve this goal. Remember that leadership is needed at all levels of the organization.

CREATING A SHARED VISION

In order to accomplish a stated goal, all members involved in reaching that goal must understand and be committed to achieving that goal. One way to achieve understanding and commitment is to include all members in the complete process. Members of effective teams feel some ownership of programs and projects when they understand goals, objectives, and/or mutually well-understood expectations and are given access to needed information and resources.

To create understanding and commitment, leaders employ skills such as clear formulation of a concept, emphasis of key points, repetition, and summarization. Multiple channels are absolutely vital to convey our message in the intricate information world we inhabit. Every listener/reader is bombarded with communication from myriad sources all day (and most of the night) long.

Types of written communication include queries, directives, memos, summaries of meeting, formal and informal letters, planning agendas, invitations, apologies, e-mail and public documents. The use of paper (hard copy) is still sometimes required for archival and legal reasons. Clear and unambiguous writing is an essential skill. Practice and seeking out of constructive feedback are essential.

Types of oral communication include interviews, formal speeches, conversation, debate, directives, briefings, and public announcements. Every successful quality engineer will master both discussion skills and presentation skills. The ability to analyze and organize information and to present this information orally will consistently reap rewards.

COMMUNICATION PROCESS

The term "to communicate" comes from the Latin *communicat(us)* meaning to impart or make common. When we communicate we try to establish a coming together or common ground with someone. We share information, ideas, and attitudes in an attempt to establish a link or joining together with another. We give or exchange thoughts, feeling, information, and ideas. However, the communicator must know something about the receiver in order to link the message with the receiver. The message must be joined from the sender to the receiver by thought, word, or deed in order to facilitate comprehension followed by action. The greater the areas of common experience and understanding that the sender and the receiver share, the greater the possibility for successful communication. This means that communication is greatly enhanced by repetitive contact and sharing.

Human communication is dynamic and ever changing. It is irreversible in that once it is transmitted and received it can never be totally forgotten or erased from memory. It is interactive in that it must be shared. It exists within a context both social and cultural, never in a vacuum. Our ability to communicate is the strongest force that makes us human beings and should be treated with utmost respect.

Aristotle

The importance of communication to human interactions has a long history dating back to the time of Aristotle in ancient Greece about 550 BCE. His book *The Rhetoric* defined rhetoric as "the faculty of discovering in any given case all the available means of persuasion." Rhetoric was the most powerful technology of his time because most communication was spoken. Carefully crafted rhetoric gradually replaced physical combat as the most effective way to persuade others to change their behavior. Decisions were made and actions were taken because of the strength of a given speech.

Although the means by which we communicate have expanded to include written, visual, and electronic means, understanding the three basic rhetorical principles as set forth by this ancient Greek scholar can help quality professionals communicate. The three interrelated and equally important dimensions of the rhetorical process are *ethos, logos,* and *pathos.* These principles are equally important to both oral and written communication.

Ethos. Often defined as credibility but has a much fuller meaning. The dimensions of credibility are competence, character, goodness, decency and trustworthiness, composure, sociability, dynamic extroversion, and a sense of purpose. (Effective communication is deep, subtle, and complex!)

Logos. Logic, evidence, sequence of thought, building up of the case in a pleasing manner that enhances comprehension. It means giving an idea order and form.

Pathos. The appeal to emotions. It implies a reaching out to our common bond of feelings and our innate sense of being human. It comprises our compassion, our values, and feelings about ourselves and others. The use of pathos has the ability to create in us a deeply felt response.

These three dimensions cannot be studied or learned in isolation because they are tied together and of equal importance in attempting to persuade another to understand and accept the message being presented. Effective communication relies on these three dimensions—credibility, logic, and emotion—being blended together in a coherent way. As a quality engineer you rely heavily on the discovery and organization of data, facts, and evidence—systematically collecting, analyzing, and organizing the material (logos). In addition, your authority, expertise, character, and reputation enhance the believability of your message (ethos). When this message is then framed to appeal to the emotional state of your receiver (pathos), you have a compelling triad.

An effective speaker is trustworthy and believable, has a well-organized, factual (coherent) message, is respectful to the listener, and appeals to their most salient feelings on the topic. All three methods of appeal—ethos, logos, and pathos—work together to promote the acceptance of the message. Once the message is accepted, cohesion (sticking-together) occurs in the mind of the listener, and the shared vision can be realized.

Active Listening

Hearing what is said is not the same as actively listening to what is said. Hearing is simply the act of perceiving the sound and is largely involuntary. Listening is a selected activity that involves the reception and the interpretation of the sound and decoding of the sound into meaning. Active listening is much more difficult than one would assume and requires effort and concentration. The sender of a message has the responsibility to use all available means to construct the message that will have the best possible opportunity to be adequately received and understood as intended. The receiver has the responsibility to be open and actively ready to receive and attempt to comprehend the message. This exchange is the essence of communication. This shared responsibility is marked by active participation on both sides.

Individuals speak at 100 to 175 words per minute but they can listen intelligently at 600 to 800 words per minute. Since it is possible to receive so much faster than the message can be produced orally there often is a tendency to allow our thoughts to drift to other things. This is why it takes effort and focus to hold attention on the message being sent. Active listening means to listen with purpose and concentration. The receiver decides to listen closely to gain information, obtain direction, understand others, solve problems, share interests, see how another feels, show support, and so on. It requires as much energy to listen actively as it does to construct and send the message.

Dimensions of Active Listening

Dimensions of active listening include listening to understand, confirm, support, clarify, and diminish defensiveness. Listening to understand will not always mean agreement. Rather it means trying to grasp fully what is being sent from the point of view, feelings, and experiences of the sender. It involves paraphrasing and perception checking, which includes saying in your own words how you have interpreted the other person's ideas and feelings and asking if your statement is correct. This is done to ensure that your understanding is accurate. Listening to confirm includes behavior that indicates to the sender that you are attending to the message and accepting the point of view expressed even though you may not agree. Your actions indicate that you value the person and the message that is being transmitted. This is frequently done while the message is being sent by nonverbal means such as looking at the sender, nodding, and positive facial expressions. Diminishing defensiveness as a listener also is accomplished nonverbally while the message is being sent by refraining from turning away, closing your eyes, agitated movement of your body, or negative facial expressions. Immediate verbal evaluations or interruptions of the message also will create defensiveness in the sender and should be avoided. Active listening requires the listener to hear the message, understand the meaning, and then verify the meaning by offering feedback both verbally and nonverbally.

Feedback

Feedback is an important component of the communication interaction. It provides the opportunity for clarification and in-depth understanding. There are five main categories of feedback, listed following in the order in which they most frequently occur in communication exchanges:

1. *Evaluation.* Making judgment about the worth, goodness, or appropriateness of the statement.

2. *Interpretation.* Paraphrasing or perception checking as a means of clarification.

3. *Support.* Confirming behavior that encourages the sender to continue to communicate.

4. *Probing.* Attempting to gain additional information, continue the discussion, or clarify a point.

5. *Understanding.* Trying to discover completely what the sender of the message intends or means by the message.

Of all these five feedback methods, evaluation is the one that must be used with the most care. Insensitive evaluation will create defensiveness in the sender and may break the communication process. There are several ways for the listener to diminish this potential defensiveness:

1. Limit negative evaluations

2. Keep evaluations honestly positive

3. Postpone specific evaluations

4. Keep evaluations tentative

5. Own your own statements

6. Ask for responses to your evaluations

Being an active listener and supplying adequate feedback provide the important other half of the communication process. It holds equal responsibility with the sender for the successful transaction. It is what allows the message to be accepted and the unifying vision to be implemented.

Chapter 7

G. Customer Relations

Define, apply, and analyze the results of customer relation measures such as quality function deployment (QFD), customer satisfaction surveys, etc. (Analyze)

Body of Knowledge I.G

Customers can be found both internally and externally to the organization, and you must find some way of communicating with your customers on a regular basis. In studies conducted for a number of years, Collins and Porras (1997) point out that the best-of-the-best companies (visionaries) in their respective industries have developed systems that transcend dependence on any single leader or great idea to build an enduring, great human institution that has lasted and will last for decades. Many of these companies have stumbled along the way but somehow find a way to come back, providing the customer or client the products or services that are wanted and/or needed. The true secret seems to be to try a lot of things, keeping those that work and stopping those that do not, and continually checking back with the customer to see if anything has changed, thus starting the process over.

CUSTOMER NEEDS AND WANTS

Your organizational objectives should be to ensure that customers want and need your products and/or services. As Perry (1998) states, "Staying in direct, face-to-face contact with customers, in their world, is the surest way to combat organizational myopia." Far too often, a system is developed and people in that system "expect" customers to conform to the way things are done by the supplier organization. This occurs everywhere from the corner grocery store to other retail outlets, from schools to manufacturing organizations. How often have you seen cartoons with the central theme of "if it wasn't for the unrealistic customers, this would be a great place to work?"

The quality engineer's job (either manufacturing or service based) is to help the organization see that the customers are their reason for existence, versus the other way around. This goes beyond just collecting a sample of information (surveys, focus group meetings, plant visits, and so on). Everyone has seen the customer survey cards at hotels and restaurants that ask about customer satisfaction. But what is the validity of such an effort when considering issues such as response rate and nonrandomness of response? A four-stage model for evaluating training events devised by Kirkpatrick (1998) (discussed in more detail in Chapter 15) would categorize this kind of data-gathering effort—and its validity—as reaction, or level one evaluation. Some consider these tools to be "smiley sheets," a pejorative term referencing the halo effect that has been noted in research resulting from the glow of the moment of the event or because the participant wants the researcher to feel good. The real question for the quality engineer should be, "What do my customers think after using the product or service for some period of time in actual real-world settings, and what are they telling other people about my organization?"

QUALITY FUNCTION DEPLOYMENT

Quality function deployment (QFD) is a powerful planning technique, perhaps the most comprehensive ever invented for quality planning. QFD is especially suited to large-scale products such as airplanes, automobiles, and major appliances. These products have heavy tooling, high design costs, and many optional features that must be selected and then produced or procured. QFD was introduced into American industry in the 1980s by the American Supplier Institute of Livonia, Michigan, which remains one of the organizations that actively promotes its usage.

Definitions and Concepts of QFD

The six key terms associated with QFD (Sullivan 1986) are:

1. *Quality function deployment.* An overall concept that provides a means of translating customer requirements into the appropriate technical requirements for each stage of product development and production (that is, marketing strategies, planning, product design and engineering, prototype evaluation, production process development, production, and sales).

2. *The voice of the customer (VOC).* The customers' requirements expressed in their own terms.

3. *Counterpart characteristics.* An expression of the customer's voice in technical language that specifies customer-required quality.

4. *Product quality deployment.* Activities needed to translate the voice of the customer into counterpart characteristics.

5. *Deployment of the quality function.* Activities needed to assure that customer-required quality is achieved; the assignment of specific quality responsibilities to specific departments. (Note: any activity needed to assure that quality is achieved is a quality function, no matter which department performs it.)

6. *Quality tables.* A series of matrices used to translate the voice of the customer into final product control characteristics.

Sometimes it is possible to incorporate all of the key relationships into a simple diagram called the *house of quality* because of its distinctive shape. Figure 7.1 shows such a diagram, which resembles a house with a pitched roof.

For comprehensive coverage of more than 30 different planning tools grouped under QFD, see King (1987). A typical project will require only a few of these. The following QFD documents are most common:

1. Customer requirements planning matrix

2. Design matrix

3. Final product characteristic deployment matrix

4. Manufacturing/purchasing matrix

5. Process plan and quality control charts

6. Operating instructions

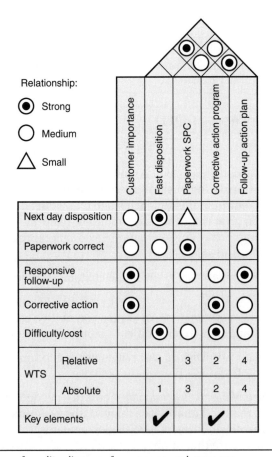

Figure 7.1   QFD house of quality diagram for a paperwork process.

Application of QFD: The Basics

By applying QFD, customers' expectations are translated into directly related job requirements. The objective is improved customer satisfaction at acceptable cost. The basic relationship is displayed in the input–output matrix shown in Figure 7.2. This matrix—only one of many in QFD—organizes the process of determining relationships between what the customers want (usually described in nontechnical terms) and how the supplier satisfies these wants. Wants fall into three categories: must have, expected to have, and would like to have. Numerical measures are highly desirable. The wants must be specified in sufficient detail to ensure they are clearly understood. Although customers may or may not be involved in setting the requirements, their satisfaction will depend on identifying and meeting their wants.

The hows are the technical details of each job. The strength of each relationship may be strong, medium, or small, as shown in Figures 7.1 and 7.3. These symbols can be converted to weights, such as strong = 5, medium = 3, and small = 1. The weights will convert to scores indicating how important each job requirement is. At the top of the requirements matrix, a correlation matrix is added to show the strengths of the relationships among the different job requirements. A small example is shown in Figure 7.1 for a paper improvement project, and a more complex example of a car door design is depicted in Figure 7.3.

QFD as a planning technique has brought significant benefits:

1. Product objectives based on customer requirements are not misinterpreted at subsequent stages.

2. Particular marketing strategies or sales points do not become lost or blurred during the translation process from marketing through planning and on to execution.

3. Important production control points are not overlooked.

4. Efficiency is increased because misinterpretations are minimized.

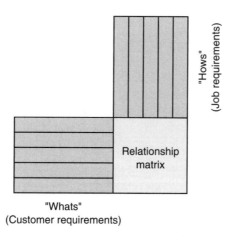

Figure 7.2   Input–output requirements matrix.

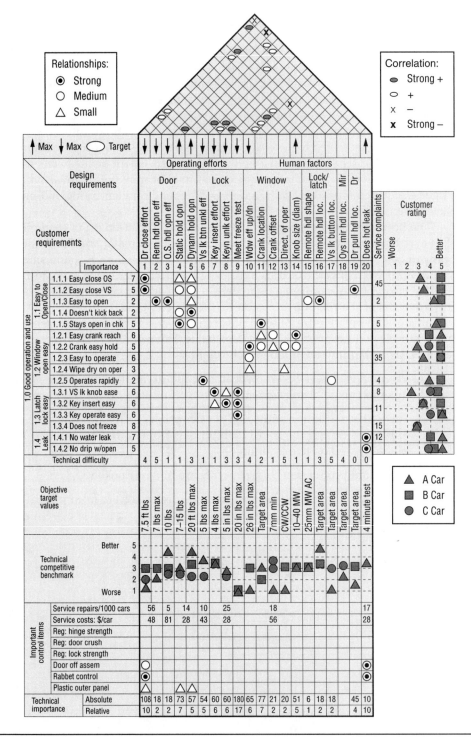

Figure 7.3   House of quality for a car door.

Customer Value Analysis

Gale and Wood (1994) describe seven tools of customer value analysis:

1. The market-perceived quality profile ("indicator of how well you are performing overall for customers in your targeted market")

2. The market-perceived price profile (a weighted indicator of how customers perceive different competitors' performance on given price attributes)

3. The customer value map (a "map that reveals a sizable cluster of business units receiving premium prices that are not fully supported by superior perceived quality")

4. The won/lost analysis (an analysis of those factors that won or lost the sale)

5. The head-to-head area chart of customer value (a "chart of customer value displaying where you are doing well and where you do worse against a single competitor")

6. The key events timeline (a chronological list of the events which changed the market's perception of performance on each quality attribute, yours and your competitor's)

7. A what/who matrix ("a method for tracking who is responsible for the actions that will make success in customer value possible")

Using these tools will "enable an organization to navigate strategically even in confusing times. . . ." Numerous factors represent value to different customers under a variety of situations. The characteristics shown in Table 7.1 illustrate different perspectives on what the customer considers important.

Table 7.1   Customer perspectives of *value*.

Characteristics—product (examples)	Performance Reasonable price Durability Safety	Serviceability Ease/flexibility of use Simplicity of design, aesthetics Ease of disposal
Characteristics—service (examples)	Responsiveness Reliability Competence Access Courtesy Communication (sensitivity, genuine interest/concern)	Credibility/image Confidentiality/security Understanding the customer Accuracy/completeness Timeliness

CUSTOMER-DRIVEN QUALITY

A growing number of approaches focus on greater understanding of and inter-action with customers. The two types of customer-driven quality, reactive and planned, are proving to be successful in improving quality but still do not guaran-tee customer satisfaction (Foster 1998). Reactive customer-driven quality (RCDQ) responds to customer requirements after the fact. Planned customer-driven qual-ity, on the other hand, is anticipatory and proactive in that it assesses customer needs and seeks methods for satisfying those needs before the fact. Any organi-zation wanting to meet customer expectations is pursuing a moving target. The reactive nature of the RCDQ approach will cause the supplier to fall behind the moving target.

Planned customer-driven quality is best accomplished using some form of strategic quality planning (SQP). This is not necessarily the same as the strategic planning process, however, and is one reason that the Malcolm Baldrige National Quality Award changed the name of the SQP category to strategic planning to counter the sense that some quality professionals had too narrow a focus on com-pany competitiveness in the marketplace.

With any given effort to become a customer-driven company, an organization needs to study what they do and how they look to their customers. One list of top 10 key characteristics of customer-focused companies includes:

1. *Total consumer experience.* The ability to look at the customer from all angles of how the organization's products and services are experienced in the real world. Look for every possible point of contact with the customer to collect information on what is happening in the field.

2. *Product hits.* Use of the Kano model to continuously delight the customer with new products and services, some of which the customer may not even have known that they wanted.

3. *Consumer loyalty.* Building a sustained momentum over time to the point where the customer will only use your product or service, even waiting, if necessary, to get the "real thing."

4. *Retailing and distribution.* Creating a win–win–win for your organization, distributors, and customers. Your distribution system is a customer as well.

5. *Brand process.* The creation of recognized products or services that are sought after in the marketplace.

6. *Logistics.* Providing just-in-time and just what is needed/wanted in the marketplace at point of usage.

7. *Build to demand.* Creating a lean process that is capable of rapid changeovers to give the customers the needed products and services as they want them (just in time). This process has to be built into the entire system from suppliers, through production to the ultimate customer.

8. *Consumer knowledge system.* Continuous information gathering of customers' expectations and wants that feed into the system; used to look for continual improvement opportunities.

9. *E-commerce.* Becoming interactive, offering distribution, selling, and constant communication with customers online.

10. *Growth.* Continually improving with faster service, better value, and higher quality to create a culture that uses creativity and innovations to improve customer satisfaction.

To summarize this chapter: there is no sure way to always satisfy or delight customers because we cannot talk to every individual customer that we have and because customers are constantly changing their minds about what they need or expect. So we must find ways to continuously talk with many customers using the techniques we can. With today's technology this should become easier, but will the quality engineer be able to ensure that the information received is good enough to make sound predictions? The challenge is to keep the process both simple and informative. (See Chapter 2 for more details on quality information systems.)

Chapter 8

H. Supplier Management

Define, select, and apply various techniques including supplier qualification, certification, evaluation, ratings, performance improvement, and so on. (Analyze)

Body of Knowledge I.H

Many years ago, companies worked under the assumption that engineers designed products and specified requirements, suppliers provided materials, manufacturing built the products, and quality control inspected the product after it was made to assure quality. This approach was inherently wasteful. Beginning in the 1940s, the use of quality standards for suppliers has gradually evolved into a system that assures quality products that meet requirements with only a limited amount of inspection by quality control personnel. MIL-Q-9858, BS 5750, industry-specific (starting in the early 1960s), and ISO 9000 standards (see Chapter 12) have each made their contribution.

Quality assurance personnel now spend greater effort assuring that quality is built into products and that conformance is achieved during production. The lines are becoming more blurred as Six Sigma programs help everyone in the organization become concerned about quality and defect prevention. The same team cooperation and close communication used internally are now being applied to supplier relations. The goal is to assure that purchased items and materials conform to requirements without the need for extensive inspection upon receipt by the purchaser and that continual improvement is being practiced (Johnson and Webber 1985).

Suppliers also can be found both internally and externally to the organization, so the best advice is that you must find some way of communicating with all of your suppliers on a regular basis.

PROCUREMENT STANDARDS AND SPECIFICATIONS

Standards and specifications are documents containing criteria that must be met, and these documents become legally binding by reference on the purchase order. They define what is being purchased. They can be in the form of engineering drawings, catalog descriptions, or other documentation. It is important that the applicable standard or specification document be incorporated into the purchase order so there is no doubt that the requirements are to be met. If they are not incorporated, there is no basis for enforcing compliance.

The purchaser need not always develop original specifications. Commercial quality specifications are available and range from detailed engineering drawings (which may include references to process specifications, such as reliability verifications and inspection requirements) to off-the-shelf items (which are defined by the characteristics on the manufacturer's data sheet or catalog). Such commercial specifications help simplify the procurement process.

SURVEY VERSUS AUDIT VERSUS SAMPLING INSPECTION

At the superficial level, surveys, audits, and inspection are all about the same—they provide internal or external customers with a degree of confidence, but not absolute assurance, that the quality of the product or process is what it should be. However, each of these tools has its own distinctive characteristics.

Survey

The survey can be defined as a broad overview of a supplier's system and/or processes that is used to evaluate the adequacy of that system or processes to produce quality products (LaFord 1986). The system survey is used to assess whether the supplier has appropriately controlled systems that will adequately prevent the manufacture of nonconforming products. The process survey is used to evaluate whether a supplier has controls in place to ensure that the process will manufacture quality products. Process controls include proper tooling, equipment, inspection, and so on.

Audit

An audit can be defined as a systematic examination of the acts and decisions with respect to quality to independently verify or evaluate compliance to the operational requirements of the quality program, specifications, or contract requirements of the product or service (American National Standard 1978a). Note that the term compliance, often meaning compliance to documented procedures, is used instead of the term adequacy. Audits of a supplier's systems or processes can only be performed at the supplier's facility. Audits of a supplier's product may be performed either at the supplier's or customer's facility.

The system audit is a documented activity performed to verify, by examination and evaluation of objective evidence, that applicable elements of the quality system are suitable and have been developed, documented, and effectively implemented in accordance with specified requirements (American National Standard 1978a). The process audit is an analysis of elements of a process and appraisal of completeness, correctness, or conditions, and probable effectiveness.

The product audit is a quantitative assessment of conformance to required product characteristics. Simply stated, the product audit verifies that the system and processes used to produce the product are capable of producing a product that conforms to the established specifications/requirements. This should not be confused with the term inspection, which concerns the acceptance or rejection of the product or lot.

Sampling Inspection

Inspection is a process of measuring, examining, testing, gauging, or otherwise comparing the unit with the applicable requirements. Sampling inspection is somewhat comparable to survey and audit; 100 percent inspection is somewhat comparable to production line operation because each and every item is subjected to it. (See Chapter 23 for inspection and sampling.)

One hundred percent inspection is required in certain highly critical processes, and in processes that produce unavoidable defects, such as semiconductor fabrication. However, both Deming and Juran point out that 100 percent inspections done by humans are usually only around 80 percent effective. Thus in today's industrial environment, 100 percent inspections are nearly always automated.

Acceptance sampling is sampling where decisions are made to accept or reject a product or service based on the results of inspected samples.

Skip-lot inspection is an acceptance sampling plan in which some lots in a series are accepted without inspection because the sampling results for a stated number of immediately preceding lots met stated criteria. Explication of this methodology is found in American National Standard, ANSI/ASQC S1-1987.

Incoming inspection is the inspection of purchased parts at the customer's facility, after the shipment of parts from the supplier, to ensure supplier compliance with specifications and contractual agreements.

Source inspection is the inspection of purchased parts at the supplier's facility by a customer representative to ensure supplier compliance with specifications and contractual agreements.

SURVEYING THE SUPPLIER

The primary purpose of a survey of a supplier or potential supplier is to ascertain whether the supplier has: adequate financial resources (evaluated by purchasing), adequate manufacturing capabilities (evaluated by manufacturing engineering), and adequate quality systems (evaluated by the quality assurance group).

In preparing for the survey, the team leader should obtain as much information about the supplier as possible. The purchasing agent can provide copies of the supplier's annual reports, credit investigation, Dun & Bradstreet reports, Internet searches, and so on. A facilities and equipment list should be obtained for review by manufacturing engineering, and a copy of the supplier's quality manual must also be reviewed prior to the survey.

The survey team may be made up of members from purchasing, manufacturing, and quality control, plus various specialists in the areas of nondestructive testing, product design, or other special processes. At times, the team may consist of only the quality professional. In the latter case, the purchasing agent usually has previously evaluated the supplier's financial status.

It is important that the team meet prior to arriving at the supplier's facility. Based on the premise that the team has reviewed all pertinent materials, the presurvey meeting is held to: (1) assure that all of the team members agree on the theme and purpose of the survey, (2) assure that the roles and responsibilities of each team member are understood by the others, (3) draft a preliminary survey agenda, and (4) select the team leader. This meeting is too important to be scheduled at the last minute in the airport or in the hotel the evening prior to the survey.

The team leader must not overlook the obvious, such as the supplier's current address, name of host individual to contact, correct time and date for the survey, and so on. It is important that the team leader verify that the supplier is ready for the survey. Often it is appropriate to advise the supplier of the proposed agenda, allowing supplier representatives to prepare for the visit.

In order to quantify the results of a survey, there must be a formalized approach to collecting and evaluating the systems observed. The primary method of quantification is for the survey team to use a checklist(s) to record survey results. Checklists commonly used cover both procurement and manufacturing/quality aspects of a supplier's organization.

The manufacturing/quality checklists often are broken into the following categories:

1. Drawing and specification control

2. Purchased material control

3. Measuring and test equipment control

4. Process control and product acceptance

5. Material storage area, packing, shipping, and record retention control

6. Quality program management

7. Statistical process control

8. Strength summary of system survey

9. Corrective action summary of system survey

10. Summary report

The manufacturing/quality categories may be expanded as needed. An amplification of the listed categories can be found in Laford (1986).

The supplier procurement checklist often is broken down into the following categories:

1. General information

2. Product information

3. Facilities and equipment information

4. Sales, shipping, and payment information

The supplier procurement checklist categories may be expanded as needed. An amplification of the list can be found in Laford (1986).

The use of scoring (numerical, alphabetical, or other regularly sequenced scores) in a checklist further enhances quantification and validity of judgments. Many professional evaluators prefer to have the supplier also score a copy of the checklist in order to better compare the customer's viewpoint with that of the supplier's.

The opening conference is get-acquainted time. The survey team members should explain why they are there, what they are going to attempt to do, and, in a general way, the sort of results they expect. Each team member should explain his or her role in the survey and in the customer's organization. The team leader also should briefly explain the nature of the customer's products or services. It is essential that all levels of supplier management understand the scope and purpose of the survey (Vendor-Vendee Technical Committee 1977).

Each supplier representative present should explain his or her role in the supplier organization. At this time, the supplier representatives also should briefly describe the nature of the products manufactured and present an overview of the company and systems used. The opening conference also is a good time for the survey team to brief the supplier on the intended products to be purchased.

A brief plant tour will acquaint the survey team with the supplier's overall operations. Following the plant tour, the team members can proceed to their respective areas for evaluation. Each area should be evaluated in detail in accordance with the checklist and point scores recorded. It is imperative that each area be evaluated in the actual area and not in the conference room or manager's office. Furthermore, by being in the appropriate area, verbal statements of compliance and quality procedures can be verified by witnessing the action being performed. The survey team should discuss any negative findings with the supplier escort who was present during the finding to reconfirm the facts prior to the closing conference with supplier top management.

Prior to the closing conference, the survey team must meet to compile the report for that conference (this is not the final report). During the closing conference, the team leader should review each category, expressing the strengths and weaknesses observed. At this time it may be possible to estimate corrective actions required for deficiencies found if they have not already been addressed.

The closing conference must be kept on a positive note, with a win–win attitude on both sides, which requires careful attention to communication strategies and can challenge the team leader's communication skills. In the closing conference, the team leader should focus on the major deficiencies found, if any, and detail appropriate corrective actions. This should be followed by a brief mention of any minor deficiencies observed. All can be lost if the survey team presents an extensive list of minor observations with a few major deficiencies intertwined.

If at all possible, the survey team should leave a draft copy of the survey report with the supplier. By doing so, any questions can be cleared up immediately. It is much more difficult to clarify misunderstandings when a copy of the final report is received a month—or more—later.

The end product of the survey or quality program evaluation should be an understandable final report. A good report effectively communicates the findings, using the original observations to support the conclusions. The report must be an honest, objective summation of the team's efforts.

The report should detail the following:

1. List all individuals present and their correct titles

2. List the areas evaluated

3. List any major deficiencies requiring written corrective action

4. List any minor deficiencies

5. A summary that states the final conclusion, for example, approval, conditional approval, or disapproval

6. A closing statement expressing appreciation for the supplier's assistance and cooperation

Survey follow-up is carried out to assure that satisfactory corrective action has been taken by a supplier that did not qualify at the time of the survey visit. The customer may have to judge if a follow-up visit is warranted. A report from the supplier, accompanied by suitable documentation of corrective actions taken, may be adequate.

SUPPLIER RATING AND EVALUATION

Rating a supplier's capabilities is a twofold process: (1) rate or evaluate the supplier's system (financial, manufacturing, and quality), and (2) rate the supplier's delivered product.

The rating of a supplier's system usually begins with the initial supplier survey (discussed earlier). Often, the initial survey is followed up with a periodic supplier resurvey, called a systems audit. The audit provides the customer with an opportunity to evaluate the supplier's systems over time so that any deterioration is noticed immediately.

The rating of a supplier's delivered product basically takes the form of recording, in some predetermined manner, the results of incoming inspections. It also can include failures caused by the supplier's delivered products that appeared during the customer's manufacturing cycle or while the product was in service.

Elements and Formulas

Supplier rating elements and formulas are as diverse as companies are. The common aspects are quality, price, and delivery.

The quality factor usually includes:

- Quality lot rating

$$\text{Quality lot rating} = \frac{\text{Number of lots rejected}}{\text{Number of lots inspected}}$$

- Quality part rating

$$\text{Quality part rating} = \frac{\text{Number of parts rejected}}{\text{Number of parts inspected}}$$

- Comparison to competition

- Complexity analysis

- Economic conditions

The delivery factor usually includes:

- Timeliness rating

- Completeness rating

The timeliness rating is based on the due date of the lot minus some demerit (for example, 10 percent) for each day the lot is early or late beyond some specified grace period or window (for example, due date ± two working days). It is important to note that if the supplier chooses the freight carrier, the system can base the due date on the date the lot is received on the customer's dock. If the customer chooses the freight carrier, however, the due date should be measured by the date shipped from the supplier.

$$\text{The completeness rating} = \frac{\text{Number of parts actually received}}{\text{Number of parts scheduled to be received}}$$

An overall rating can be derived by assigning percentages to the aforementioned aspects of quality, price, and delivery.

Quality lot rating—40 percent
Quality part rating—60 percent $\Big\}$ Equals quality rating

Comparison level—40 percent
Complexity level—30 percent $\Big\}$ Equals price rating
Economic condition—30 percent

Timeliness rating—50 percent
Competence rating—50 percent $\Big\}$ Equals delivery rating

The next step is to assign weights to the three main factors. For example:

Quality rating—40 percent
Price rating—30 percent $\Big\}$ Equals overall supplier rating
Delivery rating—30 percent

This generic example can be expanded into an elaborate computerized system. It also can be tailored for use by smaller businesses that may still have manual systems.

Supplier Monitoring

The purchasing organization usually tracks and monitors suppliers. A special supplier quality assurance (SQA) group may be formed to work with the buyer to look at suppliers' performance. Some common supplier information includes:

Defective parts per million (PPM)

Cost adjustment requests

Delivery date slippages

Performance improvement

Using metrics such as the above, a quality information system (QIS) can generate reports such as supplier profiles by select criteria. Suppliers can be ranked by PPM, improvement, or similar metrics. Preferred suppliers can then be selected using quantitative data instead of guesswork and politics.

INCOTERMS/Delivery Terms

INCOTERMS are international commercial terms used in shipping documentation that are recognized as the international standard. Ford Motor Company, for example, generally uses standard delivery terms. INCOTERMS are generally letters or abbreviations that represent a universal understanding of the parties involved, terms of sale, point of origin, destination, and party responsible given a certain condition. The purchasing department normally manages this process.

Partnering with Suppliers

Ideally, suppliers are treated as partners in satisfying customers. This requires a mature organization with objective information. Communication skills, careful fact gathering, and a good QIS are all needed to achieve this goal. You and your suppliers should keep constant communication open on many fronts to ensure that everything is working well to delight the ultimate customer.

Chapter 9

I. Overcoming Barriers to Quality Improvement

Identify barriers to quality improvement, their causes and impact, and describe methods for overcoming them. (Analyze)

Body of Knowledge I.I

A properly implemented total quality management system will have fewer non-conformities, reduced rework and scrap, lower inventory levels, reduced cycle times, greater employee satisfaction, and increased customer satisfaction. These benefits will not occur in many organizations because they are not able to overcome the barriers or obstacles to quality improvement. In a study by Salegna and Fuzel (2000), managers of TQM companies ranked 12 obstacles to implementing quality.

TWELVE OBSTACLES TO IMPLEMENTING QUALITY

These barriers or obstacles follow in order of importance.

Lack of Time to Devote to Quality Initiatives

Frequently, managers are too busy with their regular activities to take on an additional activity such as quality. Initially, senior management must provide time for employees to devote to the quality initiative. Once a program is well established, the quality activity will become part of the employee's activities.

Poor Intraorganizational Communication

All organizations communicate with their employees in one manner or another. Communications deliver the organizations values, expectations, and directions, provide information about developments, and allow feedback from all levels. The organization must encourage and provide the means for two-way communication so that information flows up as well as down the ladder.

Lack of Real Employee Empowerment

Too often, empowerment is merely lip service. Individuals should be empowered to make decisions that affect the efficiency of their process or the satisfaction of their customers. Teams need to have the proper training and, at least in the beginning, a facilitator.

Lack of Employee Trust in Senior Management

In many organizations, this obstacle will not be a problem because senior management has created an atmosphere of trust in its relationship with the employees. In other organizations, this atmosphere will have to be developed by management being honest with the employees.

Politics and Turf Issues

Differences between departments and individuals create problems. The use of multifunctional teams will help to break down long-standing barriers. Restructuring to make the organization more responsive to customer needs may be needed. An example of restructuring is the use of product or customer support teams whose members are permanently reassigned from the areas of quality, production, design, and marketing.

Lack of a Formalized Strategic Plan for Change

A formalized plan for change is necessary because individuals resist change—they become accustomed to performing a particular process and it becomes the preferred way. Management must understand and utilize these basic concepts of change:

1. People change when they want to and to meet their own needs

2. Never expect anyone to engage in behavior that serves the organization's values unless an adequate reason (why) has been given

3. For change to be accepted, people must be moved from a state of fear to trust

It is difficult for individuals to change their own behavior, and it is much more difficult for an organization. Honest two-way communication with respectful feedback increases the chances of success.

Lack of Strong Motivation

The building of a motivated work force is, for the most part, an indirect process. Management at all levels cannot cause an employee to become motivated; they must create a conducive environment for individuals to become motivated.

View of Quality Program As a Quick Fix

Frequently, the quality program is viewed as a quick fix. Quality improvement is a race that does not have a finish. Management must constantly and forever improve the system so that quality and productivity are continually and permanently improved and costs reduced.

Drive for Short-Term Financial Results

Too often, organizations focus their efforts on the quarterly financial results. Quality improvement requires an organization to have a strong future orientation and a willingness to make long-term commitments.

Lack of Leadership

In order for any organizational effort to succeed, there must be leadership. Leadership requires a substantial commitment in terms of both management time and organizational resources.

Lack of Customer Focus

Organizations need to understand the changing needs and expectations of their internal and external customers. Effective feedback mechanisms are necessary for this understanding.

Lack of a Companywide Definition of Quality

This obstacle is the least of the twelve and is easy to correct. Experienced quality professionals recommend that all areas of the organization be involved in writing the definition.

SUMMARY OF PART I

The quality profession has a human element and a technical element and in Part I we have examined the human element of quality from several different perspectives.

First, we briefly reviewed the history of quality and noted the contributions of the leading gurus over the past 80 years or so, starting with Walter Shewhart and highlighting his two greatest successors, W. Edwards Deming and Joseph M. Juran. Some major quality programs discussed were statistical process control, total quality management, lean philosophy, theory of constraints, and Six Sigma.

No matter whether one of the above names is used, a successful organization will have some kind of a system for managing its quality. One way to view the quality management system is to look at three parts: strategic planning of the vision and goals, deployment techniques for converting the vision/goals into reality, and an information system to collect, analyze, and report the data.

Deployment techniques used for selecting and managing projects include return on investment (ROI), PERT, and Gantt charts. Heavy emphasis was also given to performance measurement tools.

Next, we discussed professional ethics, including the *ASQ Code of Ethics* and legal constraints on the quality engineer.

Leadership, facilitation, and communication skill are all interrelated. For the organization to achieve its goals in a positive and efficient manner, leaders must translate vision and goals into tangible activities. Executive direction and indirect or "soft" leadership known as facilitation unleashes the energy of middle and lower-level employees. Communication skills are critical to effective leadership and facilitation, as well as to individual career success.

The final three chapters addressed the role of quality in dealing with customers, suppliers, and improvement barriers. Two typical techniques are supplier surveys, which tell us what we can expect from our suppliers, and customer surveys, which tell us what our customers think of us. Finally, the section on barriers reinforced the idea that quality improvement is a constant struggle, and the various ideas of this book must be applied again and again in order to maintain momentum toward that elusive but unobtainable goal of perfection.

Part I.I

Part II

The Quality System

Part II

A quality system is the enabling mechanism behind the quality assurance and improvement functions of any organization. It is a statement of commitment to quality and tells how quality is to be achieved. The term *system* implies functional elements, attributes, and relationships. Part I explained quality management systems and quality information systems. We first discuss "the quality system," including its elements, how it is documented, recognized standards that define or recommend quality systems, and operations that are audited for compliance.

Quality is intrinsically related to cost, and we explain the most prominent quality cost systems. Finally, we suggest that training is a quality system, and provide an overview of the role of the quality engineer in quality training.

Chapter 10

A. Elements of the Quality System

> Define, describe, and interpret the basic
> elements of a quality system, including
> planning, control, and improvement, from
> product and process design through quality
> cost systems, audit programs, and so on.
> (Evaluate)
>
> **Body of Knowledge II.A**

Every system includes inputs, outputs, activities (processes), and relationships. The elements of a quality system are the activities used to assure customer satisfaction. Typically, these activities depend on the type of organization, its structure, the market, and the particular type of product or service provided.

Quality-related activities start with identifying customer needs and extend throughout the lifecycle of the product, as depicted in Figure 10.1. The procedures and work instructions followed within each of these functional areas to achieve the stated quality objectives represent elements of the quality system. It is important to note that the suitability and effectiveness of the system as a whole is determined by the attributes of these individual elements and their relationships. Top management must establish, document, and maintain such systems with overall objectives in mind.

System elements closely correspond to the various phases in the traditional product lifecycle depicted in Figure 10.1. In other words, a quality system must cover all the activities that affect product or service quality. ISO 9004:1994 listed the following fourteen functional elements of a quality system. Although ISO 9004:1994 is obsolete, every element is still pertinent, and each of these elements is discussed elsewhere in this book.

1. *Quality in marketing.* The marketing function is an important source of information regarding the implied and stated needs of the customer, actual field performance, and the degree of customers' satisfaction with the product. Such information will help identify product problems relative to expectations and initiate corrective measures. Consequently, the marketing function is required to define

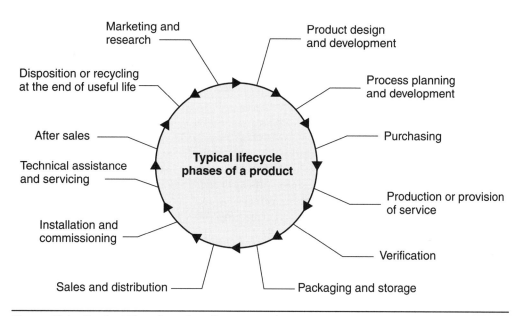

Figure 10.1   Product lifecycle and quality system elements.
Adapted from ANSI/ISO/ASQC Q9004-1-1994. Used with permission.

and document the requirements for a quality product, provide the organization with a formal statement or outline of product requirements, and establish an information feedback system for monitoring field performance on a continuous basis.

2. *Quality in specification and design.* With the customers' needs clearly identified, the design function provides the translation of these needs into technical specifications. Formal plans should be prepared and documented for identifying critical stages of the design process and assigning responsibility for each. Design reviews should be conducted at the end of each stage to identify problem areas and initiate corrective actions. All necessary measures should be taken to assure clear and definitive statements of the design requirements. Methods for evaluating conformance during production should also be specified. Design verification and validation through prototype testing or other techniques is required. Provisions should be made for periodic evaluation of the design in light of field performance data.

3. *Quality in purchasing.* The standard requires that all purchasing activities be planned and controlled by documented procedures. Successful purchase of supplies begins with clear definition of the requirements. A close working relationship with vendors and subcontractors is required to facilitate and secure continuous quality improvements. Procedures must be established for evaluating the capability of the vendors. In some cases the vendor is required to establish a demonstrated capability of meeting design requirements. If incoming inspection is to be performed, the costs involved should be considered and the vendor should be notified of the results.

4. *Quality of processes.* This element stipulates the requirements of operation under controlled conditions. The operation of processes and the operating conditions should be specified by documented work instructions. Process capability studies are required to determine the effectiveness of the process and to identify the need for improvements.

5. *Control of processes.* This is a central element in achieving conformance to design requirements. The type and sensitivity of the control technique depends on the quality characteristic involved or generated, the nature and stability of the process, and its potential capability. Control should extend over the material and parts used, tooling and any shop aids utilized, and environmental conditions. Proper identification of materials from the time of receipt to product delivery and installation is required. Statistical techniques for monitoring process variables are described in Chapter 37.

6. *Product verification.* This element addresses the allocation of test and inspection points in the process for the purpose of verifying conformance. Verification of incoming materials and products at various stages of the process prevents the unnecessary cost of further processing nonconforming units. Final product verification is performed to prevent shipping nonconforming units to customers.

7. *Control of inspection, measuring, and test equipment.* All measuring systems used in the development, production, and installation of products should be controlled. Documented procedures should be established to maintain the measuring process in a state of statistical control. The procedure includes initial calibration against a reference standard as well as periodic recall for adjustment and recalibration, and may be extended to all vendors.

8. *Control of nonconforming product.* Documented procedures for dealing with nonconforming units should be established and maintained. These procedures include steps for the identification, segregation, and review of the nonconformities. The objective is to avoid the unintended use of such units and the consequent dissatisfaction of internal and external customers.

9. *Corrective action.* A quality system should define the responsibility and authority for instituting corrective actions. These actions should be planned after identifying the root causes of the problem. Actions to eliminate these causes may involve a variety of functions such as design, purchasing, production, and quality control. The objective should be to prevent the recurrence of these causes and improve quality. Corrective action is required to monitor the effect of such actions in order to ensure that the above objectives are met.

10. *Postproduction activities.* Included here are procedures for product storage, delivery, and installation activities. These activities should prevent deterioration of product quality, secure proper identification, and safeguard against improper installation. Also, the quality system should allow for a feedback of information regarding field performance, customer satisfaction, and the initiation of corrective actions.

11. *Quality records.* These are records indicating the results of implementing the system and providing subjective means for evaluating its effectiveness. An organization is required to establish and maintain documented procedures for identification, collection, storage, retrieval, and disposition of these records. Analysis of the quality records can help identify trends in quality performance, as well as the need for and effectiveness of corrective actions. In addition, records should indicate authorized changes to the quality manual and any modifications made in the procedures or work instructions. Documentation systems are discussed in the next chapter.

12. *Personnel.* Employee training, qualification, and motivation are key factors in developing the human resources of an organization and emphasizing quality awareness among them. Documented procedures for identifying and providing training programs at all levels should be established and maintained. Periodic assessment of personnel skills and capabilities should be considered. Recognition of proper job performance and the use of motivational programs are ways in which management can support quality improvement efforts.

13. *Product safety.* Procedures are needed for identifying the safety aspects of products and processes. These aspects are best identified and considered during the design phase of the product lifecycle. Further, the rule of strict liability has created a need to plan for field failures and their legal implications. These procedures may include documenting prototype and product design evaluation testing for safety, providing adequate operational instructions with warnings against known hazards, and developing contingency plans for product recall. Failure mode and effects analysis, fault tree analysis, and hazard function analysis are all valuable tools.

14. *Use of statistical methods.* This element of the quality system is concerned with the analytical techniques used to measure, control, and improve quality throughout the product lifecycle. These include design of experiments, estimation and test of significance, control charts, and sampling inspection.

Chapter 11

B. Documentation of the Quality System

> Identify and apply quality system
> documentation components, including
> quality policies, procedures to support
> the system, configuration management
> and document control to manage work
> instructions, quality records, and so on.
> (Apply)
>
> **Body of Knowledge II.B**

Plans for achieving customer satisfaction and assuring that the quality of products or services are documented in a quality manual are sometimes referred to as the quality program, which represents the first of two major system efforts: documentation and implementation. Compliance, accuracy, and clarity are critical characteristics of documentation. A generic quality manual may be viewed as a composite document of four tiers—also known as the documentation hierarchy or pyramid—as illustrated in Figure 11.1. Starting from the top, these tiers are policies, procedures, instructions, and records.

The first tier represents a policy statement, which explains what the company stands for and what its commitments are. This is the opening statement of the quality manual, indicating the management policy and objectives for quality. There is usually a policy statement for each of the requirements of the applicable standard.

The second tier is a procedures tier, which provides an overview of how a company does its business. Direct, yet simple statements indicate who is responsible for what in achieving the requirements. In some cases the procedures will be in the quality manual but more often they will be distributed, often online.

The third tier represents work instructions, which spell out the how-to in a clear manner. An organization may choose to include detailed work instructions or exclude proprietary information. Work instructions are documented in many ways, depending on the function at hand. Format examples are in ISO/TR 10013:2001.

Document contents

Layer I
Statements of the quality policy
and objectives

Layer II
Description of the activities
needed to implement the system

Layer III
Detailed work documents

Layer IV
Results of implementing the
quality system

Figure 11.1   Tiers of the quality documentation hierarchy.

Finally, the fourth tier shows the results obtained by implementing the quality system. These results are documented and maintained to form quality records. These records provide subjective evidence that the system is being implemented and is effective. Records must be maintained for a specified time in a protected format retrievable for analysis.

A quality manual need not be partitioned into four separate parts to include the four tiers—this is only a model. Most likely, all the elements will not even be included in one document. The structure of the manual is best selected based on the nature of the organization and the applicable standard. In a small organization a separation between the work instructions and the procedures manuals may not be necessary, as it would be for a large organization. However, if the tiers are separated, it is important to provide cross-references or links between these tiers to assure effective documentation.

Upon the completion of the quality manual, a final review to determine its competence, accuracy, and clarity is undertaken. Top management should endorse the contents of the reviewed copy and authorize its release. Authorized copies of the manual should be distributed in total or by section to intended users throughout the organization. Proper distribution and control can be aided, for example, by a dedicated document control function. Parsowith (1995) identifies the following four requirements for proper document control:

1. A process is in place for the *generation of documents* that includes the writing of the policies and procedures drawings and specifications or other required documentation, approval of the contents of the documents, and the distribution of the documents.

Part II.B

2. *Documentation* fulfilling the needs of contractual or process requirements is available at all locations in which these functions are performed.

3. A process is in place for the *control of revisions* to or redistribution of documents using the same system as the original document distribution.

4. A process is in place for the *identification and removal* of obsolete documents to ensure against unintended use.

Chapter 12

C. Quality Standards and Other Guidelines

NATIONAL VERSUS INTERNATIONAL STANDARDS

The concept of national standards—which spelled out requirements for how things were to be done in the production of goods and services—grew hand in hand with the industrialization of national economies. One of the first national standards was a boiler standard, issued late in the 19th century by the American Society of Mechanical Engineers. Over time, different nations adopted standards that, while entirely appropriate to their own national needs, were in conflict with each other, which meant that a company would either have to customize its operations to different national standards, which could become very inefficient and expensive, or to forfeit the opportunity to do business in some countries.

These conflicts between different national standards naturally gave rise to the concept of international standards. Around the beginning of the 20th century, when electricity became a powerful force in many different countries, an international standards organization, the International Electrotechnical Institute, was established. This organization provided precedence for the later establishment of the International Organisation for Standardization, familiarly known as ISO. In the 1970s and 1980s, as global commerce became a matter of interest to more than 100 different countries and thousands of different companies, a major cooperative effort of international quality professionals led to the ISO 9000 family of standards.

THE ISO 9000 FAMILY

ISO 9000:2005 refers to both a family of three related standards and to one of the standards in that family. The purpose of this family is "to assist organizations, of all types and sizes, to implement and operate effective quality management systems" and consists of three standards: quality management vocabulary, requirements, and guidelines for performance.

- *ISO 9000: Quality management systems—Fundamentals and vocabulary,* provides the fundamentals and terminology of quality management systems.

- *ISO 9001: Quality management systems—Requirements,* specifies the needed requirements for an organization to provide products that aim to enhance customer satisfaction.

- *ISO 9004: Quality management systems—Guidelines for performance improvements,* suggests ways to improve organizational performance and customer satisfaction beyond the requirements of ISO 9001.

Within the ISO 9000 family, the following eight quality management principles are consistently emphasized:

1. *Customer focus.* Understand the customer's needs, meet their requirements, and strive to exceed their expectations.

2. *Leadership.* Establish unity of purpose and direction.

3. *Involvement of people.* Help people at all levels to have a sense of ownership and involvement.

4. *Process approach.* Strive to manage activities and related resources as a process.

5. *Systems approach to management.* Identify the interrelated processes and how they affect each other.

6. *Continual improvement.* Maintain the ideal of continually improving all aspects of the organization.

7. *Factual approach to decision making.* Use data and information to guide decisions.

8. *Mutually beneficial supplier relationships.* Recognize that suppliers and customers are dependent on each other and that a mutually beneficial relationship helps both to add value.

ISO 9000:2005 replaced ISO 9000:2000, which replaced ISO 9000:1994. The major changes from ISO 9000:1994 to ISO 9000:2000 are summarized by Cianfrani, Tsiakals, and West in *The ASQ ISO 9000:2000 Handbook* (2002). The details and implications of all the changes in the ISO 9000:2000 family are covered in Chapter 8 in *The ASQ ISO 9000:2000 Handbook.*

- Greater focus on the customer and customer satisfaction (clause 8.2.1)

- A new focus on the process approach (clauses 0.2, 4.1, 5.4.2, 7.1, and 8.1)

- Clarification of requirements for continual improvements (for example, clause 8.5)

- Greater emphasis on the role of top management (clause 5)

- Measurable quality objectives (clause 5.4.1)

- New requirements for data collection and analysis (clause 8.4)

- Reduced emphasis on documented procedures (clause 4.2)

- Shift in emphasis from training to providing competent people (clause 6.2)

- Consistency between ISO 9001 and ISO 9004 (clause 0.3)

- Compatibility with ISO 14000 (clause 0.4)

- Elimination of ISO 9002 and ISO 9003 (clause 1.2)

- Modification of the purpose of internal audits (clause 8.2.2)

The following sections are overviews of the three standards that make up the ISO 9000:2000 family.

ISO 9000:2005 Fundamentals and Vocabulary

This document is the language foundation for the entire worldwide system of development, implementation, auditing, and registration of ISO 9001:2008. All definitions of terms are based on many person-years of research and consultation. In all, 85 concepts and their associated terms are defined in the following 10 categories: quality, management, organization, process and product, characteristics, conformity, document, examination, audit, and measurement process. The standard differentiates between a concept and a term as follows: a *concept* is a unit of knowledge created by a unique combination of characteristics. A *term* is the verbal designation of the concept as it applies to a specific field of study.

Two criteria apply to all of the ISO 9000 terms and definitions:

1. Avoid technical language in technical descriptions.

2. Employ a coherent and harmonized vocabulary that is understood by all actual and potential users.

Because the standards are translated into many different languages, it is critical that all users have the same understanding of what the terms mean. This goal has been accomplished by having representatives from more than 100 different countries intimately involved in polishing the definitions. A good example of the need for this kind of language-specific polishing is the term *interested party*. In English, a more common term would be *stakeholder*. However, in some languages, a literal translation of stakeholder is *someone holding a stick*. Many such conflicts and ambiguities have been resolved over the years.

Part II.C

ISO 9001:2008 Requirements

This document is the set of requirements that organizations must satisfy in order to achieve ISO 9001 registration. Such registration is required in some industries and very highly regarded in many others. Over 140 countries have ISO 9001 registration programs. Many people inadvertently refer to this key document as "ISO 9000:2008." (Remember: ISO 9000 refers to a family of three documents, and also to the *Vocabulary* document; ISO 9001 refers to the requirements document.)

The standard has eight major parts, or clauses. The first three are *general* clauses:

1. *Scope.* This tells what organization(s), location(s), process(es), product(s), and so on, are covered.

2. *Normative references.* These cite other standards which, by being listed, constitute provisions of the ISO 9001 standard.

3. *Terms and definitions.* Here, reference is made to ISO 9000, which contains all definitions applicable to ISO 9001.

The remaining five are *technical* clauses and are listed here as they appear in the standard. For further details, consult the standards themselves. The five technical clauses (clauses 4–8) are:

4. *Quality management system*

    4.1 General requirements

    4.2 Documentation requirements

5. *Management responsibility*

    5.1 Management commitment

    5.2 Customer focus

    5.3 Quality policy

    5.4 Planning

    5.5 Responsibility, authority and communication

    5.6 Management review

6. *Resource management*

    6.1 Provision of resources

    6.2 Human resources

    6.3 Infrastructure

    6.4. Work environment

7. *Product realization*

    7.1 Planning of product realization

7.2 Customer-related processes

7.3 Design and development

7.4 Purchasing

7.5 Production and service provision

7.6 Control of monitoring and measuring devices

8. *Measurement, analysis and improvement*

8.1 General

8.2 Monitoring and measurement

8.3 Control of nonconforming product

8.4 Analysis of data

8.5 Improvement

ISO 9004:2000 Guidelines for Performance Improvements

Whereas ISO 9001 is compliance-based, ISO 9004 is improvement-based. All the great ideas in ISO 9004 are guidelines, not requirements. There is some controversy in the field of quality on the usefulness of ISO 9004 and it has not been widely adopted. The developers of the ISO 9000 family made ISO 9001 and ISO 9004 completely compatible in structure, so it is easy to follow any of the following three paths:

Path A. You have no present wish to be registered to ISO 9001 requirements but you want to install a powerful quality management system now, with the option to go for ISO 9001 registration later. So you build your present quality system on the guidelines of ISO 9004. Nothing you do in following the ISO 9004 guidelines will cause you trouble if you later seek ISO 9001 registration.

Path B. You are presently registered to ISO 9001 but want to upgrade to a more powerful system that leads to performance improvement. Without making any changes in your present quality management system, you can start to selectively apply the ISO 9004 guidelines.

Path C. You are not registered but want to become registered and also want to put quality improvement procedures in place that are not required for registration. You can work with ISO 9001 and ISO 9004 simultaneously, devoting to each the resources you deem appropriate to achieving your goals.

ISO 9004 uses exactly the same format, definitions, and clauses as ISO 9001. Like ISO 9001 it relies on the eight principles of quality management mentioned earlier. However, 9004 is almost twice as long as 9001. Whereas compliance to 9001 raises the issue of corrective action, the 9004 guidelines suggest how and where to go further in improving performance.

ISO 9004 contains two annexes (not present in 9001) in the form of guides for two differing approaches to improvement. The first annex is a set of guidelines for self-assessment. The second lays out a specific process for self-improvement. Either approach can work. Westcott (2003) expands on both approaches, helps management develop plans to implement ISO 9004, and provides some case studies of successful implementation. The best place to start, of course, is with the ISO 9004 standard itself.

SOME OTHER QUALITY STANDARDS

There exist a number of industry-specific standards that may have an impact on the quality engineer. The automobile, telecommunications, and biomedical industries have all created industry-specific standards that emulate ISO 9001 but impose additional requirements. The American automobile industry took the lead in creating its own industry standard with QS 9000. Later, Americans and Europeans joined forces to create the ISO/TS 16949 standard, which is mandatory for many original equipment manufacturers (OEMs). The telecommunications quality standard is TL 9000 and the biomedical quality standard is ISO 13485:2003.

These standards as well as other pertinent publications are available from ASQ Quality Press by phoning 800–248–1946 or visiting the ASQ Web site at www.asq.org/quality-press. Commentary and offers of assistance on all three of these standards can be found by entering the standard number into a Web browser search engine.

MALCOLM BALDRIGE NATIONAL QUALITY AWARD

The Malcolm Baldrige National Quality Award (MBNQA), another quality management approach, emphasizes results rather than procedures or requirements. Congress established this award in 1987 to recognize U.S. organizations for their achievements in quality and business performance and to raise awareness about the importance of quality and performance excellence as a competitive edge. The award is named in honor of Malcolm Baldrige, who was secretary of commerce at the time of his death in 1987. The award is not given for specific products or services. Awards may be given annually in each of these categories: manufacturing, service, small business, education, healthcare, nonprofit, and government.

While the Baldrige Award and the Baldrige recipients comprise the very visible centerpiece of the U.S. quality movement, a broader national quality program has evolved around the award and its criteria. A report, *Building on Baldrige: American Quality for the 21st Century*, by the private Council on Competitiveness, said, "More than any other program, the Baldrige Quality Award is responsible for making quality a national priority and disseminating best practices across the United States."

The U.S. Commerce Department's National Institute of Standards and Technology (NIST) manages the Baldrige National Quality Award Program in close cooperation with the private sector. Since its inception, several million copies of the award criteria have been distributed and there have been over 60 recipients of the award.

The Baldrige Award Criteria

The Malcolm Baldrige National Quality Award is awarded according to these criteria for performance excellence:

1. *Leadership.* Examines how senior executives guide the organization and how the organization addresses its responsibilities to the public and practices good citizenship.

2. *Strategic planning.* Examines how the organization sets strategic directions and how it determines key action plans.

3. *Customer and market focus.* Examines how the organization determines requirements and expectations of customers and markets.

4. *Information and analysis.* Examines the management, effective use, and analysis of data and information to support key organization processes and the organization's performance management system.

5. *Human resource focus.* Examines how the organization enables its workforce to develop its full potential and how the workforce is aligned with the organization's objectives.

6. *Process management.* Examines aspects of how key production/delivery and support processes are designed, managed, and improved.

7. *Business results.* Examines the organization's performance and improvement in its key business areas: customer satisfaction, financial and marketplace performance, human resources, supplier and partner performance, and operational performance. This category also examines how the organization performs relative to competitors.

Further information about the Malcolm Baldrige National Quality Award, including procedures for ordering the criteria, is available at the following Web site: www.quality.nist.gov.

Part II.C

Chapter 13

D. Quality Audits

A quality system audit, as defined by ANSI/ASQC A3-1987, is a systematic and independent evaluation of the quality system and its execution, looking at both design and performance of the system. It is a fact-finding process that compares actual results with specified standards and plans. It provides feedback for improvement. It differs from inspection, which emphasizes acceptance or rejection, and surveillance, which is ongoing continuous monitoring.

1. TYPES OF AUDITS

> Describe and distinguish between various
> types of quality audits such as product,
> process, management (system), registration
> (certification), compliance (regulatory), first,
> second, and third party, and so on. (Apply)
>
> **Body of Knowledge II.D.1**

Quality audits may be classified according to the party conducting them, their scope, and the audit method used. In general, three parties are involved in an audit: (1) the organization requesting the audit, or client, (2) the party conducting the audit, or the auditor, and (3) the organization to be audited, or the auditee.

When the auditor is an employee of the organization being audited (auditee), the audit is classified as an *internal quality audit*. For the purposes of maintaining objectivity and minimizing bias, internal auditors must be independent from the activity being audited. On the other hand, when the auditors are employees of the client or an independent organization or third party hired for the purpose, the audit is termed an *external quality audit*. In this case, the auditors are clearly independent of the auditee and are in a position to provide the client with an unbiased, objective assessment. This is the type of audit required to permit listing in a register or to meet mandatory quality requirements. However, the time required and costs involved in an external audit are much higher as compared to internal audits.

Another way to classify quality audits is by scope and extent. An audit may be as comprehensive as needed or requested by the client. The most comprehensive type of audit is the quality system audit, which examines suitability and effectiveness of the system as a whole. This involves both the documentation and implementation aspects of the quality system. Reasons for initiating a system audit may range from evaluating a potential supplier to verifying an organization's own system. Audits of specific elements of a system, processes, products, or services, are also possible. These are limited in scope and are typically referred to using a modifier preceding the term quality audit. Examples include process quality audits and product quality audits.

The method by which the quality audit is conducted provides yet another way to classify. Audits may be conducted by location or function. A location-oriented audit provides an in-depth examination of all the quality-related activities within a given location. In a function-oriented audit, an activity is examined in all the locations where the activity is carried out.

It is important to note that these classifications are not mutually exclusive and, in practice, cross-classifications of a quality audit are possible.

The following four purposes of quality audits are listed in ANSI/ISO/ASQ QE19011S-2008:

1. To meet requirements for certification to a management system standard

2. To verify conformance with contractual requirements

3. To obtain and maintain confidence in the capability of a supplier

4. To contribute to the improvement of the management system

2. ROLES AND RESPONSIBILITIES IN AUDITS

> Identify and define roles and responsibilities for audit participants such as audit team (leader and members), client, auditee, and so on. (Understand)
>
> **Body of Knowledge II.D.2**

Each of the three parties involved in an audit—the client, the auditor, and the auditee—plays a role that contributes to its success. The *client*, the party that initiates the audit, selects the auditor and determines the reference standard to be used. The client, typically the end user of the audit results, determines the type of audit needed (system, process, product, and so on) as well as its time and duration.

The selected *auditor*, whether an individual or a group, needs to adhere to the role of a third party. That is, the auditor must maintain objectivity and avoid bias in conducting the audit. The auditor must comply with any confidentiality requirements mandated by the auditee. An experienced individual is appointed as lead auditor to communicate audit requirements, manage the auditing activities, and report the results. For rules, qualifications, and evaluation criteria for an auditor, see ANSI/ISO/ASQ QE19011S-2008.

Finally, the *auditee* has the responsibility of accommodating the audit, which entails providing the auditors access to the facilities involved and copies of all relevant documentation. The auditee is also expected to provide the resources needed and select staff members to accompany the auditors.

3. AUDIT PLANNING AND IMPLEMENTATION

> Describe and apply the steps of a quality audit, from the audit planning stage through conducting the audit, from the perspective of an audit team member. (Apply)
>
> **Body of Knowledge II.D.3**

Proper planning is a key factor in achieving an efficient quality audit. Planning should be conducted with consideration of the client expectations. This includes the scope, depth, and time frame. The lead auditor has the responsibility of planning and conducting the audit and should be authorized to perform these activities.

Planning an audit, just like any other activity, should address the questions of what, when, how, and who. That is, what elements of the quality system are to be audited? Against what document or reference standard? The answers to both questions are determined by the client and should be communicated clearly to the auditee. When to start and when to conclude the audit? A schedule of the audit activities needs to be prepared and communicated to both the client and the auditee. It is the lead auditor's responsibility to inform the client of any delays, report their reasons, and update the completion date of the audit.

The method of conducting the audit also should be addressed. Working documents need to be prepared, including checklists of the elements to examine, questions to ask, and activities to monitor. A number of references provide generic checklists that can be used as templates. However, it is best to design a checklist to suit the audit at hand and its specific scope and objectives. Forms for collecting auditors' observations and the supporting evidence also should be included in the working document. Working documents typically are reviewed by an experienced auditor and approved by the lead auditor before implementation. It is recommended that the auditor explain the methods planned to the auditee. This should help the organization better prepare for the audit and ease the fear usually attached to the process.

The question of who will examine specific elements, processes, or products addresses the qualifications and experiences of the individual auditors (assessors) needed. With the client expectations in mind, the lead auditor should assign the various tasks among his or her team.

An audit is usually conducted in three steps. (1) A pre-examination or opening meeting with the auditee marks the beginning of the process. During this meeting, the lead auditor introduces team members to the senior management of the auditee and explains the objectives of the audit and the methods used. The auditee is represented by selected members of the organization who facilitate and assist in the process and submit a documented description of the quality system or element to be examined. Issues regarding proprietary information typically are addressed and resolved before starting the audit.

The next step (2) involves a suitability audit of the documented procedures against the selected reference standard. Observed nonconformities at this stage of the audit should be reported to both the client and the auditee for immediate action. The auditing process should pause to allow for corrective measures.

For the third step (3), the auditor examines in depth the implementation of the quality system. The auditor maintains records of all nonconformities observed and the supporting data. Provisions should be made in the audit plan to allow additional investigation of clues suggesting nonconformities revealed by the data collected. The auditee management should be made aware of, and acknowledge, all the nonconformities observed during the audit. This step concludes with a closing meeting with the auditee's management for a presentation of findings. In some cases, the auditor may be required to recommend corrective measures for improving the system. However, it is up to the auditee to plan and implement these measures in a way that best suits the organization.

4. AUDIT REPORTING AND FOLLOW-UP

> Identify, describe, and apply the steps of audit reporting and follow up, including the need to verify corrective action. (Apply)
>
> **Body of Knowledge II.D.4**

A final report is submitted to the client indicating the facts of the audit and conclusions regarding the ability of the subject system, element, process, or product to achieve quality objectives. Proper planning and execution of the audit facilitates the preparation of this report and provides data to support its conclusions. The lead auditor is responsible for the accuracy of the report and the validity of its conclusions. The report should be submitted to the client, who in turn is responsible for providing a copy to the auditee.

The audit final report should include, at a minimum, the following:

1. Type of audit conducted

2. Objectives of audit

3. Identification of involved parties: auditor, auditee, and third party

Part II.D.4

4. Audit team members

5. Critical nonconformities and other observations

6. Audit standards and reference documents used

7. Determination of proper corrective action(s)

8. Duration of audit

9. Audit report distribution and date

10. Audit results and recommendations

11. Audit-related records

Should the auditee initiate improvement efforts to correct nonconformities, the three parties should agree on a follow-up audit to verify the results. The plan, audit, report, and improve cycle may be repeated whenever systems and/or requirements change. The results attained provide a measure of the effectiveness of the audit. Improvement efforts also should be directed to identifying and eliminating the root causes of reported nonconformities and identifying the corrective action(s) to be taken. Root causes represent the main reason behind the occurrence of a non-conformance or an undesirable condition or status. These corrective actions may then be validated by performing tests, inspections, or even more audits.

Chapter 14

E. Cost of Quality

> Identify and apply COQ concepts, including cost categories, data collection methods and classification, and reporting and interpreting results. (Analyze)
>
> **Body of Knowledge II.E**

To achieve the most effective improvement efforts, management should ensure that the organization has ingrained in its operating principles the understanding that quality, speed, and cost are complementary—and not conflicting—objectives. Traditionally, recommendations made to management were choices between quality, speed, and cost, where they could pick two of these but not all three at once. Experience throughout the world has shown, and management is beginning to see, that this is not true. Good quality leads to increased productivity and reduced quality costs, and eventually to increased sales, market penetration, and profits.

The purpose of cost of quality (COQ) techniques is to provide a tool to management for facilitating quality program and quality improvement activities. Quality cost reports can be used to point out the strengths and weaknesses of a quality system. Improvement teams can use COQ reports to describe the monetary benefits and ramifications of proposed changes. Return-on-investment (ROI) models and other financial analyses can be constructed directly from quality cost data to justify proposals to management. Improvement team members can use this information to rank problems in order of priority. In practice, quality costs can define the activities of quality program and quality improvement efforts in a language that management can understand and act on—dollars. Any reduction in quality costs will have a direct impact on gross profit margins and can be counted immediately as pretax profit.

THE ECONOMICS OF QUALITY

The expression *the economics of quality* has contributed to some confusion surrounding the true business and economic value of quality management. Some people believe there is no *economics of quality*, that is, it is never economical to ignore quality. At the other extreme are those managers who believe it is uneconomical to have 100 percent quality. These managers feel free to make arbitrary decisions about the needed quality of a product or service, usually expressed by the term "that's good enough. "

The facts about quality management and quality costs, however, show that the real value of a quality program is determined by its ability to contribute to customer satisfaction and profits. Quality cost techniques provide tools for management in its pursuit of customer satisfaction, quality improvement, and profit contributions.

Whether for manufacturing or service, a quality cost program will lend credence to the business value of the quality management program and provide cost justification for the corrective actions demanded. Quality cost measurements provide guidance to the quality management program much as the cost accounting system does for general management. Quality cost measurements define and quantify those costs that are directly affected, both positively and negatively, by the quality management program, thus allowing quality to be managed more effectively.

Simply stated, quality costs are a measure of the costs specifically associated with the achievement or nonachievement of product or service quality—including all product or service requirements established by the company and its contracts with customers and society. More specifically, quality costs are the total of the costs incurred by: (a) investing in the prevention of nonconformances to requirements (*prevention costs*), (b) appraising a product or service for conformance to requirements (*appraisal costs*), and (c) failure to meet requirements (*failure costs*). Quality costs represent the difference between the actual cost of a product or service and what the reduced cost would be if there were no possibility of substandard service, failure of products, or defects in their manufacture.

Every company lives with significant costs that fit this description. Unfortunately, significant chunks of quality cost are normally overlooked or unrecognized simply because most accounting systems are not designed to identify them. As this is generally the case, it is not too difficult to understand why top management of most companies is more sensitive to overall cost and schedule than to quality. The interrelationship of quality, schedule, and cost, without attention to the contrary, is likely to be unbalanced in favor of schedule and cost—and often unwittingly at the expense of quality. This imbalance will continue to exist as long as the real cost of quality remains hidden among total costs. In fact, such a condition can easily set the stage for a still greater imbalance whenever the rising, but hidden, true cost of quality grows to a magnitude that can significantly affect a company's competitive position.

When the cost of quality rises without constraint, or is tolerated at too high a level, failure to expose the condition is a sign of ineffective management. Yet, it is entirely possible for this condition to exist without top management's awareness. A quality cost program can provide specific warnings against oncoming, dangerous, quality-related financial situations. An argument for needed quality improvement is always weak when it must deal in generalities and opinions but it will become unmistakably clear when a company suddenly finds itself in serious, expensive quality trouble.

On the premise that any dollar expenditure that could have been avoided will have a direct negative effect on profits, the value of clearly identifying the cost of quality should be obvious. Achieving this clarity of identification, however, is more easily said than done. A real danger lies in finding and collecting only a small portion of the costs involved and assuming it represents the total. There are as many ways of hiding costs in industry as there are people with imagination. This is an all too natural phenomenon in organizations that are never fully charged with all inefficiencies—because some inefficiencies are hidden and not measured—and thus are able to maintain an illusion of effective management.

GOAL OF A QUALITY COST SYSTEM

The goal of any quality cost system is to facilitate quality improvement efforts that will lead to operating cost reduction opportunities. The strategy for using quality costs is quite simple: (1) take direct attack on failure costs in an attempt to drive them to zero, (2) invest in the *right* prevention activities to bring about improvement, (3) reduce appraisal costs according to results achieved, and (4) continuously evaluate and redirect prevention efforts to gain further improvement.

This strategy is based on the premise that:

- For each failure there is a root cause

- Causes are preventable

- Prevention is always cheaper

In a practical sense, real quality costs can be measured and then reduced through the proper analysis of cause and effect. As failures are revealed through appraisal actions or customer complaints, they are examined for root causes and eliminated through corrective action. The further along in the operating process that a failure is discovered, that is, the nearer to product or service use by the customer, the more expensive it is to correct. Usually as failure costs are reduced, appraisal efforts also can be reduced in a statistically sound manner. The knowledge gained from this improvement can then be applied, through prevention activities or disciplines, to all new work. By minimizing quality costs, quality performance levels can be improved.

MANAGEMENT OF QUALITY COSTS

Managing quality costs begins with a general understanding and belief that improving quality performance and improving quality costs are synonymous (the economics of quality). The next step is recognizing that measurable quality improvement also can have a tangible effect on other business measures, such as sales and market share. The proviso, however, is that quality costs must be measured and must reflect cost or lost opportunities to the company.

It should be further understood that the cost of quality is a comprehensive system, not a piecemeal tool. There is a danger in responding to a customer problem only with added internal operations, such as inspections or tests. For service operations, this could mean more operators. While this may solve the immediate customer problem, the added costs may, in fact, destroy profit potential. A comprehensive quality management program will force the analysis of all associated quality costs, making these added internal costs appear clearly as just one step toward the ultimate resolution—prevention of the root cause of the problem. Quality costs should, therefore, become an integral part of any quality management program and, in turn, any quality system or quality improvement activity. Overall quality cost data will point out the potential for improvement and provide management with the basis for measuring the improvement accomplished.

Total quality costs are intended to represent the difference between the actual cost of a product or service and what the cost would be if quality was perfect. It is, according to Dr. Joseph Juran, "gold in the mine, " waiting to be extracted. When you zero in on the elimination of failure costs and then challenge the level of appraisal costs, you will not only be managing the cost of quality, you will be mining gold.

QUALITY COST CATEGORIES

To manage quality costs they must be categorized. The three major categories commonly used are prevention costs, appraisal costs, and failure costs. See Table 14.1 for a list of quality cost elements by category.

Prevention costs are the costs of all activities specifically designed to prevent poor quality in products or services. Examples are the costs of quality planning, training programs, and quality improvement projects.

Appraisal costs are the costs associated with measuring, evaluating, or auditing products or services to assure conformance to quality standards and performance requirements. These include the costs of inspection, testing, product or service audits, process audits, and calibration of measuring and test equipment.

Failure costs are those costs resulting from products or services not conforming to requirements or customer needs. They are usually divided into two types, internal and external.

1. *Internal failure costs* occur prior to delivery or shipment of the product or furnishing of a service to the customer, such as the costs of scrap, rework, material review, and so on.

2. *External failure costs* occur after delivery of the product and during or after furnishing of a service to the customer. Examples include the costs of processing customer complaints, customer returns, warranty claims, and product recalls.

Total quality cost is the sum of these costs—prevention, appraisal, and failure—and represents the difference between the actual cost of a product or service and what the reduced cost would be if there were no possibility of substandard service, failure of products, or defects in their manufacture.

IMPLEMENTATION

To implement a quality cost program, the need for the program must first be determined. This need should be presented to management in a way that will justify

Continued

Table 14.1   Quality cost elements by category.

	Prevention Costs		Appraisal Costs
1.0	**Prevention Costs**	2.0	**Appraisal Costs**
1.1	Marketing/Customer/User	2.1	Purchasing Appraisal Costs
1.1.1	Marketing Research	2.1.1	Receiving or Incoming Inspections and Tests
1.1.2	Customer/User Perception Surveys/Clinics	2.1.2	Measurement Equipment
1.1.3	Contract/Document Review	2.1.3	Qualification of Supplier Product
1.2	Product/Service/Design Development	2.1.4	Source Inspection and Control Programs
1.2.1	Design Quality Progress Reviews	2.2	Operations (Manufacturing or Service) Appraisal Costs
1.2.2	Design Support Activities	2.2.1	Planned Operations Inspections, Tests, Audits
1.2.3	Product Design Qualification Test	2.2.1.1	Checking Labor
1.2.4	Service Design Qualification	2.2.1.2	Product or Service Quality Audits
1.2.5	Field Trials	2.2.1.3	Inspection and Test Materials
1.3	Purchasing Prevention Costs	2.2.2	Set-Up Inspections and Tests
1.3.1	Supplier Reviews	2.2.3	Special Tests (Manufacturing)
1.3.2	Supplier Rating	2.2.4	Process Control Measurements
1.3.3	Purchase Order Tech Data Reviews	2.2.5	Laboratory Support
1.3.4	Supplier Quality Planning	2.2.6	Measurement (Inspection and Test) Equipment
1.4	Operations (Manufacturing or Service) Prevention Costs	2.2.6.1	Depreciation Allowances
1.4.1	Operations Process Validation	2.2.6.2	Measurement Equipment Expenses
1.4.2	Operations Quality Planning	2.2.6.3	Maintenance and Calibration Labor
1.4.2.1	Design and Development of Quality Measurement and Control Equipment	2.2.7	Outside Endorsements and Certifications
1.4.3	Operations Support Quality Planning	2.3	External Appraisal Costs
1.4.4	Operator Quality Education	2.3.1	Field Performance Evaluation
1.4.5	Operator SPC/Process Control	2.3.2	Special Product Evaluations
1.5	Quality Administration	2.3.3	Evaluation of Field Stock and Spare Parts
1.5.1	Administrative Salaries	2.4	Review of Test and Inspection Data
1.5.2	Administrative Expenses	2.5	Miscellaneous Quality Evaluations
1.5.3	Quality Program Planning		
1.5.4	Quality Performance Reporting		
1.5.5	Quality Education		
1.5.6	Quality Improvement		
1.5.7	Quality System Audits		
1.6	Other Prevention Costs		

Part II.E

Table 14.1 Quality cost elements by category. *(Continued)*

3.0	**Internal Failure Costs**
3.1	Product/Service Design Failure Costs (Internal)
3.1.1	Design Corrective Action
3.1.2	Rework Due to Design Changes
3.1.3	Scrap Due to Design Changes
3.1.4	Production Liaison Costs
3.2	Purchasing Failure Costs
3.2.1	Purchased Material Reject Disposition Costs
3.2.2	Purchased Material Replacement Costs
3.2.3	Supplier Corrective Action
3.2.4	Rework of Supplier Rejects
3.2.5	Uncontrolled Material Losses
3.3	Operations (Product or Service) Failure Costs
3.3.1	Material Review and Corrective Action Costs
3.3.1.1	Disposition Costs
3.3.1.2	Troubleshooting or Failure Analysis Costs (Operations)
3.3.1.3	Investigation Support Costs
3.3.1.4	Operations Corrective Action
3.3.2	Operations Rework and Repair Costs
3.3.2.1	Rework
3.3.2.2	Repair
3.3.3	Reinspection/Retest Costs
3.3.4	Extra Operations
3.3.5	Scrap Costs (Operations)
3.3.6	Downgraded End-Product or Service
3.3.7	Internal Failure Labor Losses
3.4	Other Internal Failure Costs

4.0	**External Failure Costs**
4.1	Complaint Investigations/Customer or User Service
4.2	Returned Goods
4.3	Retrofit Costs
4.3.1	Recall Costs
4.4	Warranty Claims
4.5	Liability Costs
4.6	Penalties
4.7	Customer/User Goodwill
4.8	Lost Sales
4.9	Other External Failure Costs

Source: ASQ Quality Costs Committee. *Principles of Quality Costs: Principles, Implementation, and Use.* 3rd ed. Ed. Jack Campanella. Milwaukee: ASQ Quality Press, 1999.

the effort and interest them in participating. To interest management, the need must be justified.

One way to do this is by establishing a trial program. It can be simple. For this purpose, only major costs need to be gathered and only readily available data need be included. Much of the required data may be available already. If necessary, some of these costs may even be estimated.

When setting up the trial program, there is no need to do everything—there's time for that later. Select a program, facility, or area of particular interest to management. The results should be sufficient to sell them on the need for the program.

Most trial runs will show eye-opening results, spectacular enough to make management sit up and take notice. They will see quality costs running as much as 20 percent or more of sales dollars (according to some studies), and opportunities for significant savings will be obvious. With top management sold on the program, getting the much-needed cooperation of the accounting people should be easy.

With management sold and with accounting ready to go, the specific quality costs to be collected must be determined. To do this, tasks must be classified as to prevention, appraisal, or failure, and listed together with the departments responsible for them. Remember that quality costs are not only incurred by the quality department.

To determine the prevention costs in the effort to prevent poor quality, such tasks performed in the company should be listed together with the departments responsible for those tasks. In a like manner, appraisal cost elements are determined by listing those tasks associated with the inspection or test of products or services for the detection of poor quality. For failure costs, determine those costs that would not have been expended if quality were perfect. If quality were perfect there would not be any rework, customer complaints needing response, or need for corrective action. Remember to divide failure costs into internal and external categories.

Quality cost elements may differ from company to company and particularly from industry to industry. However, the overall categories of prevention, appraisal, and failure are always the same.

QUALITY COST COLLECTION

Now that the specific costs to be collected have been decided on, a method to collect them must be developed. Collection of quality costs should be the responsibility of the controller. The finance and accounting department is the cost collection agency of the company, and what is being done here is collecting costs. Besides, having the controller collect the costs adds credibility to the data.

If top management is properly sold on the program, the controller will be charged with the task of heading this effort. With the help of the quality manager, the controller should review the list of costs to be collected, determine which of these are already available under the existing accounting system, and decide where additions to the existing system are needed. Sometimes, the simple addition of new cost element codes to the present charging system is sufficient. However, if necessary, the present system could be supplemented by separate inputs designed specially for this purpose.

Ideally, a complete system of cost element codes could be generated. They could be coded in such a way that the costs of prevention, appraisal, and internal and external failures could be easily distinguished and sorted (see Table 14.1). Then these codes could be entered into the labor cost collection system, together with the hours expended against the cost element or task represented by the code. The labor hours could later be easily converted to dollars.

Scrap is an exception to this system of collecting quality costs as they are incurred. All work needs to be inspected, rejected, and dispositioned first. In many companies, the existing scrap reporting documents are forwarded to estimating, where the costs of expended labor and material are estimated to the stage of completion of the scrapped items.

The accounting department should provide all collected quality costs to the quality function in a format suitable for analysis and reporting. Of course, training programs will be necessary to assure that all personnel are informed as to how to report their quality cost expenditures. The training should be repeated periodically and the collection system should be audited on a regular basis.

QUALITY COST SUMMARY AND ANALYSIS

Quality costs can be summarized in many ways, such as by company, division, facility, department, or shop. They may be summarized by program, type of program, or all programs combined. What is the best way? The decision must be based on the specific needs of the organization.

Analysis can include comparison of the total quality cost to an appropriate measurement base. Some commonly used bases are sales, cost input, and direct labor. Again, the base selected will depend on what is appropriate for the needs of the organization. Comparing quality costs to a measurement base will relate the cost of quality to the amount of work performed. An increase in quality costs with a proportionate increase in the base is normal. It is the nonproportionate change that should be of interest. The index "total quality cost over the measurement base" is the factor to be analyzed. The goal is to bring this index to a minimum through quality improvement. The index may be plotted so that trends representing present status in relation to past performance and future goals may be analyzed.

Other methods of analysis include study of the effect that changes in one category have on the other categories and on the total quality cost. For example, was the increase in prevention costs effective in reducing failure costs? And was this reduction in failure costs sufficient to cause a reduction in total quality costs? This technique can provide insight into where the quality dollar can most wisely be spent. Increases in failure costs must be investigated to determine where costs must be expended to reverse a trend and reduce the total quality cost. Losses must be defined, their causes identified, and corrective action taken to preclude recurrence.

Other existing quality systems, such as a defect reporting system, can be used in conjunction with the quality cost program to identify significant problems. The defect reporting system can help define the causes of scrap, rework, and other failure costs. While the losses are distributed among many causes, they are not uniformly distributed. A small percentage of the causes will account for a high percentage of the losses. This is the Pareto principle, where these causes are the *vital few* as opposed to the *trivial many*. Concentration on prevention of the vital few causes will achieve maximum improvement at a minimum of cost. This quality improvement tool will have the effect of improving quality while reducing costs.

QUALITY COST REPORTING

There are almost as many ways to report quality costs as there are companies reporting them because how they are reported depends on who they are reported to and what the report is trying to say. The amount of detail included in the quality cost report generally depends on the level of management the report is geared to.

To top management, the report might be a scorecard, depicting the status of the quality program through a few carefully selected trend charts—where it has been and the direction it is heading. Savings over the report period and opportunities for future savings might be identified. To middle management, the report might provide quality cost trends by department or shop to enable identification of areas in need of improvement. Reports to line management might provide detailed cost information, perhaps the results of a Pareto analysis identifying those specific areas where corrective action would afford the greatest improvement. Scrap and rework costs by shop also provide valuable information when included in reports to line management.

Again, how quality costs are reported depends to a large extent on who they are reported to and what the report is trying to say.

USING QUALITY COSTS

Once the quality cost program is implemented, it should be used by management to justify and support improvement in each major area of product or service activity. Quality costs should be reviewed for each major product line, manufacturing area, service area, or cost center. The improvement potential that exists in each individual area can then be looked at and meaningful goals can be established. The quality cost system then becomes an integral part of quality measurement. The proper balance is to establish improvement efforts at the level necessary to effectively reduce the total cost of quality, and then as progress is achieved, adjust it to where total quality costs are at the lowest attainable level. This prevents unheeded growth in quality costs and creates improved overall quality performance, reputation, and profits.

Still another benefit to be gained from a quality cost program is its ability to be used as a budgeting tool. As costs are collected against quality cost elements, a history is generated. This history can then be used to determine the average cost per element. In other words, depending on how detailed the elements are that have been established, what the organization has been spending for various functions or tasks will be identified. This information can be used as the basis for future quotes and estimates. Budgets can be established for each element. Then, going full circle, the actuals collected against these elements can be bounced against the budget amounts to determine budget variances. Action can then be initiated to bring over- or under-running elements into line.

QUALITY IMPROVEMENT AND REDUCING QUALITY COSTS

The key factor in the reduction of quality costs is quality improvement, and a key factor in quality improvement is corrective action. Quality costs do not reduce themselves. They are merely the scorecard. They can tell you where you are and where your corrective action dollar will afford the greatest return. Quality costs do identify targets for corrective action.

Once a target for corrective action is identified, through Pareto or other methods of quality cost analysis, the action necessary must be carefully determined. It must be individually justified on the basis of an equitable cost trade-off. You do not want to resolve a $500 problem with a $5000 solution. At this point, experience in measuring quality costs will be invaluable for estimating the payback on individual corrective action investments or quality improvement projects. Cost–benefit justification of corrective action and quality improvement projects should be a continuing part of the quality management program.

Some problems have fairly obvious solutions, such as the replacement of a worn bearing or a worn tool, that can be fixed immediately. Others are not so obvious, such as a marginal condition in design or processing, and are almost never discovered and corrected without the benefit of a well-organized and formal approach. Marginal conditions usually result in problems that can easily become lost in the accepted cost of doing business. Having an organized quality improvement program and corrective action system, justified by quality costs, will reveal such problems for management's visibility and action. The true value of corrective action is that you only have to pay for it once, whereas failure to take corrective action may be paid for over and over again.

QUALITY COST PRINCIPLES AND LESSONS

Traditional quality cost methods have been around a long time—about half a century. These principles still apply today and will for the foreseeable future. However, through our experiences with quality costs over that time, some useful lessons learned can be identified that can be applied in the future.

The first lesson is that speaking the language of money is essential. For a successful quality effort, the single most important element is leadership by upper management. To gain that leadership, some concepts or tools could be proposed, but that is the wrong approach. Instead, management should first be convinced that a problem exists that requires their attention and action, such as excessive costs due to poor quality. A quality cost study, particularly when coupled with a successful pilot quality improvement project, is a solid way to gain management support for a broad quality improvement effort. Excessive cost is a quality-related hot button for management. Loss of sales revenue is another.

The second lesson learned is that quality cost measurement and publication do not solve quality problems. They must be used. Improvement projects must be identified, clear responsibilities established, and resources provided to diagnose and remove the cause of problems, as well as other essential steps. New organizational machinery is needed to attack and reduce the high costs of poor quality.

The third lesson is that the scope of traditional quality costs should be expanded. Traditionally, quality costs have emphasized the cost of nonconformities. Important as this cost is, we also need to estimate the cost of inefficient processes. This includes variation of product characteristics (even on conforming products), redundant operations, sorting inspections, and other forms of non-value-added activities. Another area to be considered is the cost of lost opportunities for sales revenue.

The fourth lesson is that the traditional categories of quality costs have had a remarkable longevity. About 50 years ago, some pioneers proposed that quality costs be assigned the categories of prevention, appraisal, and failure. Many practitioners found the categories useful and even devised ingenious ways to adapt the categories beyond manufacturing, as in engineering design, and also to the service sector, as in financial services and healthcare. The principles still work today. The difference is in their additional applications.

Quality costs have expanded to become a principal management and quality improvement tool. Definitions and standards have been developed and refined along with techniques and methods for implementation. Quality cost principles and concepts have been expanded to include lessons learned over the past half century, with applications now including the software and service sectors. The quality cost program is the bridge between line and executive management. It provides a common language and a measurement and evaluation system that shows how quality pays in increased profits, productivity, and customer acceptance.

Chapter 15

F. Quality Training

> Quality Training. Identify and define key
> elements of a training program, including
> conducting a needs analysis, developing
> curricula and materials, and determining the
> program's effectiveness.
>
> **Body of Knowledge II.F**

INTRODUCTION

To keep an organization healthy, its people must be continually trained in new concepts and techniques. The late Frank Gryna epitomized the role of quality engineer as leader and trainer. In addition to the college students he helped educate and the adult workers he trained, he inspired hundreds of professionals to become passionate, skillful carriers of the quality torch as trainers. Gryna (1988) stated "the need is to extend training in quality-related matters to personnel in all functions." He stated that while U.S. companies [formerly] trained only quality-related specialists in quality, the Japanese, from the very beginning of their industrial renaissance in 1946, targeted *all* departments, and that "this difference in training contributed to a quality crisis" for the United States.

Training may be formal or informal, large scale or small. Although it is usually delivered by instructors in classrooms, training can be done through directed self-study with workbooks or computer guidance. A powerful training method in the areas of intellectual skills and human relations is mentoring. The mentor provides guidance, inspiration, and motivation. Likewise, well-structured improvement projects can include a training component. Project leaders are given special instructions to ensure that team members learn various skills as they complete the project. For details see the section on facilitation in Chapter 5.

If the training task is small, it may involve only two people: an apprentice working alongside a master. At the other extreme it may require a fully staffed training and development department with a budget in the millions. In some companies, such as McDonalds and Motorola, this department is called a corporate university, and manages dozens of instructors delivering courses, seminars, exercises, and workshops year round. The middle ground would be *you*, a quality engineer who must organize a small training program yourself, or help a task team build a larger one.

DEVELOPING A TRAINING PROGRAM

Essentially the same development process must be used, regardless of size. Many training programs are organized in five phases, as follows:

1. Assess the need for training

2. Design a curriculum, or training plan

3. Develop the lesson plans and training materials

4. Implement the plan, that is, deliver the instruction

5. Evaluate effectiveness of the training

This is called the ADDIE model, using the first letter of the first word of each phase. Some have proposed surrounding these five phases with a beginning called "customer identification" and an ending called "maintain beneficial outcomes," resulting in the CADDIEM model. Many other variations are used, as illustrated by the following success story.

Training Case Study Number One

At Tennessee Eastman Company in 1980, a companywide training program evolved from concern about poor quality attitudes. The project was reported by Hill and McClaskey (1980) (available at www.asq.org/qic).

1. *Determining the purpose.* This phase involved upper and middle management, numerous operational units, and the training department. The stated purpose was not to create a training program, but to improve overall quality performance. Only after several weeks of discussions and surveys was a training program decided on.

2. *Developing alternatives that will achieve the purpose.* Through the use of focus groups, brainstorming, and exchange of memos, several dozen alternatives were proposed. Seven were selected for further study. Two of the seven were:

   • Require position guides that include quality responsibilities

   • Create a central quality organization to coordinate development and dissemination of information and requirements.

3. *Analyzing the alternatives.* A set of five weighted criteria was developed, including such items as "chance of completion," and "flexibility of format." The alternative with the highest score was "teach about quality responsibilities."

4. *Designing the selected program.* Many elements were specified. Some typical design parameters were:

- Create awareness of quality responsibilities

- Cover total learning needs in quality awareness

- Be adaptable to specific needs

- Be used only by people requiring the knowledge

- Be portable and usable near work area

- Have a maximum length of two hours

After the design criteria were set, a survey was taken of all employees, with 40 potential courses listed. Using the survey, the task force proceeded to develop 16 new courses.

5. *Implementing the solution.* The team proceeded to write outlines and scripts, identify needed materials, and publish results, calling on others for help as needed. Teachers were selected and trained, a budget was set up, a cost tracking system was created, and the courses were put in place for delivery. The courses ran for several years with periodic updates.

6. *Evaluating the results.* Pre- and post-tests were regularly used to determine how much was learned.

NEEDS ANALYSIS

If large-scale training is contemplated, spend more time than you think necessary in assessing the needs. Stay open-minded as to possibilities. A thorough needs analysis can prevent wasting of large amounts of time and money on ineffective or inadequate training. For example, you might start out thinking a training program is needed, only to discover through needs assessment that your problem is solved by organizational realignment.

The methods of quality function deployment (QFD) are very suitable to needs assessment. One key QFD tool is the matrix chart, which can be used to organize the results of surveys and focus groups. See Chapter 7 for more details about QFD.

DEVELOPING CURRICULA AND MATERIALS

The curriculum flows naturally from the needs analysis. It states learning objectives and how they will be achieved in each training event, whether by lecturer, demonstration, role play, or other method. Suppliers, customers, or even competitors may share their curriculum ideas. Subject matter experts and training professionals need to partner in this phase because of its highly technical and subject-specific nature.

Write Lesson Plans

Once the curriculum is set, the lesson plans flow rather naturally (it helps to have experience or a good mentor). There are numerous issues to resolve, such as detailed content, sequencing, depth, breadth, review points, quizzes, and demonstrations.

Choose Training Materials

Finding suitable materials is not a problem. However, selecting from the plethora of artifacts, paper and electronic media, simulations, workbooks, role plays, and so on, might be a problem. Remember that training can be structured in many ways. Formal classrooms may be appropriate but often the best training area is actually the workplace, with carefully designed instructional aids so that training occurs as the work is done. Creativity and imagination are definitely in order.

For developing intellectual skills such as facilitation and conflict resolution, role playing is highly recommended. It is a good way to increase the learners' involvement in the process. Designing good role plays can be time-consuming. But Stolovitch (1992) explained how role plays and simulations can be developed during the learning process in certain situations. Book discussion groups can focus management attention on timely issues with little or no development cost.

A rapidly growing body of training material is now available electronically, through both video and computer. In fact these two technologies are gradually converging. A number of different organizations offer products and assistance in this exciting new area of training materials. Web search engines such as Google and Yahoo will find many entries dealing with this rapidly changing area.

Select and Train the Trainer

Both technical competence and teaching skills are mandatory! An experienced quality engineer might need special "how to teach" training, since technical competence does not ensure teaching skill. "Train the trainer" programs can be anything from a colleague giving informal mentoring to an eight-week off-site course. Remember, students must respect both teaching ability and competence for much learning to take place.

DETERMINE EFFECTIVENESS

Referring to the ADDIE model, evaluation (step 5) and needs analysis (step 1) are closely related. Both are learning experiences for the training team. It is very important for credibility to demonstrate that something useful has been accomplished. And if the outcome was poor you need to know quickly to take immediate corrective action.

Some informal evaluation can occur while the course is under way. Especially if the instructor is new, a trusted colleague or mentor can help with discussions and role play exercises, and can visit with attendees during breaks. The single most prevalent (and probably most cost-effective) form of evaluation is the pre- and post-test of knowledge.

Attendee evaluation forms (rate the instructor, rate the course) have been widely used in the past but this technique is not recommended as there is too much

Table 15.1 Five different levels of evaluation.

Level	Name	Question	Techniques
1	Reaction	How did learners feel?	Post-instruction questionnaires or interviews. Learners report impressions of instructor, curriculum, facilities, and content.
2	Learning	What did learners retain?	Pre-test and post-test, checking for gains in either knowledge or performance.
3	Behavior	Did learners change?	Assessors must collect data at the workplace to evaluate changes in skill and performance.
4	Organizational	Is the impact beyond learner?	Large-scale surveys of morale, product quality, turnover, and so on, followed by executive conferences.
5	Return on investment	Is there an effect on the bottom line?	Analyze financial data carefully constructed by professionals. Six Sigma includes this element in program evaluation.

room for subjectivity. This is known as level 1 evaluation in Donald Kirkpatrick's hierarchy (Kirkpatrick 2006), shown with one additional level in Table 15.1. The fifth level is most informative but also quite difficult and expensive to achieve.

Why Training Programs Fail

According to Gryna (1988), 10 reasons why training programs fail are:

1. Cultural resistance by line managers

2. Doubt as to the usefulness of the training

3. Lack of participation by line managers

4. Technique rather than problem orientation

5. Inadequacy of leader/instructor

6. Mixing of participant levels

7. Lack of application during the course

8. Overly complex language

9. Lack of participation by the training function

10. Operational and logistical deficiencies

Consider reason #7 in more detail. To quote Gryna, "The ideal approach is to design the course so that the participants must apply the training during the course. One of the best learning experiences is the application of the material being taught.

This was successfully done during World War II in the area of work-simplification programs. More recently, value engineering seminars often have a project included as part of the seminar. Quality circles also use the concept." In the years since Gryna published those words, the scope and effectiveness of training for quality in the United States has greatly increased.

What We Know About Adult Learners

Most training programs are directed toward adults. Knowles (1996) pointed out significant facts about how adults learn. Three of his conclusions are:

1. Adults decide for themselves what is and isn't important to learn. In order to be sure learning takes place, the trainer should state specifically what should be learned and how it relates to on-the-job performance.

2. Adults buy in to training when it is supported on the job by supervisors and management.

3. Adults who are happy in their jobs are more receptive to training; and adults who are well-trained for their jobs are happier employees.

Case Study Number Two

This case illustrates pitfalls # 4 (technique orientation), #5 (inadequacies of leader/instructor), #7 (no immediate application), and #8 (language too complex). It also demonstrates the importance of Knowles's conclusion #1 above.

The manager of an engineering design unit decided that his engineers should learn how to use statistics in their daily work. A recent PhD in statistics was recruited from a nearby university. He loved the beauty of statistics and mathematics. Without really thinking it through, he assumed that the attendees shared his own values. Since they all had engineering degrees, he knew they possessed the needed mathematical background, and he unconsciously assumed they could pick up the jargon.

Neither the instructor nor his sponsor checked to see what the attendees wanted, and so he started teaching much the same techniques and theories, using the same language, as with his undergraduate students. After two days, the grumbling became so loud that the instructor was directed to meet with lead engineers to find out what was going wrong. A complete redirection of the course was made, but half the course was over before it could be implemented, and it was impossible by then to build any rapport between instructor and class. Ultimately the effort was judged a complete failure, and the practicing engineers' prior prejudices against "statistics and statisticians" were reinforced. It was a negative experience all round and could have been prevented by more sensitive planning and understanding before the course began.

Another probable reason for the failure was a lack of awareness on the part of both instructor and sponsor of the difference between training and education, which is highlighted in Figure 15.1. The instructor was used to working in the education environment, but the sponsor was expecting a training program.

Part II.F

Training	Education
Providing skills and techniques for immediate application in a job or related (for example, lifesaving, pottery-making) situation. Generally sponsored by employers for immediate payoff.	Developing one's knowledge and understanding, with a goal of enriching one's life in an unpredictable future. Generally paid for by taxpayers, foundations, parents, and long-term student loans.

Figure 15.1 Training versus education.

A FINAL THOUGHT . . .

We leave you with this thought: in a sense, life is a process of continually alternating between two kinds of events—learning, and doing what you have learned. When you do a training event, you are also helping someone else to learn. Do it well and you enrich the learner's life as well as your own.

SUMMARY OF PART II

Part II is all about the quality system. The first three chapters of Part II address system elements, documentation, and standards/guidelines. The last three chapters address auditing, training, and cost of quality.

The quality system is an enabling mechanism that provides the framework for achieving quality. It must be formal, it must be detailed, it must be explicitly documented, and it must be understood by the people who use it.

There is more than one way to approach the design of a quality system. Two quite different approaches are the "requirements" approach of the ISO 9001 standard and the "guidelines" approach of the Baldrige Award.

ISO 9001 is a worldwide standard of requirements. It uses a controlled vocabulary spelled out in ISO 9000. It is complemented by guidelines in ISO 9004, which allows for nonrequired improvement activities. Those who wish to be registered must prepare all their materials and then submit to a formal audit verifying that they are doing what they say they are doing. The Baldrige Award program is completely voluntary and utilizes guidelines and examiners to choose national winners in various categories each year.

Quality auditing is a cousin of quality engineering. While there is overlap between the two specialties, each has its own unique role. Auditing is a critical part of maintaining a quality system.

Cost of quality concepts and tools help quality professionals justify our role in the language of top management: money. The basic concept is to track costs throughout the entire organization and then show how spending money on quality activities saves much more money in reduced failure and waste. Many tools are provided to make this quality system an effective one.

Training is essential to maintaining organizational excellence, and quality engineers may be asked to put on their training hats from time to time. Needs must be assessed and the training curriculum must then be designed. After assembling all the necessary materials and conducting the training, its effectiveness is assessed.

Part III
Product and Process Design

The five chapters in Part III cover the different elements that quality engineers use in quality initiatives involving products and processes. The areas covered in this section include classification of quality characteristics (as opposed to product defects, which are discussed in Part IV), design inputs and review elements, elements of technical drawings and specifications, design verification to ensure fitness for use, and reliability and maintainability.

Part III

Chapter 16

A. Classification of Quality Characteristics

> Define, interpret, and classify quality characteristics for new products and processes. (Evaluate).
>
> **Body of Knowledge III.A**

Quality characteristics are features that describe the fit and function of a product or process and aid in differentiating between items of a given sample or population. To differentiate items from each other, and/or to compare items to a standard, measurements and/or comparisons are used. *Variables* data are represented by direct measurement on a continuous scale. *Attributes* data are most often discrete data usually reported in the form of counts. The counts are classified by category with the most common categories being pass/fail, go/no-go, and accept/reject. (For more details on variables, attributes, and continuous and discrete data see Chapters 27, 32, and 34).

MEASUREMENT OF VARIABLES DATA

Measurement is the process of evaluating a property or characteristic of an object and describing it with a numerical or nominal value. A quality characteristic is referred to as a *variable* if it is measurable over a continuous scale. For example, in healthcare a patient's temperature can be measured with an electronic thermometer. Other examples could include measurements related to weight, length, diameter, or cost.

MEASUREMENT OF ATTRIBUTES DATA

If the quality characteristic of interest can't be directly measured, then each item under inspection is often classified into one of two or more categories. For example, items inspected may be classified as conforming or nonconforming. Each product unit is assigned one of these two labels according to inspection operation results. It is then possible to derive a numerical measure of process quality using a quantitative scale. The numerical measure is achieved by calculating the *fraction nonconforming* as the ratio between the number of units labeled as nonconforming and the total number of units inspected. When the item inspected can be classified into one of exactly two possible categories, the binomial distribution is often appropriate to model this situation. (See Chapters 27 and 32 for more details on attributes data and the binomial distribution.)

Another commonly used attribute quality characteristic is the number of nonconformities (or number of defects) observed on an item inspected. In this situation, a single item inspected may have more than one nonconformity or defect. For example, a car door panel may have more than one scratch, dent, or discoloration. These would be considered nonconformities on the single item inspected, in this case the car door panel. The number of nonconformities is often well modeled by the Poisson distribution. (See Chapters 27 and 32 for more details on number of nonconformities and the Poisson distribution.)

Limit Gages

A common method of inspection by attributes involves the use of limit gages, also known as fixed limit gages or *go/no-go gages*. Limit gages are made to sizes essentially identical with the design specification limits of the dimension to be inspected. If a specific gage can properly mate with a part, then the part can be assembled with another part whose physical boundaries do not exceed those of the gage. Consequently, the part is acceptable for assembly. Limit gages designed to identify this condition are called *go gages*. (See Figure 16.1.)

The *go* end of a go/no-go gage is designed to check the characteristic at the maximum material condition (minimum size for interior features, maximum size for exterior features). The maximum material condition produces the minimum clearance required for assembly.

The *no-go* end is designed to detect conditions of excessive clearance. It checks the characteristic at its minimum material condition. A part will not mate with a no-go gage unless the actual condition of the part feature is below the specified minimum. Thus, if the no-go gage mates with the part, then the part dimension is out of specification and the part should be rejected.

In practice, go/no-go gages are used together and often appear at opposite ends of an inspection instrument. An acceptable part should mate with the go end but should not mate with the no-go end. Parts that mate with neither or both ends do not meet design specifications and should be rejected.

Other than gauging, most methods of inspection by attributes are largely subjective and depend on the ability of human inspectors to make the right decisions. In many cases inspection by attributes involves visual characteristics, such as color, shape, or smoothness, and other visual defects.

Figure 16.1   Go/no-go gage to check the diameter of a shaft.

Chapter 17

B. Design Inputs and Review

> Identify sources of design inputs such as
> customer needs, regulatory requirements,
> etc. and how they translate into design
> concepts such as robust design, QFD, and
> Design for X (DFX, where X can mean six
> sigma (DFSS), manufacturability (DFM), cost
> (DFC), etc.). Identify and apply common
> elements of the design review process,
> including roles and responsibilities of
> participants. (Analyze)
>
> **Body of Knowledge III.B**

DESIGN BACKGROUND AND DEFINITION

Design is a term that describes the thought processes, procedures, tools, documentation, and specifications associated with products and processes. Designs are developed to document and ensure compliance with customer expectations as they relate to operational capabilities and characteristics of products and processes.

THE PRODUCT/PROCESS DEVELOPMENT LIFECYCLE

Whether for products or processes, designs progress through phases. Design phases are linked to phases within the product/process development lifecycle, wherein the product/process development lifecycle typically includes the following:

- *Definition phase.* In this phase, a problem or opportunity is clearly defined, documented, refined, and consensus on the definition is reached among stakeholders.

- *Specification phase.* In this phase, specifications are set that lead to, or provide, a product or process desired by the customer. Specifications are commonly applied to characteristics that affect the form, fit, or function of a product or process. Specifications also are commonly applied to characteristics that affect the reliability of a product or process to function in a given environment, within a given range of temperature, or for a given period of time or cycle of operation.

- *Concept phase.* In this phase, all possible solutions to solve the problem or exploit the opportunity are explored. During the concept phase, feasible solutions are identified and nonfeasible solutions are dismissed.

- *Detailed design phase.* In this phase, specifications and the most feasible concept are used as the basis for development of detailed plans for a product or process design.

- *Prototype phase.* In this phase, a working model of the detailed design is fabricated and tested in a laboratory or development environment for its ability to perform or operate as intended.

- *Production phase.* In this phase, following successful development, testing, and refinement of a prototype, production units of the design are produced in sufficient volume to satisfy customer demand. Production phase units are produced not in a laboratory or development environment as were prototype units, but are produced with tools, equipment, methods, and procedures used on the shop floor or service delivery area, and these production units are produced by regular production or service delivery personnel.

- *Distribution phase.* In this phase, the product or process enters the supply chain for sale and distribution.

- *Normal use phase.* In this phase, the product or process is released to the customer for use in its intended role or function. During normal use, products and processes require normal maintenance, repair (warranty and non-warranty), and customers frequently require technical assistance and support.

- *Obsolescence and disposal phase.* In this phase, products and processes lose their usefulness due to normal wear, catastrophic failure (planned or unplanned), introduction of enhancements to an existing design, or changes in technology. As products and processes become obsolete, the original designer must consider whether or how to provide enhancements enabling extended life and/or the designer must consider how to safely and ethically address disposal.

How a design links with the product/process development lifecycle (that is, which specific design phases are used, and how the work of various design phases are related to the product/process development lifecycle) depends completely on the model used as a basis for a design. It should be noted that there are numerous models or approaches for design, far too many models to provide an exhaustive list in this book. One model for review of designs, however, is well developed, sufficiently universal, applies to products or processes, and is known as the Systems

Engineering Technical Review Process as described in the United States Navy, Naval Air Systems Command (NAVAIR) Instruction 4355.19C (April, 2006). Available at http://www.navair.navy.mil/kms/41g.

DESIGN REVIEW

In accordance with NAVAIR Instruction 4355.19C, there are 12 phases of design review as follows:

- Initial Technical Review (ITR)
- Alternative Systems Review (ASR)
- Systems Requirements Review (SRR)
- Technology Readiness Assessment (TRA)
- System Functional Review (SFR)
- Preliminary Design Review (PDR)
- Critical Design Review (CDR)
- Test Readiness Review (TRR)
- Flight Readiness Review (FRR) (for airborne systems)
- System Verification Review/Production Readiness Review (SVR/PRR)
- Physical Configuration Audit (PCA)
- In-Service Review (ISR)

Depending on the type and complexity of the design, any or all of the design reviews may be completed. The depth of detail, analysis, and documentation should increase as the design reviews progress toward completion. Design reviews are not intended for solving design-related problems but rather to verify completion of problem-solving activities by cross-functional teams. Discovery of too many design-related problems during a design review may indicate that a design review is being conducted prematurely.

Although the product development group is responsible for creating a design, no one group can provide all the necessary assurance that the design is adequate. Therefore, design reviews should be conducted periodically by a cross-functional team until the design and process are finalized. Quality and manufacturing should be active participants in the review process. Suppliers also should participate if possible. Early sourcing commitments enable suppliers to attend the design reviews and contribute their expertise prior to investing in expensive tooling. Drawings should comply with applicable standards for drafting, dimensioning, and tolerances. At each review, the design must be considered from several different viewpoints:

- *Reliability.* Will the failure rate be sufficiently low?
- *Quality engineering.* Can the design be adequately inspected and tested?

- *Field engineering.* Are proper installation, maintenance, and user-handling features included in the design?

- *Procurement.* Can the necessary parts be acquired at acceptable costs, delivery schedules, and quality levels?

- *Materials engineering.* Will the selected materials perform as expected?

- *Tooling engineering.* Is the equipment capable of meeting the specified tolerances on a consistent basis?

- *Packaging engineering.* Can the product be shipped without damage?

- *Outside consultants.* Have appropriate outside consultants been called for when necessary?

- *Customer.* Should a customer representative participate in the design reviews for military applications and original equipment manufacturers?

- *Other design engineers.* Are other design engineers needed when there are tight tolerances to mating components or critical system interfaces?

DESIGN INPUTS

Designs for products and processes are influenced by factors known as inputs. Inputs are simply requirements placed on products and processes that relate to:

- Customer needs and expectations (for example, time of delivery, cost, performance characteristics)

- Regulatory requirements (for example, safety of end users, safety of production/service delivery personnel, use of hazardous chemicals, distribution to unauthorized personnel/vendors, control of sensitive technology)

- Patents and technology licensing (for example, protections for existing designs owned by competitors)

- Product/process capabilities

- Product/process reliability

Translating Design Inputs into Basic Design Concepts

The design inputs identified above translate into basic design concepts relevant to quality engineering, particularly when the nature of a design emphasizes a specific characteristic. When a specific characteristic is emphasized, the nature of the design may be considered "constrained" wherein the design input must either guide design efforts (such as the case with design for Six Sigma), or the design input must constrain the product or process resulting from the design (such as the case with design for cost). When a design does emphasize a specific characteristic, the design is referred to as "design for *X*," where *X* may be Six Sigma, cost, manufacturability, or reliability. Awareness of the basic design concepts and how they relate to the design process are included within the Certified Quality Engineer Body of Knowledge and are addressed as follows:

Design for Six Sigma. Design for Six Sigma (DFSS) is not to be confused with the well-known DMAIC approach to Six Sigma. While DMAIC Six Sigma focuses on solving problems in existing products or processes, DFSS focuses on eliminating problems before they occur.

Design for Cost. Design for Cost (DFC) is a design constraint that begins with cost targets as drivers of the design process. DFC differs from most commonly used traditional design processes, which typically tally development costs at the end of the design process with little regard for cost targets.

Design for Manufacturability. Design for Manufacturability (DFM) is an approach to the design of products and processes that focuses on cost-effectiveness, simplification, optimization, and mistake-proofing to enhance manufacturability. DFM applies both to the product/process design as well as the use/selection of manufacturing technology.

Design for Reliability. Design for Reliability (DFR) is an approach to design that focuses on development of products and processes able to perform under specified conditions, in a specified environment, and for specified periods of time.

Related Design Inputs and Basic Design Concepts

Quality Function Deployment. Quality Function Deployment (QFD) provides a framework for the design process that captures the "voice of the customer" (VOC) via a series of matrices. Once captured, the VOC is used to guide design efforts to ensure that customer expectations are met. See page 65 for more information on QFD.

Concurrent Engineering. Concurrent engineering is practice of the design function and associated activities by a team of engineers, technicians, management, and administrative personnel such that all aspects of the design phases are considered simultaneously.

Chapter 18

C. Technical Drawings and Specifications

Interpret technical drawings including characteristics such as views, title blocks, dimensioning, tolerancing, GD&T symbols, and so on. Interpret specification requirements in relation to product and process characteristics. (Evaluate)

Body of Knowledge III.C

DIMENSIONING AND TOLERANCING

It is expected that drawings have dimensions that provide detailed information about sizes, shapes, and the location of different components and parts. It is also expected that part and component dimensions show acceptable variation. To produce any part or component to an exact dimension is nearly impossible, except by remote chance. Variations in materials, machines, manufacturing parameters, and humans make it necessary that dimensions have acceptable variations. Such variation is referred to as *tolerance.* Higher quality requires tighter tolerances that, in turn, require more expensive and strict production and inspection procedures to obtain. There are two types of tolerances: unilateral tolerance and bilateral tolerance. Unilateral tolerance specifies allowable variation in a dimension from a basic or nominal size in one direction in relation to that basic size.

For example: $2.000^{+0.000/-0.005}$ inches describes an allowable variation only in the lower limit: unilateral tolerance. Specifications on a part with this tolerance will be 2.000 inches and 1.995 inches as desired upper and lower limits, respectively. On the other hand, $2.000^{+0.005/-0.005}$ inches describes a bilateral tolerance. It does specify a dimension with allowable variations in both directions of the basic size. Specifications on a part with such bilateral tolerance will be 2.005 inches and 1.995 inches as desired upper and lower limits, respectively.

Geometric Dimensioning and Tolerancing (GD&T)

Geometric tolerancing defines tolerances for geometric features or characteristics on a part. Figure 18.1 shows some of the geometric dimensioning symbols as defined in ANSI Y14.5M. Figure 18.2 illustrates the interpretation of a geometric tolerance on a drawing.

The limit dimensions of the simple cylindrical piece at the top of Figure 18.3 define the maximum and minimum limits of a profile for the work. The form or shape of the part may vary as long as no portions of the part exceed the maximum profile limit or are inside the minimum profile limit. If a part measures its maximum material limit of size everywhere, it should be of perfect form. This is referred to as the *maximum material condition* (MMC) and is at the low limit for a hole or slot but at the high limit for parts such as shafts, bolts, or pins.

If it is desired to provide greater control on the form than is imposed by the limit dimensions, then certain tolerances of form must be applied. In most cases, these tolerances appear in the form of notations on the drawing as is illustrated at the bottom of Figure 18.3.

Geometric Symbols

Straightness	——	Concentricity	◎
Flatness	▱	Profile of a line	⌒
Parallelism	⫽	Profile of a surface	⌓
Perpendicularity	⊥	True position	⊕
Angularity	∠	Runout	↗
Roundness	○	Total runout	↗↗
Cylindericity	⌀		

Other Symbols

Maximum material condition (MMC)	Ⓜ
Least material condition (LMC)	Ⓛ
Diameter	⌀
Datum is A	– A –

Figure 18.1   Some geometric tolerancing symbols.

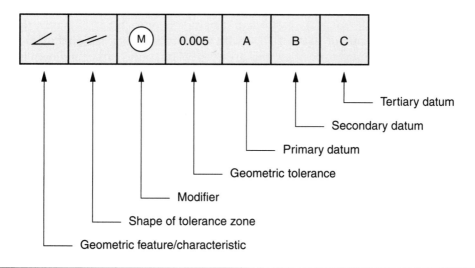

Figure 18.2 Interpretation of a geometric tolerance on a drawing.

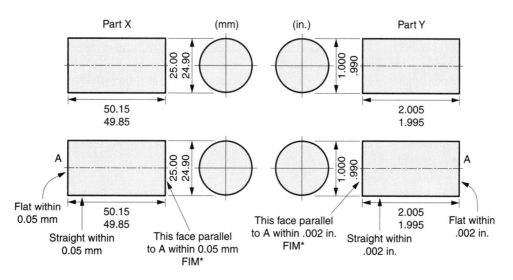

*FIM = Full indicator movement

Figure 18.3 Part drawing with and without tolerances of form.

Reprinted with permission of the Society of Manufacturing Engineers, *Manufacturing Processes and Materials*, 4th Edition, Copyright 2000.

Positional Tolerances

Positional tolerancing is a system of specifying the true position, size, or form of a part feature and the amount it may vary from the ideal. The advantage of the system is that it allows the one responsible for making the part to divide tolerances between position and size as he or she finds best. The principles are illustrated for two simple mating parts in Figure 18.4. The basic dimensions without tolerances are shown at the bottom and right side of each part. Beneath the size dimension for holes or posts is a box with the notations for positional tolerancing. Actually, a number of specifications are possible but only one set is shown here as an example. The circle and cross in the first cell of the box is the convention that says the feature has a positional tolerance.

Part I in Figure 18.4 introduces the idea of the MMC utilized in most positional tolerancing. This is designated by the letter M in a circle and means that the smallest hole (12.70 mm or .500 in.) determines the inner boundary for any hole. The "Ø 0.20 mm (.008 in.)" notation in the box specifies that the axis of any minimum-size hole must not be outside a theoretical cylinder of 0.20 mm (.008 in.) diameter around the true position. A 12.50 mm (.492 in.) diameter plug in true position will fit in any 12.70 mm (.500 in.) diameter hole with its axis on the 0.20 mm (.008 in.) diameter cylinder. Any hole that passes over such a plug is acceptable, provided that its diameter is within the high and low limits specified.

The letter "A" in the specification box designates that the theoretical cylinder bounding the hole axes must be perpendicular to the datum surface carrying the "A" flag. Features usually are referred to with three coordinate datum surfaces, but for simplicity, in this case, the holes are related only to each other and surface "A" and not to the sides of the part.

Part II of Figure 18.4 introduces the idea of zero maximum material condition specified by "Ø 0.000" before the MMC symbol. This means the axis of the largest-diameter post (12.50 mm [.492 in.]) must be exactly in the true position, but smaller sizes of posts may vary in position as long as they do not lie outside the boundary set by the largest. Thus, if the posts are held to a tolerance smaller than the 0.20 mm (.008 in.) specified, say to a tolerance of 0.05 mm (.002 in.), the difference (0.15 mm [.006 in.]) is then available for variations in post positions. The advantage of zero MMC is that only one limit of the feature, in this case the lower limit of the post diameter, needs to be checked along with position.

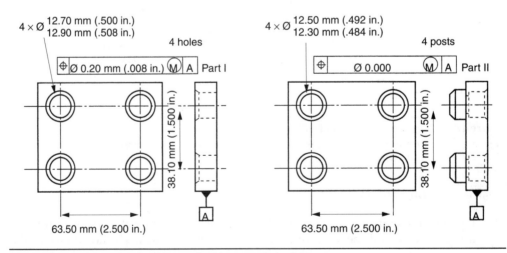

Figure 18.4 Two parts dimensioned with positional tolerances.

Chapter 19

D. Design Verification

Identify and apply various evaluations and
tests to qualify and validate the design of
new products and processes to ensure their
fitness for use. (Evaluate)

Body of Knowledge III.D

Design verification consists of a series of evaluations and tests to validate the design and ensure that it is fit for use in its intended environment. The test methods, sample sizes, and acceptance criteria should be clearly specified during conceptual planning of a product or process, and the design should be validated at each phase of the design review. When designing the tests, consider incorporating the following factors:

- Dimensional wear, material fatigue, assembly process variation

- Variation of critical characteristics throughout the range of the tolerances

- Contamination

- Environmental aging and extreme environmental conditions

- Extreme customer usage, such as maximum loads or long duty cycles

Test results should be analyzed using appropriate statistical methods, including reliability analysis. Reliability testing falls into four major categories, as delineated in MIL-STD-785B10:

- Environmental stress screening to identify early failures due to weak parts or poor workmanship

- Reliability growth tests, to be performed periodically between design conception and final production, to track the improvement of reliability and the resolution of reliability concerns

- Reliability qualification tests to provide assurance that production units will meet requirements when they become available

- Production reliability acceptance tests to periodically verify that
  production units meet specified reliability requirements

A more detailed discussion of reliability and maintainability is provided in Chapter 20. Test failures should be carefully examined to determine the failure modes. Unanticipated failure modes must be added to the design failure mode and effects analysis (DFMEA). Of course, corrective actions and design improvements must be pursued if the test results do not meet the quality goals.

Results of engineering evaluations, reliability tests, and other methods used to validate the design should be included in the design reviews. In addition, this information should be used to update the classification of quality characteristics. As is the case with many quality disciplines, the process of classifying characteristics should be iterative. Characteristics that are associated with unexpected failures may require reclassification as major or critical characteristics. Characteristics that perform as expected may be candidates for downgrading to minor characteristics. In all cases, involve the quality team in the discussions. There can be no substitute for the experience and process knowledge the team members bring to the design review process. More information on MIL-STD-785B10 can be found at http://assist.daps.dla.mil/quicksearch. Marsh (2004) provides a simple short discussion of canceled U.S. military specifications.

Chapter 20

E. Reliability and Maintainability

INTRODUCTION

This chapter focuses on estimating and predicting reliability and defines other reliability measures for repairable systems, such as maintainability and availability. Other chapters in this handbook focus on quality as a static characteristic of a product at the time it is released to the user. However, because reliability is a time-dependent quality characteristic, traditional methods for quality control cannot be used to ensure product reliability and maintainability. Finally, this chapter discusses systems, techniques, and failure models for analyzing a system in order to determine its potential failures.

Because reliability engineering is a broad field, it is impossible to cover the entire range of reliability topics in one chapter. This chapter focuses on reliability and maintainability definitions, analysis of failure data, design of systems for reliability, and maintainability and risk analysis using fault tree analysis (FTA), failure mode and effects analysis (FMEA), failure mode effects and criticality analysis (FMECA), and environmental stress screening (ESS). Reliability and maintainability as elements of product and process design will be viewed in four parts: predictive and preventive maintenance tools, reliability and maintainability indices, the bathtub curve, and reliability, safety, and hazard assessment tools.

1. PREDICTIVE AND PREVENTIVE MAINTENANCE TOOLS

> Describe and apply predictive and preventive maintenance tools and techniques to maintain and improve process and product reliability. (Analyze)
>
> **Body of Knowledge III.E.1**

Reliability is defined as the probability that a product or service will operate properly for a specified period of time (design life) under the design operating conditions. The main factors that lead to a system's failure include the system's design and configuration, the reliability of its components, the operating environment, and the interactions among environmental factors, manufacturing defects, and preventive and scheduled maintenance. Further, reliability cannot be measured at the release time of the product but can only be predicted (Elsayed 2000).

Therefore, it is extremely important to consider reliability during the design phase of a product or service because minor, major, and catastrophic failures result in economic consequences such as repairs or replacements, the loss of production or interruption of service, and potentially severe economic losses and the loss of life. Examples of major failures are:

- Failure of a major link of a telecommunications network

- Failure of a power generating unit

- Failure of software for an air traffic control system

The consequences of catastrophic failures are much more severe than minor or major failures, and may include the loss of human life and significant economic losses. Examples of catastrophic failures are:

- Explosions at the Chernobyl nuclear reactors site in the former USSR (Elsayed 1996)

- Explosion of the space shuttle Challenger in 1986

- Failure of the space shuttle Columbia in 2003

Reliability also has a great effect on consumers' perception of a manufacturer. For example, consumers' experiences with automobile recalls, repairs, and warranties affect the manufacturer's future sales. Another example shows the importance of reliability: 6.5 million tires were recalled after 46 deaths were attributed to the separation of the tread from the tire causing vehicles to skid or roll over.

Defining and Estimating Reliability

Reliability usually is defined in terms of the probability that a product or service will perform properly under specified conditions for a specified period of time.

Three important functions that are the result of traditional calculus derivations help quantify reliability: the *reliability function*, the *failure time distribution function* (sometimes referred to as the probability density function), and the *hazard rate function* (or instantaneous failure rate).

Suppose N identical components are tested. During a specified time interval t, we observe x failures and $(N - x)$ survivors. Because reliability is defined as the cumulative probability function of success, then at time t the reliability $R(t)$ is:

$$R(t) = \frac{(N - x)}{N} \qquad (20\text{--}1)$$

In other words, the *reliability function* (or survival function) at time t is the fraction of all components that have survived for a time greater than t. $R(t)$ is also used as the estimate of the probability that a randomly selected component will survive for a time greater than t. In order to describe the distribution of failures, the cumulative distribution function (cdf) of failure $F(t)$ can be defined as:

$$F(t) = \frac{x}{N} \tag{20-2}$$

(See Chapter 34 for more details on cumulative distribution functions.) The cdf given in (20–2) can be interpreted as:

- The probability that a randomly selected unit drawn from a population fails by time t, or

- The fraction of all units in the population that fail by time t.

In addition, $F(t)$ is the *complement* of $R(t)$ and

$$F(t) + R(t) = 1. \tag{20-3}$$

Equation (20–3) can be rewritten as:

$$R(t) = 1 - F(t) \tag{20-4}$$

or

$$F(t) = 1 - R(t) \tag{20-5}$$

Suppose N identical units are selected at random from a population described by $F(t)$. Then $NF(t)$ is the average (expected) number of failures through time t, and $NR(t)$ represents the average (expected) number of survivors through time t. That is, we would expect $NR(t)$ of the units to still be operational up to time t.

A probability density function (pdf) that represents the distribution of failure time can be found by taking the derivative of equation (20–5)

$$f(t) = \frac{dF(t)}{dt} = -\frac{dR(t)}{dt} \tag{20-6}$$

The hazard rate function is defined as the limit of the failure rate as the time interval approaches zero. In other words, it provides an instantaneous rate of failure at some time t. The hazard rate function (also known as the instantaneous hazard rate or failure rate function) can be expressed as:

$$h(t) = \frac{\text{Number of failures per unit time}}{\text{Number of components tested per unit time}} = \frac{f(t)}{R(t)} \tag{20-7}$$

Grouped Data

In some situations, failure times are placed into time intervals and the individual failure times are no longer preserved. In this case, the failure times become *grouped data*. The reliability, distribution function, failure density, and hazard rate are estimated from the grouped data.

Suppose we wish to estimate the four quantities given in equations (20–1), (20–2), (20–6), and (20–7) in terms of a reliability test where N identical units are tested. First, record the number of failed units (x_i) and the number of survivors ($n_i = N - x_i$) at time t_i (where $i = 1, 2, \ldots$). Next, $R(t)$, $F(t)$, $f(t)$, and $h(t)$ can be estimated as follows:

Reliability: $\hat{R}(t) = \dfrac{n_i}{N}$

Cumulative distribution function: $\hat{F}(t) = 1 - \hat{R}(t)$

Failure density: $\hat{f}(t) = \dfrac{n_i - n_{i+1}}{(t_{i+1} - t_i) \times N}$, for $t_i < t < t_{i+1}$

Hazard rate: $\hat{h}(t) = \dfrac{n_i - n_{i+1}}{(t_{i+1} - t_i) \times n_i} = \dfrac{\hat{f}(t)}{\hat{R}(t)}$, for $t_i < t < t_{i+1}$

The caret ("hat") on each term indicates an estimated quantity. There are several methods for estimating these functions if the data are ungrouped, censored, ungrouped and censored, or grouped and censored. The reader is referred to Ebeling (2005) for a complete discussion and derivations of these quantities and more.

EXAMPLE 20.1

Suppose that 300 light bulbs are subjected to a reliability test. The manufacturer would release the bulbs for distribution if the reliability of the bulb were 0.75 at 2000 hours of usage. The observed failures during 1000-hour intervals are shown in Table 20.1.

Solution:

Using the previous equations we can determine the four functions: reliability function, distribution function, probability density function (failure density), and the hazard rate function. The results are shown in Table 20.2.

To illustrate, consider the values for $i = 2$, where $1000 < t < 2000$:

Estimated reliability: $\hat{R}(t) = \dfrac{n_2}{N} = \dfrac{286}{300} = 0.95333$

Cumulative distribution function: $\hat{F}(t) = 1 - \hat{R}(t) = 1 - 0.95333 = 0.04667$

Failure density: $\hat{f}(t) = \dfrac{n_2 - n_3}{(t_3 - t_2) \times N} = \dfrac{286 - 269}{(2000 - 1000) \times 300} = 0.0000567$

Hazard rate: $\hat{h}(t) = \dfrac{n_2 - n_3}{(t_3 - t_2) \times n_2} = \dfrac{286 - 269}{(2000 - 1000) \times 286} = 0.0000594$

Continued

Continued

Table 20.1 Number of failures in the time intervals.

Upper bound (hours)	Number of failures, x
0	0
1000	14
2000	17
3000	21
4000	25
5000	31
6000	37
7000	40
8000	50
9000	65

Table 20.2 Reliability, cumulative distribution function, failure density, and hazard rate for the light bulb example.

Interval	Upper bound	Failures in the interval	Survivors	Reliability	Cumulative distribution function	Failure density	Hazard rate
i	t_i	x_i	n_i	$\hat{R}(t)$	$\hat{F}(t)$	$\hat{f}(t)$	$\hat{h}(t)$
1	0	0	300	1.00000	0.00000	0.0000467	0.0000467
2	1000	14	286	0.95333	0.04667	0.0000567	0.0000594
3	2000	17	269	0.89667	0.10333	0.0000700	0.0000781
4	3000	21	248	0.82667	0.17333	0.0000833	0.0001008
5	4000	25	223	0.74333	0.25667	0.0001033	0.0001390
6	5000	31	192	0.64000	0.36000	0.0001233	0.0001927
7	6000	37	155	0.51667	0.48333	0.0001333	0.0002581
8	7000	40	115	0.38333	0.61667	0.0001667	0.0004348
9	8000	50	65	0.21667	0.78333	0.0002167	0.0010000
10	9000	65	0	0.00000	1.00000		

These values can be easily calculated using a spreadsheet.

The reliability function, cumulative distribution function, failure density function, and hazard rate function are displayed in Figures 20.1 through 20.4, respectively. The

Continued

Continued

reliability function in Figure 20.1 indicates that the bulbs exceed the level of reliability set by the manufacturers. The distribution function in Figure 20.2 shows how unreliability grows with the passage of time. The failure density function is displayed in Figure 20.3.

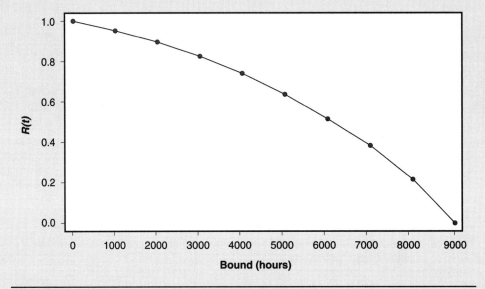

Figure 20.1   Reliability function versus time.

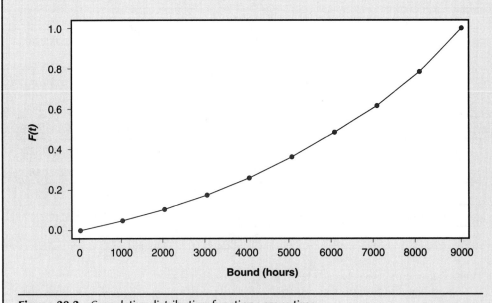

Figure 20.2   Cumulative distribution function versus time.

Continued

Continued

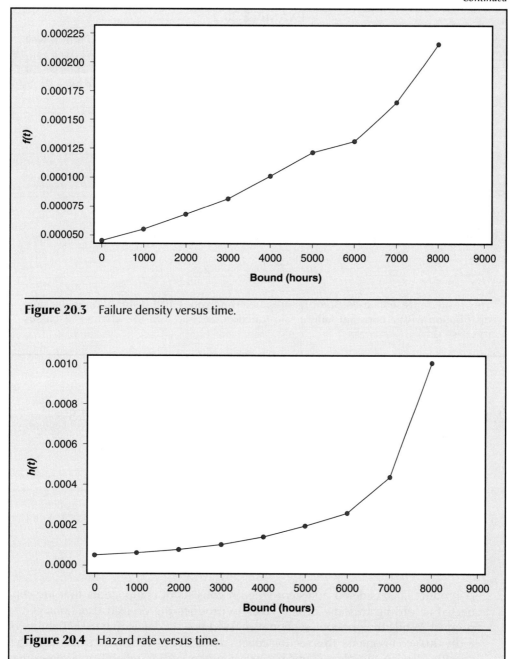

Figure 20.3   Failure density versus time.

Figure 20.4   Hazard rate versus time.

Part III.E.1

EXAMPLE 20.2

Suppose the time-to-failure information given is no longer a set of data, but now is well modeled by a particular distribution. For example, suppose the failure time is well estimated or modeled by an exponential distribution with parameter λ (see Chapter 34 for details on the exponential distribution). For this distribution the cdf is given by

$$F(t) = 1 - e^{-\lambda t}.$$

It can be shown that the pdf (failure density) is given by

$$f(t) = \lambda e^{-\lambda t}.$$

Using the relationship that $R(t) = 1 - F(t)$, we also obtain

$$R(t) = e^{-\lambda t}.$$

Finally, the hazard rate function can be shown to be

$$h(t) = \frac{f(t)}{R(t)} = \frac{\lambda e^{-\lambda t}}{e^{-\lambda t}} = \lambda.$$

This result represents a *constant* failure rate. The exponential distribution is the only distribution with a constant failure rate function. Section 3 of this chapter discusses this result.

---

2. SYSTEM RELIABILITY AND MAINTAINABILITY INDICES

> Review and analyze indices such as MTTF, MTBF, MTTR, availability, failure rate and so on. (Analyze)
>
> **Body of Knowledge III.E.2**

A product is considered a system when it consists of components that are connected according to some design rules to produce the desired functions of the product. While the previous section discussed how to determine the reliability of individual components, this section covers reliability estimates for systems with a specific focus on simple systems because complex system reliability is sometimes difficult to estimate. In complex systems such as a telecommunications network, the system is composed of units or subsystems connected in a network configuration where the arcs represent the units and the nodes represent connection points along the paths. Reliability estimates of complex systems are often simplified into an aggregation of many simple systems. Methods for estimating reliability of complex systems are given in Elsayed (1996).

This section discusses how to estimate the reliability of two kinds of simple systems, series systems and parallel systems, and addresses *k*-out-of-*n* systems and standby systems.

Series Systems

A typical series system is composed of *n* components (or subsystems) connected end-to-end. A failure of any component results in the failure of the entire system. A laser printer, for example, has several major components, such as a photoconductor drum, a laser beam, a toner station, and a paper feed system. The printer fails if any of these components fails. We depict the components graphically, with their respective reliabilities, in a block diagram in Figure 20.5.

Under the assumption that each of the component failures are independent, then the reliability of the system is the product of the reliabilities of its components. It is expressed as:

$$R_s\left(t\right) = R_1\left(t\right) \times R_2\left(t\right) ... R_n\left(t\right) \tag{20-8}$$

where $R_i(t)$ is the reliability of the *i*th component (for $i = 1, 2, \ldots n$). Equation (20–8) assumes that the components are independent, that is, the degradation of one component does not affect the failure rate of other components.

EXAMPLE 20.3

For Figure 20.5, the series reliability $R_s(t)$ is computed as follows:

$$R_s(t) = 0.96 \times 0.92 \times 0.94 \times 0.90 = 0.7472$$

The reliability of a series system is lower than its "weakest" component.

Parallel Systems

In a parallel system, components or units are connected in parallel so that the failure of one or more paths still allows the remaining path(s) to perform properly. The system fails when all units fail. Under the assumption of independence, the reliability of a parallel system $R_s(t)$ with *n* units can be estimated by:

$$R_s\left(t\right) = 1 - \left[F_1\left(t\right) \times F_2\left(t\right) \times ... \times F_n\left(t\right)\right] \tag{20-9}$$

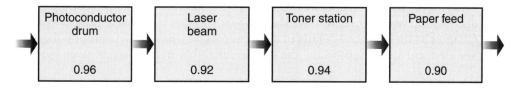

Figure 20.5   A typical series system.

or equivalently:

$$R_s(t) = 1 - \left[\left(1 - R_1(t)\right) \times \left(1 - R_2(t)\right) \times \ldots \times \left(1 - R_n(t)\right) \right] \qquad (20\text{–}10)$$

where $F_i(t)$ is the probability of failure of the ith component and $R_i(t)$ is the reliability of the ith component (for $i = 1, 2, \ldots n$). Equation (20–10) results from the relationship given in equation (20–5), that is $F_i(t) = 1 - R_i(t)$. If the components are identical and p is the probability that a component is operational (that is, $R_i(t) = p$ for all units), then the system reliability becomes

$$\begin{aligned} R_s(t) &= 1 - \left[F_1(t) \times F_2(t) \times \ldots \times F_n(t) \right] \\ &= 1 - \left[\left(1 - R_1(t)\right) \times \left(1 - R_2(t)\right) \times \ldots \times \left(1 - R_n(t)\right) \right] \\ &= 1 - \left[(1-p) \times (1-p) \times \ldots \times (1-p) \right] \\ &= 1 - (1-p)^n. \end{aligned} \qquad (20\text{–}11)$$

The reliability block diagram of a parallel system is shown in Figure 20.6. The reader is referred to Ebeling (2005) or Tobias and Trindade (1995) for complete discussion of parallel systems.

Figures 20.5 and 20.6 show what we refer to as *pure series* and *pure parallel systems*, respectively. There are many situations where the design of the system is composed of combinations of series and parallel subsystems, such as parallel-series, series-parallel, and mixed parallel.

EXAMPLE 20.4

For Figure 20.6, the parallel system reliability is computed using equation (20–10) (since the units are not identical):

$$\begin{aligned} R_s(t) &= 1 - \left[\left(1 - R_1(t)\right) \times \left(1 - R_2(t)\right) \times \ldots \times \left(1 - R_n(t)\right) \right] \\ &= 1 - \left[(1 - 0.95) \times (1 - 0.93) \times \ldots \times (1 - 0.91) \right] \\ &= 0.99969 \end{aligned}$$

---

k-out-of-*n* Systems

Sometimes the system design requires, at a minimum, *k*-out-of-*n* functioning units for the system to operate properly. This is a direct application of the *binomial distribution*, where p represents the probability of success of a component (see Chapter 34 for complete details of the binomial distribution). Assuming the units are identical and independent, the system reliability in this case is given by:

$$R_s(t) = \sum_{i=k}^{n} {}_nC_i \, p^i \left(1 - p\right)^{n-i} \qquad (20\text{–}12)$$

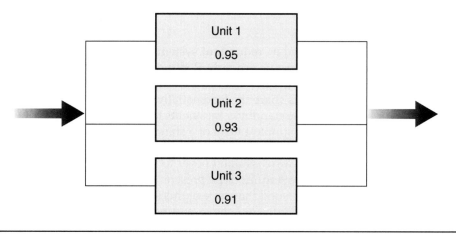

Figure 20.6   A typical parallel system.

where

$$_nC_i = \frac{n!}{i!(n-i)!}$$ and represents the number of ways i units can be chosen from a group of n units.

$$n! = n \times (n-1) \times (n-2) \times \ldots \times 1$$

$$0! = 1$$

See the discussion of the binomial distribution in Chapter 34 for on details on calculating $_nC_i$.

EXAMPLE 20.5

Suppose a system has four identical and independent components. System design requirements indicate that a minimum of two components must function for the successful operation of the system. What is the reliability of this system if each component has a reliability of 0.90?

Solution:

In this situation, $n = 4$, $k = 2$, and $p = 0.90$. Direct substitution into equation (20–12) yields the following result:

$$R_s(t) = \sum_{i=2}^{4} {}_4C_i (0.90)^i (1-0.90)^{4-i}$$

$$= {}_4C_2 (0.90)^2 (1-0.90)^2 + {}_4C_3 (0.90)^3 (1-0.90)^1 + {}_4C_4 (0.90)^4 (1-0.90)^0$$

$$= 6(0.90)^2 (1-0.90)^2 + 4(0.90)^3 (1-0.90)^1 + 1(0.90)^4 (1-0.90)^0$$

$$= 0.9963$$

Standby Systems

Parallel systems are treated as redundant systems. Only one operational path is needed for the system to operate properly. Redundancy can take other forms, such as hot standby redundancy, where all units are operating in parallel at all times. Under this design, all units share the load equally.

In standby systems, the standby components function only upon the failure of the main component. The simplest form of a standby system is the one where the components are assumed to be identical, the switch is assumed never to fail, and the standby component is also assumed never to fail while in the standby status. Deviations from these two assumptions present a variety of systems configurations whose analyses go beyond the scope of this section (see Tobias and Trinidad [1995] or Ebeling [2005]). Figure 20.7 shows a standby system with perfect switching (that is the switch will turn on the standby component instantaneously upon the failure of the main component.)

Standby system reliability with n standby components is given by

$$R(t) = e^{-\lambda t} \sum_{i=0}^{n} \frac{(\lambda t)^i}{i!} \qquad (20\text{--}13)$$

where λ is the component failure rate and t the time. If the system has only one standby component, the system reliability is given by

$$R(t) = e^{-\lambda t}\left[1 + \lambda t\right]$$

If the system has two standby components, the system reliability is given by

$$R(t) = e^{-\lambda t}\left[1 + \lambda t + \frac{(\lambda t)^2}{2!}\right].$$

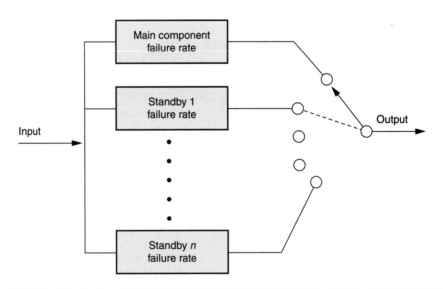

Figure 20.7　A standby system with n components in standby mode.

EXAMPLE 20.6

Suppose we have a standby system with three components in standby mode. All components are identical with a constant rate of failure of $\lambda = 0.02$. What is the system reliability at 75 hours of continuous operation?

Solution:

Substitute $n = 3$, $\lambda = 0.02$, and $t = 75$ in equation (20–13):

$$R(75) = e^{-(0.02)(75)} \sum_{i=0}^{3} \frac{(0.02 \times 75)^i}{i!}$$

$$= e^{-1.5} \sum_{i=0}^{3} \frac{(1.5)^i}{i!}$$

$$= e^{-1.5} \left[\frac{(1.5)^0}{0!} + \frac{(1.5)^1}{1!} + \frac{(1.5)^2}{2!} + \frac{(1.5)^3}{3!} \right]$$

$$= e^{-1.5} [1 + 1.5 + 1.125 + 0.84375]$$

$$= 0.2231 [4.469]$$

$$= 0.9970$$

Cold standby is another form of redundancy where the minimum number of units needed to operate the system properly share the load equally and other units are available on a standby basis but can only share the load when one or more of the operating units fail. The third type of redundancy is called warm standby. This is similar to the hot standby but not all units share the load equally. Those carrying more than 50 percent of the load are the primary units while the others are considered to be in a warm standby state. When a primary unit fails, the warm standby unit shares the load equally with the remaining primary units.

The following paragraphs present some important measures of reliability. The mean time to failure (MTTF) should not be confused with the mean time between failures (MTBF). The expected time between two successive failures is the MTTF when the system is nonrepairable. The expected time between failures, the MTBF, can be calculated when the system is repairable.

First consider n identical nonrepairable systems and observe the times to failure for them. Assume that the observed times to failure are $t_1, t_2, \ldots, t_n$. The estimated mean time to failure MTTF is:

$$\mathrm{MTTF} = \frac{1}{n} \sum_{i=1}^{n} t_i \qquad (20\text{–}14)$$

For constant failure rate the mean time to failure is:

$$\mathrm{MTTF} = \frac{1}{\lambda}$$

which can be interpreted as the reciprocal of the failure rate. It should be noted that this is only true for the constant failure rate model. The accurate method for estimating the mean time to failure for discrete time intervals is given in equation (20–14). It can be estimated by using integration for continuous time functions.

Maintainability and Availability

We have presented several measures of reliability for nonrepairable systems that include reliability function and mean time to failure. Other measures of reliability are defined for repairable systems, such as system availability (instantaneous, average up-time, inherent, operational, and achieved availabilities), mean time to repair, and maintainability. Common to all these definitions is that the system is subject to repair or replacement upon failure. Availability at time t is defined as the probability that the system is properly operating at that time. The steady state availability is the long-term availability of the system (t $\rightarrow \infty$). The steady state availability A is defined as

$$A = \frac{\text{MTBF}}{\text{MTBF} + \text{MTTR}}$$

where MTBF and MTTR are the mean time between failures and mean time to repair respectively.

MTTR is defined as the average time to repair a failure, not including waiting time for parts or tools to start the repair.

Maintainability is defined as the probability that a failed system is restored to its operational condition within a specified time.

Maintenance actions or policies can be classified as *corrective maintenance, preventive maintenance,* and *predictive maintenance* (which is also called on-condition maintenance). Maintenance actions are dependent on many factors, such as the failure rate of the machine, the cost associated with downtime, the cost of repair, and the expected life of the machine.

A *corrective maintenance policy* requires no repairs, replacements, or preventive maintenance until failures occur, which allows for maximum run time between repairs. Although a corrective maintenance policy does allow for maximum run time between repairs, it is neither economical nor efficient, as it may result in a catastrophic failure that requires extensive repair time and cost.

A *preventive maintenance policy* requires maintaining a machine according to a predetermined schedule, whether a problem is apparent or not. On a scheduled basis, machines are removed from operation, disassembled, inspected for defective parts, and repaired accordingly. Actual repair costs can be reduced in this manner, but production loss may increase if the machine is complex and requires days or even weeks to maintain. Preventive maintenance also may create machine problems where none existed before. It is important to note that preventive maintenance is only applicable when the following conditions are satisfied:

1. The cost to repair the system after its failure is greater than the cost of maintaining the system before its failure.

2. The failure rate function of the system is monotonically increasing with time. Clearly, if the system's failure rate is decreasing with time, then the system is likely to improve with time and any preventive action

or replacement is considered a waste of resources. Likewise, performing preventive maintenance when the failure rate is constant is improper, as replacing or maintaining the system before failures does not affect the probability that the system will fail in the next instant, given that it is now good (Jardine and Buzacott (1983).

The third repair policy is the *predictive maintenance policy*. Obviously, tremendous savings can result if a machine failure can be predicted and the machine can be taken off-line to make only the necessary repairs. Predictive maintenance can also be done when failure modes for the machine can be identified and monitored for increased intensity, and when the machine can be shut down at a fixed control limit before critical fault levels are reached.

Predictive maintenance results in two benefits. The first benefit is the result of taking a machine off-line at a predetermined time, which allows production loss to be minimized by scheduling production around the downtime. Since defective components can be predetermined, repair parts can be ordered and manpower scheduled for the maintenance accordingly. Moreover, sensors for monitoring the machines eliminate time spent on diagnostics, thus reducing the time to perform the actual repair. The second benefit is that only defective parts need to be repaired or replaced and the components in good working order are left as is, thus minimizing repair costs and downtime.

Three main tasks must be fulfilled for predictive maintenance. The first task is to find the condition parameter that can describe the condition of the machine. A condition parameter could be any characteristic, such as vibration, sound, temperature, corrosion, crack growth, wear, or lubricant condition. The second task is to monitor the condition parameter and to assess the current machine condition from the measured data. The final task is to determine the limit value of the condition parameter and its two components, the alarm value and the breakdown value. A running machine reaching the alarm value is an indication that the machine is experiencing intensive wear. At this point, the type and advancement of the fault must be identified in order to prepare the maintenance procedure. If a machine reaches the breakdown value, the machine must be shut down for maintenance. See Ebeling (2005) for detailed discussion of availability and maintainability.

Part III.E.3

3. THE BATHTUB CURVE AND OTHER FAILURE MODELS

Identify, define, and distinguish between the basic elements of the bathtub curve. (Analyze)

Body of Knowledge III.E.3

One of the earliest models of failure rate, the bathtub curve (see Figure 20.8), is so named because of its shape. The failure rate versus time can be divided into three regions. The first region is characterized by a decreasing failure rate with time and

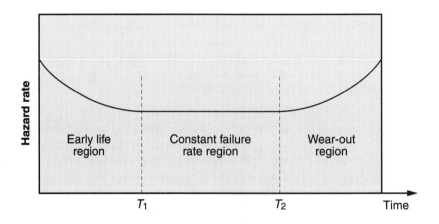

Figure 20.8 The general failure rate model (the bathtub curve).

is conventionally referred to as the infant mortality phase or the early life region of the product, component, or system during their early period of use. Experience shows that the length (0 to T_1) of this region is about 10,000 hours (approximately one year) for most electronic components. The failures in this region are usually attributed to defects in the manufacturing processes, assemblies, and shipping of the product.

The second region of the bathtub curve is the constant failure rate region, which is characterized by the inherent failure rate of the product's composite components. In this region, the failures occur randomly over time, as shown in Example 1. The third region is referred to as the wear-out region. It is characterized by an increasing failure rate over time. Most electronic components do not exhibit such a region, with the exception of electro-mechanical devices, such as relays. On the other hand, most, if not all, mechanical components that are subjected to rotating and alternating motions wear out with time. This is exemplified by the behavior of cutting tools, fatigue loading on structures, and wear-out due to friction between mating surfaces.

In Example 1, we showed a case of constant failure rate (we use hazard rate and failure rate interchangeably). This is the simplest failure model, as its probability density function and reliability function can easily be shown in the following section, whereas other failure rate models (decreasing or increasing) are sometimes difficult to obtain from their corresponding functions.

The second region in the general failure rate model (bathtub curve) shows constant failure rate. Let λ be the constant failure rate. Thus:

$$h(t) = \lambda$$

The reliability function and the probability density function are given in Equations (20–15) and (20–16) respectively:

$$R(t) = e^{-\lambda t} \tag{20–15}$$

$$f(t) = h(t)R(t) = \lambda e^{-\lambda t} \tag{20–16}$$

This is the standard exponential failure time distribution. The graphs of Equations (20–15) and (20–16), shown in Figures 20.9 and 20.10, are similar to those in Figures 20.2 and 20.3, which are obtained from actual failure data.

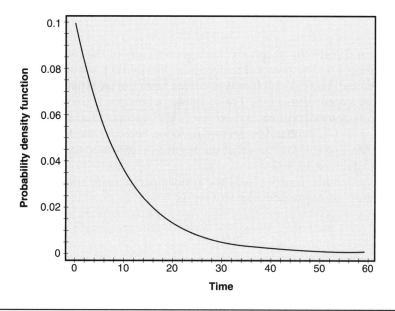

Figure 20.9   Probability density function for constant failure rate.

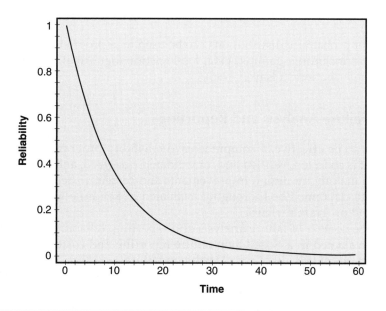

Figure 20.10   Reliability function for constant failure rate.

Part III.E.3

The first and third regions (the decreasing and increasing failure rate regions) of the general failure rate models can be described by time-dependent failure rate functions. The Weibull failure rate is the most widely used failure rate model that describes these regions. It is expressed as:

$$h(t) = \frac{\gamma}{\theta} t^{\gamma-1} \qquad (20\text{--}17)$$

where γ and θ are the shape and scale parameters of the two-parameter Weibull distribution. For discussion of the Weibull distribution, see chapter 34. The appeal of the Weibull hazard rate function comes from the fact that it can represent several other known functions. For example, when $\gamma = 1$ the Weibull hazard rate function becomes constant. When $\gamma = 2$, the resultant hazard function is linear with time and its probability density function becomes the Rayleigh distribution. Indeed, Makino (1984) shows that the normal distribution can be approximated to Weibull when $\gamma = 3.43927$.

The reliability function and the probability density function of the Weibull distribution are expressed respectively as:

$$R(t) = e^{\frac{-t\gamma}{\theta}} \qquad t > 0 \qquad (20\text{--}18)$$

and

$$f(t) = \frac{\gamma}{\theta} t^{\gamma-1} e^{\frac{-t^\gamma}{\theta}} \qquad (20\text{--}19)$$

Figures 20.11 and 20.12 demonstrate the use of the Weibull failure model to describe decreasing and increasing failure rates. Of course, the constant failure rate is also included.

Other probability distributions can be used to appropriately describe the failure times, including: gamma, beta, log-logistics, lognormal, extreme value, and normal distributions (Elsayed 1996).

Reliability Failure Analysis and Reporting

In order to be effective, a comprehensive reliability program must be based on data that is collected, verified and/or validated, analyzed, and used as the basis of decision making for design improvements and corrective action. At a minimum, reliability data must be thoroughly evaluated at key milestones such as design phase and program reviews.

In the context of failure analysis and reporting, reliability data is most commonly evaluated in a closed-loop failure reporting and corrective action system. For purposes of this chapter, a closed-loop failure reporting and corrective action system provides the means to ensure that failures are not only documented and tracked over time, but also analyzed to a sufficient depth to determine whether corrective action is required, and if so, what corrective action is necessary as determined by appropriate design engineers or a reliability review board.

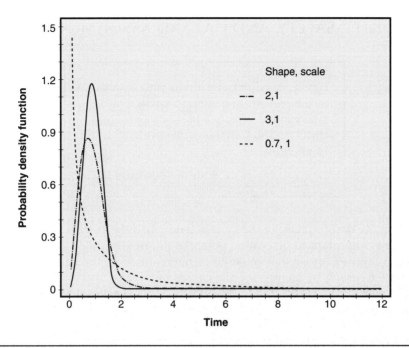

Figure 20.11   Probability density functions for the Weibull model with different shape and scale paramenters.

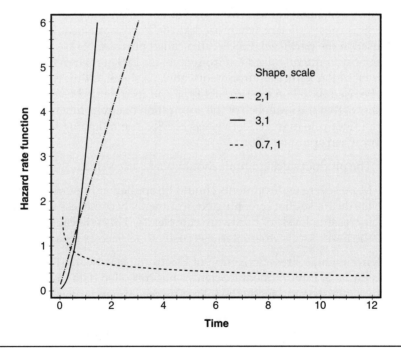

Figure 20.12   Hazard rate functions for the Weibull model with different shape and scale paramenters.

Part III.E.3

4. RELIABILITY, SAFETY, AND HAZARD ASSESSMENT TOOLS

> Define, construct, and interpret the results
> of failure mode and effects analysis (FMEA).
> failure mode, effects, and criticality analysis
> (FMECA), and fault tree analysis (FTA).
> (Analyze)
>
> **Body of Knowledge III.E.4**

During the design phase of the system, and when the system fails during operation, it is important to determine potential failures and their causes to eliminate critical failures (those that cause total interruption of the function or potential injuries to users) by identifying the causes of failures and by developing appropriate methods to reduce their effects. Several approaches that have proven to be effective in identifying potential failures are discussed here: environmental stress screening (ESS), failure mode and effects analysis (FMEA), failure mode effects and criticality analysis (FMECA), and fault tree analysis (FTA).

Environmental Stress Screening

Environmental stress screening (ESS) is a process designed to precipitate incipient defects into detectable failures by use of environmental stresses applied to hardware. ESS is most efficient when used at the lowest practical level of hardware. When used at the part level, ESS is often called burn-in.

The most frequently used environments for ESS are temperature cycling and random vibration. Other environments, such as shock, altitude, humidity, and so on, can be used based on the product type and its intended use conditions. Experience shows that the sequence of the application of environments has been found to play a minor role in the effectiveness of ESS. The following two conditions are necessary when applying ESS:

1. The product's design limit should not be exceeded.

2. More severe environments should be applied at the lower levels of the hardware so that screening environments become less severe with increasing levels of hardware complexity. This will cause failures at the lower levels where it is less costly to replace or repair.

The Environmental Stress Screening of Electronic Hardware (ESSEH) committee of the Institute of Environmental Sciences has compiled data from throughout the electronics industry and made the following recommendations:

- The optimal number of thermal cycles for electronics is 10. This number is obtained based on experience; scientific or mathematical methods are needed to obtain the "true" optimum for given test conditions and constraints.

- Random vibration is a more efficient screen than sinusoidal vibration.

- The preferred random vibration profile is the naval material command (NAVMAT) profile, which covers the frequency spectrum from 20 hertz to 2000 hertz with an overall acceleration of six grams. Studies show that the vast majority of failures with this profile occur in the first 10 minutes of the test.

It is important that a baseline experiment be conducted and analyzed during ESS to determine the optimum screening parameters.

Failure Mode and Effects Analysis

Failure mode and effects analysis (FMEA) is a team-based problem-solving tool intended to help users identify and eliminate or reduce the negative effects of potential failures before they occur in systems, subsystems, product or process design, or the delivery of a service. FMEA can be used as a stand-alone tool or as part of comprehensive quality programs such as ISO 9000, QS-9000, advanced product quality planning and control plan (APQP), or Six Sigma. Accordingly, this section discusses terminology, theory, mechanics, and applications of FMEA as it applies to product designs, process designs, and systems.

A word of caution: FMEA can be a powerful and effective tool for system, subsystem, product or process design, or service delivery improvement, but completing an FMEA has significant costs associated with it. Organizations that may be tempted to follow the results of an FMEA to implement further levels of refinement and specificity should conduct a cost/benefit analysis to ensure that FMEA is the proper tool under the circumstances.

Selecting a Standard for FMEA

There are two primary standards for FMEA, the military standard (MIL-STD 1629A) and the Society of Automotive Engineers standard (SAE J1739). Both standards are limited in scope to address only design and process FMEAs. These standards provide general FMEA forms and documents, identify criteria for the quantification of risk associated with potential failures, and provide very general guidelines on the mechanics of completing FMEAs. MIL-STD 1629A and SAE J1739 may be obtained by contacting the Department of the Navy and the Society of Automotive Engineers at www.navy.mil or www.sae.org/technical/standards, respectively.

Another useful reference is the manual *Potential Failure Effects Analysis* published by the Automotive Industry Action Group (AIAG). This manual is available at http://www.aiag.org.

Failure mode and effects analysis (FMEA) can also be implemented in other fields, such as healthcare. The *Joint Commission* recommends several resources and manuals on FMEA in healthcare which can be found at http://store.jcrinc.com/JCRStore. The interested reader is encouraged to visit the Joint Commission at http://www.jointcommission.org or the Institute for Healthcare Improvement (IHI) at http://www.ihi.org for more information about FMEA and healthcare research and accreditation.

Planning for an FMEA

Planning for an FMEA involves a series of considerations that include, as a minimum, the following:

• *Select appropriate applications for the analysis.* An FMEA may be authorized by individuals at various levels within an organization or may be required by ISO 9000, QS-9000, APQP, Six Sigma methodologies, internal quality programs, or customer requirements. However authorized or required, an FMEA is expensive to complete and should be completed only in those instances where the benefits outweigh the costs.

• *Identify and allocate resources.* These resources include FMEA team members and a reporting structure, physical space to conduct the analysis and store documentation, time, and clerical/communications support.

• *Define the scope.* Since an FMEA can be conducted at a high level (that is, the system level) or at a very detailed level (that is, the component level or service delivery level), and since a high-level FMEA may lead to additional FMEAs at more detailed levels, it is very important to set the scope of the analysis before beginning.

• *Establish expectations and deliverables.* The team-based nature of completing an FMEA means FMEA team members will have dual or multiple responsibilities and reporting structures in addition to the FMEA team. It is critical, therefore, to clearly define performance expectations for all FMEA team members and to communicate those expectations directly to appropriate supervisory or managerial personnel in reporting structures outside the FMEA team. It is equally important that all FMEA team members understand what deliverables will result from the analysis and their respective roles in developing those deliverables.

• *Establish milestones, due dates, and deadlines.* Key milestones for an FMEA include authorization for the analysis, establishment of a reporting structure, allocation of resources (particularly FMEA team members), gathering input for the analysis, completing the analysis, taking and monitoring corrective action, preparing documentation, and report-outs and debriefings. To ensure effectiveness, an FMEA should be conducted like a project from the perspective of establishing a schedule specifying due dates and deadlines for each of the major milestones.

• *Establish a single point of responsibility.* Although FMEA is a team-based analysis, sufficient practical experience supports the idea that assigning responsibility to a cross-functional team rather than a single individual is not the most effective policy. So for a variety of reasons, a single person should be assigned the responsibility of FMEA team leader, and that person needs the authority to make decisions and allocate resources to complete the FMEA as planned.

FMEA Team Members

The belief that only the one or two people closest to a system, subsystem, product or process design, or service delivery should be assigned to an FMEA violates the very intent of the analysis. FMEA is intended to be completed by team members representing a broad cross section of expertise—technical and nontechnical. For example, an FMEA team should have representation from the following functional groups, as a minimum:

- Design engineering
- Manufacturing engineering
- Production
- Quality/reliability
- Purchasing/material control
- Sales and marketing
- Customers

It cannot be overemphasized that for an FMEA to be truly effective, the viewpoints and perspectives of every functional group mentioned above must be included—particularly customers. As Palady (1997) explains, "excluding the customer's input from the FMEA will result in an incomplete list of the effects and low estimates of the severity."

Inputs to an FMEA

To prepare for an FMEA, it is necessary to gather information from several sources—and these data should be gathered prior to the initial FMEA team meeting to maximize the effectiveness of team members' time. Minimum inputs to an FMEA include:

- Process flowchart or functional block diagram
- Design specifications
- Customer requirements/specifications
- Testing data/results
- Data on similar process/design technology
- Warranty data
- Failure/rework data
- Design/configuration change data
- Prior FMEAs
- Results from quantitative analysis (DOE, SPC, process capability assessments, reliability assessments, and so on)

FMEA and Other Quality Tools

In addition to the inputs described above, other quality tools are frequently used during the completion of an FMEA. These other quality tools include, but are not limited to, the following:

- Cause-and-effect diagrams
- Process decision program charts
- Histograms
- Pareto diagrams
- Run charts
- Force-field analysis
- Fault tree diagrams
- Root cause analysis

Outputs from an FMEA

Outputs or deliverables from an FMEA include the following:

- FMEA documentation
- System, subsystem, design, process, and/or service delivery documentation
- Recommendation reports
- Corrective action reports
- Design changes
- Compliance reports
- Debriefings and presentations

Basic Steps in an FMEA

Complexity in an FMEA is directly related to the number of levels of analysis dictated by the situation or team members. At the most fundamental level, however, every FMEA consists of the same basic steps, including:

1. Identify a starting point for the analysis. A starting point will be a system, subsystem, product or process design, or service delivery system of interest.

2. Gather all relevant inputs to support the analysis. Gathering inputs for an FMEA is a milestone to be completed prior to the initial FMEA meeting. It is far more effective, both from cost and efficiency perspectives, to have all team members at meetings participating in the analysis rather than leaving meetings to gather input!

3. Identify potential failure modes such as:

   - Who would be impacted by a failure?
   - What would happen in the event of a failure?
   - When would the failure occur?

- • Where would the failure occur?

- • Why would the failure occur?

- • How would the failure occur?

4. Quantify the risk associated with each potential failure. Risk assessment is based on severity, occurrence, and detection of a potential failure.

5. Develop a corrective action plan for the most significant risks.

6. Repeat the analysis until all potential failures pose an *acceptable* level of risk. What constitutes an acceptable risk must be clearly defined by the individual or agent authorizing the FMEA.

7. Document results.

8. Report-out and/or present results.

Obtaining Risk Priority Numbers

For purposes of the FMEA, risk has three components: *severity, occurrence,* and *detection.* Each of these components is assigned a value, and the values are multiplied to produce risk priority numbers (RPN).

Severity (S)—An indicator of the severity of a failure should a failure occur. Severity is described on a 10-point scale.

Occurrence (O)—An indicator of the likelihood of a failure occurring. Occurrence is described on a 10-point scale.

Detection (D)—An indicator of the likelihood of detecting a failure once it has occurred. Detection is described on a 10-point scale.

RPNmin = 1 while RPNmax = 1000

Taking Action Based on an RPN

A common mistake in assessing FMEA risk is prioritizing corrective action based on the descending order of RPNs. Logic would suggest that the largest RPNs represent the highest risk—which is true, but only to a point. When multiplying the three risk components together, their importance relative to each other becomes obscured. Consider the following example:

	(S)	*	(O)	*	(D)	=	RPN
Potential failure 1	2		10		5		100
Potential failure 2	10		2		5		100
Potential failure 3	2		5		10		100
Potential failure 4	10		5		2		100

In each case the resulting RPN = 100, so it is unclear what potential failure to take corrective action on first. There is, however, a generally accepted strategy when taking action on an RPN, and Palady (1997) describes that strategy as follows:

Part III.E.4

1. Eliminate the occurrence

2. Reduce the severity

3. Reduce the occurrence

4. Improve detection

Applying this strategy shows how to proceed:

Eliminating occurrences would, mathematically, reorder the RPNs.

Reducing severity next would focus our attention on potential failures 2 and 4.

But then what? We still have two potential failures with the same level of risk.

Reducing occurrence as the next step in this process focuses our attention on potential failure 4, which had a higher occurrence rating than did potential failure 2.

Now our attention can turn to evaluating the remaining potential failures since potential failures 2 and 4 have been ranked as the two most important. Of the remaining two potential failures, potential failure 1 has the higher occurrence rating and is therefore ranked as the third most important potential failure, and potential failure 3 drops to the least important position by default. The rank order by which the potential failures in the above example should be investigated for corrective action is as follows:

First priority	Potential failure 4
Second priority	Potential failure 2
Third priority	Potential failure 1
Fourth priority	Potential failure 3

Do We Rate the Failure Mode or the Cause?

A common point of confusion arises when considering what is actually rated as part of the risk assessment—the actual failure itself or the cause of a given failure. It is perfectly acceptable to rate either the failure or the cause, as long as the assumption is well-documented (on actual FMEA charts, in written correspondence, and in all reports/presentations) and everyone on the FMEA team and in the reporting structure is aware of the assumption. Whether rating a failure itself or a cause of that failure, an FMEA should provide consistent results and corrective actions.

FMEAs Encountered by Quality Engineers

FMEA can be applied to the system, subsystem, design or process, or service delivery levels. A brief synopsis of each FMEA application is as follows:

- *System FMEA.* A system, or subsystem, is a collection of elements or components working together to accomplish a desired task or function. FMEA is applied at the system or subsystem level to identify potential failure modes and effects that could negatively impact system or subsystem performance. At the system or subsystem level, FMEA is focused at system or subsystem boundaries where potential failures are most likely to occur. The boundaries of interest for a system or subsystem FMEA include functional (that is, expected outcomes assuming normal operation) or operational (that is, specific outputs expected as compared to tolerances, specifications, and timing).

- *Design FMEA.* A design, or more accurately a product design, is a set of specifications that describes all aspects of a product (that is, major functions, operating parameters and tolerances, materials, dimensions, and so on). FMEA is applied to product designs as early in the product design process as is feasible to identify potential failure modes that could result from a design flaw. Design FMEAs are a normal part of key milestones in the product development process, such as concept reviews, concept approvals, preliminary design reviews, and final design reviews.

- *Process FMEA.* A process design is a set of specifications that describes all aspects of a process (that is, functional components, flow rates, process steps, equipment to be used, steps to be performed, operators or employees to be involved, and so on). Process design FMEA is applied to process designs at the earliest possible point to identify potential failure modes that could result from a design flaw. Process FMEAs, also, are a normal part of key milestones in the process development process.

- *Service delivery FMEA.* A service delivery is the completion of a set of tasks designed to meet one or more customer expectations. Service delivery FMEA is applied to service delivery designs to identify potential failure modes that, if experienced, would result in some level of dissatisfaction from customers. Service delivery FMEAs are also completed as early as possible in the design process and are a normal part of key milestones in the service delivery design process.

In most instances, the practicing quality engineer (QE) can be expected to work primarily on design and/or process FMEAs. Accordingly, this chapter will focus on design and process FMEAs, and will omit system/subsystem and service delivery FMEAs. Readers are encouraged to reference Stamatis (2003) for a detailed discussion of system/subsystem and service delivery FMEAs.

Design and Process FMEAs

Following the steps previously outlined that described the planning functions preceding an FMEA, the analysis proceeds as the FMEA team completes appropriate documentation, such as the FMEA form. For purposes of this discussion, one form applicable to either a design or process FMEA will be described. Where the criteria change between a design or process FMEA, both criteria will be provided. Figures 20.13 and 20.14 are blank FMEA forms applicable to design and process FMEA—each component of the forms will be identified and described.

Part III.E.4

Potential
Failure Mode and Effects Analysis
(Design FMEA)

System _____
Subsystem _____
Component _____   Design responsibility _____
Model year(s) vehicle(s) _____   Key date _____
Core team _____

FMEA number _____
Page ____ of ____
Prepared by _____
FMEA date (orig.) ____ (rev.) ____

Item / Function	Potential failure mode	Potential effect(s) of failure	S e v	C l a s s	Potential cause(s)/ mechanism(s) of failure	O c c u r	Current design controls	D e t e c	R. P. N.	Recommended action(s)	Responsibility and target completion date	Action results					
												Actions taken	S e v	O c c	D e t	R. P. N.	

Figure 20.13 Blank design FMEA form.

Part III.E.4

Item _____

Model year(s) vehicle(s) _____

Core team _____

Process responsibility _____

Key date _____

Potential
Failure Mode and Effects Analysis
(Process FMEA)

FMEA number _____

Page _____ of _____

Prepared by _____

FMEA date (orig.) _____ (rev.) _____

Process function	Potential failure mode	Potential effect(s) of failure	S e v	C l a s s	Potential cause(s)/ mechanism(s) of failure	O c c u r	Current process controls	D e t e c	R. P. N.	Recommended action(s)	Responsibility and target completion date	Action results				
												Actions taken	S e v	O c c	D e t e c	R. P. N.
Requirements																

Figure 20.14   Blank process FMEA form.

Heading Information and Documentation

Product or process name	Provide the formal and/or commonly used (if different) name for the product or process.
Product or process description	Provide a brief description of the product or process that is meaningful to the FMEA team members.
FMEA number	Assign an FMEA number to each FMEA for tracking and documentation purposes. There are no standards for numbering FMEAs; however, a numbering system that links the FMEA to a specific period of time and product/process family is preferred.
Design/process owner	Identify the individual or team assigned primary responsibility for the design or process for tracking and documentation purposes. This individual or team is also identified for reference, if needed, during the FMEA.
FMEA team leader	Identify the individual assigned primary responsibility for completion of the FMEA for documentation purposes. This individual is also identified so as to establish a point of contact should any stakeholder need information during or after the FMEA.
FMEA team	List each member of the FMEA team along with any key responsibilities relative to the FMEA.
FMEA date	Provide the date(s) during which the FMEA is completed to help establish a chronology of events. Revision dates should be noted here as well.
FMEA risk assessment	Indicate the basis of the risk assessment. The FMEA risk assessment may be based on either actual failures or failure causes. It is important to document the team's decision to assess risk based on failures or causes to ensure that everyone evaluating the FMEA understands exactly how risk was assessed.

Analysis Content and Documentation

DFMEA part name, number, function, or PFMEA process function	Identify the product (that is, part name, part number, and function) or process (that is, functions to be completed as part of the process).

Potential failure mode	List each of the potential failure modes associated with the design or process. Design failure modes may include dented, deformed, fractured, loosened, leaking, warped, and so on. Process failure modes may include overheating, inoperable, visual defect, and so on.
Potential effect of failure mode	For each potential failure mode, indicate the potential effect on customers or production/process personnel—it is entirely possible to have multiple effects for each potential failure mode.
Severity	Indicate the seriousness of the effect of the potential failure using the severity criteria defined in Tables 20.3 and 20.4. Note: The severity rating applies only to the effect of the potential failure.

Table 20.3 Design FMEA severity criteria.

Effect	Severity criteria	Ranking
Hazardous without warning	Very high ranking when potential failure mode affects safe operation and/or regulation noncompliance. Failure occurs without warning.	10
Hazardous with warning	Very high ranking when potential failure mode affects safe operation and/or regulation noncompliance. Failure occurs with warning.	9
Very high	Item or product is inoperable, with loss of function. Customer very dissatisfied.	8
High	Item or product is operable, with loss of performance. Customer dissatisfied.	7
Moderate	Item or product is operable, but comfort/convenience items inoperable. Customer experiences discomfort.	6
Low	Item or product is operable, but with loss of performance of comfort/convenience items. Customer has some dissatisfaction.	5
Very low	Certain characteristics do not conform. Noticed by most customers.	4
Minor	Certain characteristics do not conform. Noticed by average customers.	3
Very minor	Certain characteristics do not conform. Noticed by discriminating customers.	2
None	No effect.	1

$S \times O \times D$ = risk priority number (RPN)

Derived from Technical Standard SAE J 1739.

Reprinted by permission of The Society of Automotive Engineers (SAE).

Part III.E.4

Table 20.4   Process FMEA severity criteria.

Effect	Severity criteria	Ranking
Hazardous without warning	May endanger machine or assembly operator. Very high severity ranking when a potential failure mode affects safe operation and/ or involves noncompliance with regulation. Failure will occur without warning.	10
Hazardous with warning	May endanger machine or assembly operator. Very high severity ranking when a potential failure mode affects safe operation and/ or involves noncompliance with regulation. Failure will occur with warning.	9
Very high	Major disruption to production line. 100% of product may have to be scrapped. Item inoperable, loss of primary function. Customer very dissatisfied.	8
High	Minor disruption to production line. A portion of product may have to be sorted and scrapped. Item operable, but at reduced level. Customer dissatisfied.	7
Moderate	Minor disruption to production line. A portion of product may have to be scrapped (no sorting). Item operable, but some comfort items inoperable. Customer experiences discomfort.	6
Low	Minor disruption to production line. 100% of product may have to be reworked. Item operable, but some comfort items operable at reduced level of performance. Customer experiences some dissatisfaction.	5
Very low	Minor disruption to production line. Product may have to be sorted and a portion reworked. Minor adjustments do not conform. Defect noticed by customer.	4
Minor	Minor disruption to production line. Product may have to be reworked online, but out of station. Minor adjustments do not conform. Defect noticed by average customer.	3
Very minor	Minor disruption to production line. Product may have to be reworked online, but out of station. Minor adjustments do not conform. Defect noticed by discriminating customer.	2
None	No effect.	1

Derived from Technical Standard SAE J 1739.
Reprinted by permission of The Society of Automotive Engineers (SAE).

Classification	Classify any special characteristics that may require additional process controls. SAE J1739 identifies classifications that include critical, key, major, and significant.
Potential cause of failure mode	For each potential effect of each failure mode, identify all possible causes—it is entirely possible to have more than one cause for each potential effect.

Table 20.5 Design FMEA occurrence criteria.

Probability of failure	Possible failure rates	Ranking
Very high: Failure almost inevitable	> 1 in 2 1 in 3	10 9
High: Repeated failures	1 in 8 1 in 20	8 7
Moderate: Occasional failures	1 in 80 1 in 400 1 in 2000	6 5 4
Low: Relatively few failures	1 in 15,000 1 in 150,000	3 2
Remote: Failure is unlikely	< 1 in 1,500,000	1

Derived from Technical Standard SAE J 1739.
Reprinted by permission of The Society of Automotive Engineers (SAE).

Table 20.6 Process FMEA occurrence criteria.

Probability of failure	Possible failure rates	Ranking
Very high: Failure almost inevitable.	> 1 in 2 1 in 3	10 9
High: Generally associated with processes similar to previous processes that have often failed.	1 in 8 1 in 20	8 7
Moderate: Generally associated with processes similar to previous processes that have experienced occasional failures.	1 in 80 1 in 400 1 in 2000	6 5 4
Low: Isolated failures associated with similar processes.	1 in 15,000	3
Very low: Only isolated failures associated with almost identical processes.	1 in 150,000	2
Remote: Failure is unlikely. No failures associated with almost identical processes.	< 1 in 1,500,000	1

Derived from Technical Standard SAE J 1739.
Reprinted by permission of The Society of Automotive Engineers (SAE).

Occurrence	Indicate how frequently each failure is expected to occur using the occurrence criteria defined in Tables 20.5 and 20.6.
DFMEA design verifications or PFMEA process controls	For a design FMEA, identify the actions completed that ensure or verify the adequacy of the design. For a current process FMEA, identify the control currently in place that prevents a failure mode from occurring.

Table 20.7   Design FMEA detection criteria.

Effect	Detection criteria	Ranking
Absolute uncertainty	Design control will not and/or cannot detect a potential cause/mechanism and subsequent failure mode or there is no design control.	10
Very remote	Very remote chance the design control will detect a potential cause/mechanism and subsequent failure mode.	9
Remote	Remote chance the design control will detect a potential cause/mechanism and subsequent failure mode.	8
Very low	Very low chance the design control will detect a potential cause/mechanism and subsequent failure mode.	7
Low	Low chance the design control will detect a potential cause/mechanism and subsequent failure mode.	6
Moderate	Moderate chance the design control will detect a potential cause/mechanism and subsequent failure mode.	5
Moderately high	Moderately high chance the design control will detect a potential cause/mechanism and subsequent failure mode.	4
High	High chance the design control will detect a potential cause/mechanism and subsequent failure mode.	3
Very high	Very high chance the design control will detect a potential cause/mechanism and subsequent failure mode.	2
Almost certain	Design control will almost certainly detect a potential cause/mechanism and subsequent failure mode.	1

Derived from Technical Standard SAE J 1739.
Reprinted by permission of The Society of Automotive Engineers (SAE).

Detection	Indicate the ability of design verification or current process controls to detect a potential failure mode in the event that failure actually occurs. Use the detection criteria defined in Tables 20.7 and 20.8.
Risk priority number (RPN)	For each potential failure mode, multiply the severity (S), occurrence (O), and detection (D) assessments together. Since each scale (S, O, and D) ranges from 1 to 10, RPNmin = 1 and RPNmax = 1000.
Recommended actions	For each potential failure mode, list one or more recommended corrective actions. For further direction and guidance on prioritizing recommended corrective actions, refer to the "Taking Action Based on an RPN" section of this chapter.

Table 20.8 Process FMEA detection criteria.

Effect	Detection criteria	Ranking
Absolutely impossible	No known controls to detect failure mode.	10
Very remote	Very remote likelihood current controls will detect failure mode.	9
Remote	Remote likelihood current controls will detect failure mode.	8
Very low	Very low likelihood current controls will detect failure mode.	7
Low	Low likelihood current controls will detect failure mode.	6
Moderate	Moderate likelihood current controls will detect failure mode.	5
Moderately high	Moderately high likelihood current controls will detect failure mode.	4
High	High likelihood current controls will detect failure mode.	3
Very high	Very high likelihood current controls will detect failure mode.	2
Almost certain	Current controls will almost certainly detect a failure mode. Reliable detection controls are known with similar processes.	1

Derived from Technical Standard SAE J 1739.
Reprinted by permission of The Society of Automotive Engineers (SAE).

Individual/team responsible and completion date	For each recommended action, assign an appropriate individual or team and an expected completion date.
Actions taken	Provide a brief description of the actual actions taken and their respective action dates.
Resulting RPN analysis	Following each action taken, reiterate the severity, occurrence, and detection assessments and calculate a new resulting RPN. Actions taken based on RPNs and resulting RPNs continue until the risk assessment for each potential failure is "acceptable" to the customer and/or authorizing agent for the FMEA.

A Final Word on Taking Corrective Action

An FMEA represents an in-depth, objective, quantitative analysis of the risk associated with potential failures that result in the calculation of one or more RPNs. Once RPNs have been calculated and the FMEA team prepares to take corrective action, the analysis necessarily takes on a subjective element as FMEA team members use the risk assessment to guide prioritization of corrective actions.

As was mentioned earlier in this chapter, the most common practice is to prioritize corrective action based on RPNs. Prioritizing corrective action based solely on RPNs works effectively, however, only as long as there is a "comfortable" difference among the RPN values. When there are clusters of RPN values that are the same, or very close (that is, within 25 to 50 points), taking action based on RPNs alone is not straightforward. When there are clusters of RPN values (that is, grouping of RPN values that are the same or within a 25 to 50 point range), follow these steps to prioritize corrective action:

1. Rank the RPNs in descending order.

2. For those RPNs that cluster within a predefined range, for example, 25 to 50 points, eliminate occurrence, then reduce severity, then reduce occurrence, then improve detection.

3. Plan, take, and monitor corrective action on the largest nonclustered RPNs.

4. Plan, take, and monitor corrective action on RPN clusters as defined in step 2.

Repeat steps 3 and 4 as needed to address all potential failures identified in the analysis.

As another means of eliminating the subjectivity in prioritizing corrective actions based on RPNs, a method called criticality analysis was developed as part of MIL-STD 1629A.

Design and Process FMEA Examples

Figures 20.15 and 20.16, showing examples of design and process FMEAs, have been provided to help guide the reader through an actual analysis.

Failure Mode Effects and Criticality Analysis (FMECA)

MIL-STD 1629A defines two very important terms and concepts with respect to risk assessment:

Criticality	"A relative measure of the consequences of a failure mode and its frequency of occurrences."
Criticality Analysis	"A procedure by which each potential failure mode is ranked according to the combined influence of severity and probability of occurrence" (MIL-STD-1629A).

When criticality is considered in an FMEA, the name is changed to failure mode effects and criticality analysis (FMECA). FMECA can be a qualitative or quantitative assessment of risk that leads to a prioritization of corrective action based on severity (S) and occurrence (O) assessments. In the qualitative approach to risk assessment in FMECA, risk is categorized as frequent, reasonably probable, occasional, remote, or extremely unlikely. In the quantitative approach to risk assessment in FMECA, failure rate data, failure effect probability data, individual part failure data, and operating time data are required as input to one or more protocols as defined in Military Handbook 217.

Part III.E.4

Potential Failure Mode and Effects Analysis (Design FMEA)

System _____		FMEA number ___1234___ (1)
X Subsystem _01.03/Body closures_ (2)	Design responsibility _Body engineering_ (3)	Page __1__ of __1__
_ Component _199X/Lion 4dr/wagon_ (5)	Key date _9X 03 01 ER_	Prepared by _A. Tate—X6412—Body engr_ (4)
Model year(s)/vehicle(s) _199X/Lion 4dr/wagon_ (5)		FMEA date (orig.) _8X 03 22_ (rev.) _8X 07 14_ (7)
Core team T. Fender—Car product dev., Childers—Manufacturing, J. Ford—Assy ops (Dalton, Fraser, Henley assembly plants)		(8)

Item ⑨ Function	Potential failure mode ⑩	Potential effect(s) of failure ⑪	C l a s s ⑫	S e v	Potential cause(s)/ mechanism(s) ⑬ of failure ⑭	O c c u r ⑮	Current design controls ⑯	D e t e c ⑰	R. P. N.	Recommended action(s) ⑱⑲	Responsibility and target completion date ⑳	Action results ㉒ Actions taken ㉑	S e v	O c c	D e t	R. P. N.
Front door L.H. H8HX-0000-A	Corroded interior lower door panels	Deteriorated life of door leading to: • Unsatisfactory appearance due to rust through paint over time • Impaired function of interior door hardware	7	7	Upper edge of protective wax application specified for inner door panels is too low	6	Vehicle general durability test veh. T-118 T-109 T-301	7	294	Add laboratory accelerated corrosion testing	A Tate-Body Engrg 8X 09 30	Based on test results (Test No. 1481) upper edge spec raised 125mm	7	2	2	28
• Ingress to and egress from vehicle • Occupant protection from weather, noise, and side impact • Support anchorage for door hardware including mirror, hinges, latch, and window regulator • Provide proper surface for appearance items • Paint and soft trim					Insufficient wax thickness specified	4	Vehicle general durability testing - as above	7	196	Add laboratory accelerated corrosion testing	Combine w/test for wax upper edge verification A Tate Body Engrg 9X 01 15	Test results (Test No. 1481) show specified thickness is adequate. DOE shows 25% variation in specified thickness is acceptable	7	2	2	28
							Conduct Design of Experiments (DOE) on wax thickness									
					Inappropriate wax formulation specified	2	Physical and Chem Lab test - Report No. 1265	2	28	None						
					Entrapped air prevents wax from entering corner/edge access	5	Design aid investigation with non-functioning spray head	8	280	Add team evaluation using production spray equipment and specified wax	Body Engrg & Assy Ops 8X 11 15		7	1	3	21
					Wax application plugs door drain holes	3	Laboratory test using "worst case" wax application and hole size	1	21	None		Based on test, 3 additional vent holes provided in affected areas				
					Insufficient room between panels for spray head access	4	Drawing evaluation of spray head access	4	112	Add team evaluation using design aid buck and spray head	Body Engrg & Assy Ops	Evaluation showed adequate access	7	1	1	7

SAMPLE

Figure 20.15   Design FMEA example.

Part III.E.4

Potential
Failure Mode and Effects Analysis
(Process FMEA)

Item __Front door L.H./H8HX-000-A__ ②   Process responsibility __Body engrg./assembly operations__ ③   FMEA number __1450__ ①

Model year(s) vehicle(s) __199X/Lion 4dr/wagon__ ⑤   Key date __9X 03 01 ER__   __9X 08 26 Job #1__ ⑥   Page __1__ of __1__

Core team __A. Tate—Body engrg., J. Smith—OC, R. James—Production, J. Jones—Maintenance__   Prepared by __J. Ford—X6521—Assy ops__ ④

FMEA date (orig.) __9X 05 17__ (rev.) __9X 11 06__ ⑦   ⑧

Process function / Requirements ⑨	Potential failure mode ⑩	Potential effect(s) of failure ⑪ ⑫	Class ⑫	Sev	Potential cause(s)/mechanism(s) of failure ⑬ ⑭	Occur ⑮	Current process controls ⑯	Detec ⑰	R.P.N.	Recommended action(s) ⑱	Responsibility and target completion date ⑳	Actions taken ㉑	Sev	Occ	Det	R.P.N.
Manual application of wax inside door	Insufficient wax coverage over specified surface	Deteriorated life of door leading to: • Unsatisfactory appearance due to rust through paint over time • Impaired function of interior door hardware		7	Manually inserted spray head not inserted far enough	8	Visual check each hour-1/shift for film thickness (depth meter) and coverage	5	280	Add positive depth stop to sprayer	MFG Engrg 9X 10 15	Stop added, sprayer checked on line	7	2	5	70
										Automate spraying	Mfg Engrg 9X 12 15	Rejected due to complexity of different doors on same line				
To cover inner door, lower surfaces at minimum wax thickness to retard corrosion					Spray heads clogged • Viscosity too high • Temperature too low • Pressure too low	5	Test spray pattern at start-up and after idle periods, and preventative maintenance program to clean heads	3	105	Use Design of Experiments (DOE) on viscosity vs. temperature vs. pressure	Mfg Engrg 9X 10 01	Temp and press limits were determined and limit controls have been installed - control charts show process is in control Cpk=1.85	7	1	3	21
					Spray head deformed due to impact	2	Preventative maintenance programs to maintain head	2	28	None						
					Spray time insufficient	8	Operator instructions and lot sampling (10 doors / shift) to check for coverage of critical areas	7	392	Install spray timer	Maintenance 9X 09 15	Automatic spray timer installed - operator starts spray, timer controls shut-off control charts show process is in control Cpk=2.05	7	1	7	49

⑮⑯⑰⑱⑲⑳㉑㉒   Action results ㉒

SAMPLE

Figure 20.16   Process FMEA example.

The key result of an FMECA is a criticality matrix that ranks potential failures with respect to severity. The matrix then identifies a prioritization scheme for corrective actions based on the severity of potential failure modes. As displayed on an FMECA criticality matrix, potential failures plotted farther away from the matrix origin on a diagonal line represent higher potential risks of failure, and thus warrant increased need for corrective action.

EXAMPLE 20.7: FMECA EXAMPLE

Figure 20.17 shows an example of an FMECA for a traveling lawn sprinkler. Note that each hardware item is listed on a separate line. For each possible failure, its effect on the product is determined. Type of failure is also shown along with estimates for its probability of occurrence and for its seriousness (Gryna, Chua, and Defeo 2007).

For additional discussion of FMECA, consult Mil-Std 1629A for guidance in completing a criticality assessment.

Designing for Quality

1 = Very low (<1 in 1000)
2 = Low (3 in 1000)
3 = Medium (5 in 1000)
4 = High (7 in 1000)
5 = Very high (>9 in 1000)

T = Type of failure
P = Probability of occurrence
S = Seriousness of failure of system
H = Hydraulic failure
M = Mechanical failure
W = Wear failure
C = Customer abuse

Product HRC-1
Date Jan. 14, 2007
By S.M.

Component part number	Possible failure	Cause of failure	T	P	S	Effect of failure on product	Alternatives
Worm bearing 4224	Bearing worn	Not aligned with bottom housing	M	1	4	Spray head wobbles or slows down	Improve inspection
Zytel 101		Excessive spray head wobble	M	1	3	Spray head wobbles or slows down	Improve worm bearing
Bearing stem 4225	Excessive wear	Poor bearing/ material combination	M	5	4	Spray head wobbles and loses power	Change stem material
Brass		Dirty water in bearing area	M	5	4	Spray head wobbles and loses power	Improve worm seal area
		Excessive spray head wobble	M	2	3	Spray head wobbles and loses power	Improve operating instructions
Thrust washer 4226	Excessive wear	High water pressure	M	2	5	Spray head will stall out	Inform customer in instructions
Fulton 404		Dirty water in washers	M	5	5	Spray head will stall out	Improve worm seal design
Worm 4527	Excessive wear in bearing area	Poor bearing/ material combination	M	5	4	Spray head wobbles and loses power	Change bearing stem material
Brass		Dirty water in bearing area	M	5	4	Spray head wobbles and loses power	Improve worm seal design
		Excessive spray head wobble	M	2	3	Spray head wobbles and loses power	Improve operating instructions

Figure 20.17 Failure mode effects and criticality analysis.

Fault Tree Analysis

Fault tree analysis (FTA) is a technique for analyzing complex systems to determine potential failure modes and probabilities of their occurrences. The technique was originated by H. A. Watson of Bell Telephone Laboratories to analyze the Minuteman Launch Control System. The following steps are required in order to develop fault trees (Dhillon and Singh 1981):

1. Define the undesired event (top event) of the system under consideration

2. Thoroughly understand the system and its intended use

3. Obtain the predefined system fault condition causes and continue the fault analysis to determine the relationships that can cause them

4. Construct a fault tree of logical relationships among input fault events

To obtain quantitative results for the top event, assign failure probability, unavailability, failure, and repair rates data to basic events, provided the fault tree events are redundancy free.

Fault tree analysis requires the construction of a fault tree diagram that represents the system conditions symbolically. This requires definition of the fault tree symbols. Such symbols include, for example, AND gate, OR gate, basic fault event, and priority AND gate. AND and OR gates are summarized as follows:

AND gate—The AND gate denotes that the output event occurs if and only if all the input events occur. Its symbol is:

OR gate—The OR gate denotes that the output event occurs if any of the input events occurs. Its symbol is:

Exhaustive listings of fault tree symbols exist in specialized references (see Dhillon and Singh [1981] or Barlow, Fussell, and Singpurwalla [1975]). We demonstrate the use of FTA in the following example.

EXAMPLE 20.8

Construct a fault tree of a simple electric lamp. The top event is "no light" when the switch is turned on. This could be caused by:

1. Power failure E_1

2. Switch fails to close E_2

3. Lamp failure E_3

4. Fuse failure E_4

Furthermore, the power failure can be attributed to two events: major power failure or a fuse failure. A simple tree of these events is shown in Figure 20.18.

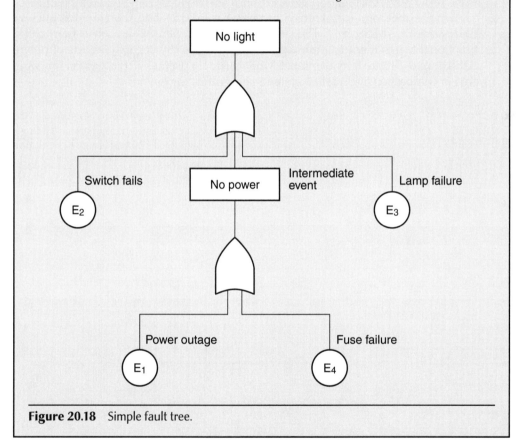

Figure 20.18   Simple fault tree.

Fault tree evaluations can be performed qualitatively or quantitatively. The qualitative evaluation determines the minimum cut sets (the minimum number of components that cause system failure) while the quantitative evaluation can be done using failure data for each component or event. The latter can be obtained from historical data or by using computer simulation. The result of the qualitative evaluation is a set of critical components and the result of the quantitative evaluation is the probability of the occurrence of the top event.

SUMMARY OF PART III

In Part III, basic definitions of reliability for both repairable and nonrepairable systems have been presented. In addition the basic relationships between the failure rate (hazard rate), probability density function, and reliability function have been developed. An example was provided to demonstrate how these functions can be obtained from failure data.

Reliability estimations of simple systems made of series, parallel, or k-out-of-n components were obtained using the reliability of individual components. Maintainability of the systems was defined and three widely used maintenance and repair policies—corrective maintenance, preventive maintenance, and predictive maintenance—were discussed. Conditions for the applicability of these policies were also discussed.

Finally, methods for identifying potential failures and their modes, such as FMEA, FMECA, ESS, and FTA, were discussed. FMEA is a tool to help cross-functional teams identify, eliminate, and/or reduce the negative effects of potential failures—before they happen. FMEA is widely used as a stand-alone tool or as part of comprehensive quality systems/programs.

Part IV

Product and Process Control

Part III presented the different elements of product and process design that include:

1. Classification of quality characteristics

2. Design inputs and design review

3. Validation and qualification methods

4. Interpretation of technical drawings and specifications

5. Determining product and process control methods

Each of these five elements is critical to ensuring proper execution of the quality planning process. However, in a typical product development effort these elements will be executed in a different sequence. Design inputs (including quality and reliability goals, cost, size, timing targets, and so on) usually will occur first. As the design is developed, periodic reviews will be conducted to ensure that the design will meet the program goals. Element (4), interpretation of technical drawings and specifications, typically is treated within the context of the design reviews. Element (1) can be initiated once the design is sufficiently detailed. Validation and qualification methods may include computer simulation, such as finite element analysis, or traditional methods such as capability studies and reliability testing of prototype parts.

Part IV

Chapter 21

A. Tools

> Define, identify, and apply product and
> process control methods such as developing
> control plans, identifying critical control
> points, developing and validating work
> instructions, etc. (Analyze).
>
> **Body of Knowledge IV.A**

In this section, product and process control methods are presented. Such methods depend on the classification of quality characteristics and the results of validation tests. See Part III for more details. Characteristics that are critical to the operation of the process or the function of the product will be subject to more intense monitoring and control.

CONTROL PLANS

Control plans are used to document and communicate the plan for monitoring and controlling the process. The control plan summarizes information from various sources into a single, handy document for quick reference on the production line. The format of the control plan is not important; standard spreadsheets are acceptable. However, the control plan should include the following elements:

- Station or operation number and process description

- Machinery, equipment, or fixtures

- Reference drawing numbers

- Product or process characteristic to be controlled (including tolerances)

- Evaluation method (gages, sensors, visual checks, and so on)

- Sample size and sample frequency

- Control method ($\bar{X}$ and R chart, check sheet, go/no-go, poka-yoke, and so on)

- Reaction plan to be followed when the control method detects a problem

The control plan is the final link in a seamless chain that begins with the design FMEA. Potential failure modes that cannot be prevented through design are carried over to the process FMEA. Some failure modes can be prevented in the process through the use of poka-yokes or reduced to very low frequency through the use of designed experiments to optimize the process. Other failure modes can be detected with high confidence. Despite our best efforts, some potential failures may still have unacceptable RPNs, and process controls must be added to monitor the process. The control plan should be checked to verify that all critical and significant characteristics identified during the design and process FMEAs are included.

At this point in the process, all nondestructive measurement systems listed on the control plan should have successfully passed the gage repeatability and reproducibility (R&R) requirement. (Gage R&R studies are discussed in Chapter 26.) Sample sizes and sample frequencies should be based on statistically sound principles. Keep in mind that the sample frequency should be often enough to enable containment of suspect product prior to shipment to the customer. The quality engineer plays a critical role in selecting the control method that is best suited for the characteristic being monitored.

Perhaps the most important aspect of the control plan methodology is the reaction plan. The reaction plan lists the steps to be taken by the operator when the control method indicates a problem. For example, what should happen when the $\bar{X}$ chart goes out of control? Unfortunately, many references and training seminars do not adequately develop this concept. The examples simply state, "adjust and recheck" or "recalibrate and recheck." Simplistic directions may lead to process tampering (overadjustment). In addition, opportunities for permanent corrective actions will be missed. (See Chapter 37 for discussion of control charts.)

Good reaction plans include four critical elements:

- Containment

- Diagnosis

- Verification

- Disposition

Containment. As soon as the problem is identified, quarantine and segregate all suspect product. This may include everything produced since the previous acceptable sample. A good inventory management system that uses the principle of first in–first out will simplify the task of containment should it ever be needed. Provide specific direction to the operator on how to accomplish containment. It also may be wise to intensify inspection until the problem is resolved.

Diagnosis. Determine the root cause of the failure. It may be necessary to ask repeatedly, "Why?" For example, if the failure occurred because the operator was not adequately trained, then ask, "Why was the operator not properly trained?" Repeat this process until an appropriate root cause is identified that will lead to a permanent corrective action. Incorporate lessons learned from previous failures to facilitate the diagnostic process. Remember that in the heat of battle common sense is not very common. Therefore, it is helpful to provide written guidance to the operator as to likely causes of the failure. In other words, specify the diagnostic steps and tests the operator should conduct during preliminary efforts to identify the root cause. If the root cause still is not identified, specify who should be called in to help, such as the product or quality engineer.

Verification. Do not assume that the corrective action resolved the problem. Prove it! Collect additional samples after the corrective change is implemented to verify that the problem is fixed. If possible, the reaction plan should specify how many additional samples are necessary before resuming normal operations.

Disposition. The obvious but nonetheless mandatory final step of the reaction plan is to determine an appropriate disposition for the material that was contained in the first step of the reaction plan. Typical dispositions include scrap, rework, sort, use as-is, and return to vendor. Written instructions are recommended for performing sorts or rework.

See Figures 21.1 and 21.2 for an example of a control plan that incorporates many of the suggestions outlined above. It was developed by a valve manufacturing company. The author uses code letters in the reaction plan section of the control plan. Detailed reaction plan instructions are provided on the second page.

Once the initial version of the control plan is released to production, the operators should take ownership of the document and treat it as a living document, constantly reviewing and updating it with new information. There also should be a feedback mechanism in the process—as new or unexpected failure modes are discovered on the line, update the control plan and feed the information back to update the FMEAs. Keeping the documentation current will facilitate the AQP process during future programs.

WORK INSTRUCTIONS

Work instructions provide detail for personnel who have direct responsibility for the operation of the process. The instructions must be documented and posted or readily accessible at the work site. Assembly instructions list each task to be performed in sequential order. Setup instructions list appropriate machine settings, such as feed rates, temperatures, and pressures. Setup instructions also should list any tasks or inspections that must be performed during production start-up to verify that the process is properly adjusted. Work instructions must be clear and understandable. Liberal use of sketches, charts, photographs, and other visual aids is strongly encouraged. The effort to eliminate opportunities for error in the process should include the work instructions. Therefore, organizations that produce a variety of similar products should consider creating unique instructions for each model, rather than using generic examples, look-up tables for bills of material, cross-referenced set-up instructions, and so forth.

Part IV.A

Soft Start-Up Valve Control Plan

Control plan number: CP714		Control plan revision level: C			Revision date: 12/01/99				
Part/assembly number/rev: 714647-H & 714648-J		Product line: Soft start air dump valve			Originator: J. Hausner				

Sta #	Process description	Machine tools/ equipment	Print no.	Characteristic specification	Evaluation measurement equipment (Methods)	Sample Size	Sample Freq.	Control method	Reaction plan code
14	Machine needle bleed port on cover	Drill press	714648	0.060" min diameter	0.60 (minus) gage pin S/N 15-50-2118	1	1 per hour	Check sheet	A
18	Pressure gage torque	Torque driver	714647 714648	20 +/– 5 IN LB	Torque gage S/N 15-50-2019	5	1 per shift	$\bar{X}$ chart	E, F
23	Body-cover screw torque	Torque driver	714647 714648	60 +/– 15 IN LB	Torque gage S/N 15-50-2120	3 per screw	2 per shift	Separate $\bar{X}$ charts	E, F
27	Solenoid assembly torque	Torque driver	209647 209648	14 +/– 7 IN LB	Torque gage S/N 15-50-2019	5	1 per shift	$\bar{X}$ chart	E, F
29	Final air test	Test tank	209647 209648	Functional test and leak check	Visual: ref. QA spec 203795 Functional: ref. assy instruction	1	100%	Go/no-go	A, B, C, D
All	All	All	209647 209648	Workmanship	Visual	1	100%	Go/no-go	See note 2

Note 1: At all times, quarantine one hour worth of product before releasing to shipping. In the event of a final test failure, the last hour of production should be set aside for possible retest. This should be done on all final test failures with the exception of porosity.

Note 2: Compare suspect unit to visual accept/reject standards. If unit is unacceptable, stop the line and follow standard four-step reaction plan: (A) contain suspect units; (B) diagnose the root cause and implement corrective action; (C) verify that the corrective action is effective; (D) disposition suspect material (sort, scrap, rework, use as-is).

Figure 21.1   Control plan example: page 1.

Part IV.A

Part IV.A

Soft Start-Up Valve Control Plan

Control plan number: CP714	Key contact: J. Hausner	Control plan revision level: C	Revision date: 12/01/99
Part/assembly number/rev: 714647-H & 714648-J	Part name/description: Soft start air dump valve HG & HJ series	Product line: Airlogic control valve series	Originator: J. Hausner

Failure mode	Reaction plan	Code
Valve fails to open	Containment: Segregate nonconforming unit and previous hour of production for MRB. Disposition: Verify that wire leads and power supply are hooked up correctly. Verify needle port diameter > 0.060". If port diameter is under spec, switch to 100% inspection for the next 50 units and notify the product engineer (PE) if another failure is found. Replace drill bit if hole is not drilled through or burrs are present. Verify that piston ring is installed and free of nicks. Verify that needle valve is open at least one complete turn. Verify that the solenoid port resistor is installed. Try another solenoid. If other tests fail, check diameter of diaphragm. Contact the PE if additional diagnosis is required. Verification: Verify that corrective action eliminates problem. Disposition: Scrap nonconforming components. Rework assemblies as necessary and retest 100% of the previous hour of production.	
Valve fails to close	Containment: Segregate nonconforming product for MRB. Diagnosis: Verify that wire leads and power supply are hooked up correctly. Verify that flow control is open. Verify that diaphragm is installed correctly and check for voids in the seal bead. Verify that the dump hole is drilled completely through bonnet. Check that the fluid resistor is in place. Try another solenoid. If solenoid sticks open, quarantine current batch and switch to a new batch of solenoids. Contact PE if further diagnosis is required to determine cause. Verification: Verify that corrective action eliminates problem. Notify PE if another failure is found on the next 50 units. Disposition: Scrap nonconforming components. Rework assembly and retest.	
Body–bonnet leak	Containment: Segregate nonconforming product for MRB. Diagnosis: Verify torque. For torque adjustments, see Reaction Code "E" below. Ensure that diaphragm is installed correctly and that there are no voids present on the bead. Verify that the bead grooves on the bonnet and body are free of nicks or porosity and the diameters are within tolerance. Verify that the milled slot on the body is within tolerance. Contact PE if further diagnosis is required. Verification: Verify that corrective action eliminates problem. Disposition: Scrap nonconforming components. Rework assembly and retest. Contact line lead or PE if there are two or more consecutive failures or three failures within one hour.	
Leak at fittings	Containment: Segregate nonconforming product for MRB. Diagnosis: Verify that fittings are installed correctly and have the correct torque applied. Verify that the threads on the fitting and assembly are free of nicks or porosity. Contact PE if further diagnosis is required. Verification: Verify that corrective action eliminates problem. Notify PE if another failure is found on the next 50 units. Disposition: Scrap nonconforming components. Rework assembly and retest.	
Torque out of spec	Containment: Segregate nonconforming product for MRB. Diagnosis: Verify torque using another torque gage. For torque adjustments, take at least 10 samples and adjust torque gun if average is more than one standard deviation away from the nominal. Notify maintenance if average is close to nominal and there are any observations out of spec. Contact PE for further diagnosis. Verification: Measure a minimum of three subgroups and verify that the process is near nominal and in control. Disposition: If undertorqued, retorque assembly. If overtorqued, replace screw(s) and retorque.	
SPC out of control, but parts in spec	Refer to QA/SPC procedure 231573. Comply with SPC procedure requirements. Document the root cause and corrective action in a note on the control chart.	

Figure 21.2   Control plan example: page 2.

Chapter 22

B. Material Control

Material control addresses the raw materials, work in process, and final products and how they are physically controlled, identified, and tracked. The first step in control is classification; the last step is disposition.

Material control is based on identification and classification. Systems, components, nonconformities, and features are all subject to classification schemes, and only after a classification has been done can the appropriate control be applied. There are many different classification factors that should be considered, including:

- Volume of production

- Complexity

- Cost

- Expected lifetime

- Amount of maintenance required

- Risk to safety and/or the environment

If the product tends to be complex, expensive, and long-lived, then a great deal of effort must be expended in developing the material control scheme. Commodity-type products may require very little in the way of material control, but even the simplest products must be controlled—in simple and inexpensive ways. Such issues as process selection, inspection method, amount of sampling, strictness of inspection, and control of deviating material must be decided with respect to the importance of each characteristic and each component. Every good quality engineer should spend some time thinking about issues of relative importance and criticality. Think about the Pareto chart (see Chapter 27 for discussion of Pareto charts). Collect data and opinions so that before production ever begins, a scheme of relative importance is clearly established.

This process requires careful study by a number of different individuals. It is an exercise in clarification, in making distinctions, and clearing up confusion. The task requires input from several different sources of expertise to assure that a balanced result is obtained. The people involved should include representatives of product design, safety, marketing, and field service.

1. MATERIAL IDENTIFICATION, STATUS, AND TRACEABILITY

> Define and distinguish these concepts, and describe methods for applying them in various situations. [Note: Product control procedures will not be tested.] (Analyze)
>
> **Body of Knowledge IV.B.1**

Identification of Materials

The only reason to identify anything is to be able to trace it. And the only reason to trace it is to be able to find out something about it later. But those are two huge reasons in today's highly technological and litigious society. Without product traceability, many manufacturers would be exposed to unacceptable risk.

Principles of Identification

Modern technology has produced a wide array of identification methods. The physical application of markings and subsequent tracking by means of scanners and sensors provide many options. It is necessary to maintain records not only of items produced and their identification but also of how the record-keeping system itself is operated and modified. After all, the storage and retrieval of information is a rapidly changing field.

One of the most effective identification methods is radio frequency identification (RFID). By using radio frequency tags, information can be provided about, for example, identification, tracking, and security.

RFID technology has been used in supply chain management, inventory tracking, and the healthcare industry. In healthcare, RFID technology has been implemented for asset management (determining where mobile medical devices are at all times, for example), patient care (determining where a patient is at all times while hospitalized), and inventory management (reducing the chance of inventory being out of stock at critical times).

Mechanics

To illustrate the mechanics of product identification, consider the case of the Sauer Danfoss Company in Ames, Iowa. This company makes moderately complex mechanical products that require 100 percent testing and periodic design modifications. They have recently improved their materials management system by creating a multifunctional task team of four people. The team collected data for two and one-half years and finally decided to scrap their existing system for tracking material, which was dependent on manual entry into paper "move tags" and then manual keying into a computer database. Determination of current status required frequent physical count of all items.

The team started all over with bar code and RFID (radio frequency identification) technologies. Now whenever an item of hardware moves, it is automatically accounted for, either by a bar code scanner or an RFID receiver. A sophisticated database system automatically processes each scan. The database maintains a variety of characteristics about each unit, including:

- Model number

- Unit number

- Date produced

- Result of test

- Date of test

- Rework record

Product identification is vital when producing complex products and often unnecessary for mundane commodities. However, a recent example of the lack of sufficient product identification and control was the Starlink seed corn problem of 2000. Starlink was a form of seed corn that was approved for growing animal feed but not for human consumption. There were inadequate controls put into place when the seed corn was sold to farmers and as a result the animal feed corn was inextricably intermixed with human-consumption corn at grain elevators throughout the Midwest. At the time they were delivering the corn, neither the farmers nor the grain elevator operators realized there was a problem. But soon, consumer groups were testing products made out of this corn, and the use of the unacceptable corn was detected. A great outcry resulted, and many losses were incurred as both types of the intermixed corn had to be converted to animal feed.

Lennox Industries, in Marshalltown, Iowa, uses a 10-digit alphanumeric product identification code. This set of ten digits allows traceability to a diverse set of factors, including the date of fabrication, the supplier of each subsystem, the product model, and the date of final assembly. Several things must be considered when setting up such a code:

- The amount of liability exposure

- The number of levels of components and subcomponents

- The process design must incorporate the ability to trace products back to their point of creation and installation

Traceability

Traceability is an explicit part of the ISO 9000 and ISO/TS 16949 standards. See paragraph 7.5.3 in ANSI/ISO/ASQ Q9001-2001, for example. Traceability is like a pedigree for a dog breed or the provenance of a painting. It allows one to find out about the past history of any item. Commodity products such as nuts and bolts have limited needs for traceability. Complex products such as automobiles must have multiple paths to trace back through many levels and many different sources. Sensitive material such as pharmaceuticals and food products must be traceable at all times. Even in the case of nuts and bolts, however, wise

Part IV.B.1

manufacturers will keep different lots segregated and identified as long as it is economically possible.

The ISO 9001 standard requires product identification and traceability, where appropriate, for recall of nonconforming product, hazardous product, or product in conflict with laws, regulations, or statutes. Product identification must be provided when required by a customer. Properly identified items must have a unique number and are tracked by their location in the process. Differences between items and lots must be distinguishable.

The place to start with traceability, that is, the ability to preserve the identity of the product and its origins, is when the process is first designed. Today, appropriate software and database designs are available. Training of workers may be required in order to create the proper climate and means to accomplish this.

Gryna (1988) listed four reasons why traceability is needed:

1. To assure that only materials and components of adequate quality enter the final product, for example, sterility of drug materials, adequate metallurgical composition, and heat treatment of structural components.

2. To assure positive identification to avoid mix-up of products that otherwise look alike.

3. To permit recall of suspected product on a precise basis. Lacking traceability programs, huge recalls of automobiles and other products have been required in the past. The number of defectives in the recalled set was often quite small.

4. To localize causes of failure and take remedial action at minimal cost.

There are other uses of traceability—such as in inventory control and scheduling. Some of these uses also affect quality. For example, use of materials on a first-in, first-out basis reduces the risk of quality deterioration of perishable materials.

Factors to Consider

- What is the cost of the product? A more expensive product requires more accountability over time, and thus better traceability.

- How long will the product last? If it is going to be around a long time, there is more concern about its origin, as new discoveries often are made of chemical characteristics and environmental effects. The discovery that asbestos was a carcinogen after its routine use for decades is a good example.

- Will the product be built into another product?

- Does the product have items or materials in it that have not been thoroughly evaluated over a long period of time?

- Is there a significant possible health hazard associated with the product?

- Are field modifications often required, with different replacement items required on different models? (Automobiles are a prime example.)

Ten items to consider in a traceability program:

1. Product category

2. Product life

3. Unit cost

4. Recall or modification in the field

5. Product complexity

6. Level of downstream traceability

7. Documents providing traceability

8. Type of identification

9. Coded versus uncoded identification

10. Method of identification—tags, name plates, ink stamps, other means

The use of a tracing code is required for efficient operation (Feigenbaum 1991). This code is established at the beginning of material flow and a traceability flowchart is established. The major activities on the flowchart include:

1. Critical component selection and listing by part number.

2. Vendor part coding (recording vendor name and date of receipt).

3. Coding internally manufactured parts, subassembly, assembly, and storage in a daily tally. At the end of the assembly line, each shipping container is date coded. This sequential coding procedure provides sufficient data to tie critical components to specific dates of receiving inspection, manufacturing, and final assembly.

4. Computerized shipping records, including date codes, customer name, and destination. Correlation of these data with tracing code numbers results in very effective traceability of critical components.

2. MATERIAL SEGREGATION

> Describe material segregation and its importance, and evaluate appropriate methods for applying it in various situations. (Evaluate)
>
> **Body of Knowledge IV.B.2**

Part IV.B.2

There are two major situations that demand disposition of nonconforming products. The first is when a product fails to pass inspection or test and a decision regarding it must be made. This is the function of the material review board (MRB), to be discussed in section 4 of this chapter. The second situation, considerably more serious, is when a problem develops after the product is out of the plant, on store shelves, in dealer showrooms, and in use by customers. Now a product recall may be required. In view of the very negative aspects of product recall, all the prior work concerning product traceability and product integrity will pay off quite handsomely in organizing the recall.

3. CLASSIFICATION OF DEFECTS

> Define, describe, and classify the seriousness of
> product and process defects. (Evaluate)
>
> **Body of Knowledge IV.B.3**

In certain types of products, more than one defect could be present and a relatively small number of minor defects could be acceptable to the customer. Product quality in these cases may be judged by the total number of defects or the number of defects per unit. Control charts for attributes are a tool that may be used for this purpose. In such cases, the objective of inspection is to determine the number of defects or nonconformities present rather than to classify units as conforming or nonconforming.

Defect and *nonconformity* are two terms that may be used synonymously in many situations. For other purposes, the definitions of both terms are slightly different. A nonconformity is defined as a failure of a quality characteristic to meet its intended level or state, occurring with severity sufficient to cause the product not to meet a specification. A defect is a nonconformity severe enough to cause the product not to satisfy normal usage requirements. Thus, the difference between the term nonconformity and the term defect is based mainly on perspective. The former is defined based on specifications, while the latter is defined based on fitness for use. The numerical result generated by inspection consists of the count of defects or nonconformities for each product unit. Often it is possible to classify the different types of defects according to their severity, and then assign a weight to each class based on the importance of the affected quality characteristic that relates to the product specifications. The selection of the weights should reflect the relative importance of the various defect categories and their likelihood of causing product failure or customer dissatisfaction. A typical seriousness classification includes four levels of defect seriousness:

1. *Critical* defect may lead directly to severe injury or catastrophic economic loss.

2. *Serious* defect may lead to injury or significant economic loss.

3. *Major* defect may cause major problems during normal use. A major defect will likely result in reducing the usability of the product.

4. *Minor* defect may cause minor problems during normal use.

See Montgomery (2009b) for discussion of defect levels.

4. MATERIAL REVIEW BOARD (MRB)

> Identify the purpose and function of an MRB, and make appropriate disposition decisions in various situations. (Analyze)
>
> **Body of Knowledge IV.B.4**

The material review board (MRB) is an appointed group of individuals with different backgrounds and expertise. Their assignment is to determine what corrective actions must be taken after nonconforming parts or components are discovered. In a larger sense, the purposes of the MRB are to determine the disposition of nonconforming parts, components, and subassemblies, determine the causes of the nonconformance of these items, and take the necessary corrective actions to prevent such nonconformance from taking place in future production.

The basic function of a material review board is to: (a) review material that does not conform to standard, (b) determine what its disposition should be, and (c) drive the development of effective corrective action to prevent recurrence.

The MRB is a broad-based reviewing agency whose membership usually consists minimally of representatives from the following:

- *Engineering.* The cognizant designer is often the representative

- *Quality assurance.* The representative is often from quality control engineering

- *Customers.* The representative may be from the customer's organization (for example, the government inspector) or from marketing

In some companies, the role of the material review board is solely one of judging fitness for use of nonconforming products. Bond (1983) discusses board composition, philosophy, and problem documentation.

In general, the MRB procedural steps can be summarized as follows: After a defect is discovered, verification by inspection may be needed. A complete description of any nonconformance is then initiated. A quality engineer picked by the MRB will review the facts and include the case in an appropriate tracking system. The MRB committee may then follow up with investigation and analysis. When done, the quality engineer takes the case again, recommending the appropriate corrective action(s) and steps for implementation.

The term *standard repair* is common within the MRB framework. It signifies a procedure where a certain type of defect(s) occurs time and time again. A standard repair procedure is then initiated, documented, and implemented for such

Part IV.B.4

Table 22.1 Standards pertaining to material review board operations.

Standard	Purpose
MIL-STD-1520C	Sets "the requirements for cost-effective corrective action and disposition system for nonconforming material"
MIL-Q-9858A	Quality program requirements, Section 6.5, Nonconforming Material, requires the contractor to establish "an effective and positive system for controlling nonconforming material"
MIL-STD-481B	Configuration control—Engineering changes
MIL-I-8500	Establishes interchangeability and replaceability requirements
ANSI/ASQ Z1.4-2003	Sampling procedures and tables for inspection by attributes
ANSI/ASQ Z1.9-2003	Sampling procedures and tables for inspection by variables for percent defectives

situations. Minor defects are most likely to be treated with a standard repair procedure. Within the context of defect classification, defects may further be classified as major or minor. Minor defects, unlike major ones, may not adversely affect the integrity of the part, component, or assembly.

In many cases, the MRB concludes that the lot containing nonconforming products should not be shipped as is. The decision, concurred with by inspection personnel, may be: sort (100 percent inspection), downgrade, repair, rework, scrap, and so on. A decision to ship also may be authorized by the MRB. In such cases, a unanimous decision should be reached by all members. The decision also should create factual data and thus an important source of information. A successful MRB program requires that the board not only make decisions about immediate disposition of rejected material, but also direct ongoing programs of root cause analysis to eliminate future rejections of the same type.

There are several military documents associated with the MRB concept. A partial list is shown in Table 22.1.

Part IV.B.4

Chapter 23

C. Acceptance Sampling

A cceptance sampling is a method for inspecting the product. Inspection can be done with screening (also called sorting or 100 percent inspection), in which all units are inspected, or with sampling. Acceptance sampling is the process of inspecting a portion of the product in a lot for the purpose of making a decision regarding classification of the entire lot as either conforming or nonconforming to quality specifications.

Whether inspection is done with screening or with sampling, the results of inspection can be used for different purposes as follows:

1. To distinguish between good lots and bad lots using acceptance sampling plans (as in incoming material inspection and final product inspection).

2. To distinguish between good products and bad products.

3. To determine the status of process control and if the process is changing. This is usually done in conjunction with control charts.

4. To evaluate process capability. In this case, inspection is used to determine if the process exhibits excessive variation and if it is approaching or exceeding the specification limits.

5. To determine process adjustment. Based on inspection results of process output, as depicted by a histogram for example, the process mean may require adjustment and/or process variation may need to be reduced. A process might require adjustment even though all the units produced to date conform to the quality standards agreed upon with the customer.

6. To rate the accuracy of inspectors or of inspection equipment by comparing the inspection results with corresponding standards. An inspection operation can result in two types of error: classification of a conforming unit as nonconforming and classification of a nonconforming unit as conforming. The probabilities of both types of error can be easily estimated using probability theory and other statistical methods.

7. To serve as a mechanism for evaluating vendors in terms of their products' quality. Vendors that consistently deliver high-quality products can receive preferred status involving reduced inspection and priority in bidding for new contracts, while vendors that do not stand up to quality requirements could be warned or discontinued altogether. This type of procedure is known as vendor qualification or vendor certification.

The last three uses of inspection might be seen as feedback about the production processes, the measurement processes, and the supplier.

SAMPLING INSPECTION VERSUS 100 PERCENT INSPECTION

Sampling provides the economic advantage of lower inspection costs due to fewer units being inspected. In addition, the time required to inspect a sample is substantially less than that required for the entire lot and there is less damage to the product due to reduced handling. Most inspectors find that selection and inspection of a random sample is less tedious and monotonous than inspection of the complete lot. Another advantage of sampling inspection is related to the supplier/ customer relationship. By inspecting a small fraction of the lot and forcing the supplier to screen 100 percent in case of lot rejection (which is the case for rectifying inspection), the customer emphasizes that the supplier must be concerned about quality. On the other hand, the variability inherent in sampling results in sampling errors: rejection of lots of conforming quality and acceptance of lots of nonconforming quality.

Acceptance sampling is most appropriate when inspection costs are high and when 100 percent inspection is monotonous and can cause inspector fatigue and boredom, resulting in degraded performance and increased error rates. Obviously, sampling is the only choice available for destructive inspection. Rectifying sampling is a form of acceptance sampling. Sample units detected as nonconforming are discarded from the lot, replaced with conforming units, or repaired. Rejected lots are subject to 100 percent screening, which can involve discarding, replacing, or repairing units detected as nonconforming.

In certain situations, it is preferable to inspect 100 percent of the product. This would be the case for critical or complex products, where the cost of making the wrong decision would be too high. Screening is appropriate when the fraction nonconforming is extremely high. In this case, most of the lots would be rejected under acceptance sampling and those accepted would be so as a result of statistical variations rather than better quality. Screening is also appropriate when the fraction nonconforming is not known and an estimate based on a large sample is needed.

1. SAMPLING CONCEPTS

> Define, describe, and apply the concepts of producer
> and consumer risk and related terms, including operating
> characteristic (OC) curves, acceptable quality limit
> (AQL), lot tolerance percent defective (LTPD), average
> outgoing quality (AOQ), average outgoing quality limit
> (AOQL), etc. (Analyze)
>
> **Body of Knowledge IV.C.1**

Sampling may be performed according to the type of quality characteristics to be inspected. There are three major categories of sampling plans: sampling plans for attributes, sampling plans for variables, and special sampling plans. It should be noted that acceptance sampling is not advised for processes in continuous production and in a state of statistical control. For these processes, Deming (1986) provides decision rules for selecting either 100 percent inspection or no inspection.

Lot-by-Lot versus Average Quality Protection

For continuing processes, sampling plans based on average quality protection have characteristics calculated from the binomial and/or Poisson distributions. For processes not considered to be continuing, sampling plans based on lot-by-lot protection have characteristics calculated from the hypergeometric distribution, which takes the lot size into consideration.

Sampling plans based on the Poisson and binomial distributions are more common than those based on the hypergeometric distribution. This is due to the complexity of calculating plans based on the hypergeometric distribution. New software on personal computers, however, may eliminate this drawback.

The Operating Characteristic Curve

No matter which type of attribute sampling plan is being considered, an important evaluation tool is the operating characteristic (OC) curve.

The OC curve allows a sampling plan to be almost completely evaluated at a glance, giving a pictorial view of the probabilities of accepting lots submitted at varying levels of percent nonconforming. The OC curve illustrates the risks involved in acceptance sampling. Figure 23.1 shows an OC curve for a sample size n of 50 drawn from an infinite lot size, with an acceptance number c of 3.

As can be seen by the OC curve, if the lot were 100 percent to specifications, the probability of acceptance P_a also would be 100 percent. But if the lot were 13.4 percent defective, there would be approximately a 10 percent probability of acceptance.

Part IV.C.1

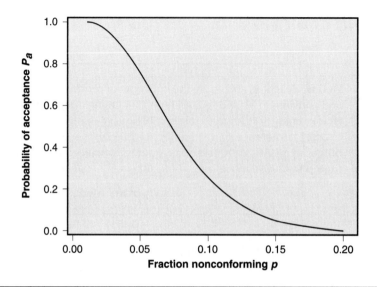

Figure 23.1   An operating characteristic (OC) curve for $n = 50$ and $c = 3$.

There are two types of OC curves to consider: (1) type A OC curves and (2) type B OC curves. Type A OC curves are used to calculate the probability of acceptance on a lot-by-lot basis when the lot is not a product of a continuous process. These OC curves are calculated using the hypergeometric distribution.

Type B OC curves are used to evaluate sampling plans for a continuous process or for a process where a lot of size N is large. These curves are based on the binomial and/or Poisson distributions when the requirements for usage are met. In general, the ANSI/ASQ Z1.4-2003 standard OC curves are based on the binomial distribution for sample sizes through 80 and the Poisson approximation to the binomial for sample sizes greater than 80.

The Poisson approximation to the binomial was often employed for calculating the probability of acceptance (P_a) when the sample sizes of interest were quite large. This approximation was used because the computations needed to calculate the binomial probabilities could be impractical.

With modern spreadsheet software, the binomial computations are no longer a problem. However, you still see Poisson approximations used for the binomial distribution, and this is acceptable.

Plotting the OC Curve

In the examples that follow, it is assumed that the process of interest is continuous (in theory). Since the process is considered continuous, the lot size is not taken into consideration in the calculations of P_a. Suppose a sample size of $n = 50$ is randomly selected from the lot. Furthermore, the lot is accepted if three or fewer nonconformances are found in the sample. To plot the OC curve, six to eight representative points for fraction nonconforming should be used to draw the continuous curve through the points.

EXAMPLE 23.1

Consider a sampling plan with $n = 50$ and an acceptable number of nonconforming units of at most three ($c = 3$). The probability of acceptance of the lot can be found for various values of p using equation (23–1). The probabilities are given in Table 23.1. The resulting OC curve is displayed in Figure 23.1 on the previous page.

Table 23.1 Probability of acceptance for various levels of fraction nonconforming.

p	P_a
0.01	0.9984
0.02	0.9822
0.03	0.9372
0.04	0.8609
0.05	0.7604
0.06	0.6473
0.07	0.5327
0.08	0.4253
0.09	0.3303
0.10	0.2503
0.15	0.0460
0.20	0.0057

The probability of acceptance P_a can be calculated using the binomial probability mass function (see Chapter 34 for complete details on the binomial distribution and the cumulative distribution function). The probability of acceptance is given by

$$P_a = P(d \le c) = \sum_{d=0}^{c} {}_nC_d p^d (1-p)^{n-d} \tag{23–1}$$

where

d = the number of nonconforming items

c = the acceptance number

p = fraction nonconforming

${}_nC_d = \dfrac{n!}{d!(n-d)!}$ and represents the number of ways that d nonconforming units can be chosen from a sample of size n.

The OC curve can be constructed similarly to the one in Figure 23.1 for various values of *p*.

The probabilities of acceptance can be calculated using the Poisson distribution (discussed in Chapter 34). The probability of acceptance is

$$P_a = P(d \le c) = \sum_{d=0}^{c} \frac{(np)^d e^{-np}}{d!}$$ (23–2)

where *np* is the mean of the binomial distribution and therefore the necessary parameter for the Poisson distribution. Complete details on the Poisson and binomial distributions can be found in Chapter 34. Furthermore, tables providing these probabilities can also be found in Appendix J for the binomial distribution and in Appendix M for the Poisson distribution.

The operating characteristic curve is useful for a number of quantities of interest. Two of those quantities are the acceptable quality limit (AQL) and the lot tolerance percent defective (LTPD).

Acceptance Sampling by Attributes

Acceptance sampling by attributes generally is used for two purposes: (1) protection against accepting lots from a continuing process whose average quality deteriorates beyond an acceptable quality level, and (2) protection against isolated lots that may have levels of nonconformances greater than can be considered acceptable. The most commonly used form of acceptance sampling plan is sampling by attributes. The most widely used standard of all attribute plans, although not necessarily the best, is ANSI/ASQ Z1.4-2003. The following sections provide more details on the characteristics of acceptance sampling and discussion of military standards in acceptance sampling.

Acceptable Quality Limit

As part of the revision of ANSI/ASQC Z1.4-1993, acceptable quality level (AQL) has been changed to acceptable quality limit (AQL) in ANSI/ASQ Z1.4-2003 and is defined as the quality level that is the worst tolerable process average when a continuing series of lots is submitted for acceptance sampling. This means that a lot that has a fraction defective equal to the AQL has a high probability (generally in the area of 0.95, although it may vary) of being accepted. As a result, plans that are based on AQL, such as ANSI/ASQ Z1.4-2003, favor the producer in getting lots accepted that are in the general neighborhood of the AQL for fraction defective in a lot.

Lot Tolerance Percent Defective

The lot tolerance percent defective (LTPD), expressed in percent defective, is the poorest quality in an individual lot that should be accepted. The LTPD has a low probability of acceptance. In many sampling plans, the LTPD is the percent defective having a 10 percent probability of acceptance.

Producer's and Consumer's Risks

There are risks involved in using acceptance sampling plans. The risks involved in acceptance sampling are: (1) producer's risk and (2) consumer's risk. These risks correspond with type I and type II errors in hypothesis testing (type I and type II errors are discussed in Chapter 35). The definitions of producer's and consumer's risks are:

Producer's risk (α). The producer's risk for any given sampling plan is the probability of rejecting a lot that is within the acceptable quality level (see ASQ [2004]). This means that the producer faces the possibility (at level of significance α) of having a lot rejected even though the lot has met the requirements stipulated by the AQL level.

Consumer's risk (β). The consumer's risk for any given sampling plan is the probability of acceptance (often 10 percent) for a designated numerical value of relatively poor submitted quality (ASQ 2004). The consumer's risk, therefore, is the probability of accepting a lot that has not met the requirements stipulated by the LTPD level.

Average Outgoing Quality

The average outgoing quality (AOQ) is the expected average quality of outgoing products, including all accepted lots, plus all rejected lots that have been sorted 100 percent and have had all of the nonconforming units replaced by conforming units. There is a given AOQ for specific fractions nonconforming of submitted lots sampled under a given sampling plan. When the fraction nonconforming is very low, a large majority of the lots will be accepted as submitted. The few lots that are rejected will be sorted 100 percent and have all nonconforming units replaced with conforming units. Thus, the AOQ will always be less than the submitted quality. As the quality of submitted lots declines in relation to the AQL, the percent of lots rejected increases in proportion to accepted lots. As these rejected lots are sorted and combined with accepted lots, an AOQ lower than the average fraction of nonconformances of submitted lots emerges. Therefore, when the level of quality of incoming lots is good, the AOQ is good; when the incoming quality is bad and most lots are rejected and sorted, the result is also good.

To calculate the AOQ for a specific fraction nonconforming and a sampling plan, the first step is to calculate the probability of accepting the lot at that level of fraction nonconforming. Then, multiply the probability of acceptance by the fraction nonconforming for the AOQ. Thus,

$$\text{AOQ} = P_a p \left[1 - \frac{n}{N} \right]$$

where N is the lot size and n is the sample size. If the desired result is a percentage, multiply by 100. If the lot size is assumed infinite (theoretically) then AOQ $\cong P_a p$.

The average outgoing quality limit (AOQL) is the maximum AOQ for all possible levels of incoming quality.

Average Outgoing Quality Limit

The AOQ is a variable dependent on the quality level of incoming lots. When the AOQ is plotted for all possible levels of incoming quality, a curve as shown in Figure 23.2 results. The average outgoing quality limit (AOQL) is the highest value on the AOQ curve.

Assuming an infinite lot size, the AOQ may be calculated as $AOQ = P_a p$. The probability of acceptance can be calculated using equation (23–1) or equation (23–2) as before. An average outgoing quality curve can be constructed for various fractions nonconforming (p) and probabilities of acceptance (P_a). The maximum AOQ is the *average outgoing quality limit* (AOQL).

Lot Size, Sample Size, and Acceptance Number

For any single sampling plan, the plan is completely described by the lot size, sample size, and acceptance number. In this section, the effect of changing the sample size, acceptance number, and lot size on the behavior of the sampling plan will be explored along with the risks of constant percentage plans.

EXAMPLE 23.2

Consider the previous example with $n = 50$, $c = 3$, and $p = 0.01$ to 0.10 by 0.01. The AOQ values are given in Table 23.2. The resulting AOQ curve is displayed in Figure 23.2. The AOQL is approximately 0.03884.

Table 23.2 AOQ levels for various levels of fraction nonconforming.

p	P_a	AOQ
0.01	0.9984	0.00998
0.02	0.9822	0.01964
0.03	0.9372	0.02812
0.04	0.8609	0.03444
0.05	0.7604	0.03802
0.06	0.6473	0.03884
0.07	0.5327	0.03729
0.08	0.4253	0.03402
0.09	0.3303	0.02973
0.10	0.2503	0.02503
0.15	0.0460	0.00690
0.20	0.0057	0.00114

The effect on the OC curve caused by changing the sample size while holding all other parameters constant is shown in Figure 23.3. The probability of acceptance changes considerably as sample size changes. The P_a for the given sample sizes for

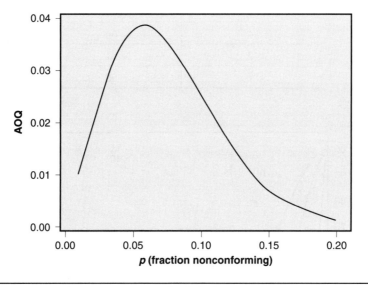

Figure 23.2 AOQ curve for $n = 50, c = 3$, and infinite lot size.

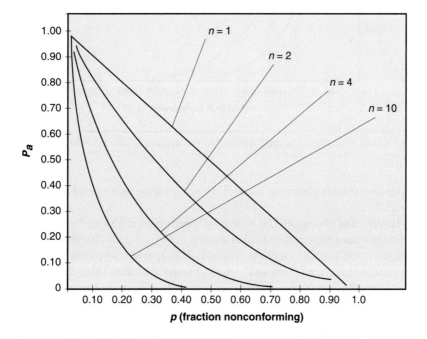

Figure 23.3 Effect on an OC curve of changing sample size (n) when accept number (c) is held constant.

Table 23.3   Probability of acceptance for various *n*.

Sample size (*n*)	Probability of acceptance (*P$_a$*%)
10	35
4	66
2	81
1	90

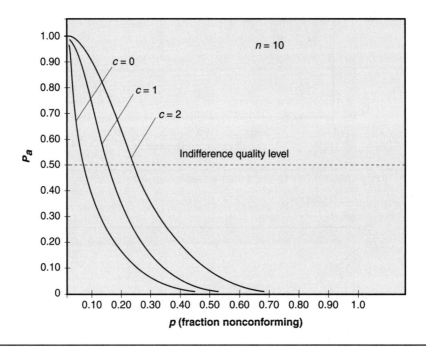

Figure 23.4   Effect of changing accept number (*c*) when sample size (*n*) is held constant.

a 10 percent nonconforming lot and an acceptance number of zero are shown in Table 23.3.

The effect of changing the acceptance number on a sampling plan while holding all other parameters constant is shown in Figure 23.4. Another point of interest is that for *c* = 0, the OC curve is concave in shape, while plans with larger acceptance numbers have a "reverse s" shape. Figure 23.4 and Table 23.4 show the effect of changing the acceptance number of a sampling plan on the indifference quality level (IQL: 50–50 chance of accepting a given percent defective).

The parameter having the least effect on the OC curve is the lot size *N*. Figure 23.5 shows the changes in the OC curve for a sample size of 10, acceptance number of 0, and lot sizes of 100, 200, and 1000. For this reason, using the binomial and

Table 23.4   Fraction defective at indifference quality level.

Sample size (n)	Acceptance number (c)	Percent defective at indifference quality level
10	2	0.26
10	1	0.17
10	0	0.07

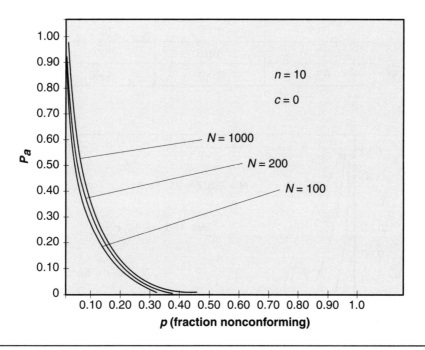

Figure 23.5   Effect of changing lot size (N) when acceptance number (c) and sample size (n) are held constant.

Poisson approximations, even when lot sizes are known (and are large compared to sample size), results in little error in accuracy. Some key probabilities of acceptance points for the three lot sizes are displayed in Table 23.5. As can be seen, the differences due to lot size are minimal.

Computing the sample size as a percentage of the lot size has a large effect on risks and protection, as shown in Figure 23.6. In this case, plans having a sample size totaling 10 percent of the lot size are shown. As can be seen, the degree of protection changes dramatically with changes in lot size, which results in low protection for small lot sizes and gives excessively large sample requirements for large lot sizes.

Table 23.5 Probability of acceptance for various lot sizes.

Fraction defective (p)	Probability of acceptance (P_a)	Lot size (N)
0.10	0.330	100
0.30	0.023	100
0.50	0.001	100
0.10	0.340	200
0.30	0.026	200
0.50	0.001	200
0.10	0.347	1000
0.30	0.028	1000
0.50	0.001	1000

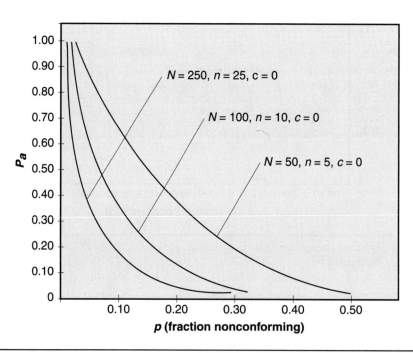

Figure 23.6 Operating characteristic curves for sampling plans having the sample size equal to 10 percent of the lot size.

2. SAMPLING STANDARDS AND PLANS

> Interpret and apply ANSI/ASQ Z1.4 and Z1.9 standards
> for attributes and variables sampling. Identify and
> distinguish between single, double, multiple, sequential,
> and continuous sampling methods. Identify the
> characteristics of Dodge-Romig sampling tables and
> when they should be used. (Analyze)
>
> **Body of Knowledge IV.C.2**

There are several types of attribute sampling plans in use, with the most common being single, double, multiple, and sequential sampling plans. The type of sampling plan used is determined by ease of use and administration, general quality level of incoming lots, average sample number, and so on.

Single Sampling Plans

When single sampling plans are used, the decision to either accept or reject the lot is based on the results of the inspection of a single sample of n items from a submitted lot. In Example 1, the OC curve and AOQ curve were calculated for a single sampling plan where $n = 50$ and $c = 3$. Single sampling plans have the advantage of ease of administration, but due to the unchanging sample size they do not take advantage of the potential cost savings of reduced or tightened inspection when incoming quality is either excellent or poor.

Double Sampling Plans

When using double sampling plans, a smaller first sample is taken from the submitted lot, and one of three decisions is made: (1) accept the lot, (2) reject the lot, or (3) draw another sample. If a second sample is to be drawn, the lot will either be accepted or rejected after the second sample. Double sampling plans have the advantage of a lower total sample size when the incoming quality is either excellent or poor because the lot is either accepted or rejected on the first sample.

EXAMPLE 23.3

A double sampling plan is to be executed as follows: take a first sample (n_1) of 75 units and set c_1 (the acceptance number for the first sample) at 0. The lot will be accepted based on the first sample results if no nonconformances are found in the first sample.

Continued

Continued

If three nonconformances are found in the first sample, the lot will be rejected based on the first sample results. If after analyzing the results of the first sample one or two nonconformances are found, take a second sample ($n_2 = 75$). The acceptance number for the second sample (c_2) is set to 3. If the combined number of nonconformances in the first and second samples is three or fewer, the lot will be accepted and if the combined number of nonconformances is four or more, the lot will be rejected. The plan is represented as follows:

Sample size	Acceptance number (c)	Rejection number (r)
$n_1 = 75$	$c_1 = 0$	$r_1 = 3$
$n_2 = 75$	$c_2 = 3$	$r_2 = 4$

OC Curve for a Double Sampling Plan

To calculate the OC curve for a double sampling plan, equation (23–1) and equation (23–2) can again be utilized. To calculate probabilities of acceptance, some arbitrary points for p are chosen to cover the range of the OC curve. The fraction defective p is then multiplied by n_1 (the first sample) or n_2 (the second sample) to determine the expected value np.

The generalized formula for calculating the probability of acceptance (P_a) is:

$$P_a = p_0 + (p_1p_2 + p_1p_1 + p_1p_0) + (p_2p_1 + p_2p_0)$$

where:

p_0 = probability of zero nonconformances in first sample

p_1p_2 = probability of one nonconformance in first sample times the probability of two nonconformances in the second sample, and so on.

EXAMPLE 23.4

For a double sampling plan where $n_1 = 75$, $c_1 = 0$, $r_1 = 3$, $n_2 = 75$, $c_2 = 3$, $r_2 = 4$, show the computations for the OC curve.

To determine the technique of plotting the OC curve, three points for p may be used (0.01, 0.04, and 0.08), although in practice six to ten should be used. The points for the OC curve are calculated using the generalized equation for each fraction nonconforming, selected as follows:

Continued

Continued

Generalized equation values	$p = 0.01$	$p = 0.04$	$p = 0.08$
p_0	0.4720	0.050	0.002
$p_1 p_0$	0.1676	0.0075	0.00003
$p_1 p_1$	0.1260	0.0222	0.000225
$p_1 p_2$	0.0471	0.0334	0.000675
$p_2 p_0$	0.0627	0.0112	0.00009
$p_2 p_1$	0.0471	0.0334	0.000675
Totals for P_a	0.9226	0.1577	0.003695

These points are used to construct the OC curve for the double sampling plan as shown in Figure 23.7.

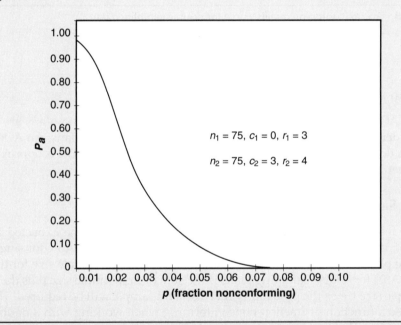

Figure 23.7   OC curve for double sampling plan where $n_1 = 75$, $c_1 = 0$, $r_1 = 3$, $n_2 = 75$, $c_2 = 3$, $r_2 = 4$.

Multiple Sampling Plans

Multiple sampling plans work in the same way as double sampling with an increase in the number of samples to be taken up to seven, according to ANSI/ASQ Z1.4-2003. In the same manner that double sampling is performed, acceptance or rejection of submitted lots may be reached before the seventh sample, depending on the acceptance/rejection criteria established for the plan.

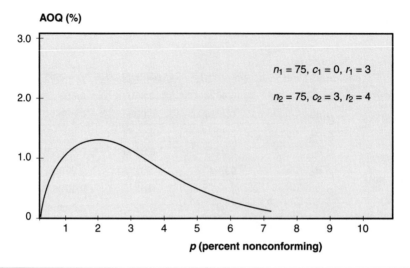

Figure 23.8 Average outgoing quality curve for double sampling plan.

AOQ and AOQL for Double and Multiple Plans

The AOQ curve and AOQL for double and multiple sampling plans are plotted and determined in the same manner as for single sampling plans. An AOQ curve for a double sampling plan is shown in Figure 23.8; the AOQL is approximately 1.3 percent.

Average Sample Number

The average sample number (ASN) is a determination of the expected average amount of inspection per lot for a given sampling plan. The ASN for single sampling plans is a constant value that is equal to the single sample size for the plan. The ASN for double sampling plans is the sum of first sample size plus the second sample size times the probability that a second sample will be required. The ASN is also a function of fraction noncomforming when working with a double sampling plan. The double sampling plan ASN formula is:

$$\text{ASN} = n_1 + n_2(P_2)$$

where:

n_1 = size of first sample

n_2 = size of second sample

P_2 = probability of requiring a second sample

EXAMPLE 23.5

The double sampling plan in the earlier section was

$$n_1 = 75 \qquad c_1 = 0 \qquad r_1 = 3$$
$$n_2 = 75 \qquad c_2 = 3 \qquad r_2 = 4$$

- A second sample is required if on the first sample one or two nonconformances are noted.

- If zero nonconformances are found in the first sample, the lot is accepted.

- If three or more nonconformances are found in the first sample, the lot is rejected.

Denote the probability of making a decision, accept or reject, on the first sample as $P(D_1)$. Then,

$$P(D_1) = P(0) + P \text{ (3 or more)}$$

$$P(0) = \text{the probability of zero nonconformances on the first sample}$$

P (3 or more) = the probability of three or more nonconformances on the first sample.

$$P_2 = 1 - P(D_1), \text{ then, ASN} = n_1 + n_2(P_2)$$

When using the Poisson table to calculate the probability of three or more nonconformances, remember that the probability of three or more nonconformances is given by:

(1 – probability of two or less nonconformances) in the sample

The average sample number will be plotted for several values of fraction nonconforming p and an ASN curve will be plotted. An example of the ASN calculation for the fraction nonconforming $p = 0.01$ is shown below. Several other points need to be plotted for other values of p. Figure 23.9 shows an ASN curve for the example.

When $p = 0.01$:

$$P(0) = \text{Probability of zero nonconformances in sample} = 0.4724$$

P (3 or more) = Probability of three or more nonconformances in sample
$$= 0.0410$$

$P(D_1)$ = Probability of a decision on the first sample (using the above
equation) $= 0.4724 + 0.0410 = 0.5134$

Then P_2 = probability of requiring a second sample $= 1 - 0.5134 = 0.4866$.

Thus the ASN is

ASN(0.01) = Average sample number for a lot quality $p = 0.01$

$$= n_1 + n_2 (P_2)$$

$$= 75 + 75 \ (0.4866) = 111.50 \text{ or } 112$$

Continued

Continued

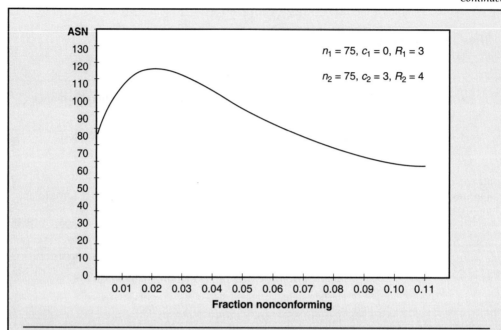

Figure 23.9 Average sample number curve for double sampling plan.

Values of ASN at different p values (ASNp) may be calculated in a similar way; the results are given below. All values are rounded to the next highest integer.

ASN(0.01) = 112   ASN(0.06) = 87

ASN(0.02) = 119   ASN(0.07) = 82

ASN(0.03) = 113   ASN(0.08) = 79

ASN(0.04) = 103   ASN(0.09) = 78

ASN(0.05) = 94   ASN(0.1) = 77

When comparing sampling plans with equal protection, double sampling plans will generally result in smaller average sample sizes when quality is excellent or poor. When quality is near the indifference level, double sampling plans will rarely result in greater ASN.

ANSI/ASQ Z1.4-2003*

ANSI/ASQ Z1.4-2003 is a revision of ANSI/ASQC Z1.4-1993 incorporating eight changes that include (ANSI/ASQ [2003]):

1. Acceptable quality level (AQL) has been changed to acceptable quality limit (AQL).

* The tables for these and other standards that appear in Chapter 23 of the previous edition of this handbook are now available on the CD-ROM accompanying this edition.

2. The definition and explanation of AQL have been changed. See the new definition of AQL above.

3. The discontinuation of inspection rule has been changed. See later sections in this chapter.

4. ANSI/ASQC A2-1987 has been changed to ANSI/ASQ A3534-2-1993.

5. ANSI/ASQC Q3 has been changed to ASQC Q3-1988.

Other than the above changes and some changes to the footnotes of some tables, all tables, table numbers, and procedures used in MIL-STD-105E (which was canceled in 1995) and ANSI/ASQC Z1.4-1993 have been retained.

ANSI/ASQ Z1.4-2003 is probably the most commonly used standard for attribute sampling plans. The wide recognition and acceptance of the plan could be due to government contracts stipulating the standard rather than its statistical importance. Producers submitting products at a nonconformance level within AQL have a high probability of having the lot accepted by the customer.

When using ANSI/ASQ Z1.4-2003, the characteristics under consideration should be classified. The general classifications are critical, major, and minor defects:

- *Critical defect.* A defect that judgment and experience indicate is likely to result in hazardous or unsafe conditions for the individuals using, maintaining, or depending on the product, or a defect that judgment and experience indicate is likely to prevent performance of the unit. In practice, critical characteristics are commonly inspected to an AQL level of 0.40 to 0.65 percent if not 100 percent inspected. One hundred percent inspection is recommended for critical characteristics if possible. Acceptance numbers are always zero for critical defects.

- *Major defect.* A defect, other than critical, that is likely to result in failure or to reduce materially the usability of the unit of product for its intended purpose. In practice, AQL levels for major defects are generally about one percent.

- *Minor defect.* A defect that is not likely to reduce materially the usability of the unit of product for its intended purpose. In practice, AQL levels for minor defects generally range from 1.5 percent to 2.5 percent.

Levels of Inspection

There are seven levels of inspection used in ANSI/ASQ Z1.4-2003: reduced inspection, normal inspection, tightened inspection, and four levels of special inspection. The special inspection levels should be used only when small sample sizes are necessary and large risks can be tolerated. When using ANSI/ASQ Z1.4-2003, a set of switching rules must be followed as to the use of reduced, normal, and tightened inspection.

The following guidelines are taken from ANSI/ASQ Z1.4-2003:

Initiation of inspection. Normal inspection level II will be used at the start of inspection unless otherwise directed by the responsible authority.

Continuation of inspection. Normal, tightened, or reduced inspection shall continue unchanged for each class of defect or defectives on successive lots or batches except where the following switching procedures require change. The switching procedures shall be applied to each class of defects or defectives independently.

Switching procedures. Switching rules are shown in Figure 23.10.

Normal to tightened. When normal inspection is in effect, tightened inspection shall be instituted when two out of five consecutive lots or batches have been rejected on original inspection (that is, ignoring resubmitted lots or batches for this procedure).

Tightened to normal. When tightened inspection is in effect, normal inspection shall be instituted when five consecutive lots or batches have been considered acceptable on original inspection.

Normal to reduced. When normal inspection is in effect, reduced inspection shall be instituted providing that all of the following conditions are satisfied:

a. The preceding 10 lots or batches (or more), as indicated by the note on ANSI/ASQ Z1.4-2003 Table VIII, have been on normal inspection and none has been rejected on original inspection.

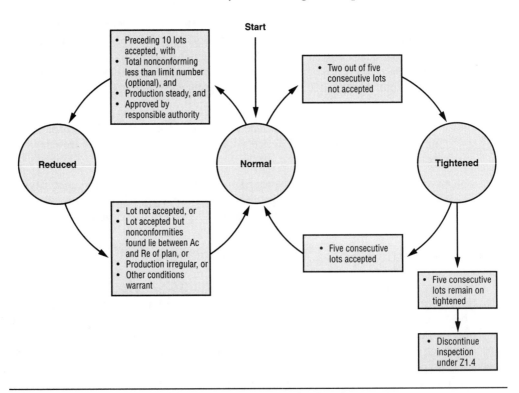

Figure 23.10   Switching rules for normal, tightened, and reduced inspection.

b. The total number of defectives (or defects) in the sample from the preceding 10 lots or batches (or such other number as was used for condition (a) above) is equal to or less than the applicable number given in Table VIII of ANSI/ASQ Z1.4-2003. If double or multiple sampling is in use, all samples inspected should be included, not "first" samples only.

c. Production is at a steady rate.

d. Reduced inspection is considered desirable by the responsible authority.

Reduced to normal. When reduced inspection is in effect, normal inspection shall be instituted if any of the following occur on original inspection:

a. A lot or batch is rejected.

b. A lot or batch is considered acceptable under reduced inspection but the sampling procedures terminated without either acceptance or rejection criteria having been met. In these circumstances, the lot or batch will be considered acceptable, but normal inspection will be reinstated starting with the new lot or batch.

c. Production becomes irregular or delayed.

d. Other conditions warrant that normal inspection shall be instituted.

Discontinuation of inspection. If the cumulative number of lots not accepted in a sequence of consecutive lots on tightened inspection reaches five, the acceptance procedures of this standard shall be discontinued. Inspection under the provisions of this standard shall not be resumed until corrective action has been taken. Tightened inspection shall then be used as "normal to tightened" above.

Types of Sampling

ANSI/ASQ Z1.4-2003 allows for three types of sampling:

1. Single sampling

2. Double sampling

3. Multiple sampling

The choice of the type of plan depends on many variables. Single sampling is the easiest to administer and perform but usually results in the largest average total inspection. Double sampling in ANSI/ASQ Z1.4-2003 results in a lower average total inspection than single sampling, but requires more decisions to be made, such as:

• Accept the lot after first sample

• Reject the lot after first sample

- Take a second sample

- Accept the lot after second sample

- Reject the lot after second sample

Multiple sampling plans further reduce the average total inspection but also increase the number of decisions to be made. As many as seven samples may be required before a decision to accept or reject the lot can be made. This type of plan requires the most administration.

A general procedure for selecting plans from ANSI/ASQ Z1.4-2003 is as follows:

1. Decide on an AQL.

2. Decide on the inspection level.

3. Determine the lot size.

4. Find the appropriate sample size code letter. See Table 1 from ANSI/ASQ Z1.4-2003.

5. Determine the type of sampling plan to be used: single, double, or multiple.

6. Using the selected AQL and sample size code letter, enter the appropriate table to find the desired plan to be used.

7. Determine the normal, tightened, and reduced plans as required from the corresponding tables.

EXAMPLE 23.6

A lot of 1750 parts has been received and are to be checked to an AQL level of 1.5 percent. Determine the appropriate single, double, and multiple sampling plans for general inspection level II.

Steps to define the plans are as follows:

4.1 Table I on page 10 of ANSI/ASQ Z1.4-2003 stipulates code letter K.

4.2 Normal inspection is applied. For code letter K, using Table II-A of ANSI/ASQ Z1.4-2003 on page 11 of the standard, a sample of 125 is specified.

4.3 For double sampling, two samples of 80 may be required. Refer to Table III-A on page 14 of the standard.

4.4 For multiple sampling, at least two samples of 32 are required and it may take up to seven samples of 32 before an acceptance or rejection decision is made. Refer to Table IV-A on page 17 of the standard.

A breakdown of all three plans follows:

Continued

Continued

Sampling plan		Sample(s) size	Ac	Re
Single sampling		125	5	6
Double sampling	First	80	2	5
	Second	80	6	7
Multiple sampling	First	32	*	4
	Second	32	1	5
	Third	32	2	6
	Fourth	32	3	7
	Fifth	32	5	8
	Sixth	32	7	9
	Seventh	32	9	10

Ac = Acceptance number
Re = Rejection number
* Acceptance not permitted at this sample size.

Dodge-Romig Tables

Dodge-Romig tables were designed as sampling plans to minimize average total inspection (ATI). These plans require an accurate estimate of the process average nonconforming in selection of the sampling plan to be used. The Dodge-Romig tables use the AOQL and LTPD values for plan selection, rather than AQL as in ANSI/ASQ Z1.4-2003. When the process average nonconforming is controlled to requirements, Dodge-Romig tables result in lower average total inspection, but rejection of lots and sorting tend to minimize the gains if process quality deteriorates.

Note that if the process average nonconforming shows statistical control, acceptance sampling should not be used. The most economical course of action in this situation is either no inspection or 100% inspection (Deming 1982). See Duncan (1986) or Montgomery (2009b) for more details on Dodge-Romig tables.

VARIABLES SAMPLING PLANS

Variables sampling plans use the actual measurements of sample products for decision making rather than classifying products as conforming or nonconforming, as in attribute sampling plans. Variables sampling plans are more complex in administration than attribute plans, thus they require more skill. They provide some benefits, however, over attribute plans. Two of these benefits are:

1. Equal protection to an attribute sampling plan with a much smaller sample size. There are several types of variables sampling plans in use, three of these being: (1) σ known, (2) σ unknown but can be estimated using sample standard deviation s, and (3) σ unknown and the range R is used as an estimator. If an attribute sampling plan sample size is determined, the variables plans previously listed can be compared as a percentage to the attribute plan.

Plan	Sample size (percent)
Attribute	100
σ unknown, range method	60
σ unknown, s estimated from sample	40
σ known	15

2. Variables sampling plans allow the determination of how close to nominal or a specification limit the process is performing. Attribute plans either accept or reject a lot; variables plans give information on how well or poorly the process is performing.

Variables sampling plans, such as ANSI/ASQ Z1.9-2003, have some disadvantages and limitations:

1. Unlike attribute sampling plans, separate characteristics on the same parts will have different averages and dispersions, resulting in a separate sampling plan for each characteristic.

2. Variables plans are more complex in administration.

3. Variables gauging is generally more expensive than attribute gauging.

In addition, for variables sampling plans it is assumed that the quality characteristic under study is normally distributed.

ANSI/ASQ Z1.9-2003

ANSI/ASQ Z1.9-2003 is a revision of ANSI/ASQC Z1.9-1993 that includes changing the term acceptable quality level (AQL) to acceptable quality limit (AQL), changing the definition and explanation of AQL, and changing the discontinuation of inspection rule, as explained previously in terms of ANSI/ASQ Z1.4-2003.

The most common standard for variables sampling plans is ANSI/ASQ Z1.9-2003, which has plans for: (1) variability known, (2) variability unknown—standard deviation method, and (3) variability unknown—range method. Using these methods, this sampling plan can be used to test for a single specification limit, a double (or bilateral) specification limit, estimation of the process average, and estimation of the dispersion of the parent population.

As in ANSI/ASQ Z1.4-2003, several AQL levels are used and specific switching procedures for normal, reduced, or tightened inspection are followed. ANSI/ASQ Z1.9-2003 allows for the same AQL value for each specification limit of double specification limit plans or the use of different AQL values for each specification limit. The AQL values are designated ML for the lower specification limit and MU for the upper specification limit.

There are two forms used for every specification limit ANSI/ASQ Z1.9-2003 plan: form 1 and form 2. Form 1 provides only acceptance or rejection criteria, whereas form 2 estimates the percent below the lower specification limit and the percent above the upper specification limit. These percentages are compared to the AQL for acceptance/rejection criteria. Figure 23.11 summarizes the structure and organization of ANSI/ASQ Z1.9-2003.

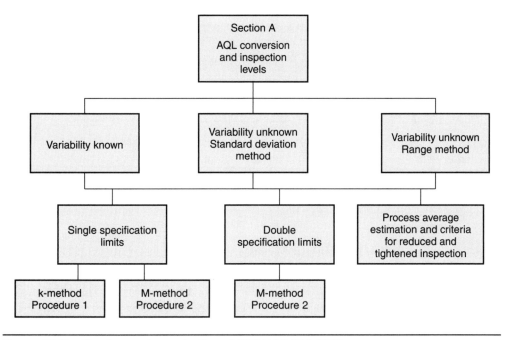

Figure 23.11   Structure and organization of ANSI/ASQ Z1.9-2003.

There are 14 AQL levels used in ANSI/ASQ Z1.9-2003 that are consistent with the AQL levels used in ANSI/ASQ Z1.4-2003. Section A of ANSI/ASQ Z1.9-2003 contains both an AQL conversion table and a table for selecting the desired inspection level. Inspection level II should be used unless otherwise specified. See Section A7.1 of the standard for further information about levels.

Table A-3 on page 7 of ANSI/ASQ Z1.9-2003 contains the OC curves for the sampling plans in Sections B, C, and D.

Section B contains sampling plans used when the variability is unknown and the standard deviation method is used. Part I is used for a single specification limit, Part II is used for a double specification limit, and Part III is used for estimation of process average and criteria for reduced and tightened inspection.

Section C contains sampling plans used when the variability is unknown and the range method is used. Parts I, II, and III are the same as Parts I, II, and III in Section B.

Section D contains sampling plans used when variability is known. Parts I, II, and III are the same as Parts I, II, and III in Section B.

Variability Unknown—Standard Deviation Method

In this section, a sampling plan is shown for the situation where the variability is not known and the standard deviation is estimated from the sample data. The sampling plan will be that for a double specification limit, and it is found in Section B of the standard with one AQL value for both upper and lower specification limits combined.

The acceptability criterion is based on comparing an estimated percent non-conforming to a maximum allowable percent nonconforming for the given AQL level. The estimated percent nonconforming is found in ANSI/ASQ Z1.9-2003 Table B-5.

The quality indices for this sampling plan are:

$$Q_U = \frac{USL - \bar{X}}{s} \text{ and } Q_L = \frac{\bar{X} - LSL}{s}$$

where

USL = upper specification limit

LSL = lower specification limit

$\bar{X}$ = sample mean

s = estimate of lot standard deviation

It should be noted that Q_L and Q_U follow a standard normal distribution since the quality characteristic being measured is assumed to be normally distributed.

The quality level of the lot is in terms of the lot percent defective. Three values are calculated: P_U, P_L, and p. P_U is an estimate of conformance with the upper specification limit P_L is an estimate of conformance with the lower specification limit, and p is the sum of P_U and P_L.

The value of p is then compared with the maximum allowable percent defective. If p is less than or equal to M (ANSI/ASQ Z1.9-2003 Table B-5) or if either Q_U or Q_L is negative, the lot is rejected, since this would be the result of $\bar{X}$ lying beyond the specification limits. Example 23.7 illustrates the above procedure.

EXAMPLE 23.7

The minimum temperature of operation for a certain device is specified as 180°F. The maximum temperature is 209°F. A lot of 40 items is submitted for inspection. Inspection level IV, normal inspection with AQL = 1 percent, is to be used. ANSI/ASQ Z1.9-2003 Table A-2 (this table can be found on the CD-ROM accompanying this book), gives code letter D, which results in a sample size of five from ANSI/ASQ Z1.9-2003 Table B-3. The results of the five measurements in degrees Fahrenheit are as follows: 197, 188, 184, 205, 201. Determine if the lot meets acceptance criteria.

Given:

- Sample size, $n = 5$

- Upper specification limit, USL = 209

- Lower specification limit, LSL = 180

- From Table B of the ANSI/ASQ Z1.9-2003 standard, we find the maximum allowable percent nonconforming (M) to be M = 3.32%

Let the random variable X represent the temperature of operation.
The steps for calculating the percent nonconforming are as follows:

Continued

Continued

1. Calculate the sample mean (see Chapter 32 for calculation of the sample mean):

$$\bar{x} = \frac{\sum_{i=1}^{n} x_i}{n} = \frac{\sum_{i=1}^{5} x_i}{5} = \frac{975}{5} = 195$$

2. Calculate the sample standard deviation (see Chapter 32 for calculation of the sample standard deviation):

$$s = \sqrt{\frac{\sum_{i=1}^{n}(x_i - \bar{x})^2}{n-1}} = 8.803$$

3. Calculate Q_U:

$$Q_U = \frac{USL - \bar{x}}{s} = \frac{209 - 195}{8.803} = 1.59$$

4. Calculate Q_L:

$$Q_L = \frac{\bar{x} - LSL}{s} = \frac{195 - 180}{8.803} = 1.70$$

From Table B-5 of the ANSI/ASQ Z1.9-2003 standard, determine the percent non-conforming:

- The percent above the upper specification limit with $n = 5$ and $Q_U = 1.59$ is 2.19%.

- The percent below the lower specification limit with $n = 5$ and $Q_L = 1.70$ is 0.66%.

The total percent nonconforming is then 2.19% + 0.66% = 2.85%.

Therefore, since our percent nonconforming (2.85%) is less than the maximum allowable (3.32%), we conclude that the lot is acceptable.

SEQUENTIAL SAMPLING PLANS

When tests are either destructive in nature or costly, it may be advantageous to use sequential sampling plans popularized by Wald (1973). These plans have the advantage of greatly reduced sample sizes while giving good protection.

To determine a sequential sampling plan, the following parameters must be defined:

α = producer's risk

AQL = acceptable quality level = p_1

β = consumer's risk

RQL = rejectable (or unacceptable) quality level = p_2; this is also referred to as limited quality level.

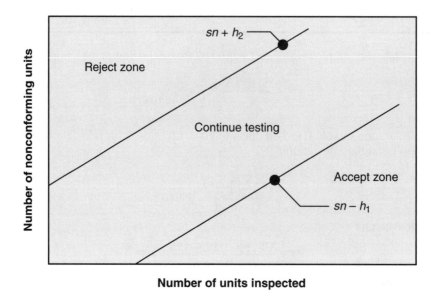

Number of units inspected

Figure 23.12 Decision areas for a sequential sampling plan.

The following example will use $\alpha = 0.05$, AQL = 0.05, $\beta = 0.1$, RQL = 0.2. This results in a plan that will have a five percent chance of rejecting a lot that is five percent nonconforming and a 10 percent chance of accepting a lot that is 20 percent nonconforming.

Figure 23.12 shows the accept, reject, and continue testing areas for a sequential sampling plan. The y-axis represents the number of nonconforming items in the sample and the x-axis represents the number of units inspected.

The equations for the acceptance and rejection zone lines are:

Reject zone line = $sn + h_2$

Accept zone line = $sn - h_1$

where:

$$n = \text{sample size}$$

$$h_1 = \frac{b}{\log\left[\dfrac{p_2(1-p_1)}{p_1(1-p_2)}\right]}$$

$$h_2 = \frac{a}{\log\left[\dfrac{p_2(1-p_1)}{p_1(1-p_2)}\right]}$$

$$s = \frac{\log\left[(1-p_1)/(1-p_2)\right]}{\log\left[\dfrac{p_2(1-p_1)}{p_1(1-p_2)}\right]}$$

$$a = \log\left[\frac{(1-\beta)}{\alpha}\right]$$

$$b = \log\left[\frac{(1-\alpha)}{\beta}\right]$$

EXAMPLE 23.8

Assume that the following values are desired for a sequential sampling plan:

$$\alpha = 0.05,\; p_1\;(\text{AQL}) = 0.05$$

$$\beta = 0.1,\; p_2\;(\text{RQL}) = 0.2$$

Then:

$$a = \log\left[\frac{1-0.10}{0.05}\right] = 1.2553$$

$$b = \log\left[\frac{1-0.05}{0.10}\right] = 0.9777$$

$$s = \frac{\log\left[(1-0.05)/(1-0.20)\right]}{\log\left[\dfrac{0.20(1-0.05)}{0.05(1-0.20)}\right]} = 0.1103$$

$$h_1 = \frac{0.9777}{\log\left[\dfrac{0.20(1-0.05)}{0.05(1-0.20)}\right]} = 1.4448$$

$$h_2 = \frac{1.2553}{\log\left[\dfrac{0.20(1-0.05)}{0.05(1-0.20)}\right]} = 1.855$$

$$\text{Reject line} = sn + h_2 = (0.1103)(n) + 1.855$$

$$\text{Accept line} = sn - h_1 = (0.1103)(n) - 1.4448$$

Points for Accept and Reject Lines*

n	Acceptance number	Rejection number	n	Acceptance number	Rejection number
1	A	B	14	0	4
2	A	B	20	0	5
3	A	3	24	1	5
4	A	3	40	2	7
5	A	3	50	4	8
6	A	3			

*Acceptance values are rounded down to the nearest integer.
Note A: Acceptance not possible when acceptance number is negative.
Note B: Rejection not possible when rejection number is greater than sample number.

Part IV.C.2

Continued

Continued

As can be seen by the preceding plan, rejecting the lot is not possible until the third sample unit and acceptance of the lot is withheld until the 14th sample unit.

Continuous Sampling Plans

Many production processes do not produce lots, and thus lot-by-lot acceptance sampling plans discussed earlier cannot be applied. In cases such as these, continuous sampling plans are developed. In continuous sampling plans, 100 percent inspection and sampling inspection are alternately applied. The most recent standard for developing continuous sampling plans is MIL-STD-1235B.

Continuous sampling plans are characterized by two parameters: i is called the clearance number or the number of conforming units under 100 percent inspection, and f is the ratio of the units inspected to the total number of units produced or passing through the inspection station.

Types of Continuous Sampling Plans

There are two different standards for continuous sampling plans:

1. *Dodge's continuous sampling plans.* These include CSP-1 and CSP-2 sampling plans. These plans take AOQL (average outgoing quality limit) as an index. That is, for every AOQL value, there are different combinations of i and f.

2. *MIL-STD-1235B.* These plans are selected using a sample size code letter and an AQL value. The standard includes CSP-1, CSP-2, CSP-F, CSP-T, and CSP-V plans.

Dodge's Continuous Sampling Plans

These include CSP-1 and CSP-2 sampling plans. These plans take AOQL (average outgoing quality limit) as a quality index.

Dodge's CSP-1 continuous sampling plans operate as follows for a selected AOQL value:

1. Start with 100 percent inspection

2. When i (clearance number) consecutive number of units are found free from nonconformities, 100 percent inspection is then substituted with sampling inspection

    2.1.   A fraction of f units is randomly selected and then inspected

        2.1.1.   If one nonconformity is found, the 100 percent inspection procedure is restarted and the cycle is repeated

Dodge's CSP-2 continuous sampling plans operate as follows for a selected AOQL value:

1. Start with 100 percent inspection

2. When *i* (clearance number) consecutive number of units are found free from nonconformities, 100 percent inspection is then substituted with sampling inspection

   2.1.   A fraction of *f* units is randomly selected and then inspected

   2.1.1.   If one nonconformity is found, the sampling inspection continues and the following procedure (2.1.2.) is initiated

   2.1.2.   The number of conforming units (after finding the nonconformity) is counted

     2.1.2.1.   If *i* consecutive number are found free of nonconformities, sampling inspection continues

     2.1.2.2.   If one nonconformity is found, 100 percent inspection is reinstated

MIL-STD-1235B

This standard uses the same parameters, *i* and *f*, as previously defined. The standard includes CSP-1, CSP-2, CSP-F, CSP-T, and CSP-V plans.

CSP-1 and CSP-2 plans operate in the same way as Dodge's CSP-1 and CSP-2 plans, but they are selected based on a sample size code letter and an AQL value as a quality index. The sample size code letter is selected based on the number of units in the production interval.

CSP-F plans work the same way as CSP-1 plans, providing alternate sequences of 100 percent and sampling inspection procedures, but the difference is that AOQL and the number of units in the production interval are used to characterize the plans in this case. Once AOQL and *f* values are selected, go to the corresponding table to read *i*, the clearance number. CSP-F is a single-level continuous sampling scheme.

CSP-T plans provide the provision of reduced sampling frequency once the product shows superior quality. The CSP-T plan works as follows:

1. Start with 100 percent inspection

2. When *i* (clearance number) consecutive number of units are found free from nonconformities, 100 percent inspection is then substituted with sampling inspection

3. A fraction of *f* units is randomly selected and then inspected

   3.1   If one nonconformity is found, the inspector reinstates 100 percent inspection

   3.2   If the inspector finds *i* consecutive units free from nonconformities, the frequency *f* is reduced to *f*/2

     3.2.1.   If one nonconformity is found, the inspector switches back to 100 percent inspection

     3.2.2.   If the inspector finds *i* consecutive units free from nonconformities, the frequency *f* is reduced to *f*/4

3.2.2.1. If one nonconformity is found, 100 percent inspection is reinstated

CSP-V plans work the same way as CSP-T plans but with reduced *i* instead of reduced *f*. The procedure is as follows:

1. Start with 100 percent inspection

2. When *i* (clearance number) consecutive number of units are found free from nonconformities, 100 percent inspection is then substituted with sampling inspection

3. A fraction of *f* units is randomly selected and then inspected

   3.1. If one nonconformity is found, the inspector reinstates 100 percent inspection

   3.2. If the inspector finds *i* consecutive units free from nonconformities, the inspection continues with inspecting the same fraction *f*

      3.2.1. If one nonconformity is found, the inspector switches back to 100 percent inspection

      3.2.2. If the inspector finds *i*/3, the sampling inspection continues with the same fraction *f*

3. SAMPLE INTEGRITY

> Identify the techniques for establishing and maintaining sample integrity. (Analyze)
>
> **Body of Knowledge IV.C.3**

Products are always at risk of contamination and misuse. Sample integrity is vital whenever sampling is done for any purpose, whether to go through a fitness program, for customer evaluation, or for destructive/nondestructive testing. In order to maintain sample integrity, carefully thought-out controls are necessary. Many people recall the murder trial of O. J. Simpson, where extremely complex and expensive DNA testing was challenged by the defense because the prosecution could not prove that the DNA sample was completely safe from any contamination at all times. While this is an extreme example, it highlights the importance of maintaining sample integrity.

Batch Control

When products are created in batches (as opposed to discrete item production or continuous processes) it is necessary to keep records on all aspects of the batch. The concept of a batch includes mixing, heating, distilling, and comparable operations. A recipe is used, and documentation that the recipe was followed is vital in all but the most trivial cases. A qualified operator must maintain a log or journal indicating the quantities and products (or identification) of each material that is inserted into the batch. The time each insertion is made is usually important, as well as the time that different inputs (heat, pressure, and so on) are applied to the batch.

Tests may be required to verify that the batch has developed the needed properties over time. The results of such tests must be tightly linked to the physical batch and to all the other records. In some cases these details can be automated but often they must be recorded manually. When the batch is finished, it must be labeled with a separate identification code from other batches. The batch (lot) number must be printed or engraved on appropriate cartons, drums, jugs, pallets, and so on. A linkage between batch number and customer name is often necessary when the product is sold, so it can be tracked through the entire distribution chain.

Change Control

Change control is a technique for dealing with relatively simple to moderately complex products to which minor changes are made that must be tracked. For example, such products as refrigerators and desktop computers may be changed slightly and new version numbers issued on the same model name/number. For warranty purposes, product repair, and replacement, it is necessary to record each time the product is changed.

Engineers must decide when a change is required and how rapidly it is to be implemented. One priority scheme is to categorize the changes as *emergency, priority,* or *routine.* An emergency change is appropriate when a hazardous condition is discovered in the present version. In such cases, no time must be lost in correcting the deficiency. A priority change is called for if there is sound economic reason to make the change promptly, but life and property are not at risk. For example, a product upgrade that reduces power consumption or maintenance could be implemented as a priority change. The final category, routine, is for changes that must be made, but need not be rushed. These are often to accommodate newly designed parts or to allow the product to have slightly more functionality—but not enough to justify an entirely new model.

Configuration Control

Configuration control is an extension of change control. The term configuration refers to how a complex product is composed of various units and subassemblies. In an evolving product with high research and development content, such as aerospace vehicles, defense weapons, and so on, the field version of the same unit of product gradually changes over time as new engines, new avionics, and new hydraulic systems are installed into existing units of product.

In order to manage such ongoing field product modifications, a lot of effort must be put into configuration control systems. This is really an adaptation of materials resource planning techniques. Extensive documentation is mandatory for proper control. Usually both computerized database records and hard-copy backup records (often at multiple locations) are required.

Two DOD standards address the subject of configuration control. DOD-STD-480A addresses the big picture, specifying that the contractor analyze the impact of an engineering change proposal (ECP). DOD-STD-481 is more narrowly focused on how the customer of the material is to handle the change. A given contract may specify one or the other.

A key principle of configuration control is to avoid changes in a given product model unless a clear and compelling benefit can be shown. Management must compare the downside of change—more complexity in the product line, more chance for confusion—against the claimed benefits: possibly reduced cost, increased performance, better safety, lower maintenance, and so on.

Part IV.C.3

Chapter 24

D. Measurement and Test

THE MEASUREMENT PROCESS

A measurement process is a repeated application of a test method using a measuring system. A test method includes requirements for a test apparatus and a well-defined procedure for using it to measure a physical property.

General Characteristics

There are three general characteristics of a measurement process (Rashed and Hamouda 1974):

1. *Realization of a test method.* If a test method specifies use of a certain kind of test apparatus, a measurement process following the test method will utilize a particular version of such test apparatus. It will also involve a specific operator who is needed to carry out preparation of specimens and measurements.

2. *Realization of a system of causes.* A system of causes is a collection of factors that may cause variability of measurements due to test apparatus, operator, test specimen, and other factors. Some causes may be explicitly involved in the test method. This realization of a system of causes defines the statistical universe of individual measurements.

3. *Capability of statistical control.* In a measurement, it is necessary to require the capability of statistical control. Capability of control means that either the measurements are obtained from an identifiable statistical universe or an orderly array of such universes, or if not, the physical causes preventing such identification may themselves be identified and, if desired, isolated and suppressed.

1. MEASUREMENT TOOLS

> Select and describe appropriate uses of inspection
> tools such as gage blocks, calipers, micrometers, optical
> comparators, etc. (Analyze)
>
> **Body of Knowledge IV.D.1**

Measurement is the process of evaluating a property or characteristic of an object and describing it with a numerical or nominal value. If the value is numerical, reflecting the extent of the characteristic, then the measurement is said to be on a quantitative scale and the actual property is referred to as a variable. Examples of variables inspection are measurements related to weight, length, temperature, and so on.

If the value assigned to each unit is other than numerical, then the measurement is on a qualitative or classification scale and is referred to as an attribute. In most inspection situations involving nominal or attribute data, there are two possible nominal values: conforming (good) and nonconforming (defective). Each product unit is assigned one of these two labels according to inspection operation results. It is also possible to derive a numerical measure from a qualitative scale. This is achieved by calculating the fraction nonconforming (fraction defective) as the ratio between the number of units labeled as nonconforming and the total number of units inspected.

The Measuring System

A measuring system should be able to provide accuracy capabilities that will assure the attainment of a reliable measurement. In general, the elements of a measuring system include the instrumentation, calibration standards, environmental influences, human operator limitations, and features of the workpiece or object being measured. Each of these elements may involve detailed studies of extended scope and thus fall beyond the purpose of this book. The design of measuring systems also involves proper analysis of cost-to-accuracy considerations (Darmody 1967).

The functional design of measuring systems can include consideration of many approaches and employment of a variety of physical phenomena useful in establishing parametric variables from the measured quantity. In linear measuring systems, the basic function may be mechanical, optical, pneumatic, electronic, radiological, or combinations of these (Darmody 1967).

Controlling Product Quality

In contrast to the rather imprecise measurements made and measurement standards used in everyday life, measurements and standards applied to manufactured parts must necessarily be extremely precise, since they must conform to definite geometric and aesthetic design specifications. The production of quality products in any manufacturing operation requires an efficient and continuous testing program, and such programs have become increasingly important in recent years.

Society has changed its attitudes, not only with respect to product safety and cost but also with respect to product reliability. Variations in product quality that were once accepted as the natural result of industrial systems are no longer tolerated. What is required today is the consistent extraction of the best technological quality available on a routine production basis. In this circumstance, testing serves two functions: to check on the performance of materials or components to obtain design data and to check on the conformity of a product to its design specifications. Testing of the latter type is commonly called inspection.

Inspection to ensure and control product quality, as performed in industry, is of two kinds:

1. Visual inspection

2. Dimensional inspection

Visual inspection, by far the more common of the two, involves visual examination by human operators for conformity to aesthetic requirements. Less common, but equally important and generally more difficult to perform adequately, is dimensional inspection. Visual and dimensional inspection are defined in the following paragraphs.

Quality, of course, cannot be inspected into a product. Quality depends on engineering and manufacturing excellence, and inspection simply determines whether or not it exists. Better inspection is not the solution to large numbers of rejects. The solution must take the form of improvements in design or in the manufacturing process.

Visual Inspection

Visual inspection takes place, even if inadvertently, each time a part is handled during its manufacture. Parts such as bearing elements that have critical aesthetic requirements may also be given a final visual inspection once manufacture is complete. Visual inspection is concerned primarily with gross appearance—the detection of surface flaws and the recognition of patterns. These functions have, to date, attracted far less attention from developers of automatic inspection systems than have the functions associated with dimensional inspection. As a consequence, the human being currently is the most efficient general-purpose flaw-detection and pattern-recognition "instrument" available to the manufacturer. Human beings have highly developed sensing and data-processing faculties. Human operators are trainable and adaptive, although they are generally somewhat less reliable and experience more downtime than their automatic-equipment counterparts. Current research in artificial intelligence will surely cause this situation to change in the future.

Dimensional Inspection

Dimensional inspection refers to the measurement of lengths and angles and, in combination, of geometric shapes and may be accomplished automatically by a machine or manually by an operator. Measurements that are taken while the product is still undergoing manufacture have a greater value than those applied to the finished product, since the former constitute process control whereas the latter are merely process verification. Obviously, it is more costly to correct or to scrap a bad product than it is to manufacture it properly in the first place.

Because dimensional measurement is very important to every manufacturing operation, much effort has historically been expended toward improving the techniques and the instrumentation involved and toward refining the standards employed.

The term "standard" has a dual meaning in the manufacturing environment. It is used to denote universally accepted specifications for devices, components, or processes, that ensure conformity and therefore interchangeability throughout a particular industry. Thus, one manufacturer's screw will fit another's nut, all makers of bricks will produce them in the same sizes, and all microscope objectives will fit all microscopes.

As used in metrology, on the other hand, a standard provides a reference for assigning a numerical value to a measured quantity. The term "measurement" implies the comparison of an unknown with a known to determine the qualitative relationship between the two. Each basic, measurable quantity has associated with it an ultimate standard that embodies the definition of a particular unit. Working standards—those used in conjunction with the various measurement-making instruments—are calibrated in terms of the particular unit definitions involved. Obviously, if measurements made at different locations are to be comparable, they must ultimately be traceable to the same standard.

Selection of the Measuring Instrument

Selection of a measuring tool or measuring instrument is based on several factors. In general, the Rule of Ten serves as a baseline for the selection process. The Rule of Ten states that inspection measurements should be better than the tolerance of a dimension by a factor of 10 and calibration standards should be better than the inspection instrument by a factor of 10. Once this rule is implemented, candidate instruments need to be evaluated based on the following criteria:

- Accuracy and precision
- Repeatability
- Sensitivity
- Resolution
- Stability and consistency
- Part or workpiece material
- Shape and dimensions of the part being measured
- Capabilities of the metrology laboratory

Measurement Technology

The following is a review of the different measurement instruments and technologies employed in common measurement practices such as length and angle measurement, surface texture measurement, and measurement of out-of-roundness.

Length and Angle Measurements

The standard environmental conditions for length measurements include a temperature of 68°F (20°C) and a barometric pressure of 760 mm Hg. Because these conditions are assumed for all precision dimensional measurements, dimensional metrology laboratories are temperature-controlled as nearly as is practical to 68°F, and thermal expansion corrections are made for any deviations that may occur. It is seldom necessary to correct for thermal expansion to achieve the accuracy required in industrial movement. Since the majority of precision parts, like the masters against which they are measured, are made of steel, it is generally safe to assume that their thermal expansion coefficients are identical and that no temperature correction need be made. Temperature corrections are also unnecessary when angles alone are measured, since a uniform temperature change cannot change the size of an angle. This will definitely change with the introduction of new materials.

Instrumentation for Dimensional Measurements

Dimensional (or linear) measuring instruments are used to measure length. They are of two types:

1. Absolute instruments

2. Comparative instruments, or comparators

Absolute instruments have their working standards built in and thus require no mastering; they are generally used for long-range measurements. Comparators are short-range devices that measure deviations between a working master and a given part. The yardstick is a crude example of the first type, and the dial indicator is an example of the second.

Table 24.1 details typical units, standards, and instruments for length and angle measurements.

Measuring instruments range from very basic tools to more sophisticated measuring machines, such as coordinate measuring machines and laser scanners. This section contains a review of those basic measuring tools that are commonly used for many applications.

These basic measuring equipment and tools include:

• Surface plates

• Micrometers

• Verniers

Table 24.1 Typical standards and instrumentation for industrial length and angle measurements.

	Length measurements	Angle measurements
Unit of measurement	Meter	Radian
Ultimate standard	Speed of light	Circle
Single-valued working standards	Length gage blocks	Angle gage blocks
Many-valued working standards	Line scales, step bars	Optical polygons, serrated-type index tables
Displacement-measuring instruments	Interferometers	Autocollimators

- Comparators
- Dial indicators
- Gage blocks
- Ring, plug, and snap gages

Basic Linear Measuring Instruments

Most of the basic or general-purpose linear measuring instruments are typified by the use of steel rulers, vernier calipers, and micrometer calipers.

Steel rulers are commonly used for linear measurements, in which the ends of a dimension being measured are aligned with graduations of the scale from which the length is read directly. A specialized type of steel ruler is the depth ruler that is used for measuring holes, slots, and so on.

Vernier calipers are used for inside or outside linear measurement. Other types of verniers include digital reading calipers that provide LCD readouts in micrometers (μm) or microinches (μin) and vernier height gages that can measure external, internal, and distance dimensions, as well as perpendicularity, flatness, straightness, centers, and diameters.

Micrometers come in various types. The measuring element of a micrometer consists of a fixed anvil and a spindle that moves lengthwise as it turns. Vernier micrometer calipers use a vernier scale on the sleeve. Digital micrometers use digital readouts to make readings faster and easier. Indicating micrometers have a built-in dial indicator to provide a positive indication of measuring pressure applied.

Angular Measuring Devices

Angular measurements use the degree as the standard unit. Angular measuring devices range from simple tools such as protractors, bevel protractors, and squares to sine bars and dividing heads. The protractor reads directly in degrees. A bevel protractor utilizes a vernier scale that shows angles as small as five or less minutes.

The sine bar is a more precise device for precision measuring and checking of angles. It consists of an accurately ground flat steel straight edge with precisely affixed round buttons that are a known distance apart and of identical diameters.

Dividing heads are either optical or mechanical devices that often are used for the circular measurement of angular spacing, common in machine tool operations.

Layout and Locating Devices

Surface plates provide a relatively accurate surface plane from which measurements can be made. Surface plates may employ a cast iron or granite surface. Granite surface plates provide better hardness, resistance to corrosion, nonmagnetic characteristics, and less response to temperature changes than cast iron surface plates.

Gages

Gages are used to determine the conformance or nonconformance of a dimension to required specifications without attempting actual measurements. Typical common functional gages are classified according to their use for checking outside dimensions, inside dimensions, or special features. Ring and snap gages are used for checking outside dimensions, plug gages are used for checking inside dimensions, and other gages are used for checking special features like tapers, threads, and splines. They normally provide a go/no-go decision on part specifications.

Go/no-go gages (also known as limit gages) are made to sizes essentially identical with the design specification limits of the dimension to be inspected. If a specific gage can properly mate with a part, then the part can be assembled with another part whose physical boundaries do not exceed those of the gage. Consequently, the part is acceptable for assembly. Limit gages designed to identify this condition are called go gages.

The "go" end of a go/no-go gage contains the reverse physical replica of the dimension inspected at the maximum material condition (minimum size for interior features, maximum size for exterior features). The maximum material condition produces the minimum clearance required for assembly.

The "no-go" end is designed to detect conditions of excessive clearance. It contains the reverse physical replica of the dimension inspected at its minimum material condition. A part will not mate with a no-go gage unless the actual condition of the part feature is below the specified minimum. Thus, if the no-go gage mates with the part, then the part dimension is incorrect and the part should be rejected.

In practice, go/no-go gages are used together and often appear at opposite ends of an inspection instrument. An acceptable part should mate with the go end but should not mate with the no-go end. Parts that mate with neither or both ends do not meet design specifications and should be rejected.

Most methods of inspection by attributes, other than gauging, are largely subjective and depend on the ability of human inspectors to make the right decision. In many cases, inspection by attributes involves visual characteristics, such as color, shape, smoothness, and other visual defects.

Dial Indicators

Dial indicators magnify the dimension deviation from a standard to which the gage is set. Dial indicators are used for many kinds of checking and gauging operations, checking machines and tools, verifying alignments, and cutter runout. Some indicators employ mechanical mechanisms for their operation and others come with a digital readout.

Comparators

Comparators normally employ dial indicators for their operation and come in different varieties: mechanical, optical, electronic, and pneumatic. Optical projectors, also known as optical comparators, employ a system in which light rays are directed against the object and then reflected back through a projection lens onto a screen. The projections are large enough to accurately measure small configurations of objects.

Gage Blocks

Gage blocks are the practical standards for length in the manufacturing industry. They are rectangular, square, or round blocks of steel, carbide, or ceramic materials. Each has two faces that are flat, level, and parallel with an accuracy and length grade, depending on the application.

Surface Texture Measurement

Surface metrology may be broadly defined as the measurement of the difference between what the surface actually is and what it is intended to be. It is treated separately from length measurement, which is concerned with the relationship of two surfaces on a workpiece. Surface measurement, however, is involved with the relationship of a surface on the workpiece to a reference that is not actually on the workpiece. The most common aspect of surface metrology is the measurement of surface roughness as an average deviation from a mean center line (Bosch 1984).

Numerical Assessment of the Surface

Of all the methods used for the numerical assessment of the surface, the following are the most widely used (Reason 1960):

1. Peak-to-valley measure

2. Mean-line measures (center line average [CLA] and root mean square [RMS])

3. Crest-line measures

4. Envelope method, in which the crest line should be defined as the locus of the center of a circle or defined radius rolling across the surface, the locus being displaced toward the surface until it contacts the crests

The international standard for the assessment of surface texture, ISO/R468, defines three parameters: R_a (CLA), R_z, and R_{max}, all measured relative to a straight mean line. These parameters are shown in Figure 24.1 and can be defined as (Spragg 1976):

1. R_a (center line average) value is the arithmetic mean of the departures of a profile from the mean line. It is normally determined as the mean result of several consecutive sample lengths L.

2. R_z (ten-point height) is the average distance between the five height peaks and five deepest valleys within the sampling length and measured perpendicular to it.

3. R_{max} is the maximum peak-to-valley height within the sampling length.

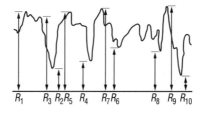

$$R_a = \frac{1}{L} \int_0^L |y| \, dL$$

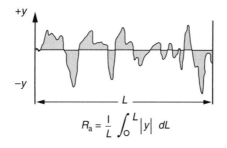

$$R_Z = \frac{(R_1 + R_3 + \dots R_9) - (R_2 + R_4 + \dots R_{10})}{5}$$

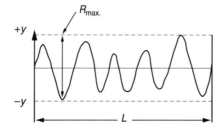

Figure 24.1 ISO/R468 surface roughness parameters.

Part IV.D.1

Other parameters of surface roughness are shown in Figure 24.2. They are defined as follows (Machinability Data Center 1980):

1. R_{tm} is the average value of R_{max}'s for five consecutive sampling lengths.

2. R_p is the maximum profile height from the mean line within the sampling length. R_{pm} is the mean value of R_p's determined over five sampling lengths.

3. PC (peak count) is the number of peak/valley pairs per inch projecting through a band of width b centered about the mean line.

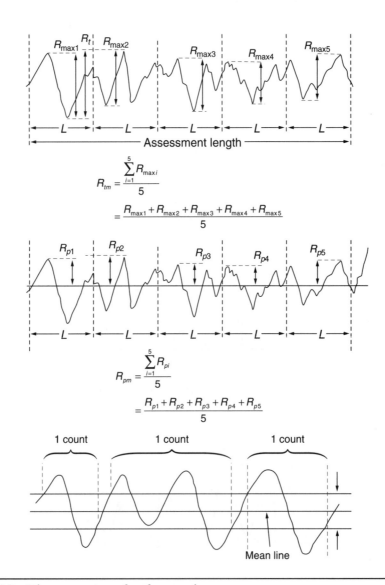

$$R_{tm} = \frac{\sum_{i=1}^{5} R_{max\,i}}{5}$$

$$= \frac{R_{max1} + R_{max2} + R_{max3} + R_{max4} + R_{max5}}{5}$$

$$R_{pm} = \frac{\sum_{i=1}^{5} R_{pi}}{5}$$

$$= \frac{R_{p1} + R_{p2} + R_{p3} + R_{p4} + R_{p5}}{5}$$

Figure 24.2   Other parameters of surface roughness.

The most common method of surface measurement is to move a stylus over the surface and measure an average electrical signal produced by a transducer attached to the stylus. Other means used less frequently include stylus profiling, where a chart record is produced instead of an average number, reflectance meters, pneumatics, and optical interference. The stylus averaging unit is the most common because it is fast, repeatable, quite easy to interpret, and relatively inexpensive (Bosch 1984).

Measurement of Roundness

Geometrically, a part can be said to be round in a given cross section if there exists within the section a point from which all points on the periphery are equidistant. In practice, however, the radius of nominally round parts tends to vary from point to point. Thus, the problem found by the metrologist is one of displaying and assessing these variations, and correctly interpreting the results (Bosch 1984).

Roundness Measurement Methods

Although many methods have been used for roundness measurement, only those that provide valid radial-deviation data lend themselves to standardization and consistent, accurate measurement of all out-of-roundness conditions. For this reason, current industry, national, and international standards primarily cover measurements taken with precision spindle-type instruments with the data recorded on a polar chart.

Precision spindle instruments include those in which the spindle supports and rotates the part with the gage tip remaining stationary, and those in which the spindle rotates the gage tip about the part, which remains stationary. Figure 24.3 illustrates these two types of out-of-roundness measurement (Drews 1978).

Part IV.D.1

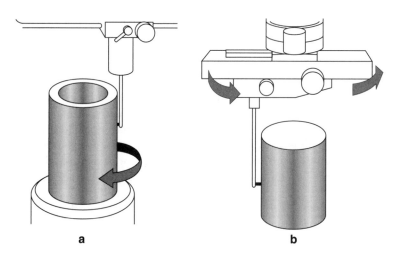

a   b

Figure 24.3   Two types of roundness–measuring instruments: (a) rotating table, (b) rotating workpiece.

The center of rotation of the precision spindle and the indicator gage tip provides a master radius to which all the radii of a cross section profile of the part are compared. It is necessary that the center of the part cross section and the spindle axis be adjusted to be concentric within narrow limits. The variations of the cross section radii from the master radius are usually recorded in a highly magnified form on a polar chart. Because the out-of-roundness value is defined as the difference between the largest and smallest radius that will just contain the measured profile, these radii must be measured from a specified center. The choice of these reference circles is arbitrary, but is chosen to fulfill some functional requirements. As shown in Figure 24.4, there are four ways in which a center can be chosen (Drews 1978):

1. Minimum radial separation (MRS) (also known as minimum zone circle [MZC])

2. Least squares circle (LSC)

3. Maximum inscribed circle (MIC)

4. Minimum circumscribed circle (MCC)

The magnified profile produced on the polar chart is evaluated by two concentric circles that just contain the profile when centered in accordance with the minimum-radial-separation center criteria. Other center criteria can be specified. For example, the concentric circles could be engraved on a transparent overlay (a more common method). The out-of-roundness value is the separation of the two concentric circles divided by the magnification setting of the instrument. The polar chart clearly shows the number and magnitude of the roundness deviations.

There are many advantages to the precision spindle methods. Accurate measurements of all types of out-of-roundness are possible and a permanent polar chart, which is easily interpreted, is provided. It is also the most accurate method of measurement available. With proper equipment, accuracies of one microinch are attainable. In addition to roundness, the equipment also permits ultraprecise measurement of centricity, squareness, flatness, and other related geometric part-feature characteristics.

Coordinate Measuring Machines

Coordinate measuring machines have become a primary means of dimensional quality control for manufactured parts of complex form, where the volume of production does not warrant the development of functional gauging. The advent of increasingly inexpensive computing power and more fully integrated manufacturing systems will continue to expand the use of these machines into an even larger role in the overall quality assurance of manufactured parts.

Coordinate measuring machines (CMMs) can most easily be defined as physical representations of a three-dimensional rectilinear coordinate system. Coordinate measuring machines now represent a significant fraction of the measuring equipment used for defining the geometry of different-shaped workpieces. Most dimensional characteristics of many parts can be measured within minutes with these machines. Similar measurements would take hours using older measuring equipment and procedures. Besides flexibility and speed, coordinate measuring machines have several additional advantages:

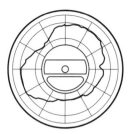

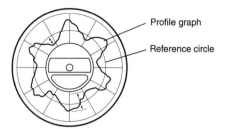

Minimum radial separation (MRS or MZC)

Two concentric circles are chosen so as to have the least radial separation and yet contain between them all of the polar trace. This radial separation is the measure of the out-of-roundness value. The radial difference between concentric circles determined by this method is numerically unique, in that by definition a smaller value cannot exist.

Least squares circle (LSC)

A theoretical circle is located with the polar profile such that the sum of the squares of the radial ordinated between the circle and the profile is a minimum. The out-of-roundness value would be determined by the sum of the maximum inward and maximum outward ordinates divided by the proper chart amplification factor.

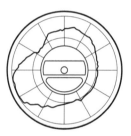

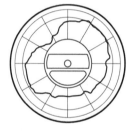

Maximum inscribed circle (MIC)

This procedure determines the center of the polar profile by the center of the largest circle that can be fitted inside the profile. From this circle the maximum outward departure of the profile denotes the out-of-roundness.

Minimum circumscribed circle (MCC)

The profile center is determined by the smallest circle that will just contain the measured profile. From the circle, the maximum inward departure of the profile can be measured; this maximum departure is the out-of-roundness.

Figure 24.4 Four ways by which a center may be chosen.

1. Different features of a part can be measured in one setup. This eliminates errors introduced due to setup changes.

2. All CMM measurements are taken from one geometrically fixed measuring system, eliminating the accumulation of errors resulting from using functional gauging and transfer techniques.

3. The use of digital readouts eliminates the necessity for the interpretation of readings, such as with the dial or vernier-type measuring scales.

4. Most CMMs have automatic data recording, which minimizes operator influence.

5. Part alignment and setup procedures are greatly simplified by using software supplied with computer-assisted CMMs. This minimizes the setup time for measurement.

6. Data can be automatically saved for further analysis.

Coordinate Measuring Machines Classification

Although coordinate measuring machines can be thought of as representations of a simple rectilinear coordinate system for measuring the dimensions of different-shaped workpieces, they naturally are constructed in many different configurations, all of which offer different advantages. CMMs provide means for locating and recording the coordinate location of points in their measuring volumes. Traditional coordinate measuring machines are classified according to their configurations, as follows (ASME 1985):

1. Cantilever configuration, in which the probe is attached to a vertical machine ram (z-axis) moving on a mutually perpendicular overhang beam (y-axis) that moves along a mutually perpendicular rail (x-axis). Cantilever configuration is limited to small and medium-sized machines. It provides for easy operator access and the possibility of measuring parts longer than the machine table.

2. Bridge-type configuration, in which a horizontal beam moves along the x-axis, carrying the carriage that provides the y-motion. In other configurations, the horizontal beam (bridge structure) is rigidly attached to the machine base and the machine table moves along the x-axis. This is called fixed bridge configuration. A bridge-type coordinate measuring machine provides more rigid construction, which in turn provides better accuracy. The presence of the bridge on the machine table makes it a little more difficult to load large parts.

3. Column-type configuration, in which a moving table and saddle arrangement provides the x and y motions and the machine ram (z-axis) moves vertically relative to the machine table.

4. Horizontal-arm configuration features a horizontal probe ram (z-axis) moving horizontally relative to a column (y-axis), which moves in a mutually perpendicular motion (x-axis) along the machine base. This configuration provides the possibility for measuring large parts. Other arrangements of horizontal-arm configuration feature a fixed horizontal-arm configuration in which the probe is attached and moving vertically (y-axis) relative to a column that slides along the machine base in the x-direction. The machine table moves in a mutually perpendicular motion (z-axis) relative to the column.

5. Gantry-type configuration comprises a vertical ram (z-axis) moving vertically relative to a horizontal beam (x-axis), which in turn moves along two rails (y-axis) mounted on the floor. This configuration provides easy access and allows the measurement of large components.

6. L-shaped bridge configuration comprises a ram (z-axis) moving vertically relative to a carriage (x-axis), which moves horizontally relative to an L-shaped bridge moving in the y-direction.

Figure 24.5 shows CMM types according to this classification. The most advanced configuration, that of the ring-bridge, is not illustrated.

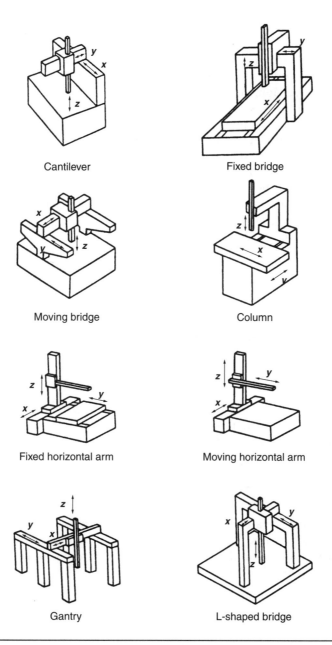

Cantilever   Fixed bridge

Moving bridge   Column

Fixed horizontal arm   Moving horizontal arm

Gantry   L-shaped bridge

Figure 24.5   Coordinate measuring machine classifications.

In addition to classifying coordinate measuring machines according to their physical configuration, they can also be classified according to their mode of operation: manually oriented, computer-assisted, or direct computer-controlled. With manual machines, the operator moves the probe along the machine's axes to establish and manually record the measurement values that are provided by digital readouts. In some machines, digital printout devices are used.

Computer-assisted coordinate measuring machines can be either manually positioned (free-floating mode) by moving the probe to measurement locations, or manually driven by providing power-operated motions under the control of the operator. In either case, data processing is accomplished by a computer. Some computer-assisted CMMs can perform some or all of the following functions: inch to metric conversion, automatic compensation for misalignment, storing of pre-measured parameters and measurement sequences, data recording, means for disengagement of the power drive to allow manual adjustments and manipulations of the machine motions, and geometric and analytical evaluations.

Direct computer-controlled CMMs use a computer to control all machine motions and measuring routines and to perform most of the routinely required data processing. These machines are operated in much the same way as CNC machine tools. Both control and measuring cycles are under program control. Off-line programming capability is also available.

The effective use of computers for CMM applications is a principal feature differentiating available CMM systems. The value of a measurement system depends a great deal on the sophistication and ease of use of the associated software and its functional capabilities. The functional capabilities of a CMM software package depend on the number and types of application programs available.

2. DESTRUCTIVE AND NONDESTRUCTIVE TESTS

> Distinguish between destructive and nondestructive measurement test methods and apply them appropriately. (Analyze)
>
> Body of Knowledge IV.D .2

Testing involves evaluation of product conformance to certain design or production requirements. In addition, the output of testing can be used to evaluate new designs during product development, to define a product's potential failure causes, in product reliability evaluation, and so on.

Testing versus Inspection

Inspection is the evaluation of product quality by comparing the results of measuring one or several product characteristics against applicable standards. From this definition it is evident that the inspection function involves a number of tasks:

1. Measurement, which could be on a qualitative or quantitative scale. The objective is to make a judgment about the product's conformance to specifications.

2. Comparison of the measurement results to specific standards that reflect the intended use of the product by the customer and the various production costs. If the product is found to be nonconforming, a decision as to whether nonconforming products are fit for use may be reached.

3. Decision making regarding the disposition of the unit inspected and, under sampling inspection, regarding the lot from which the sample was drawn.

4. Corrective action(s) in order to improve the quality of the product and/or process based on the aggregate results of inspection over a number of units.

Testing is also carried out to determine the conformity of a product by comparing the results of measuring one or several product characteristics against applicable standards. It involves similar tasks as inspection. The difference is that testing can be performed on a part, a product, a subassembly, or an assembly, while inspection is typically performed on a component or a part of a product.

Testing versus Gauging

Two terms normally associated with inspection are *gauging* and *testing*. Gauging determines product conformance with specifications with the aid of measuring instruments such as calipers, micrometers, templates, and other mechanical, optical, and electronic devices. Testing refers to the determination of the capability of an item to meet specified requirements by subjecting it to a set of physical, chemical, environmental, or other operating conditions and actions similar to or more severe than those expected under normal use.

Destructive and Nondestructive Testing

Testing might be destructive or nondestructive. In testing, the product is subjected to measuring procedures that render its usefulness to the customer. Gauging, however, is the more common form of inspection and is less costly; this operation has no effect on the product's service capability. Of course, certain product characteristics, mainly those related to failure modes, may only be observed and measured by exposing the product to conditions beyond its designed limits, such as determining the maximum current that an electronic component can carry or the maximum tensile force that a mechanical part can withstand. Most of these procedures normally are destructive testing procedures and may be performed in cases where mandatory requirements are to be met. Nondestructive testing (NDT) of products usually is performed by subjecting the product to tests such as eddy current, ultrasonic resonance, or x-ray testing.

Nondestructive Testing Techniques. Screening or 100 percent inspection can not be used when the product is subjected to a destructive testing procedure or the time involved in performing inspection is too long. Another constraint is that the cost of inspection may be too high to justify the economics of inspection. NDT techniques are more common for automated inspection or 100 percent inspection. The most common NDT techniques include:

- Eddy current testing involves the application of an AC current passing through a coil that is placed near the surface of the part to be inspected. Thus, its application is limited to conducting materials and the test results are made by comparison.

- Ultrasonic testing normally is used to check for surface defects that cause deflection of an ultrasonic wave directed on the part surface, thus giving an indication of the presence of a surface defect. For ultrasonic testing, reference standards are required.

- X-ray techniques cause the internal characteristics of the part to be displayed and thus provide information about the presence of defects, cracks, or other impurities.

- Liquid penetration is more common for detecting defects on the part surface. It is used for different part configurations and, unlike magnetic particle testing, it can be used for nonmagnetic materials. However, liquid penetration can not be used to locate subsurface discontinuities.

- Magnetic particle testing is used when the part material can be magnetized. Discovery of part defects, like cracks or discontinuities, can then be detected by the presence of paring magnetic fields. Magnetic particle testing is limited to parts made of iron, steel, or allied materials.

Other common NDT techniques include the application of some phenomenon, such as thermal, chemical, holographic inteferometry (employing interference patterns for checking surface displacements), or optical phenomena. These are used for special testing procedures and often are too expensive to be widely applied.

Part IV.D.2

Chapter 25

E. Metrology

Identify, describe, and apply metrology
techniques such as calibration systems,
traceability to calibration standards,
measurement error and its sources, and
control and maintenance of measurement
standards and devices. (Analyze)

Body of Knowledge IV.E

INTRODUCTION AND SCOPE

The science of precision measurement, usually referred to as metrology, encompasses all scientific disciplines. The word "metrology" is derived from two Greek words: metro, meaning measurement, and logy, meaning science. The term is used in a more restricted sense to mean that portion of measurement science that is often used to provide, maintain, and disseminate a consistent set of units, to provide support for the enforcement of equity in trade by weights and measurement laws, or to provide data for quality control in manufacturing (Simpson 1981).

CONTEXT OF MEASUREMENTS

A measurement is a series of manipulations of physical objects or systems according to a defined protocol that results in a number. The number is purported to uniquely represent the magnitude (or intensity) of a certain property, which depends on the properties of the test object. This number is acquired to form the basis of a decision affecting some human goal or satisfying some human object need, the satisfaction of which depends on the properties of the test subject.

These needs or goals can usefully be viewed as requiring three general classes of measurements (Simpson 1981):

1. *Technical.* This class includes those measurements made to assure dimensional compatibility, conformation to design specifications necessary for proper function, or, in general, all measurements made to ensure fitness for intended use of some object.

2. *Legal.* This class includes those measurements made to ensure compliance with a law or regulation. This class is the concern of weights and measures bodies, regulators, and those who must comply with regulations. The measurements are identical in kind with those of technical metrology but usually are embedded in a much more formal structure. Legal metrology is more prevalent in Europe than in the United States, although this is changing.

3. *Scientific.* This class includes those measurements made to validate theories of the nature of the universe or to suggest new theories. These measurements, which can be called scientific metrology (properly the domain of experimental physics), present special problems.

Standards of Measurement

The National Institute of Standards and Technology (NIST) is the American custodian of the standards of measurement. It was established by an act of Congress in 1901 although the need for such a body had been noted by the founders of the Constitution. NIST's two main campuses are in Gaithersburg, Maryland, and Boulder, Colorado, where research into the phenomenon of measurement, the properties of materials, and calibration of the reference standards submitted by laboratories from throughout the United States are carried out. The following is a generalization of the echelons of standards in the national measurement system (Rice 1986):

- *National standards.* Include prototype and natural phenomena of SI (Systems International, the worldwide system of weight and measures standards) base units and reference and working standards for derived and other units.

- *Metrology standards.* Reference standards of industrial or governmental laboratories.

- *Calibration standards.* Working standards of industrial or governmental laboratories. Frequently, there are various levels within these echelons (Mack 1976).

In order to maintain accuracy, standards in a vast industrial complex must be traceable to a single source, usually the country's national standards. Since the national laboratories of well-developed countries maintain close connections with the International Bureau of Weights and Measures, there is assurance that items manufactured to identical dimensions in different countries will be compatible (McNish 1967).

Application of precise measurement has increased so much during the past few years that it is no longer practical for a single national laboratory to perform directly all the calibrations and standardization required by a large country with a high technical development. This has led to the establishment of a considerable number of standardizing laboratories in industry and in various branches of the state and national governments (see Figure 25.1). In order that results of calibrations be uniform, the standardizing laboratories must maintain close rapport with the national laboratory. This is facilitated by the use of uniform terminology in discussing standards (McNish 1967).

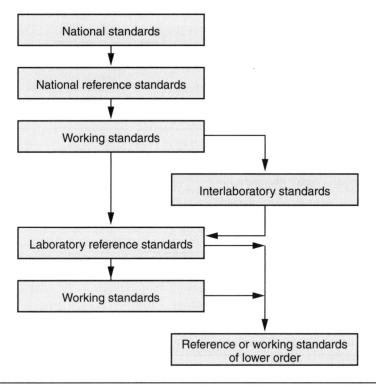

Figure 25.1   Classification of standards.

Concern with Standards

The term *standard* includes three distinct areas, all of which are of importance in metrology (NIST 1981):

1. Definitions of base units

2. Physical artifacts

3. Paper standards

Definitions of Base Units

The definitions of the base units of measurement form a reference from which all other units can be derived. These base units, together with two supplementary units related to angle measurement that are necessary to specify a complete system of units, are listed in Table 25.1. Table 25.2 gives the definitions of all the SI units listed in Table 25.1. The definitions can also be found at the NIST Web site at http://physics.nist.gov/Pubs/SP811/appenA.html. A current chart showing the relationships of all the SI units to which names have been assigned can also be found at the NIST Web site at http://ts.nist.gov/WeightsAndMeasures/Metric/pub814.cfm.

All of the SI units listed in Tables 25.1 and 25.2 are defined in terms of experiments that can be performed in any suitably equipped laboratory, except for

Table 25.1 Base units of the international system.

Quantity	Name
Length	Meter
Mass	Kilogram
Time	Second
Electric current	Ampere
Thermodynamic temperature	Kelvin
Amount of substance	Mole
Luminous intensity	Candela
Plane angle*	Radian
Solid angle*	Steradian

*Supplementary units

Table 25.2 Definitions of the SI base units.

Unit	Definition
meter–m	The distance traveled by light in a vacuum during a time interval of $1/299, 792, 458$ of a second.
kilogram–kg	A cylinder of platinum-iridium alloy kept by the International Bureau of Weights and Measures at Paris. A duplicate in the custody of the National Institute of Standards and Technology serves as the mass standard for the United States.
second–s	The duration of $9, 192, 631, 770$ cycles of the radiation associated with a specified transition of the cesium-133 atom. It is realized by tuning an oscillator to the resonance frequency of cesium-133 atoms as they pass through a system of magnets and a resonant cavity into a detector.
Ampere–A	That current which, if maintained in each of two long parallel wires separated by one meter in free space, would produce a force between the two wires (due to their magnetic fields) of 2×10^{-7} newton for each meter of length.
Kelvin–K	The fraction $1/273.16$ of the thermodynamic temperature of the triple point of water. The temperature 0 K is called absolute zero.
mole–mol	The amount of substance of a system that contains as many elementary entities as there are atoms in 0.012 kilogram of carbon-12.
candela–cd	The luminous intensity, in a given direction, of a source that emits mono-chromatic radiation of frequency 540×10^{12} (Hz) and that has a radiant intensity in that direction of 1/683 watt per steradian.
radian–rad	The plane angle with its vertex as the center of a circle that is subtended by an arc equal in length to the radius.
steradian–sr	The solid angle with its vertex at the center of a sphere that is subtended by the area of the spherical surface equal to that of a square with sides equal in length to the radius.

Source: NIST Special Publication 304A, August 1981 (used with permission).

the definition of the unit mass, the kilogram. The kilogram is the only base unit defined in terms of a physical artifact. It must therefore be carefully preserved and protected, and the unit can only be disseminated by direct comparisons with the defining artifact. The kilogram is the mass of the International Prototype of the Kilogram, which is kept at the International Bureau of Weights and Measures near Paris, France.

The standard for angle measurements is present in the form of the circle, and units of angle are defined in terms of this standard. Thus, one degree is the angle that subtends 1/360 of the circumference of a circle, and one radian is the angle that subtends $1/(2p)$ times the circumference.

Measurements of length are man-defined and man-made. Until 1960, the meter was defined as the distance, under certain specified environmental conditions, between two lines engraved on the neutral axis of the International Prototype Meter, a bar of 90 percent platinum/10 percent iridium alloy, which is preserved at the International Bureau of Weights and Measures; the Prototype Meter No. 27, whose length was known in terms of the international prototype, served as a standard for the United States. This method of defining the meter length was not entirely satisfactory, since it required periodic recalibration of the various national standards in terms of the international standard. In 1960, the Eleventh General Conference on Weights and Measures redefined the meter as a length equal to 1,650,763.73 wavelengths, in a vacuum, of the orange-red radiation corresponding to the transition between the 2p10 and 5d5 levels of the krypton-86 atom. The meter so defined is identical to that previously defined, within the limits of accuracy of the various measurements involved. The new definition provided a standard for length measurement that was based on an unchanging physical constant that could be reproduced in any properly equipped laboratory in the world. The inch is defined as 0.0254 meters.

The definition of the meter was again changed in 1975 by the General Conference of Weights and Measures. The current definition of the meter is the length of a path traveled by light in a vacuum during a time interval of 1/299,792,458 of a second. This definition for the meter thus defines the speed of light to be exactly 299,792,458 meters/second, and with this definition the meter could be realized from the wavelength of any coherent optical source whose frequency is known and the wavelength is the speed of light divided by the frequency.

Physical Artifacts

Physical artifacts are manufactured with high precision to embody a particular quantity, dimension, or feature. These include such items as gage blocks for length, standard resistors for electrical resistance, standards for cell voltage, and so on. This class of artifacts also includes high-precision analog measurement instruments that can be used as masters for reference, such as mercury in glass thermometers and dead weight testers for pressure.

Paper Standards

Paper standards are the many documents published by various technical societies and standards-writing organizations that contain specifications or generally accepted methods for making measurements.

Part IV.E

CONCEPTS IN METROLOGY

A fundamental role of the metrology and calibration process is to assign accuracy or uncertainty statements to a measurement. This can be achieved by defining characteristics of measuring system elements as well as equipment limitations.

Error in Measurement

Error in measurement is the difference between the indicated value and the true value of a measured quantity. The true value of a quantity to be measured is seldom known. Errors are classified as:

1. Random errors

2. Systematic errors

Random errors are accidental in nature. They fluctuate in a way that cannot be predicted from the detailed employment of the measuring system or from knowledge of its functioning. Sources of error such as hysteresis, ambient influences, or variations in the workpiece are typical but not all-inclusive in the random category.

Systematic errors are those not usually detected by repetition of the measurement operations. An error resulting from either faulty calibration of a local standard or a defect in contact configuration of an internal measuring system is typical but not completely inclusive in the systematic class of errors (Darmody 1967).

It is important to know all the sources of error in a measuring system, rather than merely to be aware of the details of their classification. Analysis of the causes of errors is helpful in attaining the necessary knowledge of achieved accuracy.

There are many different sources of error that influence the precision of a measuring process in a variety of ways according to the individual situation in which such errors arise. The permutation of error sources and their effects, therefore, is quite considerable. In general, these errors can be classified under three main headings:

1. Process environment

2. Equipment limitation

3. Operator fallibility

These factors constitute an interrelated three-element system for the measuring process as shown in Figure 25.2.

The requirement of any precision measuring instrument is that it should be able to represent, as accurately as possible, the dimension it measures. This necessitates that the instrument itself have a high degree of inherent accuracy. Small inaccuracies will exist, however, due to the tolerances permitted in the instrument's manufacture. These inaccuracies will influence the degree of precision attainable in its application.

The areas in which operator fallibility arise can be grouped as follows (Rashed and Hamouda 1974):

1. Identification of the measuring situation

2. Analysis of alternative methods

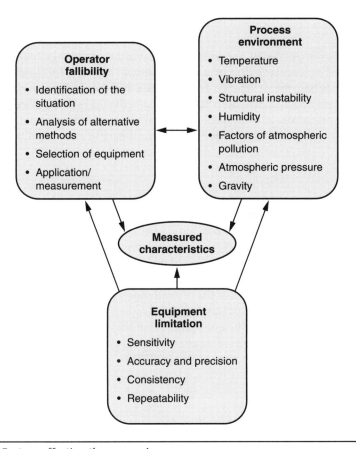

Figure 25.2   Factors affecting the measuring process.

3. Selection of equipment

4. Application (or measurement)

The identification of measuring situations becomes increasingly complex in modern metrology. As parts become smaller and more precise, greater attention has to be paid to geometric qualities such as roundness, concentricity, straightness, parallelism, and squareness. Deficiencies in these qualities may consume all of the permitted design tolerance, so that a simple dimensional check becomes grossly insufficient.

Operators have to be knowledgeable about what they have to measure and how satisfactorily the requirements of the situation will be met by the measuring instrument. Correct identification of the measuring situation will eliminate those methods unsuitable for the situation. Proper measuring equipment can therefore be selected from a smaller range of measuring process alternatives. Method analysis can then be applied to these alternatives to determine which best satisfies the situation. This usually involves examining each method for different characteristics and evaluating the relative accuracies between the different methods.

Accuracy

Accuracy is the degree of agreement of individual or average measurements with an accepted reference value or level (American Society for Testing and Materials 1977). Measurement science encompasses two basic approaches for determining conformity to measurement accuracy objectives: (1) an engineering analysis to determine all causes of error, and (2) a statistical evaluation of data after stripping or eliminating the errors revealed by the engineering analysis (Darmody 1967).

Precision

Precision is the degree of mutual agreement among individual measurements made under prescribed like conditions, or simply, how well identically performed measurements agree with each other (American Society for Testing and Materials 1977). This concept applies to a process or a set of measurements, not to a single measurement, because in any set of measurements, the individual results will scatter about the mean. Since the means of the results from groups of measurements tend to scatter less about the overall mean than individual results, reference is commonly made to the precision of a single measurement as contrasted with the precision of groups of measurements, but this is a misuse of the term. What is really meant is the precision of a set of single measurements or the precision of a set of groups of measurements (McNish 1967).

Sensitivity and Readability

The terms *sensitivity* and *readability* often are used in discussing measurement, and sometimes the concepts they involve are confused with accuracy and precision (see McNish 1967). Sensitivity and readability are primarily associated with equipment, while accuracy and precision are associated with the measuring process. The most sensitive or the most readable equipment may not always lead to the most precise or the most accurate results.

Sensitivity can be defined as the least perceptible change in dimension detected by the measuring tip and shown by the indicator. Readability is the ease of reading the instrument scale when a dimension is being measured. It is a factor that should remain constant over the full scale range.

Consistency

Consistency is another characteristic of the measuring instrument. Consistency of the reading on the instrument scale when the same dimension is being measured is necessary. This property affects the performance of the measuring instrument and, therefore, complete confidence in the accuracy of the process cannot be established in the absence of consistency.

TRACEABILITY

Traceability is a process intended to quantify a laboratory's measurement uncertainty in relationship to the national standards. It is based on analyses of error contributions present in each of the measurement transfers: the calibration of the laboratory's reference standards by NIST, the measurements made in the calibration transfers within the laboratory, and the measurements made on a product. Evidence of traceability is normally required; it may be as simple as retention of certificates and reports on calibration or as complex as reproduction of the analyses demonstrating the uncertainties claimed for the measurements (Rice 1986).

A laboratory that maintains its own reference standards (that is, it relies on no laboratory other than NIST for calibration of its standards) must continuously monitor its own performance. Measurements on check standards, intercomparisons of standards, and participation in measurement assurance programs sponsored by NIST are meant to quantify laboratory error sources, as well as to provide indications of the causes (Rice 1986).

Measurement Assurance

Measurement assurance, thought by some to relate only to methods used in the metrology or calibration laboratory to secure calibrations by NIST, is one of the more important concepts in the measurement field.

Traditionally, calibrations by NIST determine the accuracy and precision of the measuring instrument. Measurement assurance protocols (MAPs), on the other hand, are able to include not only the accuracy of the item, but also the contribution to error by the metrologist/technician, laboratory environment, and practices/procedures of the laboratory because the experiment involves measurements by participants in their own laboratories (Belanger 1980).

Measurement assurance, in addition to being a concept of importance to metrology and calibration laboratory managers, is one that should interest quality assurance personnel involved in testing and measurement. Most factory testing and measuring involves the use of equipment whose accuracy has been determined through calibration. Little, if any, consideration is given to errors that may be contributed by the test operator, by his or her instructions or procedures, or by the environments in which the equipment is operated. The application of measurement assurance can serve to reduce errors (Rice 1986).

CALIBRATION

Calibration refers to measurements where the individual values are reported, rather than to measurements indicating only that an instrument is functioning within prescribed limits. It also refers to the disciplines necessary to control measuring systems to assure their functioning within prescribed accuracy objectives.

The general calibration provisions for a measuring system include:

1. Acceptance calibration of a new system

2. Periodic calibration of the system in use or when placed in use after storage

3. Availability of standards traceable to the national standard for the unit of measure under consideration

Part IV.E

Normally, a calibration chain or pyramid of echelons is involved in the discipline of metrology control and surveillance. The levels include:

Level 1. The product tolerance or measured quantity.

Level 2. The calibration of the product measuring system.

Level 3. The calibration of the measuring system used to calibrate the product measurement system.

Level 4. Local standards, such as gage blocks or standard cells (volts), used for calibration of level 3.

Level 5. Referencing local standards of level 4 to the national standard.

Each of these levels attempts to achieve an accuracy/tolerance ratio that will satisfy requirements of the preceding level. This achievement is, of course, subject to the limitations of the state of the art, as well as cost–accuracy tradeoffs that may come into play.

The aim of all calibration activities is ascertaining that a measuring system will function to assure attainment of its accuracy objectives.

Periodic calibration of measuring and test equipment is accepted by most as necessary for measurement accuracy. A little more controversial is the question of determining the basis of the period of recalibration. There are a number of techniques in use to establish calibration intervals initially and to adjust the intervals thereafter. These methods include:

1. The same interval for all equipment in the user's inventory

2. The same interval for families of instruments (for example, oscilloscopes, gage blocks, and so on)

3. The same interval for a given manufacturer and model number

Adjustments of these initial intervals are then made for the entire inventory, individual families, or manufacturer and model numbers, respectively, based on analyses or history. A study conducted for NIST in connection with a review of government laboratory practices identifies these and other methods (Voft 1980).

Calibration Control System

A typical calibration program may involve all or most of the following tasks (Rice 1986):

1. Evaluation of equipment to determine its capability

2. Identification of calibration requirements

3. Selection of standards to perform calibration

4. Selection of methods/procedures to carry out the measurements necessary for the calibration

5. Establishment of the initial interval and the rules for adjusting the interval thereafter

6. Establishment of a recall system to assure that instruments due for calibration are returned

7. Implementation of a labeling system to visually identify the instrument's due date

8. Use of a quality assurance program to evaluate the calibration system (process, control, audit, corrective action, and so on)

Selection of the standards, methods, and procedures to carry out the calibration includes the decision relating to where the calibration will be performed.

The recall system must be designed to assure that the calibration organization and the using organization are both aware in advance that an instrument will be due for calibration.

Labeling instruments to visually display their calibration due dates is a companion feature to the recall system. Labels indicate (by dates, color codes, or similar symbols) the date the instrument is due for its next calibration. This visual identification may be used by the quality assurance organization to ensure that the instrument is not used beyond its due date.

Intervals are established in a variety of ways, as discussed previously. Principal objectives of an interval adjustment program include minimizing the potential for out-of-tolerance instruments in user areas, minimizing the costs of calibration, and assuring the required accuracy of instrumentation.

Chapter 26

F. Measurement System Analysis

Measurement system analysis consists of qualifying the measurement process, determining the adequacy of the measurement system for use, and identifying and estimating the process error. A measurement system is the entire process for obtaining measurements on some quality characteristic of interest; this process includes standards, personnel, methods of measurement, and so on.

In this chapter, definitions as well as the concept of gage repeatability and reproducibility are introduced.

TERMS AND DEFINITIONS

Systematic and Random Errors

Two important and common types of error in measurement system analysis are systematic error and random error. *Systematic errors* can be caused by human interference, poor manufacturing methods, and measuring device imperfections, for example. This error remains fairly constant over repeated measurements collected under identical conditions. The error is systematic, which results in values that are consistently above or consistently below the true or reference value of the quality characteristic.

Random errors vary arbitrarily over all measurements taken under identical conditions. Even when systematic errors have been identified and accounted for, normal random fluctuations will occur. If only random errors are present in the system, then increasing the number of measurements taken will provide a better estimate of the quality characteristic's true value.

Measurement System Error

Measurement system error with respect to measurement system analysis consists of variability that can be attributed to gage *bias, stability, linearity, repeatability,* and *reproducibility. Accuracy* of a measurement system is made up of bias, linearity, and stability. Repeatability and reproducibility are the components that describe *precision,* or measurement variation.

Accuracy

Accuracy is a qualitative term defined as the difference between the measurement taken and the actual value of the quality characteristic of interest. The three components of accuracy are bias, linearity, and stability.

Bias is defined as the difference between the observed average measurement and a reference value, and is a measure of systematic error in terms of the measurement system:

$$\text{Bias} = \text{Observed average} - \text{Reference value}$$

The observed average measurement can be found by measuring a single part multiple times or selecting several parts at random and measuring each part multiple times. The measurements should be taken under identical conditions.

EXAMPLE 26.1

Suppose three parts of different sizes are selected and the diameter of each part is measured. These parts represent the normal range of part sizes for which the measurement system is used. A reference value is known for each of the parts. Suppose each part is measured five times, with the results displayed in Table 26.1. The observed averages are calculated and the resulting bias estimated for each part.

Table 26.1   Bias and average estimates for parts of different sizes.

	Parts	1	2	3
	Reference value	2.00	3.80	5.60
	1	2.10	3.65	6.21
	2	1.88	4.00	5.40
Trials	3	1.92	3.88	5.26
	4	2.05	3.78	5.98
	5	2.01	4.10	4.93
Average		1.992	3.882	5.556
Bias		−0.008	0.082	−0.044

Hypothesis tests can be carried out to test the significance of bias (see AIAG [2002]). If bias is found to be significant, the cause for bias should be identified. Some reasons for significant bias might include (but are not limited to) an incorrect reference value, a worn measuring device, or improper calibration of or incorrect use of the measuring device.

Linearity measures how changes in the size of the part being measured will affect measurement system bias over the expected process range. Consider the previous example with three parts of different sizes. Notice that the bias estimates were quite different across the different sizes. There may be evidence of nonlinearity if as the part size increases, the bias changes significantly. Tests can be performed to determine if nonlinearity, if it exists, is significant.

Stability is a measure of how well the measurement system performs over time. It provides a measure of the change in bias over time when the same part is measured. Stability differs from linearity in that only one part, whose reference value is known (or assumed to be known), is measured at different points in time. This is to determine if the measurement system has changed over time and after many uses.

In general, accuracy provides information about *location*, or the relationship between the measurement results and reference value of the quality characteristic.

Precision

Precision is defined as the variation encountered when the same part is measured repeatedly using the same measurement system (under the same conditions). The two components of precision are repeatability and reproducibility. *Repeatability* represents the variability due to the gage or test instrument when used to measure the same part under identical conditions (that is, same operator measuring the same part). *Reproducibility,* on the other hand, represents the variability due to different operators or setups measuring the same parts using the same measuring device. Reproducibility represents the variability due to the measurement system. Both repeatability and reproducibility will be discussed in more detail in this chapter.

GAGE REPEATABILITY AND REPRODUCIBILITY*

Gage repeatability and reproducibility (R&R) studies are used to determine if a measurement system is capable for its intended purpose. If the measurement system variation is small compared to the process variation, then the measurement system is considered capable. In general, the purposes of a gage R&R study are to:

- Determine the amount of variability in the collected data that can be attributed to the measurement system in place

- Isolate the sources of variability in the measurement system

---

* In the literature, you will see the terms "gage" and "gauge" used interchangeably. Both spellings are correct and acceptable.

• Determine whether the measurement system is suitable for use in a broader project

Variance Components

When conducting a gage R&R study, it is often assumed that the "parts" and the "operators" are selected at random from larger populations. The parts are typically selected at random so that they represent the entire operating range of the process. Since the parts and operators are randomly selected, there is a measure of variability associated with each. There are situations where the parts or operators may be fixed. To illustrate, suppose the operators are really automatic gages and there are only three total for a particular process. If all three automatic gages are used, then we say that the factor "operator" is fixed. Assessing the capability of fixed factors is beyond the scope of this handbook, but additional information and references can be found in Burdick, Borror, and Montgomery (2005).

Gage variability is a function of *variance components*. Let $\sigma^2_{\text{Repeatability}}$ represent the inherent variability in the gage and $\sigma^2_{\text{Reproducibility}}$ represent the variability due to the different operators (or setups, different time periods, and so on) using the same gage. Specifically, we can write the measurement error variability as

$$\sigma^2_{\text{Measurement error}} = \sigma^2_{\text{Gage}} = \sigma^2_{\text{Reproducibility}} + \sigma^2_{\text{Repeatability}}$$

Furthermore, suppose part-to-part variability is denoted by σ^2_P. Then total variability can be written as a sum of the two variance components:

$$\sigma^2_{\text{Total}} = \sigma^2_{\text{Gage}} + \sigma^2_p$$

In a gage R&R study it is important to accurately estimate these variance components and thus adequately estimate repeatability and reproducibility. Two commonly used methods for estimating repeatability and reproducibility are: 1) the tabular method (also known as the range method) and 2) the analysis of variance method. Both methods will be presented and discussed in this section.

The Tabular Method (Range Method)

Gage R&R studies were often conducted using a *tabular method*. This method is based on information that can be obtained from control charts and using the sample ranges to estimate variability (see Chapter 34 for discussion of the sample range and Chapter 37 for discussion of control charts).

Estimating Reproducibility. The steps for estimating reproducibility using the tabular method are as follows:

1. Estimate the average measurement for each "operator."

2. Find the range of these averages (largest average – smallest average); this is called R_O (for operator range).

3. Estimate the standard deviation for reproducibility using the relationship

$$\hat{\sigma}_{\text{Reproducibility}} = \frac{R_O}{d_2}.$$

4. Estimate the variance component for reproducibility:

$$\hat{\sigma}^2_{\text{Reproducibility}} = \left(\frac{R_O}{d_2}\right)^2.$$

Estimating Repeatability. The steps for estimating repeatability are as follows:

1. Calculate the range for each part (or sample).

2. Calculate the average range across all samples; this is denoted $\bar{R}$.

3. Estimate the standard deviation for repeatability:

$$\hat{\sigma}_{\text{Repeatability}} = \hat{\sigma}_e = \frac{\bar{R}}{d_2}.$$

4. Estimate the variance component for repeatability:

$$\hat{\sigma}^2_{\text{Repeatability}} = \hat{\sigma}^2_e = \left(\frac{\bar{R}}{d_2}\right)^2.$$

Estimating Part-to-Part Variability. The steps for estimating part-to-part variability are as follows:

1. Calculate the average measurement for each part (or sample).

2. Find the range of these averages (largest average – smallest average); this is denoted R_p (for part range).

3. Estimate the standard deviation for parts:

$$\hat{\sigma}_p = \frac{R_p}{d_2}.$$

4. Estimate the variance component for parts:

$$\hat{\sigma}^2_p = \left(\frac{R_p}{d_2}\right)^2.$$

Complete details of determining values of d_2 for each of the above quantities can be found in AIAG (2002) or Barrentine (2003). Additionally, in AIAG (2002) and Barrentine (2003) you will find details of the range method.

The Analysis of Variance Method

One of the reported drawbacks to using the tabular method has been the inability to estimate any possible interaction between operators and parts (or samples).

It is often assumed that the operators are well trained and as a result there should be no significant interaction between these two factors. If, however, there is a significant interaction, this effect should be quantified and taken into consideration when providing estimates of repeatability and reproducibility. Using the tabular or range method, it is not possible to estimate the interaction between operator and part.

The analysis of variance (ANOVA) method has become a common choice for practitioners conducting gage R&R studies since the computations can be easily carried out using modern statistical software. (See Chapters 35 and 37 for discussion of interactions, factors, and the general analysis of variance method). Before presenting the ANOVA method, some basic assumptions must be discussed.

The Standard Experiment

Suppose the response of interest in a gage R&R study can easily be expressed by a random two-factor model (see Chapter 35 for more details on modeling a response, factors, and two-way ANOVA). We are interested in the factors "parts," "operators," and possibly the part-by-operator interaction (see Chapter 35 for details of two-factor interactions). A gage R&R study is to be carried out involving p parts, o operators, and r replicates. Suppose y represents the response of interest, and can be modeled as

$$y_{ijk} = \mu + P_i + O_j + (PO)_{ij} + \varepsilon_{ijk}$$

for $i = 1, 2, \ldots, p; \; j = 1, 2, \ldots, o; \; k = 1, 2, \ldots, r.$

where

y_{ijk} is the kth measurement of the ith part by the jth operator.

μ is the overall process mean.

P_i represents the effect of the ith part; we assume that P_i is a random factor that follows a normal distribution with mean zero and variance σ_P^2.

O_j represents the effect of the jth operator; we assume that O_j is a random factor that follows a normal distribution with mean zero and variance σ_O^2.

$(PO)_{ij}$ represents the part-by-operator interaction effect; we assume that $(PO)_{ij}$ is a random factor that follows a normal distribution with mean zero and variance σ_{PO}^2.

ε_{ijk} represents random error; we assume that ε_{ijk} follows a normal distribution with mean zero and variance σ_e^2.

The terms σ_P^2, σ_O^2, σ_{PO}^2, and σ_e^2 are our *variance components*. As discussed previously, gage variability is a function of these variance components. Specifically, we wrote measurement error (gage) variability as

$$\sigma_{\text{Measurement error}}^2 = \sigma_{\text{Gage}}^2 = \sigma_{\text{Reproducibility}}^2 + \sigma_{\text{Repeatability}}^2$$

But now we will use the variance components for our random factors to determine repeatability, reproducibility, and part variability. Specifically, reproducibility and repeatability variation can be written as

$$\sigma^2_{\text{Reproducibility}} = \sigma^2_{PO} + \sigma^2_O$$

and

$$\sigma^2_{\text{Repeatability}} = \sigma^2_e.$$

Part-to-part variability is given by σ^2_P. The variability of the total observed measurement is given by

$$\sigma^2_{\text{Total}} = \sigma^2_{\text{Gage}} + \sigma^2_P.$$

Estimating the Variance Components

The variance components will be estimated using the mean squares obtained from an analysis of variance table. To begin, a standard analysis of variance is conducted assuming that the two-factor standard model given earlier is valid. The reader is encouraged to review Chapter 35 for complete discussion of sum of squares, mean square, ANOVA, *p*-value, and degrees of freedom.

The procedure is as follows:

• Treat the problem as a designed experiment (see Chapter 39 for details on designed experiments).

• Conduct an analysis of variance (set up an ANOVA table—see Chapter 35).

• Use the mean square values from the ANOVA table to estimate the variance components (see Chapter 35 for discussion of mean square).

Some of the quantities from the ANOVA table are given in Table 26.2. Standard statistical software packages will provide these values so it is not necessary to carry out the calculations by hand.

Table 26.2   Necessary quantities for an analysis of variance.

Source	DF	SS	MS
Part	$p-1$	SS_p	MS_p
Operator	$o-1$	SS_o	MS_o
Part × operator	$(p-1)(o-1)$	SS_{op}	MS_{op}
Error (repeatability)	$op(n-1)$	SS_E	MS_E
Total	$opn-1$	SS_T	

The estimates of the variance components given earlier are

$$\text{Operators: } \hat{\sigma}_O^2 = \frac{\text{MS}_o - \text{MS}_{op}}{pr}$$

$$\text{Part} \times \text{operator: } \hat{\sigma}_{PO}^2 = \frac{\text{MS}_{po} - \text{MS}_E}{r}$$

$$\text{Parts: } \hat{\sigma}_P^2 = \frac{\text{MS}_p - \text{MS}_{op}}{or}$$

$$\text{Error: } \hat{\sigma}_e^2 = \text{MS}_E$$

It is possible that one or more of the variance components could result in a negative value. Some researchers have maintained that if any variance component estimate is negative, it is set equal to zero. Other researchers recommend using different approaches to estimating these quantities so that the estimates are nonnegative (see Montgomery [2009a] for more details). The variance component estimates are then used to estimate reproducibility, repeatability, part-to-part variation, as well as the total variability, using the equations given previously.

EXAMPLE 26.2

An experiment was conducted on the thermal performance of a power module for an induction motor starter. The response was thermal performance measured in degrees C per watt. Table 26.3 displays a partial list of data collected for 20 motors by six operators. Each operator measures all parts twice. The original data has been multiplied by 100 for convenience. (The original problem statement for this example came from Houf and Berman [1988].) The specification limits are LSL = 18 and USL = 58. We assume that each motor and the operators have been selected at random from larger populations. The model of interest involves operators, parts, and the operator-by-part interaction.

Table 26.3   Typical data for the gage R&R experiment.

Part	Operator 1		Operator 2		...	Operator 6	
	1	2	1	2	...	1	2
1	44	34	43	44	...	46	46
2	21	23	20	22	...	21	21
.	.	.	.	.		.	.
.	.	.	.	.	...	.	.
.	.	.	.	.		.	.
20	29	31	31	30	...	31	29

Continued

Continued

In this problem, $p = 20$, $o = 6$, and $r = 2$. We will examine results of the gage R&R study using both the tabular method and the ANOVA method. The calculations for the variance components were carried out using Minitab v15 (2007) for both methods.

Tabular Method Results

The results of the tabular method are given in Table 26.4.

The second column in Table 26.4 provides the estimates for the variance components:

- $\hat{\sigma}^2_{\text{Repeatability}} = \hat{\sigma}^2_e = 0.5678$

- $\hat{\sigma}^2_{\text{Reproducibility}} = \hat{\sigma}^2_O = 0.2607$

- $\hat{\sigma}^2_p = 54.8697$

- $\hat{\sigma}^2_{\text{Measurement error}} = \hat{\sigma}^2_{\text{Gage}} = \hat{\sigma}^2_{\text{Reproducibility}} + \hat{\sigma}^2_{\text{Repeatability}}$

$$= 0.2607 + 0.5678$$

$$= 0.8285$$

- $\hat{\sigma}^2_{\text{Total}} = \hat{\sigma}^2_{\text{Gage}} = \hat{\sigma}^2_p$

$$= 0.8285 + 54.8697$$

$$= 55.6982$$

The last column in Table 26.4 provides the percent of the total variability contributed by each source. For example, the percent contribution for "Repeatability" was found by

$$\%\text{Contribution} = \frac{\hat{\sigma}^2_{\text{Repeatability}}}{\hat{\sigma}^2_{\text{Total}}} \times 100 = \frac{0.5678}{55.6982} \times 100 = 1.02.$$

From Table 26.4, we see that the largest source of variability is differences between parts.

Table 26.4   Gage R&R estimates using the tabular method.

Source	Variance component	% contribution
Total gage R&R	0.8285	1.49
Repeatability	0.5678	1.02
Reproducibility	0.2607	0.47
Part-to-part	54.8697	98.51
Total variation	55.6982	100.00

Continued

Continued

ANOVA Method

Before estimating the variance components using the ANOVA method, we can determine if there is a statistically significant difference between parts or between operators, and if there exists a statistically significant interaction between parts and operators. An analysis of variance was carried out, with the results provided in Table 26.5.

The variance components can be estimated as follows (although generally it is not necessary to calculate these by hand):

$$\text{Operators: } \hat{\sigma}_O^2 = \frac{MS_o - MS_{po}}{pr} = \frac{13.580 - 2.060}{20(2)} = 0.288$$

$$\text{Part} \times \text{operator: } \hat{\sigma}_{PO}^2 = \frac{MS_{po} - MS_E}{r} = \frac{2.060 - 0.733}{2} = 0.6635$$

$$\text{Parts: } \hat{\sigma}_P^2 = \frac{MS_P - MS_{po}}{or} = \frac{591.479 - 2.060}{6(2)} = 49.118$$

$$\text{Error: } \hat{\sigma}_e^2 = MS_E = 0.733$$

The gage R&R estimates are then:

- $\hat{\sigma}_{Reproducibility}^2 = \hat{\sigma}_{PO}^2 + \hat{\sigma}_O^2 = 0.6635 + 0.288 = 0.9515$

- $\hat{\sigma}_{Repeatability}^2 = \hat{\sigma}_e^2 = 0.733$

- $\hat{\sigma}_{Measurement\ error}^2 = \hat{\sigma}_{Gage}^2 = \hat{\sigma}_{Reproducibility}^2 + \hat{\sigma}_{Repeatability}^2$

  $$= 0.9515 + 0.733$$

  $$= 1.6845$$

- $\hat{\sigma}_P^2 = 49.118$

- $\hat{\sigma}_{Total}^2 = \hat{\sigma}_{Gage}^2 + \hat{\sigma}_P^2$

  $$= 1.6845 + 49.118$$

  $$= 50.803$$

Table 26.5   ANOVA for the gage R&R example.

Source	DF	SS	MS	F	P
Part	19	11,238.1	591.479	287.126	0.000
Operator	5	67.9	13.580	6.592	0.000
Part × operator	95	195.7	2.060	2.810	0.000
Error (repeatability)	120	88.0	0.733		
Total	239	11,589.7			

Continued

Part IV.F

Continued

Table 26.6 Gage R&R results using the ANOVA method.

Source	Variance component	% contribution
Total gage R&R	1.6850	3.32
Repeatability	0.7333	1.44
Reproducibility	0.9515	1.87
Operator	0.288	0.57
Operator × part	0.6635	1.31
Part-to-part	49.1181	96.86
Total variation	50.8031	100.00

As with the tabular method, the variance components for the gage R&R study and the percent contribution can be found using a statistical software package such as Minitab. The results are given in Table 26.6.

The slight differences between the estimates computed by hand and those provided by the software package for the ANOVA method are strictly due to round-off error. Based on the results in Table 26.6, we see again that most of the total variability is due to differences in the parts. However, the ANOVA results in Table 26.5 show that there appears to be a significant difference between operators as well as a significant interaction between operators and parts (p-values are zero for all practical purposes—see Chapter 35 for discussion of p-values). Since there is a significant interaction between part and operator, there may be evidence that more operator training is necessary.

Comparison of the Results

It is important to more fully examine and compare the results that were obtained with these two methods. The variance component estimates for both methods are repeated in Table 26.7.

The differences between the two methods are striking. The tabular method uses sample ranges to estimate the variance components while the ANOVA method uses arguably more efficient estimates based on functions of sample variances (see Chapter 35). In addition, using the tabular method the variance component for the operator-by-part interaction could not be estimated. As a result, we obtain very different estimates for reproducibility and therefore total gage R&R. From the tabular method, total gage R&R is found to be 0.8286 while for the ANOVA method it is 1.6850.

Since many of these estimates are also used in the calculation of measures such as *signal-to-noise ratios* (SNR), *precision-to-tolerance ratios* (PTR), *discrimination ratios* (DR), and *process capability ratios*, for example, it is imperative that the variance component estimates be as reliable as possible. The example provided here illustrates that the two methods could lead to different estimates. In turn,

Table 26.7 Variance component estimates for both methods.

Source	Tabular method	ANOVA method
Total gage R&R	0.8286	1.6850
Repeatability	0.5678	0.7333
Reproducibility	0.2607	0.9515
Operator	0.2607	0.2882
Operator × part	–	0.6635
Part-to-part	54.8697	49.1181
Total variation	55.6983	50.8031

it is possible that the two methods could lead to very different conclusions about the adequacy of the measurement system. As a simple illustration, one formula for the precision-to-tolerance ratio is

$$PTR = \frac{6\hat{\sigma}_{Gage}}{USL - LSL}$$

(another form uses 5.15 in place of 6). Since $\hat{\sigma}_{Gage}$ is simply the square root of our variance component for total gage variability $\hat{\sigma}_{Gage}$, we can calculate the PTR for our example using results from both the tabular method and the ANOVA method. For the tabular method, PTR is

$$PTR = \frac{6\hat{\sigma}_{Gage}}{USL - LSL} = \frac{6\left(\sqrt{0.8286}\right)}{58 - 18} = 0.137.$$

For the ANOVA method, PTR is

$$PTR = \frac{6\hat{\sigma}_{Gage}}{USL - LSL} = \frac{6\left(\sqrt{1.6850}\right)}{58 - 18} = 0.195$$

For details on PTR, SNR, and DR, see AIAG (2002), Wheeler and Lyday (1989), or Montgomery (2009b). Woodall and Borror (2008) provide a discussion of the relationships between these measures as well.

Control Charts in Gage R&R Studies

Control charts (presented in Chapter 37) play an integral role in gage R&R studies. Control charts display information about gage capability. Consider the $\bar{X}$ and R charts for the thermal performance example (displayed in Figure 26.1). The $\bar{X}$ chart shows the gage's ability to distinguish between parts. In a gage R&R study, it is desirable for the $\bar{X}$ chart to have many out-of-control points. Each point on the $\bar{X}$ chart represents the average of the two measurements taken by

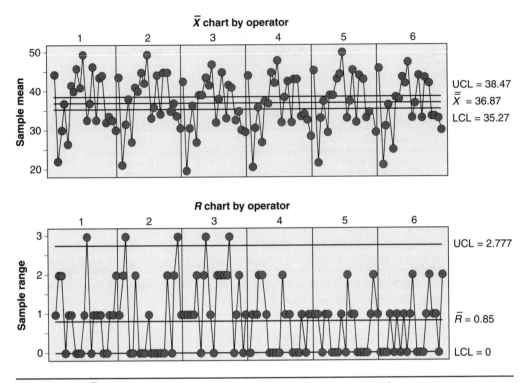

Figure 26.1 $\bar{X}$ and R control charts for the thermal performance example.

an operator on a part. Each point on the R chart represents the range between the two measurements taken by an operator on a part. There are a total of 120 samples on each chart.

The upper and lower control limits on the $\bar{X}$ control chart were determined using the average range (see Chapter 37). As a result, the $\bar{X}$ control chart reflects the within-sample variability, which is related only to gage *repeatability*. Notice that many of the points on the $\bar{X}$ control chart plot beyond the control limits (what we would usually consider evidence that our process is out of control). In a gage R&R study, this is actually desirable since it indicates that the gage is capable of discriminating between different parts. If most of the samples on this control chart plotted within the control limits, it would signify that it is difficult for the gage to clearly identify different parts. In this example, there are several points that lie within the control limits. It may be necessary to determine if these are chance occurrences or if they indicate that the gage is having difficulty discriminating between the different parts. It is not clear-cut in this example, so further investigation is most likely needed.

The R chart can provide information about special causes of variation. For example, if many of the ranges plot beyond the control limits, this could indicate problems with operator experience, training, or fatigue, which would also result in differences among operators. It is desirable for the points on the R chart to plot within the control limits. This condition signifies that the operators exhibit consistency in their use of the gage. The R chart for our example has several points outside the control limits. This is not surprising since our analysis of variance indicated that there was a significant interaction between operator and parts. Further investigation is needed.

Issues and Considerations in Gage R&R Studies

When designing a gage R&R experiment, a number of issues must be considered, such as the number of parts, the number of operators, and the number of replicates to include. There has been considerable debate about these issues. The "standard" experiment often included 10 parts, three operators, and two replicates. However, research has indicated that these recommendations may not be appropriate for many problems. Burdick and Larsen (1997) demonstrate that the lengths of confidence intervals on the variance components in a gage R&R study are significantly shortened when the number of operators is increased (see Chapter 36 for discussion on confidence intervals). They recommend at least five or six operators in a typical gage R&R study. Increasing the number of parts does not affect the confidence intervals as much as increasing the number of operators. However, it has been shown that if the practitioner has to choose between increasing the number of parts or increasing the number of replicates on each part, a greater benefit is obtained by increasing the number of parts. See the review paper by Burdick, et al. (2003) and the references within for further discussion of these issues in gage R&R experiments.

There are a number of assumptions made when using either the tabular method or the ANOVA method to carry out a gage R&R study. One such assumption involves *replication* (replication is defined and discussed in Chapters 34 and 39). In particular, it is assumed that each measurement (replicate) is made independently of one another where a unique setup or preparation of the measuring device is made before the next measurement is taken. Suppose an operator measures a part four times. If the setup of the measuring device is not changed or reset before the next measurement, then the measurements are *not* true replicates. If the measurements are taken consecutively without resetting the measuring device, then they are a type of repeated measure. The analysis to obtain the estimates of the variance components would have to be different than what has been presented here.

Another assumption related to replication is *randomization* (randomization is discussed more fully in Chapters 34 and 39). Randomization in a gage R&R study is understood to mean that the operator measures each part in random order. A part is selected at random, measured, and then the next part randomly selected and measured. The operator does not randomly select a part, take four measurements, put it back, and then select the next part. In that case, the randomization is a form of *restricted randomization* and requires estimation of repeatability and reproducibility using methods other than what has been presented previously. There are numerous applications where complete randomization or true replication is not practical or possible. In those situations, other methods would have to be employed to provide reliable estimates of the necessary variance components.

Part IV.F

Tabular Method or ANOVA Method

There are advantages and disadvantages to using either the tabular method or the ANOVA method. The tabular method is easy to carry out using ranges to estimate variance components. In addition, interpretation of the results is often intuitive for the practitioner. However, the tabular method is restricted to investigating a measurement system that involves only parts (with one operator) or parts and several operators. It does not lend itself to more complex measurement systems that may involve more than two factors (parts and operators). Furthermore, it does not adequately lend itself to dealing with systems where randomization is restricted or true replication is not possible. In general, as long as you are interested only in parts and possible operators (and not even the interaction between them), then the tabular or range method can be used—again, only if complete randomization can be guaranteed.

The ANOVA method can be more computationally intensive than the tabular method, but with modern computer software this is less of an issue. The ANOVA method is more flexible than the tabular method in that it can handle unusual experimental conditions. For example, the analysis of variance method can be used if there are more factors than just parts or operators. Suppose not only parts and operators but location on the part is also a factor to consider. In this case a *nested design* may be appropriate. The necessary variance components can be easily estimated using analysis of variance for a nested design (see Burdick, Borror, and Montgomery [2005] for details on gage R&R studies for nested designs). However, the tabular method cannot be used for this more complex experimental situation. It should also be noted that just including a third factor (not necessarily nested) and estimating variance components for the factors, all two-factor interactions, and the three-factor interaction is not possible using the tabular approach. A simple extension of the standard two-factor design can not be handled using the tabular approach.

In summary, the analysis of variance method for estimating repeatability and reproducibility is more flexible than the tabular or range method. It also uses more efficient estimates than sample ranges to obtain the necessary variance components' estimates. With modern computational capabilities, the ANOVA method is no more difficult to carry out than the range method.

For further details on gage R&R studies or measurement systems in general, please see AIAG (2002), Barrentine (2003), Borror, Montgomery, and Runger (1997), Burdick, Allen, and Larsen (2002), Burdick, Borror, and Montgomery (2003, 2005), Dolezal, Burdick, and Birch (1998), Engel and deVries (1997), Jensen (2002), Larsen (2002), Mader, Prins, and Lampe (1999), Majeske and Andrews (2002), Montgomery (2009), Montgomery and Runger (1993a, b), and Vardeman and VanValkenburg (1999).

Attribute Gage R&R Studies

Methods for assessing the capability of a quantitative measurement system as discussed in this chapter are well documented in the literature. When the measurement system involves attribute data, the standard quantitative methods are no longer appropriate. An attribute gage measurement system is appropriate when the parts or objects of interest are placed into one of two or more possible categories. The measurement of interest is the classification of the part. Several assessment statistics and approaches that deal with categorical measurements include:

1. Appraiser agreement statistics such as kappa statistics and intraclass correlation

2. The analytic method

3. Latent-class models

These three approaches can provide some measure of reproducibility or repeatability, and in some cases bias. For more details on appraiser agreement statistics, the reader is encouraged to see Banerjee, Capozzoli, McSweeney, and Sinha (1999), Bloch and Kraemer (1989), Cicchetti and Feinstein (1990), Cohen (1960), Conger (1980), de Mast and van Wieringen (2007), Feinstein and Cicchetti (1990), Fleiss (1971), and AIAG (2002). For more discussion of the analytic method or latent-class models see AIAG (2002), Agresti (1992, 1988), Agresti and Lang (1993), Banerjee, Capozzoli, McSweeney, and Sinha (1999), Boyles (2001), de Mast and van Wieringen (2004), McCaslin and Gruska (1976), Sweet, Tjokrodjojo, and Wijaya (2005), Uebersax and Grove (1990), and van Wieringen and van Heuvel (2005).

Nonmanufacturing Applications of Measurement System Analysis

In this chapter, measurement system analysis has been presented for typical manufacturing situations. There are of course numerous applications of agreement analysis in nonmanufacturing settings. Many of the kappa statistics described here originated in the medical statistics and psychometrics fields. As more quality engineers become involved in the service sector, for example, it is imperative that they understand the use of appropriate statistical methods for assessing the capability of the measurement system.

SUMMARY OF PART IV

The material in Part IV covered section IV of the ASQ Body of Knowledge (BoK) for the Certified Quality Engineer Examination (Product and Process Control). It includes the following elements:

1. Product and process control methods

2. Material control, including material identification, status, and traceability, material segregation, classification of defects, and material review board (MRB)

3. Acceptance sampling, including sampling concepts, sampling standards and plans, and sample integrity

4. Measurement and test, including measurement tools and destructive and nondestructive tests

5. Metrology

6. Measurement system analysis (MSA)

Part IV.F

Control plans are used to document and communicate the plan for monitoring and controlling the process. They summarize information from various sources into a single, handy document for quick reference on the production line. The format of the control plan is not important; standard spreadsheets are acceptable. The control plan should be checked to verify that all critical and significant characteristics identified during the design and process FMEAs are included.

Material control is an intrinsic part of quality engineering. The first step in material control always is to mark the item that must be controlled. But marking is of little value without a strong data processing system and accompanying procedures to track the items through the system. Not only individual items but also lots and sublots must be identified and kept separate. With this information in hand it is possible to efficiently conduct product recalls when necessary.

Decisions about the disposition of nonconforming material must be made in a careful and well-documented manner. Strict procedures are required to avoid reduction of outgoing quality, as well as unnecessarily wasting nonconforming materials that have some residual value. An appropriate board, such as the material review board, must be established to develop policy and to supervise the subsequent work.

Acceptance sampling has been considered one of the most widely used tools of statistical quality control. This section explored different topics in acceptance sampling, including general concepts such as lot-by-lot protection, average quality protection, producer's and consumer's risks, operating characteristic (OC) curves, definitions (AQL, LTPD, AOQ, AOQL), standard sampling schemes (ANSI/ASQ Z1.4-2003 and ANSI/ASQ Z1.9-2003) and types of acceptance sampling plans (single, double, multiple, continuous, sequential).

The general characteristics and components of the measurement process were presented. Tools and techniques for dimensional and angular measurements, surface roughness, and roundness were covered. An introduction to coordinate measuring machines and their performance also was presented, since these constitute the most advanced metrology equipment available to industry today. The section also covered different nondestructive testing techniques.

An attempt has been made to define different concepts in metrology such as calibration, traceability, and measurement errors. Metrology and measuring system terminology also was defined, such as accuracy, precision, sensitivity, and so on. A brief introduction to dimensional and geometric tolerancing also was made. Finally measurement system analysis (MSA) was presented, emphasizing gage repeatability and reproducibility (gage R&R) studies.

Part V

Continuous Improvement

Some of the most successful organizations are those in which all members believe that a part of each person's daily job is the improvement of the processes they work with. Part V describes tools and techniques for accomplishing these vital tasks. It is divided into five chapters: Quality Control Tools, which describes the seven original problem-solving tools; Quality Management and Planning Tools, which discusses what have become known as the seven new tools; Continuous Improvement Techniques, which provides an introduction to several of the broader, more systematic approaches to quality; Corrective Action; and Preventive Action.

Part V

Chapter 27

A. Quality Control Tools

> Select, construct, apply, and interpret tools such as 1) flowcharts, 2) Pareto charts, 3) cause and effect diagrams, 4) control charts, 5) check sheets, 6) scatter diagrams, and 7) histograms. (Analyze)
>
> **Body of Knowledge V.A**

Quality control tools as defined by the American Society for Quality (ASQ) and as accepted throughout the quality engineering community include:

- Flowcharts
- Pareto charts
- Cause-and-effect diagrams
- Control charts
- Check sheets
- Scatter diagrams
- Histograms

Collectively, these tools are commonly referred to as the *seven basic tools.* Kaoru Ishikawa (1985) is credited with making the following statement with respect to these tools: ". . . as much as 95 percent of all quality-related problems in the factory can be solved with seven fundamental quantitative tools."

Ishikawa's statement provides three key insights into these tools, namely that these seven tools are:

1. Applicable in problem-solving situations most commonly encountered by CQEs

2. Quantitative in nature and rely, with possibly the exception of flowcharts and cause-and-effect diagrams, on numerical data

3. Most commonly used in quality control—that is, as aids in tracking, monitoring, and analyzing data—as opposed to the planning functions associated with quality assurance

This chapter discusses six of the seven basic tools (control charts are discussed in considerable detail in Part VI). The next sections discuss six of the tools, the graphical tools, describing the purpose for each tool, information about the tool's applications and mechanics, and at least one illustration of the tool's use.

FLOWCHART

The purpose of a flowchart is to provide a graphic representation of the elements, components, or tasks associated with a process.

Applications

Flowcharts are helpful for documentation purposes and, through standardized symbols, promote a common understanding of process steps and the relationships/ dependencies among those process steps.

Flowcharts can be prepared for and used at a high level, where readers/users of the flowcharts may not be familiar with process-specific jargon or terminology. In the high-level application, flowcharts are intended to help readers/users understand what may be a complex process without providing unnecessary, and potentially confusing, detail.

Likewise, flowcharts can be prepared for and used at a detail level where readers/users have familiarity and expertise with a given process. In the detail-level application, flowcharts are intended to help readers/users perform analyses most commonly related to optimization or process improvement.

Mechanics

1. *Select a start and stop point.* A flowchart, by definition, must specify start and end points. Since it is possible to have many flowcharts describing various sections, elements, or components of a process, particularly when the process gets large and complex, start and end points for flowcharts are defined in terms of boundaries. Boundaries are naturally occurring breaks or division points that separate processes or systems at the macro level or sections, elements, or components of a process at the micro level.

2. *List major steps/tasks and decision points.* List, in sequential order, each of the major steps or tasks and decision points that occur as part of the process between the start and stop points.

3. *Use standardized graphical symbols to document the process.* Using standardized symbols, document each of the steps/tasks identified above. Placement of appropriately labeled symbols and use of arrows

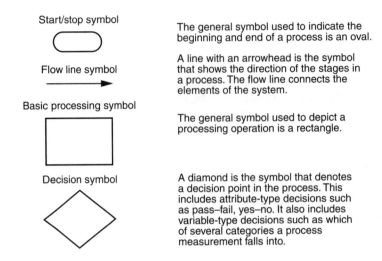

Start/stop symbol

The general symbol used to indicate the beginning and end of a process is an oval.

Flow line symbol

A line with an arrowhead is the symbol that shows the direction of the stages in a process. The flow line connects the elements of the system.

Basic processing symbol

The general symbol used to depict a processing operation is a rectangle.

Decision symbol

A diamond is the symbol that denotes a decision point in the process. This includes attribute-type decisions such as pass–fail, yes–no. It also includes variable-type decisions such as which of several categories a process measurement falls into.

Figure 27.1 Four primary flowcharting symbols.

defines the sequence of events. Four primary flowcharting symbols are depicted in Figure 27.1. While there are many symbols for flowcharting, these primary flowcharting symbols are capable of and adequate for documenting any process.

4. *Review results.* Compare the flowchart with the process to verify that the flowchart is complete and accurately describes the process. Having more than one person independently verify the flowchart is generally considered standard protocol.

Illustration

Hallock, Alper, and Karsh (2006) present a process improvement study on diagnostic testing in an outpatient healthcare facility. The purpose of the study was to determine what factors contributed to the delay of notification of test results to patients. A general flowchart for overall diagnostic testing process was presented similar to the one in Figure 27.2.

PARETO CHART

The purpose of a Pareto chart is to identify those "vital few" areas that account for the largest frequency or relative frequency in a data set and separate those vital few areas from the "trivial many."

Applications

A Pareto chart graphically depicts the "80/20 rule" originally postulated to explain economic phenomena by the Italian economist Vilfredo Pareto and later adapted for quality applications by Juran and Gryna (1980). The 80/20 rule allows

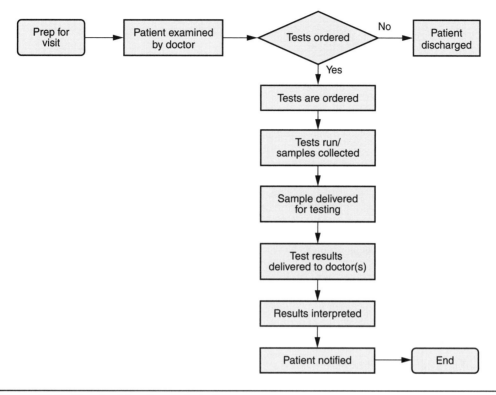

Figure 27.2 Flowchart for diagnostic testing process.

readers/users to identify and focus on the approximately 20 percent of factors (that is, columns or categories) that account for approximately 80 percent of potential problems.

Mechanics

1. *Rank order the columns or categories of data.* In a Pareto chart, columns or categories of data displayed previously as check sheets or histograms are rank ordered from the highest frequency or relative frequency on the left to the lowest frequency or relative frequency on the right.

2. *Prepare the graphic.* As the data are rearranged for display from a check sheet or histogram to a Pareto chart, the title of the chart changes, as do the column or category titles when the corresponding data are placed into different column or category locations.

3. *Calculate and place on the graphic a relative frequency line above the data columns or categories.* A relative frequency line can be calculated and placed above the data in a Pareto chart for quick assessment of the relative contribution made by each column or category.

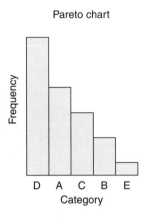

Figure 27.3 Typical Pareto chart.

Source: W. Stevenson, "Supercharging Your Pareto Analysis," *Quality Progress* (October 2000): 51–55. Used with permission.

Illustration

Figure 27.3 depicts a Pareto chart related to the specific types of problems found in the inspection of school buses (see Stevenson 2000). Each column for the tally data corresponds to an occurrence of a problem, and the columns or categories have been rank ordered as follows for the Pareto chart:

- Column D: Worn seats
- Column A: Dirty floors
- Column C: Exterior scratches
- Column B: Cracked windows
- Column E: Faulty brakes

CAUSE-AND-EFFECT DIAGRAMS

The purpose of a cause-and-effect diagram, also known as a fishbone diagram or Ishikawa diagram, is to graphically document the analysis of factors (that is, causes) that relate to a single problem or opportunity (that is, effect).

Applications

Cause-and-effect diagrams are used in problem-solving situations and in general analysis to identify factors (that is, causes) related to a problem or opportunity (that is, effect) to help the problem-solving or analysis team understand how those factors may cause the given effect, and to help the problem-solving or analysis team focus on "next steps" in process improvement.

Mechanics

1. *Select a single problem or opportunity (that is, effect).* A cause-and-effect diagram is useful for analyzing only one problem or opportunity. The problem or opportunity that is selected for analysis is documented by a keyword description or short narrative description placed in a rectangle or box, generally on the right side of the diagram. When analyzing more than one problem or opportunity, a different cause-and-effect diagram is used for each problem or opportunity.

2. *Identify the major causes of the problem or opportunity.* Cause-and-effect diagrams have been adequately described as fishbone diagrams where major causes are documented as the major bones of a fish skeleton. Major causes are generally described as they relate to people, hardware/equipment, the intended operating environment, methods, and materials. Teams should be formed to brainstorm possible causes or opportunities.

3. *Identify the minor causes associated with each major cause.* For each major cause (that is, people, hardware/equipment, environment, methods, and materials) associated with a problem or opportunity, minor causes are identified. Identification of minor causes may be graphically described as adding more structure to the fishbone skeleton. Minor causes appear graphically as "bones" attached to a major cause.

4. *Identify additional cause structure.* The analysis continues, adding detail to the fishbone structure until all causes associated with a problem or opportunity have been identified and documented. The analysis may continue until several more layers of detail have been considered and added to the diagram.

Illustration

Figure 27.4 depicts a high-level cause-and-effect diagram before detailed analysis is started. As mentioned previously, a single problem or opportunity is identified on the right side of the graphic. Major causes are normally associated with one or more of the following:

- People (personnel)
- Hardware/equipment
- Environment
- Methods
- Materials

Major causes graphically represent the major bones of a fish while minor causes represent additional structure in the diagram. Figure 27.4 generally is the starting point for a cause-and-effect analysis and, therefore, may be used as a template to help QEs begin.

Part V.A

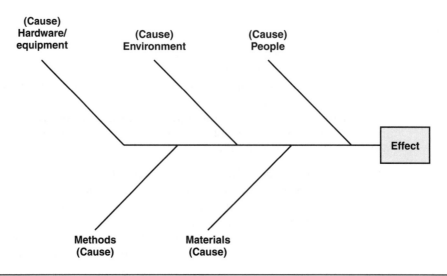

Figure 27.4 Cause-and-effect diagram/template.

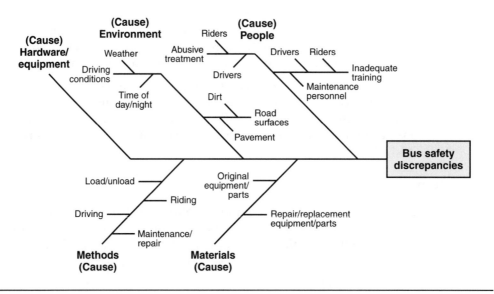

Figure 27.5 Cause-and-effect diagram: bus safety discrepancies.

Figure 27.5 illustrates a continuation of the example shown in Figure 27.4 originally conceived by Stevenson (2000).

In Figure 27.5 we see that the effect of interest is "bus safety discrepancies." We also see that the major causes of people, hardware/equipment, the intended operating environment, methods, and materials have been identified. Associated with each major cause are a series of supporting causes related to the major cause. In the major cause "environment," for example, we see that "driving conditions" is a causal factor associated with bus safety discrepancies.

Continuing with the analysis of driving conditions in the major cause of environment, we see that weather (that is, rain, snow, sleet, fog, and so on), as well as the time of day or night, can cause the effect. Road surfaces (that is, dirt or paved) also cause the effect. The analysis continues until each major cause has been investigated and enough supporting structure has been added to the diagram to identify all the causes associated with the problem or opportunity.

CHECK SHEETS

The purpose of a check sheet is to summarize, and in some cases graphically depict, a tally count of event occurrences.

Applications

A check sheet is used when readers/users are interested in counting the number of occurrences of an event, such as defects. In many instances, a check sheet will summarize count data related to certain types of defects and will provide a rough graphical representation of where in a part or process defects occur.

Mechanics

1. *Design the check sheet for a given application.* A check sheet is a tool designed for a specific application and must, therefore, include any and all information pertinent to the application. In general, the design of a check sheet should include enough administrative data to facilitate referencing and analysis. Administrative data frequently include identification of the product or process, duration of the data collection period, individuals responsible for the product or process, and individuals responsible for the data collection. A check sheet should also include space to record tally data for event occurrences, a rough graphical representation of where in the part, product, or process events occur, and a space to record remarks.

2. *Record the data.* Using the space provided to record tally data, indicate each occurrence of an event with a symbol such as an "x," check mark, circle/dot, and so on. Each event occurrence receives one mark or symbol. Check sheets also frequently identify, through a rough graphical representation, where in the part or process events occur by highlighting that portion of the rough graphical representation provided.

3. *Use the data for analysis or input to additional graphical tools.* Count data summarized on a check sheet frequently are analyzed to identify, track, or monitor defects associated with a particular area on a part or location in a process. The analysis performed on check sheet data frequently is used to trigger process improvement efforts or the data are used as input to other graphical tools, such as histograms and Pareto charts.

Part V.A

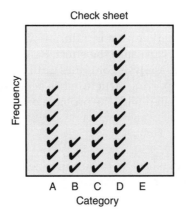

Figure 27.6 A simple check sheet.
Source: W. Stevenson, "Supercharging Your Pareto Analysis," *Quality Progress* (October 2000): 51–55. Used with permission.

Illustration

Figure 27.6 depicts tally data related to specific types of problems found during the inspection of school buses (Stevenson 2000). Each column for the tally data corresponds to an occurrence of a problem, as follows:

- Column A: Dirty floors

- Column B: Cracked windows

- Column C: Exterior scratches

- Column D: Worn seats

- Column E: Faulty brakes

There are many different types of check sheets that can be created. The user should customize the check sheet by including such information as dates, shifts, and so on, to allow for ease of interpretation. See Bothe (2001) or Montgomery (2009b) for more details.

HISTOGRAMS

The purpose of a histogram is to graphically depict the frequency of occurrence of events, where event occurrences are sorted into categories of a defined range along a continuous scale.

Applications

Histograms are helpful for displaying the distribution of event occurrences among the various columns or categories of event types. Histograms are used when it is important to see and understand how a particular set of data are distributed relative to each other, and possibly relative to a target or tolerance. The data are recorded in each column or category as they occur, and columns are not sorted by frequency.

Mechanics

1. *Determine the amount of data to be collected.* As a starting point for a histogram, it is necessary to identify approximately how much data will be collected. One data point will be collected for each event occurrence.

2. *Determine the number of columns or bins to be used.* There are many different guidelines available for determining the number of bins. For example, one recommendation is that the number of bins be approximately equal to $\sqrt{n}$, where n is the number of data points. Computer software packages use several different algorithms for determining the number of bins, including those based on Scott (1979), Freedman and Diaconis (1981), and variations of Sturges's rule (Sturges 1926).

3. *Collect and record data.* As data for a histogram are collected, they are recorded in tabular or tally form.

4. *Prepare the graphic.* To prepare the histogram for plotting data, it is necessary to provide a descriptive title for the graphic, label each axis, provide a measurement scale for each axis, label the columns, and provide a data summary.

5. *Graph the data.* Using the data summary, plot the frequency or relative frequency in each column.

It should also be noted that the histogram is often considered a large-sample graphical technique and can be unreliable for small sample sizes. Some researchers argue that the histogram should not be used for samples with less than 50 to 75 observations. For small samples, the histogram can be quite sensitive regarding the number and width of the bins chosen.

Illustration

With the increase in the use of high-strength concrete mixtures in roadway and bridge construction, quality improvement and quality assurance procedures have become an important aspect of production monitoring. Reducing the use of costly but necessary materials while maintaining a high level of quality and meeting required specifications has become increasingly important due in part to the growing demand for materials worldwide. Quality improvement tools will aid suppliers in improving the manufacturing process and reducing product variation and unnecessary waste. One important quality characteristic is the compressive strength of concrete, which is directly related to the amount of Portland cement used (there are many other variables influencing compressive strength). Figure 27.7 displays a histogram of compressive strengths for 133 samples collected for

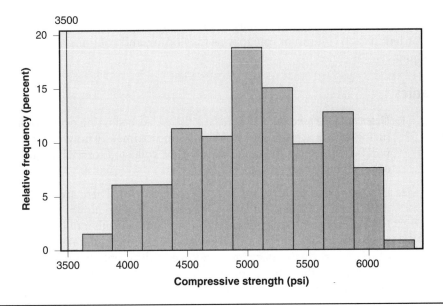

Figure 27.7 Histogram of compressive strength of concrete samples.

a particular product from one company. The minimum acceptable compressive strength in this case is 3500 psi, which is indicated on the histogram in Figure 27.7. The histogram clearly shows that quite often the strength of concrete delivered can be as much as 1500 psi to 2500 psi higher than the specified minimum. The amount of cement that could be saved by reducing the total cement content in the mixture is significant.

SCATTER DIAGRAMS

The purpose of a scatter diagram is to graphically display indications of a relation-ship between two variables.

Applications

A scatter diagram is used in the analysis of quantitative data where a QE may be interested in how a variable may perform or behave relative to another variable. The relationship being investigated is called a correlation, and Figure 27.8 identi-fies three possible relationships as positive correlation, no correlation, and nega-tive correlation. Correlation is discussed in detail in Chapter 36.

Mechanics

1. *Select two variables of interest.* The scatter diagram focuses on possible correlations between two variables. The two variables of interest should have the potential for a cause-and-effect relationship.

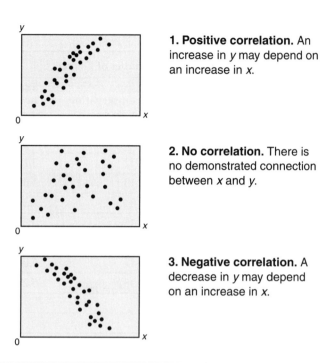

1. **Positive correlation.** An increase in *y* may depend on an increase in *x*.

2. **No correlation.** There is no demonstrated connection between *x* and *y*.

3. **Negative correlation.** A decrease in *y* may depend on an increase in *x*.

Figure 27.8   Three possible relationships identified by scatter diagrams.

2. *Set a scale for the axes.* Since one variable will be plotted on the *x*-axis while the other variable is plotted on the *y*-axis, a scale must be selected for each axis such that the data use all, or nearly all, of the scale.

3. *Collect and chart the data.* Having set up the graphic, collect and chart or plot the data in accordance with the scale specified.

4. *Evaluate the results.* Using Figure 27.8, evaluate the results to identify any relationships.

Illustration

Table 27.1 provides the data for Figure 27.9. The data provided are derived from a training analysis involving the number of hours spent in training as compared to the number of defects produced by employees who received varying amounts of training. The *x*-axis (representing training hours) documents how many hours employees spent in training. The *y*-axis (representing defects) documents tally or count data of the number of defects produced by employees who received the training.

RUN CHARTS

While run charts are not specifically identified in the QE BoK, run charts are becoming an increasingly important tool for QEs.

Part V.A

Table 27.1 Training data.

	Training Hours versus Number of Defects				
Observation	Training hours	Defects	Observation	Training hours	Defects
1	1.00	33	10	3.25	23
2	1.25	33	11	3.50	20
3	1.50	32	12	3.75	17
4	1.75	31	13	4.00	14
5	2.00	30	14	4.25	12
6	2.25	28	15	4.50	9
7	2.50	27	16	4.75	8
8	2.75	27	17	5.00	8
9	3.00	25	18	5.25	7

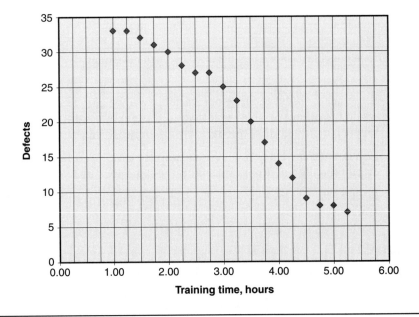

Figure 27.9 Training time versus defects.

The purpose of a run chart is to track and monitor the number of event occurrences over time.

Applications

A run chart is used to help QEs understand how a parameter or metric is behaving or performing over time. The run chart tracks and monitors a metric or parameter without regard to control limits or tolerances. In fact, it is the exclusion of control limits or tolerances that differentiates the run chart from various types of control charts.

Mechanics

1. *Select a parameter or metric of interest.* The run chart focuses on only one parameter or metric.

2. *Set a scale for the y-axis.* Once the parameter or metric has been selected, it will be graphed on the y-axis or vertical axis. A scale must, therefore, be set for the y-axis in such a manner that distributes the data throughout the scale.

3. *Identify the time intervals for the graphic.* Since the run chart displays data over time, the time frame must be meaningful for the application. Time frames such as hourly, each shift, daily, weekly, and monthly are commonly used.

4. *Collect and chart the data.* Having set up the graphic, collect and chart or plot the parameter or metric over the time intervals specified.

5. *Calculate the average.* The parameter or metric average is normally calculated for a run chart once sufficient data have been collected. A line indicating the average is plotted directly on the run chart.

Illustration

Figure 27.10 continues with an extension of the data originally introduced in Figure 27.6, considering the case of defects associated with a school bus as originally conceived by Stevenson (2000).

Stevenson originally discussed a set of data identifying 27 defects or deficiencies associated with a school bus safety inspection. It is reasonable to extend

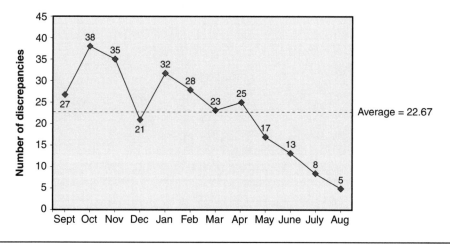

Figure 27.10   Run chart.

Stevenson's analysis by concluding that the inspection occurred at a specific time—say in September at the start of the school year.

Figure 27.10 shows that in September there were 27 defects or deficiencies recorded during a regular inspection of the school bus fleet. Since safety inspections are a regularly occurring event, it would be reasonable, interesting, and important to track and monitor the results of similar inspections as they occur monthly during the course of a school year. The results of such inspections are summarized in Figure 27.10.

Figure 27.10 indicates that safety inspections were completed each calendar month. As would be expected, the number of defects or discrepancies is higher in the beginning of the school year when the buses are used very frequently and decreases substantially later in the year when the buses are not used as frequently. The parameter of metric average in this case is 22.67 defects or discrepancies per month.

CONTROL CHARTS

As was mentioned earlier in this chapter, control charts will be thoroughly discussed in Chapter 37 of this book.

SUMMARY OF THE GRAPHICAL TOOLS

The tools discussed in this section, while helpful for quality assurance or planning, are primarily intended for quality control. In the quality control phase of production or service delivery, process optimization and improvement take over from design and development. As the transition is made from design and development to optimization and improvement, a new set of tools is needed.

Chapter 28

B. Quality Management and Planning Tools

Select, construct, apply, and interpret tools
such as 1) affinity diagrams, 2) tree diagrams,
3) process decision program charts (PDPC),
4) matrix diagrams, 5) interrelationship
digraphs, 6) prioritization matrices, and 7)
activity network diagrams. (Analyze)

Body of Knowledge V.B

The concept of quality has existed as long as people have existed. Qualities, defined as physical or nonphysical characteristics that constitute the basic nature of things, are readily accepted as part of the package that encompasses a good or a service. Shewhart (1980) captured the concept in the first part of the 20th century:

> There are two common aspects of quality, one of these has to do with the consideration of the quality of a thing as an objective reality independent of the existence of man. The other has to do with what we think, feel, or sense as a result of the objective reality—this subjective side of quality is closely linked to value.

Shewhart and others such as Deming (1986), Juran (1989), Crosby (1979), Feigenbaum (1983), Ishikawa (1985), Shingo (1986), and Taguchi (1986) have helped us understand the essence of quality and helped us bring it to the point of actionable issues. There have been, and continue to be, a number of approaches and initiatives that advocate quality as a scientific discipline. But, on the other hand, there are also many anecdotal approaches and initiatives that treat quality as an art.

Interest in tactical, in-process approaches that stress the importance of meeting substitute quality characteristics (as opposed to strategic approaches that stress true quality characteristics) helped to move the quality concept upstream from final product inspection. This evolutionary branch was eventually called *kaizen* or incremental improvement (a management-by-fact-related approach) and applied primarily in production-related processes (Imai 1986). Here, evolving practices were observed and eventually tools were identified, described, and adopted. Tools such as the seven basic tools—cause-and-effect diagram, flowcharts, check sheet, histogram, scatter diagram, Pareto analysis, and control charts—were recognized as useful.

The Japanese further expanded the quality concept in a formal sense in the late 1970s and early 1980s with what they termed the seven "new" quality tools (Mizuno 1988). This new era was based on two fundamental requirements: (1) the creation of added value over and above consumer needs, and (2) the prevention, rather than the rectification, of failure in meeting customer needs. Hence, these tools were positioned to address strategic (as opposed to tactical) quality issues. Seven tools—relations diagram, affinity diagram, systematic diagram, matrix diagram, matrix data analysis, process decision program chart (PDPC), and arrow diagram—were the result of this initiative.

In the 1990s, based on Shewhart's definition of quality, field experience/observation, and Ishikawa's (1985) concepts of true and substitute quality characteristics, Kolarik (1995) postulated a scientific framework. This framework has two major components—the experience of quality and the creation of quality: The experience of quality is a function of the fulfillment of human needs and expectations. We create quality through processes that we develop and maintain (Kolarik 1995).

The following pages describe the CQE BoK management and planning tools plus several other useful tools that help us to create quality. These pages describe, position, and illustrate a selected cross section of ten quality-related tools. The seven BoK tools are marked with an asterisk (*). The three remaining tools—process maps, process value chain diagrams, and benchmarking—are included to provide extended quality management/planning capabilities.

Affinity diagrams*

Interrelationship diagraphs*

Tree diagrams*

Process decision program charts*

Matrix diagrams*

Prioritization matrices*

Activity network diagrams*

Process maps

Process value chain diagrams

Benchmarking

These tools help to formulate and organize thoughts and ideas so that they can be leveraged directly toward quality/business improvement. More elaborate discussions of quality strategies, initiatives, and tools appear in Kolarik (1999).

AFFINITY DIAGRAMS

The purpose of an affinity diagram is to help people collect, organize, summarize, and communicate facts, opinions, and ideas.

Applications

The affinity diagram is useful when we are faced with describing, organizing, and communicating the general nature of a relatively complicated situation that can be described in terms of a large number of facts, opinions, and/or ideas. It allows us to group or cluster the facts, opinions, and/or ideas into categories with some common feature so that we can locate/classify/describe/summarize the basic issues. The affinity principle (of association and clustering) is useful in the initial stages of constructing a relationship diagram or in any situation where we desire to discover, summarize, and organize a variety of facts, opinions, and/or ideas.

Mechanics

1. *Identify a general theme.* The theme may be associated with a problem situation or an opportunity situation, or simply a situation in our physical and/or social environments.

2. *Collect facts, opinions, and ideas.* Data/information may be generated by a group of people in any number of formats. For example, we can use work teams, focus groups, groups of experts, or data/information existing in files or archives.

3. *Express and enter the data/information in a common format.* Here, we might use sticky notes on a wall, cards on a table, or computer software capable of expressing each piece of data/information in a medium that can be "moved around."

4. *Identify the groups/clusters.* Here, we identify/label/describe the groups or clusters regarding the common attribute(s) or summary characteristics that apply.

5. *Cluster the data/information pieces.* At this point we cluster or organize our data/information into cohesive groups.

6. *Repeat steps 4 and 5 to form supergroups/clusters.* It may be possible to relate two or more of the initial groups/clusters and develop a supergroup or supercluster. Supergrouping can be repeated until the facts, opinions, or ideas are suitably classified/organized.

7. *Present the results.* The final product is an organized set of facts, opinions, and ideas that make sense in terms of providing help in understanding the nature of the situation or theme from step 1.

Illustration

Figure 28.1 depicts the results of a student focus group session. The goal of the focus group was to communicate issues that were important to undergraduate students in their college program. Here we can see that a number of concerns were voiced, in no particular order, and that we have used the affinity principle to sort, organize, and isolate/label relevant issues for further action. For more

Part V.B

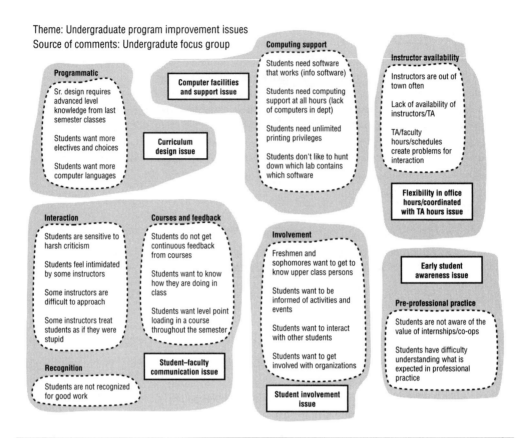

Figure 28.1 Student focus group affinity diagram.

information on affinity diagrams see Mizuno (1988), Brassard (1989), and Kolarik (1995, 1999).

INTERRELATIONSHIP DIGRAPHS

The purpose of an interrelationship digraph is to help people discover, visualize, and communicate high-level sequential and/or cause-and-effect relationships.

Applications

Constructing an interrelationship digraph is best addressed in a team environment, so as to capture a diversity of perspectives regarding sequences, effects, and causes. Typical starting points include effects or symptoms, both undesirable as well as desirable. Logical development from these effects back to potential causes is common to most relations diagramming efforts. Clustering and sequencing of causes are common to all interrelations digraphs. Boxes, circles, ovals, loops, and directional arrows are used to depict cause-to-effect flows.

In general, the interrelationship digraph helps us identify and isolate relevant causal factors concerning a situation—problem or opportunity. Ultimately it helps us understand and communicate the essence of causal or sequential relationships regarding a situation in our physical and/or social environments. It is a graphical aid in basic problem–opportunity/cause–effect discovery and relationship determination and expression, which helps us to identify and relate basic causal factors, express basic causal sequences, introduce assertions and assess or project resulting effects, and communicate critical relationships. The interrelationship digraph is one form of relationship diagram—see Brassard (1989) for details.

Mechanics

The mechanics of constructing a interrelationship diagraph generally follow the same lines as in the affinity diagram, but extend the affinity diagramming process into cause–effect and/or sequential ordering, generally indicated by arrows that connect the "boxes" or statements.

1. *Identify a general situation.* The situation may be associated with a problem or an opportunity in our physical, economic, and/or social environments.

2. *Collect facts, opinions, and ideas.* This data/information may be generated from a group of people in any number of formats. For example, we can use work teams, focus groups, or groups of experts.

3. *Express and enter the data/information in a common format.* Here, we might use sticky notes on a wall, cards on a table, or computer software capable of expressing each piece of data/information in a medium that can be "moved around."

4. *Identify the groups/clusters.* Here, we identify/label/describe the groups or clusters regarding the common attribute(s) or summary characteristics that apply and describe their relationship (as a group) to the situation at hand.

5. *Cluster the data/information pieces.* At this point, we cluster or organize our data/information into cohesive groups.

6. *Identify relations/sequences.* Once we have basic descriptions and clusters/groups, we express the relationships between these entities with arrows.

7. *Repeat steps 4, 5, and 6 to form supergroups/clusters.* It may be possible to relate two or more of the initial groups/clusters and develop a supergroup or supercluster. Supergrouping can be repeated until the facts, opinions, or ideas are suitably classified/organized. The result here is a supergroup and its description/relationship to the situation.

8. *Present the results.* The final product is an organized set of facts, opinions, and ideas that make sense in terms of providing help in understanding the nature of the situation from step 1, and summarizing the situation in a problem or opportunity format that flows logically from the facts and figures.

Part V.B

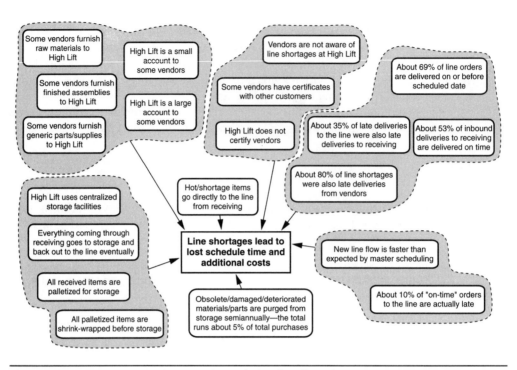

Figure 28.2   Line support subprocess interrelationship digraph.

Reproduced with permission, from W. J. Kolarik, *Creating Quality: Process Design for Results* (New York: McGraw-Hill, 1999): 450.

Illustration

The illustration in Figure 28.2 provides a relatively simple interrelationship diagraph where the situational descriptions are grouped and labeled using the affinity principle, then arrows are used to indicate convergence toward a logical, actionable conclusion. For more information on interrelationship diagraphs, see Mizuno (1988), Brassard (1989), and Kolarik (1995, 1999).

TREE DIAGRAMS

The purpose of a tree diagram is to help people discover, visualize, and communicate logical hierarchical relationships between critical events or goals/objectives and means.

Applications

Tree diagrams are useful in situations where we want to discover or define a hierarchical relationship between events—desirable or undesirable. A fault tree (FT) can be constructed to relate an undesirable "top event" or failure to a sequence of events that led to the top event. In other words, the FT depicts logical pathways from sets of basic causal events to a single undesirable result or top event. We typically use logical operators, such as AND or OR gates, to connect lower-level events with higher events. Hence, once the logic has been described, quantification can take place and risk level can be assessed.

Mechanics

Several steps are involved in the development of the FT:

1. *Identify the top event.* The top event is an undesirable event that we are motivated to prevent.

2. *Identify the next-level events.* The second-level events represent events that could lead to the top event.

3. *Develop logical relationships between the top and next-level events.* Here we use logic gates, for example, AND or OR gates, to connect the second-level events to the top event.

4. *Identify and link lower-level events.* Now, we develop the logic tree down to the lowest level desired by repeating steps 2 and 3, moving down through event sequences one level at a time.

5. *Quantify the FT (optional).* Here we develop probability of occurrence estimates for the events in the FT, and then develop a probability statement and estimate for the top event.

Illustration

Figure 28.3 presents an FT focused on unintended line shutdowns. This illustration contains OR gates that connect lower-level events with higher-level events.

A fault tree does not contain all possible failure modes or all possible fault events that could cause system failure. However, an FT is capable of considering/modeling human error, hardware and software failures, and acts of nature. It finds widespread usage in the fields of reliability, safety, and risk analysis. The FT is a more focused tool than the failure mode and effects analysis (FMEA). FMEA is sometimes used to help determine the top event in an FT. FT works well for independent events—common cause is difficult to model, especially in terms of quantification.

Other Applications

Other tree diagram formats include event trees, systematic diagrams, and goal trees, as well as concept fans. Event trees are simply tree diagrams that start with an event and work backward from the event by defining binomial response (yes or no) branches. The response branches form a hierarchy of responses that eventually lead to an outcome. A systematic diagram depicts a sequence of goals/objectives and their respective means chained together so that we can visualize our possible alternatives with respect to the accomplishment of the high-level

Part V.B

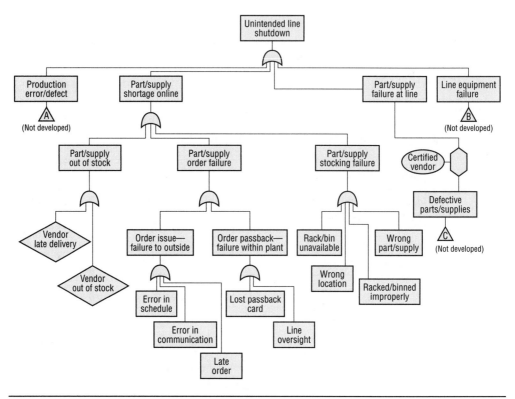

Figure 28.3 Simplified line shutdown fault tree.

Reproduced with permission, from W. J. Kolarik, *Creating Quality: Process Design for Results* (New York: McGraw-Hill, 1999): 469.

goal/objective. The goal tree is very similar to the systematic diagram in that it is built around a high-level goal that we want to accomplish. It is also similar to the FT in that it links lower-level subgoals, functions, and success trees together with logic symbols or gates that lead up to the top goal.

A concept fan is built in a tree format, but differs from the other formats significantly. The concept fan is a creativity-based tool, where we start with a purpose or functional requirement in a generic sense and expand it backward to provide alternate concepts that can accomplish the purpose or functional requirement. It is simple to construct and allows us to visualize possibilities for accomplishing our purpose early in the creative process.

Illustration

A partial goal tree is illustrated in Figure 28.4. This tree structure uses AND gates to connect goals, subgoals, and functions. Success trees are then hooked into the functions using OR gates. The essence of the goal tree is to support strategic and tactical planning by depicting paths of goal accomplishment. For more information on tree-like diagrams, see Mizuno (1988), Brassard (1989), and Kolarik (1995, 1999).

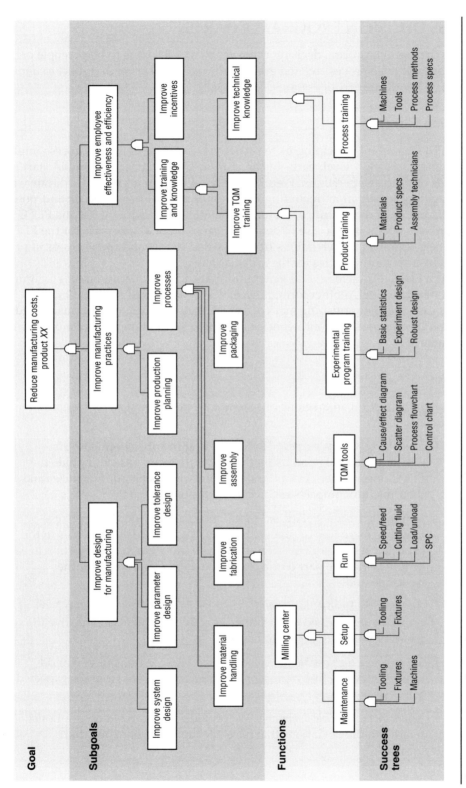

Figure 28.4   Partial manufacturing cost improvement goal tree.

Reproduced with permission, from W. J. Kolarik, *Creating Quality: Process Design for Results* (New York: McGraw-Hill, 1999): 269.

Part V.B

PROCESS DECISION PROGRAM CHARTS

The purpose of a process decision program chart (PDPC) is to help people organize and evaluate process-related events and contingencies with respect to implementation and/or early operations.

Application

The PDPC is useful in helping us to proactively evaluate or assess process implementation at a high level, early in the planning stage, or in the initial start-up phases of process operations. We may use the PDPC to argue or work our way through implementation, including events that might arise or occur and possibly disrupt our process and/or its implementation. Or we might use the PDPC to guide early operations in case of deviations from plan. The key use for the PDPC is to help us anticipate deviations from expected events and then help us to provide effective contingencies for these deviations.

The PDPC can take several general formats. One format resembles an annotated tree diagram. Another format resembles an annotated process flowchart. In either case, the distinguishing mark of a PDPC is its ability to offer the user/reader an overview of possible contingencies regarding process implementation and/or operations.

Mechanics

Although the PDPC can take one of several formats, several steps are common to all formats:

1. *Identify the process purpose.* Understanding the process purpose is critical to building and using the PDPC. This purpose will guide the PDPC development from the standpoint of possible contingencies and their resulting impacts relative to the desired outcome.

2. *Identify the basic activities and related events associated with the process.* Here, we use a tree or process flow format to place the activities in the expected sequence. This step should present a graphical depiction of activities that are part of the plan to be implemented and/or the basic operation.

3. *Annotate the basic activities and related events.* Working from step 2, we provide summarized descriptions of activities and events relative to what we normally expect to happen.

4. *Superimpose the possible (conceivable) deviations.* At this point, we add branches/events that represent identified deviations from the expected activities/events.

5. *Annotate the possible deviations.* We provide summarized descriptions relative to the deviations that have been mapped onto our chart in step 4.

6. *Identify and annotate contingency activities.* This step provides a description of the contingencies that we identify to avoid or counter the mapped deviations.

7. *Weight the possible contingencies.* At this final step, we examine the PDPC as a whole, consider the purpose, and select/mark the most appropriate contingencies. At this point we have a contingency plan—complete with our priorities for avoiding and/or dealing with possible deviations from our original implementation and/or operational plan.

Illustration

A receiving/storage/stocking subprocess is depicted in the PDPC format in Figure 28.5. This depiction provides a basic look at the existing process, with several deviations indicated: damage, shortage, salvage, expedition, and line delay. It provides a number of facts and figures. Contingency-related issues are discussed in Table 28.1 relative to possible root causes and impact. In this case, general contingencies were process improvement, process redefinition, or the status quo subprocess. For more information on PDPCs, see Mizuno (1988), Brassard (1989), and Kolarik (1995, 1999).

MATRIX DIAGRAMS

The purpose of a matrix diagram is to help people discover, visualize, and communicate relationships within a single set of factors or between two or more sets of factors.

Application

A matrix diagram typically is used to display relationships between two sets of characteristics or factors. However, it can be used to display interrelationships within one set of characteristics or factors. The typical layout is a two-dimensional matrix with the vertical dimension used to lay out one set of factors and the horizontal dimension used to lay out the other set. In the case of displaying interrelationships within one set of factors, the same factors are laid out in both the horizontal and vertical dimensions. We typically identify and document relationships within each set and between the two sets at intersection points in our graphic.

The concept of a matrix diagram is relatively simple—essentially, we develop it to help us relate sets of factors or characteristics, usually in a qualitative fashion. The actual development of a matrix diagram, however, is rather involved in terms of defining level of detail, completeness, and association. Quantification and prioritization are addressed in the Prioritization Matrices section.

In quality-related work, a primary application of the matrix diagram is to relate customer needs, demands, and expectations in the customer's language to technical characteristics of the product/process, expressed in the producer's

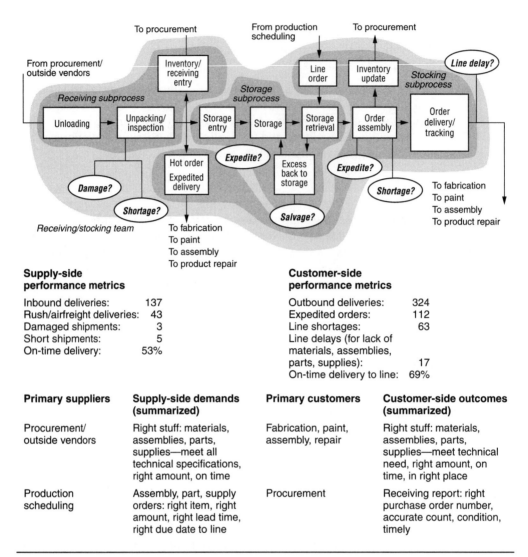

Supply-side
performance metrics

Inbound deliveries:	137
Rush/airfreight deliveries:	43
Damaged shipments:	3
Short shipments:	5
On-time delivery:	53%

Customer-side
performance metrics

Outbound deliveries:	324
Expedited orders:	112
Line shortages:	63
Line delays (for lack of materials, assemblies, parts, supplies):	17
On-time delivery to line:	69%

Primary suppliers	Supply-side demands (summarized)	Primary customers	Customer-side outcomes (summarized)
Procurement/ outside vendors	Right stuff: materials, assemblies, parts, supplies—meet all technical specifications, right amount, on time	Fabrication, paint, assembly, repair	Right stuff: materials, assemblies, parts, supplies—meet technical need, right amount, on time, in right place
Production scheduling	Assembly, part, supply orders: right item, right amount, right lead time, right due date to line	Procurement	Receiving report: right purchase order number, accurate count, condition, timely

Figure 28.5   Receiving/storage/stocking subprocesses PDPC.

Reproduced with permission, from W. J. Kolarik, *Creating Quality: Process Design for Results* (New York: McGraw-Hill, 1999): 446.

language. Figure 28.6 illustrates this particular application of a matrix diagram. This illustration contains interrelationships in the triangular appendages at the left side and the top of the matrix. Here, we use "+" and "–" symbols to represent positive and negative relationships, respectively. We use the bull's-eye, open circle, and triangle symbols to represent very strong, strong, and weak relationships between characteristics of the two sets, respectively. In this particular matrix diagram, we have included customer needs, demands, and expectations, technical definition characteristics, and competitor characteristics together.

Matrix diagrams differ in scope and detail, as well as layout format. See Mizuno (1988), Akao (1990), Day (1993), and Kolarik (1995, 1999), for details regarding the

Table 28.1 Issues, possible root causes, and general impact summary for receiving/storage/stocking PDPC.

Issue	Possible root causes	General impact
1. Our vendors are not aware of, or responsive to, our line shortage problems—why?	We do not communicate as well as we should with our vendors. Our vendors do not see High Lift as a large account. Our vendors are not capable of providing better service to us under current conditions.	More prompt deliveries from our vendors could decrease our airfreight costs and reduce our line shortages, speeding up/smoothing out our assembly subprocess. Estimated savings potential: $1.1 million per year.
2. Line flow is faster than the master schedule algorithm reflects in order issuance—why?	Our manufacturing time estimates that drive several parts of our master scheduling system were made using time estimates from our former/pre-redefinition product/production processes. Our redefined product/production processes flow better than we anticipated/estimated—provided materials, assemblies, parts, and supplies are readily available.	A lack of current reality of our present redefined processes within our scheduling algorithm is holding our production process back from realizing its full potential. Present mismatches are putting brakes on potential assembly improvement on the lines. Estimated savings potential: $1 million to $10 million per year.
3. Everything that enters receiving goes through the storage area, with the exception of "hot" items that are needed to resolve a line shortage—why?	High Lift supplies centralized storage/inventory system solutions to its customers. This concept is a part of High Lift culture and reflected in current operations. Centralized storage for all items is questionable.	Centralized storage capital as well as operational costs are running about $1.2 million per year. Material, assembly, part, and supply obsolescence costs are running at about 5% of purchased part costs or about $2 million dollars per year. Potential customers are brought in to observe the technical operations of the High Lift storage system. This demonstration is viewed as a decisive element in customers choosing High Lift. Such observation is involved with about 45% of system sales.

Reproduced with permission, from W. J. Kolarik, *Creating Quality: Process Design for Results* (New York: McGraw-Hill, 1999): 451.

Part V.B

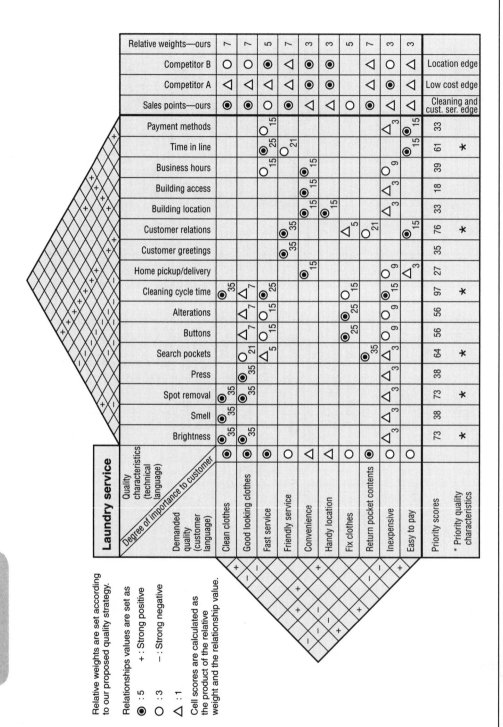

Figure 28.6 Quality function deployment matrix diagram.
Reproduced with permission, from W. J. Kolarik, *Creating Quality: Process Design for Results* (New York: McGraw-Hill, 1999): 150.

matrix diagram in general and specific quality function deployment (QFD) applications in particular.

Illustration

Figure 28.6 provides a simplified matrix diagram regarding a laundry service. Ignoring the quantification numbers in the matrix for now, we see customer demands on the left and technical quality characteristics on the top. Two interrelationship matrices appear at the left and top. Customer degrees of importance and laundry sales points appear in vertical columns. Here, critical laundry sales points include clean clothes, good-looking clothes, friendly service, and return of pocket contents. This type of matrix diagram is commonly found in QFD work.

PRIORITIZATION MATRICES

The purpose of a prioritization matrix is to help people measure/evaluate relationships from a matrix or tree analysis relative to a weighting scheme and decision criteria in order to set implementation priorities for the decisions at hand.

Application

Once we develop/identify relationships and options/alternatives such as might be developed through a relationship matrix, a relations diagram, or a tree diagram, or through some other means, we typically move into a decision mode. The prioritization matrix allows us to make relative comparisons and present our information in an organized manner so that we can support our decisions with consistent, objective, quantitative evaluation.

Prioritization typically requires two things: (1) decision criteria and (2) a means of structuring relative comparisons. Decision criteria stem from our perception of what is important. For example, economics, timeliness, physical performance, and customer service form basic categories from which to develop decision criteria. Once developed, these criteria must be assessed as to their importance within the judgment of each decision maker and collectively between decision makers. This assessment may be carried out subjectively or objectively.

In the subjective case, we as individuals draw on our past experiences and perceptions of the future and collectively use some sort of consensus/voting/ranking-based process. Methods include various types of rating/voting schemes—the Delphi method, the nominal group technique, and other methods. The matrix diagram illustration in Figure 28.6 contains two sets of rankings, one for the strength of the relationships in the body and one for the relative importance of our sales points. Together these two sets allow us to quantify the body of the matrix and develop quality characteristic scores. Hence, we can prioritize our thinking/action in terms of the more critical quality characteristics. In this case, criticality is indicated by the "*" symbol, and a total score of 60 (selected subjectively) was used as the criteria for selection.

In the objective case, we assign relative weighting values and quantitatively manipulate these values to converge to a relative priority number. Several techniques exist for objectively establishing prioritization criteria. The analytical hierarchy process (AHP) is widely described as a quantitative technique (Saaty 1982). The AHP allows a number of decision makers to integrate their priorities into a priority matrix where the decision criteria are compared as to relative importance in a pairwise fashion. The results include a decision criteria priority matrix and a corresponding alternative priority-weighted matrix. Hence, a quantitative group consensus analysis matrix emerges. From this analysis, the alternatives can be selected with the confidence that all criteria—economic, technological, and intangible factors—are integrated into the decision process. For more information on prioritization matrices, see Brassard (1989).

ACTIVITY NETWORK DIAGRAM AND ARROW DIAGRAM

The purpose of activity network diagramming is to help people sequentially define, organize, and manage a complex set of activities and events with respect to time schedule planning and implementation.

The Japanese scheduling/planning tool known as an arrow diagram is a hybrid derived from Gantt chart technology and a simplified extraction from the program evaluation research technique (PERT) and critical path method (CPM) technologies (see Kolarik [1995] and Mizuno [1988]). An arrow diagram is a network planning method that displays activities on the "arrows" as opposed to on the "nodes." An activity network diagram is a derivation of PERT, CPM, and the arrow diagram (Brassard 1989). We will describe a useful simplified version of CPM with activities on the nodes.

Application

Complex processes typically are made up from a number of activities that must be carried out in a defined sequence in order to accomplish the desired result. We use an activity/sequence list to identify and organize a set of activities as to sequence and estimated duration.

In general, each activity involved with an endeavor will be sequential, parallel, or coupled to other activities. Sequential activities require that a predecessor activity be completed before its successor can begin. Parallel activities can be undertaken and executed simultaneously. Coupled activities are executed together and hence their progression is linked together in some manner. The activity/sequence list addresses these relationships. First, each activity on the list is uniquely identified. Then, the sequence as to predecessor and successor activities is established. Finally, we estimate duration for each activity. An example activity/sequence list appears in Table 28.2.

From the activity/sequence list we construct CPM-like networks of our planned activities, allowing us to organize and display a schedule of project activities/events with regard to starting and finishing time estimates—both as a whole project and as individual activities.

In order to develop a CPM network for a project, we first identify activities and events. An activity is something that requires action of some type such as shingling a roof. An event happens at a specific time, for example, the beginning or ending point of an activity. Our critical events represent milestones—points

Table 28.2   Line support improvement process activities, sequences, and durations.

Activity description	Activity symbol	Predecessor	Duration, days
Explain change/plan to affected areas	A		2
Identify rackable/binnable items	B	A	7
Design racks/bins/storage facility modifications	C	B	21
Build/test racks/bins*	D*	C	14
Identify/inform affected vendors	E	A	4
Prepare High Lift and vendor training/certification materials	F	A	15
Gain vendors' cooperation	G	E	8
Certify/train vendors*	H*	G, F	10
Review/modify High Lift team needs	I	F	2
Train High Lift people*	J*	I	5
Modify staging facilities	K	C	12
Modify in/out facilities	L	C	14
Develop procurement scheduling/card system*	M*	F	25
Rack/bin existing bulk inventory*	N*	D, K, L	14
Stage racks/bins to line	O	N	5
Remove/salvage old storage area	P	O	20
Limited-scale operation, test/tune/mistakeproof*	Q*	H, J, M, O	30
Full-scale operations	R	Q	–

*Indicates milestone activities; milestone occurs at the end of the marked activity.

Reproduced with permission from W. J. Kolarik, *Creating Quality: Process Design for Results* (New York: McGraw-Hill, 1999): 474.

at which we reassess our progress. The activity/sequence list is a helpful tool to summarize activities, sequences, and time estimates.

Mechanics

A CPM-like network diagram is depicted in Figure 28.7. Here, we have taken the symbol, sequence, and duration information from our activity/sequence list in Table 28.2. The network flows from left to right in a time sequence. Each activity is represented by a node, that is, a circle. Within each circle we list the activity's symbol and its estimated time duration. Other information developed includes earliest start time ES, earliest completion time EC, latest start time LS, and latest completion time LC. These estimates are provided for each node/activity on the network.

The critical path is defined as the path that determines the minimum completion time for the entire project. Bold-faced arrows usually depict the critical path. If a delay occurs on any activity on the critical path, then the project duration will be increased. Hence, we watch the activities on the critical path very carefully with respect to time duration violations.

The ES and EC estimates are developed on a forward pass through the network of activities and durations. We develop the network using a start event and

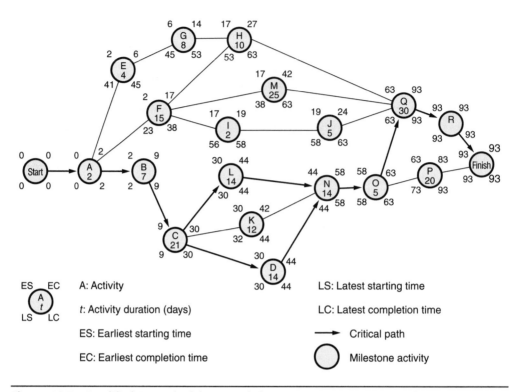

Figure 28.7 Simplified CPM schedule network–line support improvement implementation.
Reproduced with permission, from W. J. Kolarik, *Creating Quality: Process Design for Results* (New York: McGraw-Hill, 1999): 475.

a finish event. We usually start at time zero, and finish at the shortest time possible, considering our time/duration estimates. On the forward pass, we begin at the start node and develop our ES_j estimates for each node. Usually, we assume the ES_{Start} node is equal to zero. However, we could assume some positive value. Then, we develop ES_j estimates for each activity as we move from left to right (across time) through the network. Each ES_j is equal to the maximum of the EC_i estimates taken from the set of all immediate predecessor activities. Each ES_j is estimated by summing its ES_j and its duration, t_j. The EC_{Finish} node is equal to the maximum of the EC_i estimates taken from the set of all immediate predecessor activities.

The LC and LS estimates are developed on a backward pass through the network of activities. Starting at the finish node, we set the LC_{Finish} node equal to the EC_{Finish} node. We set the LS_{Finish} node equal to the LC_{Finish} node. We estimate LC_j as the minimum of the LS_i estimates taken from the set of all immediate successor activities. Each LS_j is equal to its LC_j minus its activity duration, t_j.

Tables such as Table 28.3 are constructed in order to both facilitate our network development as well as summarize our results. We usually repeat our activity descriptions, symbols, and durations. We list our ES, EC, LS, and LC estimates, which match those in our CPM network. Additionally, we include total slack, TS, and free slack, FS, estimates. In the CPM network method, we define total slack as

Table 28.3   Line support improvement scheduling details.

Activity description	Activity symbol	Duration, days	ES	EC	LS	LC	TS	FS	Critical?
Explain change/plan to affected areas	A	2	0	2	0	2	0	0	Yes
Identify rackable/binnable items	B	7	2	9	2	9	0	0	Yes
Design racks/bins/storage facility modifications	C	21	9	30	9	30	0	0	Yes
Build/test racks/bins*	D*	14	30	44	30	44	0	0	Yes
Identify/inform affected vendors	E	4	2	6	41	45	39	0	No
Prepare High Lift and vendor training/certification materials	F	15	2	17	21	36	19	0	No
Gain vendors' cooperation	G	8	6	14	45	53	39	3	No
Certify/train vendors*	H*	10	17	27	53	63	36	36	No
Review/modify High Lift team needs	I	2	17	19	56	58	39	0	No
Train High Lift people*	J*	5	19	24	58	63	39	39	No
Modify staging facilities	K	12	30	42	32	44	2	2	No
Modify in/out facilities	L	14	30	44	30	44	0	0	Yes
Develop procurement scheduling/card system*	M*	25	17	42	38	63	21	21	No
Rack/bin existing bulk inventory*	N*	14	44	58	44	58	0	0	Yes
Stage racks/bins to line	O	5	58	63	58	63	0	0	Yes
Remove/salvage old storage area	P	20	63	83	73	93	10	10	No
Limited-scale operation, test/tune/mistake-proof*	Q*	30	63	93	63	93	0	0	Yes
Full-scale operations	R		93	93	93	93	0	0	Yes

*Indicates milestone activities; milestone occurs at the end of the marked activity.

Reproduced with permission from W. J. Kolarik, *Creating Quality: Process Design for Results* (New York: McGraw-Hill, 1999): 476.

the amount of time activity j may be delayed from its earliest starting time without delaying the latest completion time of the project.

$$TS_j = LC_j - EC_j = LS_j - ES_j$$

Whenever the TS_j equals zero, we have a critical path activity.

Free slack is defined as the amount of time activity *j* may be delayed from its earliest starting time without delaying the starting time of any of its immediate successor activities:

$$FS_j = Min \{(ES_i = 1 - EC_j), (ES_i = 2 - EC_j), ..., (ES_i = \text{Last successor activity} - EC_j)\}$$

where *i* corresponds to the index for all successor activities, $i = 1, 2, ...$, last successor for activity *j*.

We can use updated CPM graphics and tables to update our plan as activities are completed. Additionally, we can project changes in subsequent activity estimates. Here we use the same basic rules that we used to develop the initial CPM network, but begin at the end of the completed event. Hence, we can generate updated ES, EC, LS, and LC estimates for the remaining activities, as well as redevelop our slack estimates. We also can determine if our critical path has changed as a result of our changes. Additional details pertaining to project planning and implementation are available in project management texts, such as Badiru and Pulat (1995).

PROCESS MAPS

The purpose of a process map is to help people discover, understand, and communicate the input-to-transformation-to-output characteristics of a process.

Application

Process flowcharts are used to map processes at any level of detail. Gross-level maps are useful in high-level planning work, while minute-level maps are useful in process control work. A flowchart depicts process flow by using a sequence of symbols and words to represent process flow components—all connected with directional line/arrows to indicate flow paths. A wide variety of processes are charted, and hence a wide variety of symbols are used. In some cases, simple box or rectangular symbols are used that are self-descriptive or annotated near the symbol. In other cases, the symbols are iconic in the sense that the symbol shape is indicative of the process element. Usually, a legend is provided to define specialized symbols. Typically, the more focused the flowchart, the more specialized the symbols.

Process mapping is performed by teams and individuals—operators, technicians, engineers, specialists, and/or managers. Diverse perspectives are gained through process mapping when an interdisciplinary team is involved with the mapping. See Kolarik (1995) for general details, Barnes (1980) for specialized charting techniques relative to classical industrial engineering, and Hughes (1995) for automatic process control–related flowcharting basics.

Mechanics

We map processes to help us understand how processes work, or how they are expected to work. Process flow mapping usually involves several steps.

1. *Establish flowchart/map purpose.* Initially, we clearly state the purpose for our charting efforts. This purpose will dictate the level of detail we need in our map.

2. *Define map boundaries.* We determine the starting and ending points for the mapping effort, relative to purpose and necessary observations.

3. *Observe process.* Next, provided the process is in operation, direct process observation/experience is necessary to develop the process map. We may also observe/map processes in other organizations through benchmarking activities.

4. *Establish gross process flow.* Here we develop/chart a process overview, depicting the production system or process in terms of major components, for example, processes or subprocesses, respectively.

5. *Develop map details.* Once we have obtained and captured the general essence of the process flow, we focus on details, cascading the level of detail down to the point where it is compatible with our purpose. Details are sequenced to represent the order/position that they occupy in the actual process.

6. *Check for validity/completeness.* Finally, we move from level to level in our maps—we examine our maps for validity and completeness. Validity checks typically involve map review as to accuracy of inputs, transformation, output, and sequence. Completeness extends to the level of detail within the target process as well as interactions with other processes.

Illustration

Figure 28.8 provides an illustration of a macro-level process map, broken out by the seven fundamental processes—market/definition, design/development,

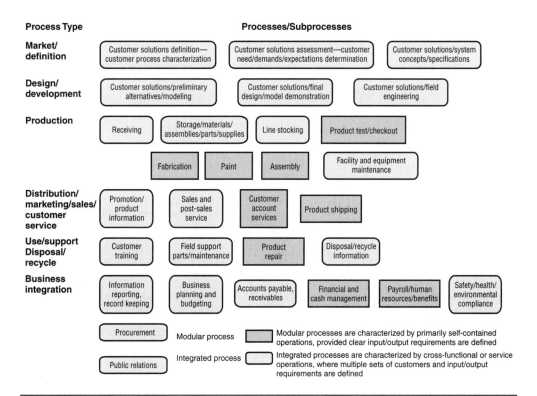

Figure 28.8 Enterprise-level process map.

Reproduced with permission, from W. J. Kolarik, *Creating Quality: Process Design for Results* (New York: McGraw-Hill, 1999): 441.

production, distribution/marketing/sales/service, use/support, disposal/recycle, and business integration. Here, we can see a global depiction of the essential processes involved in an enterprise. We can "drill down" through these fundamental processes and build more detailed process maps, sometimes resembling a PDPC in nature. Figure 28.9 provides an illustration of such a map for a visual manufacturing alternative subprocess plan. Process maps may be layered to depict a process hierarchy; see Kolarik (1999) for details.

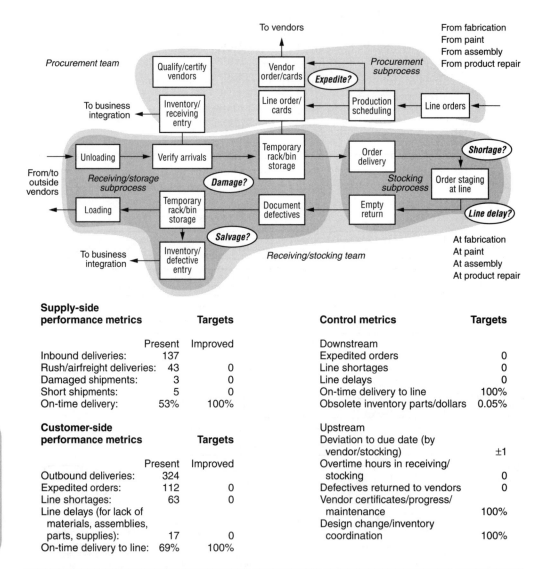

Supply-side performance metrics

	Present	Improved
Inbound deliveries:	137	
Rush/airfreight deliveries:	43	0
Damaged shipments:	3	0
Short shipments:	5	0
On-time delivery:	53%	100%

Customer-side performance metrics

	Present	Improved
Outbound deliveries:	324	
Expedited orders:	112	0
Line shortages:	63	0
Line delays (for lack of materials, assemblies, parts, supplies):	17	0
On-time delivery to line:	69%	100%

Control metrics

	Targets
Downstream	
Expedited orders	0
Line shortages	0
Line delays	0
On-time delivery to line	100%
Obsolete inventory parts/dollars	0.05%
Upstream	
Deviation to due date (by vendor/stocking)	±1
Overtime hours in receiving/ stocking	0
Defectives returned to vendors	0
Vendor certificates/progress/ maintenance	100%
Design change/inventory coordination	100%

Figure 28.9   Visual alternative–improved subprocess map/PDPC.

Reproduced with permission, from W. J. Kolarik, *Creating Quality: Process Design for Results* (New York: McGraw-Hill, 1999): 468.

PROCESS VALUE CHAIN (PVC) DIAGRAMS

The purpose of a value chain diagram is to help people depict and understand a sequence of cause-to-effect and effect-to-cause relationships between business results and outcomes and basic physical, economic, and social variables.

Application

PVC analysis links basic physical and social variables with business results so that value-added process sequences are clearly depicted. This linkage is not precise because each basic variable has its own natural/technical units of measure, for example, length, pressure, volume, or composition, while process/business results are expressed in their own units or unitless ratios, for example, production units, percent conformance, scrap rate, efficiency, cost, revenue, profit, and return on investment. Hence, PVCs have discontinuities where unitary incompatibility presents gaps and challenges. The point is to link variables related to specific process decisions and process control points to business results and vice versa as best we can. Hence, understanding as to cause–effect and time lags in moving from cause to effect become more obvious for all concerned, for example, operators, engineers, and managers.

The PVC diagram connects the business world to the technical world through a logical, sequential linkage that cascades up and down all processes and their respective subprocesses. PVC diagrams are useful for operators to see how operational decisions in the technical world ultimately impact business results. They are useful for managers/leaders to clearly see that business targets are met through a sequence of operational decisions. An efficient and effective PVC adds value to products throughout the chain.

Illustration

A generic PVC is depicted in Figure 28.10. Across the top we see basic business outputs on the right-hand side and basic inputs in the form of controlled and uncontrolled variables on the left-hand side. Transformations in the form of processes and subprocesses are depicted in the middle. The oval cycle on the bottom half of the figure shows that we develop a PVC working from one of several starting points—we may start somewhere in our outputs, the business results, and work toward inputs, the basic variables. Or, we may start somewhere in our input variables and work toward our business outputs. The focus is to understand how the processes work, and how they impact the business objectives. See Kolarik (1999) for more details regarding PVC.

VALUE STREAM MAPPING

A *value stream map* is similar to a flowchart, but includes additional information about various activities that occur at each step of the process. *Value stream mapping* (VSM) is a powerful tool based on the principles of lean and used to identify opportunities for improvement of a process and track performance. *Current-state* value stream maps provide information about the process as it is currently defined. *Future-state* value stream maps provide information about the process

Part V.B

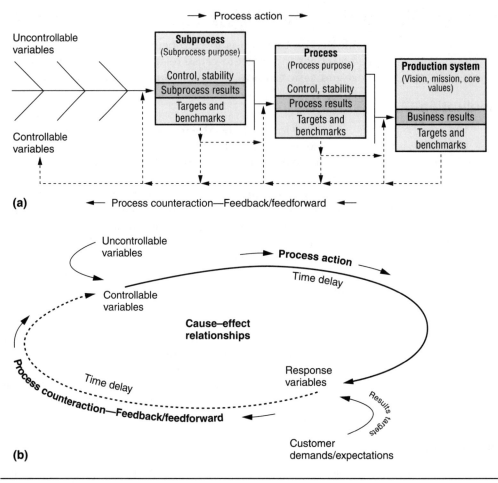

Figure 28.10   Generic production system process value chain diagram. (a) Analytical view.
(b) General systems view.

Reproduced with permission, from W. J. Kolarik, *Creating Quality: Process Design for Results* (New York: McGraw-Hill, 1999): 54.

as it could look once it has been redefined. Figure 28.11 displays a generic value stream map for a manufacturing process. Symbols used for a value stream map vary somewhat in the literature, but detailed examples can be found in Manos (2006) and Montgomery (2009b).

SIPOC DIAGRAMS

SIPOC is an acronym for:

- *Suppliers.* Those who provide inputs to the process including materials, resources, services, information, and so on.

- *Inputs.* Materials, services, resources, information, and so on.

- *Process.* Process description and listing of all key process steps.

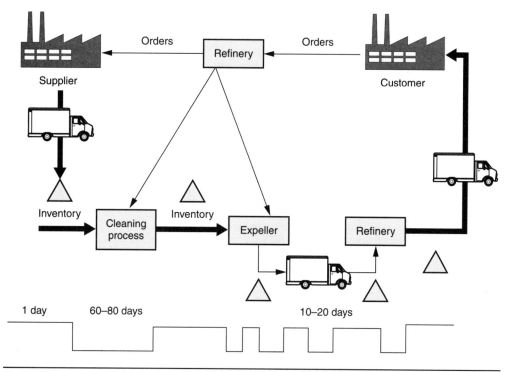

Figure 28.11   Value stream map for a manufacturing process.

- *Outputs.* Products, information, services, and so on.

- *Customers.* Those who receive the outputs. Customers may be internal or external.

The SIPOC diagram is a high-level process map used to identify the important aspects of the current process such as the process outputs and customers in order to capture the *voice of the customer.* It is a useful tool in the early stages of the DMAIC process to determine the *critical-to-quality* factors (see Chapter 29 for discussion of the DMAIC methodology). Figure 28.12 displays a simple SIPOC diagram for the process used to report and investigate work-related injuries at a manufacturing firm.

BENCHMARKING

The purpose of benchmarking is to help people learn from the work of others—seek out, study, and emulate the best practices associated with high performance/results—so as to enhance or better their own performance.

Application

We have a tendency to perceive our organization as the "best" through rather subjective arguments, for example, exhortations of various types. In reality, our perceptions may not be accurate. We may lack insight as to what is happening around us—what others are doing and the results they obtain. In essence, we lack

Part V.B

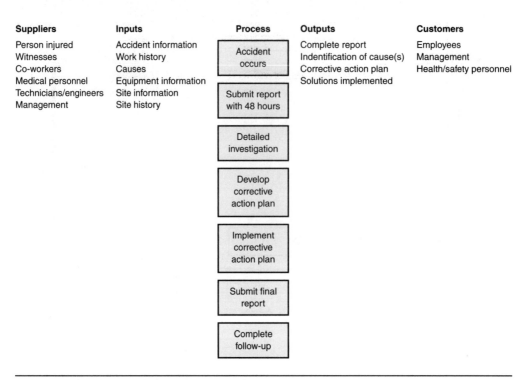

Suppliers	Inputs	Process	Outputs	Customers
Person injured	Accident information	Accident occurs	Complete report	Employees
Witnesses	Work history		Indentification of cause(s)	Management
Co-workers	Causes		Corrective action plan	Health/safety personnel
Medical personnel	Equipment information		Solutions implemented	
Technicians/engineers	Site information	Submit report with 48 hours		
Management	Site history			
		Detailed investigation		
		Develop corrective action plan		
		Implement corrective action plan		
		Submit final report		
		Complete follow-up		

Figure 28.12 SIPOC diagram for work–related injuries.

outside standards/benchmarks from which to judge our own performance. Benchmarking helps us to gain an awareness of shortfalls in our own performance, as well as to plan and implement countermeasures to enhance our performance.

Informal benchmarking is a matter of natural curiosity and always has been practiced; however, formal benchmarking was positioned as an organizational initiative at Xerox. Kerns and Nadler (1992) defined benchmarking as:

> . . . *the continuous process of measuring products, services, and practices against the toughest competitor or those companies recognized as industry leaders.*

Camp (1989, 1995) defines benchmarking as:

> . . . *the search for and implementation of best practices.*

Benchmarking encompasses four aspects: (1) analyze the operation, (2) know the competition and industry leaders, (3) incorporate the best of the best, and (4) gain superiority. The formal scope of benchmarking includes products, processes, and performance metrics.

Camp cites four types of benchmarking: internal, competitive, functional, and generic. Internal benchmarking focuses on best practices within our own organization. Competitive benchmarking provides a comparison between direct competitors. Functional benchmarking refers to comparisons of methods across organizations executing the same basic functions outside our industry. Generic process benchmarking focuses on innovative work processes in general, wherever they occur.

Benchmarking, which was also discussed in Part I, is a broad initiative. Watson (1993) describes the evolution of benchmarking in terms of generations. He cites reverse engineering as the first generation. Here we see essentially a rote copying strategy. The second generation is termed competitive benchmarking, which focuses on direct competitors. As the third generation he cites process benchmarking, where processes common to different industries are assessed for best practices. The fourth generation is termed strategic benchmarking. Here, the focus is on the strategies that a competitor or noncompetitor uses to guide their organization. The fourth level is used to feed process reengineering initiatives. A futuristic fifth level is cited as global benchmarking. Here, the focus is international in scope and deals with trade, cultural, and business process distinctions among companies. In all cases, the driving force is "profit-oriented," as addressed through three parameters: (1) quality beyond that of competitors, (2) technology before that of competitors, and (3) costs below those of competitors.

The benchmarking initiative focuses on two basic issues: (1) best practices, and (2) metrics or measurement. We recognize performance gaps and address them with improvement plans. Management commitment, communication, and employee participation are all critical elements in a benchmarking initiative. For more information on benchmarking, see Camp (1989, 1995), Kolarik (1995, 1999), and Watson (1993).

Mechanics

1. *Preplan the benchmarking initiative.* Assess and understand customer needs and the business results/outcomes desired.

2. *Plan and execute the initiative.* Identify comparative organizations and what is to be benchmarked. Determine data collection methods and collect data.

3. *Analyze the data and information collected.* Determine the current performance gap. Project future performance levels/goals into the future.

4. *Integrate the information into actionable issues.* Communicate the findings and gain acceptance within your organization. Establish functional goals that are actionable.

5. *Prepare for action and act.* Develop action plans, implement specific actions, monitor progress, and recalibrate the benchmarks.

6. *Gain maturity in benchmarking.* Attain a leadership position and integrate benchmarking practices into processes.

Benchmarking clearly is an invaluable asset in quality improvement work. It provides a perspective of how things are done within other organizations and leads to the identification of best practices and encourages the adoption of the same. However, a best practice today will undoubtedly be eclipsed by a better practice in the near future.

In many cases, we inject creative elements within/beyond current practices. These extensions require creative thinking or *breakthrough thinking*. Breakthrough

Part V.B

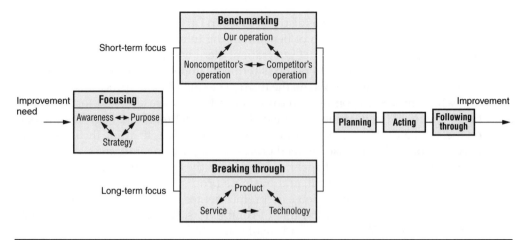

Figure 28.13 Benchmarking and breakthrough thinking.

Reproduced with permission, from W. J. Kolarik, *Creating Quality: Process Design for Results* (New York: McGraw-Hill, 1999): 164.

thinking typically is approached very differently from benchmarking. Here, we are encouraged to think "out of the box," as opposed to thinking "in the box" (for example, finding an existing best practice). Creative thinking is the only tool available that allows us to move beyond best practices.

Creativity has received considerable attention in quality improvement work (Kolarik 1995, 1999). Nadler and Hibino (1994) proposed seven principles of breakthrough thinking: (1) the uniqueness principle, (2) the purposes principle, (3) the solution-after-next principle, (4) the systems principle, (5) the limited information collection principle, (6) the people design principle, and (7) the betterment timeline principle. DeBono (1992) encourages the use of *hats* in creative thinking: the white hat—data and information, the red hat—feelings, intuition, hunches, and emotions, the black hat—pessimistic perspective, the yellow hat—optimistic perspective, the green hat—creative effort, and the blue hat—thinking process control.

Figure 28.13 depicts an overview of the integration of breakthrough thinking into a benchmarking model. From this depiction, we can see that breaking through focuses on the essence of the product, technologies (relative to both products and process), and services. The long-term focus of breakthrough thinking tends to complement the shorter-term focus of benchmarking, yielding a broad view of improvement efforts.

SUMMARY OF QUALITY MANAGEMENT AND PLANNING TOOLS

The concept of quality and our basic understanding of it have expanded and matured over the years to the point at which we now understand and appreciate the customers' role in defining the essence of quality in every product. We now see our role (as leaders, managers, engineers, and operators) as creators of quality. Hence, the process approach to creating quality has become dominant.

Part V.B

A number of quality-related initiatives and tools have been generated and touted over the past several decades. Their names come and go, but the fundamental issues of understanding and responding to our physical, social, and economic environments in terms of customer needs and expectations remain. In summary, initiatives and tools that are both effective and efficient in helping us to discover, explore, understand, plan, and act in the best interest of customers and stakeholders will always be useful.

Part V.B

Chapter 29

C. Continuous Improvement Techniques

Define, describe, and distinguish between
various continuous improvement models:
total quality management (TQM), kaizen,
plan–do–check–act (PDCA), Six Sigma,
theory of constraints (TOC), lean, etc.
(Analyze)

Body of Knowledge V.C

Quality improvement is achieved by continuously improving the production and business processes of an organization (Besterfield 1999). It is optimized by:

- Viewing all work as a process, whether it is associated with production or business activities

- Making all processes effective, efficient, and adaptable

- Anticipating changing customer needs

- Controlling in-process performance using metrics such as scrap and cycle time, and monitoring tools such as control charts

- Maintaining constructive dissatisfaction with the present level of performance

- Eliminating waste and rework wherever it occurs

- Investigating activities that do not add value to the product or service, with the aim of eliminating those activities

- Eliminating nonconformities in all phases of everyone's work, even if the increment of improvement is small

- Using benchmarking to improve competitive advantage

- Innovating to achieve breakthroughs

- Holding gains so there is no regression

- Incorporating lessons learned into future activities

- Using technical tools such as statistical process control (SPC), experimental design, benchmarking, quality function deployment (QFD), and so on

Continuous process improvement is designed to utilize the resources of the organization to achieve a quality-driven culture. Individuals must think, act, and speak quality. An organization attempts to reach a single-minded link between quality and work execution by educating its constituents to continuously analyze and improve their own work, the processes, and their work group (Langdon 1994).

Process improvement achieves the greatest results when it operates within the framework of the problem-solving method. In the initial stages of a program, quick results are frequently obtained because the solution is obvious or an individual has a brilliant idea.

There are a number of models for quality improvement. We will discuss total quality management (TQM), kaizen, PDSA (sometimes known as PDCA), reengineering, Six Sigma, theory of constraints (TOC), and the lean enterprise model.

TOTAL QUALITY MANAGEMENT (TQM)

This term, originally used at the Naval Air Systems Command, encompasses the following ideas:

- *Customer focus.* The customer determines whether a product or service is good enough.

- *Employee empowerment.* All employees must understand that continuous improvement is a part of everyone's job.

- *Leadership.* Upper management must provide the impetus and motivation for the quality programs.

This model, properly implemented, often results in an enterprise that is more productive and more competitive. Customer loyalty will improve and stakeholder value will increase.

KAIZEN

Kaizen is a Japanese word for the philosophy that defines management's role in continuously encouraging and implementing small improvements involving everyone. It is a method of continuous improvement in small increments that makes processes more efficient, effective, under control, and adaptable. Improvements are usually accomplished at little or no expense without sophisticated techniques or expensive equipment. Kaizen focuses on simplification by breaking down complex processes into their subprocesses and then improving them.

The kaizen improvement focuses on the use of:

1. Value-added and non-value-added work activities.

2. Muda, which refers to the seven classes of waste—overproduction, delay, transportation, processing, inventory, wasted motion, and defective parts.

3. Principles of motion study.

4. Principles of materials handling.

5. Documentation of standard operating procedures.

6. The five S's for workplace organization, which are five Japanese words that mean proper arrangement (seiko), orderliness (seiton), personal cleanliness (seiketso), cleanup (seiso), and discipline (shitsuke). Various authors have translated them slightly differently. The National Institute for Standards and Technology (NIST) through the Manufacturing Extension Partnership uses sort, set in order, shine, standardize, and sustain.

7. Visual management by means of (visual) displays that everyone in the plant can use for better communications.

8. Just-in-time principles to produce only the right units in the right quantities, at the right time, and with the right resources.

9. Poka-yoke to prevent or detect errors.

10. Team dynamics, which include problem solving, communication skills, and conflict resolution (Gee, McGrath, and Izadi 1996).

Kaizen relies heavily on a culture that encourages suggestions by operators who continually try to incrementally improve their job or process. An example of a kaizen-type improvement would be the change in color of a welding booth from black to white to improve operator visibility. This change results in a small improvement in weld quality and a substantial improvement in operator satisfaction. The PDSA cycle, described next, may be used to help implement kaizen concepts.

PDSA OR PDCA

The basic plan–do–study–act (PDSA) cycle, sometimes known as the plan–do–check–act (PDCA) cycle, was developed by Shewhart and is an effective improvement technique. It is sometimes called the Shewhart cycle or the Deming cycle. Figure 29.1 illustrates the cycle.

The four steps in the cycle are exactly as stated. First, plan carefully what is to be done. Next, carry out the plan (do it). Third, study the results—did the plan work as intended or were the results unexpected? Finally, act on the results by identifying what worked as planned and what did not. Using the knowledge learned, develop an improved plan and repeat the cycle. The PDSA cycle is a simple adaptation of the more elaborate problem-solving method discussed in the next section.

REENGINEERING

According to Hammer and Champy (1993), reengineering is the fundamental rethinking and radical redesign of business processes to achieve dramatic improvements in critical measures of performance. Many practitioners believe that quality improvement is associated only with incremental improvements. Nothing could

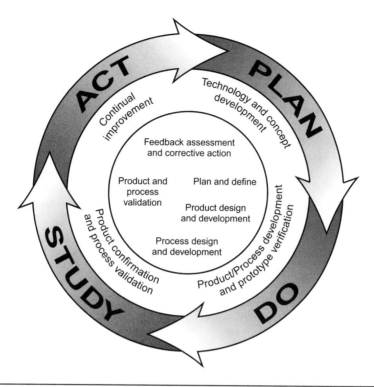

Figure 29.1 Basic plan–do–study–act cycle.

be further from the truth—for many years the Malcolm Baldrige National Quality Award has defined continuous improvement as referring to both incremental and "breakthrough" improvement. The Japanese have not only relied on kaizen but have developed policy management (hoshin kanri) and policy deployment (hoshin tenkai) in large part to produce the kind of large-scale breakthroughs that Hammer and Champy promote. Nor is this concept uniquely Japanese. Joseph Juran had a long-standing emphasis on breakthrough efforts aimed at achieving unprecedented levels of performance. Clearly there is nothing new in the reengineering concept—it has always been part of the total quality management (TQM) umbrella.

SIX SIGMA

According to Senge (1990), most organizations die before they reach the age of 40. Companies are embracing Six Sigma not only to reduce defects but also as a catalyst to change the culture of their company and impact how employees engage in their everyday work.

Utilizing a Six Sigma business strategy, organizations can understand threats and recognize new opportunities for growth, not only to survive but to actually thrive within competitive environments.

Part V.C

Quality practitioners often note that the tools of Six Sigma are not unique. It is true that most Six Sigma techniques are familiar; however, the power of properly integrating them as a total system is new. Six Sigma creates a road map for changing data into knowledge, resulting in process-focused change and bottom-line benefits for organizations. Not all organizations have achieved success with Six Sigma, which depends on the successful integration of two components: strategy and metrics.

The strategy of Six Sigma relates to how the methodology (tools and techniques) is integrated into an organization through key projects, yielding substantial benefits to an organization's bottom line. Companies experiencing success with Six Sigma have created an effective infrastructure for selecting, supporting, and executing projects. These projects are focused on achieving strategic business goals, as well as addressing the voice of the customer.

The success of Six Sigma also depends on the wise application of metrics. Unfortunately, much confusion exists relative to the metrics of Six Sigma. There is no "one size fits all" metric applicable to every project. Effective metrics are cross-functional, providing a holistic view of the process and contributing insight to the project team. A lot of resources are wasted if Six Sigma metrics are not applied wisely and subsequently used to orchestrate improvement activities. "Fire prevention" is preferred to "firefighting."

This section details the two components previously mentioned, as well as other important aspects of a successful Six Sigma implementation, including the following:

- Six Sigma needs assessment

- Six Sigma as a business strategy

- Implementing Six Sigma

- The metrics of Six Sigma

- Sustaining and communicating change

Six Sigma Needs Assessment

Organizations often become overwhelmed with day-to-day activities and lose sight of what needs to be done to make process-focused improvements or reengineering changes in order to survive the "long haul." Individuals within organizations might be aware of Six Sigma and think that the techniques could be useful to reduce the amount of firefighting activities that occur; however, they may have trouble determining where it applies and where the benefits are achievable. This type of organization requires a simple and quick approach to make a Six Sigma needs assessment.

For this situation, we suggest that people within the organization respond to the Six Sigma Needs Checklist shown in Table 29.1. Upon completion of this survey, the additional question can then be asked, "How much money are the affirmative responses costing the business annually?" An improvement opportunity often can be accurately quantified if the amount is initially determined as a percentage of the gross revenue of the organization.

Table 29.1   Six Sigma needs checklist.

Six Sigma needs checklist	Answer yes or no
Do you have multiple "fix-it" projects in a critical process area that seem to have limited or lasting impact?	
Are you aware of a problem that management or employees are encountering?	
Are you aware of any problem that a customer is having with the products/services your organization offers?	
Do you believe that primary customers might take their business elsewhere?	
Is the quality from competitive products/services better?	
Are your cycle times too long in certain process areas?	
Are your costs too high in certain process areas?	
Do you have concerns that you might be "downsized" from your organization?	
Do you have a persistent problem that you have attempted to fix in the past with limited success?	
Do you have regulatory/compliance problems?	

Source: F. W. Breyfogle III, J. M. Cupello, and B. Meadows, *Managing Six Sigma* (John Wiley & Sons, 2000). Adapted by permission of John Wiley & Sons, Inc.

Monetary estimates from this survey could be considered the perceived "cost of doing nothing" within the organization. That is, the cost to the business of not "doing Six Sigma." When this survey is conducted during a meeting of informed individuals, an even more accurate estimate for this cost can be obtained. We suggest that during this meeting, individuals describe the logic used for their vote. Consensus might then be achieved for an overall monetary estimate for the group. When consensus does not seem possible, an average of the responses can give a very good estimate.

Estimated projected benefits from Six Sigma could then be approximated as 25 percent to 50 percent of the projected monetary "cost of doing nothing." Experience has shown that full-time Six Sigma Black Belts can save on the average of $500,000–$1,000,000 annually, depending on:

- Executive-level support
- Process focus area (that is, some areas have more room for improvement than others)
- Team motivation
- Six Sigma Black Belt (that is, Six Sigma practitioner) proficiency

Six Sigma As a Business Strategy

A question we frequently hear from executives is, "How does Six Sigma fit with other corporate initiatives?" Six Sigma should not be considered just another initiative but should integrate other programs (for example, lean manufacturing and kaizen) at a higher level as part of an overall business strategy. Six Sigma should not replace other initiatives but instead create an infrastructure that offers a tactical approach to determine the best solution for a given process/situation.

Successful implementation should be viewed as an ongoing process of infusing the Six Sigma methodology into the way your employees approach their everyday work. It requires a proactive view and the commitment to evolve into a more process-oriented culture and reduce the amount of daily firefighting on strategic processes. The implementation process requires up-front work to develop awareness and generate buy-in before projects are selected. This process often displays unique characteristics in each organization; however, there are two essential elements needed for success: executive leadership and customer focus.

To date, companies achieving significant results with Six Sigma have the commitment of their executive management. Executive leadership is the foundation of any successful Six Sigma business strategy. Upper managers need to develop an infrastructure to support the changes that implementing Six Sigma will create, not only to strategic business processes but also, as previously discussed, to the culture of the organization. Past quality programs resulted in varying success because they typically did not have an infrastructure that supported change.

The results received from a Six Sigma business strategy are highly dependent on how well leaders understand the value of wise implementation of the methodology and sincerely promote it within their organization. An executive retreat can help identify true champions that will promote change and can also prioritize the actions necessary to establishing a road map to successful implementation. Through discussion and the careful planning of the process of successfully implementing Six Sigma, employees will have an easier journey to success in applying the methodology to their projects.

Establishing a customer focus mind-set within an organization goes hand in hand with creating a successful Six Sigma business strategy. The factors that are critical to your customers' success are necessary to a process improvement team's true success. Therefore, evaluating customers' perception of quality should be at the forefront of the implementation process.

Every complaint from a customer should be viewed as an opportunity for growth and increased market share—a spotlight on areas needing process improvement focus. The key to success in this initial step is to make it easy for your customers' comments to be heard. Various methods exist to obtain this valuable input, including:

- Walking the customer process
- Performing customer surveys
- Conducting personal interviews with key customers
- Establishing feedback/complaint systems
- Developing customer panels

Depending on the size of your organization and its core values, the word "customer" can take on many different definitions. When collecting feedback, care should be taken to maintain a comprehensive view of your customers. By combining external feedback with such things as internal business strategies, employee needs, and government regulations, your organization will obtain a balanced list of customer needs.

Through customer feedback, learning about what works and what does not will help to establish a mind-set of continual process improvement within your organization. Jack Welch, former CEO of GE and the most visible advocate of Six Sigma, has been quoted as saying that a business strategy alone will not generate higher quality throughout an organization.

Implementing Six Sigma

As discussed previously, Six Sigma can be a great success or failure, depending on how it is implemented. Implementation strategies can vary significantly between organizations, depending on their distinct culture and strategic business goals. After completing a needs assessment and deciding to implement Six Sigma, an organization has two basic options:

- Implement a Six Sigma program or initiative
- Create a Six Sigma infrastructure

Option 1: Implement a Six Sigma Program or Initiative. The traditional approach to deploying statistical tools within an organization has not been very effective. With this approach, certain employees (practitioners) are taught the statistical tools from time to time and asked to apply a tool on the job when needed. The practitioners might then consult a statistician if they need help. Successes within an organization might occur; however, these successes do not build upon each other to encourage additional and better use of the tools and overall methodology.

When organizations implement Six Sigma as a program or initiative, it often appears that they only have added, in an unstructured fashion, a few new tools to their toolbox through training classes. A possible extension of this approach is to apply the tools as needed to assigned projects. However, the selection, management, and execution of projects are not typically an integral part of the organization. These projects, which often are created at a low level within the organization, do not have the blessing of upper management; hence, resistance is often encountered when the best solution directly affects another group that does not have buy-in to the project. In addition, there typically is no one assigned to champion projects across organizational boundaries and facilitate change.

A program or initiative does not usually create an infrastructure that leads to bottom-line benefits through projects tied to the strategic goals of the organization. As a program or initiative, Six Sigma risks becoming the "flavor of the month" and will not capture the buy-in necessary to reap a large return on the investment in training. With this approach, employees may end up viewing Six Sigma as a program similar to total quality management (TQM) and other quality programs that may have experienced only limited success within their organization.

Even if great accomplishments occur through the individual use of statistical tools within organizations, there is often a lack of visibility of the benefits to upper management. A typical missing element for success with this approach is management buy-in. Because of this lack of visibility, practitioners often have to fight for funds and may be eliminated whenever the times get rough financially. Effective use of statistical tools often does not get recognized and the overall company culture is not affected. For true success, executive-level support is needed that asks the right questions and leads to the wise application of statistical tools and other Six Sigma methodologies across organizational boundaries.

Option 2: Create a Six Sigma Infrastructure. Instead of focusing on the individual tools, it is best when Six Sigma training provides a process-oriented approach that teaches practitioners a methodology to select the right tool, at the right time, for a predefined project. Training of Six Sigma practitioners (Black Belts) utilizing this approach typically consists of four weeks of training over four months, where students work on their projects during the three weeks between training sessions.

Deploying Six Sigma as a business strategy through projects instead of tools is the more effective way to benefit from the time and money invested in Six Sigma training. Consider the following benefits of Six Sigma deployment via projects that have executive management support:

- Offers bigger impact through projects tied to bottom-line results

- Utilizes the tools in a more focused and productive way

- Provides a process/strategy for project management that can be studied and improved

- Increases communications between management and practitioners via project presentations

- Facilitates the detailed understanding of critical business processes

- Gives employees and management views of how statistical tools can be of significant value to organizations

- Allows Black Belts to receive feedback on their project approach during training

- Deploys Six Sigma with a closed-loop approach, creating time for auditing and incorporating lessons learned into an overall business strategy

A project-based approach relies heavily on a sound project selection process. Projects should be selected that meet the goals of an organization's business strategy. Six Sigma can then be utilized as a road map to effectively meet those goals. Once strategic projects are selected, many practitioners (Black Belts) have found a "21-step integration of tools" road map helpful in developing a plan for specific projects.

Initially, companies might have projects that are too large or perhaps are not chosen because of their strategic impact to the bottom line. Frustration with the first set of projects can be vital experience that motivates improvement in the second phase. Six Sigma is a long-term commitment. Treating deployment as a process allows objective analysis of all aspects of the process, including project selection and scoping. Utilizing lessons learned and incorporating them into subsequent waves of an implementation plan creates a closed feedback loop and real opportunities for improvement. Deploying Six Sigma through projects can lead to dramatic bottom-line benefits if the organization invests the time and executive energy necessary to implement Six Sigma as a business strategy!

The Metrics of Six Sigma

Much confusion exists relative to the metrics of Six Sigma. The sigma level (that is, sigma–quality level) sometimes used as a measurement within a Six Sigma program includes a $\pm 1.5\sigma$ value to account for "typical" shifts and drifts of the mean, where σ is the standard deviation of the process. This sigma–quality level relationship is not linear. In other words, a percentage unit improvement in parts per million (ppm) defect rate (or defect per million opportunity [dpmo] rate) does not equate to the same percentage improvement in the sigma–quality level.

Figure 29.2 shows the sigma–quality level associated with various services (considering the 1.5σ shift of the mean). From this figure, we note that the sigma–quality level of most services is about four sigma, while "world class" is considered six.

Figures 29.3, 29.4, and 29.5 illustrate various aspects of a normal distribution as it applies to Six Sigma program measures and the implication of the 1.5σ shift. Figure 29.3 illustrates the basic measurement concept of Six Sigma, where parts are to be manufactured consistently and well within their specification range. Figure 29.4 shows the number of parts per million (ppm) that would be outside the specification limits if the data were centered within these limits and had various standard deviations. Figure 29.5 extends Figure 29.3 to noncentral data relative to specification limits, where the mean of the data is shifted by 1.5σ. Figure 29.6 shows

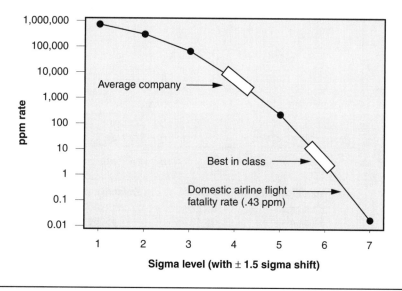

Figure 29.2   Implication of sigma–quality level. Parts per million (ppm) rate for part or process step, considers a 1.5σ shift of the mean where only 3.4 ppm fail to meet specifications at a six sigma quality level.

Source: F. W. Breyfogle III, *Implementing Six Sigma* (John Wiley & Sons, 1994). Adapted by permission of John Wiley & Sons, Inc.

Part V.C

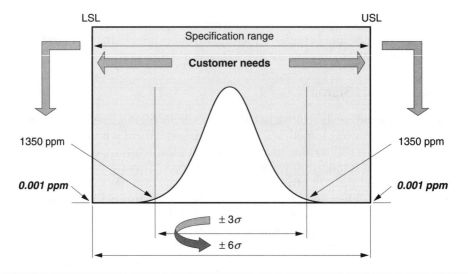

Figure 29.3 Normal distribution curve illustrates three sigma and six sigma parametric conformance.

Copyright of Motorola, used with permission.

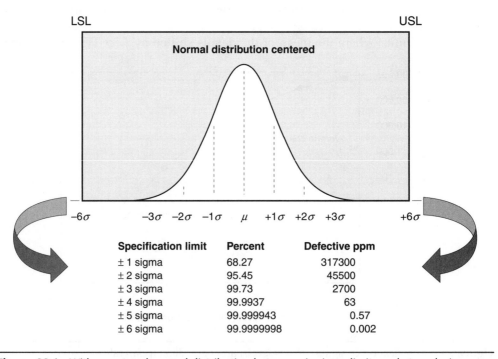

Specification limit	Percent	Defective ppm
± 1 sigma	68.27	317300
± 2 sigma	95.45	45500
± 3 sigma	99.73	2700
± 4 sigma	99.9937	63
± 5 sigma	99.999943	0.57
± 6 sigma	99.9999998	0.002

Figure 29.4 With a centered normal distribution between six sigma limits, only two devices per billion fail to meet the specification target.

Copyright of Motorola, used with permission.

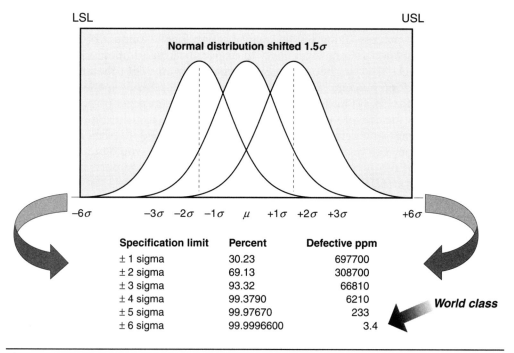

Figure 29.5   Effects of a 1.5σ shift where only 3.4 ppm fail to meet specifications.
Copyright of Motorola, used with permission.

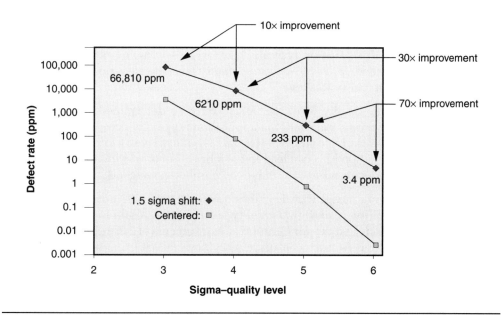

Figure 29.6   Defect rates (ppm) versus sigma–quality level.
Source: F. W. Breyfogle III, *Implementing Six Sigma* (John Wiley & Sons, 1994). Adapted by permission of John Wiley & Sons, Inc.

Part V.C

the relationship of ppm defect rates versus sigma–quality level for a centered and 1.5σ shifted process, along with a quantification for the amount of improvement needed to change a sigma level. Refer to Appendix E for additional Z-values.

To achieve this basic goal of a Six Sigma program might then be to produce at least 99.99966 percent "quality" at the "process step" and part level within an assembly (that is, no more than 3.4 defects per million parts or process steps if the process mean were to shift by as much as 1.5σ). If, for example, there was on the average one defect for an assembly that contained 40 parts and four process steps, practitioners might consider that the assembly would be at a four sigma quality level from Figure 29.6, since the number of defects in parts per million is: $(1 \div 160)(10^6) = 6250$.

Problems that can occur using the sigma–quality level metric include:

• The improvement from 4.1 to 4.2 sigma–quality level is not the same as improvement from 5.1 to 5.2 sigma–quality level.

• Determining the number of opportunities for any given process can be dramatically different between individuals.

• A sigma–quality level metric can be deceiving. For example, one process might have a 50 percent defective unit rate and a sigma–quality level much greater than six, while another process might have a 0.01 percent defective unit rate and have a sigma–quality level much worse than six. To illustrate this, first consider the counting of opportunities for failure within a computer chip as junctions and "components." The sigma–quality level metric for this situation typically leads to a very large number of opportunities for failure for a given computer chip; hence, a very high sigma–quality level is possible even when the defective rate per unit is high. Compare this situation to another situation where there are only a very small number of components or steps required for a process. The sigma–quality level metric for this situation typically leads to a very low number of opportunities for failure; hence, a very low sigma–quality level metric is possible even when the defective rate per unit is low.

• The sigma–quality level metric can only be determined when there are specifications. Service/transactional applications typically do not have specifications like manufacturing does. When a sigma–quality level is forced on a service/transactional situation, this can lead to the fabrication of specifications and alterations of these "specifications" to "make the numbers look good."

Another Six Sigma metric that describes how well a process meets requirements is process capability. A six sigma–quality level process is said to translate to process capability index values for C_p and C_{pk} requirements of 2.0 and 1.5 respectively. Unfortunately, there is much confusion with these values, even though the following basic equations for these metrics are simple:

$$C_p = \frac{USL - LSL}{6\sigma}$$

$$C_{pk} = \min\left(\frac{USL - \mu}{3\sigma}, \frac{\mu - LSL}{3\sigma}\right)$$

where USL is the upper specification limit, LSL is the lower specification limit, and σ is standard deviation. Computer programs often will not even give the same answer for a given set of data. Some programs consider the standard deviation to be short-term, while others consider standard deviation to be long-term. There are many ways to estimate standard deviation. Breyfogle (1999) describes eight different approaches. Process capability indices are discussed in Chapter 38.

It is best not to force a sigma–quality metric on the various groups and/or projects within an organization. It is most important to use the right metric for any given situation. However, we believe that the sigma–quality level metric should be included, along with the other Six Sigma metrics, in all Six Sigma training. The positive, negative, and controversial aspects of each Six Sigma metric should be covered within the training so that organizations can more effectively communicate with their customers and suppliers. Often, customers and suppliers ask the wrong questions relative to Six Sigma and other metrics. When people understand the pluses and minuses of each metric, then they can work with their customers and/or suppliers to direct their efforts toward the best metric for a given situation, rather than reacting to issues that result from mandated metrics that make no sense.

The training people receive in Six Sigma should lead them to the right metric for a given situation. As depicted in Figure 29.7, in addition to devising a business strategy, organizations wanting success with Six Sigma must be able to understand, select, and communicate Six Sigma metrics, including: sigma-quality levels, C_p, C_{pk}, P_p, and P_{pk}, rolled throughput yield (RTY*), defects per million opportunities (dpmo), cost of poor quality (COPQ), and "30,000-foot level" control charts.

---

* Technical note: Calculation of rolled throughput yield.

Reworks within an operation comprise what is termed the "hidden factory." Rolled throughput yield measurements can give visibility to process steps that have high defect rates and/or rework needs. One way to find rolled throughput yield is: First determine yield for all process operations. Multiply these process operation yields together. A cumulative throughput yield up through a process step can be determined by multiplying the yield of the current step by the yields of previous steps.

Rolled throughput yield (YRT or RTY) can be calculated from the number of defects per unit (DPU) using the relationship:

$$Y_{RT} = e^{-DPU}$$

To understand this relationship, consider that the probability of observing exactly *x* events in the Poisson situation is given by the Poisson probability density function (PDF):

$$P(X = x) = \frac{e^{-\lambda}\lambda^x}{x!} = \frac{e^{-np}(np)^x}{x!} \qquad x = 0,1,2,3\ldots$$

where *e* is a constant approximately equal to 2.71828, *x* is the number of occurrences, and λ can equate to a sample size multiplied by the probability of occurrence (that is, *np*). It then follows that

$$Y_{RT} = P(X = 0) = e^{-\lambda} = e^{\frac{-D}{U}} = e^{-DPU},$$

where *D* is defects, *U* is unit, and *DPU* is defects per unit.

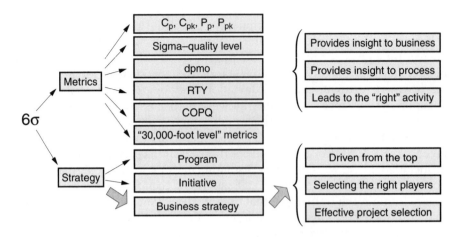

Figure 29.7 Six Sigma metrics and implementation strategy.

Care must be taken that the training an organization receives in Six Sigma metrics is not "sugar coated" or avoided. In addition to the careful selection of metrics, Six Sigma training also should address the effective use of statistical methodologies, providing insight into how one can best determine what truly is causing a problem.

SUSTAINING AND COMMUNICATING CHANGE

Many companies attempt to improve products with numerous small changes or "tweaks" to their current processes; however, changes frequently are not documented and the associated results not reported. Substantial results are rarely obtained with this half-hearted method of change. When employees in this type of corporate culture hear of a new initiative such as Six Sigma, they wonder what will be different.

In today's constantly changing marketplace, companies that are able to embrace change in a focused and proactive manner are leaders in their field. Companies who not only master the technical side of Six Sigma but also overcome the cultural challenges associated with change can realize significant bottom-line benefits.

Launching a Six Sigma business strategy is an excellent opportunity to assess current culture in an organization. Consider the following questions:

- How has your company historically dealt with change initiatives?

- Does your company often make changes that do not last?

- How effective are your project teams?

- Are you frequently focusing on the same problem?

- How do your employees attack problems and conduct their daily work?

- What is required within your company culture to make continual process improvement a lasting change?

- What will prevent your company from achieving success with Six Sigma?

By evaluating the key cultural drivers and restraints to embracing Six Sigma, organizations can develop plans that enhance the key drivers and mitigate the critical restraints.

A common key driver of sustaining Six Sigma change that is often overlooked is communication plans. Company leaders usually implement Six Sigma because they possess a clear vision of what their company can achieve. Frequently, however, they do not realize the power behind effectively communicating this vision throughout the corporation. Executives need to get everyone engaged and speaking the language of Six Sigma. A shared vision of how Six Sigma fits the strategic needs of the business should be created. A communication plan should be carefully considered and executed with enthusiasm. If successful, it will be your biggest ally in key stakeholder buy-in.

Creating and implementing Six Sigma does not guarantee tangible benefits within an organization. However, when Six Sigma is implemented wisely as a business strategy accompanied by effective metrics, as illustrated in Figure 29.7, organizations can yield significant bottom-line benefits. Through the wise implementation of Six Sigma, the successes of individual projects can build upon each other, gaining the sustained attention of executive management and resulting in a corporate culture change from a reactive or firefighting environment to a learning organization.

THE DMAIC PROCESS

DMAIC is a data-driven quality strategy used to improve processes. It is an integral part of a Six Sigma initiative, but in general can be implemented as a stand-alone quality improvement procedure or as part of other process improvement initiatives such as lean. DMAIC is an acronym for the five phases that make up the process. Briefly, the phases are

- *Define* the problem, improvement activity, opportunity for improvement, the project goals, and customer (internal and external) requirements.

- *Measure* process performance.

- *Analyze* the process to determine root causes of variation, poor performance (defects).

- *Improve* process performance by addressing and eliminating the root causes.

- *Control* the improved process and future process performance.

The DMAIC process easily lends itself to the project approach to quality improvement encouraged and promoted by Juran. There are many tools used at each step of the process, most of which are described in this handbook. The reader is encouraged to consult additional resources for detailed discussion of the DMAIC process, Six Sigma quality initiatives, and the numerous tools used. See, for example, the ASQ Web site at www.asq.org, Britz and Emerling (2000), Hahn, Doganaksoy,

Part V.C

and Stanard (2001), Hoerl (2001), Hoerl and Snee (2002), Snee and Hoerl (2007), Montgomery (2009b), and the numerous references within these sources.

THEORY OF CONSTRAINTS

Theory of constraints is a problem-solving methodology that focuses on the weakest link in a chain of processes. Usually the constraint is the process that is slowest. Flow rate through the system can not increase unless the rate at the constraint increases. Theory of constraints lists five steps to system improvement:

1. *Identify.* Find the process that limits the effectiveness of the system. If throughput is the concern then the constraint often will have work in process (WIP) awaiting action.

2. *Exploit.* Use kaizen or other methods to improve the rate of the constraining process.

3. *Subordinate.* Adjust (or subordinate) the rates of other processes in the chain to match that of the constraint.

4. *Elevate.* If the system rate needs further improvement, the constraint may require extensive revision (or elevation). This could mean investment in additional equipment or new technology.

5. *Repeat.* If these steps have improved the process to the point where it is no longer the constraint, the system rate can be further improved by repeating these steps with the new constraint.

The strength of the theory of constraints is that it employs a systems approach, emphasizing that improvements to individual processes will not improve the rate of the system unless they improve the constraining process.

LEAN ENTERPRISE

Achieving what is known as a lean enterprise requires a change in attitudes, procedures, processes, and systems. It is necessary to "zoom out" and look at the flow of information, knowledge, and material throughout the organization. In any organization there are multiple paths through which products, documents, and ideas flow. The process of applying lean thinking to such a path can be divided into the following steps:

1. *Produce a value stream map (VSM).* This is also referred to as a value chain diagram. This diagram is described in detail by Rother and Shook (1999). It has boxes labeled with each step in the process. Information about timing and inventory is provided near each process box. Figure 29.8 shows an example of a value stream map. Some symbols that are used on value stream maps include:

 = inventory—originally a tombstone shape indicating dead material.

 = supermarket where employees can pick needed parts. Supermarkets are usually replenished by stockroom staff.

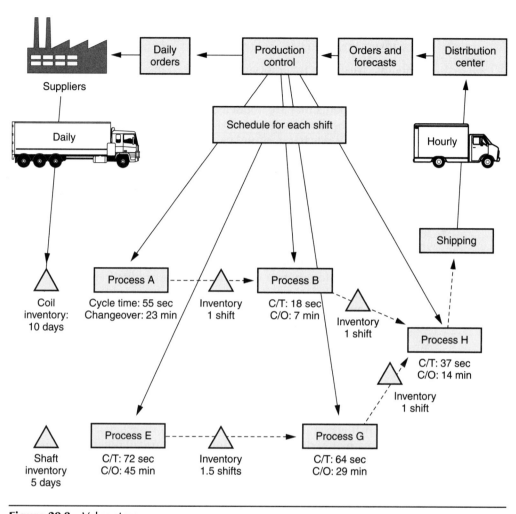

Figure 29.8 Value stream map.

Y = Kanban post where cards or other visual signals are displayed.

👓 = visual signal used to make stocking decisions.

⎍⎍ = graph of value-added versus non-value-added times.

2. *Analyze all inventory notations with an eye toward reduction or elimination.* Inventory tends to increase costs because:

• Storage space may be expensive (rubber awaiting use in a tire factory is stored at 120°F; wood inventory may need to have humidity control).

• Quality may deteriorate (rust, spoilage, and so on)

- Design changes may be delayed as they work their way through the inventory.

- Money invested in inventory could be used more productively elsewhere.

- Quality problems that are not detected until a later stage in the process will be more expensive to correct if an inventory of defective products has accumulated.

One company refers to its racks of safety stock as the "wall of shame."

3. *Analyze the entire value stream for unneeded steps.* These steps are called non-value-added activities.

4. *Determine how the flow is driven.* Strive to move toward value streams in which production decisions are based on the pull of customer demand. In a process where pull-based flow has reached perfection, a customer order for an item would trigger the production of all the component parts for that item. These components would arrive, be assembled, and delivered in a time interval that would satisfy the customer. In many situations this ideal has not been reached and the customer order will be filled from finished goods inventory. The order will, however, trigger activities back through the value chain that produce a replacement part in finished goods inventory before it is needed by a customer.

5. *Extend the value stream map upstream into suppliers' plants.* New challenges occur regarding compatibility of communication systems. The flow of information, material, knowledge, and money are all potential targets for lean improvements.

When beginning the process, pick a narrow focus—do not try to boil the ocean as the saying goes.

Continuous Flow Manufacturing

The traditional manufacturing strategy is to study the marketplace to obtain a forecast of sales of various products. This forecast is used as a basis for orders that are issued to suppliers and to departments responsible for fabrication and assembly. This is referred to as a *push system*. One major problem with this strategy is that if the forecast is imperfect, products are produced that are not wanted by customers and/or products that customers want are not available. A second major problem with the forecast-based strategy is the increasing expectation of customers for exactly the product they want exactly when they want it. These two problems have led to a response by manufacturers that is sometimes called *mass customization*. As illustrated by the automotive industry, a customer order of a vehicle with choices among dozens of options with perhaps hundreds of possible combinations can not be accurately forecast. Instead, the customer order initiates the authorization to build the product. This is referred to as a "pull" system because the pull of the customer instead of the push of the forecast activates the system.

Rather than producing batches of identical products, a pull-oriented organization produces a mix of products with the mix of features that customers order. In the ideal pull system, the receipt of the customer order initiates orders for the component parts to be delivered to the assembly line at scheduled times. The mixture of features of the components as they continuously flow to and through the line result in exactly the product the customer needs. Making this happen in a reasonable amount of time would have been unthinkable only a few years ago.

When a pull system is in a state of perfection, each activity moves a component through the value stream so that it arrives at the next activity at the time it is needed. Achieving and maintaining this may require a great deal of flexibility in allocating resources to various activities. Cross-training of personnel is essential. The resulting flexibility and system nimbleness permits reduction of WIP.

Non-Value-Added Activities

Some functions perform activities that do not change the form or function of the product or service. The customer is not willing to pay for these activities. These activities are labeled non-value-added. A classic example is rework. The customer expects to pay for the printing of a document, for instance, but does not want to pay for corrections caused by supplier error. A key step in making an organization more lean is the detection and elimination of non-value-added activities.

In searching for non-value-added activities the operative guideline should be "question everything." Steps that are assumed to be necessary are often rife with opportunities for improvement. Team members not associated with a process will often provide a fresh eye and ask the impertinent questions.

Some authors list seven or eight categories of waste or *muda* as it is referred to in some sources. These lists usually include overproduction, excess motion, waiting, inventory, excess movement of material, defect correction, excess processing, and lost creativity. The following paragraphs examine the causes and results of each of these wastes.

Overproduction is defined as making more than is needed or making it earlier or faster than is needed by the next process. The principal symptom of overproduction is excess work in process (WIP). Companies adopt overproduction for various reasons including long setup times, unbalanced workload, and a just-in-case philosophy. One company maintains a six-month supply of a particular small part because the machine that produces it is unreliable. In some cases accounting methods have dictated that machines overproduce to amortize their capital costs. All WIP should be continuously scrutinized for possible reduction or elimination.

Excess motion can be caused by poor workplace layout including awkward positioning of supplies and equipment. This results in ergonomic problems, time wasted searching for or moving supplies or equipment, and often in reduced quality levels. "Kaizen events" have been effectively used to focus a small short-term team on improvements in a particular work area. The team must include personnel with experience at the positions involved as well as those with similar functions elsewhere. In addition it is essential to include people with the authority to make decisions. Such teams have made startling changes in two to five days of intense activity.

Waiting typically is caused by such events as delayed shipments, long setup time, or missing people. This results in waste of resources and perhaps more importantly demoralization of personnel. Setup time reduction efforts and total productive maintenance are partial answers to this problem. Cross-training of personnel so that they can be effectively moved to other positions is also helpful in some cases. Most important, of course, is carefully laid and executed scheduling.

Inventory is wasteful when inventories of raw materials, finished goods, or work in process are maintained, costs are incurred for environmental control, record keeping, storage and retrieval, and so on. These functions add no value to the customer. Of course some inventory may be necessary, but if a competitor finds ways to reduce costs by reducing inventory, business may be lost. One of the most tempting times to let inventory levels rise is when a business cycle is in the economic recovery phase. Instead of increasing inventories based on forecasts, the proper strategy is to synchronize production to increase with actual demand. Similarly, production or administrative functions that use more space or other resources than necessary increase costs without adding value. The overused analogy of the sea of inventory shown in Figure 29.9 illustrates how excess inven-

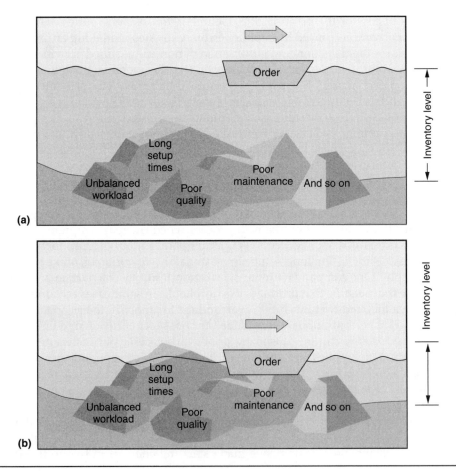

Figure 29.9 A sea of inventory often hides unresolved problems.

tory makes it possible to avoid solving other problems. As the level of inventory is lowered, some problems will rear their ugly heads and need to be solved before further progress is possible.

Excess movement of material as indicated by large conveyor systems, huge fleets of fork lifts, and so on, makes production more costly and complex, often reducing quality through handling and storing. Poor plant layout is usually to blame. Plants with function-oriented departments (such as all lathes together and all presses together) require excessive material movement. A better plan is to gather equipment together that is used for one product or product family. This may mean having a manufacturing cell contain several types of equipment requiring personnel with multiple skills. Many companies have had success with cells that form a C shape as shown in Figure 29.10 because they can be staffed in several ways. If demand for the cell's output is high, six people could be assigned there, one per machine. If demand is very low, one person could move from machine to machine producing parts one at a time.

Defect correction is non-value-added because the effort required to fix the defective part is wasted. Typical causes of defects are poor equipment maintenance, poor quality system, poor training and/or work instructions, and poor product design. Lean thinking demands a vigorous look at these and other causes in order to continuously reduce defect levels.

Excess processing is often difficult to recognize. Sometimes entire steps in the value chain are non-value-added. A steel stamping operation produces a large volume of parts before they are scheduled for painting, which may cause the practice of dipping parts in an oil solution to prevent rust as they wait to be painted. As the paint schedule permits, the parts are degreased and painted. The customer is unwilling to pay for the dip/degrease activities because they do not enhance the product. The best solution in this case is to schedule the pre-paint activities so that the parts are painted immediately upon production. This solution may require smaller batch sizes and improved communication procedures, among

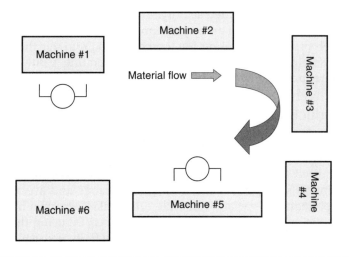

Figure 29.10   C-shaped manufacturing cell.

other things. The purpose of the grinding step that often follows a welding operation is to remove some of the weld imperfections. Improving the welding process may reduce or eliminate the need for grinding. In this case, the unnecessary grinding would be classified as excessive processing. Excessive processing can occur in the office as well as on the plant floor. Information from customer purchase orders (POs) is sometimes entered into a database and the order itself is filed as a backup hard copy to resolve any later disagreements. A recent study by one company revealed the fact that the hard copies—although they are occasionally pulled from files and initialed, stamped, stapled, and so on—really serve no useful purpose. The company now discards the PO once the information has been entered. The processes of filing, storing, and maintaining these records required one-half person performing non-value-added activity.

Lost creativity is perhaps the most unfortunate waste. Most manufacturing employees have ideas that would improve processes if implemented. Standard organizational structures sometimes seem designed to suppress such ideas. Union/management divides seem almost impossible to bridge. Lean thinking recognizes the need to involve employees in teams that welcome and reward their input. These teams must be empowered to make changes in an atmosphere that accepts mistakes as learning experiences. The resulting improved morale and reduced personnel turnover impact the bottom line in ways that no accountant has calculated.

There are, of course, gray areas where the line between valued-added and non-value-added may not be obvious. One such area is inspection and testing. A process may be so incapable that its output needs to be inspected to prevent defective parts from entering downstream processes. It could be argued that this inspection is a value-added activity because the customer does not want defective products. The obvious solution is to work on the process, making it capable and rendering the inspection activity unnecessary. Most authorities would agree that this inspection is non-value-added. On the other hand, a gas furnace manufacturer must fire test every furnace in order to comply with Canadian Standards Association (CSA) requirements. Customers are willing to pay for the CSA listing, so this test step is a value-added activity.

Studies have shown that an overwhelming percent of lead time is non-value-added, much of it spent waiting for the next step. Yet over the years efforts to decrease lead time often have focused on accelerating value-added functions rather than reducing or eliminating non-value-added functions.

Cycle Time Reduction

Another aspect of the value chain that should be studied is the cycle time. Cycle time is displayed below each process in Figure 29.8. It is defined as the amount of time required to complete the named activity for one product or service. If the cycle time is variable it is useful to show a range and average on the value stream map. Reducing variation in cycle time makes a system more predictable. Sometimes the cycle time variation can be reduced by using the cycle times of sub-activities instead. For example, suppose the activity consists of using a word processor to modify a standard bid form. Sub-activities might include inserting client information, listing proposed budget, detailing alternatives, and so on. The total time to prepare the bid might vary a great deal while the time required to accomplish each sub-activity should show less variation. The activities performed should be continuously studied in an effort to eliminate non-value-added components and find better and faster ways to complete the value-added components. Techniques that have been successfully applied to accomplish these goals are variously called kaizen methods, kaizen blitz, rapid continuous improvement (RCI), and similar names. The usual procedure is to form a small team that is given a process to improve and a limited time frame, often only a few days. The team should include the people who perform the targeted activity, outsiders who can provide a fresh perspective, as well as people who are authorized to approve changes. The team observes the process and raises questions about its various parts. Typical questions might include:

- Why is that stored there? Is there a better place to put it?

- Why do things in that order?

- Would a different table height work better?

- Could your supplier (internal or external) provide a better service? Does your supplier know what you need?

- Are you providing your customer, whether internal or external, with the best possible services?

- Do you know what your customer needs?

- Should parts of this activity be performed by the customer or the supplier?

- Are there steps that can be eliminated?

- Is there enough light, fresh air, and so on, to do the job efficiently?

- Would another tool, software package, or other material be more helpful?

- Are tools conveniently and consistently stored?

- Can the distance the person and/or product moves be reduced?

- Should this activity be moved closer to the supplier or customer?

- How many of these items should be kept on hand?

- Would it help to do this activity in less space?

In other words, the team questions everything about the process and its environment. Kaizen activity usually results in making several small improvements. In many situations the team actually implements a change and studies the result before making a recommendation.

Cycle time must not be confused with takt time. Takt time is determined by customer demand. Its formula is

$$\text{Takt time} = (\text{time available}) \div (\text{units required})$$

Part V.C

For example if 284 units are to be produced in a shift consisting of 27,000 seconds, then

$$\text{Takt time} = 27{,}000 \div 284 \cong 95 \text{ seconds.}$$

That is, the system must average one unit every 95 seconds. To meet this demand rate, the cycle time for each process must be less than 95 seconds. So the basic relationship between cycle time and takt time is

$$\text{Cycle time} \leq \text{takt time}$$

If cycle time exceeds takt time, more than one person is needed. To approximate the number of people required, use the following formula:

$$\text{Number of people required} = \frac{\text{cycle time}}{\text{takt time}}$$

Takt time is recalculated whenever the production schedule is changed. In the example, if 312 units are scheduled, the takt time is reduced to 87 seconds. Adjustments to cycle times, possible by adding people or equipment, may be necessary.

Lean Tools

In a *visual factory*, locations for tools, inventory, safety equipment, and so on, are clearly marked and identified. Signs and floor paint designate traffic patterns and storage locations. Information needed by personnel to perform their functions is readily available. Monitors display current information about the activity.

A *kanban* system may be used to simplify and improve resupply procedures. In a typical two-bin kanban arrangement, as the first bin is emptied, the user signals roving resupply personnel. The signal is usually visual and may be placement of a card that came with the bin, turning on a light, or just displaying the empty bin. The resupply employee gathers the information on supplies needed and replenishes the bins. Sometimes the bins are resupplied from a stockroom although often it is from a closer supply point sometimes referred to as the supermarket. In some cases, bins are replenished directly by an outside vendor. The entire string of events occurs routinely, often with no paperwork. The result is smoother flow and less inventory.

A *poka-yoke* device is designed to prevent errors. Suppose several people place documents in four separate trays depending on document type. A kaizen team discovered that a person sorts the trays at the end of the day because about five percent of the documents are in the wrong tray even though signs clearly state document type. The team recommended printing the documents on different colored paper and also printing the signs on the corresponding paper color. This reduced the number of misplaced documents to 0.7 percent and made the sorting job much easier. Figure 29.11 illustrates a poka-yoke device used to ensure that round and square tubing items are placed in the correct containers.

Poka-yoke methods are helpful in reducing the occurrence of rare events. A manufacturer finds that about one in 2000 of its assemblies shipped is missing one

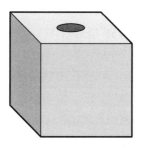 

Figure 29.11   A poka-yoke technique ensures that the round and square parts are placed in correct containers. Neither part will fit through the hole in the top of the incorrect container.

of its 165 components. A poka-yoke technique was used to eliminate this defect. The manufacturer now bar codes each component and scans serial number and component bar codes as each component is added to the assembly. The software is written so that the printer at the shipping department will not print a shipping label if any component is missing. Another poka-yoke example involves the selection of the correct part from several bins with similar contents. As the product reaches the workstation, its bar code is read. Light beams crisscross the front of the bins. If the operator reaches into the wrong bin, as determined from the bar code, the conveyor stops until appropriate corrections have been made.

The lean tool called *standard work* states that each activity should be performed the same way every time. The application of this principle can help reduce variation in cycle time and produce a better, more consistent product or service and can also simplify downstream activities. The best procedure is to have the people involved with the activity reach a consensus regarding the standard method and agree to use it. The agreed-upon method should be documented and easily available to all involved. Charts and posters in the work area often are used to reinforce the method. These documents must be updated as continuous improvements are made.

Lean thinking is built on timely satisfaction of customer demand, which means there must be a system for quickly responding to changes in customer requirements. In metal-forming industries it was common practice to produce thousands of parts of a particular type before changing the machine's dies and producing thousands of another part. This often produced vast inventories of work in process and the associated waste. These procedures were justified because changing machine dies took several hours. The time required to change over from one part to another is displayed on the value chain map below each process. The system used to reduce changeover time and improve timely response to demand is called *single minute exchange of dies* (SMED). Shigeo Shingo is given credit for developing the SMED concept and using it in the Toyota Production System. The goal is to reduce the time from the last good part of one type to the first good part of the successive run. The initial application of SMED often requires considerable resources in special staging tables and die storage areas, among others. Activities done while the machine is down are referred to as *internal activities* versus the *external activities*

Part V.C

**EXAMPLE 29.1: APPLICATION OF SMED TO
A PHOTOGRAPHY OPERATION**

Formerly the procedure for changing cameras required several steps:

1. Shoot last good picture with camera A.

2. Remove camera A and its power supply and place in storage cupboard.

3. Remove type A tripod.

4. Remove type A lighting and reflectors.

5. Install type B lighting and reflectors.

6. Install type B tripod. Measure distance to subject with tape measure.

7. Locate camera B in cupboard and install it and its power supply.

8. Shoot first good picture with camera B.

A team working to reduce changeover time designed a fitting so both cameras could use the same tripod. Purchasing extra cables made it possible to avoid moving power supplies. More flexible lighting reflectors were designed so one set would work with all cameras. Taped marks on the floor now show where to locate tripod feet to avoid the necessity of using a tape measure.

Another alternative would be to obtain a more versatile camera that would not need to be changed.

---

performed in preparation for or follow-up to the die change. Shingo's method is to move as many activities from internal to external as possible. A useful technique is to make a video recording of a typical changeover and have involved personnel use it to identify internal activities that can be converted to external activities. Positioning correct tooling, equipment, and manpower should all be done in external time. Activities that don't involve die changes also need to be nimble in their response to changing customer requirements. This can be achieved through analysis of the changeover process.

An assembly department that produced three different models spent considerable time converting the assembly line from one model to another. They found that three different assembly lines worked best for them. They now switch models by walking across the room. Opportunities to apply SMED concepts abound in many businesses and industries. Recognizing and developing these opportunities depend on the creativity and perseverance of the people involved.

Total Productive Maintenance

In order for lean systems to work, all equipment must be ready to quickly respond to customer needs. This requires a system that foresees maintenance needs and takes appropriate action. A total productive maintenance (TPM) system uses historical data, manufacturer's recommendations, reports by alert operators, diagnostic tests, and other techniques to schedule maintenance activity so that machine downtime can be minimized. Total productive maintenance goes beyond keeping everything running, however. A TPM system includes continuous improvement initiatives as it seeks more effective and efficient ways to predict and diagnose problems.

Chapter 30

D. Corrective Action

Identify, describe, and apply elements of the corrective action process including problem identification, failure analysis, root cause analysis, problem correction, recurrence control, verification of effectiveness, etc. (Evaluate)

Body of Knowledge V.D

Corrective and preventive actions often are best taken using a problem-solving method. Problem-solving methods (also called the scientific method) have many variations depending, to some extent, on the use; however, they are all similar. The seven phases of corrective action are shown in Figure 30.1, which also shows the relationship to the PDSA cycle. The phases are integrated in that they are all dependent on the previous phase. Continuous improvement is the objective and these phases are the framework to achieving that objective.

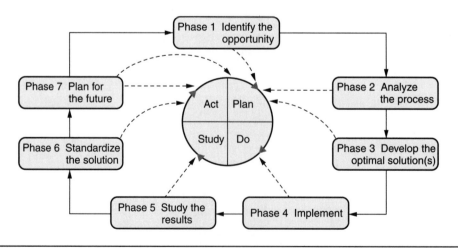

Figure 30.1   The seven phases of corrective action.

PHASE 1: IDENTIFY THE OPPORTUNITY (PROBLEM IDENTIFICATION)

The objective of this phase is to identify and prioritize opportunities for improvement. It consists of three parts: identify the problem, form the team (if one is not in existence), and define the scope.

Problem identification answers the question, "What are the problems?" The answer leads to those problems that have the greatest potential for improvement and have the greatest need for solution. Problems can be identified from a variety of inputs, such as:

- Pareto analysis of repetitive external alarm signals, such as field failures, complaints, returns, and others

- Pareto analysis of repetitive internal alarm signals (for example, scrap, rework, sorting, and the 100 percent test)

- Proposals from key insiders (managers, supervisors, professionals, and union stewards)

- Proposals from suggestion schemes

- Field study of users' needs

- Data on performance of competitors (from users and from laboratory tests)

- Comments of key people outside the organization (customers, suppliers, journalists, and critics)

- Findings and comments of government regulators and independent laboratories

- Customer surveys

- Employee surveys

- Brainstorming by work groups

Problems identified provide opportunities for improvement. For a condition to qualify as a problem, it must meet the following three criteria:

1. Variable performance from an established standard

2. Deviation from the perception and the facts

3. The cause is unknown; if we know the cause, there is no problem

Identifying problems for improvement is not difficult, as there often are many more than can be analyzed. The quality council or work group must prioritize them using the following selection criteria:

1. Is the problem important and not superficial? Why?

2. Will problem solution contribute to the attainment of goals?

3. Can the problem be defined clearly using objective measures?

In selecting its initial improvement opportunity, a work group should find one that gives the maximum benefit for the minimum amount of effort.

The second part of phase 1 is to form a team. If the team is a natural work group or one where members already work together, then this part is complete. If the problem is of a multifunctional nature, as most are, then the team should be selected and directed by the quality council to address the improvement of a specific process. The team leader is then selected and becomes the owner of the process improvement. Goals and milestones are established.

If the improvement strategy is the repair or refinement of an existing process, an individual, rather than a team, may be assigned.

The third part of phase 1 is to define the scope. Failure in problem solving is frequently caused by poor definition of the problem. A problem well stated is half solved. Criteria for a good problem statement are as follows:

- It clearly describes the problem as it currently exists and is easily understood

- It states the effect—what is wrong, when it happens, and where it is occurring, not why it is wrong or who is responsible

- It focuses on what is known, what is unknown, and what needs to be done

- It uses facts and is free of judgment

- It emphasizes the impact on the customer

An example of a well-written problem statement is:

As a result of a customer satisfaction survey, a sample of 150 billing invoices showed that 18 had errors that required one hour to correct.

This example statement describes the current state. We might also wish to describe the desired state, such as "Reduce billing errors by 75 percent."

In addition to the problem statement, this phase requires a comprehensive charter for the team. The charter specifies:

1. *Authority.* Who authorized the team?

2. *Objective and scope.* What are the expected outputs and specific areas to be improved?

3. *Composition.* Who are the team members and process and subprocess owners?

4. *Direction and control.* What are the guidelines for the internal operation of the team?

5. *General.* What are the methods to be used, the resources, and the specific milestones?

PHASE 2: ANALYZE THE CURRENT PROCESS

The objective of this phase is to understand the process and how it is currently performed. Key activities are to define process boundaries, outputs and customers, inputs and suppliers, and process flow, determine levels of customer satisfaction and measurements needed, gather data, and identify root causes.

The first step is for the team to develop a process flow diagram. A flow diagram translates complex work into an easily understood graphic description. This activity often is an eye-opening experience for the team, because it is rare that all members of the team understand the entire process.

Next, the target performance measures are defined. Measurement is fundamental to meaningful process improvements. If something cannot be measured, it cannot be improved. There is an old saying that what gets measured gets done. The team will determine if the measurements needed to understand and improve the process are presently being used; if new ones are needed, they will:

- Establish performance measures with respect to customer requirements

- Determine data needed to manage the process

- Establish regular feedback with customers and suppliers

- Establish measures for quality/cost/timelines of inputs and outputs

Once the target performance measures are established, the team can collect all available data and information. If these data are not enough, then additional new information is obtained. Gathering data: (1) helps confirm that a problem exists, (2) enables the team to work with facts, (3) makes it possible to establish measurement criteria for a baseline, and (4) enables the team to measure the effectiveness of an implemented solution. It is important to collect only needed data and to get the right data for the problem. The team should develop a plan that includes input from internal and external customers and ensures that the plan answers the following questions:

1. What problem or operation do we wish to learn about?

2. What are the data used for?

3. How much data is needed?

4. What conclusions can be drawn from the collected data?

5. What action should be taken as a result of the conclusion?

Data can be collected by a number of different methods, such as check sheets, computers with application software, data-collection devices like hand-held gages, or an online system.

The team will identify the customers and their requirements and expectations as well as the inputs, outputs, and interfaces of the process. Also, they will systematically review the procedures currently being used. Common items of data and information are:

- Customer information, such as complaints and surveys

- Design information, such as specifications, drawings, function, bills of materials, costs, design reviews, field data, service, and maintainability

- Process information, such as routing, equipment, operators, raw material, and component parts and supplies

- Statistical information, such as average, median, range, standard deviation, skewness, kurtosis, and frequency distribution

- Quality information, such as Pareto diagrams, cause-and-effect diagrams, check sheets, scatter diagrams, control charts, histograms, process capability, acceptance sampling, run charts, life testing, inspection steps, and operator and equipment matrix analysis

- Supplier information, such as process variation, on-time delivery, and technical competency

The cause-and-effect diagram is particularly effective in this phase. Determining all of the causes requires experience, brainstorming, and a thorough knowledge of the process. It is an excellent starting point for the project team. One word of caution—the object is to seek causes, not solutions. Therefore, only possible causes, no matter how trivial, should be listed.

It is important to identify the root cause. This activity can sometimes be determined by voting. It is a good idea to verify the most likely cause because a mistake here can lead to the unnecessary waste of time and money by investigating possible solutions to the wrong cause. Some verification techniques are:

1. Examine the most likely cause in regard to the problem statement

2. Recheck all data that support the most likely cause

3. Check the process when it is performing satisfactorily versus when it is not by using the who, where, when, how, what, and why approach

4. Utilize an outside authority who plays "devil's advocate" with the data, information, and reasoning

5. Use experimental design, Taguchi's quality engineering, and other advanced techniques to determine the critical factors and their levels

6. Save a portion of the data used in the analysis to confirm during verification

Once the root cause is determined, the next phase can begin.

PHASE 3: DEVELOP THE OPTIMAL SOLUTION(S) (CORRECTION)

The objectives of this phase are establishing potential and feasible solutions and recommending the best solution to improve the process. Once all the information is available, the project team begins its search for possible solutions. Frequently, more than one solution is required to remedy a situation. Sometimes the solutions are quite evident from a cursory analysis of the data.

In this phase, creativity plays the major role and brainstorming is the principal technique. Brainstorming on possible solutions requires not only a knowledge of the problem but innovation and creativity.

There are three types of creativity: (1) create new processes, (2) combine different processes, or (3) modify the existing process. The first type is innovation in its highest form, such as the invention of the transistor. Combining two or more processes is a synthesis activity to create a better process. It is a unique combination of what already exists. This type of creativity relies heavily on benchmarking. Modification involves altering a process that already exists so that it does a better job. It succeeds when managers utilize the experience, education, and energy of empowered work groups or project teams. There is not a distinct line between the three types—they overlap (Rother and Shook 1999).

Creativity is the unique quality that separates mankind from the rest of the animal kingdom. Most of the problems that cause inefficiency and ineffectiveness in organizations are simple problems. There is a vast pool of creative potential available to solve these problems. Quality is greatly improved because of the finding and fixing of a large number of problems, and morale is greatly increased because it is enormously satisfying to be allowed to create (Mallette 1993).

Areas for possible change include the number and length of delays, bottlenecks, equipment, timing and number of inspections, rework, cycle time, and materials handling. Consideration should be given to simultaneously combining, eliminating, rearranging, and executing the process steps.

Once possible solutions have been determined, evaluation or testing of the solutions comes next. As mentioned, more than one solution can contribute to the situation. Evaluation and/or testing determines which of the possible solutions has the greatest potential for success and the advantages and disadvantages of these solutions. Criteria for judging the possible solutions include such things as cost, feasibility, effect, resistance to change, consequences, and training. Solutions also may be categorized as short range and long range. At a minimum, the solution must prevent reoccurrence.

Control charts give us the ability to evaluate possible solutions. Whether the idea is good, poor, or has no effect is evident from the chart.

PHASE 4: IMPLEMENT CHANGES

Once the best solution is selected, it can be implemented. The objectives of this phase are preparing the implementation plan, obtaining approval, and implementing the process improvements.

Although the project team usually has some authority to institute remedial action, more often than not the approval of the quality council or other appropriate authority is required. If such is the case, a written and/or oral report is given.

The contents of the implementation plan report must fully describe:

- Why it will be done

- How it will be done

Part V.D

- When it will be done

- Who will do it

- Where it will be done

The report will designate required actions, assign responsibility, and establish implementation milestones. The length of the report is determined by the complexity of the change. Simple changes may require only an oral report, whereas others require a detailed written report.

After approval by the quality council, it is desirable to obtain the advice and consent of departments, functional areas, teams, and individuals that may be affected by the change. A presentation to these groups will help gain support from those involved in the process and provide an opportunity for feedback with improvement suggestions.

The final element of the implementation plan is the monitoring activity that answers the following:

- What information will be monitored or observed and what resources are required?

- Who will be responsible for taking the measurements?

- Where will the measurements be taken?

- How will the measurements be taken?

- When will the measurements be taken?

Measurement tools such as run charts, control charts, Pareto diagrams, histograms, check sheets, and questionnaires are used to monitor and evaluate the process change.

PHASE 5: STUDY THE RESULTS

The objective of this phase is monitoring and evaluating the change by tracking and studying the effectiveness of the improvement efforts through data collection and review of progress. It is vital to institutionalize meaningful change and ensure ongoing measurement and evaluation efforts to achieve continuous improvement.

The team should meet periodically during this phase to evaluate the results to see that the problem has been solved or if fine-tuning is required. In addition, they will wish to see if any unforeseen problems have developed as a result of the changes. If the team is not satisfied, then some of the phases will need to be repeated.

PHASE 6: STANDARDIZE THE SOLUTION (RECURRENCE CONTROL)

Once the team is satisfied with the change, it must be institutionalized by positive control of the process, process certification, and operator certification. Positrol (positive control) assures that important variables are kept under control. It specifies the what, who, how, where, and when of the process and is an updating of the monitoring activity. Standardizing the solution prevents backsliding. Table 30.1 gives an illustration of a few variables of a wave soldering process.

In addition, the quality peripherals—the system, environment, and supervision—must be certified. The partial checklist in Table 30.2 provides the means to initially evaluate the peripherals and periodically audit them to ensure that the process will meet or exceed customer requirements for the product or service.

Finally, operators must be certified to know what to do and how to do it for a particular process. Also needed is cross-training in other jobs within the process to ensure next-customer knowledge and job rotation. Total product knowledge is also desirable. Operator certification is an ongoing process that must occur periodically.

Table 30.1   Positrol of a wave soldering process.

What	Specs	Who	How	Where	When
An 880 flux	0.864 g ± 0.0008	Lab technician	Specific gravity meter	Lab	Daily
Belt speed	ft/min ± 10%	Process technician	Counter	Board feed	Each change
Preheat temperature	220° ± 5°	Automatic	Thermocouple	Chamber entrance	Continuous

Table 30.2   Checklist for process certification.

Quality system	Environment	Supervision
Authority to shut down line	Water/air purity	Coach, not boss
Preventive maintenance	Dust/chemical control	Clear instructions
Visible, audible alarm signals	Temperature/humidity control	Combining tasks
Foolproof inspection	Electrostatic discharge	Encourage suggestions
Neighbor and self-inspection	Storage/inventory control	Feedback of results

PHASE 7: PLAN FOR THE FUTURE (EFFECTIVENESS ASSESSMENT)

This phase has the objective of achieving improved levels of process performance. Regardless of how successful initial improvement efforts are, the improvement process must continue. Everyone in the organization is involved in a systematic long-term endeavor to constantly improve quality by developing processes that are customer-oriented, flexible, and responsive.

A key activity is to conduct regularly scheduled reviews of progress by the quality council and/or work group. Management must establish the systems to identify areas for future improvement and to track performance with respect to internal and external customers. They also must track changing customer requirements.

Continuous improvement means not being satisfied with merely doing a good job or process but striving to improve that job or process. It is accomplished by incorporating process measurement and team problem solving in all work activities. TQM tools and techniques are used to improve quality, delivery, and cost. We must continuously strive for excellence by reducing complexity, variation, and out-of-control processes.

Lessons learned in problem solving, communications, and group dynamics, as well as technical know-how, must be transferred to appropriate activities within the organization.

Chapter 31

E. Preventive Action

> Identify, describe, and apply various
> preventive action tools such as error-
> proofing/poka-yoke, robust design, etc., and
> analyze their effectiveness. (Evaluate)
>
> **Body of Knowledge V.E**

The problem-solving method discussed in the previous chapter often may be useful for preventive actions. The function of quality engineers has moved from that of detection of defects to prevention. The concept of preventive action has been around for many years and has been practiced extensively in Japan, where it has the name poka-yoke. There are five categories of preventive systems: fail-safe devices, magnification of senses, redundancy, countdown, and special checking and control devices.

Many kinds of fail-safe devices are used to ensure that problems or abnormalities in processes will be discovered in a manner that will maintain a safe working environment and ensure that quality is not compromised. See Table 31.1.

Magnification of senses is used to increase the power of human seeing, hearing, smelling, feeling, tasting, and muscle power. Some examples are optical magnification, multiple visual and audio signals, remote-controlled viewing of a

Table 31.1 Types of fail-safe devices.

Type of fail-safe device	Device function
Interlocking sequences	Ensure that the next operation can not start until the previous operation is successfully completed
Alarms and cutoffs	Activate if there are any abnormalities in the process
All-clear signals	Activate when all remedial steps have been taken
Foolproof work-holding devices	Ensure that a part can be located in only one position
Limiting mechanisms	Ensure that a tool cannot exceed a certain position or amount

hazardous process, robotic placement of parts or tools, and use of pictures rather than words.

Redundancy is the use of additional activities as a quality safeguard. Multiple-identity codes, such as bar and color codes, are used to prevent product mix-ups. Redundant actions and approvals require two individuals working independently. Audit review and checking procedures assure that plans are being followed. Design for verification utilizes special designs, such as holes for viewing, to determine if the product or process is performing satisfactorily. Multiple test stations may check a number of attributes, such as those that occur on a high-speed production line.

Another category is countdown, which structures sensing and information procedures to parallel the operating procedures in order to check each step. The most familiar example of this category of error-proofing is the launching of a space vehicle. It also has been effectively used in surgical operations and in welding.

The last category is special checking and control devices. A familiar example is the computer checking of credit card numbers whereby invalid numbers are rejected and instant feedback provided.

There are five error-proofing principles: elimination, replacement, facilitation, detection, and mitigation. Elimination of the possible error occurs when the process or product is redesigned so that the error can no longer occur. Replacement is a change to a more reliable process. Facilitation occurs when the process is made easier to perform and, therefore, more reliable. Detection occurs when the error is found before the next operation. Mitigation minimizes the effect of the error.

VERIFYING THE EFFECTIVENESS OF PREVENTIVE ACTIONS

It is not enough merely to plan and execute preventive actions. In accordance with the PDSA and PDCA models, the effectiveness of preventive actions must be verified. Such verification can be difficult, however, since preventive actions that are effective eliminate problems before they occur. In this respect, verification of preventive actions is completed by ensuring that problems for which preventive actions have been planned and executed have not, in fact, recurred.

ROBUST DESIGN

A product or process is called robust if its function is relatively unaffected by variation in the environment in which it operates.

EXAMPLE 31.1

A laundry appliance must operate correctly with a variety of water chemistry and cleaning products as well as variations in temperature, humidity and other factors.

EXAMPLE 31.2

An automobile must function correctly under various weather conditions as well as variation in operator techniques.

EXAMPLE 31.3

The process of assembling a bid must be performed in an area where frequent interruptions, phone calls, and so on, occur. In order to make certain that all 23 required elements of the bid document are included, 23 color-coded trays are set out with the appropriate form in each tray before the document is assembled.

EXAMPLE 31.4

The raw material for a punching process has a wide variation in thickness, in other words the process operates in an environment of thickness variation. This results in unacceptable burrs on some parts. One solution is to impose a tighter thickness specification on the raw material supplier. The robust design solution might be a new die that would prevent burrs regardless of the thickness.

SUMMARY OF PART V

Part V described a broad spectrum of tools that have proved helpful in continuous improvement efforts. The novice practitioner may feel overwhelmed by the array of options. The best advice is, rather than study the tools and memorize their individual traits, to identify a problem and try to use one or more of the tools in its solution. Experience with these tools provides a depth of understanding never attainable from the written word alone.

Part VI

Quantitative Methods and Tools

Part VI

This part covers eight topics in data analysis that CQEs must understand and routinely employ: collecting and summarizing data, quantitative concepts, probability distributions, statistical decision making, relationships between variables, statistical process control, process and performance capability, and the design and analysis of experiments.

Chapter 32

A. Collecting and Summarizing Data

T his chapter covers seven aspects related to collecting and summarizing data: types of data, measurement scales, data collection methods, data accuracy, descriptive statistics, graphical methods for depicting relationships, and graphical methods for depicting distributions.

1. TYPES OF DATA

> Types of Data: Define, classify, and compare discrete (attributes) and continuous (variables) data. (Apply)
>
> **Body of Knowledge VI.A.1**

There are two types of data encountered in practice: *discrete data* and *continuous data*.

Discrete (count) data are obtained when the characteristic being studied can only take on certain values and is countable. For example, number of nonconforming units in a lot, pass/fail data, or number of successes per trial. Another example would be the number of scratches on an object. In this case the possible values are 0, 1, 2, . . ., a so-called countably infinite set. In quality control, discrete data are referred to as *attribute* data.

Continuous (variables) data are obtained when the characteristic being studied can take on any value over an interval of numbers. For example, the length of a part can be any value above zero. Between each two values on a continuous scale there are infinitely many other values. For example, between 2.350 inches and 2.351 inches the values 2.3502 inches, 2.35078 inches, and so on, occur.

2. MEASUREMENT SCALES

> Define, describe, and use nominal, ordinal,
> interval, and ratio scales. (Apply)
>
> **Body of Knowledge VI.A.2**

There are four types of measurement scales: nominal, ordinal, interval, and ratio.

Nominal scales classify data into categories with no order implied, such as an equipment list of presses, drills, and so on. Sometimes we assign zero and one to represent, say, a conforming or nonconforming item; however, the numbers have no meaning in terms of order.

Ordinal scale refers to positions in a series where order is important, but precise differences between values are not defined. For example, on the Mohs hardness scale of 10 minerals, talc has a hardness of one, fluorite has a hardness of four, and topaz has a hardness of eight. However, topaz is harder than fluorite, but not twice as hard. Another example might be survey responses such as strongly dissatisfied, dissatisfied, neutral, satisfied, and strongly satisfied, which can be scaled as 1, 2, 3, 4, 5.

Interval scales have meaningful differences but no absolute zero. In this case, ratios are not meaningful. An example is temperature measured in degrees Fahrenheit (F). In this case, 20 degrees F is not twice as warm as 10 degrees F. Although the Fahrenheit scale has a zero, it is not an absolute zero. That is, the zero value does not signify that there is an absence of temperature. Data on an interval scale can be added and subtracted but can not be multiplied or divided.

Ratio scales have meaningful differences and an absolute zero exists. One example of a ratio scale is length in inches because zero length is defined as having no length, and 20 inches is twice as long as 10 inches. Heat in degrees Kelvin (K) is another example of a ratio scale because zero degrees K is defined as having no heat and 10 degrees K has twice as much heat as five degrees K.

3. DATA COLLECTION METHODS

> Describe various methods for collecting data,
> including tally or check sheets, data coding,
> automatic gaging, etc., and identify their
> strengths and weaknesses. (Apply)
>
> **Body of Knowledge VI.A.3**

Raw data: .127 .125 .123 .123 .120 .124 .126 .122 .123 .125 .121 .123 .122 .125
.124 .122 .123 .123 .126 .121 .124 .121 .124 .122 .126 .125 .123

Value	Tally
.120	I
.121	III
.122	IIII
.123	IIIIIII
.124	IIII
.125	IIII
.126	III
.127	I

Figure 32.1 Example of tally or check sheet.

Tally or Check Sheet

A tally or check sheet consists of a column of potential values usually shown from smallest to largest. As measurements are read, a tally mark is placed next to the appropriate value. Although no sophisticated analysis is provided, the tally sheet is very simple to use and understand. An illustration of such a sheet is shown in Figure 32.1. The data represent a sample of diameters from a drilling operation.

Automatic Gauging

Data also may be collected by automatic gauging equipment. Potential advantages of this approach include improved precision as well as reduction of labor, time, error rates, and costs. When considering automated inspection, CQEs must pay attention to the possibility of high initial costs, including the possibility of part redesign to adapt the part to the constraints of the measurement system. If the measured values are fed directly into a database, care must be taken to make certain that the communication link is reliable and free of noise.

Data Coding

Coding data can simplify recording and analysis.

Sometimes it is useful to code data using an algebraic transformation. Suppose a set of data has mean μ and standard deviation σ (see section 5 of this chapter for more details on μ and σ). A new set of data may be formed using the formula

---

EXAMPLE 32.1

A dimension has values that range from 1.031 to 1.039. For convenience it is useful to code these numbers using digits from 1 to 9 so that:

$$1 \rightarrow 1.031$$

$$2 \rightarrow 1.032 \text{ and so on.}$$

$y = ax + b$. That is, each element of the new set is formed by multiplying an element of the original set by a, then adding b. The mean μ_y and standard deviation σ_y of the new set are:

$$\mu_y = a\mu + b \qquad \sigma_y = |a|\sigma$$

For further information on the affect of algebraic transformations, see Hogg and Tanis (1997).

4. DATA ACCURACY

> Describe the characteristics or properties of data (e.g., source/resource issues, flexibility, versatility, etc.) and various types of data errors or poor quality such as low accuracy, inconsistency, interpretation of data values, and redundancy. Identify factors that can influence data accuracy, and apply techniques for error detection and correction. (Apply)
>
> **Body of Knowledge VI.A.4**

Common Causes of Errors

The best data collection and analysis techniques can be defeated if the data have errors. Common causes of errors include:

- Units of measure that are not defined (for example, feet or meters?).
- Similarity of handwritten characters (for example, 2 or Z?).
- Inadequate measurement system.
- Rounding (generally should only be done at last stage of computation).
- Batching input versus real-time input.
- Inadequate use of validation techniques.
- Multiple points of data entry.
- Poor instructions or training.
- Ambiguous terminology (for example, calendar or fiscal year? day ends at 3 PM or midnight?). For example, the NASA team working with the Mars rovers uses the term *sol* to designate a Martian day to avoid confusion with earth days. (Apparently yestersol refers to the previous Martian day.)

Strategies to Avoid Data Errors

Use strategies like these to minimize error:

- Have a carefully constructed data collection plan.
- Maintain a calibration schedule for data collection equipment.
- Conduct gage repeatability and reproducibility (R&R) studies on data collection equipment.
- Record appropriate auxiliary information regarding units, time of collection, conditions, measurement equipment used, name of the data recorder, and so on.
- Use appropriate statistical tests to identify potential outliers.
- If data are transmitted or stored digitally, use an appropriate redundant error-correction system.
- Provide clear and complete instruction and training.

If data are obtained through sampling, the sampling procedure must be appropriately designed. Some of the different techniques that can be used to establish a well-designed sampling strategy are discussed in the following paragraphs.

Random Sampling

Simple random sampling is a procedure by which each item has an equal probability of being selected as part of the sample. One way to do this is to assign each item a number and create a set of numbered tags so that each tag number corresponds to exactly one item. The tags are thoroughly stirred in a container and one is drawn out. The number on the tag identifies which item is selected as part of the sample. If the population size is quite large, making up tags can be unreasonable. In this situation, *random numbers* generated by calculators or computer software such as Excel can be used to select the elements of the sample.

Stratified Sampling

If the population of parts to be sampled is naturally divided into groups, it might be desirable to use *stratified sampling*. For example, suppose 300 of the parts came from Cleveland, 600 came from Chicago, and 100 came from Green Mountain. A stratified sample of size 50 could be formed by randomly selecting 15 items from the Cleveland batch, 30 from the Chicago batch, and five from Green Mountain. In other words, each group makes up a proportional part of the stratified sample.

Sample Homogeneity

Sample homogeneity refers to the need to select a sample so that it represents just one population. Sample homogeneity is desirable regardless of the type of sampling. In the case of the stratified sampling procedure, the population consists of the original 1000 parts, and stratification is used to help ensure that the sample represents the various strata.

When selecting the data collection scheme for time-related data, the entire sample should be collected at the same time in the process so that it comes from the population being produced at 9:00 AM, not that produced at 9:15 AM, which may be a different population. In fact, the purpose of a control chart is to use sampling to determine whether the population produced at one time is different from the other populations sampled.

5. DESCRIPTIVE STATISTICS

Describe, calculate, and interpret measures of central tendency and dispersion (central limits theorem) and construct and interpret frequency distributions including simple, categorical, grouped, ungrouped, and cumulative. (Evaluate)

Body of Knowledge VI.A.5

The two principal types of statistical studies are *descriptive* and *inferential*. The purpose of descriptive statistics is to present data in a way that will facilitate understanding. Some important statistics that can be used to describe a set of data include:

- A measure of the center of the population or a sample

- A measure of the variability (measure of the spread of the data) for the population or a sample

- A graphical display (displaying overall shape) of the data.

Center, spread, and shape are key to understanding data and the process that generated them. The next few paragraphs discuss these attributes. (Complete definitions and discussion of population, sample, parameters, and statistics are provided in Chapter 34.)

Measures of Central Tendency

Three ways to quantify the center of a data set are the *mean* (or average), *median*, and *mode*.

The *mean* is the arithmetic average of a set of data or observations. The mean is also referred to as a "balancing point" for the set of observations. Suppose the data in a sample of size n are denoted by $x_1, x_2, x_3, \ldots, x_n$. The *sample mean*, denoted $\bar{x}$ (read "x-bar"), is given by

$$\bar{x} = \frac{x_1 + x_2 + x_3 + \ldots + x_n}{n} = \frac{\sum_{i=1}^{n} x_i}{n}.$$

EXAMPLE 32.2

Emergency room waiting times are continually increasing. One factor that was identified as affecting wait time was turnaround time for basic blood analysis. Turnaround times (in minutes) for 10 such tests on one particular day are:

| 62 | 68 | 72 | 60 | 50 | 58 | 58 | 49 | 66 | 70 |

The average turnaround time is

$$\overline{x} = \frac{62+68+72+60+50+58+58+49+66+70}{10}$$

$$= 61.3 \text{ min.}$$

If the data represent the entire population of interest, then the average is the *population mean* and commonly denoted by μ. Suppose there are N observations in the population. The *population mean* is

$$\mu = \frac{x_1 + x_2 + x_3 + \ldots + x_N}{N}$$

$$= \frac{\sum_{i=1}^{N} x_i}{N}$$

EXAMPLE 32.3

An accident investigator has been contracted by a large tire company to investigate accidents where the company's tire may have been at fault. The investigator was contracted by this company for a total of six months before the company determined that his work was unacceptable. At the time his contract was terminated, the investigator had submitted a total of eight invoices for time spent at accident scenes. The amounts for each invoice are:

| $4390 | $3285 | $1582 | $725 | $3001 | $2971 | $463 | $8923 |

Since these invoice amounts are the *only* amounts for this investigators' work for the tire company, they represent the *entire population of amounts*. Therefore, the average invoice amount will be the population mean:

$$\mu = \frac{x_1 + x_2 + x_3 + \ldots + x_N}{N}$$

$$= \frac{4390+3285+1582+725+3001+2971+463+8923}{8} = \$3167.50$$

The *median* is that value that divides *ordered* data into two equal parts—half of the data lies at or below that value and half of the data lies above that value. Suppose we have a sample of size n. If the sample contains an odd number of observations, the sample median is the central value. If there is an even number of observations, the median is the average of the two central values. The *location* of the median for *n* observations is $(n + 1)/2$. The sample median is often denoted by *M*.

EXAMPLE 32.4

Consider the turnaround times for blood analysis given in Example 32.2, now written in increasing order:

| 49 | 50 | 58 | 58 | 60 | 62 | 66 | 68 | 70 | 72 |

Since there are $n = 10$ observations in the data set, the location of the median is $(10 + 1)/2 = 5.5$. Therefore, the median is the average of the fifth and sixth observations from the smallest in the data set:

$$M = \frac{60+62}{2}$$
$$= 61 \text{ min.}$$

The *sample mode* is the observation that occurs most often in the sample. There can be more than one mode for a set of data. For example, the mode for the blood analysis turnaround times is 58 minutes, since it occurs more often than any other observation.

As with the mean, the population median and population mode can be determined if the entire population is known. The mean and median are the most commonly used measures of the center.

One final note on measures of the center: the median is known as a *resistant* measure of the center while the mean is not a resistant measure. The median is often used as the measure of the center for data that involves prices, salaries, or any data that may naturally contain extreme observations. The median is resistant to the influence of these extreme observations.

EXAMPLE 32.5

Housing prices in Glendale, Arizona, vary over a wide range. Suppose five houses on the market in May 2008 were listed at the following prices:

| $54,900 | $75,000 | $79,000 | $101,500 | $386,000 |

The average house price for this set of data is $139,280. Does the average appear to represent the sample of data itself? The price of $139,280 lies above all but one house price. The median house price for this set of data is $79,000. The average was pulled toward the extreme value of $386,000 while the median was not influenced by this particular value.

Now suppose we discovered that the house priced $386,000 was reduced to $345,000. All other housing prices remained constant at the time of the data collection. With this reduction, the sample mean house price is now $131,080; the sample median house price remains at $79,000. Therefore, the median was resistant to the change in price while the mean was not resistant.

Measures of Variability (Spread)

Measures of variability describe the spread of the data around the center or central point of the distribution of the data. Three common measures of variation are the *range, variance,* and *standard deviation.*

The *sample range* is the difference between the maximum value (max) and the minimum value (min) in the sample. The sample range is often denoted by R and given by:

$$R = \text{max} - \text{min}$$

For example, the sample range for the turnaround times given previously is $R = 72 - 49 = 23$ minutes.

The *sample variance* is a measure of the variability based on the deviations of the actual observations from the mean. Suppose we have a sample of size n with observations $x_1, x_2, \ldots, x_n$. The sample variance is

$$s^2 = \frac{\sum_{i=1}^{n}\left(x_i - \bar{x}\right)^2}{n-1}.$$

EXAMPLE 32.6

Consider the blood analysis turnaround times (in minutes) given in Example 32.2:

49	50	58	58	60	62	66	68	70	72

The sample average was found to be $\bar{x} = 61.3$ minutes. The sample variance is

$$s^2 = \frac{\sum_{i=1}^{n}\left(x_i - \bar{x}\right)^2}{n-1}$$

$$= \frac{(49-61.3)^2 + (50-61.3)^2 + \ldots + (72-61.3)^2}{10-1}$$

$$= 7.89 \text{ min}^2.$$

The *population variance,* denoted by σ^2, can be determined if the data from the entire population are given. Suppose the population consists of N observations and the population mean is given by μ. The population variance is

$$\sigma^2 = \frac{\sum_{i=1}^{N}\left(x_i - \mu\right)^2}{N}.$$

Notice that the unit of measure of the variance is the square of the unit of measure of the original data and the mean. It is more convenient to have summary statistics (such as the measure of the center and measure of variability) in the same unit of measure as the original data. The measure of variability that is in the same unit of measure as the original data and mean is the *standard deviation*. The standard deviation is simply the positive square root of the variance. The sample standard deviation is

$$s = \sqrt{\frac{\sum_{i=1}^{n}\left(x_i - \bar{x}\right)^2}{n-1}}$$

and the population standard deviation is

$$\sigma = \sqrt{\frac{\sum_{i=1}^{N}\left(x_i - \mu\right)^2}{N}}.$$

For example, the sample standard deviation for the blood analysis turnaround times is

$$s = \sqrt{7.89} = 2.81 \text{ minutes.}$$

Shape of the Data

The shape of the sample or population refers to the form the data takes on when it is plotted in a graphical display. Graphical displays include but are not limited to dot plots, box-and-whisker plots, and stem-and-leaf plots (histograms are presented in Chapter 27). For example, a dot plot (also known as a dot diagram) for the blood analysis turnaround times is shown in Figure 32.2. The display reveals the spread of the data as well as possible outliers. This and other graphical displays will be discussed later in this chapter as well as in Chapter 34.

There are numerous possible shapes that data can assume. Consider Figure 32.3. Figure 32.3a represents a histogram of the diameters from a drilling operation given in Section 3 of this chapter. The shape of this distribution is *symmetric (bell-shaped)* and there do not appear to be any potential outliers or unusual observations. Figure 32.3b displays lifetime data of a manufactured part. The lifetime data follows a skewed distribution, specifically a *right-skewed distribution*. Figure 32.3c displays data representing time to show symptoms in rats that have been subjected to a particular treatment. This is a left-skewed distribution. Finally, Figure 32.3d represents a bimodal distribution. This type of distribution has many applications, but sometimes this shape can indicate a mixed distribution of data (data may be coming from two different distributions).

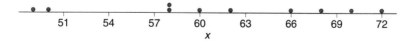

Figure 32.2   Dot plot of blood analysis turnaround times.

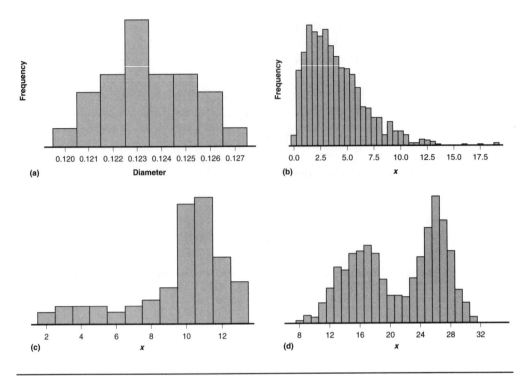

Figure 32.3   Histograms of variously-shaped distributions.

Frequency and Cumulative Frequency Distributions

A frequency distribution is a compact summary of data collected. The frequency distribution can be displayed in table form, in graphical form, or some functional form. An *ungrouped frequency distribution* in table form displays the individual observations and the number of times that each value appears in the data set. A frequency distribution of the diameters from the drilling operation is given in Table 32.1.

The *cumulative frequency distribution* contains the observations themselves as well as the frequency of the occurrence of the current and preceding observations. The cumulative frequency distribution of the diameters from the drilling operation is given in the last column in Table 32.1.

Grouped Frequency Distributions

Another way to present the diameter data from the previous example would be to group the measurements together as shown in Table 32.2.

Categorical Frequency Distributions

If the data represent numbers of items in *nonnumerical* groups or categories, a *categorical frequency distribution* is used. An example of a categorical frequency

Table 32.1   Frequency and cumulative frequency distributions for the ungrouped diameter data.

Measurement	Frequency	Cumulative frequency
0.120	1	1
0.121	3	4
0.122	4	8
0.123	7	15
0.124	4	19
0.125	4	23
0.126	3	26
0.127	1	27

Table 32.2   Frequency and cumulative frequency distributions for grouped diameter data.

Group	Frequency	Cumulative frequency
0.120–0.121	4	4
0.122–0.123	11	15
0.124–0.125	8	23
0.126–0.127	4	27

Table 32.3   Categorical frequency distribution of manufacturing defects.

Defect type	Frequency
Chip	3
Scratch	5
Ink smear	4
Fold mark	7
Tear	2

distribution is displayed in Table 32.3 for several important types of defects in a manufacturing process.

Cumulative frequency distributions do not make sense when the groups are categories where order does not matter.

Frequency distributions and cumulative frequency distributions provide a simple way to quickly examine the variability of data around the center. These distributions also aid in the calculation of statistics from the data such as the sample mean and sample standard deviation. In addition, data from the frequency and cumulative frequency distributions can easily be displayed graphically, such as in a histogram.

The Central Limit Theorem

A frequent question in the minds of quality engineers is the validity of $\bar{x}$ control charts when the population is not normally distributed (see Chapter 34 for discussion of the normal distribution). An important statistical principle in this situation is the *central limit theorem*. It states that

> *The distribution of sample averages will tend toward a normal distribution as the sample size n approaches infinity.*

The central limit theorem guarantees at least approximate normality for the distribution of sample averages, even if the population from which the sample is drawn is not normally distributed. A more specific definition of the central limit theorem will be given in Chapter 34.

For example, because the $\bar{x}$ control chart involves plotting averages, the central limit theorem implies that normality is (approximately) guaranteed. The approximation improves as the sample size n increases. In some cases, the approximation will be applicable for sample sizes as small as 10. In other situations the required sample size for the approximation to be valid can be quite large (say, $n > 100$). Finally, if the underlying distribution of the data does not depart significantly from the normal distribution, sample sizes as small as $n = 3$ can be appropriate. For details on the normality assumption in statistical process control see Montgomery (2009b).

6. GRAPHICAL METHODS FOR DEPICTING RELATIONSHIPS

> Construct, apply, and interpret diagrams and charts such as stem-and-leaf plots, box-and-whisker plots, etc. [Note: Run charts and scatter diagrams are covered in V.A].
> (Analyze)
>
> **Body of Knowledge VI.A.6**

Stem and Leaf Plot

A stem and leaf plot is constructed much like the tally column shown previously, except that the last digit of the data value is recorded instead of the tally mark. This kind of diagram often is used when the data are grouped. Consider the example shown in Figure 32.4.

Data: .18 .24 .21 .17 .36 .34 .19 .25 .18 .22 .37 .24 .42 .33 .48 .56
.47 .55 .26 .38 .54 .19 .24 .42 .44 .11 .39

Units are 0.00

Measurement	Tally	Stem and leaf	Ordered stem and leaf
0.10–0.19	llllll	1 | 8 7 9 8 9 1	1 | 1 7 8 8 9 9
0.20–0.29	lllllll	2 | 4 1 5 2 4 6 4	2 | 1 2 4 4 4 5 6
0.30–0.39	llllll	3 | 6 4 7 3 8 9	3 | 3 4 6 7 8 9
0.40–0.49	lllll	4 | 2 8 7 2 4	4 | 2 2 4 7 8
0.50–0.59	lll	5 | 6 5 4	5 | 4 5 6

Figure 32.4 Stem and leaf diagrams.

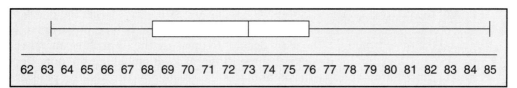

62 63 64 65 66 67 68 69 70 71 72 73 74 75 76 77 78 79 80 81 82 83 84 85

Figure 32.5 Box-and-whisker diagram.

The stem and leaf diagram conveys more information than the tally column or the associated histogram. Note that the ordered stem and leaf sorts the data and permits easy determination of the median.

Box Plots (Box-and-Whisker Diagrams)

A sorted data set may be divided into four approximately equal subsets separated by three boundary points called quartiles. The quartiles are denoted Q_1, Q_2, and Q_3. Q_2 is defined as the median. Q_1 is usually defined as the median of the values less than or equal to Q_2. Q_3 is median of the values greater than or equal to Q_2. The inter-quartile range or IQR is Q_3-Q_1. The box plot (also called a box-and-whisker diagram), developed by Professor John Tukey of Princeton University, uses the high and low values of the data as well as the quartiles. This is illustrated in Figure 32.5. Some software packages, rather than extending the "whiskers" to the maximum and minimum values, terminate them at $1.5 \times$ IQR above Q_3 and $1.5 \times$ IQR below Q_1. Values beyond these whiskers are designated "potential outliers."

The data after sorting: 63, 65, 67, 69, 71, 71, 75, 76, 76, 76, 81, 85

Low value is 63, high value is 85, $Q_1 = 68$, $Q_2 = 73$, and $Q_3 = 76$

Note that quartiles need not be values in the data set itself. The box plot of these data is shown in Figure 32.5.

Figure 32.6 shows how the shape of the dot plot is reflected in the box plot. Box plots can be used to mine information from a database. In this hypothetical

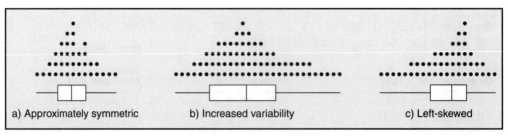

a) Approximately symmetric   b) Increased variability   c) Left-skewed

Figure 32.6 Box plots.

example, a stainless steel casting has a tight tolerance on the machined inside diameter. The quality team has heard a number of proposed fixes. Some people believe the problem is caused by a slightly out-of-round condition on a cross section of the casting. Others feel there is a taper and still others insist the problem is too much part-to-part variation. The question is, "Which type of variation is giving the most trouble?" The team decides to measure the ID at three angles (12 o'clock, 2 o'clock, and 4 o'clock) at three different locations along the bore (top, middle, and bottom) on five different pieces. The resultant data and box plots are shown in Figure 32.7.

The box plots in Figure 32.7 show that the largest source of variation is part-to-part. The Pareto principle says that the part-to-part variation should be attacked first. Furthermore, any improvements in out-of-round or taper may be masked by the large part-to-part variation. How would the box plot have looked if out-of-round or taper had been the principal source of variation?

7. GRAPHICAL METHODS FOR DEPICTING DISTRIBUTIONS

> Construct, apply, and interpret diagrams such as normal probability plots, Weibull plots, etc. [Note: Histograms are covered in V.A]. (Analyze)
>
> **Body of Knowledge VI.A.7**

Graphical displays of data are important tools that can help determine important properties of the data. Using graphical displays, the overall shape, location of the center, and measure of variability can be approximately estimated. These displays can also be used to possibly determine the type of distribution that the data may follow. One graphical display that can be used for determining the type of distribution the data may follow is the *probability plot*.

	Part #1			Part #2			Part #3			Part #4			Part #5		
	T	M	B	T	M	B	T	M	B	T	M	B	T	M	B
12	.998	.992	.996	.984	.982	.981	.998	.998	.997	.986	.987	.986	.975	.980	.976
2	.994	.996	.994	.982	.980	.982	.999	.998	.997	.985	.986	.986	.975	.976	.974
4	.996	.994	.995	.984	.983	.980	.996	.996	.996	.984	.985	.984	.978	.980	.974

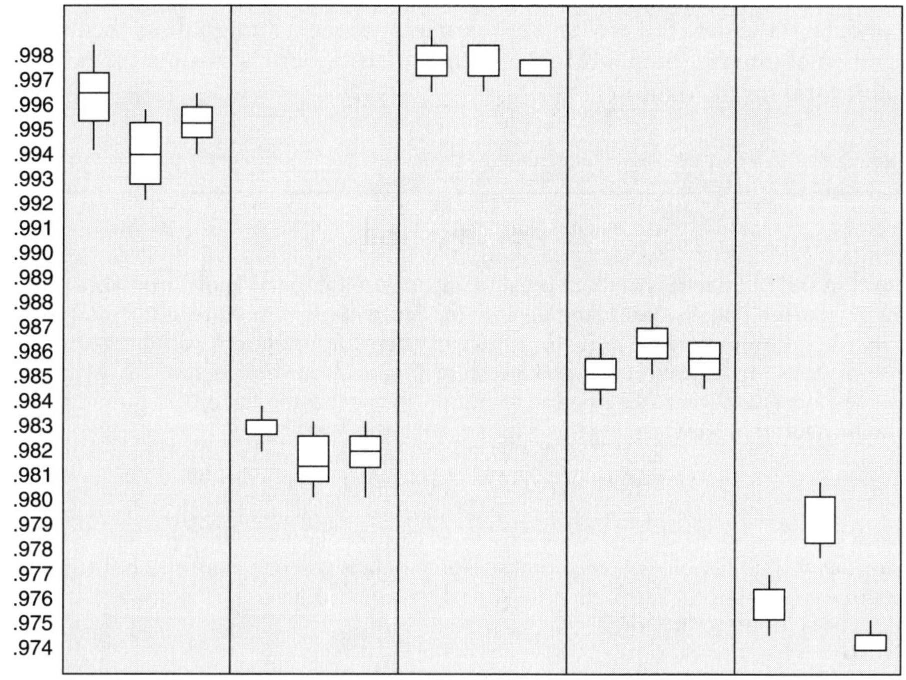

Figure 32.7   Multiple box plot example.

Probability Plotting

The probability plot displays the actual data on the *x*-axis plotted against *percentiles* based on the hypothesized or assumed distribution of interest on the *y*-axis. For example, the normal probability plot displays the actual data against percentiles from a normal distribution. If the data fall—at least approximately—along a straight line, then the data is said to be approximately normally distributed. Probability plots can be constructed for many distributions including the normal, lognormal, Weibull, and exponential. Two of the more commonly used are the normal and Weibull probability plots.

Normal Probability Plot

The assumption of at least approximate normality is often necessary to satisfactorily apply many statistical tests. The normal probability plot can be used to determine if a given set of data come from a population that is normally distributed. In general, the data are plotted on a probability plot where the vertical axis has been scaled according to a normal distribution. It is unnecessary to create these plots manually. Most statistical software packages will generate these plots for any set of data. If the data fall at least approximately along a straight line, then the distribution of interest (in this case the normal distribution) is assumed to be a reasonable form for the data.

EXAMPLE 32.7

Sumithra and Bhattacharya (2008) present a study on the toasting of corn flakes. Appropriately toasted flakes possess the desired moisture content, texture, and color. In their study, the authors investigated the effect of three independent variables—moisture content, toasting temperature, and toasting time—on several responses of interest. One response was the force needed to puncture the toasted flake. The puncture force data (measured in Newton) for this experiment are:

5.34, 6.62, 2.90, 2.07, 5.87, 4.02, 3.45, 2.24, 3.80, 3.80,

2.27, 6.62, 3.95, 4.12, 2.95, 2.80, 2.81, 2.80, 2.90, 2.95

A normal probability plot of the puncture force data is given in Figure 32.8. The data do not appear to fall along a straight line. The normal distribution is probably not a reasonable model for puncture force.

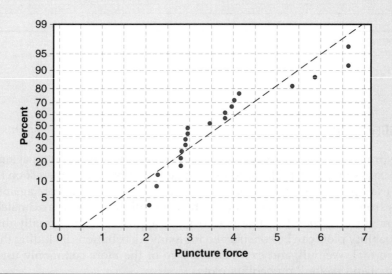

Figure 32.8   Normal probability plot of puncture force for toasted corn flakes.

Weibull Probability Plot

The Weibull probability plot is used to determine if a particular set of data follows a Weibull distribution. The Weibull distribution is often used in reliability problems (the Weibull distribution will be discussed in more detail in Chapter 34). Similarly to the normal probability plot, the Weibull probability plot uses Weibull probability paper, and the actual data are plotted against a percentile that is based on the Weibull distribution. The Weibull probability plot is more difficult to construct by hand than the normal probability plot and will not be outlined here. Many statistical packages have the capability to construct Weibull probability plots.

EXAMPLE 32.8

The following data represent the life of a particular part used in the semiconductor manufacturing industry. Fifteen parts are selected at random and their life (in hours) recorded when the parts are in use. The data are:

479.23, 43.17, 3219.41, 558.46, 56.00, 705.37, 12.02, 280.42,
3867.95, 6672.37, 8494.07, 1220.94, 66.92, 2078.13, 6431.02

It is important to determine the distribution that the data may follow. The Weibull distribution could be investigated. The Weibull probability plot for this set of data is shown in Figure 32.9.

The data fall along a straight line. Therefore, the data appear to follow a Weibull distribution. The Weibull distribution appears to be valid for this set of data.

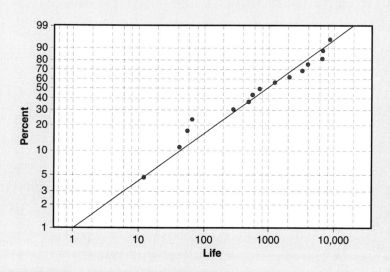

Figure 32.9   Weibull probability plot for life of a part.

Comments on Probability Plotting

Interpretation of probability plots can be subjective. One person may interpret the data as normally distributed, for example, while someone else examining the same plot could say that they are not normally distributed. The closer the data fall along a straight line, the more evidence there is that the distribution of interest is reasonable for that particular set of data. If the plot exhibits curvature or an "S" shape, then other distributions should possibly be investigated. Goodness-of-fit tests are often more reliable approaches to determining the appropriateness of a particular distribution.

Chapter 33

B. Quantitative Concepts

This chapter lays the foundation for understanding how to draw statistical conclusions and how to apply probability terms and concepts.

1. TERMINOLOGY

> Define and apply quantitative terms, including population, parameter, sample, statistic, random sampling, expected value, etc. (Analyze)
>
> **Body of Knowledge VI.B.1**

A *population* is the entirety of all items or units being studied. A *sample* is a subset of items or measurements selected from the larger population. Since it is often impractical to obtain information on all the items or units in the population, we acquire information on a subset of them in order to draw conclusions about the rest.

A *parameter* is a characteristic of a population. It is a quantity that describes characteristics of a population; for example, mean (μ), standard deviation (σ), correlation coefficient (ρ), or fraction nonconforming (p). Often the value of the population parameter is unknown and must be estimated. A *statistic* is a characteristic of a sample and is an estimator of a population parameter. A representative sample is taken from the population and summary statistics calculated such as the average or mean ($\bar{x}$), standard deviation (s), correlation coefficient (r), or fraction nonconforming ($\hat{p}$). In this case, $\bar{x}$ is an estimator for μ.

Probability is a numerical measure representing the likelihood that a particular outcome will occur. The probability that a particular event occurs is a number between zero and one inclusive. For example, if a lot consisting of 100 parts has four nonconforming parts, we would say the probability that a randomly selected part will be nonconforming is 0.04 or four percent.

The concepts can be summarized in the following example.

EXAMPLE 33.1

The thickness of a printed circuit board (PCB) is an important characteristic. If the thickness does not meet specification, the circuit board is reworked or scrapped. The average thickness of the PCB is assumed to be 0.0630 inches (that is, $\mu = 0.0630$). Thickness of 25 randomly chosen PCBs is measured and the average thickness is found to be 0.06314 inches (that is, $\bar{x} = 0.06314$ inches). It is determined that the probability that the sample average diameter (for a sample size of 25) should have been 0.06314 inches or larger is 0.0105.

In this particular problem:

- The *population* is all printed circuit boards manufactured by this company with this process.

- The *sample* is the 25 randomly chosen printed circuit boards.

- The *parameter* is the population average or mean μ and is assumed to be $\mu = 0.0630$ inches.

- The *statistic* is the sample average or sample mean $\bar{x}$, calculated using the sample of 25 printed circuit boards, which was found to be $\bar{x} = 0.06314$ inches.

- A *probability* associated with this sample is 0.0105.

---

2. DRAWING STATISTICAL CONCLUSIONS

Distinguish between numeric and analytical studies. Assess the validity of statistical conclusions by analyzing the assumptions used and the robustness of the technique used. (Evaluate)

Body of Knowledge VI.B.2

Numeric Studies

The purpose of inferential statistics is to infer (arrive at a conclusion by reasoning from evidence) properties of a population through analysis of a sample. This type of study is sometimes referred to as a numeric study. These studies are valid only if the sample is from a stable underlying population. For example, if a control chart is used on a stable process, the data from the chart can be used to conduct a capability study for the material produced while the chart was in use. This *capability study* infers information about the process population based on the sample used for the control chart, and would therefore be a numeric study.

Analytical Studies

Sample data may also be used to study either stable or non-stable processes with the goal of process improvement, which may involve the use of knowledge, experience, creativity, and basic science. Such a study is not numeric because rather than infer properties of the population, the study seeks to determine the causes that impact the process. Inferential methods are inappropriate because the underlying population is often not stable and the goal is to change it rather than determine its characteristics. W. Edwards Deming called these analytical studies. A control chart, when used to take action on the process to maintain statistical control, is an example of a tool for analytical study.

In Chapter 35 a number of statistical tests are described. Each has assumptions or conditions that must be met in order for the test to be valid. It is critical that a test's assumptions or conditions are satisfied before applying the test. In some cases the discussion accompanying the statistical test may state that the test is *robust* to minor deviations from the assumptions or conditions. For example, if one of the conditions of a test is that the population be normal, the test may be robust to minor deviations in this condition. This means that even if the population is almost normal, the test could be applied, with caution about the precision of the conclusion. Needless to say, decisions in situations like this require judgment and experience.

3. PROBABILITY TERMS AND CONCEPTS

> Describe and apply concepts such as independence, mutually exclusive, multiplication rules, complementary probability, joint occurrence of events, etc. (Apply)
>
> **Body of Knowledge VI.B.3**

Basic Definitions

Before discussing probability and probability rules, it is important to define terms that describe the experiment under study. In this context, *experiment* refers to a *random* experiment where different outcomes could be obtained even if the experiment is repeated under identical conditions.

Sample Spaces and Events

The *sample space* is the set of all possible outcomes of an experiment or a set of conditions (this is also referred to as the *universal set* in set theory). The sample space is usually denoted by the capital letter *S*. If the outcomes are finite or countably infinite, then the sample space is considered discrete. If the outcomes are values over an interval of real numbers, then the sample space is considered continuous. (Further discussion of continuous and discrete random variables and distributions is given in Chapter 34.) An *event* is a subset of the sample space and is often denoted by a capital letter such as A, B, C, and so on. If an outcome x is an element or outcome in A, for example, we write this as $x \in$ A. To illustrate these concepts, consider an experiment where a single piston ring for an automobile motor is randomly selected from a lot and classified as conforming (C) or nonconforming (N). The sample space for this experiment is $S = \{C, N\}$. If we are only interested in the event where the piston ring is nonconforming (call this event E), this event would be $E = \{N\}$. As a second illustration, suppose the experiment was to determine how long it takes a worker to complete a task (in minutes). Let x represent the time to complete the task. The sample space consists of all positive real numbers. This can be written as $S = \{x | x > 0\}$. If the event or sample space has no outcomes in it, then we say it is the empty set, denoted $\emptyset$.

Set Operations

It is often of interest to combine events to form other events in which we are interested. There are three basic *set operations* used to create new events of interest:

- The *union* of two events A and B is that event consisting of all outcomes contained in A, in B, or in both. The union is denoted as A $\cup$ B (read "A or B").

- The *intersection* of two events A and B is that event consisting of all outcomes that are contained in both A and B. The intersection is denoted as A $\cap$ B (read "A and B")

- The *complement* of any event in a sample space is an event that contains all the outcomes in the sample space that are *not* in the event itself. The complement of an event A is denoted as A′ (read "A complement" or "not A"). Other notation used to represent the complement of an event includes $\tilde{A}$, A^c, and sometimes $\overline{A}$. We will use the prime notation, A′.

It should be noted that if the intersection of any two events results in the empty set (that is, A $\cap$ B = $\emptyset$), then those two events are called *mutually exclusive*.

EXAMPLE 33.2

A simple illustration involves the rolling of a single, fair six-sided die. In this random experiment, the sample space is $S = \{1, 2, 3, 4, 5, 6\}$. Suppose A is the event where the outcome on a single roll is an even number; so A = $\{2, 4, 6\}$. Suppose B is the event where the outcome on a single roll is greater than 3; so B = $\{4, 5, 6\}$. In this situation:

- A $\cup$ B = $\{2, 4, 5, 6\}$

Continued

Continued

- $A \cap B = \{4, 6\}$
- $A' = \{1, 3, 5\}$, $B' = \{1, 2, 3\}$
- $A \cap A' = \emptyset$ (and $B \cap B' = \emptyset$); the intersection of an event and its complement is *always* the empty set
- $A \cup A' = S$ (and $B \cup B' = S$); the union of any event and its complement *always* equals the sample space

Probability

As stated previously, *probability* is a numerical measure that represents the likelihood that a particular outcome will occur. The probability that a particular event occurs is a number between zero and one inclusive. The probability of an event, say E, is written as P(E).

If the elements of E are mutually exclusive, then P(E) is equal to the sum of the probabilities of the outcomes that make up that event. To illustrate, suppose an event E contains elements a, b, c, d, and e; that is, E = {a, b, c, d, e}. Then the probability of event E would be

$$P(E) = P(a) + P(b) + P(c) + P(d) + P(e).$$

Suppose there are N possible mutually exclusive outcomes in an experiment, all equally likely to occur (such as in the rolling of a fair six-sided die). The probability of any one outcome would then be $1/N$. Another way to look at probability is as a relative frequency. That is, the probability of an outcome would be the number of times that outcome occurs divided by the total number of possible outcomes.

Probability Rules

Consider a sample space S and two events A and B from that sample space. Then

1. $P(S) = 1$
2. $0 \leq P(A) \leq 1$
3. $P(A') = 1 - P(A)$
4. If two events A and B are mutually exclusive, then $P(A \cap B) = 0$.

An important result of rule 4 is sometimes referred to as a *special addition rule* for mutually exclusive events, and is given as

$$P(A \cup B) = P(A) + P(B).$$

In other words, when two events are mutually exclusive, the probability that an outcome in event A will occur, an outcome in event B will occur, or an outcome in both A and B will occur can be found by adding the individual probabilities of each event.

EXAMPLE 33.3

Suppose the number of medication errors that occur for a patient at a particular hospital have the following probabilities:

Number of medication errors	0	1	2	3
Probability	0.90	0.07	0.02	0.01

Let A be the event of at most one medication error occurring, that is, A = {0, 1}. Let B be the event where exactly two medication errors occur; that is, B = {2}. We note that these events are mutually exclusive. For this situation:

- $P(A) = P(0) + P(1) = 0.90 + 0.07 = 0.97$
- $P(B) = 0.02$
- $P(A') = 1 - P(A) = 1 - 0.97 = 0.03$
- $P(A \cap B) = 0$
- $P(A \cup B) = P(A) + P(B) = 0.97 + 0.02 = 0.99$

General Addition Rule

The special addition rule given above applies only to experiments where the two events of interest have no outcomes in common (mutually exclusive). When the events are *not* mutually exclusive, a more general addition rule applies:

$$P(A \cup B) = P(A) + P(B) - P(A \cap B)$$

EXAMPLE 33.4

Cellular phones are put through several inspections before being shipped to the customer. Two defect types are of significant importance: critical (C) and major (M) defects. Phones with either critical or major defects are completely reworked. Using recent inspection data, it was determined that two percent of the cell phones have critical defects only, five percent have major defects only, and one percent have both critical *and* major defects. The manufacturer wants to know what percent of all phones would require complete rework.

In this situation, the information given is:

- $P(C) = 0.02$
- $P(M) = 0.05$
- $P(C \text{ and } M) = P(C \cap M) = 0.01$

Complete rework is necessary if the phone has critical *or* major defects or both. This is the event C ∪ M. The percent of all phones needing rework is then given by P(C ∪ M). Using the addition rule, the percent of phones needing rework would be

Continued

Continued

$$P(C \cup M) = P(C) + P(M) - P(C \cap M)$$
$$= 0.02 + 0.05 - 0.01$$
$$= 0.06.$$

Based on this information, roughly six percent of the cell phones will need rework.

Table 33.1 Contingency table of part color and part size.

	Red	Yellow	Green	Blue	Totals
Small	16	21	14	19	70
Medium	12	11	19	15	57
Large	18	12	21	14	65
Totals	46	44	54	48	192

Contingency Tables

Suppose each part in a lot is one of four colors—red (R), yellow (Y), green (G), or blue (B)—and one of three sizes—small (S), medium (M), or large (L). These attributes can be displayed in a *contingency table* like the one in Table 33.1. (Contingency tables are also used to determine statistical independence of characteristics. This application is discussed in Chapter 35.)

It is often useful to include the row and column totals for calculating quantities of interest, such as probabilities. The total number of parts ($N = 192$) is written in the bottom right-hand corner of the table. The row and column totals provide a great deal of information about the categories of interest. For example, the column total for red is 46. This indicates that the total number of red parts (regardless of size) in the lot is 46. In addition, the row total for medium parts is 57, which means that the total number of medium parts (regardless of color) is 57. The entries in each cell of the table itself (not including the row and column totals) represent the number of parts that have both characteristics. For example, 16 parts are both small *and* red.

EXAMPLE 33.5

We want to determine several probabilities using the contingency table given as Table 33.1. Assume that one of the parts is selected at random.

The probability that the part is small would be

$$P(S) = \frac{70}{192} = 0.365.$$

Continued

Part VI.B.3

Continued

The probability that the part is red would be

$$P(R) = \frac{46}{192} = 0.240.$$

The probability that the part is small *and* red would be

$$P(S \cap R) = \frac{16}{192} = 0.083.$$

The probability that the part is small *or* red would be

$$P(S \cup R) = P(S) + P(R) - P(S \cap R)$$
$$= 0.365 + 0.240 - 0.083$$
$$= 0.522.$$

Using the same formulas, the probability that a randomly selected part is yellow would be P(Y) = 0.229. The probability that the part is red or yellow would be

$$P(R \cup Y) = P(R) + P(Y) - P(R \cap Y)$$
$$= 0.240 + 0.229 - 0$$
$$= 0.469$$

Notice that the events "red" and "yellow" are mutually exclusive (a part cannot be both red and yellow). We could have used the special addition rule to find this probability:

$$P(R \cup Y) = P(R) + P(Y)$$
$$= 0.240 + 0.229$$
$$= 0.469$$

Conditional Probability

We will begin the discussion of conditional probability with an example.

EXAMPLE 33.6

Continuing with the previous example, suppose the selected part is *known* to be green. With this knowledge, what is the probability that the part is large?

Solution:

It is a given that the part is one of the 54 green parts. Now, the number of the 54 green parts that are large is 21. Therefore, the probability that a part will be large, given that it is green would be 21/54 = 0.389.

Example 33.6 involves conditional probability. It is referred to as conditional probability since it is conditioned on the fact that the part is green. In the example, the "probability that the part is large given that it is green" is denoted P(L|G). It is useful to remember that the category to the right of the | sign represents the *given* condition.

Formal Definition. Suppose there are two events A and B. The probability that event A occurs given that event B has already occurred is

$$P(A \mid B) = \frac{P(A \cap B)}{P(B)}.$$

EXAMPLE 33.7

Using the information given in Table 33.1, find:

a. The probability that a part is small given that it is blue

b. The probability that a small part is blue

c. The probability that a green part is red

Solution:

a. $P(S \mid B) = \dfrac{P(S \cap B)}{P(B)} = \dfrac{19}{48} = 0.396$

b. The given condition is that the part is small. Given that the part is small, the probability that it is blue is

$$P(B \mid S) = \frac{P(B \cap S)}{P(S)} = \frac{19}{70} = 0.271.$$

Note that $P(B \cap S) = P(S \cap B)$.

c. $P(R \mid G) = \dfrac{P(R \cap G)}{P(G)} = \dfrac{0}{54} = 0$

Note that red and green are mutually exclusive, so $P(R \cap G) = 0$.

General Multiplication Rule

If the practitioner has any two of the three probabilities needed to calculate the conditional probability given earlier, the third unknown probability can be found. The conditional probability can be rewritten as

$$P(A \cap B) = P(A \mid B)P(B).$$

This is sometimes referred to as the *general multiplication rule*. Verifying that this formula is valid will aid in understanding this concept.

EXAMPLE 33.8

Using the contingency table given as Table 33.1, it is known that the probability a part is red and medium is

$$P(R \cap M) = \frac{12}{192} = 0.0625.$$

Using the general multiplication rule, we would get the same result:

$$P(R \cap M) = P(R \mid M)P(M) = \frac{12}{57}\left(\frac{57}{192}\right) = \frac{12}{192} = 0.0625$$

Independence and the Probability of Independent Events

Events are said to be *independent* if the occurrence of one event does not depend on the occurrence or lack of occurrence of another (or preceding) event. The probability of two independent events occurring can be found by multiplying the individual probabilities of each event. If two events A and B are independent of one another, then the probability of both event A and event B occurring is

$$P(A \cap B) = P(A) \times P(B)$$

For more than two independent events, the independence rule can be extended as

$$P(A \cap B \cap C \cap ...) = P(A) \times P(B) \times P(C) \times ...$$

EXAMPLE 33.9

Assume that the probability that a blood specimen contains high levels of lead contamination is 0.05. Levels of contamination from one person to the next (thus, one sample to the next) are assumed to be independent. If two such samples are analyzed, then the probability that both will contain high levels of contamination is

$$
\begin{aligned}
P(\text{both contaminated}) &= P(\text{1st contaminated} \cap \text{2nd contaminated}) \\
&= P(\text{1st contaminated}) \times P(\text{2nd contaminated}) \\
&= (0.05)(0.05) \\
&= 0.0025
\end{aligned}
$$

Conditional Probability and Independence

Recall that conditional probability is given by

$$P(A \mid B) = \frac{P(A \cap B)}{P(B)}.$$

If two events A and B are known to be independent, then P(A∩B) = P(A)P(B). Therefore, if two events are independent, the probability that event A occurs given that event B has already occurred would be

$$P(A \mid B) = \frac{P(A \cap B)}{P(B)} = \frac{P(A)P(B)}{P(B)} = P(A).$$

In other words, knowing that event B has occurred does not affect the probability that event A will occur. In situations where objects or items are selected at random, one after the other, the items are said to be independent if the first item chosen is placed back into the group before the second item is chosen (with replacement).

EXAMPLE 33.10

A box holds 129 parts, of which six are defective. A part is randomly drawn from the box and placed in a fixture. A second part is then drawn from the box. This is referred to as drawing without replacement. What is the probability that the *second* part is defective (note that there is no condition on the first part chosen)? Let D_i represent the event where the *i*th part chosen is defective and let G_i represent the event where the *i*th part is good.

Solution:

We are looking for $P(D_2)$. There are two mutually exclusive events that can result in a defective part on the second draw: good on first draw and defective on second or else defective on first and defective on second. Symbolically these two events are $(G_1 \cap D_2)$ or else $(D_1 \cap D_2)$. The first step is to find the probability for each of these events. By the general multiplication rule:

$$P(G_1 \cap D_2) = P(G_1)P(D_2 \mid G_1) = \frac{123}{129}\left(\frac{6}{128}\right) = 0.045$$

and

$$P(D_1 \cap D_2) = P(D_1)P(D_2 \mid D_1) = \frac{6}{129}\left(\frac{5}{128}\right) = 0.002$$

Since the two events $(G_1 \cap D_2)$ and $(D_1 \cap D_2)$ are mutually exclusive, we can use the special addition rule in order to find the probability that the second part is defective:

$$P(D_2) = 0.045 + 0.002 = 0.047$$

EXAMPLE 33.11

Consider the information given in Example 33.10. When drawing two parts at random without replacement, what is the probability that one will be good (call this G without a subscript) and one defective (call this D without a subscript)?

Continued

Continued

Solution:

Drawing one good and one defective can occur in two mutually exclusive ways:

$$P(G \cap D) = P(G_1 \cap D_2) + P(G_2 \cap D_1)$$

From the previous example we know that $P(G_1 \cap D_2) = 0.045$. Use the general multiplication rule to find $P(G_2 \cap D_1)$:

$$P(G_2 \cap D_1) = P(D_1)P(G_2 | D_1) = \frac{6}{129}\left(\frac{123}{128}\right) = 0.045$$

Therefore, the probability that one randomly selected part will be good and one will be defective is

$$P(G \cap D) = 0.045 + 0.045 = 0.090.$$

Summary of Key Probability Rules

For events A and B:

Special addition rule: $P(A \cup B) = P(A) + P(B)$ (Use only if A and B are mutually exclusive)

General addition rule: $P(A \cup B) = P(A) + P(B) - P(A \cap B)$ (Always true)

Special multiplication rule: $P(A \cap B) = P(A)P(B)$ (Use only if A and B are independent)

General multiplication rule: $P(A \cap B) = P(A)P(B|A)$ (Always true)

Conditional probability: $P(B|A) = P(A \cap B)P(A)$

Mutually exclusive (or disjoint):

1. A and B are mutually exclusive if they cannot occur simultaneously.

2. If A and B are mutually exclusive, then $P(A \cap B) = 0$.

3. If A and B are mutually exclusive, then $P(A \cup B) = P(A) + P(B)$.

Independence:

1. A and B are independent events if the occurrence of one does not change the probability that that other occurs.

2. If A and B are independent events, then $P(B|A) = P(B)$ (or $P(A|B) = P(A)$).

3. If A and B are independent events, then $P(A \cap B) = P(A)P(B)$.

Sampling Distribution of the Sample Mean

Another important statistical principle refers to the distribution of sample means. The sample mean is a statistic calculated from a sample of data. Since the sample mean can take on different values for different samples taken from the same population, the sample mean is a *random variable*. As a random variable, the sample mean has its own distribution. The distribution of the sample mean is referred to as the *sampling distribution of the sample mean*. An important statistical principle states:

If samples of size n *are randomly drawn from a population with mean μ and standard deviation σ, then the distribution of sample means has the following properties:*

- *Its mean, denoted $\mu_{\bar{x}}$, is equal to the population mean: $\mu_{\bar{x}} = \mu$*

- *Its variance, denoted $\sigma_{\bar{x}}^2$, is equal to the population variance divided by the sample size* n*:*

$$\sigma_{\bar{x}}^2 = \frac{\sigma^2}{n}$$

- *Its standard deviation is equal to the positive square root of the variance:*

$$\sigma_{\bar{x}} = \frac{\sigma}{\sqrt{n}}$$

Also, the standard deviation of the sampling distribution of $\bar{x}$ is referred to as the standard error.

EXAMPLE 33.12

A process with mean $\mu = 1.27$ and standard deviation $\sigma = 0.17$ is monitored with a control chart using samples of size five. Compute the centerline and approximate the upper and lower control limits for the $\bar{x}$ control chart. Assume that the underlying distribution is normally distributed. (Normal distributions will be discussed in more detail in Chapter 34).

Solution

The points on the control chart are means of samples taken from the process's population. Therefore, the centerline for the control chart is : $\mu_{\bar{x}} = \mu = 1.27$. Sometimes, you will see the control limit formulas use the notation : $\mu_{\bar{x}}$ instead of : $\mu_{\bar{x}}$. Conventional control limits are : $\mu_{\bar{x}} \pm 3\sigma_{\bar{x}}$. The standard error is

$$\sigma_{\bar{x}} = \frac{\sigma}{\sqrt{n}} = \frac{0.17}{\sqrt{5}} = 0.076.$$

Continued

Continued

So, the control limits are

$$\mu_{\bar{x}} \pm 3\sigma_{\bar{x}} = 1.27 \pm 3(0.076)$$
$$= 1.27 \pm 0.228$$

or

$$(1.042, 1.498).$$

Expected Value

The *expected value* of any experiment is that value we would expect to be the average response in the long run if the experiment could be run indefinitely.

To illustrate, when flipping a coin there is a 50/50 chance of getting heads or tails. In other words, we would expect heads to appear 50 percent of the time and we would expect tails to appear 50 percent of the time. Thus, in tossing an honest coin, the *expected value* for the fraction of heads obtained would be 1/2. This rarely happens in real life. There are nearly always a few more or a few less heads than tails. But if we tossed the coin a thousand times, the number of heads divided by the number of tosses would be very close to 1/2, and even closer if we tossed it 100,000 times.

In theory, the expected value of any single observation x_i taken from a random sample is equal to the mean of the population μ from which the observation has come. The notation is given as $E(x_i) = \mu$. In essence, this states that an unknown value x_i from some population of interest would be expected to be equal to the true population mean.

EXAMPLE 33.13

A part is selected at random from a population. The true diameter of this population of parts is believed to be 12 mm (that is, $\mu = 12$). Therefore, without actually measuring the part selected at random, we would *expect* the diameter to be 12 mm (that is, $E(x_i) = 12$).

Now, the expected value of the *sample mean* is also μ, the mean of the population. The notation for expected value of the sample mean is $E(\bar{x})$ such that

$$E(\bar{x}) = \mu$$

for a sample of size n.

Example 33.14 summarizes the use of expected value and standard error of the mean.

EXAMPLE 33.14

A sample of 100 parts is selected at random from a population. The true diameter of the population of parts is believed to be 12 mm ($\mu = 12$) with a standard deviation of 0.05 mm (that is, $\sigma = 0.05$). Therefore, we would in theory *expect* the sample of 100 parts to have an average diameter of 12 mm or

$$E(\bar{x}) = \mu = 12.$$

The standard error of the sample mean is found as

$$\sigma_{\bar{x}} = \frac{\sigma}{\sqrt{n}} = \frac{0.05}{\sqrt{100}} = 0.005.$$

The value 0.005 represents the variability associated with the 100 parts chosen at random.

Expected value will be further discussed in Chapter 34 on probability distributions.

Chapter 34

C. Probability Distributions

This chapter focuses on the two kinds of distributions: continuous distributions and discrete distributions. Both distributions will be discussed in this chapter.

- *Continuous distributions* are used when the parameter being measured can be expressed on a continuous scale. Examples include the diameter of piston rings, tensile strength, output voltage, and so on.

- *Discrete distributions* are used when the parameter being measured takes on only certain values, such as integers 0, 1, 2, ... Examples include the number of defects or the number of nonconformities.

1. CONTINUOUS DISTRIBUTIONS

Define and distinguish between these distributions: normal, uniform, bivariate normal, exponential, lognormal, Weibull, chi square, Student's *t*, *F*, etc. (Analyze)

Body of Knowledge VI.C.1

Before commencing discussion of the continuous distributions, two important concepts must be introduced: the probability density function (pdf) and the cumulative density function (cdf). These are also referred to as probability distribution functions and cumulative distribution functions.

Probability Density Function

Probability density functions are mathematical expressions that describe the probability distribution of a continuous random variable. The pdf is denoted by $f(x)$. In most cases, the probabilities associated with some random variable can be described by a probability density function. Figure 34.1 represents a probability

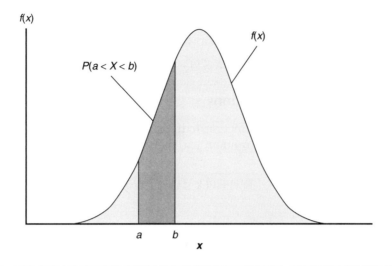

Figure 34.1   A probability density function for a random variable X.

density function for a random variable X. The x-axis represents all possible values of the random variable; the y-axis represents the probability density function $f(x)$. Suppose we wish to find the probability that our random variable X would lie between two real numbers a and b (that is, P(a < X < b)). Graphically, this probability is the shaded area under the curve $f(x)$ and between the X values of a and b (see Figure 34.1).

Definition of a Probability Density Function. For any continuous random variable X, the probability density function $f(x)$ is a function with the following properties:

   a. $f(x) \geq 0$

   b. $\int_{-\infty}^{\infty} f(x)dx = 1$

   c. $P(a \leq X \leq b) = \int_{a}^{b} f(x)dx$; this is the area under the curve $f(x)$ and between the values a and b

The first property (property a) guarantees that all probability values are nonnegative. The second property (property b) can be compared to the concept of sample space given in Chapter 32. That is, the total area under the curve must equal one (or 100 percent) and can be verified by integrating $f(x)$ over all real numbers. Property c simply describes how the probability that X will lie between two real numbers a and b can be determined by integrating $f(x)$ over the range [a, b]. Although it may seem complicated, calculus is not necessary to find most of the probabilities that we need in quality engineering. Tables with probabilities for specific distributions are available as well as software that routinely calculates these probabilities. It should be noted that for continuous distributions, the probability that the random variable *equals* some *specific* value is always zero, that is $P(X = a) = 0$. As a result

$$P(a \leq X \leq b) = P(a < X \leq b) = P(a \leq X < b) = P(a < X < b).$$

Cumulative Distribution Functions

A cumulative distribution function (cdf) is denoted by $F(x)$ and describes the cumulative probability for a random variable X:

$$F(x) = P(X \leq x) = \int_{-\infty}^{x} f(v)dv$$

The cdf can be used to find probabilities of interest for the random variable X. Suppose a and b are any real numbers where $a < b$. Then:

- $P(X < a) = F(a)$
- $P(a < X < b) = P(X < b) - P(X < a) = F(b) - F(a)$
- $P(X > a) = 1 - P(X < a) = 1 - F(a)$

Normal Distribution

An important family of continuous distributions is the *normal distribution*. The normal distribution is a symmetric, bell-shaped distribution. The parameters of the normal distribution are the population mean μ and the population variance σ^2. The normal distribution is depicted in Figure 34.2.

The centerline represents the mean of the distribution. Graphically, the standard deviation is the distance between the centerline and the point at which the down slope of the curve meets the up slope of the curve (that is, point of inflection).

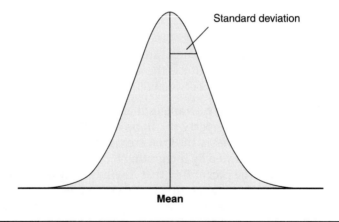

Figure 34.2 Probability density function (pdf) for the normal distribution.

A property of normal distributions is that the area under the curve represents *probability* (or percentage or proportion). The probability can be determined using the standard normal curve table in Appendix F. In a normal distribution, a Z-score for a random variable X is defined as the number of standard deviations between X and the mean of the distribution. Specifically,

$$Z = \frac{X - \mu}{\sigma}.$$

To illustrate, suppose X follows a normal distribution with mean $\mu = 20$ and standard deviation $\sigma = 4$. The Z-score for an X value of 14 would be

$$Z = \frac{X - \mu}{\sigma} = \frac{14 - 20}{4} = -1.5$$

That is, the value of 14 is 1.5 standard deviations *below* the population mean of 20.

By transforming the original random variable into a Z-score, we are able to find probabilities without having to use calculus.

Standard Normal Distribution

If a random variable is normally distributed with mean $\mu = 0$ and variance $\sigma^2 = 1$, it is called a *standard normal random variable* and often denoted as Z. Probabilities for the standard normal distribution are given in Appendix F. The values in this table are the cumulative probabilities $P(Z \le z)$, where the capital letter Z represents a random variable and the lower case letter z is a real number. The cumulative probabilities in Appendix F can be used to find any probability of interest involving a random variable that is normally distributed. Some examples illustrating the use of Appendix F follow.

EXAMPLE 34.1

Let Z be a random variable that follows a standard normal distribution. Find the probability that Z will be less than 2.5.

Solution:

The probability of interest is $P(Z < 2.5)$. This probability is shown graphically in Figure 34.3. It shows that the probability we are interested in is the area to the *left* of 2.5.

In Appendix F, the values of Z are written down the left-hand column and across the top of the table. The entries in the body of the table are the cumulative probabilities, $P(Z \le z)$. In this example our z value is 2.5. In the table, read down the left-hand column to find the value 2.5, then across until you reach the column heading of 0 (since the value in the second decimal place of our z value is 0). The entry in the body of the table for the row of 2.5 and the column of 0 is 0.9938. Therefore, the probability that the random variable Z is less than 2.5 is 0.9938.

Continued

Continued

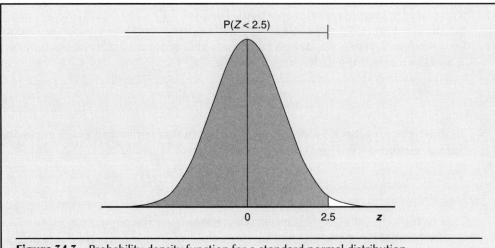

Figure 34.3   Probability density function for a standard normal distribution.

EXAMPLE 34.2

Find the probability that the random variable Z is greater than –2.5.

Solution:

The probability of interest is $P(Z > -2.5)$. From the table in Appendix F, the probability given in the body of the table for –2.5 is 0.0062. But the probabilities in this table are the probabilities that Z is at most that value. That is, $P(Z < -2.5) = 0.0062$, and we want $P(Z > -2.5)$. To find this probability, use the result that the total area under the curve (total probability) must equal 1. Therefore, if $P(Z < -2.5) = 0.0062$, then $P(Z > -2.5) = 0.9938$. More generally, we can find this probability as follows:

$$P(Z > -2.5) = 1 - P(Z < -2.5) = 1 - 0.0062 = 0.9938$$

EXAMPLE 34.3

Find the probability that Z lies between 1.42 and 2.33.

Solution:

The probability of interest is $P(1.42 < Z < 2.33)$. The probability is displayed graphically in Figure 34.4.

The area (thus the probability) of interest lies under the curve and between 1.42 and 2.33, as illustrated in Figure 34.4. The probability of interest can be found using the cumulative probabilities from Appendix F and subtraction:

$$P(1.42 < Z < 2.33) = P(Z < 2.33) - P(Z < 1.42) = 0.9901 - 0.9222 = 0.0679$$

Continued

Continued

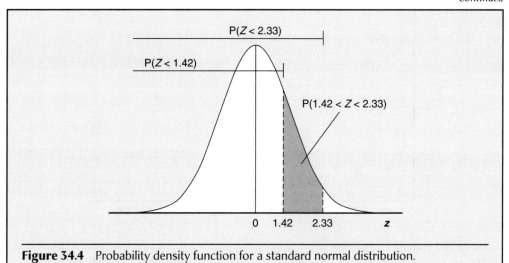

Figure 34.4   Probability density function for a standard normal distribution.

We can now find the probability for any normal random variable by using a simple transformation.

Definition. If X is a random variable that follows a normal distribution with mean μ and variance σ^2, then the random variable Z, where

$$Z = \frac{X - \mu}{\sigma},$$

is also normally distributed with a mean $\mu = 0$ and variance $\sigma^2 = 1$. That is, Z is a random variable that follows a standard normal distribution.

EXAMPLE 34.4

A product-fill operation produces net weights that are normally distributed with mean μ = 8.06 ounces and standard deviation $\sigma = 0.37$ ounces. Estimate the percent of the containers that have a net weight less than 7.08 ounces.

Solution:

Let X represent the weight of the containers. The probability of interest is $P(X < 7.08)$. Transform X into the random variable Z using the relationship

$$Z = \frac{X - \mu}{\sigma},$$

then from Appendix F find the appropriate probability.

$$P(X < 7.08) = P\left[\frac{X - \mu}{\sigma} < \frac{7.08 - 8.06}{0.37}\right] = P(Z < -2.65) = 0.0040$$

This indicates that approximately 0.40 percent of the containers have a net weight less than 7.08 ounces. This can also be stated as the probability that a randomly selected container will have a net weight less than 7.08 is approximately 0.0040.

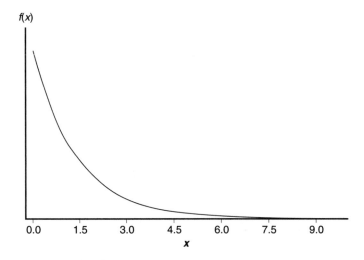

Figure 34.5 Probability density function for an exponentially distributed random variable.

Exponential Distribution

The *exponential distribution* is a continuous probability distribution often used to model problems in reliability. In particular, the exponential distribution models the time or distance between successive events (such as failures) when the events follow a Poisson distribution. The Poisson distribution is often a reasonable model of defects in material or the number of failures in systems. (The Poisson distribution for discrete data will be discussed in the next section.) When we wish to determine the average time between failures, we calculate the inverse of the average number of failures or defects. For example, if there are an average of 0.69 failures per hour, then the mean time between failure (MTBF) is $1/0.69 = 1.45$ hours. Figure 34.5 displays an exponential distribution with a mean of 1.45.

Definition. Suppose X represents the time or distance between successive events of a Poisson process with mean λ (where $\lambda > 0$). The random variable X is said to be an exponential random variable with parameter λ. The pdf for X is

$$f(x) = \lambda e^{-\lambda x}, \text{ for } x \geq 0.$$

Definition. The cumulative density function for an exponentially distributed random variable X is given by

$$F(x) = P(X \leq x) = 1 - e^{-\lambda x}, \text{ for } x \geq 0.$$

EXAMPLE 34.5

The time between calls to a customer service center is an exponentially distributed random variable with a mean time between calls of two minutes. What is the probability that the next phone call will be received in the next one minute?

Continued

Continued

Solution:

Let X represent the time between phone calls received at the customer service center. X follows an exponential distribution with parameter $\lambda = 0.5$ (recall that the mean of an exponential distribution is $1/\lambda$ and the mean in this case is two minutes; thus $\lambda = 1/2 = 0.5$). The probability of interest is $P(X < 1)$ and can be found using the cdf for the exponential:

$$P(X < 1) = F(1) = 1 - e^{-0.5(1)} = 1 - 0.6065 = 0.3935$$

Therefore, the probability that the next phone call will be received within the next minute is 0.3935.

Expected Value and Variance

Suppose the random variable X follows an exponential distribution with parameter λ. The mean (expected value) of X is

$$\mu = E(X) = \frac{1}{\lambda}.$$

The variance of X is

$$\sigma^2 = V(X) = \frac{1}{\lambda^2}.$$

Weibull Distribution

The Weibull distribution is a commonly used distribution in areas such as reliability. The Weibull is extremely flexible in modeling failure distributions that can take on many different shapes. Let X represent a random variable that follows a Weibull distribution. The pdf for the Weibull distribution is:

$$f(x) = \left(\frac{\beta}{\theta}\right)\left(\frac{x - \gamma}{\theta}\right)^{\beta - 1} e^{-\left(\frac{x-\gamma}{\theta}\right)^{\beta}}, \text{ for } x > 0$$

where

β is the shape parameter ($\beta > 0$)

θ is the scale parameter ($\theta > 0$)

γ is a threshold parameter ($\gamma > 0$)

This pdf is referred to as a *three-parameter* Weibull distribution. The threshold parameter allows the user to model a distribution that can not practically begin at zero. It simply shifts the beginning point away from zero. The pdf for the Weibull distribution with $\beta = 1.2$ and $\theta = 20$ is displayed in Figure 34.6.

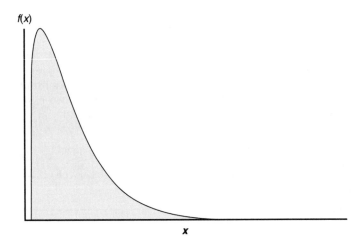

Figure 34.6 Probability density function for the Weibull distribution.

The cdf for a random variable that follows a three-parameter Weibull distribution with parameters β, θ, and γ is

$$P(X \leq x) = F(x) = 1 - e^{-\left(\frac{x-\gamma}{\theta}\right)^{\beta}}$$

The cdf can be used to easily find probabilities associated with the Weibull distribution.

Expected Value and Variance. The expected value for the Weibull distribution is

$$E(X) = \mu = \gamma + \theta \Gamma\left(\frac{1}{\beta} + 1\right)$$

where

$$\Gamma\left(\frac{1}{\beta} + 1\right)$$

is a gamma function (see Montgomery and Runger [2006] or Devore [2007] for discussion of the gamma function). The variance for the Weibull distribution is

$$Var(X) = \sigma^2 = \theta^2 \left[\Gamma\left(\frac{2}{\beta} + 1\right) - \Gamma\left(\frac{2}{\beta} + 1\right)^2\right]$$

The beauty of the Weibull function is that it takes on many shapes depending on the value of β. For example, when $\beta = 1$, the function is exponential and when $\beta = 3.5$ the function is approximately the normal distribution. If the threshold parameter is set equal to zero (that is, $\gamma = 0$), then the three-parameter Weibull reduces to the *two-parameter* Weibull distribution—another commonly used distribution in reliability. The Weibull function is sometimes used for reliability data when the underlying distribution is unknown. This is discussed in more detail in Chapter 20.

Continuous Uniform Distribution

The *continuous uniform distribution* is one that has a flat probability distribution between two points a and b. That is, if each value of the random variable has the same probability of occurring, the distribution is called the uniform distribution. The plot of a uniform distribution has a horizontal line as its upper boundary. An example is given in Figure 34.7.

The pdf for the continuous uniform distribution on the interval $[a, b]$ is

$$f(x) = \begin{cases} \dfrac{1}{b-a}, & a \le x < b \\ 0, & \text{otherwise} \end{cases} .$$

The cdf is

$$P(X < x) = F(x) = \begin{cases} 0, & x < a \\ \dfrac{(x-a)}{(b-a)} & a \le x < b \\ 1 & b \le x \end{cases} .$$

The cdf can easily be used to find probabilities associated with the uniform distribution using the relationships shown previously in this section.

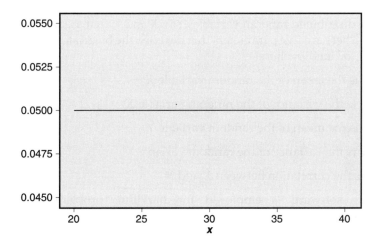

Figure 34.7   Continuous uniform probability distribution.

EXAMPLE 34.6

The thickness of a manufactured airplane part is uniformly distributed between 2.2 and 2.8 millimeters. We would like to find the probability that the thickness is less than 2.6 millimeters.

Solution:

Let X represent the thickness of the airplane part. We want to find $P(X < 2.6)$.

Since we are looking for X less than some value, we have $P(X < 2.6) = F(2.6)$. Since the number that we are interested in (2.6) lies between the endpoints 2.2 and 2.8, we will use $F(X) = (x - a)/(b - a)$ from the cdf. The probability that the thickness is less than 2.6 millimeters is

$$P(X < 2.6) = F(2.6) = (2.6 - 2.2)/(2.8 - 2.2) = 0.667.$$

Expected Value and Variance. The expected value (mean) and variance for a continuous uniform distribution over the interval $[a, b]$ are

$$E(X) = \mu = \frac{a + b}{2}$$

$$V(X) = \sigma^2 = \frac{(b - a)^2}{12}$$

Bivariate Normal Distribution

If there are two variables of interest (such as length and width), each of which is normally distributed, the resulting distribution is called *bivariate normal*. The bivariate normal distribution can be used to describe the distribution of two normally distributed random variables, say X and Y, that are not necessarily independent. There are five parameters that describe the bivariate normal distribution: μ_X, μ_Y, σ_X^2, σ_Y^2, and ρ where:

- μ_X is the mean of the random variable X
- σ_X^2 is the variance of the random variable X
- μ_Y is the mean of the random variable Y
- σ_Y^2 is the variance of the random variable Y
- ρ is the correlation between X and Y

Computer software is employed for handling problems involving these distributions.

The bivariate normal distribution can be illustrated through the following example.

EXAMPLE 34.7

The inside and outside diameters of a particular type of tubing are important character-istics to be measured. Let X represent the inside diameter of the tubing and let Y repre-sent the outside diameter of the tubing. The inside and outside diameters are assumed to be normally distributed but not independent. For this problem, $\mu_X = 26$, $\mu_Y = 39$, $\sigma_X^2 = 0.16$, $\sigma_Y^2 = 0.09$, and the correlation between the inside and outside diameters is assumed to be $\rho = 0.96$.

It is important that the diameters both meet the specifications of several custom-ers. Suppose the specifications for one particular customer for X are 25.2 to 26.4 and the specifications of Y are 38.5 to 40.9. The probability that *both* dimensions are within specifications at the same time is P(25.2 < X < 26.4, 38.5 < Y < 40.9) = 0.7922. This value was calculated using computer software.

Lognormal Distribution

If a variable X follows a normal distribution, then the variable $Y = e^X$ follows a *log-normal* distribution. This distribution has applications in modeling life spans for products, response time, time-to-failure data, as well as certain economic vari-ables. Some important properties of the lognormal distribution are:

- It assumes only *positive* values

- It is a right-skewed distribution

- It is the distribution of the random variable whose logarithm follows the *normal* distribution

Suppose X follows a *normal* distribution with mean μ_X and variance σ_X^2, and $Y = e^X$. We then say that Y follows a *lognormal* distribution with the following mean and variance:

$$\mu_Y = E(Y) = e^{\mu_X + (1/2)\sigma_X^2}$$

$$V(Y) = \sigma_Y^2 = e^{2\mu_X + \sigma_X^2}(e^{\sigma_X^2} - 1)$$

When the data follow a lognormal distribution, a transformation of data can be done to make the data follow a normal distribution so we can then find probabili-ties, construct confidence intervals, and conduct tests of hypotheses (all of which depend on the assumption that the logged data follow a *normal* distribution).

Sampling Distributions

A *sampling distribution* is the probability distribution of a sample statistic. The following sampling distributions are used in the inferential statistics chapters to follow. Each of the following sampling distributions can be defined in

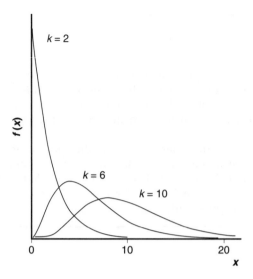

Figure 34.8   Several chi-square distributions.

terms of normally distributed random variables. Their theoretical bases are introduced here.

Chi-Square (χ^2) Distribution. Suppose Z_1, Z_2, Z_3, . . . , Z_k are independent standard normal random variables. Then the random variable

$$\chi^2 = Z_1^2 + Z_2^2 + Z_3^2 + \ldots + Z_k^2$$

follows a *chi-square distribution* with k degrees of freedom. The probability density function for the chi-square distribution is

$$f(x) = \frac{1}{2^{k/2}\Gamma\left(\dfrac{k}{2}\right)} x^{(k/2)-1} e^{-x/2}, \text{ for } x > 0.$$

The expected value and variance for the chi-square distribution are $\mu = k$ and $\sigma^2 = 2k$, respectively. Several chi-square distributions are displayed in Figure 34.8.

Student's t Distribution. Let Z be a standard normal random variable and W be a χ^2 random variable with k degrees of freedom where Z and W are statistically independent. Then the random variable T defined as

$$T = \frac{Z}{\sqrt{\dfrac{W}{k}}}$$

has a probability density function given by

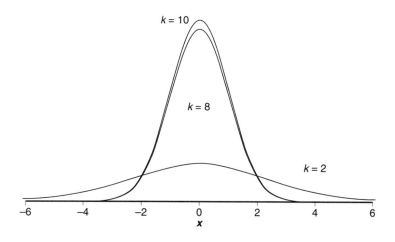

Figure 34.9   Probability density functions for three t distributions.

$$f(t) = \frac{\Gamma\left(\dfrac{k+1}{2}\right)}{\sqrt{\pi k}\,\Gamma\left(\dfrac{k}{2}\right)} \times \frac{1}{\left[\dfrac{t^2}{k}+1\right]^{(k+1)/2}}, \quad \text{for } -\infty < t < \infty,$$

which follows a t distribution with k degrees of freedom. For $k > 1$, the mean and variance for the t distribution are $\mu = 0$ and $\sigma^2 > 1$. For $k = 1$, the t distribution is a *Cauchy* distribution, which has no mean or variance. Figure 34.9 displays t distributions for various degrees of freedom. The t distribution is very similar to the standard normal distribution since both are symmetric, bell-shaped, and have $\mu = 0$. However, the tails of the t distribution are heavier than the standard normal; in other words, there is more probability in the tails (extreme values) of the t distribution than in the standard normal distribution. Notice that as the degrees of freedom go to infinity the form of the Student's t distribution becomes the standard normal distribution.

F *Distribution*. Suppose Y and W are independent chi-square random variables with k_1 and k_2 degrees of freedom, respectively. Then the random variable

$$F = \frac{Y / k_1}{W / k_2}$$

is said to follow an F distribution with k_1 and k_2 degrees of freedom.

Summary of Continuous Distributions

Table 34.1 summarizes the pdf, mean, and variance for certain continuous distributions.

Table 34.1   pdf, mean, and variance for certain continuous distributions.

Distribution	pdf ($f(x)$)	Mean	Variance
Normal	$\dfrac{1}{\sqrt{2\pi}\sigma}e^{-\frac{(x-\mu)^2}{2\sigma^2}}$	μ	σ^2
Exponential	$\lambda e^{-\lambda x}$	$\dfrac{1}{\lambda}$	$\dfrac{1}{\lambda^2}$
Weibull (three-parameter)	$\left(\dfrac{\beta}{\theta}\right)\left(\dfrac{x-\gamma}{\theta}\right)^{\beta-1}e^{-\left(\frac{x-\gamma}{\theta}\right)^{\beta}}$	$\gamma+\theta\Gamma\left(\dfrac{1}{\beta}+1\right)$	$\theta^2\left[\Gamma\left(\dfrac{2}{\beta}+1\right)-\Gamma\left(\dfrac{2}{\beta}+1\right)^2\right]$
Uniform	$\dfrac{1}{b-a}$	$\dfrac{a+b}{2}$	$\dfrac{(b-a)^2}{12}$

2. DISCRETE DISTRIBUTIONS

> Define and distinguish between these distributions: binomial, Poisson, hypergeometric, multinomial, etc. (Analyze)
>
> **Body of Knowledge VI.C.2**

Typical applications for discrete distributions in quality engineering include situations where the variable of interest is either the number of nonconformities or the number of nonconforming units in a sample. The variable represents a count and would have to be zero or a positive whole number. It should also be noted that for discrete distributions the term probability density function is not often used. Instead, the mathematical expression that describes the probability distribution for a discrete distribution is referred to as a *probability mass function* (pmf). The cumulative distribution function (cdf) also exists for discrete distributions.

Binomial

The *binomial distribution* can be applied in situations where the experiment can result in only one of two possible outcomes, for example, good/bad, go/no-go, with/without, conforming/nonconforming, success/failure. In addition, the outcome on one run of the experiment (often referred to as a *trial*) does not affect the outcome on subsequent trials, that is, the trials are said to be independent. The outcomes are often referred to as a *success* or *failure*. Examples include number of heads on 50 flips of a fair coin or the number of manufactured parts that are out of specification. In one type of problem that is frequently encountered, the engineer needs to determine the probability of obtaining a certain number of nonconforming units in a sample.

The necessary conditions for a random variable to follow the binomial distribution are:

1. There are a fixed number of observations or trials n.

2. The n trials are independent.

3. Each trial results in one of two possible outcomes (success or failure).

4. The probability of a success is denoted by p; the probability of a failure is then $1 - p$. The probability of a success is assumed constant trial to trial.

Suppose an experiment consists of n independent trials. Let X represent the number of successes in n trials. Furthermore, let p be the probability of success in one trial. Then the probability of getting x successes in n trials is described by the pmf

$$f(x) = P(X = x) = {}_nC_x p^x (1-p)^{n-x}$$

where

x is the number of successes, with a probability of each success given by p.

The number of failures is then $n - x$, where $1 - p$ is the probability of a failure.

The combination ${}_nC_x$ represents the number of ways x successes can occur in n trials, where

$$_nC_x = \binom{n}{x} = \frac{n!}{x!(n-x)!} \text{ and } n! = n(n-1)(n-2)...1.$$

EXAMPLE 34.8

Ten manufactured parts are randomly selected from a batch where it is believed that the percent nonconforming is 15 percent. It is important to determine the probability that exactly two out of the 10 manufactured parts will be nonconforming. We will define a success to be a nonconforming part. Let X represent the number of nonconforming parts. In this scenario, $n = 10$, $x = 2$, and $p = 0.15$. Then

$$_nC_x = {}_{10}C_2 = \binom{10}{2} = \frac{10!}{2!(10-2)!} = 45$$

and

$$P(X = 2) = {}_{10}C_2 (0.15)^2 (1-0.15)^{10-2}$$
$$= 45(0.0225)(0.85)^8$$
$$= 0.2759.$$

The probability that a sample of size 10 will have exactly two nonconforming parts is approximately 0.2759.

EXAMPLE 34.9

Consider the previous example. Suppose now we are interested in the probability of finding less than two nonconforming parts. If X represents the number of nonconforming parts, the probability that less than two nonconforming parts will be found in the sample is $P(X < 2)$.

Solution:

The value 2 is not included in this event of interest. So we can rewrite the probability equivalently as

$$P(X < 2) = P(X \le 1) = P(X = 0) + P(X = 1).$$

In this case, the binomial formula must be applied twice:

$$P(X < 2) = P(X \le 1) = P(X = 0) + P(X = 1)$$

$$= {}_{10}C_0(0.15)^0(1 - 0.15)^{10-0} + {}_{10}C_1(0.15)^1(1 - 0.15)^{10-1}$$

$$= 1(1)(0.85)^{10} + 10(0.15)(0.85)^9$$

$$= 0.1969 + 0.3474$$

$$= 0.5443$$

The probability that less than two parts out of 10 will be nonconforming is approximately 0.5443.

Expected Value and Variance. The expected value and variance for a random variable X that follows a binomial distribution with n trials and probability of success p are

$$E(X) = \mu = np$$

$$V(X) = \sigma^2 = np(1 - p).$$

Poisson Distribution

When observations take place over a continuum, such as time or space, then we do not have a finite series of discrete trials. For example, how often does a machine require adjustment, or how many nonconformities occur in a unit of fabric?

The necessary conditions for a random variable to follow a Poisson distribution are:

1. The counts or occurrences are independent of each other.

2. The probability that a count occurs in an interval is the same for *all* intervals of that size or length.

Let λ be a parameter representing the mean number of counts over an interval. Let X represent the number of counts in the interval. Then the probability that x counts occur in an interval is described by the probability mass function

$$f(x) = P(X = x) = \frac{e^{-\lambda}\lambda^x}{x!}, \text{ for } x = 0, 1, 2, \ldots$$

where $e = 2.71828 \ldots$.

EXAMPLE 34.10

The serious accident rate in a company is three per year. The probability there will be at most one serious accident during the next year is as follows. The probability of interest is $P(X \leq 1) = P(X = 0) + P(X = 1)$.

$$P(X \leq 1) = P(X = 0) + P(X = 1)$$

$$= \frac{e^{-3}3^0}{0!} + \frac{e^{-3}3^1}{1!}$$

$$= 0.05 + 0.149$$

$$= 0.199$$

Therefore, the probability that at most one serious accident will occur during the next year is approximately 0.2.

Expected Value and Variance. The expected value and variance for a random variable X that follows a Poisson distribution with parameter λ are

$$E(X) = \mu = \lambda$$

$$V(X) = \sigma^2 = \lambda.$$

Hypergeometric Distribution

When sampling from a finite population where independence is not assumed (for example, drawing cards without replacement from a deck of 52 cards, or selecting a sample of items from an isolated lot), then the probability changes with each observation.

The *hypergeometric distribution* is used when items are drawn without replacement from a population of interest. Specifically, the items are not returned to the population before the next item (or items) is/are drawn. It is often used for samples taken from small populations. The items must fall into one of two categories such as conforming or nonconforming. Recall that the binomial distribution assumes either an infinite population or sampling with replacement (independent events). There can be a considerable difference when the population is small (results will be similar when the total population is large).

Suppose we have a finite population of size N from which a sample of size n is drawn (without replacement). Furthermore, let A represent the number of nonconforming units in the population and let x represent the number of nonconforming units in the sample. The probability of obtaining x nonconforming items in a sample of size n for this situation is given by

$$f(x) = \frac{\binom{A}{x}\binom{N-A}{n-x}}{\binom{N}{n}}$$

where the combinations are:

$\binom{A}{x}$ is the number of ways of choosing x nonconforming units from A total possible nonconforming units.

$\binom{N-A}{n-x}$ is the number of ways of choosing $(n-x)$ conforming units from a total of $(N-A)$ conforming units in the population.

$\binom{N}{n}$ is the number of ways of choosing a sample of size n from a population of size N.

EXAMPLE 34.11

The risk of implanting a biomedical device that may be nonconforming is important to quantify. Several assumptions must be made in order to obtain an accurate estimate of the risk, such as to whether or not devices have the same failure rate, how long the devices are stored before implantation, and so on. In addition, the number of nonconforming medical devices in a population of devices often has to be estimated using prior knowledge and/or previous data. For one of these biomedical devices manufactured by a local company, there has been one known failure after implantation within the last month. Based on prior information, it is assumed that out of 200 devices there are three that are nonconforming. If 30 medical devices are randomly selected out of the 200 devices, what is the probability that exactly one device will be nonconforming? For this situation, $N = 200$, $n = 30$, $A = 3$, and $x = 1$, and the probability of interest is $P(X = 1)$:

$$P(X = 1) = \frac{\binom{3}{1}\binom{200-3}{30-1}}{\binom{200}{30}} = 0.3281$$

The probability of selecting a sample of 30 devices and one is nonconforming is 0.3281.

Expected Value and Variance. The expected value and variance for the hypergeometric distribution with parameters N, A, n, x are

$$E(X) = \mu = np$$

$$V(X) = \sigma^2 = np(1-p)\left(\frac{N-n}{N-1}\right)$$

where $p = A/N$.

Multinomial Distribution

The multinomial distribution is used when an experiment consisting of n trials could result in *more* than two possible outcomes; the outcome is placed into one of several categories. For example, a randomly selected part could be classified as good, fair, or poor. Another example could be when a nonconforming part is found from a manufacturing process; it could be due to machine wear, temperature, or a problem with raw material.

Geometric and Pascal Distributions

The *geometric distribution* involves independent trials that can result in one of only two possible outcomes, similar to the binomial distribution. However, for the geometric distribution the number of trials is not fixed. The random variable X represents the number of trials until the first success is obtained. An example would be determining the probability that x acceptable parts are produced before the first nonconforming part is generated.

The geometric distribution is a special case of a more general distribution known as the *Pascal distribution* (also known as the *negative binomial distribution*). For the geometric distribution, sampling is terminated once the first success is obtained. For the Pascal distribution, sampling is terminated only after a fixed number of successes r has been obtained. Obviously, when $r = 1$ we have the special case of the geometric distribution.

Summary of Discrete Distributions

The following rules can be applied for some of the key discrete distributions including the binomial, Poisson, and hypergeometric distributions:

- Use with binary information (yes/no, conforming/nonconforming) and for nonconformities.

- Use the hypergeometric when $n > 5\%N$ and when the sample is taken without replacement.

- Use the binomial when the sample is taken with replacement or when $n < 5\%N$ and the sample is taken without replacement.

- Use the Poisson when there can be more than one nonconformity per item or as an approximation for the binomial when $n > 100$ and $np < 10$.

Table 34.2 summarizes the pmf, mean, and variance for certain discrete distributions.

Table 34.2   pmf, mean, and variance for certain discrete distributions.

Distribution	pmf ($f(x)$)	Mean	Variance
Binomial	$_nC_x p^x (1-p)^{n-x}$	np	$np(1-p)$
Poisson	$\dfrac{e^{-\lambda}\lambda^x}{x!}$	λ	λ
Hypergeometric	$\dfrac{\dbinom{A}{x}\dbinom{N-A}{n-x}}{\dbinom{N}{n}}$	np	$np(1-p)\left(\dfrac{N-n}{N-1}\right)$

GENERAL FORM OF EXPECTED VALUE AND VARIANCE

For many of the distributions described in this chapter the specific expected value and variance were provided. In this section are formulas for expected value and variance for discrete and continuous distributions.

Continuous Distributions

The expected value of a continuous random variable X with pdf $f(x)$ is

$$E(X) = \mu_X = \int_{-\infty}^{\infty} xf(x)dx.$$

The variance of a continuous random variable X with pdf $f(x)$ is

$$V(X) = \sigma_X^2 = \int_{-\infty}^{\infty} (x-\mu_X)^2 f(x)dx.$$

Discrete Distributions

The expected value of a discrete random variable X with pmf $f(x)$ is

$$E(X) = \mu_X = \sum xf(x)$$

for all outcomes x from the distribution. Remember, $f(x)$ describes the probability that x will occur.

The variance of a discrete random variable X with pmf $f(x)$ is

$$V(X) = \sigma_X^2 = \sum (x-\mu)^2 f(x).$$

As shown previously, the standard deviation for a random variable X, discrete or continuous, is the positive square root of the variance.

EXAMPLE 34.12

Suppose the number of medication errors for a patient at a hospital have the following probability mass function (written in table form):

Number of medication errors X	0	1	2	3
Probability	0.90	0.07	0.02	0.01

The expected number of medication errors would be

$$E(X) = \mu_X = \sum xf(x) = 0(0.90) + 1(0.07) + 2(0.02) + 3(0.01) = 0.14$$

The variance of the number of medication errors would be

$$V(X) = \sum (x - \mu)^2 f(x)$$
$$= (0 - 0.14)^2(0.90) + (1 - 0.14)^2(0.07) + (2 - 0.14)^2(0.02) + (3 - 0.14)^2(0.01)$$
$$= 0.2204$$

CENTRAL LIMIT THEOREM REVISITED

In Chapter 32 a very general statement about the central limit theorem was provided. With the introduction of the sampling distribution of the sample mean and a description of the normal distribution, more specific details of the central limit theorem are given here.

Definition

Suppose $X_1, X_2, \ldots, X_n$ is a random sample taken from a distribution with mean μ and variance σ^2. If n is sufficiently large, then the sample mean $\bar{X}$ follows approximately a normal distribution with $\mu_{\bar{X}} = \mu$ and variance $\sigma_{\bar{X}}^2 = \sigma^2/n$.

Notice that the definition does not state that the underlying distribution from which the sample is drawn must be normally distributed. The true form of the distribution does not have to be normally distributed as long as the sample size is sufficiently large. There have been several recommended cutoffs for large n including $n > 30$ or $n > 40$.

However, if the underlying distribution is normal, then the large n requirement is not necessary. In this case, the sampling distribution of $\bar{X}$ will also follow a normal distribution with mean $\mu_{\bar{X}} = \mu$ and variance $\sigma_{\bar{X}}^2 = \sigma^2/n$.

Practical Use of the Central Limit Theorem

An important application of the central limit theorem described here has been in calculating probabilities associated with the sample mean. In addition, it is important in statistical inference, statistical process control, process capability analysis, and so on, as we will see in the remaining chapters.

Recall that if a random variable X follows a normally distributed random variable with mean μ and variance σ^2, then the random variable

$$Z = \frac{X - \mu}{\sigma}$$

will follow a standard normal distribution with $\mu = 0$ and $\sigma^2 = 1$. By the central limit theorem stated above,

$$Z = \frac{\bar{X} - \mu_{\bar{x}}}{\sigma_{\bar{x}}} = \frac{\bar{X} - \mu}{\sigma / \sqrt{n}}$$

also follows a standard normal distribution with $\mu = 0$ and $\sigma^2 = 1$. Using this result, we can find probabilities associated with the sample mean.

EXAMPLE 34.13

Recall the product-fill operation example given earlier in this chapter where the product-fill operation produces net weights that are normally distributed with mean $\mu = 8.06$ ounces and standard deviation $\sigma = 0.37$ ounces.

a. What is the probability that a randomly selected container will weigh less than 7.08 ounces?

b. What is the probability that a sample of nine randomly selected containers will have an average net weight less than 7.08 ounces?

Solution:

Let X represent the weight of the containers.

a. The probability of interest is $P(X < 7.08)$. Transform X into the random variable Z using the relationship

$$Z = \frac{X - \mu}{\sigma},$$

then from Appendix F find the appropriate probability.

$$P(X < 7.08) = P\left[\frac{X - \mu}{\sigma} < \frac{7.08 - 8.06}{0.37}\right] = P(Z < -2.65) = 0.0040$$

Therefore, the probability that a randomly selected container will have a net weight less than 7.08 is approximately 0.0040. (Note that this is the same answer we found previously.)

b. The probability of interest here is $P(\bar{X} < 7.08)$. Transform $\bar{X}$ into the random variable Z using the relationship

$$Z = \frac{\bar{X} - \mu}{\sigma / \sqrt{n}} :$$

Continued

Continued

$$P(\bar{X} < 7.08) = P\left(\frac{\bar{X} - \mu}{\sigma / \sqrt{n}} < \frac{7.08 - 8.06}{0.37 / \sqrt{9}} \right) = P\left(Z < -7.95 \right) = 0$$

Therefore, it would be very unlikely that a random sample of nine such containers would have an average net weight less than 7.08 ounces.

Note: In the previous example, the value $z = -7.95$ is not given in the standard normal table in Appendix F. The table values only extend from -3.59 to 3.59. If the z value is not on the table, it does not mean that it is not a possible value. When the value of z is not on the table, the probability of interest will be practically zero or one, depending on the area of interest under the curve and the sign on the z-value. For example, the $P(Z < -7.95) \cong 0$, $P(Z > -7.95) \cong 1$, $P(Z < 7.95) \cong 1$, $P(Z > 7.95) \cong 0$.

Part VI.C.2

Chapter 35

D. Statistical Decision Making

1. POINT ESTIMATES AND CONFIDENCE INTERVALS

> Define, describe, and assess the efficiency
> and bias of estimators. Calculate and
> interpret standard error, tolerance intervals,
> and confidence intervals. (Evaluate)
>
> **Body of Knowledge VI.D.1**

Point Estimation

Suppose an estimate is needed for the average coating thickness of a population of 1000 circuit boards received from a supplier. Rather than measure all 1000 boards, randomly select a sample of 40 for measurement. Suppose that the average coating thickness of these 40 boards is 0.003 and the standard deviation of the 40 coating measurements is 0.005. The estimate for the average coating thickness on the entire lot of 1000 is then around 0.003. This value is called the *point estimate*. In this case the sample mean is a *point estimator* of the population mean (recall the definitions of population mean, sample mean, parameter, and statistic given in Chapter 33).

Efficiency, Bias, and Standard Error of Estimators

To find information about a population of interest, it is important to be able to obtain information about the *parameters* that describe the population. Recall that parameters would include the population mean μ and population variance σ^2, for example. It is important to be able to estimate the parameters using information acquired from a sample taken from the population. A statistic, such as the sample mean, is used as a point estimator for a parameter, in this case the population mean (keep in mind that statistic refers to a value obtained from a sample and parameter is a characteristic of a population).

The point estimator is said to be *unbiased* if the expected value of the point estimator is equal to the parameter that it is estimating. Consider the sample and population means. If a sample consists of n observations, $X_1, X_2, \ldots, X_n$, taken from a normal population, then the sample mean $\bar{X}$ is known to be an unbiased estimator of the population mean μ, that is, $E(\bar{X}) = \mu$. It can also be shown that the sample variance s^2 for the same situation (n observations taken from a normal distribution) is an unbiased estimator for the population variance σ^2, that is $E(s^2) = \sigma^2$. However, the sample standard deviation s is *not* an unbiased estimator for σ, yet the bias is often negligible for all but very small sample sizes.

There is sometimes more than one possible unbiased point estimator for a parameter. One point estimator for a parameter is said to be more *efficient* than another if the variance of the point estimator is smaller than the variance of its competitor. As a simple example, consider a random sample of observations, $X_1, X_2, \ldots, X_n$, taken from a population with mean μ and variance σ^2. The sample mean $\bar{X}$ is one point estimator for the population mean μ. However, any one observation X_i is also a possible point estimator for μ. Recall from Chapter 33 that the variance of the sampling distribution of $\bar{X}$ is σ^2/n (that is, $V(\bar{X}) = \sigma_{\bar{X}}^2 = \sigma^2/n$) and the variance of a single observation from a population with variance σ^2 is simply σ^2 (that is, $V(X_i) = \sigma^2$). Since $V(\bar{X}) < V(X_i)$, $\bar{X}$ is said to be a more efficient point estimator than X_i for μ.

The *standard error* (s.e.) of a statistic was briefly introduced in Chapter 33. In general, the standard error of a point estimator provides a measure of precision of the estimate and is simply the square root of the variance of the point estimator. For example, we know that the variance of the sampling distribution of the point estimator $\bar{X}$ is σ^2/n. The standard error is then $\sigma/\sqrt{n}$. You sometimes see this written as s.e. $(\bar{X}) = \sigma/\sqrt{n}$.

When we calculate a statistic of interest, such as the sample mean, from real populations of interest we know that this estimate is not exactly equal to the true population mean. We could select 15 different samples of the same size n from the same population, calculate 15 sample means, and most if not all of them would be different. So which of the 15 would be the best estimate? Well, any one of the sample means would be an appropriate estimate of the population mean. As the sample size n increases, our estimates become more precise. If we were to use the entire population, our estimate would be perfect, but that is rarely found in practice. In nearly all cases, the sample means will be different even though they are drawn from the same population. The *variability* in the estimates needs to be quantified somehow.

Confidence Intervals

In this section we will present:

- Confidence intervals for a single population mean μ

- Confidence intervals for a single population variance σ^2

- Confidence intervals for a single population standard deviation σ

- Confidence intervals for a single population proportion p.

In the example given at the beginning of this chapter, is the population mean exactly 0.003? Almost surely not, due to sampling error. To capture information about a parameter, we need to quantify the variability in this estimate and then report it in a meaningful way. One type of estimation that can be used is called interval estimation. One of the most useful interval estimation approaches is constructing *confidence intervals* on the parameter of interest.

In general, a confidence interval on a population parameter depends on:

- A point estimate for the parameter of interest

- An estimate of the standard error of the point estimate

- A stated level of confidence, denoted by $1 - \alpha$ (also called the *confidence coefficient*)

- In some cases, an idea of the distribution of the underlying population, at least approximately

For example, suppose I wish to construct a 95 percent confidence interval on a population mean μ (complete details and discussion of confidence intervals will be presented later in this chapter). I would take a random sample from the population, calculate the necessary statistics (for example, sample mean and sample variance—if population variance is not known), and construct an interval on μ using the sample information (and some other information). Suppose I found the 95 percent confidence interval on μ to be $16 \leq \mu \leq 22$. This is much more informative than just reporting that the sample mean was found to be $\bar{x} = 19$.

General Form of the Confidence Interval. The general form of a $100(1 - \alpha)\%$ two-sided confidence interval for any population parameter (we will denote it as θ) is

$$L \leq \theta \leq U$$

where

L = lower endpoint of the confidence interval

U = upper endpoint of the confidence interval

θ = parameter of interest, such as μ or σ

$1 - \alpha$ = confidence coefficient (level of confidence)

Interpretation of the Confidence Interval. There are two general interpretations of the results from a confidence interval: the *probabilistic* interpretation and the *practical* interpretation.

Probabilistic Interpretation. The *probabilistic interpretation* of the confidence level would be the proportion of all confidence intervals constructed on that parameter (under repeated sampling and identical conditions) that would contain the true parameter. For example, a 95 percent confidence interval on μ would be interpreted as the percent of all confidence intervals constructed (under repeated sampling and identical conditions) that would contain the population mean μ. Consider a normal population with known mean $\mu = 25$ from which 20 samples of size $n = 100$ are selected. Twenty 95 percent confidence intervals on μ are constructed, with the following results:

(24.4713, 25.6473)   (24.0548, 25.2308)

(24.5202, 25.6962)	(23.9702, 25.1461)
(24.3994, 25.5754)	(24.8004, 25.9763)
(24.1861, 25.3620)	(24.4020, 25.5780)
(24.7750, 25.9510)	(23.8412, 25.0172)
(24.0617, 25.2377)	(24.4872, 25.6632)
(24.2578, 25.4337)	(24.4695, 25.6455)
(24.0038, 25.1798)	(25.0248, 26.2008)
(24.1231, 25.2991)	(24.4982, 25.6742)
(24.2900, 25.4659)	(24.1859, 25.3619)

What percent of these confidence intervals contain the true population mean μ = 25? In this scenario, 19 out of 20 (or 95 percent) of the confidence intervals constructed contain the true population mean μ = 25. That also means that five percent of all intervals constructed would not contain the true population mean.

Practical Interpretation. Since the true parameter value, such as the population mean μ, is usually unknown in practice, the probabilistic interpretation may not be very useful. Additionally, we often only have one sample of data, not 20. The *practical interpretation* of a confidence interval constructed in this situation would be a statement of degree of belief that the confidence interval contains the true μ. For example, we are 95 percent confident that the 95 percent confidence interval will contain the true population mean μ.

It should be noted that the practical interpretation should never be misconstrued as saying that the "probability that the confidence interval contains the true value μ is 0.95." Remember, the true value of the population mean μ exists but is unknown. Therefore, when we construct a confidence interval on μ, then either the interval contains the true value of μ (probability of 1) or not (probability of 0).

Next, confidence intervals involving single samples will be covered.

Confidence Intervals for a Single Population Mean μ. In this section, the presentation of confidence intervals on a population mean will be divided into two cases:

1. Confidence intervals on μ when the population variance σ^2 is assumed known

2. Confidence intervals on μ when the population variance σ^2 is assumed unknown

Case 1: Population Variance σ^2 Is Assumed Known. Let $X_1, X_2, \ldots, X_n$ represent a random sample taken from a normal distribution with known variance σ^2 but unknown population mean μ. From Chapter 34, we know that the sampling distribution of $\bar{X}$ is normally distributed with mean μ and variance σ^2/n. And

$$Z = \frac{\bar{X} - \mu}{\sigma / \sqrt{n}}$$

follows a standard normal distribution. It can be shown that a general $100(1 - \alpha)\%$ confidence interval on μ is given by

$$\bar{x} - z_{\alpha/2}\frac{\sigma}{\sqrt{n}} \leq \mu \leq \bar{x} + z_{\alpha/2}\frac{\sigma}{\sqrt{n}}$$

where

$\bar{x}$ = sample mean

n = sample size

$\dfrac{\sigma}{\sqrt{n}}$ = standard error of the mean

$z_{\alpha/2}$ = multiple of the standard error of the mean, which determines the width of the interval. It is a direct result of the level of confidence $1 - \alpha$ and is found using the *standard normal distribution*. The subscript $\alpha/2$ is the area to the *right* of the number $z_{\alpha/2}$ under the standard normal curve.

EXAMPLE 35.1

A manufacturing process has been running in control for some length of time. The quality characteristic of interest is diameter of the manufactured part (measured in mm). It is believed there may have been a shift in the process mean due to the change of a raw material. A sample of 25 items is randomly selected from the process, measured, and the sample average found to be 103 mm. The in-control process average has been 102 mm, which is nominal. The standard deviation during the time the process was believed to be in control was three mm. The customer wants to construct a 95 percent confidence interval on the true process mean to determine if the process has shifted away from nominal.

Solution:
The necessary information is:

- $\bar{x} = 103$.

- $\sigma = 3$.

- $n = 25$.

- $1 - \alpha = 0.95$, and solving for α, we get $\alpha = 0.05$. This value is necessary to find the multiple $z_{\alpha/2}$ from the standard normal table.

From the standard normal table in Appendix F with $\alpha = 0.05$, $z_{\alpha/2} = z_{0.05/2} = z_{0.025} = 1.96$. The resulting 95 percent confidence interval is then

$$103 - 1.96\frac{3}{\sqrt{25}} \leq \mu \leq 103 + 1.96\frac{3}{\sqrt{25}}$$

$$103 - 1.176 \leq \mu \leq 103 + 1.176$$

$$101.824 \leq \mu \leq 104.176$$

With a high degree of confidence, we can say 101.824 mm $\leq \mu \leq$ 104.176 mm. Since the nominal value of 102 mm is contained in this interval, there is insufficient evidence to conclude at the 95 percent level of confidence that the process mean has not shifted.

EXAMPLE 35.2

Reconsider the previous example. What conclusions could be reached if the level of confidence were changed to 0.90?

Solution:

With all other information held constant, the only change is in the multiple $Z_{\alpha/2}$. In this case $1 - \alpha = 0.90$, so $\alpha = 0.10$ and $z_{\alpha/2} = z_{0.10/2} = z_{0.05} = 1.645$. The 90 percent confidence interval is then

$$103 - 1.645 \frac{3}{\sqrt{25}} \leq \mu \leq 103 + 1.645 \frac{3}{\sqrt{25}}$$

$$103 - 0.987 \leq \mu \leq 103 + 0.987$$

$$102.013 \leq \mu \leq 103.987.$$

With a high degree of confidence, we can say 102.013 mm $\leq \mu \leq$ 103.987 mm. Since the nominal value of 102 mm lies outside this interval, there is sufficient evidence to conclude that the process mean has shifted. In fact, we would conclude based on this data that the process mean has shifted upward. Notice that the nominal value of 102 mm lies just outside the lower bound of the confidence interval. Whether or not this shift would result in corrective action should be determined by personnel familiar with the manufacturing process.

Examine the 95 percent and 90 percent confidence intervals for the previous examples. Decreasing the confidence level from 95 percent to 90 percent decreased the length of the confidence interval. Decreasing (increasing) the level of confidence—while all other quantities remain constant—will always result in a decrease (increase) in the length of the confidence interval.

Determining the Sample Size. There are many situations where the practitioner would like to know how large a sample is needed in order to estimate a population mean with some level of precision. This information can be obtained using the $100(1 - \alpha)\%$ confidence interval and making some reasonable assumptions.

The length of the confidence interval,

$$\bar{x} - z_{\alpha/2} \frac{\sigma}{\sqrt{n}} \leq \mu \leq \bar{x} + z_{\alpha/2} \frac{\sigma}{\sqrt{n}},$$

provides a measure of *precision* of estimation. The *margin of error* in the confidence interval formula is

$$z_{\alpha/2} \frac{\sigma}{\sqrt{n}}.$$

This quantity provides information about the *accuracy* of the confidence interval. That is, when $\bar{x}$ is used as the estimate for μ, the error

$$E = |\bar{x} - \mu|$$

will be at most

$$z_{\alpha/2} \frac{\sigma}{\sqrt{n}}.$$

So, if

$$E = z_{\alpha/2} \frac{\sigma}{\sqrt{n}}$$

is an upper bound on the amount of error the practitioner is willing to live with, an appropriate sample size can be determined. That is, for a given level of confidence, an assumed value of σ, and a margin of error E one is willing to live with, a minimum sample size can be found using the relationship

$$E = Z_{\alpha/2} \frac{\sigma}{\sqrt{n}}$$

and solving for *n*:

$$n \geq \left[\frac{\sigma Z_{\alpha/2}}{E} \right]^2$$

If the value of *n* is not an integer, round up to the nearest integer.

EXAMPLE 35.3

Suppose the turnaround time for basic blood analysis for the emergency room at a local hospital is of interest. A goal is to be able to estimate the true average turnaround time μ. Specifically, it is of interest to obtain an estimate that is within three minutes of the true average turnaround time with 95 percent confidence. Based on prior information it is assumed that $\sigma = 8$ min. How many turnaround times should be obtained in order to estimate the true average turnaround time and meet the requirements stated? That is, what is *n*?

Solution:

First, note that the problem states that the estimate is "within three minutes of the true average. . . . " This implies that we will allow the estimate to be at most three minutes less than the true average or at most three minutes greater than the true average. In this case, the margin of error we are willing to live with is $E = 3$ min. The level of confidence is 95 percent so $1 - \alpha = 0.95$, $\alpha = 0.05$, and $z_{\alpha/2} = z_{0.025} = 1.96$. With $\sigma = 8$ min, the minimum sample size needed is

$$n \geq \left[\frac{\sigma Z_{\alpha/2}}{E} \right]^2 = \left[\frac{8(1.96)}{3} \right]^2 = [5.227]^2 = 27.32.$$

Therefore, to meet the requirements of 95 percent confidence, a margin of error of no more than three minutes, and $\sigma = 8$ min, the minimum number of times to obtain would be $n = 28$.

Case 2: Population Variance σ^2 Is Assumed Unknown. Suppose the population of interest is normally distributed with unknown mean μ and unknown variance σ^2. Let $X_1, X_2, \ldots, X_n$ be a random sample taken from the population, and let the sample mean and variance be denoted by $\bar{x}$ and s^2. When σ is unknown, it can be estimated by s. Furthermore, if the sample size n is small, the standard normal distribution is no longer an appropriate distribution for the sample mean. In its place we will use Student's t distribution (recall the t distribution from Chapter 34).

Definition. Let $X_1, X_2, \ldots, X_n$ be a random sample taken from a normal population, and let the sample mean and variance be denoted by $\bar{x}$ and s^2. The random variable:

$$T = \frac{\bar{X} - \mu}{s/\sqrt{n}}$$

follows a t distribution with $k = n - 1$ degrees of freedom. It should be noted that the t distribution is defined by its degrees of freedom, which are directly related to the sample size n. As the degrees of freedom go to infinity, the t distribution approaches the standard normal distribution. The degrees of freedom are of particular interest. The degrees of freedom for T is $n - 1$. This is a direct result of using s^2 as an estimate for σ^2. Recall that the sample variance is based on the deviations $x_1 - \bar{x}, x_2 - \bar{x}, \ldots, x_n - \bar{x}$, and that

$$\sum_{i=1}^{n}\left(x_i - \bar{x}\right) = 0.$$

Since

$$\sum_{i=1}^{n}\left(x_i - \bar{x}\right) = 0,$$

this implies that if we specify $n - 1$ of these deviations, the nth deviation is automatically determined (it can not vary freely). That is, only $n - 1$ of these deviations can vary freely. The degrees of freedom for the t distribution represent the number of deviations that can vary freely.

It can be shown that the $100(1 - \alpha)\%$ confidence interval on the population mean μ is given by

$$\bar{x} - t_{\alpha/2,k}\frac{s}{\sqrt{n}} \leq \mu \leq \bar{x} + t_{\alpha/2,k}\frac{s}{\sqrt{n}}$$

where $t_{\alpha/2,k}$ is the multiple of the standard error of the mean $(s/\sqrt{n})$ and determines the width of the interval. It is a direct result of the level of confidence $1 - \alpha$ and is found using Student's t distribution. The subscript $\alpha/2$ is the area to the *right* of the number $t_{\alpha/2,k}$ that we need, and $k = n - 1$ is the degrees of freedom for a particular problem. Probabilities and values for the t distribution are given in Appendix P.

EXAMPLE 35.4

A study on the effect the type of joystick has on powered wheelchair driving performance was conducted. In the study, one type of joystick used was a position-sensing joystick. Suppose eight subjects are asked to use a position-sensing joystick, and the time to complete a predetermined task is recorded (in minutes). The results are:

$$30.7, 31.2, 26.1, 29.4, 34.6, 26.8, 33.1, 25.5$$

Assume that time to complete the task is well approximated by a normal distribution. The investigators would like to construct a 95 percent confidence interval on the true time to complete the task using the position-sensing joystick.

Solution:

First, we need to calculate the values $\bar{x}$ and s:

$$\bar{x} = \frac{\sum_{i=1}^{n} x_i}{n} = 29.675$$

$$s = \sqrt{\frac{\sum_{i=1}^{n}(x_i - \bar{x})^2}{n-1}} = 3.3363$$

For a level of confidence of 95 percent, $1 - \alpha = 0.95$, and solving for α, we get $\alpha = 0.05$. The degrees of freedom for this problem is $k = n - 1 = 7$. These values are necessary to find the multiple $t_{\alpha/2,k}$ from the t distribution. From the t distribution table in Appendix P, with $\alpha = 0.05$, $t_{\alpha/2,k} = t_{0.025,7} = 2.306$. The resulting 95 percent two-sided confidence interval is then

$$29.675 - 2.365 \frac{3.3363}{\sqrt{8}} \leq \mu \leq 29.675 + 2.365 \frac{3.3363}{\sqrt{8}}$$

$$= 29.675 - 2.790 \leq \mu \leq 29.675 + 2.790$$

$$= 26.89 \leq \mu \leq 32.47.$$

With a high degree of confidence we believe the true time to perform the task using the position-sensing joystick lies between 26.89 minutes and 32.47 minutes.

In the previous example the sample size was small, $n = 8$. In cases where the sample size is small (cutoffs have often been $n < 30$ or $n < 40$), the population is known to be normally distributed, and the population variance is unknown, the t distribution is an appropriate distribution. In cases where the sample size is sufficiently large, the population is known to be normally distributed, and the population variance is unknown, the standard normal distribution or the t distribution could be used. Again, the t distribution and standard normal distribution are approximately of the same form as the sample size n goes to infinity.

Large-Sample Confidence Interval on μ (σ^2 Unknown). Now in addition to the population mean and population variance being unknown, assume that the underlying distribution is not necessarily normally distributed. In this situation, if the sample size is large, then the central limit theorem applies and the $100(1 - \alpha)\%$ confidence interval

$$\bar{x} - z_{\sigma/2} \frac{s}{\sqrt{n}} \leq \mu \leq \bar{x} + z_{\sigma/2} \frac{s}{\sqrt{n}}$$

can be used. However, if the sample size is small and the underlying distribution is decidedly nonnormally distributed, then nonparametric methods should be used to construct the confidence interval.

Statistical Tolerance Intervals. Consider a population of manufactured steel rods. Suppose the diameters of these steel rods follow a normal distribution with mean $\mu = 25$ mm and standard deviation $\sigma = 4$ mm. Then the interval $(\mu - 1.96\sigma, \mu + 1.96\sigma) = (17.16, 32.84)$ would capture the diameters of 95 percent of the steel rods. This is a result of the fact that 95 percent of the area under the normal curve would lie between -1.96 and 1.96.

In many situations, μ and σ are unknown and are estimated using $\bar{x}$ and s. The interval $(\bar{x} - 1.96s, \bar{x} + 1.96s)$ may not actually contain 95 percent of the values in the population (since there is variability in the estimates in this case, there is no guarantee that the tolerance interval will contain 95 percent of the values). The solution to the problem is to replace 1.96 with some value that will make the resulting interval contain 95 percent of the values with a high level of confidence. This interval is referred to as a *tolerance interval.*

Definition. Suppose we wish to capture at least $\tau\%$ of the values in a normal distribution with a $100(1 - \alpha)\%$ level of confidence. The appropriate two-sided *tolerance interval* is

$$\bar{x} - Ks, \bar{x} + Ks$$

where K is a tolerance interval factor found in Appendix D. Only selected values of K are given in the table, in particular for 99 percent of the population for 90 percent, 95 percent, and 99 percent levels of confidence.

EXAMPLE 35.5

Suppose the time to complete a task is of interest. A sample of $n = 10$ times are collected and it is found that $\bar{x} = 31.50$ and $s = 2.764$. Time to complete the task is assumed to be normally distributed. Suppose we want to find a tolerance interval for time that includes 99 percent of the values in the population with 95 percent confidence.

From Table D with $n = 10$ and confidence level of 0.95 we find $K = 4.433$. The resulting tolerance interval is

$$(\bar{x} - Ks, \bar{x} + Ks) = (31.50 - 4.433(2.764), 31.50 + 4.433(2.764)) = (19.25, 43.75)$$

We can be 95 percent confident that at least 99 percent of all times to complete the task are between 19.25 minutes and 43.75 minutes.

Confidence Intervals on a Population Variance σ^2. As stated previously, the sample variance s^2 can be used as the point estimate for the population variance σ^2. The sample standard deviation s can be used as the point estimate for σ. Suppose instead of relying on a point estimate of σ^2, we can construct a confidence interval. Assume a normally distributed population from which a random sample $X_1, X_2, \ldots, X_n$ is selected.

The $100(1 - \alpha)\%$ two-sided confidence interval on the population variance σ^2 is given by

$$\frac{(n-1)s^2}{\chi^2_{\alpha/2,k}} < \sigma^2 < \frac{(n-1)s^2}{\chi^2_{1-\alpha/2,k}}$$

where $\chi^2_{\alpha/2,k}$ and $\chi^2_{1-\alpha/2,k}$ are values obtained from the chi-square distribution with $\alpha/2$ and $(1 - \alpha/2)$ being the areas under the chi-square curve and to the *right* of the value of interest to be put into the confidence interval. Again, $k = n - 1$ is the degrees of freedom. Table values of the chi-square distribution are given in Appendix K. (Recall the chi-square distribution from Chapter 34.)

EXAMPLE 35.6

A heart rate stress test was administered to 10 men. The heart rates (in beats per minute [bpm]) were recorded. The average heart rate was found to be $\bar{x} = 100$ bpm with a standard deviation of $s = 16.2$ bpm. A confidence interval was constructed on the mean heart rate and it is now desired to construct a 95 percent confidence interval on the variance in heart rate.

Solution:

The necessary information is:

$s^2 = (16.2 \text{ bpm})^2 = 262.44 \text{ bpm}^2$

$k = n - 1 = 9$

$1 - \alpha = 0.95$, therefore $\alpha = 0.05$ and the corresponding chi-square values obtained from a chi-square table are

$$\chi^2_{\alpha/2,k} = \chi^2_{0.05/2,9} = \chi^2_{0.025,9} = 19.023$$

$$\chi^2_{1-\alpha/2,k} = \chi^2_{1-0.05/2,9} = \chi^2_{0.975,9} = 2.700.$$

The resulting 95 percent two-sided confidence interval on the population variance is

$$\frac{(10-1)262.44}{19.023} < \sigma^2 < \frac{(10-1)262.44}{2.700}$$

$$= 124.16 < \sigma^2 < 874.80.$$

We are highly confident that the true population variance in heart rate lies within 124.16 bpm² and 874.80 bpm².

Confidence Intervals on a Population Standard Deviation σ. An approximate confidence interval on the population standard deviation σ can easily be found by taking the square of the bounds on the population variance. An approximate $100(1 - \alpha)\%$ confidence interval on σ is given by

$$\sqrt{\frac{(n-1)s^2}{\chi^2_{\alpha/2,k}}} < \sigma < \sqrt{\frac{(n-1)s^2}{\chi^2_{1-\alpha/2,k}}}.$$

EXAMPLE 35.7

Reconsider the previous example. A 95 percent confidence interval on the standard deviation of heart rate is

$$\sqrt{124.16} < \sqrt{\sigma^2} < \sqrt{874.80}$$
$$11.14 < \sigma < 29.58.$$

We are highly confident the true population standard deviation will lie between 11.14 bpm and 29.58 bpm.

Confidence Intervals on a Population Proportion p. The population proportion p often represents the fraction nonconforming or fraction of defective items in a population of items. Since it is often impossible or impractical to find the exact value of p, a point estimate is used to estimate the true proportion. A sample proportion denoted $\hat{p}$ will be used as a point estimate for p. The sample proportion is calculated using

$$\hat{p} = \frac{x}{n}$$

where x is the number of successes out of n trials. If n is sufficiently large, then it can be shown that the random variable

$$Z = \frac{\hat{p} - p}{\sqrt{\frac{p(1-p)}{n}}}$$

follows a standard normal distribution. This relationship allows for the development of a confidence interval on the true population proportion of interest.

A $100(1 - \alpha)\%$ confidence interval on a population proportion p is given by

$$\hat{p} - z_{\sigma/2}\sqrt{\frac{\hat{p}(1-\hat{p})}{n}} \leq p \leq \hat{p} + z_{\sigma/2}\sqrt{\frac{\hat{p}(1-\hat{p})}{n}}.$$

EXAMPLE 35.8

Billing statements for 1000 patients discharged from a particular hospital were randomly selected for errors. Out of the 1000 billing statements, 102 were found to contain errors. Using this information, it is desired to construct a 99 percent confidence interval on the true proportion of billing statements with errors.

Solution:

In this problem, a "success" is a billing statement with errors. Therefore, $X = 102$ and $n = 1000$. The sample proportion is then

$$\hat{p} = \frac{102}{1000} = 0.102$$

and provides our best estimate for the true proportion of billing statements with errors. The corresponding 99 percent confidence interval is

$$\hat{p} - z_{\alpha/2}\sqrt{\frac{\hat{p}(1-\hat{p})}{n}} \le p \le \hat{p} + z_{\alpha/2}\sqrt{\frac{\hat{p}(1-\hat{p})}{n}}$$

$$0.102 - 2.576\sqrt{\frac{0.102(1-0.102)}{1000}} \le p \le 0.102 + 2.576\sqrt{\frac{0.102(1-0.10)}{1000}}$$

$$0.077 \le p \le 0.127$$

With a high degree of confidence, we believe the true proportion of billing statements that contain errors would be between 7.7 percent and 12.7 percent.

Note: The procedure outlined here for the population proportion assumes that the normal distribution is a good approximation to the binomial. That is, the parameter of interest is a proportion that is well modeled by the binomial distribution, but if the sample size is large enough, the normal distribution is a good approximation to the binomial.

Recommendations have been that $np \ge 5$ and $np(1 - p) \ge 5$. However, if the sample size is small, the confidence interval given previously may not be a good approximation. If the sample size is small, then the binomial distribution should be used to find the multiple of the standard error in the confidence interval instead of the standard normal distribution. Agresti and Coull (1998) present an alternative form of a confidence interval for small n. (In addition see Devore [2007].)

2. HYPOTHESIS TESTING

Define, interpret, and apply hypothesis tests for means, variances, and proportions. Apply and interpret the concepts of significance level, power, type I and type II errors. Define and distinguish between statistical and practical significance. (Evaluate)

Body of Knowledge VI.D.2

The hypothesis test, another tool used in inferential statistics, is closely related to confidence intervals, a relationship that is illustrated in this section. Textbooks tend to treat hypothesis tests as somewhat more formal procedures. Many list seven or eight steps to be followed for each type of test. Although not all books agree on the steps themselves, this list is fairly generic:

1. State the null hypotheses (H_0) and alternative hypothesis (H_a).

2. Choose the level of significance α.

3. Determine the rejection region for the statistic of interest.

4. Calculate the test statistic.

5. Decide whether the null hypothesis should be rejected.

6. State the conclusion in terms of the original problem.

General descriptions of each step are provided.

1. Write the assumption that is claimed to be true in a *null hypothesis.* The null hypothesis is denoted by H_0. This is the statement that we are assuming to be true and we are trying to find evidence against. For example, from past experience the average time to complete a task is five minutes, and we would like to test this claim. The null hypothesis would be H_0: $\mu = 5$.

State the *alternative hypothesis.* The notation for the alternative hypothesis is usually H_a. If the null hypothesis is rejected, then an alternative must be provided. The *alternative* hypothesis contains the statement that we would eventually like to support (we can support the alternative only if the null hypothesis is rejected). For example, suppose we wish to show that the average time to complete a task is actually longer than five minutes. The alternative hypothesis would be H_a: $\mu > 5$.

2. Choose the *level of significance* for the test. The *significance level* (denoted α) is the probability of making the mistake of rejecting the null hypothesis when it is in fact true. This type of mistake is called a *type I error* (as opposed to a *type II error,* which is the mistake of not rejecting the null hypothesis when it is in fact false). The probability of committing a type I error should be small (that is, $\alpha \leq 0.10$) and should be set before performing the test. The significance level α is the same α used in the level of confidence in constructing confidence intervals (recall that $1 - \alpha$ is the level of confidence, so α is the level of significance). Choosing the level of significance is sometimes an economic decision. It is established based on how expensive a particular mistake may be (this expense is not necessarily monetary, but could also include personal injury or loss of life).

3. Determine the *rejection region.* The rejection region consists of all those values of the test statistic for which the null hypothesis would be rejected. The rejection region is determined by the stated level of significance and the alternative hypothesis. *Critical values* are those values that determine the rejection region (they are cutoff values for the test statistic—to be discussed next).

4. Calculate the *test statistic.* The test statistic is simply a statistic (such as the sample mean or sample variance) that has been *transformed* in order to compare this value to some standard (critical values). An example of a test statistic would be a sample mean $\bar{X}$ transformed into a Z-score. The Z-score would be used to determine if the null hypothesis could be rejected.

5. Compare the test statistic to the critical value. If the test statistic falls within the rejection region, then the null hypothesis would be rejected. Large test statistic values (in absolute value) will provide evidence against the null hypothesis. It is important to note that rejecting the null hypothesis is a strong claim. It takes significant evidence to reject the claim associated with H_0. As a result of using a small level of significance, rejecting the null hypothesis is a *strong claim*. Failing to reject the null hypothesis is a *weak claim*. That is, by failing to reject the null hypothesis, we can not say that the claim is true, just that we did not have sufficient evidence to reject the claim.

6. Once it has been determined whether or not the null hypothesis can be rejected, the results are written in terms of the problem statement.

The following hypothesis tests will be presented in this section:

- Hypothesis tests for a single population mean μ

- Hypothesis tests for a single population variance σ^2

- Hypothesis tests for a single population standard deviation σ

- Hypothesis tests for a single population proportion p

Hypothesis Tests for a Single Population Mean μ

Let μ_0 be a real value that is hypothesized or assumed to be the true value of the population mean μ. There are three types of hypothesis tests:

$H_0: \mu \leq \mu_0$	$H_a: \mu > \mu_0$	(Right-tailed test)
$H_0: \mu \geq \mu_0$	$H_a: \mu < \mu_0$	(Left-tailed test)
$H_0: \mu = \mu_0$	$H_a: \mu \neq \mu_0$	(Two-tailed test)

As with confidence intervals, there are two cases under study:

1. Hypothesis tests on μ when the population variance σ^2 is assumed known

2. Hypothesis tests on μ when the population variance σ^2 is unknown

Case 1. Hypothesis Tests on μ When the Population Variance σ^2 Is Assumed Known. Assume that the underlying population of interest is normally distributed with known population variance σ^2. Let $X_1, X_2, \ldots, X_n$ be a random sample from the population, and let $\bar{X}$ represent the sample mean. An appropriate test statistic for this situation is

$$z_0 = \frac{\bar{X} - \mu_0}{\sigma / \sqrt{n}}.$$

The rejection region depends on the alternative hypothesis and level of significance α:

Alternative hypothesis	Reject H_0 if
$H_a: \mu > \mu_0$	$z_0 > z_\alpha$
$H_a: \mu < \mu_0$	$z_0 < -z_\alpha$
$H_a: \mu \neq \mu_0$	$z_0 < -z_{\alpha/2}$ or $z_0 > z_{\alpha/2}$

EXAMPLE 35.9

A vendor claims that the average weight of a shipment of parts is 1.84 kg. The customer randomly chooses 64 parts and finds that the sample has an average weight of 1.88 kg. Suppose that the standard deviation of the population is known to be 0.3 kg. Using a level of significance of 0.05, we want to test the hypothesis that the true average weight of the shipment is 1.84 kg. We assume that the weights are normally distributed.

Solution:

Since the population standard deviation is known, the standard normal distribution is used. In addition, since the problem statement gives no indication as to whether the true mean weight is less than or greater than 1.84 kg, a two-sided hypothesis test is appropriate. The steps are as follows:

1. The null and alternative hypotheses are

    $H_0: \mu = 1.84$ $H_a: \mu \neq 1.84$.

2. The level of significance is $\alpha = 0.05$.

3. There are two areas for the rejection region since we have a two-tailed test. The critical values are found from a standard normal table with $\alpha = 0.05$:

    $$z_{\alpha/2} = z_{0.05/2} = z_{0.025} = 1.96 \text{ and } -z_{\alpha/2} = -1.96.$$

    Therefore, reject the null hypothesis if the test statistic is greater than 1.96 or less than −1.96.

4. The test statistic is calculated to be:

    $$z_0 = \frac{\bar{x} - \mu_0}{\sigma/\sqrt{n}} = \frac{1.88 - 1.84}{0.30/\sqrt{64}} = 1.07$$

    (Note: This test statistic says the following: the sample mean is roughly 1.07 standard deviations away from the population mean. Is this a large difference? The next step tells us how large is large.)

5. Comparing 1.07 to the critical values in step 4, we see that −1.96 < 1.07 < 1.96. Since the test statistic, 1.07, does not fall into the rejection region, we can not reject the null hypothesis at the 0.05 level of significance. We failed to reject the null hypothesis (weak claim).

6. There is insufficient evidence to conclude that the true mean weight of the shipment is not 1.84.

Case 2. Hypothesis Tests on μ When the Population Variance σ^2 Is Unknown.
Assume that the underlying population of interest is normally distributed with
unknown population variance σ^2. Let $X_1, X_2, \ldots, X_n$ be a random sample from
the population and let $\bar{X}$ represent the sample mean. If the sample size is small, an
appropriate test statistic for this situation is

$$t_0 = \frac{\bar{X} - \mu_0}{s / \sqrt{n}},$$

which follows a t distribution with $k = n - 1$. The rejection region depends on the
alternative hypothesis and level of significance α:

Alternative hypothesis	Reject H_0 if
$H_a: \mu > \mu_0$	$t_0 > t_{\alpha,k}$
$H_a: \mu < \mu_0$	$t_0 < -t_{\alpha,k}$
$H_a: \mu \neq \mu_0$	$t_0 < -t_{\alpha/2,k}$ or $t_0 > t_{\alpha/2,k}$

It is important to note here that the fact that the null hypothesis is not rejected
does not mean it is true. It only indicates that with this sample of data we could
not find evidence against the null hypothesis. If a second sample of data is taken,
it is possible that the null hypothesis could be rejected.

EXAMPLE 35.10

A cutoff saw has been producing parts with a mean length of 4.125 mm. A new blade is
installed and we want to know whether the mean has decreased. We select a random
sample of 20 parts, measure the length of each part, and find the mean length to be
4.120 mm and the sample standard deviation to be 0.008 mm. Assume that the population is normally distributed. Using a significance level of 0.10, determine whether the
mean length has decreased. Since the population standard deviation is unknown, the
t-test will be used.

Solution:

1. The null and alternative hypotheses are

   $H_0: \mu = 4.125$ $H_a: \mu < 4.125$.

2. The level of significance is $\alpha = 0.10$.

3. There is only one rejection region since this is a left-tailed test (again, this is based
   on the alternative hypothesis). The critical value is found from the t distribution
   table in Appendix P with $\alpha = 0.10$: $t_{\alpha,k} = t_{0.10,19} = 1.328$. Therefore, reject the null
   hypothesis if the test statistic is less than -1.328 (since the alternative hypothesis is
   "less than").

4. The test statistic is calculated to be:

   $$t_0 = \frac{\bar{X} - \mu_0}{s / \sqrt{n}} = \frac{4.120 - 4.125}{0.008 / \sqrt{20}} = -2.80$$

Continued

Continued

5. Comparing –2.80 to the critical value in step 4, we see that –2.80 < –1.328. Since the test statistic falls into the rejection region, we can reject the null hypothesis at the 0.10 level of significance (strong claim).

6. There is sufficient evidence to indicate that the average length of the part has decreased.

Table 35.1   Summary of situations outlined for testing the population mean.

Assumption	Distribution	Test statistic
σ^2 known, population normally distributed	Standard normal distribution	$z_0 = \dfrac{\bar{x} - \mu_0}{\sigma / \sqrt{n}}$
σ^2 unknown and n small ($n \leq 30$), population normally distributed	t distribution	$t_0 = \dfrac{\bar{x} - \mu_0}{s / \sqrt{n}}$
σ^2 unknown and n large (often $n > 30$), population not necessarily normal	Standard normal distribution or t distribution*	$z_0 = \dfrac{\bar{x} - \mu_0}{s / \sqrt{n}}$ or $t_0 = \dfrac{\bar{x} - \mu_0}{s / \sqrt{n}}$

* Recall that as n goes to infinity ($n \rightarrow \infty$), the form of the t distribution becomes indistinguishable from the standard normal distribution.

A summary of the situations outlined for testing the population mean are shown in Table 35.1 (assume the underlying population is normally distributed).

Hypothesis Tests on a Population Variance σ^2

The hypothesis testing procedure can be applied in the case of testing a standard or hypothesized value of the population variance. For example, we may be interested in testing the claims that a particular population variance is eight. The null hypothesis is $H_0: \sigma^2 = 8$. Assume that the underlying distribution is normal. Let σ_0^2 be a real value that is hypothesized or assumed to be the true value of the population variance σ^2. There are three types of hypothesis tests on a population variance:

$H_0: \sigma^2 \leq \sigma_0^2$ 　　 $H_a: \sigma^2 > \sigma_0^2$ 　　 (Right-tailed test)

$H_0: \sigma^2 \geq \sigma_0^2$ 　　 $H_a: \sigma^2 < \sigma_0^2$ 　　 (Left-tailed test)

$H_0: \sigma^2 = \sigma_0^2$ 　　 $H_a: \sigma^2 \neq \sigma_0^2$ 　　 (Two-tailed test)

The chi-square distribution introduced in Chapter 34 is an appropriate distribution for testing a population variance. The test statistic is given by

$$\chi_0^2 = \frac{(n-1)s^2}{\sigma_0^2}.$$

The test statistic follows a chi-square distribution with $k = n - 1$ degrees of freedom, where:

- s^2 is the sample variance for a sample taken from the population of interest.

- σ_0^2 is the hypothesized value of the variance.

- n = sample size chosen from the population of interest.

The test of hypothesis steps outlined earlier also apply to this situation.

Alternative hypothesis	Reject H_0 if
H_a: $\sigma^2 > \sigma_0^2$	$\chi_0^2 > \chi_{\alpha,k}^2$
H_a: $\sigma^2 < \sigma_0^2$	$\chi_0^2 < \chi_{1-\alpha,k}^2$
H_a: $\sigma^2 \neq \sigma_0^2$	$\chi_0^2 < \chi_{1-\alpha/2,k}^2$ or $\chi_0^2 > \chi_{\alpha/2,k}^2$

The critical values for the chi-square distribution can be found in Appendix K.

EXAMPLE 35.11

A process has been running for some time with a variance of 6.25 for a critical dimension. In an effort to improve throughput, a methods engineer increases the drive motor speed. A sample of 13 items is randomly selected from the new process. The variance of the critical dimension in this sample is found to be 6.82. Is there sufficient evidence to conclude that the true process variance has increased? Use $\alpha = 0.05$. Assume that the critical dimension follows a normal distribution.

Solution:

1. The null and alternative hypotheses are

   H_0: $\sigma^2 = 6.25$ H_1: $\sigma^2 > 6.25$.

2. The level of significance is $\alpha = 0.05$.

3. Since this is a right-tailed test, we would reject the null hypothesis if the test statistic is greater than $\chi_{\alpha,k}^2 = \chi_{0.05,12}^2 = 21.026$.

4. The test statistic is calculated to be

$$\chi_0^2 = \frac{(n-1)s^2}{\sigma_0^2} = \frac{(13-1)6.82}{6.25} = 13.1.$$

5. Since $13.1 < 21.026$, we would not reject the null hypothesis (weak claim).

6. There is insufficient evidence to conclude that the variance for this critical dimension has increased significantly at the 0.05 level of significance.

Hypothesis Testing on a Population Proportion p

The hypothesis testing procedure is applied in this case testing a standard or hypothesized value of a population proportion. For example, we may be interested in testing the claim that a particular population proportion is 0.50. The null hypothesis is then H_0: $p = 0.50$.

Assume that the underlying distribution is normal. Let p_0 be a real value that is hypothesized or assumed to be the true value of the population proportion. There are three types of hypothesis tests on a population proportion:

H_0: $p \leq p_0$	H_a: $p > p_0$	(Right-tailed test)
H_0: $p \geq p_0$	H_a: $p < p_0$	(Left-tailed test)
H_0: $p = p_0$	H_a: $p \neq p_0$	(Two-tailed test)

It should be noted that you will often see the null hypothesis written simply as H_0: $p = p_0$ for each of the three cases. Either notation is acceptable.

For sufficiently large sample sizes, the normal approximation to the binomial distribution is valid and the test statistic

$$z_0 = \frac{\hat{p} - p_0}{\sqrt{\dfrac{p_0(1 - p_0)}{n}}}$$

follows a standard normal distribution where

$\hat{p}$ = sample proportion for a sample taken from the population of interest. By definition:

$$\hat{p} = \frac{x}{n}$$

x represents the number of successes out of a sample size of (number of trials) n

p_0 = hypothesized value of the population proportion.

If the sample sizes are relatively small, then the appropriate hypothesis test to use is based directly on the binomial distribution. See Devore (2007) for more details on small-sample tests.

The rejection region depends on the alternative hypothesis and level of significance α:

Alternative hypothesis	Reject H_0 if
H_a: $p > p_0$	$z_0 > z_\alpha$
H_a: $p < p_0$	$z_0 < -z_\alpha$
H_a: $p \neq p_0$	$z_0 < -z_{\alpha/2}$ or $z_0 > z_{\alpha/2}$

Part VI.D.2

EXAMPLE 35.12

Billing statements for discharged patients from a particular hospital sometimes contain errors. It is believed that the percentage of billing statements that contain errors is 15 percent. Out of 1000 billing statements that are randomly selected from the population, 102 were found to contain errors. Based on this information, can we conclude that the proportion of billing statements that contain errors is actually less than 15 percent? Use a 10 percent level of significance.

Solution:

For this problem:

- p = the true proportion of billing statements with errors.

- x = number of statements with errors, so $x = 102$.

- n = sample size, so $n = 1000$.

- The sample proportion is then $\hat{p} = \dfrac{x}{n} = \dfrac{102}{1000} = 0.102$.

1. The null and alternative hypotheses are

   H_0: $p = 0.15$ and H_a: $p < 0.15$.

2. The level of significance is $\alpha = 0.10$

3. Since this is a left-tailed test, reject the null hypothesis if the test statistic is less than $-z_\alpha = -z_{0.10} = -1.28$.

4. The test statistic is

$$z_0 = \frac{\hat{p} - p_0}{\sqrt{\dfrac{p_0(1 - p_0)}{n}}} = \frac{0.102 - 0.15}{\sqrt{\dfrac{0.15(1 - 0.15)}{1000}}} = -4.25.$$

5. Since $-4.25 < -1.28$, we would reject the null hypothesis in favor of the alternative at the 0.10 level of significance (strong claim).

6. There is sufficient evidence to conclude that the true percentage of statement errors is less than 15 percent.

Hypothesis Tests and Confidence Intervals for Two Population Means μ_1, μ_2

There are many important cases that involve comparing two populations of interest, such as comparing two processes, two vendors, and so on. Of interest here is testing the difference in two population means, $\mu_1 - \mu_2$. One test in particular is that of no difference between the two populations $\mu_1 - \mu_2 = 0$.

Either the standard normal distribution or Student's t distribution can be used. If the population variances are known, use the standard normal distribution. If the population variances are unknown and the sample sizes are relatively small, use Student's t distribution.

The basic assumptions are as follows:

- $X_1, X_2, \ldots, X_{n1}$ is a random sample from a population with mean μ_1 and variance σ_1^2.

- $Y_1, Y_2, \ldots, Y_{n2}$ is a random sample from a population with mean μ_2 and variance σ_2^2.

- The two samples are independent of each other.

A good point estimator for $\mu_1 - \mu_2$ would be the difference between the two sample means, $\bar{X} - \bar{Y}$. The expected value and variance for this point estimator are

$$E\left(\bar{X} - \bar{Y}\right) = \mu_1 - \mu_2$$

and

$$V\left(\bar{X} - \bar{Y}\right) = \sigma_{\bar{X} - \bar{Y}}^2 = \frac{\sigma_1^2}{n_1} + \frac{\sigma_2^2}{n_2}.$$

If we assume that populations are normally distributed, then $\bar{X} - \bar{Y}$ will also be normally distributed. Therefore, the random variable

$$Z = \frac{\left(\bar{X} - \bar{Y}\right) - \left(\mu_1 - \mu_2\right)}{\sqrt{\dfrac{\sigma_1^2}{n_1} + \dfrac{\sigma_2^2}{n_2}}}$$

follows a standard normal distribution. As a result, hypothesis tests and confidence intervals can be constructed on the parameter $\mu_1 - \mu_2$.

Hypothesis Test on $\mu_1 - \mu_2$, with Population Variances Known

Let Δ_0 be a real value that represents the difference between μ_1 and μ_2 that is of interest to be tested. Specifically, the null hypothesis would be $H_0: \mu_1 - \mu_2 = \Delta_0$. For the test of no difference, $\Delta_0 = 0$. The hypothesis tests are as follows:

Null hypothesis: $H_0: \mu_1 - \mu_2 = \Delta_0$

Test statistic: $Z_0 = \dfrac{\left(\bar{X} - \bar{Y}\right) - \Delta_0}{\sqrt{\dfrac{\sigma_1^2}{n_1} + \dfrac{\sigma_2^2}{n_2}}}$

Alternative hypothesis	Reject H_0 if
$H_a: \mu_1 - \mu_2 > \Delta_0$	$z_0 > z_\alpha$
$H_a: \mu_1 - \mu_2 < \Delta_0$	$z_0 < -z_\alpha$
$H_a: \mu_1 - \mu_2 \neq \Delta_0$	$z_0 < -z_{\alpha/2}$ or $z_0 > z_{\alpha/2}$

The null hypothesis does not always have to be $\mu_1 - \mu_2 = \Delta_0$; it could be $\leq$ or $\geq$ also. We will use the null hypothesis of H_0: $\mu_1 - \mu_2 = \Delta_0$.

Example 35.13 illustrates the use of hypothesis testing for the differences between two population means. The steps for the hypothesis tests are identical to the six steps outlined earlier.

EXAMPLE 35.13

Two different formulations of gasoline are being tested to study their road octane numbers. Formulation 1 has a variance of octane number of $\sigma_1^2 = 1.45$ while the variance for formulation 2 is $\sigma_2^2 = 1.5$. Ten samples ($n_1 = 10$) are selected from formulation 1 and fifteen samples ($n_2 = 15$) are selected from formulation 2. For sample 1, the average octane number was found to be $\bar{x} = 89$ and for sample 2 the average octane number was found to be $\bar{y} = 91$. Is there significant evidence to indicate that a difference exists between the two formulations? Use a 0.05 level of significance.

Solution:

The parameter of interest is the difference in average octane number, $\mu_1 - \mu_2$. Since there is no indication that $\mu_1 > \mu_2$ or $\mu_1 < \mu_2$, a two-sided test is used.

1. H_0: $\mu_1 - \mu_2 = 0$ H_1: $\mu_1 - \mu_2 \neq 0$.

2. $\alpha = 0.05$.

3. Since this is a two-tailed test and $\alpha = 0.05$, we will reject the null hypothesis if the test statistic is less than $-z_{\alpha/2}$ or greater than $z_{\alpha/2}$, where $z_{\alpha/2} = z_{0.025} = 1.96$.

4. The test statistic is

$$Z_0 = \frac{(\bar{x} - \bar{y}) - \Delta_0}{\sqrt{\dfrac{\sigma_1^2}{n_1} + \dfrac{\sigma_2^2}{n_2}}} = \frac{(89 - 91) - 0}{\sqrt{\dfrac{1.45}{10} + \dfrac{1.5}{15}}} = -4.04.$$

5. Since $-4.04 < -1.96$, we reject the null hypothesis (strong claim).

6. We conclude there is a significant difference in average octane number for the two formulations at the 0.05 level of significance.

Confidence Interval on $\mu_1 - \mu_2$

A $100(1 - \alpha)$% confidence interval on the parameter $\mu_1 - \mu_2$ is given by

$$\left(\bar{X} - \bar{Y}\right) - Z_{\alpha/2}\sqrt{\frac{\sigma_1^2}{n_1} + \frac{\sigma_2^2}{n_2}} \leq \mu_1 - \mu_2 \leq \left(\bar{X} - \bar{Y}\right) + Z_{\alpha/2}\sqrt{\frac{\sigma_1^2}{n_1} + \frac{\sigma_2^2}{n_2}}.$$

EXAMPLE 35.14

Reconsider the formulation problem given in the previous example. The 95 percent confidence interval on $\mu_1 - \mu_2$ is

$$\left(\bar{X} - \bar{Y}\right) - Z_{\alpha/2}\sqrt{\frac{\sigma_1^2}{n_1} + \frac{\sigma_2^2}{n_2}} \leq \mu_1 - \mu_2 \leq \left(\bar{X} - \bar{Y}\right) + Z_{\alpha/2}\sqrt{\frac{\sigma_1^2}{n_1} + \frac{\sigma_2^2}{n_2}}$$

$$(89 - 91) - 1.96\sqrt{\frac{1.45}{10} + \frac{1.5}{15}} \leq \mu_1 - \mu_2 \leq (89 - 91) + 1.96\sqrt{\frac{1.45}{10} + \frac{1.5}{15}}$$

$$-2.97 \leq \mu_1 - \mu_2 \leq -1.03.$$

We are highly confident that the true difference between the average octane numbers lies between –2.97 and –1.03. Note that the hypothesized value $\Delta_0 = 0$ given in the null hypothesis of the previous problem is not contained in this interval. Therefore, we would again say there is a significant difference in the two population means (that is, we would reject the null hypothesis).

Hypothesis Test on $\mu_1 - \mu_2$, with Population Variances Unknown

If the sample sizes are relatively large, regardless of the underlying distributions of the populations of interest, we can use the standard normal distribution as in the case of known variances. The sample variances are used as estimates of the population variances.

If the sample sizes are relatively small and the underlying distributions are normally distributed, then the t distribution can be used to conduct hypothesis tests and construct confidence intervals. There are two cases for this situation: 1) the population variances are unknown but assumed roughly equal, and 2) the population variances are unknown and not necessarily equal. The three basic assumptions given earlier still hold for the following methods. Let s_1^2 represent the variance for sample 1 and s_2^2 represent the variance for sample 2.

Case 1. $\sigma_1^2 = \sigma_2^2 = \sigma^2$ (The population variances are unknown but assumed roughly equal.) Since s_1^2 and s_2^2 estimate the same common variance σ^2, yet the sample variances may not be equal, we can combine the sample variances to obtain a single point estimate for σ^2. This is commonly called the *pooled variance*:

$$s_p^2 = \frac{(n_1 - 1)s_1^2 + (n_2 - 1)s_2^2}{n_1 + n_2 - 2}$$

The pooled standard deviation can be found by taking the square root of the pooled variance. An appropriate test statistic for the hypothesis $H_0: \mu_1 - \mu_2 = \Delta_0$ is

$$t_0 = \frac{\left(\bar{X} - \bar{Y}\right) - \Delta_0}{s_p\sqrt{\frac{1}{n_1} + \frac{1}{n_2}}},$$

which follows a t distribution with $k = n_1 + n_2 - 2$.

Hypothesis Test

Null hypothesis: $H_0: \mu_1 - \mu_2 = \Delta_0$

Test statistic:
$$t_0 = \frac{(\bar{x} - \bar{y}) - \Delta_0}{s_p \sqrt{\dfrac{1}{n_1} + \dfrac{1}{n_2}}}$$

Alternative hypothesis	Reject H₀ if
$H_a: \mu_1 - \mu_2 > \Delta_0$	$t_0 > t_{\alpha,k}$
$H_a: \mu_1 - \mu_2 < \Delta_0$	$t_0 < -t_{\alpha,k}$
$H_a: \mu_1 - \mu_2 \neq \Delta_0$	$t_0 < -t_{\alpha/2,k}$ or $t_0 > t_{\alpha/2,k}$

where $k = n_1 + n_2 - 2$ is the total degrees of freedom.

EXAMPLE 35.15

Two vendors of a valve diaphragm present significantly different cost quotations. The wall thickness is the critical quality characteristic. Use the following data to determine whether the average thickness of the products from vendor 1 is greater than that from vendor 2. Assume that the populations are normally distributed and that the samples are independent. Furthermore, the population variances are unknown but assumed to be equal. The test is to be conducted at the 0.05 significance level. The wall thickness measurements for both vendors are:

Vendor 1:	86	82	91	88	89	85	88	90	84	87	88	83	84	89
Vendor 2:	79	78	82	85	77	86	84	78	80	82	79	76		

Solution:

The necessary summary statistics are:

Vendor 1: $\bar{x} = 86.7$ $s_1 = 2.76$ $n_1 = 14$

Vendor 2: $\bar{y} = 80.5$ $s_2 = 3.26$ $n_2 = 12$

Since the population variances are unknown but assumed equal, the pooled variance and pooled standard deviation should be calculated:

$$s_p^2 = \frac{(n_1 - 1)s_1^2 + (n_2 - 1)s_2^2}{n_1 + n_2 - 2} = \frac{(14 - 1)(2.76)^2 + (12 - 1)(3.26)^2}{14 + 12 - 2} = 9$$

$$s_p = \sqrt{9} = 3$$

The parameter of interest is the difference in average wall thickness, $\mu_1 - \mu_2$.

1. $H_0: \mu_1 - \mu_2 = 0$ $H_a: \mu_1 - \mu_2 > 0$.

Continued

Continued

2. $\alpha = 0.05$.

3. Since this is a right-tailed test and $\alpha = 0.05$, we will reject the null hypothesis if the test statistic is greater than $t_{\alpha,k}$ where from Appendix P we find $t_{\alpha,k} = t_{0.05,24} = 1.711$.

4. The test statistic is:

$$t_0 = \frac{(\bar{x} - \bar{y}) - \Delta_0}{s_p\sqrt{\dfrac{1}{n_1} + \dfrac{1}{n_2}}} = \frac{(86.7 - 80.5) - 0}{3\sqrt{\dfrac{1}{14} + \dfrac{1}{12}}} = 5.25.$$

5. Since $5.25 > 1.711$, we reject the null hypothesis (strong claim).

6. We conclude that the average thickness of the products from vendor 1 is greater than that from vendor 2 at the 0.05 level of significance.

Confidence Interval on $\mu_1 - \mu_2$. A $100(1 - \alpha)\%$ two-sided confidence interval on the parameter $\mu_1 - \mu_2$ is given by

$$(\bar{X} - \bar{Y}) - t_{\alpha/2,k}(s_p)\sqrt{\frac{1}{n_1} + \frac{1}{n_2}} \leq \mu_1 - \mu_2 \leq (\bar{X} - \bar{Y}) + t_{\alpha/2,k}(s_p)\sqrt{\frac{1}{n_1} + \frac{1}{n_2}}.$$

It is important to note that the test statistic based on the t distribution is robust to the common variance assumption. In addition, it is not necessarily a good idea to do formal testing on the equality of two variances (see Box [1954]).

Case 2. $\sigma_1^2 \neq \sigma_2^2$ (The population variances are unknown and not necessarily equal.) The main differences between this case and case 1 are the calculation of the test statistic and the calculation of the degrees of freedom. Since the population variances are not necessarily equal, s_1^2 and s_2^2 do not estimate a common population variance; s_1^2 is an estimate for σ_1^2, and s_2^2 is an estimate of σ_2^2, and they can be used directly in the test statistic

$$t_0 = \frac{(\bar{X} - \bar{Y}) - \Delta_0}{\sqrt{\dfrac{s_1^2}{n_1} + \dfrac{s_2^2}{n_2}}}.$$

The test statistic follows a t distribution with degrees of freedom:

$$v = \frac{\left(\dfrac{s_1^2}{n_1} + \dfrac{s_2^2}{n_2}\right)^2}{\dfrac{\left(s_1^2/n_1\right)^2}{n_1 - 1} + \dfrac{\left(s_2^2/n_2\right)^2}{n_2 - 1}},$$

which is rounded down if it is not an integer value. The same six-step procedure used in case 1 is used for this case. It is important to note that this procedure should be used only if the two variances are very different.

A $100(1 - \alpha)\%$ two-sided confidence interval on the parameter $\mu_1 - \mu_2$ is given by

$$\left(\bar{X} - \bar{Y}\right) - t_{\alpha/2,v}\sqrt{\frac{s_1^2}{n_1} + \frac{s_1^2}{n_2}} \le \mu_1 - \mu_2 \le \left(\bar{X} - \bar{Y}\right) + t_{\alpha/2,v}\sqrt{\frac{s_1^2}{n_1} + \frac{s_1^2}{n_2}}.$$

Hypothesis Tests and Confidence Intervals for Two Population Proportions p_1, p_2

There are many situations in which we would like to determine if two populations differ with respect to some proportion of successes or failures. For example, we may wish to determine if two machines from the same process are producing the same proportion of nonconforming items. The hypothesis could be H_0: $p_1 - p_2 = 0$ where p_1 is the proportion of successes from population 1 and p_2 is the proportion of successes from population 2. The estimates of p_1 and p_2 are, respectively,

$$\hat{p}_1 = \frac{x_1}{n_1}, \ \hat{p}_2 = \frac{x_2}{n_2}$$

where

n_1 is the size of the sample chosen from population 1

n_2 is the size of the sample chosen from population 2

x_1 is the number of successes out of a sample of size n_1

x_2 is the number of successes out of a sample of size n_2

The parameter of interest is the difference in the two population proportions $p_1 - p_2$. The point estimator for this parameter is $\hat{p}_1 - \hat{p}_2$. The expected value and variance for the point estimator are

$$E\left(\hat{p}_1 - \hat{p}_2\right) = p_1 - p_2$$

and

$$V\left(\hat{p}_1 - \hat{p}_2\right) = \sigma_{\hat{p}_1 - \hat{p}_2}^2 = \frac{p_1(1-p_1)}{n_1} + \frac{p_2(1-p_2)}{n_2}.$$

If $\hat{p}_1$ and $\hat{p}_2$ both follow normal distributions, then the random variable

$$z_0 = \frac{(\hat{p}_1 - \hat{p}_2) - (p_1 - p_2)}{\sqrt{\dfrac{p_1(1-p_1)}{n_1} + \dfrac{p_2(1-p_2)}{n_2}}}$$

follows a standard normal distribution. Under the assumption that the null hypothesis (H_0: $p_1 - p_2 = 0$) is true, then the random variable Z can be written as

$$z_0 = \frac{(\hat{p}_1 - \hat{p}_2) - 0}{\sqrt{\hat{p}(1-\hat{p})\left(\dfrac{1}{n_1} + \dfrac{1}{n_2}\right)}}$$

where $\hat{p}$ is the proportion resulting from the combination of the two samples (estimate of the overall proportion when we are testing $p_1 = p_2$). The formula is

$$\hat{p} = \frac{x_1 + x_2}{n_1 + n_2}.$$

Hypothesis Test

Null hypothesis: H_0: $p_1 - p_2 = 0$

Test statistic: $z_0 = \dfrac{(\hat{p}_1 - \hat{p}_2) - 0}{\sqrt{\hat{p}(1-\hat{p})\left(\dfrac{1}{n_1} + \dfrac{1}{n_2}\right)}}$

The alternative hypotheses and rejection regions are

Alternative hypothesis	Reject H_0 if
H_a: $p_1 - p_2 > 0$	$z_0 > z_\alpha$
H_a: $p_1 - p_2 < 0$	$z_0 < -z_\alpha$
H_a: $p_1 - p_2 \neq 0$	$z_0 < -z_{\alpha/2}$ or $z_0 > z_{\alpha/2}$

EXAMPLE 35.16

Two machines produce the same parts. A random sample of 1500 parts from machine 1 has 36 that are nonconforming, and a random sample of 1680 parts from machine 2 has 39 that are nonconforming. Is there evidence to suggest that machine 1 has a higher nonconforming rate than machine 2? Test at the 0.01 level of significance.

Solution:

For this problem:

- p_1 represents the proportion of nonconforming units produced by machine 1.

- p_2 represents the proportion of nonconforming units produced by machine 2.

- $\hat{p}_1$ is the sample proportion estimating p_1; it is

$$\hat{p}_1 = \frac{x_1}{n_1} = \frac{36}{1500} = 0.024.$$

Continued

Continued

- $\hat{p}_2$ is the sample proportion estimating p_2; it is found to be

$$\hat{p}_2 = \frac{x_2}{n_2} = \frac{39}{1680} = 0.0232.$$

- $\hat{p}$ is the proportion resulting from the combination of the two samples (estimate of the overall proportion when we are testing $p_1 - p_2 = 0$). It is found to be

$$\hat{p} = \frac{x_1 + x_2}{n_1 + n_2} = \frac{36 + 39}{1500 + 1680} = \frac{75}{3180} = 0.0236.$$

The parameter of interest is the difference in the two population proportions $p_1 - p_2$.

1. The null and alternative hypotheses are

    $H_0: p_1 - p_2 = 0$ $\qquad$ $H_a: p_1 - p_2 > 0$.

2. The level of significance is 0.01.

3. Since this is a right-tailed test, we will reject the null hypothesis if the test statistic is greater than $z_\alpha = z_{0.01} = 2.33$.

4. The test statistic is

$$z_0 = \frac{(\hat{p}_1 - \hat{p}_2)}{\sqrt{\hat{p}(1-\hat{p})\left(\frac{1}{n_1} + \frac{1}{n_2}\right)}} = \frac{(0.024 - 0.0232)}{\sqrt{0.0236(1-0.0236)\left(\frac{1}{1500} + \frac{1}{1680}\right)}} = 0.148.$$

5. Since $0.148 < 2.33$, we can not reject the null hypothesis (weak claim).

6. There is insufficient evidence to conclude that machine 1 has a higher nonconforming rate than machine 2 at the 0.01 level of significance.

A $100(1 - \alpha)\%$ confidence interval on the parameter $p_1 - p_2$ is

$$(\hat{p}_1 - \hat{p}_2) - z_{\alpha/2}\sqrt{\hat{p}(1-\hat{p})\left(\frac{1}{n_1} + \frac{1}{n_2}\right)} \leq p_1 - p_2 \leq (\hat{p}_1 - \hat{p}_2) + z_{\alpha/2}\sqrt{\hat{p}(1-\hat{p})\left(\frac{1}{n_1} + \frac{1}{n_2}\right)}.$$

Hypothesis Tests and Confidence Intervals for Two Population Variances σ_1^2, σ_2^2

A test on the variances of two populations can be used to determine if the variance of one is greater than the other. For example, the null hypothesis could be $H_0: \sigma_1^2 = \sigma_2^2$ where σ_1^2 is the variance of population 1 and σ_2^2 is the variance of population 2. This test uses the F distribution presented in Chapter 34.

Let $Y_1, Y_2, \ldots, Y_{n1}$ be a random sample from a normal distribution with variance σ_1^2 and $W_1, W_2, \ldots, W_{n2}$ be a random sample from a normal distribution with variance σ_2^2. Furthermore, assume that the samples are independent of each other and s_1^2 and s_2^2 are the sample variances for Y_i's and W_j's, respectively. The random variable

$$F = \frac{s_1^2 / \sigma_1^2}{s_2^2 / \sigma_2^2}$$

follows an F distribution with $k_1 = n_1 - 1$ and $k_2 = n_2 - 1$ degrees of freedom.

Hypothesis Test

Null hypothesis: $H_0: \sigma_1^2 = \sigma_2^2$

Test statistic: $F_0 = s_1^2/s_2^2$

The alternative hypotheses and rejection regions are

Alternative hypothesis	Reject H_0 if
$H_a: \sigma_1^2 > \sigma_2^2$	$F_0 > F_{\alpha,k_1,k_2}$
$H_a: \sigma_1^2 < \sigma_2^2$	$F_0 < F_{1-\alpha,k_1,k_2}$
$H_a: \sigma_1^2 \neq \sigma_2^2$	$F_0 < F_{1-\alpha/2,k_1,k_2}$ or $F_0 > F_{\alpha/2,k_1,k_2}$

The critical values for the F distribution can be found in Appendices G, H, and I. The notation F_{α,k_1,k_2} is the F value with area of α to its right, k_1 represents the numerator degrees of freedom, and k_2 represents the denominator degrees of freedom. A probability from this table represents the area under the curve and to the *right* of the F value of interest. For example, for a 0.05 level of significance with $k_1 = 15$ and $k_2 = 5$ degrees of freedom, the F value would be $F_{0.05, 15, 5} = 4.62$. The F table provides values for specific values of α (level of significance). To find critical values when the area to the right is $1 - \alpha$, such as $F_{1-\alpha,k_1,k_2}$, we have to use the following relationship:

$$F_{1-\alpha,k_1,k_2} = \frac{1}{F_{\alpha,k_2,k_1}}$$

To illustrate, suppose we want to find a critical value for a left-tailed test where $k_1 = 10$, $k_2 = 8$, and $\alpha = 0.05$. Then $F_{1-\alpha,k_1,k_2} = F_{0.95,10,8}$ and

$$F_{0.95,10,8} = \frac{1}{F_{0.05,8,10}} = \frac{1}{3.07} = 0.326.$$

EXAMPLE 35.17

Two chemical companies can supply a particular material. The concentration of an element in this material is important. The mean concentration for both suppliers is approximately the same, but we suspect that the variability in concentration may differ between the two companies. The standard deviation of concentration in a random sample of $n_1 = 10$ batches produced by company 1 is $s_1 = 3.8$ g/l, while for company 2, a random sample of $n_2 = 16$ batches yields $s_2 = 4.2$ g/l. Using a level of significance of 0.10, we would like to determine if there is sufficient evidence to conclude that the two population variances differ.

Continued

Continued

Solution:

Let:

- σ_1^2 be the population variance of the element concentration in the material from company 1

- σ_2^2 be the population variance of the element concentration in the material from company 2

1. The null and alternative hypotheses are

   H_0: $\sigma_1^2 = \sigma_2^2$ H_1: $\sigma_1^2 \neq \sigma_2^2$.

2. The level of significance is $\alpha = 0.10$.

3. There are two rejection regions since we have a two-tailed test. Furthermore, the degrees of freedom are $k_1 = n_1 - 1 = 9$ and $k_2 = n_2 - 1 = 15$. The critical values are

   $$F_{\alpha/2, k_1, k_2} = F_{0.05, 9, 15} = 2.59$$

   and

   $$F_{0.950, 9, 15} = \frac{1}{F_{\alpha/2, k_2, k_1}} = \frac{1}{F_{0.05, 15, 9}} = \frac{1}{3.01} = 0.332.$$

   Therefore, reject the null hypothesis if the test statistic is less than 0.332 or greater than 2.59.

4. The test statistic is

   $$F_0 = \frac{s_1^2}{s_2^2} = \frac{(3.8)^2}{(4.2)^2} = 0.819.$$

5. Since $0.332 < 0.819 < 2.59$, we can not reject the null hypothesis at the 0.10 level of significance (weak claim).

6. There is insufficient evidence to conclude that the variances of the element concentration in this material from the two suppliers are not equal.

A $100(1 - \alpha)\%$ two-sided confidence interval on the parameter σ_1^2/σ_2^2 is given by

$$\frac{s_1^2}{s_2^2} F_{1-\alpha/2, k_1, k_2} \leq \frac{\sigma_1^2}{\sigma_2^2} \leq \frac{s_1^2}{s_2^2} F_{\alpha/2, k_1, k_2}.$$

The confidence interval on the ratio of the two variances can be used to determine if there is a significant difference between the two variances. In hypothesis testing we assume the null hypothesis is true, that is, H_0: $\sigma_1^2 = \sigma_2^2$. We can rewrite this equality as

$$\frac{\sigma_1^2}{\sigma_2^2} = 1.$$

When constructing a two-sided confidence interval on the ratio of the two variances, we would reject the null hypothesis if the value 1 is not contained within that interval. For example, the 95 percent two-sided confidence interval on the ratio of variances of the previous example is

$$0.217 \leq \frac{\sigma_1^2}{\sigma_2^2} \leq 2.555.$$

Therefore, we are highly confident that the true ratio of the variances lies between 0.217 and 2.555. Since this interval contains the value 1, we would conclude based on our samples that there is no statistically significant difference between the two variances.

The *p*-value Approach to Hypothesis Testing

In this chapter, hypothesis testing has been presented using the *critical value* (or *fixed significance level) approach* and rejection regions. Critical values are determined based on a stated level of significance (α), among other quantities. The critical value approach is somewhat lacking for two reasons: 1) it does not completely quantify the degree to which a null hypothesis is rejected or not rejected, and 2) it imposes a specific significance level on the practitioner or others making the decision.

For example, suppose a right-tailed test on a population mean with $\alpha = 0.05$ was carried out. It was reported that the critical value found from the *t* table was $t = 2.306$, and the null hypothesis was rejected—but you are not told the value of the test statistic itself. If you are given no further information, can you determine what the test statistic value might have been? Obviously the value of the test statistic was greater than 2.306 (since the null hypothesis was rejected), but by how much? There is no indication of whether the test statistic was 2.310 or 10.310 given just this information. In addition, the decision was based on a specific level of significance. If a 0.05 level of significance is used, but after conducting the test it is determined that a 0.01 level of significance should have been used, new critical values must be determined. In many engineering problems, an acceptable level of significance may be known, but not in every situation.

A second approach that offers some measure of the degree to which the test statistic is significant involves the use of *p-values*. A *p*-value is the smallest level of significance at which the null hypothesis would be rejected. It can be thought of as how likely it is that we should have obtained that value of the test statistic or more extreme (more extreme than the value of the test statistic we did get if the null hypothesis is really true). A small *p*-value is evidence against the null hypothesis in favor of the alternative.

For example, suppose we are testing H_0: $\mu = 50$ against H_a: $\mu > 50$ and the test statistic is found to be $z_0 = 2.47$. The *p*-value for this test would be $P(Z > 2.47) = 0.0068$. That is, the probability that we should have obtained a test statistic of 2.47 or more extreme (in this case larger than 2.47, since we have a right-tailed test) if H_0: $\mu = 50$ is true, is 0.0068. This is a highly unlikely event. It is highly unlikely that we should have obtained a test statistic of 2.47 if the mean really is 50. But we did get a test statistic of 2.47, so what went wrong? Remember that the claim $\mu = 50$ is a hypothesis that can be proven incorrect (based on collected data). Therefore, the null hypothesis is probably false.

Decision. If a level of significance is predetermined (but it does not have to be) then the decisions would be as follows:

- If p-value < α, reject H_0.

- If p-value > α, do not reject H_0.

Using the p-value approach allows the practitioner flexibility in making decisions. If the significance level is changed for a particular test, no new calculations need to be done in order to make a decision. The p-value will not change for a test even if the level of significance does.

The p-value is easy to interpret, and most computer software packages will report a p-value for a hypothesis test. Reconsider the wall thickness example for two competing vendors given in Example 35.15. The data and some of the results are given here:

Vendor 1:	86	82	91	88	89	85	88	90	84	87	88	83	84	89
Vendor 2:	79	78	82	85	77	86	84	78	80	82	79	76		

The parameter of interest is the difference in average wall thickness, $\mu_1 - \mu_2$ and the hypotheses are H_0: $\mu_1 - \mu_2 = 0$ and H_1: $\mu_1 - \mu_2 > 0$. The level of significance was $\alpha = 0.05$, and we concluded that since our test statistic (5.25) was greater than the critical value (1.711), we would reject the null hypothesis.

The problem was worked again, this time using a statistical software package, with the following output:

Two-sample T for Vendor1 versus Vendor2

Difference = mu (Vendor1) – mu (Vendor2)

T-Test of difference = 0 (vs >): T-Value = 5.27 **P-Value = 0.000 DF = 24**

The p-value is given in bold and reported to be 0.000 (this value is most likely some extremely small number very close to zero; so for all practical purposes, the p-value is zero). Since the p-value < α (that is, 0.000 < 0.05), we would reject the null hypothesis. What is telling about the p-value is that we could easily change the level of significance and be able to make a decision without having to do any further calculations. The p-value will remain 0.000 regardless of the level of significance.

The six-step hypothesis testing procedure given in this chapter would also apply when using p-values. The steps would be:

1. State H_0 and H_a.

2. State α (optional).

3. Calculate the test statistic.

4. Find the p-value.

5. Reject or do not reject H_0; if α is given, then reject H_0 if p-value $< \alpha$, otherwise do not reject H_0.

6. State your conclusions in terms of the problem statement.

The smaller the p-value, the stronger the evidence against the null hypothesis and in favor of the alternative hypothesis. It is important to note that the p-value approach and the critical value approach will lead to the same conclusion for the same problem. This is true as long as all quantities and assumptions are identical when using both approaches. Finally, with all of the procedures given in this chapter, it is recommended that the calculations be done using a reliable statistical software package.

Statistical versus Practical Significance

In some situations, it may be possible to detect a statistically significant difference between two populations when there is no practical difference. In hypothesis testing, the goal is to make a decision about a claim or hypothesis. The decision as to whether or not the null hypothesis is rejected in favor of the alternative hypothesis is based on a sample taken from the population of interest. If the null hypothesis is rejected, we say there is statistically significant evidence against the null hypothesis in favor of the alternative hypothesis. But statistical significance does not imply practical significance. Rejecting the null hypothesis in favor of the alternative hypothesis by a very small margin may be the result of a relatively large sample size. Large sample sizes will almost always lead to rejection of the null hypothesis.

Illustration. Consider an automobile manufacturer's claim that one particular make of car averages 31 miles per gallon on the highway. A consumer group tests 75 cars of the same make under identical conditions and finds the average to be 30.6 miles per gallon. We could conduct a hypothesis test of H_0: $\mu = 31$ versus H_a: $\mu < 31$. The sample average is $\bar{x} = 30.6$. If we are able to reject H_0 in favor of H_a, we say there is *statistically significant* evidence to indicate that the true average is less than 31 mpg. But, is 30.6 really different from 31 in the practical sense? In this situation, a statistical significance was found, but not necessarily a practical significance in the difference between the hypothesized value (31 mpg) and the estimated value (30.6 mpg).

Rejecting the null hypothesis in favor of the alternative hypothesis by a very small margin may be the result of a relatively large sample size. Again, larger sample sizes can often result in statistically significant results even though the difference may not be of practical significance. In summary, a rejected null hypothesis implies statistical significance but not necessarily practical significance. Some practitioners prefer using confidence intervals for making decisions since they allow one to see if a practical difference exists.

Significance Level, Power, Type I and Type II Errors

Since every hypothesis test uses samples to infer properties of a population based on analysis of a sample, there is some chance that although the analysis is flawless the conclusion may be incorrect. These sampling errors are not errors in the usual sense because they can not be corrected (without using 100 percent sampling with no measurement errors). The two possible types of errors that can occur in hypothesis testing are the type I error and type II error briefly introduced earlier in this chapter.

A *type I error* occurs when a true null hypothesis is rejected. The probability of committing a type I error is denoted α—the *significance level* in hypothesis testing. The critical values for a hypothesis testing procedure are based on a predetermined level of significance. That is, the maximum allowable probability of rejecting a true null hypothesis (α) is fixed for a particular problem. A *type II error* occurs when a false null hypothesis is not rejected. The probability of committing a type II error is denoted β. A summary of the possible decisions and errors are given in the following table:

		Result of Hypothesis Test	
		Reject H_0	Fail to reject H_0
H_0 is actually	True	Type I error	No error
	False	No error	Type II error

Again,

α = P(type I error) = P(rejecting H_0 when in fact H_0 is true)

β = P(type II error) = P(failing to reject H_0 when in fact H_0 is false).

In general, it is desirable to have small α and β, but there is often a trade-off. For a fixed sample size in hypothesis testing, decreasing α will result in an increase in β. Because of the manner in which the null and alternative hypotheses are specified in hypothesis testing, it is generally true that committing a type I error is more serious than committing a type II error. Therefore, controlling the probability of committing a type I error (setting α) is often a higher priority than controlling the probability of committing a type II error. In fact, it is difficult to specify an exact value of β since that would require knowing the true value of the parameter being tested.

The *power* of a hypothesis test is defined as the probability of correctly rejecting a false null hypothesis. The power is given by $1 - \beta$, since β is the probability of failing to reject the null hypothesis when it is false. The power provides some measure of the test's ability to detect differences. This ability to detect differences is often referred to as the *sensitivity* of the hypothesis test.

3. PAIRED-COMPARISON TESTS

> Define and use paired-comparison
> (parametric) hypothesis tests, and interpret
> the results. (Apply)
>
> **Body of Knowledge VI.D.3**

Paired-comparison hypothesis testing involves a two-sample t-test for two samples that are believed to be *dependent*, that is, when an observation from one sample can be logically paired with an observation from the other sample. The pairing of two observations is based on some characteristic they have in common. By pairing the data when necessary, we can reduce the effect of the common characteristic that may influence the results.

To illustrate, 40 people are placed on the same diet program. Each person is weighed on day 1 (before weight), put through the program, then weighed again at the end of the program (after weight). The difference in the person's before weight and after weight is recorded. This is a *paired comparison*—pairing each individual person's before weight with their after weight (it would not make sense to compare the before weight of person X with the after weight of person Y, due to individual differences in people).

When Should Pairing Be Used?

The data from two samples should be paired when there is a *logical* relationship between the two observations. The following set of data represents heart rates (in beats per minute) for individuals who used two types of exercise equipment, A and B.

A	161	172	166	189	180
B	155	191	187	174	171

There is no indication of whether the heart rates recorded involved five people using both types of equipment or ten people—five using type A and five using type B. *There is no indication that the data should be paired from equipment A to equipment B.* Consider the next set of data, again representing the heart rates of people who used the exercise equipment:

Person	1	2	3	4	5
A	161	172	166	189	180
B	155	191	187	174	171

Now we have more information that indicates the heart rates have a characteristic in common. Since basal heart rates vary a great deal from person to person, we would pair the heart rates by person in order to minimize the effect of individual differences. Therefore, if a significant difference is found, there is a better chance that the difference is due to the type of equipment and not the person using it. If there is any indication that the data should be paired in a particular problem, then pairing should be done (that is, if in doubt, pair the data).

Procedure for Paired Comparisons

Suppose we have n independently selected pairs given by $(X_1, Y_1), (X_2, Y_2), \ldots, (X_n, Y_n)$. Furthermore, let $E(X_i) = \mu_1$ and $E(Y_i) = \mu_2$. The paired-comparison test is a test conducted on the differences between the two groups. Define the differences as $D_i = X_i - Y_i$ for all n pairs. Assume the differences D_i are normally distributed with the following parameters:

- Mean difference μ_D, where $\mu_D = \mu_1 - \mu_2$
- Variance of the differences σ^2_D

For a sample of n independently selected pairs (X_i, Y_i), let d_i $(i = 1, 2, \ldots, n)$ represent the actual differences from the sample. The sample mean $\bar{d}$ and sample standard deviation s_d for the differences are

$$\bar{d} = \frac{\sum_{i=1}^{n} d_i}{n}$$

and

$$s_d = \sqrt{\frac{\sum_{i=1}^{n}\left(d_i - \bar{d}\right)}{n-1}}.$$

It is important to note that once the differences are calculated, the paired t-test is equivalent to the t-test for a single population mean presented earlier. The test statistic that will be used for the paired t-test is

$$t_0 = \frac{\bar{d}}{s_d / \sqrt{n}},$$

which follows a t distribution with $k = n - 1$ degrees of freedom. The six-step procedure for conducting a paired t-test is:

1. State the null and alternative hypotheses for the problem. We will restrict ourselves to the case of no difference between the two populations. That is, $H_0: \mu_D = 0$, and the alternative hypothesis can be one of the three possible alternatives given earlier $(H_a: \mu_D < 0, \mu_D > 0, \text{ or } \mu_D \neq 0)$.

2. State the level of significance.

3. Find the rejection region.

4. Calculate the test statistic, t_0.

5. Compare the test statistic t_0 to the critical value found in step 3. If the test statistic falls into the rejection region, then reject the null hypothesis (strong claim). If the test statistic does not fall into the rejection region, then state that there is insufficient evidence to reject the null hypothesis (weak claim).

6. State the conclusions in terms of the problem statement.

EXAMPLE 35.18

Consider the study on two types of exercise equipment given earlier. The following set of data represents heart rates (in beats per minute) for individuals who used the two types of exercise equipment, A and B. The last row represents the differences in heart rate for each person, $d_i = A_i - B_i$ for $i = 1, 2, \ldots, 5$.

Person	1	2	3	4	5
A	161	172	166	189	180
B	155	191	187	174	171
$d_i = A_i - B_i$	6	−19	−21	15	9

Is there a significant difference in heart rate due to the type of exercise equipment used? Use a 0.05 level of significance. We will assume that the differences follow a normal distribution.

Solution:

- Let μ_1 represent the mean heart rate after using equipment A.

- Let μ_2 represent the mean heart rate after using equipment B.

- The logical pairing involves the differences in heart rates for both types of equipment by person. There are $n = 5$ heart rates in each sample.

- Let μ_D represent the true mean difference between the two populations $\mu_D = \mu_1 - \mu_2$.

The necessary summary statistics are

$$\bar{d} = \frac{\sum\limits_{i=1}^{n} d_i}{n} = \frac{6 + (-19) + (-21) + 15 + 9}{5} = -2.0$$

and

$$s_d = \sqrt{\frac{\sum\limits_{i=1}^{n}(d_i - \bar{d})^2}{n-1}}$$

$$= \sqrt{\frac{(6-(-2.0))^2 + (-19-(-2.0))^2 + (-21-(-2.0))^2 + (15-(-2.0))^2 + (9-(-2.0))^2}{5-1}} = 16.76.$$

Continued

Continued

The steps are:

1. $H_0: \mu_D = 0$ $H_a: \mu_D \neq 0$.

2. $\alpha = 0.05$.

3. Since this is a two-tailed test, reject H_0 if the test statistic is less than $-t_{\alpha/2,k}$ or greater than $t_{\alpha/2,k}$ where $t_{\alpha/2,k} = t_{0.025,4} = 2.776$.

4. Calculate the test statistic:

$$t_0 = \frac{\bar{d}}{s_D / \sqrt{n}} = \frac{-2.0}{16.76 / \sqrt{5}} = -0.27.$$

5. Since $-2.776 < -0.27 < 2.776$, we can not reject the null hypothesis (weak claim).

6. There is insufficient evidence to conclude that the type of exercise equipment significantly affects heart rate at the 0.05 level of significance.

A $100(1 - \alpha)$% two-sided confidence interval on the parameter μ_D is given by

$$\bar{d} - t_{\alpha/2,k}\left(\frac{s_d}{\sqrt{n}}\right) \leq \mu \leq \bar{d} + t_{\alpha/2,k}\left(\frac{s_d}{\sqrt{n}}\right).$$

4. GOODNESS-OF-FIT TESTS

> Define and use chi square and other goodness-of-fit tests, and interpret the results. (Apply)
>
> **Body of Knowledge VI.D.4**

Chi-square and other goodness-of-fit tests help determine whether a discrete sample has been drawn from a known population. The probability distribution may be of a specific form, such as the Poisson, binomial, geometric, and so on, or it may be simply a table of outcomes and their assumed probabilities. For example, suppose that all rejected products have exactly one of four types of nonconformities (that render them nonconforming) and *historically* they have been distributed as follows:

Nonconformity	Percent of nonconforming products
Paint run	16%
Paint blister	28%
Decal crooked	42%
Door cracked	14%
Total	100%

Data on rejected parts for a randomly selected week in the current year are:

Nonconformity	Number of nonconforming products
Paint run	27
Paint blister	60
Decal crooked	100
Door cracked	21
Total	208

The question we need to answer: Is the distribution of nonconformity types different from the historical distribution? The test that answers this question is referred to as the χ^2 *goodness-of-fit test.* To get a feel for this test, construct a table that displays the number of nonconforming units that would be *expected* in each category if the sample exactly followed the historical percentages (the historical percentages are used as estimates of the probabilities that the nonconformities are present on the product). The expected number will be referred to as the *expected frequency.* The expected frequency is found by multiplying the total number of items in the sample n by the probability for a particular category.

Nonconformity	Observed frequency (O_i)	Probability (p_i)	Expected frequency (E_i) [$E_i = np_i$]
Paint run	27	0.16	33.28
Paint blister	60	0.28	58.24
Decal crooked	100	0.42	87.36
Door cracked	21	0.14	29.12
Total	$n = 208$	1	

The question to be decided is whether the difference between the *expected frequencies* and *observed frequencies* is sufficiently large. If the difference is large, there may be significant evidence to conclude that the distribution the current sample came from is not the same as the historical distribution; we may even have enough evidence to conclude that the historical (assumed) distribution is no longer valid.

The test statistic that can be used to determine if the assumed distribution is still valid is

$$\chi_0^2 = \sum_{i=1}^{k} \frac{\left(O_i - E_i\right)^2}{E_i}.$$

It can be shown that the test statistic follows a chi-square distribution with $k - 1$ degrees of freedom (where k = number of categories). Let p_i represent the proportion of the population that falls into the ith category, for $i = 1, 2, \ldots, k$. Let $p_{i,0}$ represent the hypothesized value of p_i. The null and alternative hypotheses would be:

H_0: $p_1 = p_{1,0}$; $p_2 = p_{2,0}$; $\ldots$, $p_k = p_{k,0}$

H_a: $p_i \neq p_{i,0}$ for at least one $i = 1, 2, \ldots, k$

The procedure for conducting a goodness-of-fit test is as follows:

1. H_0: $p_1 = p_{1,0}$; $p_2 = p_{2,0}$; $\ldots$, $p_k = p_{k,0}$

   H_a: $p_i \neq p_{i,0}$ for at least one $i = 1, 2, \ldots, k$.

2. State the level of significance α.

3. Determine the rejection region. For this test the critical value is $\chi_{\alpha,k-1}^2$.

4. Calculate the test statistic:

$$\chi_0^2 = \sum_{i=1}^{k} \frac{\left(O_i - E_i\right)^2}{E_i}.$$

5. If $\chi_0^2 \geq \chi_{\alpha,k-1}^2$, reject H_0; otherwise do not reject H_0.

6. State the conclusions in terms of the problem statement.

EXAMPLE 35.19

We will complete the goodness-of-fit test for the problem involving nonconforming products using a five percent level of significance.

1. H_0: $p_1 = 0.16$; $p_2 = 0.28$; $p_3 = 0.42$; $p_4 = 0.14$

   H_a: $p_i \neq p_{i,0}$ for at least one $i = 1, 2, \ldots, 4$

2. $\alpha = 0.05$.

3. For this test the critical value is $\chi_{\alpha,k-1}^2 = \chi_{0.05,3}^2 = 7.815$.

4. Calculate the test statistic:

$$\chi_0^2 = \sum_{i=1}^{k} \frac{\left(O_i - E_i\right)^2}{E_i} = \frac{(27 - 33.28)^2}{33.28} + \frac{(60 - 58.24)^2}{58.24} + \frac{(100 - 87.36)^2}{87.36} + \frac{(21 - 29.12)^2}{29.12}$$

$$= 5.33$$

Continued

Continued

> 5. Since 5.33 < 7.815, we can not reject H_0 (weak claim).
>
> 6. We conclude that the data is consistent with the assumed historical probabilities at the 0.05 level of significance.

The chi-square goodness-of-fit test is valid as long as the expected frequencies are not too small. Some recommendations for a minimum value have included 3, 4, and 5. Other recommendations have been that some of the expected frequencies can be as small as 1 or 2 as long as most of expected frequencies exceed 5. For more details on other applications of the chi-square test and further recommendations see Devore (2007), Montgomery and Runger (2006), and Vining and Kowalski (2006).

5. ANALYSIS OF VARIANCE (ANOVA)

> Define and use ANOVAs and interpret the results. (Analyze)
>
> Body of Knowledge VI.D.5

One-Way ANOVA

If we are interested in comparing more than two samples, the previous tests are not valid. Suppose we want to compare a populations. Sometimes the populations are referred to as treatments or levels of a factor. Let $\mu_1, \mu_2, \ldots, \mu_a$ represent the means for the populations. The goal is to determine if the treatments applied significantly affect the outcome or response of interest.

EXAMPLE 35.20

Alternative energy sources to traditional fossil fuels are in high demand. Several variables are believed to influence the conversion of waste vegetable oil into biodiesel fuel. One variable of interest is the amount of catalyst (%) at three levels—0.6, 1.0, and 1.4—used in the conversion process. The response of interest is conversion rate (wt%) (larger values indicate that more of the waste vegetable oil was successfully converted into useable biodiesel fuel). The experiments are conducted in random order and with the following results:

Continued

Continued

	Catalyst (%)	
0.6	**1.0**	**1.4**
71.34	84.62	78.33
76.11	78.21	76.89
73.16	82.39	71.42
76.02	76.55	76.60

In this study:

- Some questions of interest are: Does the amount of catalyst have a significant effect on the conversion rate? If so, which catalyst amount will result in a high conversion rate?

- Catalyst is the *factor of interest* or *independent variable*.

- The factor of interest (catalyst) has three *levels* (0.6%, 1.0%, and 1.4%). You will also see levels referred to as *treatments* or *groups*. In this example, we would say there are three treatments applied or three groups being studied.

- Conversion rate is the *response of interest* (or *dependent variable*).

- There are four *replicates* ($n = 4$) for each level of catalyst.

Assumptions. Three important assumptions for the use of a one-way analysis of variance are:

1. The observations follow a normal distribution (that is, the populations are normally distributed).

2. The observations are independent.

3. The treatments have constant variance (homogeneity of variances).

In summary, the treatment distributions (populations) for all *a* treatments should be normally distributed each with the same variance σ^2. An additional assumption that is not always included deals with the number of replicates. It is not necessary that each level of the factor or treatment have the same number of replicates. But large differences in the number of observations from group to group can affect the validity of the analysis. We assume that the number of replicates *n* will be equal or near equal for all treatments. For more details see Devore (2007), Montgomery and Runger (2006), and Vining and Kowalski (2006).

It should be noted that the analysis of variance procedure outlined next is fairly robust to slight departures from these assumptions. The assumptions should always be verified. This is discussed later in this section.

General Notation and Methods

Suppose we have one factor of interest with *a* levels of that factor (we could also say there are *a* treatments being compared.) Let Y_{ij} represent the *j*th response in the *i*th treatment where $i = 1, 2, \ldots, a$ and $j = 1, 2, \ldots, n$. For example, the third observation for the second treatment (catalyst amount = 1.0%) given earlier would be denoted $y_{23} = 82.39$. There are a total of $a \times n$ observations in the experiment. A general table of results could be set up as:

		Treatment		
	1	2	. . .	a
	y_{11}	y_{21}	. . .	y_{a1}
	y_{12}	y_{22}	. . .	y_{a2}
			. . .	
	y_{1n}	y_{2n}	. . .	y_{an}
Totals	$y_{1.}$	$y_{2.}$	$y_{a.}$	$y_{..}$
Averages	$\bar{y}_{1.}$	$\bar{y}_{2.}$	$\bar{y}_{a.}$	$\bar{y}_{..}$

where

$y_{i.}$ = the sum of the n observations in the ith treatment (the dot subscript indicates summation over the subscript it replaces)

$y_{..}$ = the sum of all $a \times n$ observations

$\bar{y}_{i.}$ = average of the n observations in the ith treatment

$\bar{y}_{..}$ = average of all $a \times n$ observations

The hypotheses of interest are

H_0: $\mu_1 = \mu_2 = \ldots = \mu_a$

H_1: at least two of the means differ (that is, $\mu_i \neq \mu_j$)

The quantities needed to determine if a significant difference exists among the treatments (or levels of the factor) are the sum of squares and the degrees of freedom.

Sums of Squares and Degrees of Freedom

The *total sum of squares,* denoted SS_T, is an important quantity that provides a measure of the *total overall variability* in the response:

$$SS_T = \sum_{i=1}^{a}\sum_{j=1}^{n}\left(y_{ij} - \bar{y}_{..}\right)^2$$

where y_{ij} is a single observation and $\bar{y}_{..}$ is the average of all $a \times n$ responses. The total sum of squares can be partitioned into two sources of variability: variability due to the treatments applied ($SS_{Treatments}$) and variability due to error or unknown sources (SS_E). In other words:

$$SS_T = SS_{Treatments} + SS_E$$

The *sum of squares due to treatments* ($SS_{Treatments}$) is a portion of the total sum of squares (SS_T). It is a quantity that measures the proportion of total variability that can be explained by or that is due to the different treatments applied:

$$SS_{\text{Treatments}} = n \sum_{i=1}^{a} \left(\bar{y}_{i.} - \bar{y}_{..} \right)^2$$

The *error sum of squares* (SS_E) is that portion of the total sum of squares (SS_T) that represents the inherent variability. This is variability that is not due to the treatments applied or levels used. In conducting an experiment involving a single factor we assume that all variables (other than the treatments) that could possibly influence the response are held constant; any variability that can not be attributed to the treatment is said to be error. Under these conditions the "leftover" variability is considered inherent. For example, if temperature is known to possibly influence conversion rate in our previous example, but temperature is not of interest at this point, we would hold temperature (this is the temperature of a water bath in the reaction experiment) at a constant and only vary the factor that is of interest (such as catalyst). The error sum of squares can be found by subtraction:

$$SS_E = SS_T - SS_{\text{Treatments}}$$

It is important to note that if we are trying to show that the treatments cause a significant effect on the response, then we want the variability due to treatments to be large as compared to the inherent variability. It is desirable to have the variability due to error or unknown sources to be as small as possible (that is, we want SS_E to be small).

A *ratio* involving the $SS_{\text{Treatments}}$ and SS_E is used to reject or not reject the hypothesis of interest that all treatment means are equal:

$$H_0: \mu_1 = \mu_2 = \ldots = \mu_a$$

This ratio involving the $SS_{\text{Treatments}}$ and SS_E, (whose exact calculations will be shown next) should be significantly large in order to reject the null hypothesis. A large value of the ratio indicates that most of the total variability is attributed to the treatments applied and is not just variability due to error. If the error variability was comparable to (or larger than) the variability due to treatments, this would indicate that there is very little difference in treatments applied and that most of the variability is uncontrollable.

Degrees of freedom are associated with each source of variability. The degrees of freedom are necessary values in the computation of a test statistic and are as follows:

- The total degrees of freedom are $an - 1$

- For a treatments, the degrees of freedom are $a - 1$.

- The degrees of freedom for error are $a(n - 1)$.

- Notice that the total degrees of freedom can be partitioned into degrees of freedom for treatments and degrees of freedom for error:

$$an - 1 = a - 1 + a(n - 1)$$

The degrees of freedom are used in the ratio involving the sums of squares discussed previously. The sum of squares divided by the appropriate degrees of freedom provides a measure of variability adjusted for sample size and number of treatments in the study. These resulting measures are referred to as *mean squares*

(MS). Under H_0, they are estimates of the error variance. The *mean square for treatments* is

$$MS_{Treatments} = \frac{SS_{Treatments}}{a-1}.$$

The *error mean square* is

$$MS_E = \frac{SS_E}{a(n-1)}.$$

Now, we can directly compare the two mean squares. If $MS_{Treatments} > MS_E$, then there may be evidence that the treatments have a significant affect on the response. The ratio of the mean squares can be used as a test statistic to make a decision about rejecting or not rejecting the null hypothesis H_0. The ratio is our test statistic, denoted by F_0:

$$F_0 = \frac{MS_{Treatments}}{MS_E}$$

which can be shown to follow an F distribution with $k_1 = a - 1$, and $k_2 = a(n - 1)$ degrees of freedom. If F_0 is large, then we may have evidence that the different treatments significantly affect the response of interest.

Recall the section on testing two population variances. The F distribution was appropriate for modeling the ratio of two variances. Therefore we will compare the test statistic F_0 to an appropriate critical value found from the F distribution (Appendices G, H, and I). The appropriate critical value is given by $F_{\alpha,a-1,a(n-1)}$ where α is the probability of a type I error, discussed in previous sections, $a - 1$ is the degrees of freedom for the numerator of F_0, and $a(n - 1)$ is the degrees of freedom for the denominator of F_0. Therefore, if $F_0 > F_{\alpha,a-1,a(n-1)}$, we will reject the null hypothesis and conclude that the treatments or levels are significantly different at the α level of significance. We only reject the null hypothesis for large F_0 since a large ratio indicates that the variability due to the treatments is larger than the variability due to error (that is, $MS_{Treatments} >> MS_E$).

p-values

The *p*-values discussed previously can also be calculated for the F test given here. The same interpretation would apply: if the *p*-value $< \alpha$, then reject the null hypothesis, otherwise do not reject the null hypothesis. *P*-values are easy to interpret and provided by most statistical software packages when conducting an analysis of variance.

The degrees of freedom (df), sum of squares (SS), mean squares (MS), F value, and *p*-value are often summarized in an analysis of variance (ANOVA) table. The table for a one-way ANOVA is shown as Table 35.2.

The calculations and the resulting ANOVA table can be easily obtained using modern computer software or the formulas given in this section. Software packages that have statistical capabilities will automatically report some form of this ANOVA table.

Table 35.2 One-way ANOVA table.

Source of variability	df	SS	MS	F	p-value
Treatments	$a - 1$	$SS_{Treatments}$	$MS_{Treatments}$	F_0	$P(F > F_0)$
Error	$a(n - 1)$	SS_E	MS_E		
Total	$an - 1$	SS_T			

We will now return to our conversion rate of biodiesel fuel example presented at the beginning of this section. In this example, we will only set up the null and alternative hypotheses and present the results of an ANOVA table obtained using a commercially available and reliable statistical package.

EXAMPLE 35.21

The data are reproduced here with the factor of interest (treatments) being amount of catalyst (%) and the response conversion rate. Is there significant evidence to conclude that amount of catalyst significantly affects the conversion rate?

Catalyst (%)		
0.6	**1.0**	**1.4**
71.34	84.62	78.33
76.11	78.21	76.89
73.16	82.39	71.42
76.02	76.55	76.60

Solution:

The null and alternative hypotheses are

$H_0: \mu_1 = \mu_2 = \mu_3$

H_a: at least two μ_i are different, for $i \neq j$.

Before a formal analysis is conducted on the data, it is often informative to display the results graphically. The box plot is one such appropriate graphical display. Box plots for catalyst amount are shown in Figure 35.1.

Based on the box plots, it appears that the catalyst amount of 1.0 percent results in higher conversion rates than either 0.6 percent or 1.4 percent. There does not appear to be a difference in conversion rate between catalyst amounts of 0.6 percent and 1.4 percent. Since interpretation of the graphical displays can be subjective, a more formal analysis such as an analysis of variance would be more reliable. The analysis of variance table is:

Source of variability	df	SS	MS	F	p-value
Catalyst	2	84.92	42.46	4.50	0.044
Error	9	85.01	9.45		
Total	11	169.93			

Continued

Continued

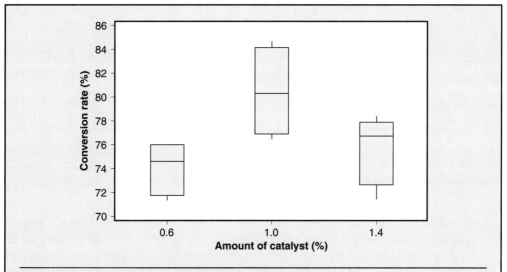

Figure 35.1   Box plots for catalyst amount.

The *p*-value is reported as 0.044. Since the *p*-value is small, we can reject the null hypothesis and conclude that there is evidence that amount of catalyst affects the conversion rate of waste vegetable oil into biodiesel fuel.

At this point, the assumptions given earlier should be verified. Some simple tools can be used to verify that the normality and constant variance assumptions are valid. To assess normality, a normal probability plot of the observations can be constructed. A simple method for assessing constant variance is to examine the standard deviations of each treatment. A quick and dirty rule of thumb is that the constant variance assumption is plausible as long as the largest treatment standard deviation is not much more than two times the smallest treatment standard deviation. (See Devore [2007] for more details on these and other methods.) More formal methods for assessing constant variance involve analyzing residuals. These methods will be discussed in later chapters.

In order to adequately assess independence we must have the order in which the data were collected. Without the order, it is difficult to determine the validity of the independence assumption. In addition, if the experiment was conducted randomly (carried out randomly) it is often assumed that this randomization will minimize any dependency among the observations.

Two-Way ANOVA

The *two-way ANOVA* hypothesis test can be used when there are two factors of interest in the experiment. In our biodiesel fuel example there was one factor (catalyst amount) with three levels. When more than one factor is under investigation in an experiment, a factorial experiment should be used. A *factorial experiment* is one where all possible combinations of the factor levels are investigated.

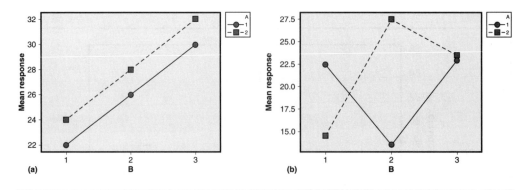

Figure 35.2   Interaction plots of factors A and B.

To illustrate, suppose we have two factors A and B with levels *a* and *b*, respectively. In a full-factorial experiment, there would be *ab* total combinations, which are the treatments of interest. We would be interested in differences among the levels of factor A, the differences among the levels of factor B, and whether there exists a possible *interaction* between the two factors. An interaction between factors can be demonstrated graphically. Figure 35.2 represents the interaction plots of two factors A and B, where A has two levels (*a* = 2) and B has three levels (*b* = 3). Figure 35.2a indicates that there is no significant interaction between factors A and B. Notice that as we move across the levels of factor B, the levels of factor A maintain identical patterns. Figure 35.2b on the other hand indicates a significant interaction between factors A and B. Notice that by changing from level 1 to level 2 of factor A, the response is quite different. By changing the level of factor A, and keeping factor B at level 2, for example, the response has changed.

When analyzing two-factor experiments, the effects to be analyzed are the main effects of factor A, the main effects of factor B, and the interaction between them.

EXAMPLE 35.22

Reconsider the biodiesel fuel example given earlier; now a second factor is of interest. Along with catalyst, the temperature of the water bath for the process is also of interest. There are two temperatures, 30°C and 60°C. Two replicates of each combination of catalyst and temperature are recorded, with the following results:

		Catalyst (%)		
		0.6	1.0	1.4
Temperature	30	75.22, 76.81	83.10, 79.55	69.24, 71.64
	60	77.01, 75.39	75.33, 72.67	72.00, 74.57

In this study:

- Some questions of interest are: Does the amount of catalyst have a significant effect on conversion rate? Does temperature have a significant

Continued

Continued

effect on conversion rate? Is there a significant interaction between temperature and the amount of catalyst?

- Catalyst and temperature are the *factors of interest* or *independent variables.*

- The factor "catalyst" has three *levels* (0.6 percent, 1.0 percent, and 1.4 percent). The factor "temperature" has two *levels* (30°C and 60°C).

- Conversion rate is the *response of interest* (or *dependent variable*).

- There are two *replicates* ($n = 2$) for each combination of catalyst and temperature.

Sums of Squares, Mean Squares, and the ANOVA Table

Suppose we have two factors of interest, A and B, with a and b levels, respectively. Furthermore, suppose there are n replicates for each combination ab. The total sum of squares (SS_T) can be calculated for the two-way table and it can be partitioned into four sources of variability:

$$SS_T = SS_A + SS_B + SS_{AB} + SS_E$$

where SS_A is the sum of squares for factor A, SS_B is the sum of squares for factor B, SS_{AB} is the sum of squares for the interaction AB, and SS_E is the error sum of squares. The mean squares can be calculated and an ANOVA table created (see Table 35.3).

The numerator and denominator degrees of freedom needed to find the appropriate critical value or calculate the p-value will vary depending on which factor is being tested. Consider factor A: the correct degrees of freedom needed to find the appropriate critical value are $(a - 1)$, $ab(n - 1)$ (that is, the degrees of freedom for the numerator of F_0 and the degrees of freedom for the denominator of F_0). As with the one-way ANOVA, the F-statistic measures the ratio between the effect

Table 35.3 Two-way ANOVA table.

Source of variability	df	SS	MS	F	p-value
Factor A	$a - 1$	SS_A	MS_A	$F_0 = \dfrac{MS_A}{MS_E}$	$P(F > F_0)$
Factor B	$b - 1$	SS_B	MS_B	$F_0 = \dfrac{MS_B}{MS_E}$	$P(F > F_0)$
AB interaction	$(a - 1)(b - 1)$	SS_{AB}	MS_{AB}	$F_0 = \dfrac{MS_{AB}}{MS_E}$	$P(F > F_0)$
Error	$ab(n - 1)$	SS_E	MS_E		
Total	$abn - 1$	SS_T			

and the experimental error. If the variation due to the effect is a sufficiently large multiple of the error, the effect is considered statistically significant. Using *p*-values, this would mean reject the null hypothesis if *p*-value < α.

EXAMPLE 35.23

Reconsider the conversion rate example with two factors of interest, catalyst and temperature. The resulting ANOVA table is shown in Table 35.4.

Using *p*-values, we would conclude that the amount of catalyst has a significant affect on the conversion rate (*p*-value = 0.009). But there is insufficient evidence to conclude that temperature has a significant affect on the conversion rate (*p*-value = 0.209). Finally, it appears that there is a significant interaction between catalyst and temperature (*p*-value = 0.016).

The interaction plot is shown in Figure 35.3. There is a clear indication that a significant interaction exists between temperature and catalyst. If the goal is to maximize conversion rate, it appears that 1.0 percent catalyst and a temperature of 30°C would be a good choice.

Table 35.4 ANOVA table for conversion rate example with two factors of interest.

Source of variability	df	SS	MS	F	p-value
Catalyst	2	72.104	36.0520	11.63	0.009
Temperature	1	6.149	6.1490	1.98	0.209
Catalyst × temperature interaction	2	55.635	27.8174	8.97	0.016
Error	6	18.598	3.0996		
Total	11	152.486			

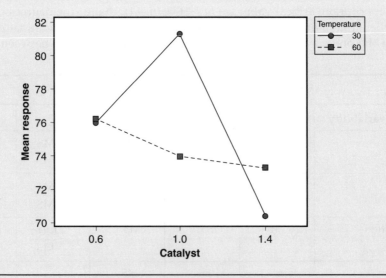

Figure 35.3 Interaction plot for temperature and catalyst.

The details of the general notation and formulas will not be presented here, but the reader is encouraged to see Devore (2007), Montgomery and Runger (2006), Montgomery, Runger, and Hubele (2006), or Vining and Kowalski (2006).

Number of Replicates

As a final note on the two-way analysis of variance, it is important to realize that if each combination of the factors consists of only one observation ($n = 1$), you can not estimate the two-factor interaction. When $n = 1$, there will not be enough degrees of freedom left over for error, the important quantity MS_E can not be estimated, and MS_E is needed to calculate the test statistic. If it is acceptable to only estimate the main factors (A and B), then the interaction is removed (not tested) and the SS_{AB} and degrees of freedom for the interaction are moved into error. If the interaction is possibly important, then it is recommended that at least two replicates for each combination of factors are collected.

6. CONTINGENCY TABLES

Define, construct, and use contingency tables to evaluate statistical significance. (Analyze)

Body of Knowledge VI.D.6

In this section, a test concerning count data will be presented. Suppose a sample of n items has been collected and each item can be classified into two different categories at the same time. Data that can be classified according to two different criteria (or factors) can be displayed in a *two-way contingency table*. In cases such as this, it may often be of interest to determine whether the two categories are statistically *independent* of one another. For example, consider the population of high school graduates. We may want to determine if the hourly wage for an entry-level job is independent of graduating from high school.

Description

Suppose there are r levels of factor 1 and c levels of factor 2. Each criterion can have several different levels. An $r \times c$ *contingency table* could be written as:

		Columns			
		1	2	...	c
	1	O_{11}	O_{12}	...	O_{1c}
Rows	2	O_{21}	O_{22}	...	O_{2c}
	:	:	:	...	:
	r	O_{r1}	O_{r2}	...	O_{rc}

where

The r rows represent the levels of the first factor.

The c columns represent the levels of the second factor.

O_{ij} represents the number of observations that fall into category i of factor 1 and category j of factor 2, where $i = 1, 2, \ldots, r$ and $j = 1, 2, \ldots c$.

EXAMPLE 35.24

A company operates two machines on three different shifts. The company wants to determine if machine breakdowns that occur during operation are *independent* of the shift on which the machine is used. The data are recorded in a 2×3 contingency table.

Machine	Shift		
	1	2	3
1	30	40	20
2	30	40	10

In this study:

- $r = 2$, the number of machines

- $c = 3$, the number of shifts

- O_{ij} represents the number of breakdowns that occur on the ith machine when used on the jth shift. For example $O_{12} = 40$. Therefore, 40 breakdowns have been recorded on machine 1 when it was used on the second shift.

We are interested in determining whether the two factors are independent of one another.

Hypothesis Test for Independence

The *expected frequencies* are calculated based on the assumption that the two factors of interest are independent of one another. Denote the expected frequencies as E_{ij} (for $i = 1, 2, \ldots, r$ and $j = 1, 2, \ldots, c$). Calculate the expected frequencies for each entry in the contingency table using $E_{ij} = na_ib_j$, where

- n = total number of observations; that is, $n = O_{11} + O_{12} + \ldots + O_{rc}$

- a_i is the *probability* that a randomly selected observation will fall into the ith category of factor 1 (the row factor) and is found using the following formula:

$$a_i = \frac{\sum_{j=1}^{c} O_{ij}}{n}$$

(Summing over the columns for the ith row)

- b_j is the *probability* that a randomly selected observation will fall into the jth category of factor 2 (the column factor) and is found using the following formula:

$$b_j = \frac{\sum_{i=1}^{r} O_{ij}}{n}$$

(Summing over the rows for the jth column)

If the two factors are independent, then we would expect the observed frequency and the expected frequency for each cell to be similar. This assumption can be tested using the test statistic

$$\chi_o^2 = \sum_{i=1}^{r} \sum_{j=1}^{c} \frac{(O_{ij} - E_{ij})^2}{E_{ij}},$$

which follows a chi-square distribution with $(r - 1)(c - 1)$ degrees of freedom. The test statistic can be compared to a critical value from the chi-square distribution with $(r - 1)(c - 1)$ degrees of freedom and a significance level α. The critical value is denoted $\chi_{\alpha,(r-1)(c-1)}^2$. If our test statistic is greater than the critical value, we say there is enough evidence to conclude that the two factors are not independent. The test is valid as long as the expected frequency of each cell is at least five.

EXAMPLE 35.25

A company operates two machines on three different shifts. The company wants to determine if machine is *independent* of shift. The data are recorded in a 2 × 3 contingency table.

Machine	Shift		
	1	2	3
1	30	40	20
2	30	40	10

Solution:

Calculate the expected frequency for each cell, where $n = 30 + 40 + 20 + 30 + 40 + 10 = 170$. The row probabilities (probabilities associated with the machines) are

Machine 1: $a_1 = (30 + 40 + 20)/170 = 0.53$

Machine 2: $a_2 = (30 + 40 + 10)/170 = 0.47$.

The column probabilities (probabilities associated with the shifts) are

Machine 1: $b_1 = (30 + 30)/170 = 0.353$

Continued

Continued

Machine 2: $b_2 = (40 + 40)/170 = 0.47$

Machine 3: $b_3 = (20 + 10)/170 = 0.177$.

The expected frequencies for all six cells are

$E_{11} = na_1b_1 = 170(0.53)(0.353) = 31.8$ $\qquad$ $E_{21} = na_2b_1 = 170(0.47)(0.353) = 28.2$

$E_{12} = na_1b_2 = 170(0.53)(0.47) = 42.35$ $\qquad$ $E_{22} = na_2b_2 = 170(0.47)(0.47) = 37.55$

$E_{13} = na_1b_3 = 170(0.53)(0.177) = 16$ $\qquad$ $E_{23} = na_2b_3 = 170(0.47)(0.177) = 14$.

The expected frequencies are summarized in the following table:

Machine	Shift		
	1	2	3
1	31.8	42.35	16
2	28.2	37.55	14

The test statistic is

$$\chi_0^2 = \sum\sum \frac{(O_{ij} - E_{ij})^2}{E_{ij}}$$

$$= \frac{(30-31.8)^2}{31.8} + \frac{(40-42.35)^2}{42.35} + \frac{(20-16)^2}{16} + \frac{(30-28.2)^2}{28.2} + \frac{(40-37.55)^2}{37.55} + \frac{(10-14)^2}{14}$$

$$= 2.65.$$

With $\alpha = 0.05$ and degrees of freedom $(r-1)(c-1) = 2$, the critical value is $\chi^2_{\alpha,(r-1)(c-1)} = \chi^2_{0.05,2} = 5.99$. Since $2.65 < 5.99$, the hypothesis of independence can not be rejected. Breakdown of a particular machine appears to be independent of which shift is using the machine.

Chapter 36

E. Relationships Between Variables

Thischapter covers three kinds of relationships between variables: linear regression, simple linear correlation, and time-series analysis.

1. LINEAR REGRESSION

> Calculate the regression equation for simple regressions and least squares estimates. Construct and interpret hypothesis tests for regression statistics. Use regression models for estimation and prediction, and analyze the uncertainty in the estimate. [Note: Non-linear models and parameters will not be tested.] (Analyze)
>
> **Body of Knowledge VI.E.1**

Linear regression models are important statistical tools developed to relate two or more variables of interest. This relationship often takes the form of a linear equation or linear model. In this section, simple linear regression is presented. Simple linear regression is the situation where there are exactly two variables:

- One independent variable (often denoted by x)

- One dependent variable (often denoted by y)

EXAMPLE 36.1

When data have been collected relating two variables, it is often useful to find an equation that models the relationship. Then the value of the dependent variable can be predicted for a given value of the independent variable. For example, suppose a chemical engineer is investigating the relationship between the operating temperature of a

---

Continued

Continued

process and product yield. In this case, it might be useful to control the operating temperature (independent variable) in order to control or predict yield (dependent variable). For this example, eight readings are taken, although in an actual application more data would be desirable.

Temperature, °C (x)	115	125	135	145	155	165	175	185
Yield, % (y)	62	64	69	77	78	81	82	88

The first step in the investigation is to plot the data, as in Figure 36.1, to determine if it seems reasonable to approximate it with a straight line.

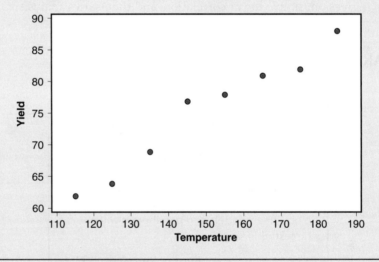

Figure 36.1   Scatter plot of temperature and yield.

Although a perfect straight line can not be drawn through these points in Example 36.1, the trend looks linear. The next step is to find an equation that best fits the data. Before creating regression lines for particular problems, some assumptions and basic definitions must be presented.

Notation and Definitions

Reconsider the scatter plot in Figure 36.1. The scatter plot indicates that the two variables may be *linearly related*. This is indicated by the fact that the observations fall approximately along a straight line. A *simple linear regression model* is one that models a linear relationship between the response of interest y and an independent (explanatory or regressor) variable x:

$$y = \beta_0 + \beta_1 x + \varepsilon$$

where β_0 and β_1 are called *regression coefficients* and ε represents a *random error term* (recall that the data will rarely lie exactly along a straight line, so when a straight line is fit to the data, there will be some *error*).

Definitions. Let $x_1, x_2, \ldots, x_n$ represent real values of the independent variable (also called an *explanatory* variable) and $y_1, y_2, \ldots, y_n$ represent real values of the dependent variable (also called the response). The sample consists of n pairs of data $(x_1, y_1), (x_2, y_2), \ldots, (x_n, y_n)$. The general model given above can be written in terms of the individual observations:

$$y_i = \beta_0 + \beta_1 x_i + \varepsilon_i, \text{ for } i = 1, 2, \ldots, n$$

For the simple linear regression model:

- The *coefficients* β_0 and β_1 are *parameters* that define the mathematical relationship between the independent and dependent variables. β_0 is the intercept and β_1 is the slope.

- The *intercept* is the value of y when $x = 0$. This is the height at which the regression line crosses the y-axis.

- The *slope* represents the change in the response for every one unit change in the independent variable x.

Given a series of values for an independent variable x and the corresponding dependent variable y, we can calculate point estimates for β_0 and β_1. The point estimates are denoted b_0 and b_1. Once the point estimates are obtained, a *fitted regression line* can be given by

$$\hat{y}_i = b_0 + b_1 x_i$$

where $\hat{y}_i$ is the *predicted value* of the response for a given value of the independent variable.

Estimating the Parameters β_0 and β_1

The statistics b_0 and b_1 need to be calculated in such a way that the resulting fitted line will provide predicted values that will be close to the actual value for each value of x. One method for calculating b_0 and b_1 is based on minimizing the *error* between the actual value of y and the predicted value of y for each pair of data, that is, $e_i = y_i - \hat{y}_i$. This is an appropriate method since a goal of simple linear regression is to make predictions after fitting a model between the independent variable and the response. A method frequently employed is the *least squares method*. The formulas for finding b_1 and b_0 are as follows:

$$b_1 = \frac{S_{xy}}{S_{xx}}$$

$$b_0 = \bar{y} - b_1 \bar{x}$$

where

$$S_{xy} = \frac{\sum_{i=1}^{n}(x_i - \bar{x})(y_i - \bar{y})}{n} = \sum_{i=1}^{n} x_i y_i - \frac{\left(\sum_{i=1}^{n} x_i\right)\left(\sum_{i=1}^{n} y_i\right)}{n}$$

$$S_{xx} = \frac{\sum_{i=1}^{n}(x_i - \bar{x})^2}{n} = \sum_{i=1}^{n} x_i^2 - \frac{\left(\sum_{i=1}^{n} x_i\right)^2}{n}.$$

These are often referred to as the *least squares estimates*. These formulas result in estimates that will give us a best-fitting line. By best fitting, we mean that the line with these estimates for the coefficients will result in the smallest *error sum of squares*.

Error Sum of Squares

Let e_i represent the error associated with the ith observation $e_i = y_i - \hat{y}_i$ for $i = 1, 2, \ldots, n$ (a realized value of the error is referred to as a *residual*). We want a fitted line that will minimize the n errors as much as possible. More specifically, we want to find the fitted regression line that will minimize the quantity

$$\sum_{i=1}^{n} e_i^2$$

(the error sum of squares). The formulas for b_0 and b_1 given previously result in a fitted line that will make this quantity as small as possible. In fact, there are no other estimates of β_0 and β_1 that will result in a smaller error sum of squares!

EXAMPLE 36.2

Reconsider the yield example given earlier. Temperature is the independent variable x and yield is the response y. We want to fit a regression line relating temperature to yield.

Temperature, °C (x)	115	125	135	145	155	165	175	185
Yield, % (y)	62	64	69	77	78	81	82	88

The necessary calculations for b_1 and b_0 are:

$n = 8$

$$\sum_{i=1}^{8} x_i = 115 + 125 + \ldots + 185 = 1200 \qquad \sum_{i=1}^{8} x_i^2 = 115^2 + 125^2 + \ldots + 185^2 = 184{,}200$$

Continued

Continued

$$\sum_{i=1}^{8} y_i = 62 + 64 + \ldots + 88 = 601 \qquad \sum_{i=1}^{n} x_i y_i = 115(62) + 125(64) + \ldots + 185(88) = 91,695$$

$$\bar{x} = 150 \qquad \bar{y} = 75.13$$

Calculate b_1 and b_0:

$$S_{xy} = \sum_{i=1}^{n} x_i y_i - \frac{\left(\sum_{i=1}^{n} x_i\right)\left(\sum_{i=1}^{n} y_i\right)}{n} = 91,695 - \frac{(1200)(601)}{8} = 1545$$

$$S_{xx} = \sum_{i=1}^{n} x_i^2 - \frac{\left(\sum_{i=1}^{n} x_i\right)^2}{n} = 184,200 - \frac{(1200)^2}{8} = 4200$$

$$b_1 = \frac{S_{xy}}{S_{xx}} = \frac{1545}{4200} = 0.37$$

$$b_0 = \bar{y} - b_1 \bar{x} = 75.13 - 0.37(150) = 19.63$$

The final fitted regression line is then

$$\hat{y} = 19.63 + 0.37x.$$

The fitted regression line is plotted along with the original data in Figure 36.2.

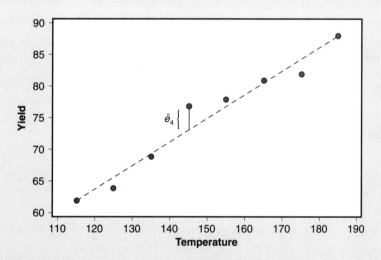

Figure 36.2   Scatter plot and fitted regression line for the yield data.

The fitted regression line represents the predicted value $\hat{y}$ for each value of x. Graphically, the residuals mentioned earlier are the vertical differences between the actual value of y and the predicted value of y for each value of x. See Figure 36.2. The vertical line represents the residual for $x_4 = 145$ ($\hat{e}_4 = y_4 - \hat{y}_4 = 77 - 73.28 = 3.72$).

Hypothesis Testing in Simple Linear Regression

Fitting a simple linear regression model involves a sample of data. As a result there will naturally be some error in the estimates of the coefficients, β_0 and β_1. Recall that when we are estimating a population mean with a sample mean there is some variability in this estimate. The same is true for the point estimates of the coefficients b_0 and b_1. The expected value and variance of the point estimate of β_0 are

$$E(b_0) = \beta_0$$

$$V(b_0) = \sigma^2 \left[\frac{1}{n} + \frac{\bar{x}^2}{S_{xx}} \right].$$

The expected value and variance for the point estimate of β_1 are

$$E(b_1) = \beta_1$$

$$V(b_1) = \frac{\sigma^2}{S_{xx}}$$

where S_{xx} was defined previously and σ^2 is the error variance (also referred to as the process variability). An estimate of σ^2 is

$$\hat{\sigma}^2 = \frac{SS_E}{n-2}$$

where $n - 2$ is the error degrees of freedom and SS_E represents the error sum of squares defined previously:

$$SS_E = \sum_{i=1}^{n} (y_i - \hat{y}_i)^2 = \sum_{i=1}^{n} e_i^2$$

The *standard errors* for b_0 and b_1 would be

$$\text{s.e.}(b_0) = \sqrt{V(b_0)} = \sqrt{\sigma^2 \left[\frac{1}{n} + \frac{\bar{x}^2}{S_{xx}} \right]}$$

$$\text{s.e.}(b_1) = \sqrt{V(b_1)} = \sqrt{\frac{\sigma^2}{S_{xx}}}.$$

An important test in simple linear regression is a test on the coefficient β_1. In particular, a test on the significance of regression would involve testing $\beta_1 = 0$. If $\beta_1 = 0$, then

$$y = \beta_0 + \beta_1 x + \varepsilon$$

$$= \beta_0 + \varepsilon,$$

which indicates no significant linear relationship between x and y.

Hypothesis Test on the Slope β_1. A *t*-test can be used to test for significance of regression. The hypotheses of interest are

$H_0: \beta_1 = 0$

$H_a: \beta_1 \neq 0.$

The test statistic would be

$$t_0 = \frac{b_1 - 0}{\sqrt{\dfrac{\hat{\sigma}^2}{S_{xx}}}}.$$

A large value of t_0 would lead to rejection of the null hypothesis. An appropriate critical value is $t_{\alpha/2,n-2}$, found from the *t* table in Appendix P. If a *p* value is calculated, the null hypothesis would be rejected if the *p* value is small (*p* value $< \alpha$) and would indicate a significant linear relationship between x and y.

Hypothesis Test on the Intercept β_0. A *t*-test can also be conducted on the intercept β_0. The hypotheses of interest are

$H_0: \beta_0 = 0$

$H_a: \beta_0 \neq 0.$

The test statistic would be

$$t_0 = \frac{b_0 - 0}{\sqrt{\hat{\sigma}^2 \left[\dfrac{1}{n} + \dfrac{\bar{x}^2}{S_{xx}} \right]}}.$$

A large value of t_0 would lead to rejection of the null hypothesis. An appropriate critical value is $t_{\alpha/2,n-2}$ found from the *t* table in Appendix P. If a *p* value is calculated, the null hypothesis would be rejected if the *p* value is small (*p* value $< \alpha$).

The calculations do not need to be done by hand. A statistical software package can be used to carry out all the necessary calculations.

EXAMPLE 36.3

Reconsider the yield and temperature example given earlier. The hypotheses of interest are

$$H_0: \beta_1 = 0 \text{ versus } H_a: \beta_1 \neq 0$$

and

$$H_0: \beta_0 = 0 \text{ versus } H_a: \beta_0 \neq 0.$$

The output from a particular statistical package for this problem is:

```
Predictor     Coef   SE Coef      T       P
Constant    19.946     4.735    4.21   0.006
x          0.36786   0.03120   11.79   0.000
```

Continued

Continued

The output can be interpreted as follows:

- The row "Constant" is the hypothesis test on the intercept: H_0: $\beta_0 = 0$ versus H_a: $\beta_0 \neq 0$.

- The row "x" is the hypothesis test on the slope: H_0: $\beta_1 = 0$ versus H_a: $\beta_1 \neq 0$.

- The column labeled "Coef" contains the point estimates for each parameter, that is, $b_0 = 19.946$ and $b_1 = 0.036786$.

- The column labeled "SE Coef" provides the standard error of each estimate, that is, s.e.$(b_0) = 4.735$ and s.e.$(b_1) = 0.0312$.

- The column labeled "T" represents the test statistic for the intercept and slope; $t_0 = 4.21$ (test on the intercept) and $t_0 = 11.79$ (test on the slope).

- The last column, labeled "P," contains the p value for each parameter.

The p value for testing $\beta_1 = 0$ is 0.000. Since this value is small, we can reject the hypothesis that $\beta_1 = 0$ and conclude that the slope is not zero. That is, there appears to be a statistically significant linear relationship between temperature and yield.

The test on the intercept $\beta_0 = 0$ also indicates that the intercept is significant. If we fail to reject the null hypothesis $\beta_0 = 0$, it is often left to the practitioner to determine if it makes practical sense to leave the intercept in the model.

100(1 – α)% Confidence Intervals on the Slope and Intercept. The $100(1 - \alpha)\%$ two-sided confidence interval on the intercept is given by

$$b_0 - t_{\alpha/2,n-2}\text{s.e.}(b_0) \leq \beta_0 \leq b_0 + t_{\alpha/2,n-2}\text{s.e.}(b_0).$$

The $100(1 - \alpha)\%$ two-sided confidence interval on the slope is given by

$$b_1 - t_{\alpha/2,n-2}\text{s.e.}(b_1) \leq \beta_1 \leq b_1 + t_{\alpha/2,n-2}\text{s.e.}(b_1).$$

EXAMPLE 36.4

For the yield and temperature example, we wish to construct 95 percent confidence intervals on the slope and intercept. In this case, the value $t_{\alpha/2,n-2} = t_{0.025,6} = 2.447$ and the resulting confidence intervals are

$$b_0 - t_{\alpha/2,n-2}\text{s.e.}(b_0) \leq \beta_0 \leq b_0 + t_{\alpha/2,n-2}\text{s.e.}(b_0)$$

$$19.96 - 2.447(4.735) \leq \beta_0 \leq 19.96 + 2.447(4.735)$$

$$8.37 \leq \beta_0 \leq 31.55$$

and

$$b_1 - t_{\alpha/2,n-2}\text{s.e.}(b_1) \leq \beta_0 \leq b_1 + t_{\alpha/2,n-2}\text{s.e.}(b_1)$$

$$0.37 - 2.447(0.0312) \leq \beta_1 \leq 0.37 - 2.447(0.0312)$$

$$0.29 \leq \beta_1 \leq 0.47.$$

Continued

The confidence intervals do not contain zero, so we have evidence to indicate that the slope and intercept are both nonzero. Again, since the 95 percent confidence interval on β_1 does not contain zero, we have evidence to indicate that there is a significant linear relationship between temperature and yield.

The Analysis of Variance Approach

The analysis of variance (ANOVA) can also be used to test for significance of regression. The null and alternative hypotheses of interest are H_0: $\beta_1 = 0$ and H_a: $\beta_1 \neq 0$. Note that only the test on the slope will determine significance of regression. The total sum of squares (SS_T) is a measure of the total variability. SS_T can be partitioned into two sources of variability: the regression line we have fit and error. This is similar to the total sum of squares discussed in Chapter 35. The *error sum of squares* (also referred to as the residual sum of squares) defined in this chapter is a measure of the unexplained variability in the responses y. The variability due to the regression model that we have fit is the *regression sum of squares* (SS_R). The partition is

$$SS_T = SS_R + SS_E$$

where

$$SS_T = S_{yy} = \frac{\sum_{i=1}^{n}(y_i - \bar{y})}{n} = \sum_{i=1}^{n} y_i^2 - \frac{\left(\sum_{i=1}^{n} y_i\right)^2}{n}$$

$$SS_R = \sum_{i=1}^{n}(\hat{y}_i - \bar{y})^2$$

and

$$SS_E = \sum_{i=1}^{n}(y_i - \hat{y}_i)^2 = \sum_{i=1}^{n} e_i^2.$$

It is desirable to have the regression sum of squares be large in comparison to the error sum of squares. A large value of SS_R would indicate that most of the variability in the response can be explained by the regression model that has been fit. As in Chapter 35, we have to take into account the sample size and adjust the sum of squares using the appropriate degrees of freedom. An ANOVA table can be constructed (see Table 36.1).

Table 36.1   ANOVA table for testing significance of regression.

Source	df	SS	MS	F	p value
Regression	1	SS_R	$MS_R = SS_R/1$	$F_0 = MS_R/MS_E$	$P(F > F_0)$
Error	$n-2$	SS_E	$MS_E = SS_E/(n-2)$		
Total	$n-1$	SS_T			

If critical values are used, we would reject the null hypothesis if $F_0 > F_{\alpha,1,n-2}$. The critical value is found from the F table in Appendix H.

EXAMPLE 36.5

The ANOVA table for the yield and temperature example is given below. The null and alternative hypotheses are

$H_0: \beta_1 = 0$

$H_a: \beta_1 \neq 0$.

Source	df	SS	MS	F	p-value
Regression	1	568.34	568.34	138.98	0.000
Error	6	24.54	4.09		
Total	7	592.87			

Since the *p* value is zero, we would reject the null hypothesis and conclude again that there is a statistically significant linear relationship between yield and temperature. If critical values are used, the critical value is $F_{0.05, 1, 6} = 5.99$ (assuming a 0.05 level of significance). Since 138.98 > 5.99, we again reject the null hypothesis.

The analysis of variance is useful not only for testing the significance of regression, but also provides an estimate of $\hat{\sigma}^2$. Specifically, $\hat{\sigma}^2 = MS_E$. In this problem $\hat{\sigma}^2 = MS_E = 4.09$.

Assumptions in Regression Analysis

There are a number of assumptions in linear regression. For the most part, the least squares approach, and the results or conclusions drawn from the data, are fairly *robust* to these assumptions, that is, it takes a substantial deviation from the norm to affect the results. The assumptions for the least squares approach to regression analysis are:

1. The errors e_i are independent.

2. The errors e_i are normally distributed with mean zero.

3. The errors e_i have constant variance σ^2.

The assumptions can be checked using residual analysis. Residuals plotted against the fitted values $\hat{y}$ or against the independent variable x can provide some information about the validity of the constant variance assumption. A normal probability plot of residuals can be used to assess the assumption of normality. The independence assumption can be verified by examining a plot of the residuals against the time sequence—if the time sequence is known. With the exception of the normal probability plot of the residuals, all residual plots should exhibit no obvious patterns in the residuals. If the residuals fall along a straight line in the normal probability plot, then the normality assumption is assumed to be valid. Caution should be used when interpreting residual plots for small sets of data. For small sample sizes, patterns on residual plots can often occur by chance. Keep in mind that the least squares method is fairly robust to slight departures from these assumptions.

Prediction of Observations

The fitted regression model is often used to make predictions of new or future observations for the response. Let x_0 be a value of the independent variable. The point estimator of the new value, y_0, is given by

$$\hat{y}_0 = b_0 + b_1 x_0.$$

For example, suppose we wish to predict the yield for a temperature of 150 degrees Celsius. The predicted value of the yield would be:

$$\hat{y}_0 = 19.9 + 0.37x_0$$
$$= 19.9 + 0.37(150)$$
$$= 75.4\%.$$

Because the value is a single point estimate calculated from sample data, there is variability or error in this prediction. It is sometimes of interest to construct an interval estimate for a future observation. A prediction interval provides a measure of the estimate and error of prediction. For complete details on prediction intervals see Devore (2007), Montgomery and Runger (2006), Montgomery, Runger, and Hubele (2006), Neter, Kutner, Nachtsheim, and Wasserman (1996), or Vining and Kowalski (2006).

2. SIMPLE LINEAR CORRELATION

Calculate the correlation coefficient and its confidence interval, and construct and interpret a hypothesis test for correlation statistics. [Note: Serial correlation will not be tested.] (Analyze)

Body of Knowledge VI.E.2

Correlation measures the strength of the *linear* relationship between two variables. A linear relationship exists between two variables if as one variable increases the other increases or decreases. Graphically, this will be seen if the values of the two variables plot along a straight line. Recall the discussion on the bivariate normal distribution given in Chapter 33. One of the parameters that defined the bivariate normal pdf was the *population correlation coefficient* ρ. The population correlation coefficient is often unknown and can be estimated using sample data. Suppose x and y are jointly normally distributed random variables. The sample correlation coefficient, denoted r, can be used as the estimate of the population correlation coefficient ρ. The sample correlation coefficient is

$$r = \frac{S_{xy}}{\sqrt{S_{xx}}\sqrt{S_{yy}}}$$

where

$$S_{xy} = \frac{\sum_{i=1}^{n}(x_i - \bar{x})(y_i - \bar{y})}{n} = \sum_{i=1}^{n}x_i y_i - \frac{\left(\sum_{i=1}^{n}x_i\right)\left(\sum_{i=1}^{n}y_i\right)}{n}$$

$$S_{xx} = \frac{\sum_{i=1}^{n}(x_i - \bar{x})^2}{n} = \sum_{i=1}^{n}x_i^2 - \frac{\left(\sum_{i=1}^{n}x_i\right)^2}{n}$$

$$S_{yy} = \frac{\sum_{i=1}^{n}(y_i - \bar{y})^2}{n} = \sum_{i=1}^{n}y_i^2 - \frac{\left(\sum_{i=1}^{n}y_i\right)^2}{n}.$$

The sample correlation coefficient r measures the strength of the *linear relationship* and has the following properties:

- $-1 \leq r \leq 1$; the closer the value is to -1 or 1, the stronger the linear relationship.
  - If r is negative, that indicates that as one variable is increasing, the other is decreasing.
  - If r is positive, that indicates that both variables are increasing or both variables are decreasing.
- If $r = 0$, then there is no linear relationship between the two variables.
- r has no units attached to it, such as pounds, inches, feet, and so on.

Figure 36.3 illustrates two variables x and y. Figure 36.3a displays two random variables that are *positively correlated*. In this case, the value of r is positive and near 1. Figure 36.3b displays two random variables that are *negatively correlated*. In this case the value of r is negative and near -1. Figure 36.3c displays two variables that are not linearly related at all. In this situation, there does appear to be some relationship between x and y, but it is not linear. Therefore, the correlation coefficient r would be zero.

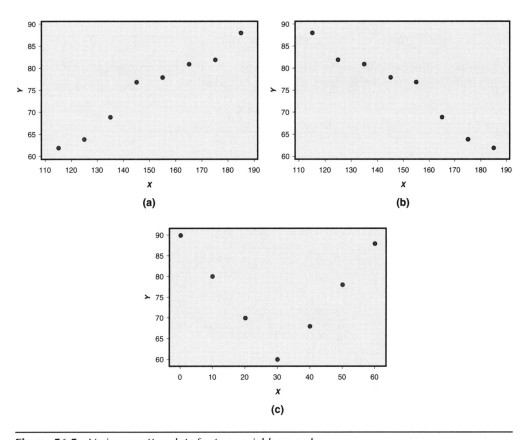

Figure 36.3   Various scatter plots for two variables x and y.

There is a direct relationship between the correlation coefficient and the slope of a model. The sign on the correlation coefficient is the same as the sign on the slope. Also,

$$r = b_1 \left(\frac{S_{xx}}{SS_T} \right)^2.$$

There is some subjectiveness in the interpretation of the correlation coefficient estimate. If $-0.6 \leq r \leq 0.6$ for example, there is not always agreement as to whether or not the association between the two variables is significantly correlated. A t-test on the population correlation coefficient can be conducted to determine the statistical significance of the correlation. For complete details on testing the significance of the population correlation coefficient see Devore (2007), Montgomery and Runger (2006), Montgomery, Runger, and Hubele (2006), or Neter, Kutner, Nachtsheim, and Wasserman (1996).

EXAMPLE 36.6

Consider the temperature and yield example again. For this problem the sums of squares needed to determine the sample correlation coefficient are

$$S_{xy} = \sum_{i=1}^{n} x_i y_i - \frac{\left(\sum_{i=1}^{n} x_i\right)\left(\sum_{i=1}^{n} y_i\right)}{n} = 91,695$$

$$S_{xx} = \sum_{i=1}^{n} x_i^2 - \frac{\left(\sum_{i=1}^{n} x_i\right)^2}{n} = 184,200$$

$$S_{yy} = \sum_{i=1}^{n} y_i^2 - \frac{\left(\sum_{i=1}^{n} y_i\right)^2}{n} = 45,743$$

resulting in

$$r = \frac{S_{xy}}{\sqrt{S_{xx}}\sqrt{S_{yy}}} = \frac{91,695}{\sqrt{184,200}\sqrt{45,743}} = 0.998.$$

The sample correlation coefficient of 0.998 indicates that there is a very strong positive linear relationship between temperature and yield.

Coefficient of Determination

The *coefficient of determination* R^2 gives a measure of how adequate the current regression model is for a particular set of data. It is the proportion of the total variability in the response that can be explained by the regression line. The coefficient of determination is simply the square of the correlation coefficient r. (We often use the notation R^2 for this value even though correlation coefficient is denoted by lower case r.) Since $-1 \le r \le 1$ then $0 \le R^2 \le 1$. The coefficient of determination can be calculated by

$$R^2 = \frac{SS_R}{SS_T} = 1 - \frac{SS_E}{SS_T}.$$

EXAMPLE 36.7

For the yield and temperature problem, the coefficient of determination is

$$R^2 = \frac{SS_R}{SS_T} = \frac{568.34}{592.87} = 0.959.$$

We would conclude that approximately 95.9 percent of the total variability in the response (yield) can be explained by the regression model involving temperature.

Multiple Linear Regression

Multiple least-squares linear regression is an extension of simple linear regression. The response variable Y is a function of several independent variables $x_1, x_2, \ldots, x_k$. The equation for the multiple linear regression is

$$y = \beta_0 + \beta_1 x_1 + \beta_2 x_2 + \ldots + \beta_k x_k + \varepsilon$$

where

β_0 represents the intercept.

$\beta_1, \beta_2, \ldots, \beta_k$ are the coefficients of the independent variables, $x_1, x_2, \ldots, x_k$.

ε_i represents the inherent variability in the process.

A fitted regression model would be given as

$$\hat{y} = b_0 + b_1 x_1 + b_2 x_2$$

where b_0 is an estimate for β_0, b_1 is an estimate for β_1, and b_2 is an estimate for β_2.

EXAMPLE 36.8

An article in the *Journal of Agricultural Engineering Research* (2001, p. 275) describes the modeling of damage susceptibility of peaches to several independent variables. Two independent variables that are believed to impact peach damage are the height at which the peach is dropped (mm) and peach density (g/cm³). Data that are typical of this type of experiment are as follows:

y	x_1	x_2
7.22	371.05	0.99
4.24	315.02	1.11
8.50	550.10	0.97
9.32	400.00	1.02
5.87	336.00	0.96
7.12	361.10	0.95
8.04	499.24	1.01
6.62	403.58	1.00
10.06	482.33	1.04
8.96	451.65	0.98

The multiple regression line for this set of data is (found using a statistical software package)

$$\hat{y} = 5.4 + 0.016 x_1 - 4.48 x_2$$

where $b_0 = 5.4$, $b_1 = 0.016$, and $b_2 = -4.48$.

T-tests were conducted on the parameters of interest β_0, β_1, and β_2, and it was determined that peach density (x_2) is insignificant (p value > 0.10). Regression analysis was

Continued

Continued

carried out again but this time relating only height dropped (x_1) and damage (y). (Note that the intercept is also found insignificant, but the researchers determined that it is appropriate to leave it in.) The final fitted model is

$$\hat{y} = 0.66 + 0.016x_1.$$

The fitted model may be useful for predicting damage, but further analysis is necessary. The coefficient of determination was calculated for the final fitted model and found to be 52.9 percent. That is, approximately 53 percent of the total variability in damage can be explained by the fitted regression line involving only drop height. Although peach density is not a significant variable for damage, there may be other independent variables that should be investigated. Residual analysis should also be done for this problem.

For complete details on multiple regression, see Devore (2007), Montgomery and Runger (2007), Montgomery, Runger, and Hubele (2006), Neter, Kutner, Nachtsheim, and Wasserman (1996), or Vining and Kowalski (2006).

Causal Relationship

As a final note on regression analysis, finding a fitted regression line statistically significant does not imply a *causal* relationship between the independent and dependent variables. Two variables could be linearly related and have a very strong association, but this does not infer that one variable *caused* the change in the other variable. Causation could only be concluded if a designed experiment were conducted for a particular problem.

3. TIME-SERIES ANALYSIS

> Define, describe, and use time-series analysis including moving average, and interpret time-series graphs to identify trends and seasonal or cyclical variation. (Analyze)
>
> **Body of Knowledge VI.E.3**

Time series analysis in mathematical statistics involves mathematical techniques for determining cycles and trends in data. The two specific tools discussed in this section are:

- Moving average smoothing
- Trend analysis

Moving average smoothing and *trend analysis* are two methods of analyzing data. There are other methods, but those are beyond the scope of this discussion.

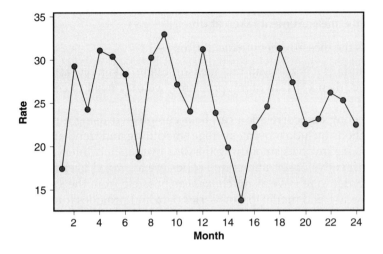

Figure 36.4 Run chart for NMCM rate.

Run Charts

Run charts display a plot of data obtained on sequential samples taken from a process. This plot has an *x*-axis of sequence or time. The *y*-axis is that of the measurement taken on the sample. For example, the rate of not mission-capable equipment or systems due to maintenance issues (NMCM) is important to monitor. Figure 36.4 displays the monthly NMCM rates over a two-year period.

Note that in this case we can see that there might be some sort of cycle present in the NMCM rate. The process may not have a random pattern of NMCM rates around the average rate. We have to know the scale or time period of the *x*-axis very well in order to correctly interpret the run chart.

The *control chart* discussed in Chapter 37 is a special type of the run chart. The control chart has a center or central line (the mean) drawn in to facilitate our eyes seeing the data move back and forth across this line. When the measurement for one sample tends to be dependent on the measurement for the previous sample, these data are called *autocorrelated*. As will be shown in Chapter 37, one assumption necessary for control charts to be valid is that the observations are independently distributed. When *autocorrelation* is present in the data, standard control charts do not work well in monitoring the process. Suppose there are *n* measurements taken in some time sequence. A measure of *sample autocorrelation* is given by

$$r_k = \frac{\sum_{t=1}^{n-k}(x_t - \overline{x})(x_{t-k} - \overline{x})}{\sum_{t=1}(x_t - \overline{x})^2}, \text{ for } k = 1, 2, \ldots, K$$

where

k represents the number of time periods between measurements

$\overline{x}$ is the average of all measurements

x_t is the measurement taken at time t

x_{t-k} is the measurement taken at time $t - k$.

For example, if it is believed that measurements taken one after another are auto-correlated, then $k = 1$. In many problems, we may need to compute r_k for several values of k.

Detecting autocorrelation can be accomplished using a number of methods. Two methods include moving average smoothing and trend analysis. *Moving average smoothing* involves smoothing the data over a short interval of time. In particular, consecutive observations in a series are averaged over a chosen window of time in order to remove as much *noise* as possible from the system. *Trend analysis* fits a general trend model to time series data and provides forecasts. Some models commonly fit include the linear, quadratic, exponential, and S-curve. Both methods work well when no seasonal component is present in the data.

For complete details of time-series analysis see Montgomery, Jennings, and Kulahci (2008). For discussion of autocorrelation with respect to statistical process control see Montgomery (2009b).

Chapter 37

F. Statistical Process Control (SPC)

This chapter covers eight aspects of statistical process control: objectives and benefits, common and special causes, selection of variable, rational sub-grouping, control charts, control chart analysis, pre-control charts, and short-run SPC.

1. OBJECTIVES AND BENEFITS

> Identify and explain objectives and benefits of SPC such as assessing process performance. (Understand)
>
> **Body of Knowledge VI.F.1**

Statistical process control (SPC) is quantitative problem solving, consisting of diagnostic techniques to assist in locating problem sources and prescriptive techniques to help solve problems. Many of these techniques are based on statistical principles.

A process is any repeatable sequence of events or operations leading to either a tangible or intangible outcome. The use of SPC will show that a process is 1) in statistical control, that is, the process variation appears to be random or 2) out of statistical control, that is, the process exhibits nonrandom variation. SPC also makes it possible to determine whether or not the process is improving.

SPC is a tool for communicating information to engineering, product operations, and quality control personnel. The principal elements of a successful SPC framework are analysis—to understand the process, methods—to measure the process, and leadership—to change the process.

A number of benefits can be attributed to SPC. Continuous improvement and maintenance of quality and productivity can be achieved, and through the SPC process complexity can be reduced. By identifying and reducing process complexity, errors will be reduced and productivity improved through the substitution of sampling for 100 percent inspection. SPC also provides a common internal language for management, supervision, quality assurance/control, and product operations to discuss problems, solutions, decisions, and actions.

2. COMMON AND SPECIAL CAUSES

> Describe, identify, and distinguish between these types of causes. (Analyze)
>
> **Body of Knowledge VI.F.2**

Every process has variation. The sources of process variation can be divided into two categories: special and common. *Common cause variability* is that which is inherent in the process and generally is not controllable by process operators. Examples of common causes include variation in raw materials and variation in ambient temperature and humidity. In the case of service processes, common causes typically include such things as variation in input data, variations in customer load, and variation in computer operations. Some authors refer to common cause variation as *natural variation*.

Special causes of variation include unusual events that when detected can usually be removed or adjusted. Examples include tool wear, gross changes in raw materials, and broken equipment. Special causes are sometimes called *assignable* causes.

A principal problem in process management is the separation of special and common causes. If the process operator tries to adjust a process in response to common cause variation, the result is usually more variation rather than less. This is sometimes called *overadjustment* or *overcontrol*. If a process operator fails to respond to the presence of a special cause of variation, this cause is likely to produce additional process variation. This is referred to as *underadjustment* or *undercontrol*.

The principal purpose of control charts is to help the process operator recognize the presence of special causes so that appropriate action can be taken. Control charts are discussed in detail in the sections that follow.

3. SELECTION OF VARIABLE

> Identify and select characteristics for monitoring by control chart. (Analyze)
>
> **Body of Knowledge VI.F.3**

When a control chart is to be used, a variable (or variables) must be selected for monitoring. In a new process, there may be many different *quality characteristics* to monitor. However, as the process becomes more stable, the number of monitored characteristics will most likely be reduced.

Sometimes the variable of interest is the most critical dimension of the product. Contractual requirements with a customer sometimes specify the variable(s) to be monitored via a control chart. If the root cause of the assignable variation is known, an input variable, such as voltage or air pressure, may be monitored. It is possible to monitor several variables on separate control charts. But it is also useful to monitor two or more characteristics using a single control chart (multivariate control chart). Ultimately, the selection of the quality characteristic to be charted depends on experience and judgment.

4. RATIONAL SUBGROUPING

Define and apply the principles of rational subgrouping. (Apply)

Body of Knowledge VI.F.4

The selection of samples is important in the construction of control charts. The method used to select samples for a control chart must be logical or rational. In general, *rational subgrouping* involves selecting samples such that if assignable causes of variation are present in the system, there should be a greater probability of variation between successive samples while the variation within the sample is kept small.

Samples frequently consist of parts that are produced successively or consecutively by the same process, to minimize the within-sample variation. The next sample is chosen later so that any process shifts that have occurred will be displayed on the chart as between-sample variation. Choosing the rational subgroup requires care to make sure the same process is producing each item.

There are instances where it is more appropriate to select the sample *over the entire interval* since the last sample was chosen. This approach to rational subgrouping is effective in detecting shifts that may occur between samples taken consecutively. The sample represents all units produced since the last sample was taken. In general, the subgroup is a random sample of units selected over the entire interval since the last subgroup was selected.

Caution should be used when interpreting control charts where the subgroups are units randomly selected over an interval. It is possible to make even an out-of-control process appear to be in control simply by increasing the interval between selected units.

5. CONTROL CHARTS

> Identify, select, construct, and use various control charts, including $\bar{X}-R$, $\bar{X}$ range (ImR or XmR), moving average and moving range (MAMR), p, np, c, u, and CUSUM charts. (Analyze)
>
> **Body of Knowledge VI.F.5**

Control charts can be used for monitoring many quality characteristics:

- Monitoring individual observations or subgroups for continuous data.

- Control charts for continuous data in subgroups are used in pairs to monitor for changes or trends in location and dispersion.

- Control charts for discrete data can be used to detect increases in the number of nonconforming units, nonconformities per unit, or proportions.

Control charts are the most common tool for monitoring a quality characteristic of interest. Dr. Walter A. Shewhart introduced the concept of control charts in the 1920s. Because of his work, several control charts monitoring a single quality characteristic of interest are referred to as Shewhart control charts.

In this section, control charts for variables data and attributes data will be presented. The control charts to be discussed are:

- $\bar{x}$ and R control charts

- $\bar{x}$ and s control charts

- Individuals control charts

- Fraction nonconforming control charts

- Control charts for nonconformities

For each of these control charts, an assumption that must be satisfied is that the data being monitored follow a normal distribution. The Shewhart control charts are sensitive to this assumption. If the normality assumption is violated, the overall performance of these charts can be very poor and result in incorrect signals.

Control Limits

Control limits are calculated based on data from the process. Formulas for control limits and examples of each are given in this section. The formulas are repeated in Appendix B. Several constants are needed in the formulas. These appear as subscripted letters such as A_2. The values of these constants are given in Appendix C. When calculating control limits it is prudent to collect as much data as practical.

Table 37.1 General notation for subgroup data.

Subgroup, i	Measurements	$\bar{x}_i$	R_i
1	$x_{11}, x_{21}, \ldots, x_{n1}$	$\bar{x}_1$	R_1
2	$x_{12}, x_{22}, \ldots, x_{n2}$	$\bar{x}_2$	R_2
3	$x_{13}, x_{23}, \ldots, x_{n3}$	$\bar{x}_3$	R_3
$\vdots$	$\vdots$	$\vdots$	$\vdots$
m	$x_{1m}, x_{2m}, \ldots, x_{nm}$	$\bar{x}_m$	R_m
		$\bar{\bar{x}} = \dfrac{\sum_{i=1}^{m} \bar{x}_i}{m}$	$\bar{R} = \dfrac{\sum_{i=1}^{m} R_i}{m}$

Many authorities specify at least 25 samples. The examples in the following sections use fewer samples for simplicity. It is desirable for the sample size to be held constant if possible.

Variables Control Charts

The most commonly used control charts for variables (continuous) subgroup data are the $\bar{x}$ and R charts and the $\bar{x}$ and s charts. The $\bar{x}$ chart monitors the mean of the process while the R chart and s chart monitor the process variability. The $\bar{x}$ chart is used for monitoring of the process mean in conjunction with either the R chart or s chart and process variability.

Suppose there are m subgroups each of size n chosen at random from a particular process (see Table 37.1). The sample mean and range for each subgroup are also given in Table 37.1.

The statistic $\bar{\bar{x}}$ is the grand average and is the best estimate of the true process mean μ. $\bar{R}$ is the average range and will be used to estimate the process variability and construct control charts. The upper control limit (UCL), centerline (CL), and lower control limit (LCL) for the $\bar{x}$ control chart are

$$UCL = \bar{\bar{x}} + A_2 \bar{R}$$

$$CL = \bar{\bar{x}}$$

$$LCL = \bar{\bar{x}} - A_2 \bar{R}.$$

The upper control limit (UCL), centerline (CL), and lower control limit (LCL) for the R control chart are

$$UCL = D_4 \bar{R}$$

$$CL = \bar{R}$$

$$LCL = D_3 \bar{R}.$$

A_2, D_3, and D_4 are constants that depend on the sample size n. They can be found in Appendix C. Derivations of these constants can be found in Montgomery (2009b).

EXAMPLE 37.1

The turnaround time for CBC analysis from the laboratory to the emergency room at a local hospital is an important quality characteristic to be monitored. Turnaround times were recorded over 20 days in a one-month period. Four specimens were randomly selected per day and the turnaround times (in minutes) recorded. The times as well as the subgroup averages and ranges are given in Table 37.2. The grand average and average range are given in the last row of Table 37.2.

From Appendix C with $n = 4$, we find $A_2 = 0.729$, $D_3 = 0$, and $D_4 = 2.282$. The control limits for the $\bar{x}$ control chart are

$$UCL = \bar{\bar{x}} + A_2\bar{R} = 71.39 + 0.729(27.05) = 91.11$$

$$CL = \bar{\bar{x}} = 71.39$$

$$LCL = \bar{\bar{x}} - A_2\bar{R} = 71.39 - 0.729(27.05) = 51.67.$$

Table 37.2 Turnaround times for CBC analysis.

Day	x_1	x_2	x_3	x_4	$\bar{x}_i$	R_i
1	83	49	65	78	68.75	34
2	81	77	75	76	77.25	6
3	71	67	44	58	60.00	27
4	92	53	93	74	78.00	40
5	75	58	90	51	68.50	39
6	70	79	87	49	71.25	38
7	74	50	68	45	59.25	29
8	80	66	75	64	71.25	16
9	80	63	72	81	74.00	18
10	90	77	92	64	80.75	28
11	75	51	89	74	72.25	38
12	64	65	88	59	69.00	29
13	97	57	88	76	79.50	40
14	84	62	55	68	67.25	29
15	76	63	70	66	68.75	13
16	62	68	66	55	62.75	13
17	73	77	91	83	81.00	18
18	65	65	84	46	65.00	38
19	73	64	84	71	73.00	20
20	75	88	65	93	80.25	28
					$\bar{\bar{x}} = 71.39$	$\bar{R} = 27.05$

Continued

Continued

The control limits for the R control chart are

$$UCL = D_4\bar{R} = 2.282(27.05) = 61.73$$

$$CL = \bar{R} = 27.05$$

$$LCL = D_3\bar{R} = 0(27.05) = 0.$$

The $\bar{x}$ and R control charts for turnaround times are displayed in Figure 37.1.

There are no points that plot outside the control limits on either chart. There also do not appear to be any obvious patterns on the $\bar{x}$ control chart. The process appears to be in control. More discussion of interpretation of control charts is provided in Section 6 of this chapter.

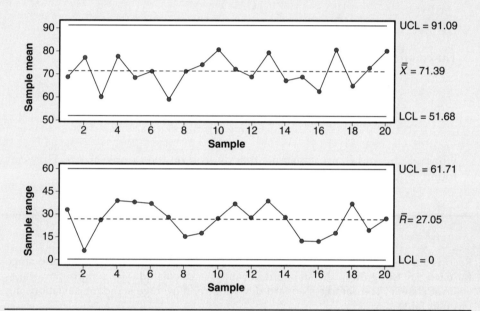

Figure 37.1 $\bar{x}$ and R control charts for turnaround times.

$\bar{x}$ and s Charts. Whenever possible, the sample standard deviation should be used instead of the range in estimating the process variability. When the sample size n is large, say $n > 10$, the sample standard deviation is a better estimate of the true process standard deviation than is the range. As n increases, the range R loses statistical efficiency and becomes less precise. The sample standard deviation is also a better estimator for the process standard deviation for nonconstant sample sizes.

The $\bar{x}$ and s control chart's development is similar to development of the $\bar{x}$ and R control chart. In this case, the subgroup standard deviation is calculated instead of the range. Suppose $x_{i1}, x_{i2}, \ldots, x_{in}$ represent a sample of size n for any subgroup i. The formula for the sample standard deviation of subgroup i is

$$s_i = \sqrt{\frac{\sum_{j=1}^{n}(x_{ij} - \bar{x})^2}{n-1}}.$$

The average standard deviation for all m subgroups is

$$\bar{s} = \frac{\sum_{i=1}^{m} s_i}{m}.$$

The control limits and centerline for the $\bar{x}$ control chart are then

$$UCL = \bar{\bar{x}} + A_3\bar{s}$$

$$CL = \bar{\bar{x}}$$

$$LCL = \bar{\bar{x}} - A_3\bar{s}.$$

The control limits and centerline for the s chart are

$$UCL = B_4\bar{s}$$

$$CL = \bar{s}$$

$$LCL = B_3\bar{s}$$

where A_3, B_3, and B_4 are constants that depend on the sample size n. They can be found in Appendix C.

EXAMPLE 37.2

Reconsider the turnaround time data from the previous example. Instead of the range for each day (subgroup), the standard deviation is calculated. The subgroup averages will not change. The sample standard deviations and average standard deviations are given in Table 37.3.

The control limits and centerline for the $\bar{x}$ control chart are

$$UCL = \bar{\bar{x}} + A_3\bar{s} = 71.39 + 1.628(11.97) = 90.88$$

$$CL = \bar{\bar{x}} = 71.39$$

$$LCL = \bar{\bar{x}} - A_3\bar{s} = 71.39 - 1.628(11.97) = 51.90.$$

The control limits and centerline for the s chart are

$$UCL = B_4\bar{s} = 2.266(11.97) = 27.12$$

$$CL = \bar{s} = 11.97$$

$$LCL = B_3\bar{s} = 0(11.97) = 0$$

where $A_3 = 1.628$, $B_3 = 0$, and $B_4 = 2.266$, from Appendix C with $n = 4$. The $\bar{x}$ and s control charts are displayed in Figure 37.2.

Continued

Continued

Table 37.3   Turnaround times for CBC analysis.

Day	x_1	x_2	x_3	x_4	$\bar{x}_i$	s_i
1	83	49	65	78	68.75	15.20
2	81	77	75	76	77.25	2.63
3	71	67	44	58	60.00	11.97
4	92	53	93	74	78.00	18.81
5	75	58	90	51	68.50	17.52
6	70	79	87	49	71.25	16.38
7	74	50	68	45	59.25	13.94
8	80	66	75	64	71.25	7.54
9	80	63	72	81	74.00	8.37
10	90	77	92	64	80.75	13.00
11	75	51	89	74	72.25	15.73
12	64	65	88	59	69.00	12.94
13	97	57	88	76	79.50	17.29
14	84	62	55	68	67.25	12.37
15	76	63	70	66	68.75	5.62
16	62	68	66	55	62.75	5.74
17	73	77	91	83	81.00	7.83
18	65	65	84	46	65.00	15.51
19	73	64	84	71	73.00	8.29
20	75	88	65	93	80.25	12.69
					$\bar{\bar{x}} = 71.39$	$\bar{s} = 11.97$

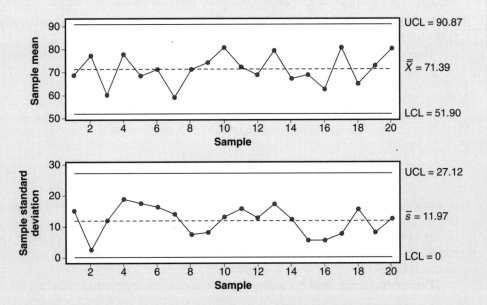

Figure 37.2 $\bar{x}$ and s control charts for CBC analysis turnaround times.

The process appears to be in control since there are no obvious trends or patterns and points plot within the control limits on both charts.

Further interpretation of these and other control charts will be presented in Section 6 of this chapter.

Individuals Control Charts

Many practical applications exist in which the subgroup consists of a single observation ($n = 1$). Examples include very slow processes or processes in which the measurement is very expensive to obtain, such as with destructive tests. An *individuals control chart* (I control chart) for variable data is appropriate for this type of situation.

The individuals control chart uses the *moving range* of two successive subgroups to estimate process variability (see Montgomery [2009b] for a detailed discussion of moving range and individuals control charts in general). The moving range is given by

$$MR_i = |x_i - x_{i-1}|.$$

For m subgroups of size $n = 1$ each, $m - 1$ moving ranges are defined as $MR_2 = |x_2 - x_1|$, $MR_3 = |x_3 - x_2|, \ldots, MR_m = |x_m - x_{m-1}|$. The *average moving range* is simply

$$\overline{MR} = \frac{\sum_{i=2}^{m} MR_i}{m-1}.$$

Division is done by $m - 1$ since only $m - 1$ moving range values are calculated (there is no moving range for subgroup 1). Control charts are constructed for the individual observations (x chart) and the moving range of the subgroups (MR chart).

The control limits and centerline of the x (or individuals) control chart are

$$UCL = \bar{x} + 3\frac{\overline{MR}}{d_2}$$

$$CL = \bar{x}$$

$$LCL = \bar{x} - 3\frac{\overline{MR}}{d_2}$$

where d_2 is a constant that depends on the number of observations used to calculate the moving range for each subgroup (that is, $n = 2$). Values for d_2 can be found in Appendix C. The control chart for individuals is constructed by plotting the actual observation x_i, the control limits, and the centerline against the subgroup (or time) order.

The control limits and centerline for the moving range control chart are

$$UCL = D_4 \overline{MR}$$

$$CL = \overline{MR}$$

$$LCL = D_3 \overline{MR}$$

where D_3 and D_4 are constants found in Appendix C for $n = 2$. The moving range control chart is constructed by plotting the $m - 1$ moving ranges, the control limits, and the centerline against the subgroup (or time) order.

EXAMPLE 37.3

Packages of a particular instant dry food are filled by a machine and weighed. The weights (in ounces) for 15 successive packages have been collected and are displayed in Table 37.4. The engineer wishes to determine whether the filling process is indeed in control.

The moving ranges are calculated using $MR_i = |x_i - x_{i-1}|$. To illustrate, consider the first moving range at subgroup 2:

$$MR_2 = |x_2 - x_1| = |19.92 - 19.85| = 0.07$$

The remaining moving ranges are calculated accordingly and are given in Table 37.4. The control limits and centerline for the individuals chart with moving ranges of size 2 are

$$UCL = 19.954 + 3\frac{0.39}{1.128} = 20.991$$

$$CL = 19.954$$

$$LCL = 19.954 - 3\frac{0.39}{1.128} = 18.917.$$

The control limits and centerline for the moving range chart are

$$UCL = 3.267(0.39) = 1.274$$

$$CL = 0.39$$

$$LCL = 0(0.39) = 0.$$

Table 37.4   Weights for dry food packages.

Bottle	Weight (x_i)	Moving range
1	19.85	—
2	19.92	0.07
3	19.93	0.01
4	19.26	0.67
5	20.36	1.10
6	19.96	0.40
7	19.87	0.09
8	19.80	0.07
9	20.40	0.60
10	19.98	0.42
11	20.17	0.19
12	19.81	0.36
13	20.21	0.40
14	19.64	0.57
15	20.15	0.51
	$\bar{x} = 19.954$	$\overline{MR} = 0.39$

Continued

Continued

The control charts for individual observations and for the moving range are displayed in Figure 37.3.

Examining these control charts, the process does not appear to be out of statistical control.

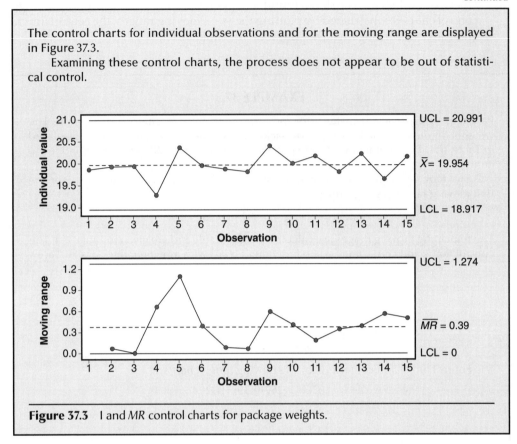

Figure 37.3   I and *MR* control charts for package weights.

It is important to note that the moving range control chart can not be interpreted in the same way as the *R* chart presented earlier, with respect to patterns or trends. Patterns or trends identified on the moving range chart do not necessarily indicate that the process is out of control. The moving ranges are *correlated* (recall $MR_i = |x_i - x_{i-1}|$). There is a natural dependency between successive MR_i values.

Attributes Control Charts

Attributes control charts are used for discrete or count data. There are many scenarios where the quality characteristic of interest is simply a classification of the measurement into a single category. For example, manufactured products may be measured but only classified as defective/nondefective, conforming/nonconforming, or pass/fail. Other situations may involve monitoring the number of nonconformities on an item. For example, billing statements may be examined for errors such as incorrect name, missing information, and incorrect amounts or type of service identified. Variables control charts are not appropriate for many of these situations. Control charts for data that can be *classified* are *attributes control charts.* The following attributes control charts will be discussed:

- Fraction nonconforming control charts (*p* charts)
- Number nonconforming control charts (*np* charts)
- Control charts for nonconformities (*c* and *u* control charts)

Definitions and Notation. Explanation of important notation and definitions is in order before presenting the various control charts. For the fraction nonconforming control charts, the quality characteristic of interest can be placed into one of exactly two categories. These categories may be pass/fail, conforming/nonconforming, and so on. For simplification, the term nonconforming will be used as a general reference regardless of the final categories to be used. The notation to be used is as follows:

- *n*—number of items examined (lot size, sample size).
- *m*—number of subgroups.
- *X*—the number of nonconforming items found in the sample of size *n*, where $X \leq n$.
- *p*—probability that any one item of interest will be nonconforming. This parameter is often unknown and must be estimated.
- $\hat{p}$—is the sample fraction nonconforming. By definition,

$$\hat{p} = \frac{X}{n}$$

and is calculated for each of the *m* subgroups.

- $\bar{p}$ is the average fraction nonconforming. By definition,

$$\bar{p} = \frac{\sum_{i=1}^{m} \hat{p}_i}{m}$$

and is an estimate of *p*, defined above.

The p Chart. The *p* chart is used to monitor the proportion nonconforming directly. The control limits and centerline (when *p* is unknown) are

$$UCL = \bar{p} + 3\sqrt{\frac{\bar{p}(1-\bar{p})}{n}}$$

$$CL = \bar{p}$$

$$LCL = \bar{p} - 3\sqrt{\frac{\bar{p}(1-\bar{p})}{n}}.$$

The control limits, centerline, and individual sample fraction nonconforming $\hat{p}_i$ are plotted against the subgroup number m. If any of the fraction nonconforming lie outside the control limits, the process is considered out of control. Patterns or trends would also be an indication of possible out-of-control situations.

EXAMPLE 37.4

A small bank collects data on the number of weekly account activities that are recorded in error. Over a 12-week period 1000 account activities are randomly selected and examined for the number that are in error. The bank would like to monitor the proportion of errors being committed, by establishing control charts.

The fraction in error $\hat{p}_i$ for each week must be computed. The fraction in error for each week is given in Table 37.5 for $n = 1000$. The average fraction in error $\bar{p}$ is found to be

$$\bar{p} = \frac{\sum_{i=1}^{12} \hat{p}_i}{12} = 0.01042.$$

The control limits and centerline for the p chart are

$$UCL = \bar{p} + 3\sqrt{\frac{\bar{p}(1-\bar{p})}{n}} = 0.01042 + 3\sqrt{\frac{0.01042(1-0.01042)}{1000}} = 0.020052$$

$$CL = 0.01042$$

$$LCL = \bar{p} - 3\sqrt{\frac{\bar{p}(1-\bar{p})}{n}} = 0.01042 - 3\sqrt{\frac{0.01042(1-0.01042)}{1000}} = 0.00078.$$

The resulting p chart is displayed in Figure 37.4. There is a single point that plots beyond the upper control limit. This point should be investigated to determine if it is truly an unusual point. If it is found to be unusual and the assignable cause identified, the point

Table 37.5 Account activities in error.

Week	Accounts in error	$\hat{p}_i$
1	6	0.006
2	11	0.011
3	4	0.004
4	10	0.010
5	5	0.005
6	30	0.030
7	9	0.009
8	8	0.008
9	12	0.012
10	7	0.007
11	12	0.012
12	11	0.011

Continued

Continued

can be removed and the centerline and control limits recalculated. Suppose in this case that the cause for the outlier in week 6 was identified and a revised control chart constructed. The revised control chart is shown in Figure 37.5. Notice that the control limits and centerline have been updated while the fraction in error for week 6 is still plotted on the graph. On a revised control chart, the removed point is used only as a placeholder.

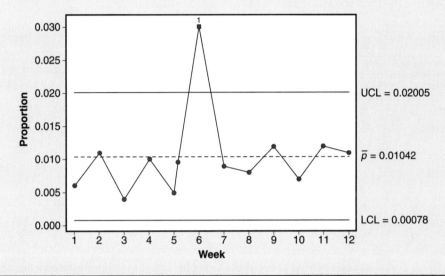

Figure 37.4   *p* chart for accounts in error.

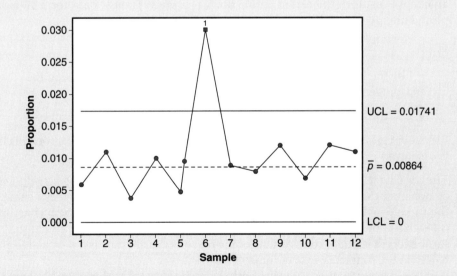

Figure 37.5   Revised *p* chart for accounts in error.

Part VI.F.5

Table 37.6 Surgical site infection rates.

Month	Surgeries	Surgical infection
1	57	8
2	62	6
3	66	1
4	57	2
5	69	2
6	63	6
7	55	10
8	56	6
9	54	9
10	62	3
11	65	4
12	69	5

It is not necessary that the sample sizes be equal for all subgroups. For example, suppose surgeries that result in surgical site infections are monitored at a particular hospital. Suppose that the number of surgeries each month is examined and those resulting in surgical infections recorded. Typical data for a 12-month period are given in Table 37.6.

The sample size is variable, and there are two ways to calculate the control limits:

- Use the same formulas for the control limits given earlier, using the average sample size as an estimate for n.

- Use the actual sample sizes and construct varying control limits.

For the surgical infection rates, varying control limits were used. The control chart is displayed in Figure 37.6.

The np Chart. The *np* chart is a variation of the *p* chart, with the *actual number* of nonconforming items plotted on the chart. The *np* chart and the *p* chart for the same problem will provide identical information. That is, if the *p* chart indicates that a process is out of control, then the *np* chart will also indicate that the same process is out of control. One of the reasons the *np* chart is an attractive alternative to the *p* chart is ease of interpretation.

The average fraction nonconforming $\bar{p}$ is the only value that must be estimated before constructing the control limits. The average fraction nonconforming can be found without having to calculate the sample fraction nonconforming values ($\hat{p}_i$). For the *np* chart, the average fraction nonconforming can be calculated as

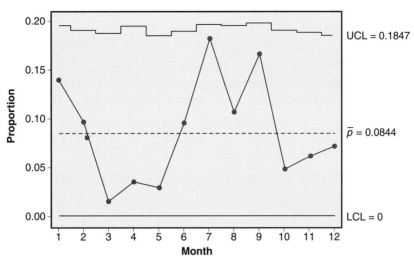

Tests performed with unequal sample sizes

Figure 37.6   *p* chart for surgical site infection rate using varying sample sizes.

$$\bar{p} = \frac{\sum\limits_{i=1}^{m} X_i}{mn}.$$

The control limits and centerline are then

$$UCL = n\bar{p} + 3\sqrt{n\bar{p}(1-\bar{p})}$$

$$CL = n\bar{p}$$

$$LCL = n\bar{p} - 3\sqrt{n\bar{p}(1-\bar{p})}.$$

The control limits, centerline, and the number of nonconforming items X_i are plotted against the subgroup. Interpretation of the chart is identical to that of the *p* chart.

EXAMPLE 37.5

Reconsider the accounts in error from the previous example. The average fraction in error was found to be $\bar{p} = 0.01042$. The control limits and centerline for the *np* control chart are

$$UCL = n\bar{p} + 3\sqrt{n\bar{p}(1-\bar{p})} = 1000(0.01042) + 3\sqrt{1000(0.01042)(1-0.01042)} = 20.05$$

$$CL = n\bar{p} = 100(0.01042) = 10.42$$

$$LCL = n\bar{p} - 3\sqrt{n\bar{p}(1-\bar{p})} = 1000(0.01042) - 3\sqrt{1000(0.01042)(1-0.01042)} = 0.787$$

Continued

Part VI.F.5

Continued

The *np* control chart is displayed in Figure 37.7. As with the *p* chart, the *np* chart indicates that the process is out of statistical control.

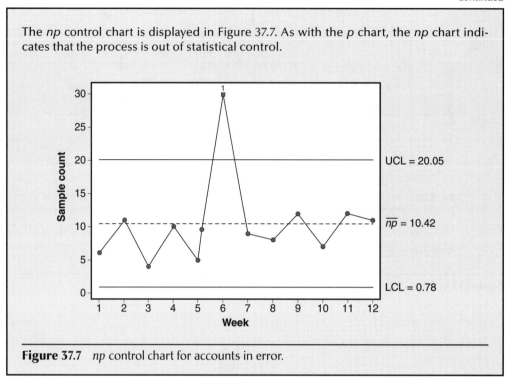

Figure 37.7 *np* control chart for accounts in error.

Control Charts for Nonconformities. Control charts for nonconformities are similar to those for the number of nonconforming items, discussed in the previous subsection. The *p* chart and *np* chart represent the fraction of nonconforming items. When the variable of interest is the number of nonconformities per unit, the *p* and *np* charts are not appropriate. For *p* and *np* charts, we noted that the number of nonconforming units could not exceed the number of units being investigated in the subgroup, that is, $X \leq n$. For monitoring *nonconformities*, there is no such restriction. In this case, nonconformities are counted *per unit*. There could be an infinite (countably infinite) number of *nonconformities* on a unit or units. For example, billing statements may be examined for errors such as incorrect name, missing information, incorrect amounts, or wrong type of service identified. More than one of these errors may occur on any one statement. Control charts for nonconformities are the *c* chart and the *u* chart.

The c Chart. If the subgroup size *n* is constant from subgroup to subgroup, the *c* chart is an appropriate control chart for nonconformities. For the *c* chart:

- *n* = number of units inspected, sample size (this can be size $n = 1$ or greater).
- *m* = number of subgroups.

- X = number of nonconformities per unit inspected or per subgroup.

- $\bar{c}$ = average number of nonconformities:

$$\bar{c} = \frac{\sum_{i=1}^{m} X_i}{m}$$

The control limits and centerline for the c chart are

$$UCL = \bar{c} + 3\sqrt{\bar{c}}$$

$$CL = \bar{c}$$

$$LCL = \bar{c} - 3\sqrt{\bar{c}}.$$

EXAMPLE 37.6

Billing statements for a local hospital are being examined for errors. Twenty billing statements are randomly chosen each day over a 24-day period and examined for missing information, incorrect amounts, and wrong type of service identified. The number of errors (nonconformities) is given in Table 37.7.

The average number of errors is

$$\bar{c} = \frac{\sum_{i=1}^{m} X_i}{m} = \frac{4 + 18 + \ldots + 10}{24} = 10.29.$$

Table 37.7 Errors on hospital billing statements.

Day	Number of errors	Day	Number of errors
1	4	13	10
2	18	14	13
3	14	15	3
4	7	16	12
5	7	17	17
6	8	18	13
7	16	19	9
8	6	20	17
9	10	21	9
10	12	22	9
11	9	23	6
12	8	24	10

Continued

Continued

The control limits and centerline for the c chart are

$$UCL = \bar{c} + 3\sqrt{\bar{c}} = 10.29 + 3\sqrt{10.29} = 19.91$$

$$CL = \bar{c} = 10.29$$

$$LCL = \bar{c} - 3\sqrt{\bar{c}} = 10.29 - 3\sqrt{10.29} = 0.67.$$

The c chart is displayed in Figure 37.8. The process appears to be in statistical control.

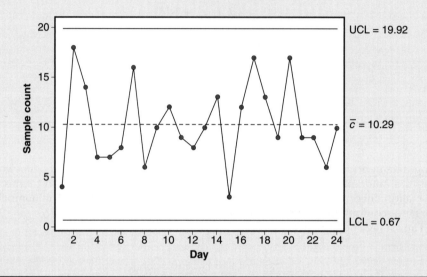

Figure 37.8 c chart for number of billing errors.

The u Chart. The c chart monitors the number of nonconformities. The u chart, on the other hand, monitors the *average* number of nonconformities. As with the p and np charts, the resulting c and u charts for constant sample size will provide identical results. It is not necessary for the sample size to be constant from subgroup to subgroup for the u chart. Let u_i be the average number of nonconformities for the ith subgroup ($i = 1, 2, \ldots, m$), where

$$u_i = \frac{X_i}{n}.$$

Also, let $\bar{u}$ represent the overall average number of nonconformities per unit, that is,

$$\bar{u} = \frac{\sum_{i=1}^{m} u_i}{m}.$$

The control limits and centerline for average number of nonconformities are

$$UCL = \bar{u} + 3\sqrt{\frac{\bar{u}}{n}}$$

$$CL = \bar{u}$$

$$LCL = \bar{u} - 3\sqrt{\frac{\bar{u}}{n}}.$$

The control limits, centerline, and u_i are plotted on the control chart against the subgroup.

EXAMPLE 37.7

Reconsider the errors on billing statements example discussed previously. The average number of nonconformities u_i for each day is given in Table 37.8.

The overall average number of nonconformities per unit is then

$$\bar{u} = \frac{\sum_{i=1}^{m} u_i}{m} = \frac{0.20 + 0.90 + \ldots + 0.50}{24} = 0.515.$$

The control limits and centerline for the *u* chart are

$$UCL = \bar{u} + 3\sqrt{\frac{\bar{u}}{n}} = 0.515 + 3\sqrt{\frac{0.515}{20}} = 0.996$$

$$CL = \bar{u} = 0.515$$

$$LCL = \bar{u} - 3\sqrt{\frac{\bar{u}}{n}} = 0.515 - 3\sqrt{\frac{0.515}{20}} = 0.033.$$

Table 37.8 Billing statement errors for a 24-day period.

Day	Number of errors	u_i	Day	Number of errors	u_i
1	4	0.20	13	10	0.50
2	18	0.90	14	13	0.65
3	14	0.70	15	3	0.15
4	7	0.35	16	12	0.60
5	7	0.35	17	17	0.85
6	8	0.40	18	13	0.65
7	16	0.80	19	9	0.45
8	6	0.30	20	17	0.85
9	10	0.50	21	9	0.45
10	12	0.60	22	9	0.45
11	9	0.45	23	6	0.30
12	8	0.40	24	10	0.50

Continued

Continued

The *u* control chart is displayed in Figure 37.9. Again, the process does not appear to be out of statistical control.

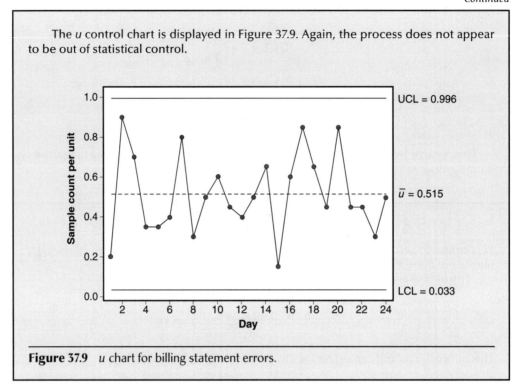

Figure 37.9   *u* chart for billing statement errors.

Cumulative Sum Control Charts

So far, Shewhart control charts for monitoring various processes have been presented. Shewhart control charts are known to be poor at detecting small shifts in the process mean because they are based only on the current observation (see Gan [1991], Hawkins [1981, 1993], Lucas [1976], Montgomery [2008b], and Woodall and Adams [1993]). An alternative to the use of Shewhart control charts is the *cumulative sum* (CUSUM) *control chart*. The CUSUM control chart has been shown to be more sensitive to small shifts in the process because it is based on the current observation and the most recent past observations.

Page (1961) first introduced the cumulative sum control chart. The control chart plots the *cumulative sums of deviations* of the observations from a target value. That is, the CUSUM control chart plots the quantity

$$C_i = \sum_{j=1}^{i} \left(\bar{x}_j - \mu_0 \right)$$

against the subgroup *i* where

C_i is the cumulative sum of deviations up to and including the ith sample

$\bar{x}_j$ is the mean of the jth sample

μ_0 is the target value for the process average

As long as the process average remains at the target value μ_0, then the cumulative sums C_i will be approximately zero. If the process shifts away from the target mean, then C_i will increase in absolute value.

Since the CUSUM chart uses information from the current and recent past observations, it can detect small shifts in the process more quickly than a standard Shewhart chart. CUSUM control charts can be used for subgroup data or individuals data. In addition, there have been applications for both variables and attributes data. The two-sided tabular CUSUM control chart for individuals will be presented here. One-sided CUSUM charts can be constructed if the interest is in a particular direction, downward or upward, but not necessarily both.

Tabular Form of the CUSUM. The *tabular* form of the two-sided CUSUM chart involves two statistics, C_i^+ and C_i^-. C_i^+ represents the cumulative sum of deviations above the target mean and is referred to as the one-sided upper CUSUM. C_i^- is the cumulative sum of deviations below the target mean and is referred to as the one-sided lower CUSUM. C_i^+ and C_i^- are calculated as

$$C_i^+ = \max\left[0, x_1 - (\mu_0 + K) + C_0^+\right]$$

$$C_i^- = \min\left[0, x_i - (\mu_0 - K) + C_0^-\right]$$

where x_i is the ith observation. C_i^+ and C_i^- are initially set at C_0^+ and C_0^-. The constant K is a reference value and calculated as

$$K = \frac{|\mu_1 - \mu_0|}{2}$$

where μ_0 is the target mean and μ_1 is the out-of-control mean that we are interested in detecting. If μ_1 is unknown, we can let $K = k\sigma$ where σ is the process standard deviation and k is some constant chosen so that a particular shift is detected. To illustrate, suppose a shift from target of 1.5 standard deviations is important to detect. That is, we want to detect a shift from μ_0 to $\mu_0 - 1.5\sigma$ or to $\mu_0 + 1.5\sigma$. In this case, $K = 1.5\sigma$. If the process standard deviation is not known, it must be estimated from the data provided.

The values of C_i^+ and C_i^- for each sample are plotted on a two-sided CUSUM control chart. If either value plots outside a stated decision interval $(-H, H)$, the process is considered out of control. H should be chosen after careful consideration. There are many possible values for H, but a common setting is $H = 5\sigma$. It has been shown that this decision value results in a low false alarm rate for the process under study. For further discussion of the design of CUSUM control charts see Hawkins (1993) or Woodall and Adams (1993).

EXAMPLE 37.8

Packages of a particular instant dry food are filled by a machine and weighed. The weights (in ounces) for 24 successive packages have been collected and are displayed in Table 37.9. The target mean weight is $\mu_0 = 20$ ounces. From past experience, it is believed that the process standard deviation is $\sigma = 0.20$ ounces. If the process mean shifts from this target by one-half of the process standard deviation, then the filling process is deemed out of control. The engineer would like to design a two-sided CUSUM control chart and determine whether the process is indeed in control at the target $\mu_0 = 20$ ounces.

Some of the known or assumed quantities are:

$\mu_0 = 20$ ounces

$\sigma = 0.20$ ounces

$K = 0.5\sigma = 0.5(0.20) = 0.10$

$H = 5\sigma = 5(0.20) = 1$

The CUSUM values C_i^+ and C_i^- are compared to the decision interval $(-H, H) = (-1, 1)$. If any cumulative sum falls outside the interval $(-1, 1)$, the process is considered to be out of control. To illustrate these calculations, consider the first observation, $x_1 = 20.26$ ounces. Initially, $C_0^+ = C_0^- = 0$, and as previously shown, $K = 0.1$. The first cumulative sums are

$$C_1^+ = \max\left[0, x_1 - (\mu_0 + K) + C_0^+\right]$$
$$= \max[0, 20.26 - (20 + 0.1) + 0]$$
$$= \max[0, 0.16]$$
$$= 0.16$$

$$C_1^- = \min\left[0, x_i - (\mu_0 - K) + C_0^-\right]$$
$$= \min[0, 20.26 - (20 - 0.1) + 0]$$
$$= \min[0, -0.36]$$
$$= 0.$$

Table 37.9 Weights for dry food packages.

Package	Weight (x_i)	Package	Weight (x_i)
1	20.26	13	20.30
2	19.97	14	19.77
3	19.76	15	20.40
4	19.72	16	19.98
5	19.69	17	19.91
6	19.85	18	20.18
7	19.96	19	20.08
8	20.03	20	20.05
9	20.06	21	20.20
10	19.71	22	19.90
11	19.68	23	19.95
12	19.94	24	20.12

Continued

Continued

The remaining CUSUMs can be calculated similarly, but it is recommended that the calculations be done using a spreadsheet package or modern statistical package. Notice that both cumulative sums are within the decision interval (–1, 1), so the process has *not* signaled out of control at this point. The CUSUM chart is shown in Figure 37.10.

The CUSUMs plot well within the decision interval, so there does not appear to have been a shift of 0.5σ from the target value of 20 ounces.

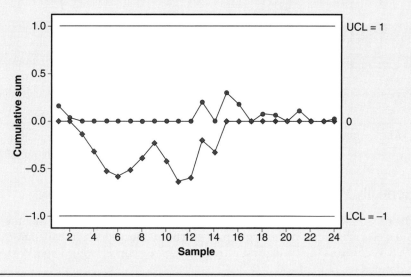

Figure 37.10   CUSUM chart for package weight.

V-Mask Approach. The previous example was an illustration of the tabular CUSUM. A second method is the use of a V-mask, presented by Barnard (1959). The V-mask for the package weight example is given in Figure 37.11.

A cumulative sum is calculated for each sample and plotted on the chart. The V-mask is constructed in such a way that if the process has not shifted out of control, all CUSUMs should plot within the V. Figure 37.11 indicates that the package-filling process does not appear to have shifted out of control. This approach can be more difficult to implement although some modern statistical packages will construct the V-mask for particular problems. For more details on the V-mask approach and its drawbacks see Montgomery (2009b).

Part VI.F.5

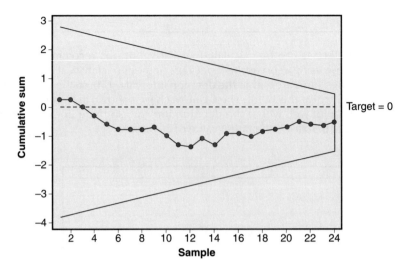

Figure 37.11 V-mask for package weight.

Exponentially Weighted Moving Average Control Charts

The *exponentially weighted moving average* (EWMA) control chart, like the CUSUM, is a good chart for detecting small shifts in the process mean parameter. The EWMA control chart was first introduced by Roberts (1959). The EWMA statistic is defined as

$$z_i = \lambda x_i + (1 - \lambda)z_{i-1}$$

where λ is a weight and $0 < \lambda \le 1$, x_i is the current observation, and z_{i-1} is the previous EWMA statistic. Initially, $z_0 = \mu_0$, the process target mean. If the process target mean is not known, then $\bar{x}$ is used as the initial value.

Like the CUSUM, the EWMA includes information from recent past observations as well as the current observation x_i. Control limits can be placed on the values of z_i. If one or more of the z_i values fall outside the control limits, then the process is considered to be out of statistical control. The control limits for the EWMA for large values of i are

$$\text{UCL} = \mu_0 + L\sigma\sqrt{\left(\frac{\lambda}{2-\lambda}\right)}$$

$$\text{LCL} = \mu_0 - L\sigma\sqrt{\left(\frac{\lambda}{2-\lambda}\right)}$$

where L is the width of the control limits. The values of L and λ can significantly impact the performance of the chart. Small values of λ work well in practice ($0.05 \le \lambda \le 0.25$) with values of L between $2.6 \le L \le 3$ (see Crowder [1989], Lucas and Saccucci [1990], and Montgomery [2009b]).

EXAMPLE 37.9

Reconsider the 24 packages being filled by a machine and weighed in the previous example. The package weights are displayed in Table 37.9. The target mean weight is $\mu_0 = 20$ ounces. From past experience, it is believed that the process standard deviation is $\sigma = 0.20$ ounces. We would like to construct an EWMA control chart for these data using $\lambda = 0.10$ and $L = 2.7$. The EWMA statistic is

$$z_i = \lambda x_i + (1 - \lambda)z_{i-1}$$
$$= 0.10x_i + (1 - 0.10)z_{i-1}$$
$$= 0.10x_i + 0.90z_{i-1}.$$

To illustrate the calculation of the EWMA statistic for each observation, consider the first observation, $x_1 = 20.26$ ounces. If we initialize the process using $z_0 = \mu_0 = 20$, z_1 is found to be

$$z_1 = 0.10x_i + 0.90z_0$$
$$= 0.10(20.26) + 0.90(20)$$
$$= 20.026.$$

The remaining EWMA statistics are calculated similarly. The control limits and centerline are

$$\text{UCL} = \mu_0 + L\sigma\sqrt{\left(\frac{\lambda}{2 - \lambda}\right)} = 20 + 2.7(0.2)\sqrt{\left(\frac{0.10}{2 - 0.10}\right)} = 20.12$$
$$\text{CL} = 20$$
$$\text{LCL} = \mu_0 - L\sigma\sqrt{\left(\frac{\lambda}{2 - \lambda}\right)} = 20 - 2.7(0.2)\sqrt{\left(\frac{0.10}{2 - 0.10}\right)} = 19.88.$$

The control limits and the EWMA statistics z_i are plotted on the EWMA control chart in Figure 37.12. The process appears to be in control since all EWMA statistics fall within the control limits.

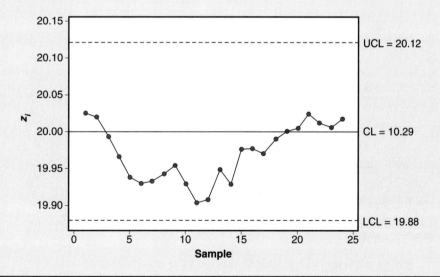

Figure 37.12   EWMA control chart for package weight.

Patterns and Trends on the CUSUM and EWMA

Patterns and trends on the CUSUM and EWMA control charts do not necessarily indicate an out-of-control process. The statistics plotted on the charts are correlated since they are functions of not only the current observation but also recent past observations. As such, patterns can be expected even with an in-control process.

Choosing a Control Chart

The choice of which control chart to use in a particular problem depends on the process under investigation. Shewhart control charts are easy to construct and interpret but they are less effective at detecting small shifts in the process parameter. It has also been shown that Shewhart control charts are very sensitive to the assumption of normality (see Borror, Montgomery, and Runger [1999]). That is, if the underlying distribution of the process is nonnormal, then Shewhart charts can often signal out-of-control when in fact the process is in control. CUSUM and EWMA control charts are quite robust to departures from normality and are better at detecting small shifts in the process than the Shewhart charts.

Moving Average Control Chart

The *moving average* (MA) *control chart* is similar to the EWMA in that it uses a moving average of a certain span (not necessarily consecutive observations). However, the moving average is an unweighted average of the observations. Suppose there are n observations, $x_1, x_2, \ldots, x_n$ selected from the process with mean μ_0 and standard deviation σ. Furthermore, suppose a moving average of span w is of interest. The moving average statistic at time i can be written as

$$MA_i = \frac{x_i + x_{i-1} + \ldots + x_{i-w+1}}{w}$$

The values of MA_i are plotted on a control chart with control limits and centerline:

$$UCL = \mu_0 + \frac{3\sigma}{\sqrt{w}}$$

$$CL = \mu_0$$

$$LCL = \mu_0 - \frac{3\sigma}{\sqrt{w}}$$

The moving average chart may be suitable for the following situations:

- When data are collected periodically or it may take some time to produce a single item

- When it may be desirable to dampen the effects of overcontrol

- When it may be necessary to detect smaller shifts in the process than with a comparable Shewhart chart

6. CONTROL CHART ANALYSIS

> Read and interpret control charts, use rules
> for determining statistical control. (Evaluate)
>
> **Body of Knowledge VI.F.6**

A critical tool in the analysis of charted data is the process log. The process log may be a separate document or it may be maintained as part of the control chart itself. Entries in the log should include all changes in the process and its environment, including maintenance, raw materials, adjustments, tooling, fixturing, and so on.

Each of the control limit formulas discussed in the previous section uses data from the process. Although it is not always obvious from the formulas, the upper and lower limits are placed at $\pm 3\sigma$ from the average. The use of three-sigma limits is a direct result of the underlying assumption of normality. It can be shown that if the underlying distribution is normal, then approximately 99.7 percent of all the data will lie within three standard deviations of the mean. Therefore, if an observation falls beyond three standard deviations from the mean, that observation would be flagged as unusual since the probability of this occurring is 0.003 and may be an indication of an out-of-control process. Since the Shewhart control charts are based on the normality assumption, it is common to use three standard deviations in the construction of the control limits for these charts. For the EWMA control chart, if $L = 3$ and $\lambda = 1$, then the control limits would reduce to the standard Shewhart control limits. But it has been shown that values other than $L = 3$ and $\lambda = 1$ can result in well-performing control charts, especially for detecting small shifts in the process parameter.

It should be noted that the probability of a point falling inside or outside three standard deviations is somewhat theoretical because no process runs as if its output were randomly selected numbers from some historical distribution. It is enough to say that when a point falls outside the control limits, the probability is quite high that the process has changed. When the probability is very high that a point *did not* come from the distribution used to calculate the control limits, the process is said to be *out of statistical control*. Unfortunately, this is often abbreviated to "out of control," which seems to imply some wild action on the part of the process. In reality, the out-of-statistical-control condition is often very subtle and would perhaps not be detected without the control chart. This, in fact, is one of the main values of the control chart: it detects changes in a process that would not otherwise be noticed. This may permit adjustment or other action on the process before serious damage is done.

One of the hazards of using a control chart without proper training is the tendency to react to a point that is not right on target by adjusting the process, even though the chart does not indicate that the process has changed. If an adjustment is made whenever a point is not exactly on target, it may tend to destabilize a stable process. In the ideal situation, a process should not need adjustment except when the chart indicates it is out of statistical control. Dr. W. E. Deming states that "The function of a control chart is to minimize the net economic loss from . . . overadjustment and underadjustment." (Deming 1986)

Rules for Determining Statistical Control

A number of events are very unlikely to occur unless the process has changed, and thus serve as statistical indicators of process change. The lists of rules that reflect these statistical indicators vary somewhat from textbook to textbook, but two of the most widely used lists of rules are the eight rules used by the software package Minitab and the six rules listed by the Automotive Industry Action Group (AIAG) in its SPC manual.

The eight Minitab rules are:

1. One point more than 3σ from the centerline (either side)

2. Nine points in a row on the same side of the centerline

3. Six points in a row, all increasing or all decreasing

4. Fourteen points in a row, alternating up and down

5. Two out of three points more than 2σ from the centerline (same side)

6. Four out of five points more than 1σ from the centerline (same side)

7. Fifteen points in a row within 1σ of the centerline (either side)

8. Eight points in a row more than 1σ from the centerline (either side)

The AIAG in the third edition of its SPC manual lists a "Summary of Typical Special Cause Criteria" that is identical to Minitab's list except for rule 2, which says:

2. Seven points in a row on one side of the centerline

The AIAG SPC manual emphasizes that ". . . the decision as to which criteria to use depends on the process being studied/controlled." CQEs may find it useful to generate additional tests for particular situations. If, for instance, an increase in values represents a safety hazard, it would not be necessary to wait for the specified number of successively increasing points to take action. The $\pm 3\sigma$ location for the control limits is somewhat arbitrary and could conceivably be adjusted based on the economic trade-off between the costs of not taking action when an out-of-control condition occurs and taking action when an out-of-control condition has not occurred. Deming has stated, however, that moving the control limits up and down can be a source of additional problems, and it would be better in most cases to put that energy into reducing variation.

Sensitizing rules should always be used with caution. Although sensitizing rules can improve a Shewhart chart's ability to detect small shifts, they can seriously degrade the performance of the chart when the process is indeed in control. Control chart performance is often measured by the *average run length* (ARL), which is defined as the number of cycles, time periods, or samples that elapse before the process signals out-of-control. If the process is in control, we want the average run length to be large. If the process is out of control, a small average run length is desirable. When several sensitizing rules are used simultaneously on a control chart, the in-control average run length can become unacceptably small. For example, suppose that independent process data are being monitored using a standard Shewhart control chart. For an in-control process, the average run length is approximately 370. However, the Shewhart control chart with Western Electric rules (Western Electric [1956]) has an in-control average run length of approximately 91 (see Champ and Woodall [1987]). That is, even if the process is in statistical control, the sensitizing rules may lead to more false alarms than the standard Shewhart control chart with no sensitizing rules.

The important issue, of course, is not the exact wording of the rules so much as the action that takes place once the unusual event has occurred. The first step always should be to ascertain that the point is calculated and plotted correctly. If possible, a double check should be made on the measurement itself. For variables charts, the range section should be analyzed first. Increases in the range values represent increased variation between the readings within an individual sample. Possible causes include bearings, tooling, or fixtures. In the case of cutoff operations, for instance, if the part is pushed against a backstop for measurement, the backstop could have become "rubbery." Changes in the averages chart represent some sort of shift in the process. Frequent causes are tool wear, changes in raw materials, and changes in measurement systems or process parameters such as machine settings, voltages, pneumatic pressure, and so on. It is useful to construct a list of things to check when certain chart characteristics occur. Such a list can come from a discussion among experienced personnel as well as from data from a process log.

In some cases the events on the "out of control" lists represent improved situations. For instance, the process is considered out of control if too many points are in the middle third of the control limit area. Recall that the control chart tests are used to help determine whether the current values come from the distribution that was used to calculate the control limits. If too many points are grouped around the centerline, the points probably come from a different distribution. The process should be investigated to determine what changed and to see whether this change can be perpetuated. If a log is maintained for the process, it may be possible to find changes that correspond to the time that the improvement occurred. Experience is the best teacher when it comes to chart interpretation. Efforts should be made to document a body of knowledge about each process.

Finally, note that a control chart is really a graphical hypothesis test. The null hypothesis is that the process has not changed, and as each point is plotted, the chart is examined to determine whether there is sufficient evidence to reject the null hypothesis and conclude that the process has changed. The significance level varies somewhat with the chart test employed.

7. PRE-CONTROL CHARTS

> Define and describe how these charts differ
> from other control charts and how they
> should be used. (Apply)
>
> **Body of Knowledge VI.F.7**

A *pre-control chart* is sometimes used in place of a control chart or until sufficient data are collected to construct a control chart. An important difference between pre-control charts and control charts is that the upper and lower pre-control limits are calculated from the tolerance limits rather than from data from the process. Thus the pre-control chart is not *statistical* in the sense that the distribution of the current process is not being compared to some historic distribution.

A fairly standard way to construct the pre-control (PC) limits is to multiply the value of the tolerance (upper specification limit – lower specification limit) by 0.25. Then subtract the resulting value from the upper specification limit to form the upper PC limit and add it to the lower specification limit to form the lower PC limit.

As parts are measured, their values are compared to the PC limits and appropriate action is taken based on rules such as these:

1. If the first part is outside the specification limits, adjust the process.

2. If a part is inside the specification limits but outside PC limits, measure the next part.

3. If two successive parts are outside PC limits, adjust the process.

4. If five successive parts are inside PC limits, consider switching to less frequent measuring.

There has been much debate about the use of pre-control charts. Some of the advantages and disadvantages of precontrol charts follow.

Advantages

- Pre-control charts are easy to implement and interpret.

- Pre-control charts can be very useful in initial setup operations in determining whether product being produced is centered between the tolerances.

Disadvantages

- Pre-control does not provide information about how variability can be reduced if necessary or how the process can be brought back into control.

- Pre-control charts should only be used for processes whose process capability ratio (to be discussed in the next section) is greater than one. If the capability of the process is very poor, then pre-control charts will signal that the process should be stopped and assignable causes found. But low capability does not necessarily indicate that any assignable causes are actually present. That is, unnecessary tampering will most likely occur in this case.

- The small sample sizes used in pre-control will greatly reduce the chart's ability to detect moderate to large shifts.

EXAMPLE 37.10

The specification for a dimension is 5.000 ± 0.010.

   The tolerance is 0.020, so 25 percent of the tolerance is 0.005. Therefore, the upper PC limit would be placed at 5.005 and the lower PC limit at 4.995, as indicated in Figure 37.13.

   The actions to be taken at each of the lettered points in Figure 37.13 are:

A. Adjust process

B. Measure another part

C. Measure another part

D. Measure another part

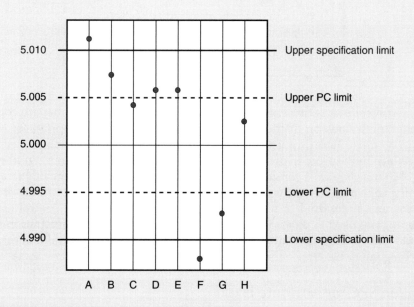

Figure 37.13   Example of a pre-control chart.

Continued

Continued

E. Adjust process

F. Adjust process

G. Measure another part

H. Measure another part

Various authors provide additional rules. The principal advantage of pre-control is that it is simpler than standard control charts. The main disadvantage is that it is not statistically based. When the pre-control rules indicate that the process should be adjusted, there is not necessarily a high probability that the process has changed. This may lead to overadjustment and decreased stability of the process. For this reason, there is some controversy over the use of pre-control, with Montgomery (2009b) stating that "This author believes that pre-control is a poor substitute for standard control charts and would never recommend it in practice."

The material presented here can be found in greater detail in Ledolter and Burrill (1999) and in an article by Ledolter and Swersey (1997).

8. SHORT-RUN STATISTICAL PROCESS CONTROL

Identify, define, and use short-run SPC rules. (Apply)

Body of Knowledge VI.F.8

The control charts presented to this point apply to processes that are considered long, continuous production runs. These charts are not appropriate for *short production runs*. Short production runs are commonplace and include processes that produce built-to-order product or quick turnaround production. Short-run control charts should be considered when data are collected infrequently or aperiodically. They may be used with historical target or target values, attribute or variable data, and individual or subgrouped averages. Standardized control charts are commonly used to monitor short production runs. A simple illustration for attribute data will be presented. For complete details on short production runs, see Montgomery (2009b).

Short-Run SPC for Attribute Data

The short-run control charts for attribute data are actually *standardized control charts*. The attribute for the control chart of interest is *standardized* and plotted on a control chart. To illustrate, consider the standardized value using the number of nonconformities (that is, c chart). The standardized value is

$$Z_i = \frac{c_i - \bar{c}}{\sqrt{\bar{c}}},$$

which follows a standard normal distribution. The following properties of *all* standardized control charts will apply:

- Each data point is standardized.

- The standardized random variable Z_i has a standard normal distribution.

- The centerline for all standardized charts is zero.

- The control limits for all of the standardized charts are –3 and 3.

EXAMPLE 37.11

Nonconformities are counted on 10 printed circuit boards. The boards come from a short production run. The nonconformities are given in Table 37.10.

A short-run c chart is appropriate for this situation. To construct the short-run control chart on the number of nonconformities, we first calculate the average number of nonconformities $\bar{c}$, then calculate the standardized values

$$Z_i = \frac{c_i - \bar{c}}{\sqrt{\bar{c}}}.$$

For this problem, $\bar{c} = 25/10 = 2.5$ (where there are a total of 25 nonconformities and 10 boards). The standardized values are then found using

$$Z_i = \frac{c_i - 2.5}{\sqrt{2.5}}.$$

To illustrate, the standardized value for the first circuit board is

$$Z_1 = \frac{c_1 - 2.5}{\sqrt{2.5}} = \frac{4 - 2.5}{\sqrt{2.5}} = 0.95.$$

Table 37.10 Number of nonconformities for printed circuit boards.

Printed circuit board	Number of nonconformities
1	4
2	0
3	1
4	3
5	6
6	3
7	1
8	0
9	5
10	2
Total	25

Continued

Continued

The remaining standardized values are calculated similarly. The short-run *c* chart is shown in Figure 37.14. The process does not appear to be out of statistical control.

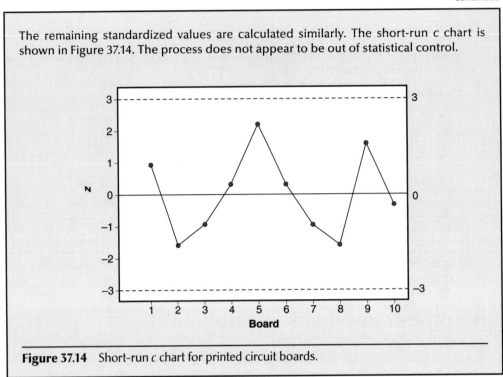

Figure 37.14   Short-run *c* chart for printed circuit boards.

There are a number of methods for constructing control charts for short production runs. The EWMA and CUSUM control charts can be very effective in this situation. See Hawkins and Olwell (1998) for more details on the CUSUM approach for short production runs.

Chapter 38

G. Process and Performance Capability

T his chapter addresses four aspects of process and performance capability: process capability studies, process performance versus specifications, process capability indices, and process performance indices.

1. PROCESS CAPABILITY STUDIES

> Define, describe, calculate, and use process capability studies, including identifying characteristics, specifications, and tolerances, developing sampling plans for such studies, establishing control, etc. (Analyze)
>
> **Body of Knowledge VI.G.1**

The purpose of a capability study is to determine whether a process is capable of meeting certain requirements. Capability of a process can be evaluated through determination of a probability distribution, its shape, center, and spread. Tools such as histograms, probability plots, and stem-and-leaf plots can be used to evaluate process capability without having stated specification limits for the quality characteristic of interest.

Process capability is often investigated with respect to given specifications. In theory, a capability study should be performed for every product dimension and every quality characteristic. In practice, however, people familiar with a process usually are able to identify the few characteristics that merit a full capability study, usually the characteristics that experience has shown to be difficult to hold to specification. For example, suppose a customer requires certain process outputs to be 45 to 55, such as:

- The arrival time for a delivery vehicle must be between 45 and 55 minutes after the hour.

- Manufactured pumps must produce between 45 psi and 55 psi.

- The plating thickness must be from 45 to 55 mm.

In these instances, the 45 to 55 requirement is called the specification, which typically is inclusive of the endpoints.

Bothe (1999) identifies six major activities as parts of a process capability study:

1. Verifying process stability

2. Estimating process parameters

3. Measuring process capability

4. Comparing actual capability to desired capability

5. Making a decision concerning process changes

6. Reporting the results of the study with recommendations

These six areas are not unique and may require several different methods to complete any one activity. For example, control charts and designed experiments can be implemented to estimate process capability. In addition, Montgomery (2009b) recommends the use of histograms and probability plotting in addition to process capability ratios (presented in this section) as techniques useful in determining the capability of a process.

The first step in conducting a capability study is to verify that the process is stable. A *stable* process can be thought of as a process without special causes of variation present. Process stability can be determined by using a control chart. The process is considered to be stable if the chart shows that no special causes are present after an appropriate number of points have been plotted. A key phrase in the previous sentence is "appropriate number of points." Although authorities disagree on the number of points needed, 20 to 30 points are commonly used. However, the more points you plot, the higher the confidence you can have in the stability conclusion.

The second step in conducting a capability study is to determine whether it is reasonable to assume that the process data come from a normal distribution. To do this, a normal probability plot or histogram could be constructed using the original readings (not the averages) from the control chart. If the histogram looks normal, with most points grouped around a single peak and fairly symmetric tails on each side, you may assume that the data constitutes a sample drawn from an approximately normal population. Using a normal probability plot, we conclude that the normality assumption is satisfied if the data fall along a straight line. Again, the more data you use, the greater the confidence you can have in this conclusion. The normality assumption is absolutely necessary in order for the results of a process capability study (process capability ratios, discussed next) to be considered valid. If the data are nonnormal, a transformation to induce normality may be necessary. Kotz and Lovelace (1998) also discuss process capability indices that can be used for nonnormal distributions. For information about a hypothesis test for normality, refer to Devore (2007) or Montgomery and Runger (2006).

If the data are normally distributed, the next step is to use the normal distribution to estimate process capability. The most common method is to use the data from a control chart to estimate μ and σ. The sampling plan is then the same as that used for the control chart. Once the chart exhibits statistical control, the values of $\bar{\bar{x}}$ and R calculated from the control chart are used in the capability analysis formulas.

2. CALCULATING PROCESS PERFORMANCE VERSUS SPECIFICATIONS

> Distinguish between natural process limits and specification limits, and calculate percent defective. (Analyze)
>
> **Body of Knowledge VI.G.2**

In this section the capability of a process in relation to specification limits will be investigated. The capability of a process could be described by the fraction of units that fall outside the specification limits. To illustrate, consider the following example.

EXAMPLE 38.1

A dimension has specifications of 2.125 ± 0.05. Data from the process indicate that the distribution is normally distributed, and the $\bar{x}$ and R control chart indicates that the process is stable. The control chart used a sample of size five and it is found that $\bar{\bar{x}} = 2.1261$ and $\bar{R} = 0.0055$. We wish to determine what fraction of the manufactured product will have this particular dimension outside the specification limits.

Solution:

Let X represent the dimension of the quality characteristic of interest. What we are looking for is the fraction of the manufactured product that will have this particular dimension outside the specification limits; this can be written as $P(2.120 < X < 2.130)$. Since X is normally distributed, we can use the standard normal distribution to determine this fraction. The best point estimate for μ is $\bar{\bar{x}} = 2.1261$. The point estimate for process standard deviation σ is given by the formula

$$\hat{\sigma} = \frac{\bar{R}}{d_2} = \frac{0.0055}{2.326} = 0.00236.$$

The constant d_2 can be found in Appendix C for $n = 5$.
The estimated fraction that *does* conform to specifications is

$$P(2.120 < X < 2.130) = P\left(\frac{2.120 - 2.1261}{0.00236} < \frac{X - \bar{\bar{x}}}{\hat{\sigma}} < \frac{2.130 - 2.1261}{0.00236} \right)$$

$$= P(-2.58 < Z < 1.65)$$

$$= P(Z < 1.65) - P(Z < -2.58)$$

$$= 0.9505 - 0.0049$$

$$= 0.9456.$$

Therefore, the fraction that is *nonconforming* is $1 - 0.9456 = 0.0544$. Approximately 5.44 percent of the products will fall outside specification for this quality characteristic.

Control Limits, Specification Limits, and Natural Tolerance Limits

It should be noted that there is a significant difference between control limits, specification limits, and natural tolerance limits. Control limits are determined by the natural tolerance of the process while specification limits are determined externally—usually by management, engineers, customers, and so on. There is no relationship between specification limits and control limits. Suppose we are monitoring the sample mean $\bar{x}$ where the population of interest is normally distributed with mean μ and standard deviation σ. The different limits could be written as:

Natural limits: $\mu \pm 3\sigma$

Control limits: $\bar{x} \pm 3\dfrac{\sigma}{\sqrt{n}}$

Specification limits: [LSL , USL] (determined externally)

3. PROCESS CAPABILITY INDICES

> Define, select, and calculate C_p, C_{pk}, C_{pm}, and C_r, and evaluate process capability.
> (Evaluate)
>
> **Body of Knowledge VI.G.3**

Various capability indices have been developed to try to quantify process capability in a single number. The stability and normality requirements discussed earlier must be met for these measures to be effective. Four such indices are C_p, C_r, C_{pk}, and C_{pm}.

C_p

C_p compares the tolerance (the width of the engineering specifications) with the natural process tolerance. C_p is given by

$$C_p = \frac{USL - LSL}{6\sigma}$$

where LSL is the lower specification limit and USL is the upper specification limit. The true process standard deviation σ is usually unknown and must be estimated from the sample data. We can use the sample standard deviation s or $\hat{\sigma} = \bar{R}/d_2$ if control charts are used in the analysis. The estimate of C_p is

$$\hat{C}_p = \frac{USL - LSL}{6\hat{\sigma}}.$$

Consider the previous example involving a quality characteristic with specification limits set at 2.125 ± 0.05 and $\hat{\sigma} = 0.00236$. Our estimate of C_p is

$$\hat{C}_p = \frac{USL - LSL}{6\hat{\sigma}} = \frac{2.130 - 2.120}{6(0.00236)} = 0.706.$$

Generally, it is desirable for $C_p > 1$. Based on this analysis, the process does not appear to be capable.

C_r

The C_r measure is simply the inverse of C_p, that is, $C_r = 1/C_p$. An estimate of C_r is

$$\hat{C}_r = \frac{6\hat{\sigma}}{USL - LSL}.$$

A simple interpretation of C_r is the percentage of the tolerance (or specification band) that is used up by the process. Consider our example again where it was found that $\hat{C}_p = 0.706$. Then $\hat{C}_r = 1/0.706 = 1.416$. This ratio is sometimes referred to as the capability ratio, and smaller values are better.

C_{pk}

The capability measure C_{pk} penalizes a process whose mean is off center. C_{pk} takes into account process centering and is given by

$$C_{pk} = \min\left[\frac{USL - \mu}{3\sigma}, \frac{\mu - LSL}{3\sigma}\right].$$

It is desirable to have a value of $C_{pk} > 1$, which indicates that the process exceeds the stated minimum requirement. An estimate of C_{pk} is

$$\hat{C}_{pk} = \min\left[\frac{USL - \bar{\bar{x}}}{3\hat{\sigma}}, \frac{\bar{\bar{x}} - LSL}{3\hat{\sigma}}\right].$$

For our example,

$$\hat{C}_{pk} = \min\left[\frac{USL - \bar{\bar{x}}}{3\hat{\sigma}}, \frac{\bar{\bar{x}} - LSL}{3\hat{\sigma}}\right]$$

$$= \min\left[\frac{2.130 - 2.1261}{3(0.00236)}, \frac{2.1261 - 2.120}{3(0.00236)}\right]$$

$$= \min\left[0.551, 0.862\right]$$

$$= 0.551.$$

Historically, a C_{pk} value of 1.0 or larger was considered capable. This would be equivalent to stating that the natural process limits lie inside the tolerance limits.

More recently, quality requirements have become more stringent, and many customers require C_{pk} values of 1.33, 1.66, or 2.00.

C_{pm}

The previous measure C_{pk} was developed to take into account centering of the process. However, studies have shown that a large value of C_{pk} does not necessarily indicate that the location of the process mean is centered between the LSL and USL. A measure was developed to provide a better measure of centering. This measure is denoted by C_{pm} and given by

$$C_{pm} = \frac{USL - LSL}{6\left[\sigma^2 + (\mu - T)^2\right]}.$$

An estimate is then

$$\hat{C}_{pm} = \frac{USL - LSL}{6\left[\hat{\sigma}^2 + (\bar{\bar{x}} - T)^2\right]}$$

where T is the process target. Again, the estimates of μ and σ are obtained from control charts.

The point estimators for the capability indices given in this section each have some degree of error or variability associated with them. It has been recommended that confidence intervals on the process capability indices be constructed to quantify the precision associated with the point estimators. The reader is encouraged to see Kotz and Lovelace (1998) for complete details of the point estimators for and confidence intervals on these and other capability indices.

4. PROCESS PERFORMANCE INDICES

> Define, select, and calculate P_p and P_{pk} and evaluate process performance. (Evaluate)
>
> **Body of Knowledge VI.G.4**

Performance indices provide a picture of current process operation and have been used for comparison and prioritization of improvement efforts. Two such performance indices are P_p and P_{pk}. The performance indices have been recommended for use when the process is *not* in statistical control. The formulas for P_p and P_{pk} are equivalent to those for C_p and C_{pk}, respectively, except that the sample standard deviation

$$s = \sqrt{\frac{\sum_{i=1}^{n}(x_i - \bar{x})^2}{n-1}}$$

is used instead of σ.

The Automotive Industry Action Group (AIAG) and the American National Standards Institute (ANSI) recommend the use of P_p and P_{pk} when the process is not in control. This is a somewhat controversial position because an out-of-control process is by definition unpredictable. Montgomery (2009b) states, "The process performance indices P_p and P_{pk} are actually more than a step backwards. They are a waste of engineering and management effort—they tell you nothing." Wheeler (2005) disagrees with Montgomery and uses P_p and P_{pk} to calculate what he refers to as the effective cost of production. The reader is encouraged to see Kotz and Lovelace (1998) for more discussion on performance and capability indices.

Short-Term versus Long-Term Process Capability

In general, the longer the time span over which the data are collected, the more valid the capability analysis. The analysis of data collected over a few hours can provide information about the process during those hours and may be useful for comparison purposes during process improvement efforts. Using control charts for process capability allows for the evaluation of both short-term process capability and long-term process capability. For example, $\bar{x}$ and R charts provide both instantaneous variability and variability over time.

Nonnormal Data Transformations (Process Capability for Nonnormal Data)

Once again, verifying the normality of a process is important. If the underlying distribution is not normal, the indices described in this chapter may not be valid. Various transformations and alternative indices have been proposed when the distribution is nonnormal. See Kotz and Lovelace (1998), Luceño (1996), Montgomery (2009b), and Rodriquez (1992) for details on dealing with nonnormality and process capability.

Chapter 39

H. Design and Analysis of Experiments

Experiments are an essential part of research and process and product development. It is important to correctly design and implement any experiment to obtain statistically valid results. All experiments can be considered "designed" experiments, but some of them may be designed poorly. Positive results can be achieved when a statistically designed experiment is developed and implemented correctly. Some of the results of a good experimental design include:

- Improvement in process yield

- Reduction in process variability (closer conformance to nominal or target requirements is often achieved)

- Reduction in design and development time

- Reduction in operation costs

Before discussing the actual design and implementation of valid experiments, some important terminology must be introduced.

1. TERMINOLOGY

> Define terms such as dependent and independent variables, factors, levels, response, treatment, error, and replication. (Understand)
>
> **Body of Knowledge VI.H.1**

This section provides definitions for several important basic terms.

Dependent Variable (Response)

In experimental design, the dependent variable or response is the result or outcome of interest of the experiment. For example, yield of a process, time to complete a task, taste score, and so on.

Independent Variables (Factors)

In experimental design these variables, sometimes referred to as *treatments* or *factors*, are chosen by the experimenter or practitioner to determine what effect, if any, they will have on the outcome of the experiment.

Examples:

- Type of gasoline (such as standard, plus, or super)

- Condensation temperature and its effect on yield

- Carbonation level in a test of a soft-drink taste

- Supplier of raw material in a manufacturing process

Factors can be *quantitative* (for example, temperature, amount of fertilizer per acre) or *qualitative* (for example, technician, different additives, supplier, or type of keyboard).

There may be more than one factor under investigation in any one experiment. In addition, factors can take on one of a number of roles. For example, *control factors* are process inputs to be controlled in actual production. These factors can be adjusted in practice to affect the output of a process. *Noise factors,* on the other hand, can be controlled during the experiment, but are allowed to vary naturally in actual production. These factors are difficult to control in practice and can introduce variability into the response of interest. Understanding the effect of noise factors on the response can aid in reducing this variability in practice while not completely removing it. Examples of noise factors can include humidity within a manufacturing plant, ambient temperature, how a product is actually used in practice, and so on.

Levels

Levels in experimental design refers to the levels of the factors. For example, temperature levels of 200, 300, and 400°C; cooking times of one hour or two hours; two suppliers, A and B; and percent additive of 0.2, 0.5, and 0.8 percent.

Treatment

A *treatment* in experimental design refers to a combination of the levels of each factor assigned to an experimental unit. This is sometimes called a *treatment combination*. To illustrate, consider an experiment on the breaking strength of a material. Two factors of interest are the machine (M1, M2, M3) on which the material is produced and the technician (T1, T2) using the machine. One treatment combination would be technician 2 using machine 1 (T2M1). "Treatment" is a term left over from the early days of experimental design and its roots in agricultural experimentation.

Factorial Designs

Factorial designs are those where all treatment combinations of the factors are carried out. Suppose an experiment involves three factors, A, B, and C, with three, five, and two levels investigated, respectively. A full-factorial design would consist of $3 \times 5 \times 2 = 30$ treatment combinations.

Error

Error in experimental design has several meanings. In any experimental situation, error could represent errors in experimentation, errors of measurement, variation in materials or factors in general, or the effect of noise factors on the response, for example. *Experimental error* is the variability that is observed when a treatment combination is repeated, that is, replicated.

Replication

In experimental design, *replication* is the repetition of the basic experiment. This would involve a complete reset of the factor levels and repeating the experiment. Replication will provide an estimate of experimental error and leads to more precise estimates of the factor effects. It should be noted that multiple measurements of a treatment combination do not necessarily constitute replication. There is a significant difference between true replication and *repeated measures.*

Putting It All Together

The objective of a designed experiment is to generate knowledge about a product or process. The experiment seeks to find the effect a set of independent variables has on a set of dependent variables. Mathematically this relationship can be denoted $y = f(x) + \varepsilon$, where x is an independent variable and y is the dependent variable (although there will most likely be more than one independent variable). For example, suppose a machine operator who can adjust the feed, speed, and coolant temperature wishes to find the settings that will produce the best surface finish. The feed, speed, and coolant temperature are the *independent variables* or *factors*. Surface finish is the *dependent variable* or *response* and its value depends on the values of the independent variables. Independent variables may also be thought of as input variables, and dependent variables as output variables. There may be additional independent variables, such as the hardness of the material or humidity of the room, that have an effect on the dependent variable. Other factors, such as hardness or humidity, are considered *noise factors* since they may induce variability in the surface finish but can not necessarily be controlled in actual production. In this example, the experimental design may specify that the speed will be set at 1300 rev/min for part of the experiment and at 1800 rev/min for the remainder. These values are referred to as the *levels* of the speed factor. The team decides to test each factor at two levels, as follows:

- Feed (F): 0.01 and 0.04 in/rev

- Speed (S): 1300 and 1800 rev/min

- Coolant temperature (C): 100° and 140° F

A full-factorial design for the three factors will be used. A full-factorial experiment tests all possible combinations of levels and factors, using one run for each combination. The total number of combinations is given by L^F where F represents the number of factors of interest each with L levels. In this situation, the number of treatment combinations is $2^3 = 8$. The team develops a data collection sheet listing those eight experiments with room for recording five replicates ($n = 5$) for each run (see Figure 39.1).

As the data are collected, the values are recorded as shown in Figure 39.2. These data are also referred to as the response values since they show how the process or product responds to various treatments.

Note that the five values for a particular run are not all the same. This may be due to drift in the factor levels, variation in the measurement system, and/or the influence of noise factors. The variation observed in the readings for a particular run is referred to as *experimental error*. If the number of replications is decreased, the calculation of experimental error is less accurate although the experiment has a lower total cost. If all the factors that impact the dependent variable are included in the experiment and all measurements are exact, replication is not needed and a very efficient experiment could be conducted. Thus, the accurate determination of experimental error and cost are competing design properties.

Run #	Feed	Speed	C temp	1	2	3	4	5
1	0.01	1300	100					
2	0.01	1300	140					
3	0.01	1800	100					
4	0.01	1800	140					
5	0.04	1300	100					
6	0.04	1300	140					
7	0.04	1800	100					
8	0.04	1800	140					

Figure 39.1 A 2^3 full-factorial data collection sheet.

Run #	Feed	Speed	C temp	1	2	3	4	5
1	0.01	1300	100	10.1	10.0	10.2	9.8	9.9
2	0.01	1300	140	3.0	4.0	3.0	5.0	5.0
3	0.01	1800	100	6.5	7.0	5.3	5.0	6.2
4	0.01	1800	140	1.0	3.0	3.0	1.0	2.0
5	0.04	1300	100	5.0	7.0	9.0	8.0	6.0
6	0.04	1300	140	4.0	7.0	5.0	6.0	8.0
7	0.04	1800	100	5.8	6.0	6.1	6.2	5.9
8	0.04	1800	140	3.1	2.9	3.0	2.9	3.1

Figure 39.2 A 2^3 full-factorial data collection sheet with data entered.

Run #	Feed	Speed	C temp	Average surface finish reading
1	0.01	1300	100	10
2	0.01	1300	140	4
3	0.01	1800	100	6
4	0.01	1800	140	2
5	0.04	1300	100	7
6	0.04	1300	140	6
7	0.04	1800	100	6
8	0.04	1800	140	3

Figure 39.3 A 2^3 full-factorial data collection sheet with run averages.

Once the data are collected as shown in Figure 39.2, it may be useful to find the average of the five replication responses for each run. These averages are shown in Figure 39.3.

2. PLANNING AND ORGANIZING EXPERIMENTS

> Define, describe, and apply the basic elements of designed experiments, including determining the experiment objective, selecting factors, responses, and measurement methods, choosing the appropriate design, etc. (Analyze)
>
> **Body of Knowledge VI.H.2**

Planning and organizing a designed experiment is just as important as conducting the experiment and analyzing the results. Some of the important steps in planning and organizing experiments include

1. State the objective

2. Choose the factors and responses

3. Define measurement methods

4. Choose an appropriate design

The team making these types of choices and decisions should include engineers, technicians, management, customers, statisticians, and others who have firsthand knowledge of and experience with the process under study. It is important to ensure that the experiment is conducted as planned. Errors that occur as the experiment is carried out or errors in the measurements could deliver invalid results.

When preparing to conduct an experiment, the first consideration is, "What question are we seeking to answer?" In the example illustrated in the previous section the objective was to find the combination of process settings that minimize the surface finish reading.

Objective

The objective of a designed experiment is considered the goal of the experiment. Recognition of and statement of the problem is the first step in designing a successful experiment. Although stating the objective of the problem may seem obvious, it is not always given due consideration in the initial stages of planning the experiment.

Choice of Factors

The response (or responses) of interest are the outputs to be measured. The responses should represent all aspects of quality, productivity, and functionality. What factors might significantly affect the response? In most processes we could measure a very large number of variables of which only a few have any real impact on the response. Initially, many factors should be included and screening experiments carried out to eliminate those factors that do not significantly affect the response. One task in designing an experiment is to maximize the chance of including the significant variables in the design and leaving out those that have little impact.

The levels of the factors should also be given serious consideration. The span or scope of the experimental conditions will have an impact on one's ability to determine the significance of a factor. For example, should the range of temperature be from 100° C to 200° C or 125° C to 175° C for a particular problem? If the range is too narrow, important effects could be completely missed.

Responses and Measurement Methods

Once the objective of the experiment has been determined and factors and levels selected, an appropriate measurement system is chosen. The measurement method is determined by the response that has been decided on. For example, if the outcome measured is placed into one of several possible categories (categorical data), the response that will be modeled or used in the analysis would be quite different than if the measured outcome is continuous. The measurement system must be appropriate for the type of response of interest and can only be determined by people familiar with the process and output. Regardless of the type of response, methods exist that can adequately address these issues. This is discussed in Section 3 of this chapter.

Choice of Design

Once the objective of the experiment has been decided on, the factors, levels, and responses determined, and the method of measurement chosen, the next step is to choose the type of design to be used. The choice of design will depend on the previous steps (stating the objective, choosing factors, levels, and responses, and determining the measurement method). Other important considerations include the size of the design that is acceptable, the number of replicates, the run order of the design, and whether or not blocking is involved. Many standard statistical packages aid the practitioner in determining an appropriate design. In choosing the appropriate design, the objective of the experiment should always be kept in mind. Therefore, rather than designing a massive experiment involving many variables and levels, it is usually best to begin with more modest screening designs whose purpose is to determine the variables and levels that need further study.

3. DESIGN PRINCIPLES

> Define and apply the principles of power and sample size, balance, replication, order, efficiency, randomization, blocking, interaction, and confounding. (Apply)
>
> **Body of Knowledge VI.H.3**

Once the experiment is planned and carried out, and the outcomes recorded, appropriate analysis is necessary to make final decisions on factors, factor settings, and prediction. Some analysis techniques are described at the end of this section.

Randomization

Randomization in experimental design is the ordering of the treatment combinations in a sequence that will reduce the effect of uncontrolled variables that might affect the dependent variable. Randomization will reduce the effect of unwanted nuisance factors that are not part of the experiment but may influence the results.

Returning to the surface finish example given earlier, there are eight treatments with five replications per treatment. This produces 40 tests or treatments. The tests from this design should be performed in random order. This would be referred to as a *completely randomized design.* For the surface finish example, suppose the machine used in the process has some temperature effect; that is, machine temperature increases the longer the machine is running and can possibly affect the surface finish. Furthermore, suppose the treatment combinations are carried out in the order they appear in Figure 39.1. If machine temperature does have an affect on surface finish, and the factor "feed rate" is found to be statistically significant, we can not be sure whether the significant effect is really due to the change in feed rate or due to the temperature of the machine. These two factors could very well be confounded. *Confounding* in experimental design is the term used to signify that the effect of one independent variable is indistinguishable from the effect of another independent variable or combination of independent variables (interactions). The 40 tests in the surface finish example may be randomized in two possible ways:

1. Number the tests from one to 40 and randomize those numbers to obtain the order in which tests are performed. This is referred to as a completely randomized design.

2. Randomize the run order, but once a run is set up, make all five replicates for that run.

Although it usually requires more time and effort, the first method is better. To see that this is true, suppose time of day is a noise factor such that products made before noon are different from those made after noon. By randomizing, the time effect of when the product is made is minimized. In this way, if significant effects of the factors are identified, we are more confident that the effect is due to the changes made in the controllable factors than outside, often uncontrollable, factors.

Blocking/Local Control of Error

There are many instances when a factor may affect the response of interest but it is not a factor in which we are interested. These factors are often referred to as *nuisance* factors. For example, suppose the 40 tests in the surface finish example can not be conducted during one shift, but must be carried out over two shifts. In addition, it is believed that the shift may have an effect on surface finish. The team would be concerned about the impact the shift difference could have on the results.

Randomization can often reduce the effects of a nuisance factor when there is no way of controlling this factor in practice. If the nuisance factor is known and can be controlled for purposes of experimentation, then the factor can be taken into account during testing. A technique called *blocking* can be used to eliminate the effect of the nuisance factor. By removing the influence of this factor, the statistical analysis is more likely to reveal whether the factor of interest is truly significant or not. The simplest form of blocking is pairing used to compare two dependent samples (see Chapter 35 for discussion of paired comparisons).

Blocking is one form of R. A. Fisher's concept of *local control of error.* In general, local control refers to grouping experimental units in such a way that units within the group are homogeneous. This type of control aids in eliminating the variability or noise due to inactive or extraneous factors. Local control also includes the use of covariates when blocking is not possible in an experiment.

Interactions

An *interaction* in experimental design describes the change in the response when two or more factors are interdependent. Interactions are discussed in some detail in Chapter 35 and also further in this chapter with respect to factorial designs.

Efficiency

The purpose for conducting a statistically designed experiment is to gain as much relevant information as possible with a minimum amount of cost (cost would include time, money, resources, and so on). Therefore, it is important to construct and carry out an *efficient* designed experiment. An efficiently designed experiment is one that will include the minimum number of runs and minimize the amount of resources, personnel, and time that are utilized. Most statistically designed experiments are efficient and economical. Experiments that are not statistically designed are often expensive and inefficient and can often result in waste of resources.

Analysis of Results

Designed experiments, when conducted properly, can lead to very reliable results that provide insight into the important factors and optimal level settings. Properly designed experiments and the results of appropriate analysis easily lend themselves to sequential experimentation for more detailed understanding and modeling of the process. The analysis of the results involves some very straightforward but important steps:

- *Exploratory and graphical analysis.* Simple plots and tables of the data can provide insight into the process.

- *Model fitting.* Mathematical models of the form $y = f(x) + \varepsilon$ are built and provide a relationship between the response and the independent variables.

- *Fine-tuning the model.* Not all independent variables will be significantly related to the response. Several analysis steps can be taken to remove terms from the fitted model that have no significant effect on the response.

- *Model diagnostics.* Assumptions should be verified. The use of plots (such as residual plots) is useful in this step.

- *Refine the model.* This step is necessary if any of the assumptions are violated. Model refitting may be necessary, or a new form of the model investigated.

In the next several sections various basic designs and analysis techniques are presented. Complete details on these and other aspects of experimental designs can be found in Montgomery (2009a).

4. ONE-FACTOR EXPERIMENTS

> Construct one-factor experiments such as completely randomized, randomized block, and Latin square designs, and use computational and graphical methods to analyze the significance of results. (Analyze)
>
> **Body of Knowledge VI.H.4**

One-factor experiments were first introduced in Chapter 35 when analysis of variance was introduced. In that presentation, the analysis approach for a single factor with several levels (we also referred to this as comparing several treatments) was outlined. The same analysis of variance approach is used when analyzing data from designed experiments.

We will now introduce a slightly different form of the model than given previously. The reader will often see both of these models in the literature, so both are presented in this handbook.

Analysis of Variance for One-Factor Experiments

As discussed in Chapter 35, if we are interested in comparing more than two levels for a single factor, we must use an appropriately designed experiment and analyze it with analysis of variance (ANOVA) techniques. It is assumed that the experiment has been carried out as a completely randomized design.

A general model for the response of interest y involving a levels (or treatments) each with n replicates can modeled as

$$y_{ij} = \mu + \tau_i + \varepsilon_{ij}$$

$$\text{for } i = 1, 2, \ldots, a \text{ and } j = 1, 2, \ldots, n$$

where

y_{ij} = jth observation from the ith factor level.

μ = overall mean.

τ_i is the parameter representing the effect of the ith factor level.

ε_{ij} is the error associated with the jth observation from the ith factor level.

In a one-factor design and corresponding experiment, we are trying to determine if there is a significant difference among the a factor levels. Since τ_i represents the ith factor level and we assume that factor levels do not affect the response differently from one another, our null hypothesis to be tested is

$$H_0: \tau_1 = \tau_2 = \ldots = \tau_a = 0$$

against the alternative

$$H_a: \tau_i \neq 0 \text{ for at least one } i.$$

The analysis of variance approach presented in Section 5 of Chapter 35 applies to the one-factor experimental design, with the model and hypotheses of interest written in a different form. We will now turn our attention to one-factor experiments where blocking should be included.

Randomized Block Designs

Often in one-factor experiments there may be a nuisance factor that may have some influence on the results. This factor is considered a blocking factor and should be included when carrying out the design and analyzing the results. We are not interested in determining whether the levels of the blocking factor are significantly different, but the factor should be included in the experimental design nonetheless. In general, for randomized block designs:

- The blocking factor is not modeled as being involved in an interaction with the treatments. Including the blocking factor reduces its effect on the response. This will allows for estimation of factor (independent variable)–level effects.

- We are interested in determining whether the factor levels are statistically significantly different, but we are not interested in determining whether the levels of the *blocking factor* are statistically significantly different. There is already some reason to believe that the blocking factor would influence the results.

- If we do not include the blocking variable in a designed experiment and it should be included, we could reach incorrect conclusions about the factor we are investigating.

General Model and Notation

Suppose we have *a* levels of the factor of interest (or treatments), *b* levels of the blocking factor, and a response denoted *y*. A general model for the response of interest is

$$y_{ij} = \mu + \tau_i + \beta_j + \varepsilon_{ij}$$

for $i = 1, 2, \ldots, a$ and $j = 1, 2, \ldots, b$

where

y_{ij} = the response for the *i*th factor level and the *j*th level of the blocking factor.

μ = overall mean.

τ_i = the parameter representing the effect of the *i*th level of the factor of interest.

β_j = the parameter representing the effect of the *j*th level of the blocking factor.

ε_{ij} = the error associated with the *i*th level of the factor of interest and the *j*th level of the blocking factor.

In a randomized block design and corresponding experiment, we are trying to determine if there is a significant difference among the *a* levels of the factor of interest. The null hypothesis of interest is

$$H_0: \tau_1 = \tau_2 = \ldots = \tau_a = 0$$

against the alternative

$$H_a: \tau_i \neq 0 \text{ for at least one } i.$$

A general display of the data is given below.

Treatment	Blocks				Treatment totals
	1	2	...	b	
1	y_{11}	y_{12}	...	y_{1b}	$y_{1.}$
2	y_{21}	y_{22}	...	y_{2b}	$y_{2.}$
⋮	⋮	⋮	⋮	⋮	⋮
a	y_{a1}	y_{a2}	...	y_{ab}	$y_{a.}$
Block totals	$y_{.1}$	$y_{.2}$	...	$y_{.b}$	$y_{..}$

where

- The totals are the sum across that particular row or column.

- $y_{..}$ is the sum of all the observations in the entire experiment.

- The total number of observations is given by $N = a \times b$.

Note that in this illustration there is exactly one observation per cell (that is, a single replicate, $n = 1$).

The following formulas are necessary to carry out an analysis for any randomized block design with one treatment of interest and one blocking factor. The same notation as presented earlier will be used here to maintain consistency. In randomized block designs, the total sum of squares can be partitioned as follows:

$$SS_T = SS_{Factor} + SS_{Block} + SS_E$$

The total sum of squares SS_T is given by

$$SS_T = \sum_{i=1}^{a} \sum_{j=1}^{b} \left(y_{ij} - \overline{y}_{..} \right)^2 = \sum_{i=1}^{a} \sum_{j=1}^{b} y_{ij}^2 - \frac{y_{..}^2}{N}$$

where y_{ij} is a single observation. The total degrees of freedom are $N - 1$.

The *sum of squares due to different factor levels* SS_{Factor} (this was also referred to as $SS_{Treatments}$ in Chapter 35) is a portion of SS_T that represents the variability explained by or due to the factor levels themselves:

$$SS_{Factor} = b \sum_{i=1}^{a} \left(\overline{y}_{i.} - \overline{y}_{..} \right)^2 = \frac{1}{b} \sum_{i=1}^{a} y_{i.}^2 - \frac{y_{..}^2}{N}$$

The degrees of freedom for the factor of interest would be $a - 1$.

The *sum of squares due to different levels of the blocking factor* SS_{Block} is the portion of the SS_T that represents the variability explained by or due to the different block levels themselves:

$$SS_{Block} = a\sum_{j=1}^{b}\left(\overline{y}_{.j} - \overline{y}_{..}\right)^2 = \frac{1}{a}\sum_{j=1}^{b} y_{.j}^2 - \frac{y_{..}^2}{N}$$

The degrees of freedom for the blocking factor are $b - 1$.

The *error sum of squares* SS_E is that portion of the SS_T that represents the inherent variability and can be found by subtraction:

$$SS_E = SS_T - SS_{Factor} - SS_{Block}$$

The degrees of freedom for error are $(a - 1)(b - 1)$.

As before, the sums of squares will be converted into mean square quantities and the appropriate test statistics calculated. An analysis of variance table can be constructed to summarize the test.

Analysis of Variance (ANOVA) Table

The ANOVA table for a randomized block design is shown as Table 39.1.

As with the completely randomized design, reject the null hypothesis if $F_0 > F_{\alpha, a-1, (a-1)(b-1)}$ where α is the level of significance, the numerator degrees of freedom are $a - 1$, and the denominator degrees of freedom are $(a - 1)(b - 1)$. In addition, p values can be used.

Table 39.1   ANOVA table for a randomized block design.

Source of variation	SS	df	MS	F	p value
Factor	SS_{Factor}	$a - 1$	$MS_{Factor} = \dfrac{SS_{Factor}}{a-1}$	$F_0 = \dfrac{MS_{Factor}}{MS_E}$	$P(F > F_0)$
Block	SS_{Block}	$b - 1$	$MS_{Block} = \dfrac{SS_{Block}}{b-1}$		
Error	SS_E	$(a-1)(b-1)$	$MS_{Error} = \dfrac{SS_E}{(a-1)(b-1)}$		
Total	SS_T	$N - 1$			

EXAMPLE 39.1

Four washing solutions are to be compared to study their effectiveness in retarding bacteria growth on a particular type of produce. The analysis is conducted in a lab and the experiment is carried out over a three-day period. The results are recorded and given in the following table:

Continued

Continued

Solution	Day 1	Day 2	Day 3
1	21	11	12
2	22	21	13
3	31	17	21
4	15	12	8

In this experiment:

- The treatment or factor is washing solution. The goal is to determine if there is a statistically significant difference between the four types of solution.

- The blocking factor is "day." Day is the blocking factor because it is believed that the day on which the measurements are taken is a source of variability. It is not a goal to determine if there is a statistically significant difference between the days. We believe that the day does make a difference and that is the reason we used it as a block.

- We are not interested in interactions between the washing solution and the day.

There are three levels of the blocking factor "day," so $b = 3$. There are four levels of washing solution, thus $a = 4$. An analysis of variance will be conducted to determine whether there is any statistically significant difference between washing solutions. We will test at the five percent level of significance. The hypotheses of interest would be:

H_0: $\tau_1 = \tau_2 = \tau_3 = \tau_4 = 0$

H_a: $\tau_i \neq 0$ for at least one $i = 1, 2, 3, 4$

The appropriate sums of squares and degrees of freedom can be found using the formulas given previously. The resulting ANOVA table is given in Table 39.2. The analysis of variance was carried out using a reliable statistical software package.

The p value is less than our stated level of significance, so the null hypothesis is rejected and we conclude that there is a statistically significant difference between the four washing solutions. The type of washing solution appears to have a significant effect on retarding bacteria growth.

Table 39.2   ANOVA table for the washing solution example.

Source of variation	df	SS	MS	F	p value
Washing solution	$4 - 1 = 3$	218.0	$\dfrac{218.0}{3} = 72.67$	$\dfrac{72.67}{11.08} = 6.56$	0.025
Day	$3 - 1 = 2$	171.5	$\dfrac{171.5}{2} = 85.75$		
Error	$(4 - 1)(3 - 1) = 6$	66.5	$\dfrac{66.5}{6} = 11.08$		
Total	$12 - 1 = 11$	456.0			

Multiple comparison techniques can be carried out to determine which washing solution is better at retarding (minimizes) bacteria growth.

The Importance of Blocking

Blocking can be very important in a designed experiment. If there is an indication that an underlying (nuisance) factor exists that will influence the response of interest, then it should be included in the experiment as a blocking factor. If a nuisance factor is influencing the response and it is not included in the designed experiment as a blocking factor, then the final conclusion (reject or not reject the null hypothesis) could be incorrect. Consider the washing solution example again, but without "day" as the blocking factor.

EXAMPLE 39.2

Suppose "day" was not included in the experiment as the blocking factor in the previous example. The experiment would contain only the factor of interest (washing solution) and becomes a one-factor experimental design. The data table would look like the following:

Solution	Growth		
1	21	11	12
2	22	21	13
3	31	17	21
4	15	12	8

where

- There is one factor, the washing solutions with four levels, that is $a = 4$.

- There are three observations for each type of solution, that is $n = 3$.

The hypotheses of interest are the same as if the blocking factor had been included:

$H_0: \tau_1 = \tau_2 = \tau_3 = \tau_4 = 0$

$H_a: \tau_i \neq 0$ for at least one $i = 1, 2, 3, 4$

Using the same level of significance, $\alpha = 0.05$, we can calculate the sum of squares and construct the ANOVA table for a one-factor experimental design (completely randomized design). Here, $a = 4$, $n = 3$, and $N = an - 1 = 12 - 1 = 11$. The ANOVA table is given in Table 39.3.

Since the p value is quite large ($0.139 > 0.05$), we do not reject the null hypothesis and conclude that there is *no significant difference* between the four washing solutions.

Continued

Continued

Table 39.3 ANOVA table for the washing solution example without blocking.

Source of variation	df	SS	MS	F	p value
Washing solution	$4 - 1 = 3$	218.0	$\dfrac{218.0}{3} = 72.67$	$\dfrac{72.67}{29.8} = 2.44$	0.139
Error	$4(3 - 1) = 8$	238.0	$\dfrac{238.0}{8} = 29.8$		
Total	$12 - 1 = 11$	456.0			

Remarks

The two previous examples demonstrate the importance of considering a possible blocking factor. If there is some underlying factor influencing the response and this factor is not taken into consideration, then the results of the experimental design could be incorrect. If there is any doubt about whether or not a nuisance factor is influencing the results, then it would be in the experimenter's best interest to include the factor in the experiment and carry out a randomized block design. It is important to note that once the experiment has been carried out with blocking included, we *can not* reanalyze the experiment as if it were not blocked.

Finally, a residual analysis should be conducted in order to test the assumption that the observations are normally and independently distributed with equal variance across factor levels. If there is a serious violation of one or more of the assumptions, a transformation may be necessary. Other methods for dealing with violated assumptions can be found in Devore (2007), Montgomery (2009a), Montgomery and Runger (2006), or Vining and Kowalski (2006).

5. FULL-FACTORIAL EXPERIMENTS

> Construct full-factorial designs and use computational and graphical methods to analyze the significance of results. (Analyze)
>
> **Body of Knowledge VI.H.5**

In full-factorial experiments all possible combinations of the levels of factors are investigated. The two-factor factorial was introduced in Chapter 35 when discussing the two-way ANOVA. Consider an experiment that involves exactly two factors of interest, A and B, where there are a levels of factor A, b levels of factor B, and n replicates at each combination of A and B. The general model that would describe the response of interest y is given as

$$y_{ijk} = \mu + \tau_i + \beta_j + (\tau\beta)_{ij} + \varepsilon_{ijk}$$

$$\text{for } i = 1, 2, \ldots, a; \; j = 1, 2, \ldots, b; \text{ and } k = 1, 2, \ldots, n$$

where

y_{ijk} = the kth response at the combination of the ith level of A and the jth level of B

μ = the overall mean effect

τ_i = the parameter for the effect of the ith level of A

β_j = the parameter for the effect of the jth level of B

$(\tau\beta)_{ij}$ = the parameter for the effect of the ijth level of the interaction between A and B

ε_{ijk} = the error

We are interested in the following hypotheses:

H_0: $\tau_1 = \tau_2 = \ldots = \tau_a = 0$ (no significant difference between the levels of factor A)

H_a: $\tau_i \neq 0$, for at least one i

H_0: $\beta_1 = \beta_2 = \ldots = \beta_b = 0$ (no significant difference between the levels of factor B)

H_1: $\beta_j \neq 0$, for at least one j

H_0: $(\tau\beta)_{11} = (\tau\beta)_{12} = \ldots = (\tau\beta)_{ab} = 0$ (no significant interaction between A and B)

H_a: $(\tau\beta)_{ij} \neq 0$ for at least one i or one j.

The sums of squares, degrees of freedom, mean squares, test statistics, and p values can be calculated using a reliable statistical software package. The resulting ANOVA table would look like Table 39.4.

It should be noted that the analysis of variance approach is not the only method for testing the significance of the effects and interactions. If each factor has exactly two levels, it is common to examine the results of t-tests on the coefficients representing each factor and interaction. To build a model as recommended, t-tests can be very useful.

Randomized Block Designs and Factorial Designs

Before presenting the details of factorial designs at two levels, a distinction should be made between a randomized block design and a two-factor full-factorial design. For example, in an experiment involving two factors A and B, we would be interested in:

- Differences between the levels of factor A

- Differences between the levels of factor B

- Whether a significant interaction between A and B exists

Table 39.4   ANOVA table for two-factor factorial experiment.

Source of variation	df	SS	MS	F	p
Factor A	$a-1$	SS_A	$MS_A = \dfrac{SS_A}{a-1}$	$F_0 = \dfrac{MS_A}{MS_E}$	$P(F > F_0)$
Factor B	$b-1$	SS_B	$MS_B = \dfrac{SS_B}{b-1}$	$F_0 = \dfrac{MS_B}{MS_E}$	$P(F > F_0)$
AB interaction	$(a-1)(b-1)$	SS_{AB}	$MS_{AB} = \dfrac{SS_{AB}}{(a-1)(b-1)}$	$F_0 = \dfrac{MS_{AB}}{MS_E}$	$P(F > F_0)$
Error	$ab(n-1)$	SS_E	$MS_E = \dfrac{SS_E}{ab(n-1)}$		
Total	$abn-1$	SS_T			

When is a design that involves two factors a randomized block design and when is it a factorial design? The distinction between the two types of designs comes from the information that is to be gained from conducting the experiment. For instance, consider an experiment that involves two factors. The type of design to use can be determined if the following remarks are kept in mind.

Use a randomized block design if:

- There is no interest in whether or not significant differences exist between levels of one of the factors (this is the blocking factor). There is some belief that this factor influences the result and by blocking we minimize its influence.

- There is little likelihood that there is an interaction between the two factors involved in the study.

Use a factorial design if:

- There is an interest in determining the differences between the levels of both factors.

- There is an interest in determining whether or not a significant interaction between the two factors exists.

Of course there are other considerations before conducting the experiment. In addition, it is quite possible to have an experiment that involves more than one factor of interest and one or more blocking factors. Designs sometimes used for experiments involving one independent variable and two blocking factors are referred to as *Latin square designs*.

Two-Level Factorial Designs

A special type of factorial design that receives a great deal of attention is a design where all factors are run at exactly two levels. If there are k factors, then we would say the design is a 2^k factorial design. The number of experimental runs (or observations) is 2^k. For example, consider the surface finish illustration given earlier. There are three factors of interest: feed rate, speed, and coolant temperature, each at two levels. A full-factorial design consists of $2^3 = 8$ runs or treatment combinations.

The two levels of each factor can be coded as –1 and 1, the low and high level of each factor, respectively. Consider an experiment with two factors A and B, each at two levels:

	A	B
Low	–1	–1
High	1	1

There would be a total of four combinations, and we would like to determine if A, B, or AB are significant. The combinations can be written in the following table. To obtain the column for the levels of the AB interaction, multiply column A and column B.

Run	A	B	AB	Responses
1	–1	–1	1	$y_{11}, y_{12}, \ldots$
2	–1	1	–1	$y_{21}, y_{22}, \ldots$
3	1	–1	–1	$y_{31}, y_{32}, \ldots$
4	1	1	1	$y_{41}, y_{42}, \ldots$

Suppose there are two replicates for each run and the average response is calculated. Geometrically, we can display the data on a square for the factors as shown in Figure 39.4.

Each corner of the square represents a run or treatment combination. The values at the corners represent the average response of each combination. For example, at the low level of A and the high level of B the average response is 24.5.

Standard analysis techniques can be applied to the special case of factors with only two levels. We will examine the estimation of the main factors and interaction using an example.

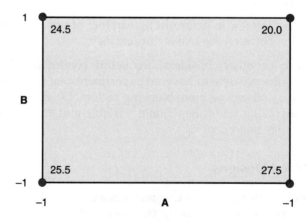

Figure 39.4 All possible combinations of two factors A and B, with two levels each.

EXAMPLE 39.3

In an article by Lee and Awbi (2004), the authors discuss the effect internal partitioning of office space has on room air ventilation. In the design of modern office buildings, it is important to consider the air quality in a room. For office buildings it is desirable to construct a highly energy-efficient building, often with an open-space floor plan. With open-space construction, internal partitions are introduced to design the office to fit the current needs of the company. With internal partitioning, the layout can easily be restructured for different occupants. However, the air ventilation system is designed for open-space rooms. When interferences are introduced (such as office furniture, wall partitions, and so on) the air quality can be significantly affected. In the study on the effect of internal partitioning on room air quality, three factors are of interest: partition location (PL), partition height (PH), and gap underneath (GU). The partition locations are chosen at 40 percent and 60 percent of the room length from the left end of the room. The partition heights are chosen as 60 percent and 80 percent of the room height. The factor "gap underneath" represents the space between the floor and the bottom of the partition. Gap is set at zero percent of the room height and 10 percent of the room height. One response of interest is ventilation effectiveness ε_v, a scaleless quantity that is a function of contamination concentration. Larger values of ε_v indicate better ventilation effectiveness. The tests are conducted on a small scale model test room with the length, width, and height of the room measured in meters. The factors and their levels are given as

Factor	Low level (–1)	High level (+1)
Partition length (A)	40%	60%
Partition height (B)	60%	80%
Gap underneath (C)	0%	10%

Suppose a similar experiment was conducted using these factors to test their effect on ventilation effectiveness. The design used was a 2^3 factorial in two replicates, with results given in Table 39.5 (factors are coded). A complete randomization of the treatments for all 16 runs was carried out.

Table 39.5   Partitioning effect on ventilation effectiveness.

Treatment	A	B	C	ε_v
1	–1	–1	–1	2.227, 1.874
2	1	–1	–1	2.134, 2.252
3	–1	1	–1	1.470, 1.404
4	1	1	–1	2.091, 2.270
5	–1	–1	1	2.073, 1.825
6	1	–1	1	2.162, 2.480
7	–1	1	1	1.615, 1.558
8	1	1	1	2.157, 2.169

Continued

Continued

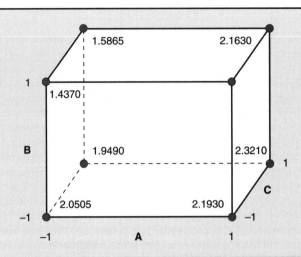

Figure 39.5 Cube plot for partition length, partition height, and gap underneath.

Graphically, we can display the results using the average response for each treatment. Figure 39.5 displays a cube plot for the three factors: partition length (A), partition height (B), and gap underneath (C).

Main Effects

The main effect provides a measure of how each individual factor (main factors such as A, B, and C) affects the response as we move from one level of the factor to the next. The *estimated effect* for each factor is simply the difference in the average response at the high level of the factor and the average response at the low level of the factor. For example, consider the estimated effect of gap underneath. The average response at the high level (+1) of C (gap underneath) is

$$C_{+1} = \frac{2.073+1.825+2.162+2.480+1.615+1.558+2.157+2.169}{8} = 2.005.$$

The average at the low level (–1) of C is

$$C_{-1} = \frac{2.227+1.874+2.134+2.252+1.470+1.404+2.091+2.270}{8} = 1.965.$$

The estimated effect of GU on ventilation effectiveness is then

$$ee(C) = C_{+1} - C_{-1} = 2.005 - 1.965 = 0.04.$$

(The term "estimated effect" is denoted by ee). The estimated effect for C shows that as the gap underneath the partition is changed from zero percent to 10 percent, the average ventilation effectiveness increases by 0.04. The estimated effects of partition length and partition height are calculated similarly and found to be 0.46 and –0.29, respectively. Main effects plots can be useful for examining the change in the factor effects from the low to high levels. Main effects plots for partition length, partition height, and gap underneath are displayed in Figure 39.6.

Continued

Continued

It appears that there is a significant difference between the levels of factor A and the levels of factor B, but not necessarily between the levels of factor C.

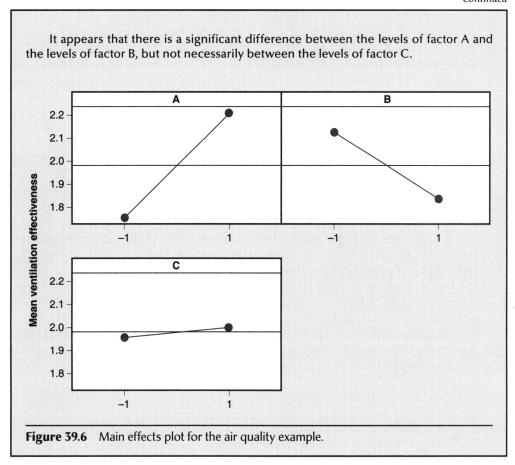

Figure 39.6   Main effects plot for the air quality example.

Using this definition of main effect, the larger the absolute value of the main effect, the more influence that factor has on the quality characteristic. It is possible that the perceived difference between high and low results is not statistically significant. This would occur if the experimental error is so large that it would be impossible to determine whether the difference between the high and low levels is due to a real difference in the dependent variable or due to experimental error. This may be determined by using ANOVA procedures and/or t-tests.

For analysis of data from an experiment, the null hypothesis is that changing the factor level does not make a difference in the dependent variable. The *α-risk* is the probability that the analysis will show that there is a significant difference when there is not. The *β-risk* is the probability that the analysis will show that there is no significant difference when there is. The power of the experiment is defined as $1 - \beta$, so the higher the power of the experiment, the lower the β-risk. In general, a higher number of replications or a larger sample size provides a more precise estimate of experimental error, which in turn reduces the β-risk.

Interaction Effects

As discussed previously, interactions may exist between the factors of interest, and this interaction effect must be determined as was done with the main effects. The interactions in our example include the two-factor interactions and the three-factor interaction: partition length by partition height (AB), partition length by gap underneath (AC), partition height by gap underneath (BC), and partition length by partition height by gap underneath (ABC).

Again, we want to find the average difference in the response between the high and low level of each interaction. What is considered a "high" and "low" level for an interaction? The levels of the interactions are simply the results of the levels of the main effects. In coded form we can label the high and low levels of each interaction simply by multiplying the levels of each factor involved in the interaction. For example, if A is set at its low level (A = –1) and B is set at its high level (B = 1), then the corresponding level of the interaction AB would be –1 (since –1 × 1 = –1). This is simply a label that is convenient for determining the low and high levels of each interaction and is a result of the geometry of the design. The table of *contrasts* for the main effects and interactions for the 2^3 full-factorial design is given as Table 39.6. Notice that any column multiplied by itself results in a column of +1's only. When a column consists of 1's only, it is called the *identity column* and denoted I. For example, A × A = I.

The estimated effects of the interactions can be easily calculated. For example, the average response at the high level of the interaction AB (partition length and partition height) is

$$AB_{+1} = \frac{2.227+1.874+2.091+2.270+2.073+1.825+2.157+2.169}{8} = 2.086.$$

The average response at the low level of AB is

$$AB_{-1} = \frac{2.134+2.252+1.470+1.404+2.162+2.480+1.615+1.558}{8} = 1.884.$$

Table 39.6 Main effect and interaction table of contrasts for the ventilation example.

Treatment	A	B	C	AB	AC	BC	ABC	ε_v
1	–1	–1	–1	1	1	1	–1	2.227, 1.874
2	1	–1	–1	–1	–1	1	1	2.134, 2.252
3	–1	1	–1	–1	1	–1	1	1.470, 1.404
4	1	1	–1	1	–1	–1	–1	2.091, 2.270
5	–1	–1	1	1	–1	–1	1	2.073, 1.825
6	1	–1	1	–1	1	–1	–1	2.162, 2.480
7	–1	1	1	–1	–1	1	–1	1.615, 1.558
8	1	1	1	1	1	1	1	2.157, 2.169

The estimated effect of the AB interaction is then

$$ee(AB) = AB_{+1} - AB_{-1} = 2.086 - 1.884 = 0.202.$$

The remaining interaction effects can be estimated similarly. The estimated effects for all of the main effects and interactions are given in Table 39.7.

Interaction plots are often useful for examining the two-factor interactions. Recall that interaction plots are discussed in Chapter 35. The interaction plots for our example are given in Figures 39.7 through 39.9.

Based on the interaction plots, it is possible that a significant interaction exists between partition length (A) and partition height (B). There may be a significant interaction between partition height (B) and gap underneath (C), but that is not definitive. Lastly, there does not appear to be a significant interaction between partition length (A) and gap underneath (C). Again, the plots may be somewhat subjective (especially in Figure 39.8), and more statistically-based evidence is needed.

Table 39.7   Estimated effects for the air quality example.

Factor	Estimated effect (ee)	Factor	Estimated effect (ee)
A	0.456	BC	0.016
B	−0.287	AC	0.026
C	0.040	ABC	−0.099
AB	0.202		

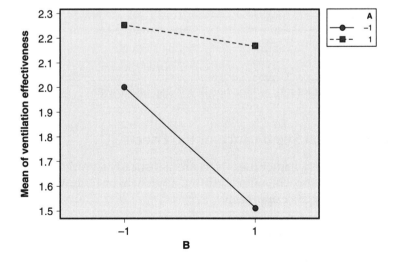

Figure 39.7   Interaction plot for partition length and partition height.

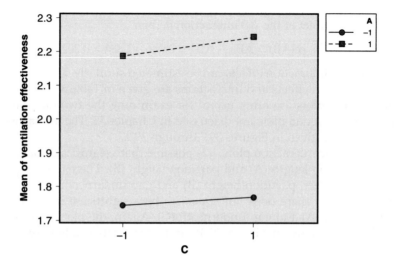

Figure 39.8 Interaction plot for partition length and gap underneath.

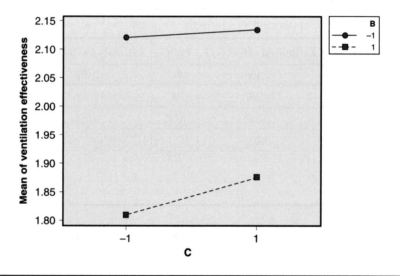

Figure 39.9 Interaction plot for partition height and gap underneath.

Testing for Statistical Significance of the Effects

We can determine whether the effects are statistically significant using the analysis of variance approach, a model-fitting approach, or both. We will first look at the analysis of variance approach.

Analysis of Variance Approach

In the analysis of variance approach, sums of squares are calculated for each effect and the experimental error. The degree of freedom for factors with exactly two

Part VI.H.5

levels (–1, +1) is 1 (the number of levels minus 1 as with all factorial designs). The sums of squares for each factor can be found easily using the estimated effects and can be shown to be

$$SS_{Factor} = n2^{k-2}(ee)^2$$

where n is the number of replicates and k is the number of factors. Test statistics can be calculated for each factor and each interaction. All of this information can be summarized in an analysis of variance table. The ANOVA table for our example is given in Table 39.8, where degrees of freedom for error are $2^k(n-1)$ and total degrees of freedom are $n2^k - 1$. Based on the results of the analysis of variance, it appears that factors A and B and the interaction AB are significant. This is evident by the small p values for each of these terms. Based on these results, the analysis should be carried out again but with only the significant terms included. The results for the new analysis are given in Table 39.9. Again, the main effects of A and B and the interaction AB are statistically significant. From the ANOVA table we also see that $\hat{\sigma}^2 = MS_E = 0.01832$.

Table 39.8 ANOVA table for the ventilation example.

Source	df	SS	MS	F	p
A	1	0.84135	0.84135	39.48	0.000
B	1	0.32862	0.32862	15.42	0.004
C	1	0.00628	0.00628	0.29	0.602
AB	1	0.16221	0.16221	7.61	0.025
AC	1	0.00098	0.00098	0.05	0.836
BC	1	0.00278	0.00278	0.13	0.727
ABC	1	0.03930	0.03930	1.84	0.211
Error	8	0.17048	0.02131		
Total	15	1.55199			

Table 39.9 ANOVA table for the ventilation example.

Source	df	SS	MS	F	p
A	1	0.84135	0.84135	45.93	0.000
B	1	0.32862	0.32862	17.94	0.001
AB	1	0.16221	0.16221	8.86	0.012
Error	12	0.21982	0.01832		
Total	15	1.55199			

We can determine which levels of the factors will result in large values for ventilation effectiveness. More details on determining these levels are provided later in this chapter.

We will now present the model-fitting approach. The model-fitting approach is simply the regression analysis procedure described in Chapter 36. It is used to fit a model relating the dependent variable (response) and independent variables (factors). Multiple linear regression was briefly introduced in Chapter 36.

Model-Fitting Approach

Model fitting (regression analysis) and ANOVA are not necessarily separate approaches. An analysis of variance is often reported when the regression approach is used to study the effects of the factors and interactions on the response. A model relating the independent variables and dependent variable (response) can be given by

$$y = \beta_0 + \beta_1 x_1 + \beta_2 x_2 + \ldots + \beta_k x_k + \varepsilon$$

where y is the response of interest and $x_1, x_2, \ldots, x_k$ represent the independent variables. In our factorial designs, the independent variables are our factors such as A, B, C, and the interactions among the factors AB, AC, BC, and ABC. To illustrate, we can let x_1 represent factor A, x_2 represent factor B, and so on. Note that the convention to let $x_1 x_2$ represent the AB interaction, for example, is used. The coefficients β_i on each term can be tested using t-tests as done in Chapter 36. The null hypothesis of interest is H_0: $\beta_i = 0$ for all i. Results of the t-test for the air quality example are given in Table 39.10.

The "Effect" column displays the estimated effects for the main effects and interactions. Based on the p values for the t-tests we again conclude that partition length, partition height, and the interaction between the two factors are significant. The analysis should be rerun involving only the terms found significant. A model relating ventilation effectiveness to partition length, partition height, and

Table 39.10 t-tests for factors and interactions for the air quality example.

Term	Effect	Coef	SE Coef	t	p
Constant	—	1.9851	0.03649	54.39	0.000
A	0.4586	0.2293	0.03649	6.28	0.000
B	−0.2866	−0.1433	0.03649	−3.93	0.004
C	0.0396	0.0198	0.03649	0.54	0.602
AB	0.2014	0.1007	0.03649	2.76	0.025
AC	0.0156	0.0078	0.03649	0.21	0.836
BC	0.0264	0.0132	0.03649	0.36	0.727
ABC	−0.0991	−0.0496	0.03649	−1.36	0.211

the interaction can now be fit. The column labeled "Coef" provides the estimates of the coefficients in the regression model

$$\hat{y} = 1.9851 + 0.2293x_1 - 0.1433x_2 + 0.1007x_1x_2$$

where x_1 represents partition length, x_2 represents the partition height, and x_1x_2 represents the interaction between the two factors. It should also be noted that the coefficient estimates are one-half of the estimated effects. The fitted model above is in coded form. That is, if we want to make predictions for certain levels of the factors, we would use the notation $(-1, 1)$ to plug into the equation. For example, if we wanted to predict the ventilation effectiveness for the low levels of A and B, we would let $x_1 = -1$ and $x_2 = -1$ in our fitted model:

$$\hat{y} = 1.9851 + 0.2293x_1 - 0.1433x_2 + 0.1007x_1x_2$$

$$= 1.9851 + 0.2293(-1) - 0.1433(-1) + 0.1007(-1)(-1)$$

$$= 2.0$$

The model can also be written in terms of the actual levels of the factors. It is recommended that the model fitting be done using a reliable statistical software package. The model using the actual levels can be shown to be

$$\hat{y} = 7.208 - 0.0829A - 0.0907B + 0.0015AB.$$

The predicted value when partition length and partition height are at their low levels is found by replacing A and B with the actual levels of the factors. For A at its low level (40) and B at its low level (60), the predicted value is

$$\hat{y} = 7.208 - 0.0829A - 0.0907B + 0.0015AB$$

$$= 7.208 - 0.0829(40) - 0.0907(60) + 0.0015(40)(60)$$

$$= 2.05.$$

The difference between this estimate and the one from the model in coded units is due strictly to round-off error. Either model can be used to fit the data. In addition, the actual levels in this example are left as percentage values such as 40 and not converted to decimal form such as 0.40. This was only by choice. Using a statistical package we could have stated the lower level and upper level of partition length as 0.40 and 0.60, respectively, but we chose to use 40 and 60. The same main effects and interaction would still be found to be significant.

Residual Analysis

Once the model has been refined so that it contains only those terms that are statistically significant, the three assumptions of normality, independence, and constant variance should be investigated. If the order in which the treatments were carried out was not recorded, the independence assumption will be difficult to verify. Hopefully, by randomizing all 16 runs while all extraneous factors are held constant there is no significant problem with dependency. Again, it is desirable to actually be able to check this assumption.

Recall that the residuals are defined as $e_i = y_i - \hat{y}_i$ where the predicted values are found as shown previously. The 16 residuals can be calculated and analyzed through residual plots. The normal probability plot of the residuals is shown in Figure 39.10. The residuals appear to fall along a straight line, so the normality assumption does not appear to be violated. The residuals plotted against the significant factors are displayed in Figure 39.11 and Figure 39.12. There does not appear to be a problem with constant variance across the factor level.

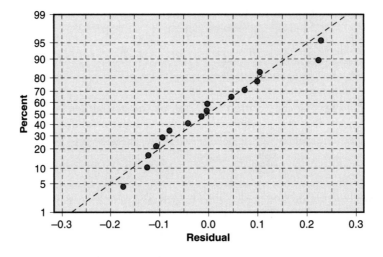

Figure 39.10   Normal probability plot of the residuals for the air quality example.

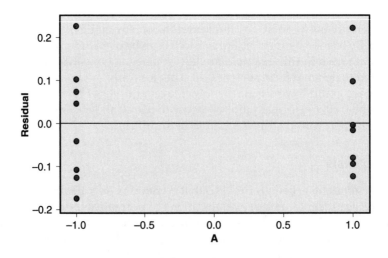

Figure 39.11   Residuals plotted against levels of factor A (partition length).

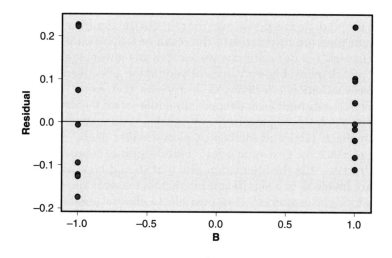

Figure 39.12   Residuals plotted against factor B (partition height).

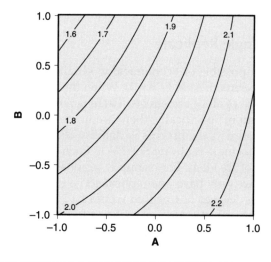

Figure 39.13   Contour plot for the air quality example.

Determining the Optimal Settings of the Important Factors

Now that the significant terms are identified and the necessary assumptions have been shown to be satisfied, the next step is to determine the optimal settings for the significant factors. In our example, a goal is to maximize the ventilation effectiveness. There are several ways to determine these settings. We will discuss two graphical methods.

A useful graphical display of the fitted model is a *contour plot*. The contour plot for our fitted model in coded form is shown in Figure 39.13. A contour plot displays the predicted response over the range of the significant factors. Notice that the contour lines are *curved*; this is the result of a significant interaction between the two factors. For our example, we see that the lower right-hand corner of the contour plot displays higher values of ventilation effectiveness. If the goal is to maximize ventilation effectiveness, it appears that factor A (partition length) should be set at its high level (60 percent) while factor B (partition height) should be set at its low level (60 percent).

Main effects plots and interaction plots are also useful graphical displays of the results. Since the two main effects found significant are involved in a significant interaction, it is the interaction plot that should be examined. In fact, if the factors are involved in a significant interaction but only the main effects plots of these factors are examined, it is possible to choose less-than-optimal settings of the factors. Recall the interaction plot of factors A and B displayed in Figure 39.7. On this figure we see that the highest ventilation effectiveness occurs at the low level of B (partition height) and high level of A (partition length).

The reader is encouraged to consult Devore (2007), Montgomery and Runger (2006), Montgomery, Runger, and Hubele (2006), or Vining and Kowalski (2006) for more details on methods for determining acceptable levels of the significant factors.

2^k Designs with a Single Replicate

Often it is not possible or economical to obtain more than a single replicate for a designed experiment (that is, $n = 1$). When this is the case it is not possible to test the significance of all of the effects. There is no *internal estimate* of error since there is no replication. Specifically, there are no degrees of freedom left over for error in order to estimate the process variability σ^2. The total degrees of freedom for a design with a single replicate are $2^k - 1$. Each main effect and interaction is given one degree of freedom. For example, suppose that in our ventilation effectiveness example we only have one replicate. The total number of runs would be eight and the total degrees of freedom would be $2^k - 1 = 8 - 1 = 7$. Furthermore, there are three main effects (A, B, and C) and four interactions (AB, AC, BC, and ABC). Since every effect has one degree of freedom, all of the degrees of freedom are used. There are no degrees of freedom for error. *t*-tests and the analysis of variance method can not be carried out.

To address this issue, there are several approaches that can be employed. The approaches are often based on the *sparsity-of-effects principle*. That is, an assumption is made that some higher-order interactions are *negligible* (orders higher than two-factor interactions) and the system being investigated is believed to be dominated by the main effects and the low-order interactions. Under this assumption the degrees of freedom for the higher-order interactions are pooled into error degrees of freedom. Any sums of squares these interactions may have had get pooled into error sum of squares.

If there is any indication that one or more of the higher-order interactions is significant, then the pooling approach is not appropriate. A different method of analysis that is often used is examination of a normal probability plot of the estimated effects. This approach was suggested by Daniels (1959) and is available in most statistical software packages. Effects that are not significant (or are negligible) are said to be normally distributed with mean zero and variance σ^2. When plotted on a normal probability plot, estimated effects that are negligible will tend to fall along a straight line. The negligible effects are pooled into error and the degrees of freedom assigned to error.

EXAMPLE 39.4

Consider the air quality scenario presented earlier. Suppose that only one replicate was obtained for each of the eight runs. Data typical of this experiment are shown in Table 39.11.

The estimated effects for the main factors and all of the interactions can still be calculated using the formulas given previously. The estimated effects are then plotted on a normal probability plot (sometimes a standardized value of the effects will be plotted). The normal probability plot of the estimated effects is displayed in Figure 39.14.

Table 39.11 A single replicate of the air quality example.

Treatment	A	B	C	AB	AC	BC	ABC	ε_v
1	−1	−1	−1	1	1	1	−1	2.135
2	1	−1	−1	−1	−1	1	1	2.015
3	−1	1	−1	−1	1	−1	1	1.520
4	1	1	−1	1	−1	−1	−1	1.999
5	−1	−1	1	1	−1	−1	1	1.998
6	1	−1	1	−1	1	−1	−1	2.103
7	−1	1	1	−1	−1	1	−1	1.624
8	1	1	1	1	1	1	1	2.135

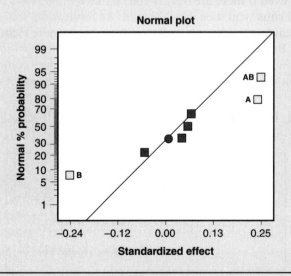

Figure 39.14 Normal probability plot of the estimated effects for the air quality example.

Continued

Continued

The normal probability plot of the effects (the effects have been "standardized") indicates that the main effects A and B and the interaction AB may be significant. An analysis could then be carried out on A, B, and AB. An analysis is conducted on the three terms with all other terms pooled into error. The results of *t*-tests on the effects are shown in Table 39.12.

Model fitting and residual analysis can be completed similarly to the case of more than one replicate. An analysis of variance can also be conducted with A, B, and the AB interaction as the only terms in the model.

Table 39.12 *t*-test results for the air quality example.

Term	Effect	Coef	SE Coef	*t*	*p*
Constant	—	1.9411	0.02953	65.72	0.000
A	0.2438	0.1219	0.02953	4.13	0.015
B	−0.2432	−0.1216	0.02953	−4.12	0.015
AB	0.2512	0.1256	0.02953	4.25	0.013

Remarks

The methods and procedures outlined in this section can be used for any number of factors at two levels each. A drawback to the use of 2^k full-factorial designs is that the design size becomes prohibitively large as the number of factors increases. For example, even if there are only seven factors each at two levels, the number of experimental runs would be $2^7 = 128$, without replication. It is not unusual, especially in screening experiments, to have six, seven, or more factors of interest being investigated. In these cases, it is often very useful to run experiments involving *fractions* of the full-factorial design. These designs are commonly referred to as *fractional factorial designs* and are discussed in the next section.

6. TWO-LEVEL FRACTIONAL FACTORIAL EXPERIMENTS

Construct two-level fractional factorial designs (including Taguchi designs) and apply computational and graphical methods to analyze the significance of results. (Analyze)

Body of Knowledge VI.H.6

Fractional factorial designs are those where only a fraction of the full-factorial design is used. Fractional factorial designs are economic alternatives to the full-factorial designs as the number of factors increases. Screening experiments often involve a large number of factors, so full-factorials are not always practical or economical.

Half-Fractions of 2^k Designs

Half-fractions of a 2^k are designs that consist of half of the standard 2^k design. Half-fractions are usually denoted 2^{k-1} (one-half of the $2^k = 2^k/2 = 2^{k-1}$).

EXAMPLE 39.5

Consider an experiment with six factors each at two levels. A full-factorial design consists of $2^6 = 64$ combinations or runs. A full 2^6 experimental design is in many instances prohibitively large. However, 32 experimental runs may be more economical. In this case, we can choose one-half of the runs from the full 2^6. The resulting design is referred to as a 2^{6-1} design. Runs selected from the full-factorial are not chosen at random. More on this later in this section.

Higher-Level Fractional Factorials

In some instances, a half-fraction may still be too large and impractical. It may be more economical to use designs that are one-fourth the size of the full-factorial or possibly one-eighth the size of the full-factorial. The general notation for a fractional factorial design is denoted as 2^{k-p} where 2^p represents the fraction of the full-factorial.

EXAMPLE 39.6

A screening experiment is going to be conducted involving 10 factors each at two levels. A full-factorial design with a single replicate would still require $2^{10} = 1024$ runs. The experimenters can afford to do no more than 40 runs initially for screening. A fraction of the full-factorial that could be used and still meet the size requirements would be a 2^{10-5} design, which would require only 32 experimental runs ($2^{10-5} = 2^5 = 32$).

Design Resolution

When conducting an experiment with k factors, we are not only interested in the significance of each factor, but also the interactions between the factors. If a full-factorial could be implemented, then all main effects of interest and all two-factor interactions are fully estimable. However, when employing fractional factorial designs, the design size is reduced, and not all the interactions of interest may be estimable separately from main effects or other interactions. Some of the interactions and/or main effects may be *confounded* or *aliased* with one another, making it difficult to determine which factor or interaction is truly significant.

EXAMPLE 39.7

A study is going to be conducted involving three factors each at two levels. Suppose we can only afford to conduct four treatments and not the eight that would make up a full 2^3 factorial design. A half-fraction of the 2^3 design would seem like a natural choice and would be called a 2^{3-1} design. A 2^{3-1} design as well as all columns for the interactions are given in Table 39.13.

Notice that the column for factor C and the column for the AB interaction are identical. We would say that factor C is aliased or confounded with the AB interaction, that is, C = AB. Also notice in the table that the column for the ABC interaction contains only the high level of the interaction. We would say that ABC is the equal to the identity column (I = ABC).

Table 39.13 Contrasts for a 2^{3-1} design.

Run	A	B	C	AB	AC	BC	ABC
1	–1	–1	1	1	–1	–1	1
2	1	–1	–1	–1	–1	1	1
3	–1	1	–1	–1	1	–1	1
4	1	1	1	1	1	1	1

The identity column will be very useful in fractional factorial designs. If any column in the design is multiplied by the identity column, the result is the original column. For example, A × I = A. The ABC interaction is a *generator* and would be used to generate the column for one of the main factors. ABC is often referred to as a *word*.

An important characteristic of fractional factorial designs is the *defining relation*. The defining relation is one that contains all possible "words" whose signs do not change in the experiment. For example, from Table 39.13 we see that the interaction column ABC consists of all +1's. Therefore, ABC would be a word in the defining relation. Since it is the only column with the signs unchanged, it is the only word in the defining relation. In this problem, our defining relation would be I = ABC. All aliases are found through the defining relation. For example, the alias for factor A is

$$A \cdot I = A \cdot ABC = BC.$$

Therefore, factor A is aliased with the BC interaction. The other aliases are found similarly:

$$B \cdot I = B \cdot ABC = AC$$

$$C \cdot I = C \cdot ABC = AB$$

The configuration in Table 39.13 guarantees that none of the main factors have identical columns (therefore they are not aliased or confounded with one another). But main effects are aliased with two-factor interactions. If it is believed that the AB interaction may be significant, then a different design (with more runs) would have to be used.

The 2^{3-1} design is said to be of *resolution III*. Resolution III designs are those where main effects are aliased with two-factor interactions. More on this later in this section.

Resolution IV designs or higher are desirable, since they guarantee that the main effects will be clear of (not aliased with) other main effects and clear of two-factor interactions. The obvious drawback to resolution IV designs is that two-factor interactions are aliased with other two-factor interactions. Suppose we carry out the 2^{4-1} design, analyze the results, and determine that all main effects and the two-factor interaction AB are found to be statistically significant. With resolution IV designs, we do not know for sure that AB is truly significant or if the two-factor interaction it is aliased with (here AB = CD) is significant. There are methods for breaking these aliases that involve adding a subset of new experimental runs. See Box, Hunter, and Hunter (2006) or Montgomery (2009a) for more details on breaking these aliases (also referred to as "de-aliasing").

EXAMPLE 39.8

A study is going to be conducted involving four factors each at two levels. Suppose we can only afford to conduct eight treatments and not the 16 that would make up a full 2^4 factorial design. A half-fraction of the 2^4 design would seem like a natural choice. The half-fraction of the 2^4 is the 2^{4-1} design and would contain $2^3 = 8$ runs. One possible fraction is displayed in Table 39.14.

Table 39.14 Half-fraction of a 2^4 factorial design.

Run	A	B	C	D
1	–1	–1	–1	–1
2	1	–1	–1	1
3	–1	1	–1	1
4	1	1	–1	–1
5	–1	–1	1	1
6	1	–1	1	–1
7	–1	1	1	–1
8	1	1	1	1

Continued

In this study a full 2^3 design was constructed for factors A, B, and C. Column D was generated from the three-factor interaction ABC, that is, D = ABC. In this example ABC is the generator and the defining relation is I = ABCD. This design is said to be of *resolution IV*. Resolution IV designs are those where main effects are aliased with three-factor interactions, and two-factor interactions are aliased with other two-factor interactions. Using the defining relation I = ABCD we can obtain all of the aliases. For the main effects:

$$A = BCD$$

$$B = ACD$$

$$C = ABD$$

$$D = ABC$$

For the two-factor interactions:

$$AB = AB \cdot I = AB \cdot ABCD = CD$$

$$AC = AC \cdot I = AC \cdot ABCD = BD$$

$$AD = AD \cdot I = AD \cdot ABCD = BC$$

The following are some of the properties for experimental design:

1. Resolution III designs have main effects confounded with two-factor interactions.

2. Resolution IV designs have main effects confounded with three-factor interactions and two-factor interactions confounded with each other.

3. Resolution V designs have two-factor interactions confounded with three-factor interactions only.

EXAMPLE 39.9

Consider an experiment involving six factors where only 16 runs can be used. A full-factorial design in 16 runs is a 2^4 design. Our design is referred to as a 2^{6-2} fractional factorial design.

We could construct a 2^4 full-factorial design for four of the six factors, but the remaining two factor columns would have to be *generated*. Let A, B, C, D, E, and F represent the six factors. Suppose a full-factorial design is constructed for A, B, C, and D. It can be shown that two generators needed for E and F could be E = ABC and F = BCD. The resulting defining relation would be I = ABCE = BCDF = ADEF. The last "word," ADEF, is found by multiplying the two original generators, ABCE and BCDF (see Box, Hunter, and Hunter [2006] or Montgomery [2009a] for more details). The resolution of this design is IV.

In general, the resolution of a design can always be determined from a complete defining relation. By definition, the resolution of a design is equal to the length of the smallest word in the defining relation. For example, consider a 2^{7-2} design with factors A, B, C, D, E, F, and G. The complete defining relation for this design can be shown to be

$$I = ABCDF = ABDEG = CEFG.$$

The length of the smallest word is four, so the design is of resolution IV.

There are numerous approaches and methods involving fractional factorial designs. The reader is encouraged to see Box, Hunter, and Hunter (2006), Ledolter and Swersey (2007), and Montgomery (2009a) for complete details and examples of full and fractional factorial designs and their applications.

Taguchi Robustness Concepts

Robustness means resistance to the effect of variation of some factor. For example, if brand A chocolate bar is very soft at 100° F and brittle at 40° F, and brand B maintains the same level of hardness at these temperature extremes, it could be said that brand B is more robust to temperature changes in this range. If a painting process produces the same color on moist wood as dry wood, the color is robust to variation in moisture content. The changes in temperature and humidity are referred to as noise. Producing products that are robust to noise of various kinds is clearly desirable. The Japanese engineer Genichi Taguchi is credited with developing techniques for improving robustness of products and processes.

One approach to improving robustness is illustrated in Table 39.15. As usual, the average value for each run is calculated and is labeled $\bar{y}$. In addition, the standard deviation of the values in the run is calculated and shown in the column labeled "S."

Now the experimenter can complete the usual main effects calculations to determine the levels of each of the factors that will optimize the response value y. In addition, the main effects calculations can be run using the values in the S

Table 39.15 Example using signal-to-noise ratio.

A	B	C	Replications				$\bar{y}$	S
−	−	−	34	29	38	25	31.5	5.7
−	−	+	42	47	39	38	41.5	4.0
−	+	−	54	41	48	43	46.5	5.8
−	+	+	35	31	32	34	33.0	1.8
+	−	−	62	68	63	69	65.5	3.5
+	−	+	25	33	36	21	28.8	6.9
+	+	−	58	54	58	60	57.5	2.5
+	+	+	39	35	42	45	40.3	4.3

column to find the levels of each of the factors that will minimize the S value. If these two combinations of levels do not agree, then a compromise between optimizing the response and minimizing the variation must be made. One way to approach the compromising process is through what Taguchi called the signal-to-noise ratio. If it is desirable to maximize y, the signal-to-noise ratio may be calculated for each run using

$$S/N = \frac{\bar{y}}{S}.$$

The main effects may then be calculated, using the S/N ratios to find the best levels for each factor. If, instead, it is desirable to make y as small as possible, the signal-to-noise ratio can be defined as

$$S/N = \frac{1}{\bar{y}S}.$$

If it is desirable to make y as close to some nominal value N as possible, the signal-to-noise ratio can be defined as

$$S/N = \frac{1}{|\bar{y} - N|S}.$$

Note that the signal-to-noise ratio is an attempt to find a useful compromise between two competing goals, optimizing y and minimizing S. It does not necessarily accomplish either of these goals, so it should be used with a bit of judgment. See Box (1988) for more details discussing signal-to-noise ratios and how a significant factor could go undetected when significant changes occur in both the average and variance.

Another technique Taguchi used for improving robustness is called the inner/outer array design. In this procedure, the uncontrollable factors—those factors that the experimenter either can not or chooses not to control—are placed in separate columns next to the controllable factors, as shown in Table 39.16.

In this example, hardness of the steel and the ambient temperature are the uncontrollable factors. These factors could conceivably be controlled by putting the machine in an environmental enclosure and putting a tighter specification on the steel, but the experimenter chooses not to do either of these. Instead, anticipated extremes of hardness and ambient temperature are used for the experiment to determine settings of the controllable variables that will minimize variation in the output quality characteristic.

When the first run of the design in Table 39.16 is executed, the feed, speed, and coolant temperature are all set at their low levels. One part is made with low-hardness steel and low ambient temperature, and the value of the quality characteristic is entered in the spot labeled "a." When all 32 values have been entered, the averages and standard deviations are calculated. In this inner/outer array approach, the design intentionally causes perturbations in the uncontrollable factors to find level combinations for the controllable factors that will minimize

Table 39.16 Illustration of inner and outer arrays.

Inner array			Outer array						
			Hardness	−	−	+	+		
Feed	Speed	Coolant temp.	Ambient temp.	−	+	−	+	$\bar{y}$	S
−	−	−		a					
−	−	+							
−	+	−							
−	+	+							
+	−	−							
+	−	+							
+	+	−							
+	+	+							

the variation in the quality characteristics under the anticipated hardness and ambient temperature variation.

Motivation for the use of crossed-array designs is simple. All control-by-noise interactions can be estimated clear of any other factors or interactions. If control-by-noise interactions are significant, then it may be possible to find settings of the controllable variables that are *robust* to variations in the uncontrollable variables. As a result, it may be possible to minimize the variability transmitted by the noise factors to the response. If no control-by-noise interactions are found significant, then there is *no robust design problem*.

There are drawbacks to the used of crossed-array designs. As the number of control and/or noise variables increases, the number of runs needed becomes excessive. In addition, even with a large number of runs the crossed-array designs do not readily accommodate potentially important control-by-control interactions.

Combined array designs are an efficient alternative to the crossed-array designs presented by Taguchi. Combined array designs are those that combine the controllable and uncontrollable variables into a single design array, such as a 2^k or 2^{k-p} design. There are a number of possible combined array designs that are highly efficient for the robust design problem, allowing for estimation of the control-by-control interactions and control-by-noise interactions.

For more discussion on the merits and drawbacks to Taguchi's approach to robust design see, for example, Nair (1992), Box, Bisgaard, and Fung (1988), Hunter (1985), Montgomery (2009a), Myers and Montgomery (2002), and Pignatiello and Ramberg (1992).

Designed Experiments and Statistical Control

There has been considerable debate about the use of designed experiments in industry if the process under investigation is not known to be in statistical control. Some researchers have argued that the process must be in statistical control before conducting legitimate industrial experiments while others have argued that statistical control is not necessary. Research by R. A. Fisher first published in 1925 showed that statistical control was not a prerequisite for implementing designed experiments when replication, blocking, and randomization are key components of the experimentation. Arguments have been made to the effect that Fisher's results, while applicable in agricultural experiments, do not apply in industrial settings.

Anyone involved in conducting experiments should read the article and discussion that appeared in *Quality Engineering* (volume 20, no. 2, 2008). Statistical control and designed experiments are discussed in detail by Søren Bisgaard, with discussion of his article provided by G. Geoffrey Vining, Thomas P. Ryan, George E. P. Box, Donald J. Wheeler, and Douglas C. Montgomery. The article and discussions are a must read for practitioners and researchers alike and provide numerous references for further reading.

SUMMARY OF PART VI

The methods and tools presented in Part VI, although complex in their details, provide a basis for what is sometimes referred to as *management by fact.* The proper use of this content will permit the user to determine how best to collect and analyze data so that sound decisions are possible.

Part VII
Appendices

Appendix A

ASQ Certified Quality Engineer (CQE) Body of Knowledge

T he topics in this Body of Knowledge include subtext explanations and the cognitive level at which the questions will be written. This information will provide useful guidance for both the Exam Development Committee and the candidate preparing to take the exam. The subtext is not intended to limit the subject matter or be all-inclusive of that material that will be covered in the exam. It is meant to clarify the type of content that will be included on the exam. The descriptor in parentheses at the end of each entry refers to the maximum cognitive level at which the topic will be tested. A complete description of cognitive levels is provided at the end of this document.

I. *Management and Leadership* (15 Questions)

A. *Quality Philosophies and Foundations*
Explain how modern quality has evolved from quality control through statistical process control (SPC) to total quality management and leadership principles (including Deming's 14 points), and how quality has helped form various continuous improvement tools including lean, six sigma, theory of constraints, etc. (Remember)

B. *The Quality Management System (QMS)*

1. *Strategic planning.* Identify and define top management's responsibility for the QMS, including establishing policies and objectives, setting organization-wide goals, supporting quality initiatives, etc. (Apply)

2. *Deployment techniques.* Define, describe, and use various deployment tools in support of the QMS: benchmarking, stakeholder identification and analysis, performance measurement tools, and project management tools such as PERT charts, Gantt charts, critical path method (CPM), resource allocation, etc. (Apply)

3. *Quality information system (QIS).* Identify and define the basic elements of a QIS, including who will contribute data, the kind of data to be managed, who will have access to the data, the level of flexibility for future information needs, data analysis, etc. (Remember)

C. *ASQ Code of Ethics for Professional Conduct.* Determine appropriate behavior in situations requiring ethical decisions. (Evaluate)

D. *Leadership Principles and Techniques.* Describe and apply various principles and techniques for developing and organizing teams and leading quality initiatives. (Analyze)

E. *Facilitation Principles and Techniques.* Define and describe the facilitator's role and responsibilities on a team. Define and apply various tools used with teams, including brainstorming, nominal group technique, conflict resolution, force-field analysis, etc. (Analyze)

F. *Communication Skills.* Describe and distinguish between various communication methods for delivering information and messages in a variety of situations across all levels of the organization. (Analyze)

G. *Customer Relations.* Define, apply, and analyze the results of customer relation measures such as quality function deployment (QFD), customer satisfaction surveys, etc. (Analyze)

H. *Supplier Management.* Define, select, and apply various techniques including supplier qualification, certification, evaluation, ratings, performance improvement, etc. (Analyze)

I. *Barriers to Quality Improvement.* Identify barriers to quality improvement, their causes and impact, and describe methods for overcoming them. (Analyze)

II. *The Quality System* (15 Questions)

A. *Elements of the Quality System.* Define, describe, and interpret the basic elements of a quality system, including planning, control, and improvement, from product and process design through quality cost systems, audit programs, etc. (Evaluate)

B. *Documentation of the Quality System.* Identify and apply quality system documentation components, including quality policies, procedures to support the system, configuration management and document control to manage work instructions, quality records, etc. (Apply)

C. *Quality Standards and Other Guidelines.* Define and distinguish between national and international standards and other requirements and guidelines, including the Malcolm Baldrige National Quality Award (MBNQA), and describe key points of the ISO 9000 series of standards and how they are used. [Note: Industry-specific standards will not be tested.] (Apply)

D. *Quality Audits*

1. *Types of audits.* Describe and distinguish between various types of quality audits such as product, process, management (system), registration (certification), compliance (regulatory), first, second, and third party, etc. (Apply)

2. *Roles and responsibilities in audits.* Identify and define roles and responsibilities for audit participants such as audit team (leader and members), client, auditee, etc. (Understand)

3. *Audit planning and implementation.* Describe and apply the steps of a quality audit, from the audit planning stage through conducting the audit, from the perspective of an audit team member. (Apply)

4. *Audit reporting and follow up.* Identify, describe, and apply the steps of audit reporting and follow up, including the need to verify corrective action. (Apply)

E. *Cost of Quality (COQ).* Identify and apply COQ concepts, including cost categories, data collection methods and classification, and reporting and interpreting results. (Analyze)

F. *Quality Training.* Identify and define key elements of a training program, including conducting a needs analysis, developing curricula and materials, and determining the program's effectiveness. (Apply)

III. *Product and Process Design* (25 Questions)

A. *Classification of Quality Characteristics.* Define, interpret, and classify quality characteristics for new products and processes. [Note: The classification of product defects is covered in IV.B.3.] (Evaluate)

B. *Design Inputs and Review.* Identify sources of design inputs such as customer needs, regulatory requirements, etc. and how they translate into design concepts such as robust design, QFD, and Design for X (DFX, where X can mean six sigma (DFSS), manufacturability (DFM), cost (DFC), etc.). Identify and apply common elements of the design review process, including roles and responsibilities of participants. (Analyze)

C. *Technical Drawings and Specifications.* Interpret technical drawings including characteristics such as views, title blocks, dimensioning, tolerancing, GD&T symbols, etc. Interpret specification requirements in relation to product and process characteristics. (Evaluate)

D. *Design Verification.* Identify and apply various evaluations and tests to qualify and validate the design of new products and processes to ensure their fitness for use. (Evaluate)

E. *Reliability and Maintainability*

1. *Predictive and preventive maintenance tools.* Describe and apply these tools and techniques to maintain and improve process and product reliability. (Analyze)

2. *Reliability and maintainability indices.* Review and analyze indices such as, MTTF, MTBF, MTTR, availability, failure rate, etc. (Analyze)

3. *Bathtub curve.* Identify, define, and distinguish between the basic elements of the bathtub curve. (Analyze)

4. *Reliability/safety/hazard assessment tools.* Define, construct, and interpret the results of failure mode and effects analysis (FMEA), failure mode, effects, and criticality analysis (FMECA), and fault tree analysis (FTA). (Analyze)

IV. *Product and Process Control* (32 Questions)

A. *Tools.* Define, identify, and apply product and process control methods such as developing control plans, identifying critical control points, developing and validating work instructions, etc. (Analyze)

B. *Material Control*

1. *Material identification, status, and traceability.* Define and distinguish these concepts, and describe methods for applying them in various situations. [Note: Product recall procedures will not be tested.] (Analyze)

2. *Material segregation.* Describe material segregation and its importance, and evaluate appropriate methods for applying it in various situations. (Evaluate)

3. *Classification of defects.* Define, describe, and classify the seriousness of product and process defects. (Evaluate)

4. *Material review board (MRB).* Identify the purpose and function of an MRB, and make appropriate disposition decisions in various situations. (Analyze)

C. *Acceptance Sampling*

1. *Sampling concepts.* Define, describe, and apply the concepts of producer and consumer risk and related terms, including operating characteristic (OC) curves, acceptable quality limit (AQL), lot tolerance percent defective (LTPD), average outgoing quality (AOQ), average outgoing quality limit (AOQL), etc. (Analyze)

2. *Sampling standards and plans.* Interpret and apply ANSI/ASQ Z1.4 and Z1.9 standards for attributes and variables sampling. Identify and distinguish between single, double, multiple, sequential, and continuous sampling methods. Identify the characteristics of Dodge-Romig sampling tables and when they should be used. (Analyze)

3. *Sample integrity.* Identify the techniques for establishing and maintaining sample integrity. (Analyze)

D. *Measurement and Test*

1. *Measurement tools.* Select and describe appropriate uses of inspection tools such as gage blocks, calipers, micrometers, optical comparators, etc. (Analyze)

2. *Destructive and nondestructive tests.* Distinguish between destructive and nondestructive measurement test methods and apply them appropriately. (Analyze)

E. *Metrology.* Identify, describe, and apply metrology techniques such as calibration systems, traceability to calibration standards, measurement error and its sources, and control and maintenance of measurement standards and devices. (Analyze)

F. *Measurement System Analysis (MSA).* Calculate, analyze, and interpret repeatability and reproducibility (Gage R&R) studies, measurement correlation, capability, bias, linearity, etc., including both conventional and control chart methods. (Evaluate)

V. *Continuous Improvement* (30 Questions)

A. *Quality Control Tools.* Select, construct, apply, and interpret tools such as 1) flowcharts, 2) Pareto charts, 3) cause and effect diagrams, 4) control charts, 5) check sheets, 6) scatter diagrams, and 7) histograms. (Analyze)

B. *Quality Management and Planning Tools.* Select, construct, apply, and interpret tools such as 1) affinity diagrams, 2) tree diagrams, 3) process decision program charts (PDPC), 4) matrix diagrams, 5) interrelationship digraphs, 6) prioritization matrices, and 7) activity network diagrams. (Analyze)

C. *Continuous Improvement Techniques.* Define, describe, and distinguish between various continuous improvement models: total quality management (TQM), kaizen, plan-do-check-act (PDCA), six sigma, theory of constraints (TOC), lean, etc. (Analyze)

D. *Corrective Action.* Identify, describe, and apply elements of the corrective action process including problem identification, failure analysis, root cause analysis, problem correction, recurrence control, verification of effectiveness, etc. (Evaluate)

E. *Preventive Action.* Identify, describe, and apply various preventive action tools such as error-proofing/poka-yoke, robust design, etc., and analyze their effectiveness. (Evaluate)

VI. *Quantitative Methods and Tools* (43 Questions)

A. *Collecting and Summarizing Data*

1. *Types of data.* Define, classify, and compare discrete (attributes) and continuous (variables) data. (Apply)

2. *Measurement scales.* Define, describe, and use nominal, ordinal, interval, and ratio scales. (Apply)

3. *Data collection methods.* Describe various methods for collecting data, including tally or check sheets, data coding, automatic gaging, etc., and identify their strengths and weaknesses. (Apply)

4. *Data accuracy.* Describe the characteristics or properties of data (e.g., source/resource issues, flexibility, versatility, etc.) and various types of data errors or poor quality such as low accuracy, inconsistency, interpretation of data values, and redundancy. Identify factors that can influence data accuracy, and apply techniques for error detection and correction. (Apply)

5. *Descriptive statistics.* Describe, calculate, and interpret measures of central tendency and dispersion (central limit theorem), and construct and interpret frequency distributions including simple, categorical, grouped, ungrouped, and cumulative. (Evaluate)

6. *Graphical methods for depicting relationships.* Construct, apply, and interpret diagrams and charts such as stem-and-leaf plots, box-and-whisker plots, etc. [Note: Run charts and scatter diagrams are covered in V.A.] (Analyze)

7. *Graphical methods for depicting distributions.* Construct, apply, and interpret diagrams such as normal probability plots, Weibull plots, etc. [Note: Histograms are covered in V.A.] (Analyze)

B. *Quantitative Concepts*

1. *Terminology.* Define and apply quantitative terms, including population, parameter, sample, statistic, random sampling, expected value, etc. (Analyze)

2. *Drawing statistical conclusions.* Distinguish between numeric and analytical studies. Assess the validity of statistical conclusions by analyzing the assumptions used and the robustness of the technique used. (Evaluate)

3. *Probability terms and concepts.* Describe and apply concepts such as independence, mutually exclusive, multiplication rules, complementary probability, joint occurrence of events, etc. (Apply)

C. *Probability Distributions*

1. *Continuous distributions.* Define and distinguish between these distributions: normal, uniform, bivariate normal, exponential, lognormal, Weibull, chi square, Student's t, F, etc. (Analyze)

2. *Discrete distributions.* Define and distinguish between these distributions: binomial, Poisson, hypergeometric, multinomial, etc. (Analyze)

D. *Statistical Decision-Making*

1. *Point estimates and confidence intervals.* Define, describe, and assess the efficiency and bias of estimators. Calculate and interpret standard error, tolerance intervals, and confidence intervals. (Evaluate)

2. *Hypothesis testing.* Define, interpret, and apply hypothesis tests for means, variances, and proportions. Apply and interpret the concepts of significance level, power, type I and type II errors. Define and distinguish between statistical and practical significance. (Evaluate)

3. *Paired-comparison tests.* Define and use paired-comparison (parametric) hypothesis tests, and interpret the results. (Apply)

4. *Goodness-of-fit tests.* Define and use chi square and other goodness-of-fit tests, and interpret the results. (Apply)

5. *Analysis of variance (ANOVA).* Define and use ANOVAs and interpret the results. (Analyze)

6. *Contingency tables.* Define, construct, and use contingency tables to evaluate statistical significance. (Analyze)

E. *Relationships Between Variables*

1. *Linear regression.* Calculate the regression equation for simple regressions and least squares estimates. Construct and interpret hypothesis tests for regression statistics. Use regression models for estimation and prediction, and analyze the uncertainty in the estimate. [Note: Non-linear models and parameters will not be tested.] (Analyze)

2. *Simple linear correlation.* Calculate the correlation coefficient and its confidence interval, and construct and interpret a hypothesis test for correlation statistics. [Note: Serial correlation will not be tested.] (Analyze)

3. *Time-series analysis.* Define, describe, and use time-series analysis including moving average, and interpret time-series graphs to identify trends and seasonal or cyclical variation. (Analyze)

F. *Statistical Process Control (SPC)*

1. *Objectives and benefits.* Identify and explain objectives and benefits of SPC such as assessing process performance. (Understand)

2. *Common and special causes.* Describe, identify, and distinguish between these types of causes. (Analyze)

3. *Selection of variable.* Identify and select characteristics for monitoring by control chart. (Analyze)

4. *Rational subgrouping.* Define and apply the principles of rational subgrouping. (Apply)

5. *Control charts.* Identify, select, construct, and use various control charts, including $\bar{X} - R$, $\bar{X} - s$, individuals and moving range (ImR or XmR), moving average and moving range (MamR), p, np, c, u, and CUSUM charts. (Analyze)

6. *Control chart analysis.* Read and interpret control charts, use rules for determining statistical control. (Evaluate)

7. *Pre-control charts.* Define and describe how these charts differ from other control charts and how they should be used. (Apply)

8. *Short-run SPC.* Identify, define, and use short-run SPC rules. (Apply)

G. *Process and Performance Capability*

1. *Process capability studies.* Define, describe, calculate, and use process capability studies, including identifying characteristics, specifications, and tolerances, developing sampling plans for such studies, establishing statistical control, etc. (Analyze)

2. *Process performance vs. specifications.* Distinguish between natural process limits and specification limits, and calculate percent defective. (Analyze)

3. *Process capability indices.* Define, select, and calculate C_p, C_{pk}, C_{pm}, and C_r, and evaluate process capability. (Evaluate)

4. *Process performance indices.* Define, select, and calculate P_p and P_{pk} and evaluate process performance. (Evaluate)

H. *Design and Analysis of Experiments*

1. *Terminology.* Define terms such as dependent and independent variables, factors, levels, response, treatment, error, and replication. (Understand)

2. *Planning and organizing experiments.* Define, describe, and apply the basic elements of designed experiments, including determining the experiment objective, selecting factors, responses, and measurement methods, choosing the appropriate design, etc. (Analyze)

3. *Design principles.* Define and apply the principles of power and sample size, balance, replication, order, efficiency, randomization, blocking, interaction, and confounding. (Apply)

4. *One-factor experiments.* Construct one-factor experiments such as completely randomized, randomized block, and Latin square designs, and use computational and graphical methods to analyze the significance of results. (Analyze)

5. *Full-factorial experiments.* Construct full-factorial designs and use computational and graphical methods to analyze the significance of results. (Analyze)

6. *Two-level fractional factorial experiments.* Construct two-level fractional factorial designs (including Taguchi designs) and apply computational and graphical methods to analyze the significance of results. (Analyze)

LEVELS OF COGNITION
BASED ON *BLOOM'S TAXONOMY*—REVISED (2001)

In addition to *content* specifics, the subtext for each topic in this BoK also indicates the intended *complexity level* of the test questions for that topic. These levels are based on "Levels of Cognition" (from *Bloom's Taxonomy*—Revised, 2001) and are presented below in rank order, from least complex to most complex.

Remember

Recall or recognize terms, definitions, facts, ideas, materials, patterns, sequences, methods, principles, etc.

Understand

Read and understand descriptions, communications, reports, tables, diagrams, directions, regulations, etc.

Apply

Know when and how to use ideas, procedures, methods, formulas, principles, theories, etc.

Analyze

Break down information into its constituent parts and recognize their relationship to one another and how they are organized; identify sublevel factors or salient data from a complex scenario.

Evaluate

Make judgments about the value of proposed ideas, solutions, etc., by comparing the proposal to specific criteria or standards.

Create

Put parts or elements together in such a way as to reveal a pattern or structure not clearly there before; identify which data or information from a complex set is appropriate to examine further or from which supported conclusions can be drawn.

Appendix B
Control Limit Formulas

VARIABLES CHARTS

$\bar{x}$ and R chart: *Averages Chart*: $\bar{\bar{x}} \pm A_2\bar{R}$ *Range Chart*: $\text{LCL} = D_3\bar{R}$ $\text{UCL} = D_4\bar{R}$

$\bar{x}$ and s chart: *Averages Chart*: $\bar{\bar{x}} \pm A_3\bar{s}$ *Std. Dev. Chart*: $\text{LCL} = B_3\bar{s}$ $\text{UCL} = B_4\bar{s}$

Individuals and Moving Range Chart (two-value moving window):

Individuals Chart: $\bar{x} \pm 2.66\bar{R}$ *Moving Range*: $\text{UCL} = 3.267\bar{R}$

Moving Average and Moving Range (two-value moving window):

Moving Average: $\bar{\bar{x}} \pm 1.88\bar{R}$ *Moving Range*: $\text{UCL} = 3.267\bar{R}$

ATTRIBUTES CHARTS

p chart: $\bar{p} \pm 3\sqrt{\dfrac{\bar{p}(1-\bar{p})}{n}}$

np chart: $n\bar{p} \pm 3\sqrt{n\bar{p}(1-\bar{p})}$

c chart: $\bar{c} \pm 3\sqrt{\bar{c}}$

u chart: $\bar{u} \pm 3\sqrt{\dfrac{\bar{u}}{n}}$

Appendix C

Constants for Control Charts

Subgroup size n	A_2	d_2	D_3	D_4	A_3	C_4	B_3	B_4	E_2	A_2 for median charts
2	1.880	1.128	0	3.267	2.659	0.798	0	3.267	2.660	1.880
3	1.023	1.693	0	2.574	1.954	0.886	0	2.568	1.772	1.187
4	0.729	2.059	0	2.282	1.628	0.921	0	2.266	1.457	0.796
5	0.577	2.326	0	2.114	1.427	0.940	0	2.089	1.290	0.691
6	0.483	2.534	0	2.004	1.287	0.952	0.030	1.970	1.184	0.548
7	0.419	2.704	0.076	1.924	1.182	0.959	0.118	1.882	1.109	0.508
8	0.373	2.847	0.136	1.864	1.099	0.965	0.185	1.815	1.054	0.433
9	0.337	2.970	0.184	1.816	1.032	0.969	0.239	1.761	1.010	0.412
10	0.308	3.078	0.223	1.777	0.975	0.973	0.284	1.716	0.975	0.362

Appendix D

Statistical Tolerance Factors
for at Least 99 Percent of the Population

("*k*-Values")

	One-sided tolerance Confidence level				Two-sided tolerance Confidence level		
n	0.90	0.95	0.99	*n*	0.90	0.95	0.99
10	3.532	3.981	5.075	10	3.959	4.433	5.594
11	3.444	3.852	4.828	11	3.849	4.277	5.308
12	3.371	3.747	4.633	12	3.758	4.150	5.079
13	3.310	3.659	4.472	13	3.682	4.044	4.893
14	3.257	3.585	4.336	14	3.618	3.955	4.737
15	3.212	3.520	4.224	15	3.562	3.878	4.605
16	3.172	3.463	4.124	16	3.514	3.812	4.492
17	3.136	3.415	4.038	17	3.471	3.754	4.393
18	3.106	3.370	3.961	18	3.433	3.702	4.307
19	3.078	3.331	3.893	19	3.399	3.656	4.230
20	3.052	3.295	3.832	20	3.368	3.615	4.161
21	3.028	3.262	3.776	21	3.340	3.577	4.100
22	3.007	3.233	3.727	22	3.315	3.543	4.044
23	2.987	3.206	3.680	23	3.292	3.512	3.993
24	2.969	3.181	3.638	24	3.270	3.483	3.947
25	2.952	3.158	3.601	25	3.251	3.457	3.904
30	2.884	3.064	3.446	30	3.170	3.350	3.733
40	2.793	2.941	3.250	40	3.066	3.213	3.518
50	2.735	2.863	3.124	50	3.001	3.126	3.385

Appendix E

Standard Normal Distribution for Selected Z-Values

Z	Area to left of Z	Area to right of Z	Parts per million right of Z
0	0.5000000	0.5000000	500000.0002
0.1	0.5398279	0.4601721	460172.1045
0.2	0.5792597	0.4207403	420740.3128
0.3	0.6179114	0.3820886	382088.6425
0.4	0.6554217	0.3445783	344578.3034
0.5	0.6914625	0.3085375	308537.5326
0.6	0.7257469	0.2742531	274253.0649
0.7	0.7580364	0.2419636	241963.5785
0.8	0.7881447	0.2118553	211855.3339
0.9	0.8159399	0.1840601	184060.0917
1	0.8413447	0.1586553	158655.2598
1.1	0.8643339	0.1356661	135666.1015
1.2	0.8849303	0.1150697	115069.7317
1.3	0.9031995	0.0968005	96800.5495
1.4	0.9192433	0.0807567	80756.71126
1.5	0.9331928	0.0668072	66807.22879
1.6	0.9452007	0.0547993	54799.28945
1.7	0.9554346	0.0445654	44565.43178
1.8	0.9640697	0.0359303	35930.26551
1.9	0.9712835	0.0287165	28716.49286
2	0.9772499	0.0227501	22750.06204
2.1	0.9821356	0.0178644	17864.35742
2.2	0.9860966	0.0139034	13903.39891
2.3	0.9892759	0.0107241	10724.08106
2.4	0.9918025	8.1975289×10^{-3}	8197.528869
2.5	0.9937903	6.2096799×10^{-3}	6209.679859
2.6	0.9953388	4.6612218×10^{-3}	4661.221783

Continued

Continued

Z	Area to left of Z	Area to right of Z	Parts per million right of Z
2.7	0.9965330	3.4670231E-03	3467.023053
2.8	0.9974448	2.5551906E-03	2555.190642
2.9	0.9981341	1.8658801E-03	1865.88014
3	0.9986500	1.3499672E-03	1349.967223
3.1	0.9990323	9.6767124E-04	967.6712356
3.2	0.9993128	6.8720208E-04	687.2020808
3.3	0.9995165	4.8348254E-04	483.4825366
3.4	0.9996630	3.3698082E-04	336.9808229
3.5	0.9997673	2.3267337E-04	232.6733737
3.6	0.9998409	1.5914571E-04	159.1457138
3.7	0.9998922	1.0783015E-04	107.8301454
3.8	0.9999276	7.2372434E-05	72.37243427
3.9	0.9999519	4.8115519E-05	48.11551887
4	0.9999683	3.1686035E-05	31.68603461
4.1	0.9999793	2.0668716E-05	20.66871577
4.2	0.9999866	1.3354097E-05	13.35409733
4.3	0.9999915	8.5460212E-06	8.546021191
4.4	0.9999946	5.4169531E-06	5.416953054
4.5	0.9999966	3.4008031E-06	3.400803062
4.6	0.9999979	2.1146434E-06	2.114643376
4.7	0.9999987	1.3023157E-06	1.302315654
4.8	0.9999992	7.9435267E-07	0.794352669
4.9	0.9999995	4.7986955E-07	0.479869547
5	0.9999997	2.8710500E-07	0.287105
5.1	0.9999998	1.7012231E-07	0.170122314
5.2	0.9999999	9.9834400E-08	0.0998344
5.3	0.9999999	5.8022066E-08	0.058022066
5.4	1.0000000	3.3396123E-08	0.033396123
5.5	1.0000000	1.9036399E-08	0.019036399
5.6	1.0000000	1.0746217E-08	0.010746217
5.7	1.0000000	6.0076532E-09	0.006007653
5.8	1.0000000	3.3260517E-09	0.003326052
5.9	1.0000000	1.8235793E-09	0.001823579
6	1.0000000	9.9012187E-10	0.000990122

Appendix F

Areas under Standard Normal Distribution to the Left of Z-Values

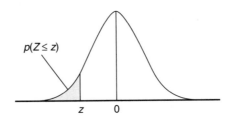

$p(Z \le z)$

z	−0.09	−0.08	−0.07	−0.06	−0.05	−0.04	−0.03	−0.02	−0.01	−0.00
−3.5	0.0002	0.0002	0.0002	0.0002	0.0002	0.0002	0.0002	0.0002	0.0002	0.0002
−3.4	0.0002	0.0003	0.0003	0.0003	0.0003	0.0003	0.0003	0.0003	0.0003	0.0003
−3.3	0.0003	0.0004	0.0004	0.0004	0.0004	0.0004	0.0004	0.0005	0.0005	0.0005
−3.2	0.0005	0.0005	0.0005	0.0006	0.0006	0.0006	0.0006	0.0006	0.0007	0.0007
−3.1	0.0007	0.0007	0.0008	0.0008	0.0008	0.0008	0.0009	0.0009	0.0009	0.0010
−3.0	0.0010	0.0010	0.0011	0.0011	0.0011	0.0012	0.0012	0.0013	0.0013	0.0013
−2.9	0.0014	0.0014	0.0015	0.0015	0.0016	0.0016	0.0017	0.0018	0.0018	0.0019
−2.8	0.0019	0.0020	0.0021	0.0021	0.0022	0.0023	0.0023	0.0024	0.0025	0.0026
−2.7	0.0026	0.0027	0.0028	0.0029	0.0030	0.0031	0.0032	0.0033	0.0034	0.0035
−2.6	0.0036	0.0037	0.0038	0.0039	0.0040	0.0041	0.0043	0.0044	0.0045	0.0047
−2.5	0.0048	0.0049	0.0051	0.0052	0.0054	0.0055	0.0057	0.0059	0.0060	0.0062
−2.4	0.0064	0.0066	0.0068	0.0069	0.0071	0.0073	0.0075	0.0078	0.0080	0.0082
−2.3	0.0084	0.0087	0.0089	0.0091	0.0094	0.0096	0.0099	0.0102	0.0104	0.0107
−2.2	0.0110	0.0113	0.0116	0.0119	0.0122	0.0125	0.0129	0.0132	0.0136	0.0139
−2.1	0.0143	0.0146	0.0150	0.0154	0.0158	0.0162	0.0166	0.0170	0.0174	0.0179
−2.0	0.0183	0.0188	0.0192	0.0197	0.0202	0.0207	0.0212	0.0217	0.0222	0.0228
−1.9	0.0233	0.0239	0.0244	0.0250	0.0256	0.0262	0.0268	0.0274	0.0281	0.0287
−1.8	0.0294	0.0301	0.0307	0.0314	0.0322	0.0329	0.0336	0.0344	0.0351	0.0359
−1.7	0.0367	0.0375	0.0384	0.0392	0.0401	0.0409	0.0418	0.0427	0.0436	0.0446
−1.6	0.0455	0.0465	0.0475	0.0485	0.0495	0.0505	0.0516	0.0526	0.0537	0.0548
−1.5	0.0559	0.0571	0.0582	0.0594	0.0606	0.0618	0.0630	0.0643	0.0655	0.0668

Continued

Continued

z	−0.09	−0.08	−0.07	−0.06	−0.05	−0.04	−0.03	−0.02	−0.01	−0.00
−1.4	0.0681	0.0694	0.0708	0.0721	0.0735	0.0749	0.0764	0.0778	0.0793	0.0808
−1.3	0.0823	0.0838	0.0853	0.0869	0.0885	0.0901	0.0918	0.0934	0.0951	0.0968
−1.2	0.0985	0.1003	0.1020	0.1038	0.1056	0.1075	0.1093	0.1112	0.1131	0.1151
−1.1	0.1170	0.1190	0.1210	0.1230	0.1251	0.1271	0.1292	0.1314	0.1335	0.1357
−1.0	0.1379	0.1401	0.1423	0.1446	0.1469	0.1492	0.1515	0.1539	0.1562	0.1587
−0.9	0.1611	0.1635	0.1660	0.1685	0.1711	0.1736	0.1762	0.1788	0.1814	0.1841
−0.8	0.1867	0.1894	0.1922	0.1949	0.1977	0.2005	0.2033	0.2061	0.2090	0.2119
−0.7	0.2148	0.2177	0.2206	0.2236	0.2266	0.2296	0.2327	0.2358	0.2389	0.2420
−0.6	0.2451	0.2483	0.2514	0.2546	0.2578	0.2611	0.2643	0.2676	0.2709	0.2743
−0.5	0.2776	0.2810	0.2843	0.2877	0.2912	0.2946	0.2981	0.3015	0.3050	0.3085
−0.4	0.3121	0.3156	0.3192	0.3228	0.3264	0.3300	0.3336	0.3372	0.3409	0.3446
−0.3	0.3483	0.3520	0.3557	0.3594	0.3632	0.3669	0.3707	0.3745	0.3783	0.3821
−0.2	0.3859	0.3897	0.3936	0.3974	0.4013	0.4052	0.4090	0.4129	0.4168	0.4207
−0.1	0.4247	0.4286	0.4325	0.4364	0.4404	0.4443	0.4483	0.4522	0.4562	0.4602
0.0	0.4641	0.4681	0.4721	0.4761	0.4801	0.4840	0.4880	0.4920	0.4960	0.5000

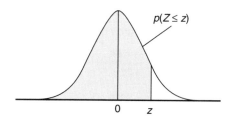

$p(Z \le z)$

0   z

z	0.00	0.01	0.02	0.03	0.04	0.05	0.06	0.07	0.08	0.09
0.0	0.5000	0.5040	0.5080	0.5120	0.5160	0.5199	0.5239	0.5279	0.5319	0.5359
0.1	0.5398	0.5438	0.5478	0.5517	0.5557	0.5596	0.5636	0.5675	0.5714	0.5753
0.2	0.5793	0.5832	0.5871	0.5910	0.5948	0.5987	0.6026	0.6064	0.6103	0.6141
0.3	0.6179	0.6217	0.6255	0.6293	0.6331	0.6368	0.6406	0.6443	0.6480	0.6517
0.4	0.6554	0.6591	0.6628	0.6664	0.6700	0.6736	0.6772	0.6808	0.6844	0.6879
0.5	0.6915	0.6950	0.6985	0.7019	0.7054	0.7088	0.7123	0.7157	0.7190	0.7224
0.6	0.7257	0.7291	0.7324	0.7357	0.7389	0.7422	0.7454	0.7486	0.7517	0.7549
0.7	0.7580	0.7611	0.7642	0.7673	0.7704	0.7734	0.7764	0.7794	0.7823	0.7852
0.8	0.7881	0.7910	0.7939	0.7967	0.7995	0.8023	0.8051	0.8078	0.8106	0.8133
0.9	0.8159	0.8186	0.8212	0.8238	0.8264	0.8289	0.8315	0.8340	0.8365	0.8389
1.0	0.8413	0.8438	0.8461	0.8485	0.8508	0.8531	0.8554	0.8577	0.8599	0.8621

Continued

Continued

z	0.00	0.01	0.02	0.03	0.04	0.05	0.06	0.07	0.08	0.09
1.1	0.8643	0.8665	0.8686	0.8708	0.8729	0.8749	0.8770	0.8790	0.8810	0.8830
1.2	0.8849	0.8869	0.8888	0.8907	0.8925	0.8944	0.8962	0.8980	0.8997	0.9015
1.3	0.9032	0.9049	0.9066	0.9082	0.9099	0.9115	0.9131	0.9147	0.9162	0.9177
1.4	0.9192	0.9207	0.9222	0.9236	0.9251	0.9265	0.9279	0.9292	0.9306	0.9319
1.5	0.9332	0.9345	0.9357	0.9370	0.9382	0.9394	0.9406	0.9418	0.9429	0.9441
1.6	0.9452	0.9463	0.9474	0.9484	0.9495	0.9505	0.9515	0.9525	0.9535	0.9545
1.7	0.9554	0.9564	0.9573	0.9582	0.9591	0.9599	0.9608	0.9616	0.9625	0.9633
1.8	0.9641	0.9649	0.9656	0.9664	0.9671	0.9678	0.9686	0.9693	0.9699	0.9706
1.9	0.9713	0.9719	0.9726	0.9732	0.9738	0.9744	0.9750	0.9756	0.9761	0.9767
2.0	0.9772	0.9778	0.9783	0.9788	0.9793	0.9798	0.9803	0.9808	0.9812	0.9817
2.1	0.9821	0.9826	0.9830	0.9834	0.9838	0.9842	0.9846	0.9850	0.9854	0.9857
2.2	0.9861	0.9864	0.9868	0.9871	0.9875	0.9878	0.9881	0.9884	0.9887	0.9890
2.3	0.9893	0.9896	0.9898	0.9901	0.9904	0.9906	0.9909	0.9911	0.9913	0.9916
2.4	0.9918	0.9920	0.9922	0.9925	0.9927	0.9929	0.9931	0.9932	0.9934	0.9936
2.5	0.9938	0.9940	0.9941	0.9943	0.9945	0.9946	0.9948	0.9949	0.9951	0.9952
2.6	0.9953	0.9955	0.9956	0.9957	0.9959	0.9960	0.9961	0.9962	0.9963	0.9964
2.7	0.9965	0.9966	0.9967	0.9968	0.9969	0.9970	0.9971	0.9972	0.9973	0.9974
2.8	0.9974	0.9975	0.9976	0.9977	0.9977	0.9978	0.9979	0.9979	0.9980	0.9981
2.9	0.9981	0.9982	0.9982	0.9983	0.9984	0.9984	0.9985	0.9985	0.9986	0.9986
3.0	0.9987	0.9987	0.9987	0.9988	0.9988	0.9989	0.9989	0.9989	0.9990	0.9990
3.1	0.9990	0.9991	0.9991	0.9991	0.9992	0.9992	0.9992	0.9992	0.9993	0.9993
3.2	0.9993	0.9993	0.9994	0.9994	0.9994	0.9994	0.9994	0.9995	0.9995	0.9995
3.3	0.9995	0.9995	0.9995	0.9996	0.9996	0.9996	0.9996	0.9996	0.9996	0.9997
3.4	0.9997	0.9997	0.9997	0.9997	0.9997	0.9997	0.9997	0.9997	0.9997	0.9998
3.5	0.9998	0.9998	0.9998	0.9998	0.9998	0.9998	0.9998	0.9998	0.9998	0.9998

Appendix G

F Distribution $F_{0.10}$

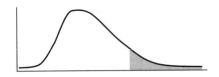

F distribution $F_{0.10}$

	Numerator degrees of freedom										
	1	**2**	**3**	**4**	**5**	**6**	**7**	**8**	**9**	**10**	**11**
1	39.86	49.50	53.59	55.83	57.24	58.20	58.91	59.44	59.86	60.19	60.47
2	8.53	9.00	9.16	9.24	9.29	9.33	9.35	9.37	9.38	9.39	9.40
3	5.54	5.46	5.39	5.34	5.31	5.28	5.27	5.25	5.24	5.23	5.22
4	4.54	4.32	4.19	4.11	4.05	4.01	3.98	3.95	3.94	3.92	3.91
5	4.06	3.78	3.62	3.52	3.45	3.40	3.37	3.34	3.32	3.30	3.28
6	3.78	3.46	3.29	3.18	3.11	3.05	3.01	2.98	2.96	2.94	2.92
7	3.59	3.26	3.07	2.96	2.88	2.83	2.78	2.75	2.72	2.70	2.68
8	3.46	3.11	2.92	2.81	2.73	2.67	2.62	2.59	2.56	2.54	2.52
9	3.36	3.01	2.81	2.69	2.61	2.55	2.51	2.47	2.44	2.42	2.40
10	3.29	2.92	2.73	2.61	2.52	2.46	2.41	2.38	2.35	2.32	2.30
11	3.23	2.86	2.66	2.54	2.45	2.39	2.34	2.30	2.27	2.25	2.23
12	3.18	2.81	2.61	2.48	2.39	2.33	2.28	2.24	2.21	2.19	2.17
13	3.14	2.76	2.56	2.43	2.35	2.28	2.23	2.20	2.16	2.14	2.12
14	3.10	2.73	2.52	2.39	2.31	2.24	2.19	2.15	2.12	2.10	2.07
15	3.07	2.70	2.49	2.36	2.27	2.21	2.16	2.12	2.09	2.06	2.04
16	3.05	2.67	2.46	2.33	2.24	2.18	2.13	2.09	2.06	2.03	2.01
17	3.03	2.64	2.44	2.31	2.22	2.15	2.10	2.06	2.03	2.00	1.98
18	3.01	2.62	2.42	2.29	2.20	2.13	2.08	2.04	2.00	1.98	1.95
19	2.99	2.61	2.40	2.27	2.18	2.11	2.06	2.02	1.98	1.96	1.93
20	2.97	2.59	2.38	2.25	2.16	2.09	2.04	2.00	1.96	1.94	1.91
21	2.96	2.57	2.36	2.23	2.14	2.08	2.02	1.98	1.95	1.92	1.90
22	2.95	2.56	2.35	2.22	2.13	2.06	2.01	1.97	1.93	1.90	1.88
23	2.94	2.55	2.34	2.21	2.11	2.05	1.99	1.95	1.92	1.89	1.87
24	2.93	2.54	2.33	2.19	2.10	2.04	1.98	1.94	1.91	1.88	1.85
25	2.92	2.53	2.32	2.18	2.09	2.02	1.97	1.93	1.89	1.87	1.84
26	2.91	2.52	2.31	2.17	2.08	2.01	1.96	1.92	1.88	1.86	1.83
27	2.90	2.51	2.30	2.17	2.07	2.00	1.95	1.91	1.87	1.85	1.82
28	2.89	2.50	2.29	2.16	2.06	2.00	1.94	1.90	1.87	1.84	1.81
29	2.89	2.50	2.28	2.15	2.06	1.99	1.93	1.89	1.86	1.83	1.80
30	2.88	2.49	2.28	2.14	2.05	1.98	1.93	1.88	1.85	1.82	1.79
40	2.84	2.44	2.23	2.09	2.00	1.93	1.87	1.83	1.79	1.76	1.74
60	2.79	2.39	2.18	2.04	1.95	1.87	1.82	1.77	1.74	1.71	1.68
100	2.76	2.36	2.14	2.00	1.91	1.83	1.78	1.73	1.69	1.66	1.64

Denominator degrees of freedom

Continued

F distribution $F_{0.10}$ *(continued)*

		12	13	14	15	16	17	18	19	20	21	22
Numerator degrees of freedom												
	1	60.71	60.90	61.07	61.22	61.35	61.46	61.57	61.66	61.74	61.81	61.88
	2	9.41	9.41	9.42	9.42	9.43	9.43	9.44	9.44	9.44	9.44	9.45
	3	5.22	5.21	5.20	5.20	5.20	5.19	5.19	5.19	5.18	5.18	5.18
	4	3.90	3.89	3.88	3.87	3.86	3.86	3.85	3.85	3.84	3.84	3.84
	5	3.27	3.26	3.25	3.24	3.23	3.22	3.22	3.21	3.21	3.20	3.20
	6	2.90	2.89	2.88	2.87	2.86	2.85	2.85	2.84	2.84	2.83	2.83
	7	2.67	2.65	2.64	2.63	2.62	2.61	2.61	2.60	2.59	2.59	2.58
	8	2.50	2.49	2.48	2.46	2.45	2.45	2.44	2.43	2.42	2.42	2.41
	9	2.38	2.36	2.35	2.34	2.33	2.32	2.31	2.30	2.30	2.29	2.29
	10	2.28	2.27	2.26	2.24	2.23	2.22	2.22	2.21	2.20	2.19	2.19
	11	2.21	2.19	2.18	2.17	2.16	2.15	2.14	2.13	2.12	2.12	2.11
	12	2.15	2.13	2.12	2.10	2.09	2.08	2.08	2.07	2.06	2.05	2.05
	13	2.10	2.08	2.07	2.05	2.04	2.03	2.02	2.01	2.01	2.00	1.99
Denominator degrees of freedom	14	2.05	2.04	2.02	2.01	2.00	1.99	1.98	1.97	1.96	1.96	1.95
	15	2.02	2.00	1.99	1.97	1.96	1.95	1.94	1.93	1.92	1.92	1.91
	16	1.99	1.97	1.95	1.94	1.93	1.92	1.91	1.90	1.89	1.88	1.88
	17	1.96	1.94	1.93	1.91	1.90	1.89	1.88	1.87	1.86	1.86	1.85
	18	1.93	1.92	1.90	1.89	1.87	1.86	1.85	1.84	1.84	1.83	1.82
	19	1.91	1.89	1.88	1.86	1.85	1.84	1.83	1.82	1.81	1.81	1.80
	20	1.89	1.87	1.86	1.84	1.83	1.82	1.81	1.80	1.79	1.79	1.78
	21	1.87	1.86	1.84	1.83	1.81	1.80	1.79	1.78	1.78	1.77	1.76
	22	1.86	1.84	1.83	1.81	1.80	1.79	1.78	1.77	1.76	1.75	1.74
	23	1.84	1.83	1.81	1.80	1.78	1.77	1.76	1.75	1.74	1.74	1.73
	24	1.83	1.81	1.80	1.78	1.77	1.76	1.75	1.74	1.73	1.72	1.71
	25	1.82	1.80	1.79	1.77	1.76	1.75	1.74	1.73	1.72	1.71	1.70
	26	1.81	1.79	1.77	1.76	1.75	1.73	1.72	1.71	1.71	1.70	1.69
	27	1.80	1.78	1.76	1.75	1.74	1.72	1.71	1.70	1.70	1.69	1.68
	28	1.79	1.77	1.75	1.74	1.73	1.71	1.70	1.69	1.69	1.68	1.67
	29	1.78	1.76	1.75	1.73	1.72	1.71	1.69	1.68	1.68	1.67	1.66
	30	1.77	1.75	1.74	1.72	1.71	1.70	1.69	1.68	1.67	1.66	1.65
	40	1.71	1.70	1.68	1.66	1.65	1.64	1.62	1.61	1.61	1.60	1.59
	60	1.66	1.64	1.62	1.60	1.59	1.58	1.56	1.55	1.54	1.53	1.53
	100	1.61	1.59	1.57	1.56	1.54	1.53	1.52	1.50	1.49	1.48	1.48

Continued

F distribution $F_{0.10}$ (continued)

		Numerator degrees of freedom										
		23	**24**	**25**	**26**	**27**	**28**	**29**	**30**	**40**	**60**	**100**
	1	61.94	62.00	62.05	62.10	62.15	62.19	62.23	62.26	62.53	62.79	63.01
	2	9.45	9.45	9.45	9.45	9.45	9.46	9.46	9.46	9.47	9.47	9.48
	3	5.18	5.18	5.17	5.17	5.17	5.17	5.17	5.17	5.16	5.15	5.14
	4	3.83	3.83	3.83	3.83	3.82	3.82	3.82	3.82	3.80	3.79	3.78
	5	3.19	3.19	3.19	3.18	3.18	3.18	3.18	3.17	3.16	3.14	3.13
	6	2.82	2.82	2.81	2.81	2.81	2.81	2.80	2.80	2.78	2.76	2.75
	7	2.58	2.58	2.57	2.57	2.56	2.56	2.56	2.56	2.54	2.51	2.50
	8	2.41	2.40	2.40	2.40	2.39	2.39	2.39	2.38	2.36	2.34	2.32
	9	2.28	2.28	2.27	2.27	2.26	2.26	2.26	2.25	2.23	2.21	2.19
	10	2.18	2.18	2.17	2.17	2.17	2.16	2.16	2.16	2.13	2.11	2.09
Denominator degrees of freedom	11	2.11	2.10	2.10	2.09	2.09	2.08	2.08	2.08	2.05	2.03	2.01
	12	2.04	2.04	2.03	2.03	2.02	2.02	2.01	2.01	1.99	1.96	1.94
	13	1.99	1.98	1.98	1.97	1.97	1.96	1.96	1.96	1.93	1.90	1.88
	14	1.94	1.94	1.93	1.93	1.92	1.92	1.92	1.91	1.89	1.86	1.83
	15	1.90	1.90	1.89	1.89	1.88	1.88	1.88	1.87	1.85	1.82	1.79
	16	1.87	1.87	1.86	1.86	1.85	1.85	1.84	1.84	1.81	1.78	1.76
	17	1.84	1.84	1.83	1.83	1.82	1.82	1.81	1.81	1.78	1.75	1.73
	18	1.82	1.81	1.80	1.80	1.80	1.79	1.79	1.78	1.75	1.72	1.70
	19	1.79	1.79	1.78	1.78	1.77	1.77	1.76	1.76	1.73	1.70	1.67
	20	1.77	1.77	1.76	1.76	1.75	1.75	1.74	1.74	1.71	1.68	1.65
	21	1.75	1.75	1.74	1.74	1.73	1.73	1.72	1.72	1.69	1.66	1.63
	22	1.74	1.73	1.73	1.72	1.72	1.71	1.71	1.70	1.67	1.64	1.61
	23	1.72	1.72	1.71	1.70	1.70	1.69	1.69	1.69	1.66	1.62	1.59
	24	1.71	1.70	1.70	1.69	1.69	1.68	1.68	1.67	1.64	1.61	1.58
	25	1.70	1.69	1.68	1.68	1.67	1.67	1.66	1.66	1.63	1.59	1.56
	26	1.68	1.68	1.67	1.67	1.66	1.66	1.65	1.65	1.61	1.58	1.55
	27	1.67	1.67	1.66	1.65	1.65	1.64	1.64	1.64	1.60	1.57	1.54
	28	1.66	1.66	1.65	1.64	1.64	1.63	1.63	1.63	1.59	1.56	1.53
	29	1.65	1.65	1.64	1.63	1.63	1.62	1.62	1.62	1.58	1.55	1.52
	30	1.64	1.64	1.63	1.63	1.62	1.62	1.61	1.61	1.57	1.54	1.51
	40	1.58	1.57	1.57	1.56	1.56	1.55	1.55	1.54	1.51	1.47	1.43
	60	1.52	1.51	1.50	1.50	1.49	1.49	1.48	1.48	1.44	1.40	1.36
	100	1.47	1.46	1.45	1.45	1.44	1.43	1.43	1.42	1.38	1.34	1.29

Appendix H

F Distribution $F_{0.05}$

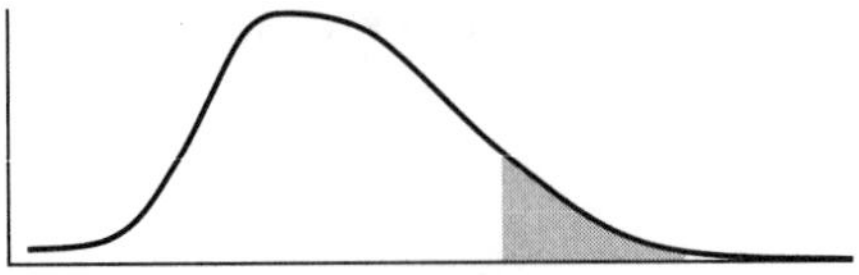

***F* distribution $F_{0.05}$**

Denominator degrees of freedom	Numerator degrees of freedom: 1	2	3	4	5	6	7	8	9	10	11
1	161.4	199.5	215.7	224.6	230.2	234.0	236.8	238.9	240.5	241.9	243.0
2	18.51	19.00	19.16	19.25	19.30	19.33	19.35	19.37	19.38	19.40	19.40
3	10.13	9.55	9.28	9.12	9.01	8.94	8.89	8.85	8.81	8.79	8.76
4	7.71	6.94	6.59	6.39	6.26	6.16	6.09	6.04	6.00	5.96	5.94
5	6.61	5.79	5.41	5.19	5.05	4.95	4.88	4.82	4.77	4.74	4.70
6	5.99	5.14	4.76	4.53	4.39	4.28	4.21	4.15	4.10	4.06	4.03
7	5.59	4.74	4.35	4.12	3.97	3.87	3.79	3.73	3.68	3.64	3.60
8	5.32	4.46	4.07	3.84	3.69	3.58	3.50	3.44	3.39	3.35	3.31
9	5.12	4.26	3.86	3.63	3.48	3.37	3.29	3.23	3.18	3.14	3.10
10	4.96	4.10	3.71	3.48	3.33	3.22	3.14	3.07	3.02	2.98	2.94
11	4.84	3.98	3.59	3.36	3.20	3.09	3.01	2.95	2.90	2.85	2.82
12	4.75	3.89	3.49	3.26	3.11	3.00	2.91	2.85	2.80	2.75	2.72
13	4.67	3.81	3.41	3.18	3.03	2.92	2.83	2.77	2.71	2.67	2.63
14	4.60	3.74	3.34	3.11	2.96	2.85	2.76	2.70	2.65	2.60	2.57
15	4.54	3.68	3.29	3.06	2.90	2.79	2.71	2.64	2.59	2.54	2.51
16	4.49	3.63	3.24	3.01	2.85	2.74	2.66	2.59	2.54	2.49	2.46
17	4.45	3.59	3.20	2.96	2.81	2.70	2.61	2.55	2.49	2.45	2.41
18	4.41	3.55	3.16	2.93	2.77	2.66	2.58	2.51	2.46	2.41	2.37
19	4.38	3.52	3.13	2.90	2.74	2.63	2.54	2.48	2.42	2.38	2.34
20	4.35	3.49	3.10	2.87	2.71	2.60	2.51	2.45	2.39	2.35	2.31
21	4.32	3.47	3.07	2.84	2.68	2.57	2.49	2.42	2.37	2.32	2.28
22	4.30	3.44	3.05	2.82	2.66	2.55	2.46	2.40	2.34	2.30	2.26
23	4.28	3.42	3.03	2.80	2.64	2.53	2.44	2.37	2.32	2.27	2.24
24	4.26	3.40	3.01	2.78	2.62	2.51	2.42	2.36	2.30	2.25	2.22
25	4.24	3.39	2.99	2.76	2.60	2.49	2.40	2.34	2.28	2.24	2.20
26	4.23	3.37	2.98	2.74	2.59	2.47	2.39	2.32	2.27	2.22	2.18
27	4.21	3.35	2.96	2.73	2.57	2.46	2.37	2.31	2.25	2.20	2.17
28	4.20	3.34	2.95	2.71	2.56	2.45	2.36	2.29	2.24	2.19	2.15
29	4.18	3.33	2.93	2.70	2.55	2.43	2.35	2.28	2.22	2.18	2.14
30	4.17	3.32	2.92	2.69	2.53	2.42	2.33	2.27	2.21	2.16	2.13
40	4.08	3.23	2.84	2.61	2.45	2.34	2.25	2.18	2.12	2.08	2.04
60	4.00	3.15	2.76	2.53	2.37	2.25	2.17	2.10	2.04	1.99	1.95
100	3.94	3.09	2.70	2.46	2.31	2.19	2.10	2.03	1.97	1.93	1.89

Continued

F distribution *F*_{0.05} *(continued)*

		12	13	14	15	16	17	18	19	20	21	22
	1	243.9	244.7	245.4	245.9	246.5	246.9	247.3	247.7	248.0	248.3	248.6
	2	19.41	19.42	19.42	19.43	19.43	19.44	19.44	19.44	19.45	19.45	19.45
	3	8.74	8.73	8.71	8.70	8.69	8.68	8.67	8.67	8.66	8.65	8.65
	4	5.91	5.89	5.87	5.86	5.84	5.83	5.82	5.81	5.80	5.79	5.79
	5	4.68	4.66	4.64	4.62	4.60	4.59	4.58	4.57	4.56	4.55	4.54
	6	4.00	3.98	3.96	3.94	3.92	3.91	3.90	3.88	3.87	3.86	3.86
	7	3.57	3.55	3.53	3.51	3.49	3.48	3.47	3.46	3.44	3.43	3.43
	8	3.28	3.26	3.24	3.22	3.20	3.19	3.17	3.16	3.15	3.14	3.13
	9	3.07	3.05	3.03	3.01	2.99	2.97	2.96	2.95	2.94	2.93	2.92
	10	2.91	2.89	2.86	2.85	2.83	2.81	2.80	2.79	2.77	2.76	2.75
	11	2.79	2.76	2.74	2.72	2.70	2.69	2.67	2.66	2.65	2.64	2.63
	12	2.69	2.66	2.64	2.62	2.60	2.58	2.57	2.56	2.54	2.53	2.52
	13	2.60	2.58	2.55	2.53	2.51	2.50	2.48	2.47	2.46	2.45	2.44
	14	2.53	2.51	2.48	2.46	2.44	2.43	2.41	2.40	2.39	2.38	2.37
	15	2.48	2.45	2.42	2.40	2.38	2.37	2.35	2.34	2.33	2.32	2.31
	16	2.42	2.40	2.37	2.35	2.33	2.32	2.30	2.29	2.28	2.26	2.25
	17	2.38	2.35	2.33	2.31	2.29	2.27	2.26	2.24	2.23	2.22	2.21
	18	2.34	2.31	2.29	2.27	2.25	2.23	2.22	2.20	2.19	2.18	2.17
	19	2.31	2.28	2.26	2.23	2.21	2.20	2.18	2.17	2.16	2.14	2.13
	20	2.28	2.25	2.22	2.20	2.18	2.17	2.15	2.14	2.12	2.11	2.10
	21	2.25	2.22	2.20	2.18	2.16	2.14	2.12	2.11	2.10	2.08	2.07
	22	2.23	2.20	2.17	2.15	2.13	2.11	2.10	2.08	2.07	2.06	2.05
	23	2.20	2.18	2.15	2.13	2.11	2.09	2.08	2.06	2.05	2.04	2.02
	24	2.18	2.15	2.13	2.11	2.09	2.07	2.05	2.04	2.03	2.01	2.00
	25	2.16	2.14	2.11	2.09	2.07	2.05	2.04	2.02	2.01	2.00	1.98
	26	2.15	2.12	2.09	2.07	2.05	2.03	2.02	2.00	1.99	1.98	1.97
	27	2.13	2.10	2.08	2.06	2.04	2.02	2.00	1.99	1.97	1.96	1.95
	28	2.12	2.09	2.06	2.04	2.02	2.00	1.99	1.97	1.96	1.95	1.93
	29	2.10	2.08	2.05	2.03	2.01	1.99	1.97	1.96	1.94	1.93	1.92
	30	2.09	2.06	2.04	2.01	1.99	1.98	1.96	1.95	1.93	1.92	1.91
	40	2.00	1.97	1.95	1.92	1.90	1.89	1.87	1.85	1.84	1.83	1.81
	60	1.92	1.89	1.86	1.84	1.82	1.80	1.78	1.76	1.75	1.73	1.72
	100	1.85	1.82	1.79	1.77	1.75	1.73	1.71	1.69	1.68	1.66	1.65

Numerator degrees of freedom spans the column headers 12–22. The leftmost vertical label reads **Denominator degrees of freedom**.

Continued

F distribution F₀.₀₅ *(continued)*

		23	24	25	26	27	28	29	30	40	60	100
Denominator degrees of freedom	1	248.8	249.1	249.3	249.5	249.6	249.8	250.0	250.1	251.1	252.2	253.0
	2	19.45	19.45	19.46	19.46	19.46	19.46	19.46	19.46	19.47	19.48	19.49
	3	8.64	8.64	8.63	8.63	8.63	8.62	8.62	8.62	8.59	8.57	8.55
	4	5.78	5.77	5.77	5.76	5.76	5.75	5.75	5.75	5.72	5.69	5.66
	5	4.53	4.53	4.52	4.52	4.51	4.50	4.50	4.50	4.46	4.43	4.41
	6	3.85	3.84	3.83	3.83	3.82	3.82	3.81	3.81	3.77	3.74	3.71
	7	3.42	3.41	3.40	3.40	3.39	3.39	3.38	3.38	3.34	3.30	3.27
	8	3.12	3.12	3.11	3.10	3.10	3.09	3.08	3.08	3.04	3.01	2.97
	9	2.91	2.90	2.89	2.89	2.88	2.87	2.87	2.86	2.83	2.79	2.76
	10	2.75	2.74	2.73	2.72	2.72	2.71	2.70	2.70	2.66	2.62	2.59
	11	2.62	2.61	2.60	2.59	2.59	2.58	2.58	2.57	2.53	2.49	2.46
	12	2.51	2.51	2.50	2.49	2.48	2.48	2.47	2.47	2.43	2.38	2.35
	13	2.43	2.42	2.41	2.41	2.40	2.39	2.39	2.38	2.34	2.30	2.26
	14	2.36	2.35	2.34	2.33	2.33	2.32	2.31	2.31	2.27	2.22	2.19
	15	2.30	2.29	2.28	2.27	2.27	2.26	2.25	2.25	2.20	2.16	2.12
	16	2.24	2.24	2.23	2.22	2.21	2.21	2.20	2.19	2.15	2.11	2.07
	17	2.20	2.19	2.18	2.17	2.17	2.16	2.15	2.15	2.10	2.06	2.02
	18	2.16	2.15	2.14	2.13	2.13	2.12	2.11	2.11	2.06	2.02	1.98
	19	2.12	2.11	2.11	2.10	2.09	2.08	2.08	2.07	2.03	1.98	1.94
	20	2.09	2.08	2.07	2.07	2.06	2.05	2.05	2.04	1.99	1.95	1.91
	21	2.06	2.05	2.05	2.04	2.03	2.02	2.02	2.01	1.96	1.92	1.88
	22	2.04	2.03	2.02	2.01	2.00	2.00	1.99	1.98	1.94	1.89	1.85
	23	2.01	2.01	2.00	1.99	1.98	1.97	1.97	1.96	1.91	1.86	1.82
	24	1.99	1.98	1.97	1.97	1.96	1.95	1.95	1.94	1.89	1.84	1.80
	25	1.97	1.96	1.96	1.95	1.94	1.93	1.93	1.92	1.87	1.82	1.78
	26	1.96	1.95	1.94	1.93	1.92	1.91	1.91	1.90	1.85	1.80	1.76
	27	1.94	1.93	1.92	1.91	1.90	1.90	1.89	1.88	1.84	1.79	1.74
	28	1.92	1.91	1.91	1.90	1.89	1.88	1.88	1.87	1.82	1.77	1.73
	29	1.91	1.90	1.89	1.88	1.88	1.87	1.86	1.85	1.81	1.75	1.71
	30	1.90	1.89	1.88	1.87	1.86	1.85	1.85	1.84	1.79	1.74	1.70
	40	1.80	1.79	1.78	1.77	1.77	1.76	1.75	1.74	1.69	1.64	1.59
	60	1.71	1.70	1.69	1.68	1.67	1.66	1.66	1.65	1.59	1.53	1.48
	100	1.64	1.63	1.62	1.61	1.60	1.59	1.58	1.57	1.52	1.45	1.39

Numerator degrees of freedom

Appendix I

F Distribution $F_{0.01}$

F distribution $F_{0.01}$

		1	2	3	4	5	6	7	8	9	10	11
						Numerator degrees of freedom						
Denominator degrees of freedom	1	4052	4999	5404	5624	5764	5859	5928	5981	6022	6056	6083
	2	98.5	99	99.16	99.25	99.3	99.33	99.36	99.38	99.39	99.4	99.41
	3	34.12	30.82	29.46	28.71	28.24	27.91	27.67	27.49	27.34	27.23	27.13
	4	21.2	18	16.69	15.98	15.52	15.21	14.98	14.8	14.66	14.55	14.45
	5	16.26	13.27	12.06	11.39	10.97	10.67	10.46	10.29	10.16	10.05	9.963
	6	13.75	10.92	9.78	9.148	8.746	8.466	8.26	8.102	7.976	7.874	7.79
	7	12.25	9.547	8.451	7.847	7.46	7.191	6.993	6.84	6.719	6.62	6.538
	8	11.26	8.649	7.591	7.006	6.632	6.371	6.178	6.029	5.911	5.814	5.734
	9	10.56	8.022	6.992	6.422	6.057	5.802	5.613	5.467	5.351	5.257	5.178
	10	10.04	7.559	6.552	5.994	5.636	5.386	5.2	5.057	4.942	4.849	4.772
	11	9.646	7.206	6.217	5.668	5.316	5.069	4.886	4.744	4.632	4.539	4.462
	12	9.33	6.927	5.953	5.412	5.064	4.821	4.64	4.499	4.388	4.296	4.22
	13	9.074	6.701	5.739	5.205	4.862	4.62	4.441	4.302	4.191	4.1	4.025
	14	8.862	6.515	5.564	5.035	4.695	4.456	4.278	4.14	4.03	3.939	3.864
	15	8.683	6.359	5.417	4.893	4.556	4.318	4.142	4.004	3.895	3.805	3.73
	16	8.531	6.226	5.292	4.773	4.437	4.202	4.026	3.89	3.78	3.691	3.616
	17	8.4	6.112	5.185	4.669	4.336	4.101	3.927	3.791	3.682	3.593	3.518
	18	8.285	6.013	5.092	4.579	4.248	4.015	3.841	3.705	3.597	3.508	3.434
	19	8.185	5.926	5.01	4.5	4.171	3.939	3.765	3.631	3.523	3.434	3.36
	20	8.096	5.849	4.938	4.431	4.103	3.871	3.699	3.564	3.457	3.368	3.294
	21	8.017	5.78	4.874	4.369	4.042	3.812	3.64	3.506	3.398	3.31	3.236
	22	7.945	5.719	4.817	4.313	3.988	3.758	3.587	3.453	3.346	3.258	3.184
	23	7.881	5.664	4.765	4.264	3.939	3.71	3.539	3.406	3.299	3.211	3.137
	24	7.823	5.614	4.718	4.218	3.895	3.667	3.496	3.363	3.256	3.168	3.094
	25	7.77	5.568	4.675	4.177	3.855	3.627	3.457	3.324	3.217	3.129	3.056
	26	7.721	5.526	4.637	4.14	3.818	3.591	3.421	3.288	3.182	3.094	3.021
	27	7.677	5.488	4.601	4.106	3.785	3.558	3.388	3.256	3.149	3.062	2.988
	28	7.636	5.453	4.568	4.074	3.754	3.528	3.358	3.226	3.12	3.032	2.959
	29	7.598	5.42	4.538	4.045	3.725	3.499	3.33	3.198	3.092	3.005	2.931
	30	7.562	5.39	4.51	4.018	3.699	3.473	3.305	3.173	3.067	2.979	2.906
	40	7.314	5.178	4.313	3.828	3.514	3.291	3.124	2.993	2.888	2.801	2.727
	60	7.077	4.977	4.126	3.649	3.339	3.119	2.953	2.823	2.718	2.632	2.559
	100	6.895	4.824	3.984	3.513	3.206	2.988	2.823	2.694	2.59	2.503	2.43

Continued

F distribution *F*0.01 *(continued)*

		12	13	14	15	16	17	18	19	20	21	22
						Numerator degrees of freedom						
	1	6107	6126	6143	6157	6170	6181	6191	6201	6208.7	6216.1	6223.1
	2	99.42	99.42	99.43	99.43	99.44	99.44	99.44	99.45	99.448	99.451	99.455
	3	27.05	26.98	26.92	26.87	26.83	26.79	26.75	26.72	26.69	26.664	26.639
	4	14.37	14.31	14.25	14.2	14.15	14.11	14.08	14.05	14.019	13.994	13.97
	5	9.888	9.825	9.77	9.722	9.68	9.643	9.609	9.58	9.5527	9.5281	9.5058
	6	7.718	7.657	7.605	7.559	7.519	7.483	7.451	7.422	7.3958	7.3721	7.3506
	7	6.469	6.41	6.359	6.314	6.275	6.24	6.209	6.181	6.1555	6.1324	6.1113
	8	5.667	5.609	5.559	5.515	5.477	5.442	5.412	5.384	5.3591	5.3365	5.3157
	9	5.111	5.055	5.005	4.962	4.924	4.89	4.86	4.833	4.808	4.7855	4.7651
	10	4.706	4.65	4.601	4.558	4.52	4.487	4.457	4.43	4.4054	4.3831	4.3628
	11	4.397	4.342	4.293	4.251	4.213	4.18	4.15	4.123	4.099	4.0769	4.0566
Denominator degrees of freedom	12	4.155	4.1	4.052	4.01	3.972	3.939	3.91	3.883	3.8584	3.8363	3.8161
	13	3.96	3.905	3.857	3.815	3.778	3.745	3.716	3.689	3.6646	3.6425	3.6223
	14	3.8	3.745	3.698	3.656	3.619	3.586	3.556	3.529	3.5052	3.4832	3.463
	15	3.666	3.612	3.564	3.522	3.485	3.452	3.423	3.396	3.3719	3.3498	3.3297
	16	3.553	3.498	3.451	3.409	3.372	3.339	3.31	3.283	3.2587	3.2367	3.2165
	17	3.455	3.401	3.353	3.312	3.275	3.242	3.212	3.186	3.1615	3.1394	3.1192
	18	3.371	3.316	3.269	3.227	3.19	3.158	3.128	3.101	3.0771	3.055	3.0348
	19	3.297	3.242	3.195	3.153	3.116	3.084	3.054	3.027	3.0031	2.981	2.9607
	20	3.231	3.177	3.13	3.088	3.051	3.018	2.989	2.962	2.9377	2.9156	2.8953
	21	3.173	3.119	3.072	3.03	2.993	2.96	2.931	2.904	2.8795	2.8574	2.837
	22	3.121	3.067	3.019	2.978	2.941	2.908	2.879	2.852	2.8274	2.8052	2.7849
	23	3.074	3.02	2.973	2.931	2.894	2.861	2.832	2.805	2.7805	2.7582	2.7378
	24	3.032	2.977	2.93	2.889	2.852	2.819	2.789	2.762	2.738	2.7157	2.6953
	25	2.993	2.939	2.892	2.85	2.813	2.78	2.751	2.724	2.6993	2.677	2.6565
	26	2.958	2.904	2.857	2.815	2.778	2.745	2.715	2.688	2.664	2.6416	2.6211
	27	2.926	2.872	2.824	2.783	2.746	2.713	2.683	2.656	2.6316	2.609	2.5886
	28	2.896	2.842	2.795	2.753	2.716	2.683	2.653	2.626	2.6018	2.5793	2.5587
	29	2.868	2.814	2.767	2.726	2.689	2.656	2.626	2.599	2.5742	2.5517	2.5311
	30	2.843	2.789	2.742	2.7	2.663	2.63	2.6	2.573	2.5487	2.5262	2.5055
	40	2.665	2.611	2.563	2.522	2.484	2.451	2.421	2.394	2.3689	2.3461	2.3252
	60	2.496	2.442	2.394	2.352	2.315	2.281	2.251	2.223	2.1978	2.1747	2.1533
	10	2.368	2.313	2.265	2.223	2.185	2.151	2.12	2.092	2.0666	2.0431	2.0214

Continued

F distribution $F_{0.01}$ *(continued)*

<table>
<thead>
<tr><th colspan="12">Numerator degrees of freedom</th></tr>
<tr><th></th><th>23</th><th>24</th><th>25</th><th>26</th><th>27</th><th>28</th><th>29</th><th>30</th><th>40</th><th>60</th><th>100</th></tr>
</thead>
<tbody>
<tr><td>1</td><td>6228.7</td><td>6234.3</td><td>6239.9</td><td>6244.5</td><td>6249.2</td><td>6252.9</td><td>6257.1</td><td>6260.4</td><td>6286.4</td><td>6313</td><td>6333.9</td></tr>
<tr><td>2</td><td>99.455</td><td>99.455</td><td>99.459</td><td>99.462</td><td>99.462</td><td>99.462</td><td>99.462</td><td>99.466</td><td>99.477</td><td>99.484</td><td>99.491</td></tr>
<tr><td>3</td><td>26.617</td><td>26.597</td><td>26.579</td><td>26.562</td><td>26.546</td><td>26.531</td><td>26.517</td><td>26.504</td><td>26.411</td><td>26.316</td><td>26.241</td></tr>
<tr><td>4</td><td>13.949</td><td>13.929</td><td>13.911</td><td>13.894</td><td>13.878</td><td>13.864</td><td>13.85</td><td>13.838</td><td>13.745</td><td>13.652</td><td>13.577</td></tr>
<tr><td>5</td><td>9.4853</td><td>9.4665</td><td>9.4492</td><td>9.4331</td><td>9.4183</td><td>9.4044</td><td>9.3914</td><td>9.3794</td><td>9.2912</td><td>9.202</td><td>9.13</td></tr>
<tr><td>6</td><td>7.3309</td><td>7.3128</td><td>7.296</td><td>7.2805</td><td>7.2661</td><td>7.2528</td><td>7.2403</td><td>7.2286</td><td>7.1432</td><td>7.0568</td><td>6.9867</td></tr>
<tr><td>7</td><td>6.092</td><td>6.0743</td><td>6.0579</td><td>6.0428</td><td>6.0287</td><td>6.0156</td><td>6.0035</td><td>5.992</td><td>5.9084</td><td>5.8236</td><td>5.7546</td></tr>
<tr><td>8</td><td>5.2967</td><td>5.2793</td><td>5.2631</td><td>5.2482</td><td>5.2344</td><td>5.2214</td><td>5.2094</td><td>5.1981</td><td>5.1156</td><td>5.0316</td><td>4.9633</td></tr>
<tr><td>9</td><td>4.7463</td><td>4.729</td><td>4.713</td><td>4.6982</td><td>4.6845</td><td>4.6717</td><td>4.6598</td><td>4.6486</td><td>4.5667</td><td>4.4831</td><td>4.415</td></tr>
<tr><td>10</td><td>4.3441</td><td>4.3269</td><td>4.3111</td><td>4.2963</td><td>4.2827</td><td>4.27</td><td>4.2582</td><td>4.2469</td><td>4.1653</td><td>4.0819</td><td>4.0137</td></tr>
<tr><td>11</td><td>4.038</td><td>4.0209</td><td>4.0051</td><td>3.9904</td><td>3.9768</td><td>3.9641</td><td>3.9522</td><td>3.9411</td><td>3.8596</td><td>3.7761</td><td>3.7077</td></tr>
<tr><td>12</td><td>3.7976</td><td>3.7805</td><td>3.7647</td><td>3.7501</td><td>3.7364</td><td>3.7238</td><td>3.7119</td><td>3.7008</td><td>3.6192</td><td>3.5355</td><td>3.4668</td></tr>
<tr><td>13</td><td>3.6038</td><td>3.5868</td><td>3.571</td><td>3.5563</td><td>3.5427</td><td>3.53</td><td>3.5182</td><td>3.507</td><td>3.4253</td><td>3.3413</td><td>3.2723</td></tr>
<tr><td>14</td><td>3.4445</td><td>3.4274</td><td>3.4116</td><td>3.3969</td><td>3.3833</td><td>3.3706</td><td>3.3587</td><td>3.3476</td><td>3.2657</td><td>3.1813</td><td>3.1118</td></tr>
<tr><td>15</td><td>3.3111</td><td>3.294</td><td>3.2782</td><td>3.2636</td><td>3.2499</td><td>3.2372</td><td>3.2253</td><td>3.2141</td><td>3.1319</td><td>3.0471</td><td>2.9772</td></tr>
<tr><td>16</td><td>3.1979</td><td>3.1808</td><td>3.165</td><td>3.1503</td><td>3.1366</td><td>3.1238</td><td>3.1119</td><td>3.1007</td><td>3.0182</td><td>2.933</td><td>2.8627</td></tr>
<tr><td>17</td><td>3.1006</td><td>3.0835</td><td>3.0676</td><td>3.0529</td><td>3.0392</td><td>3.0264</td><td>3.0145</td><td>3.0032</td><td>2.9204</td><td>2.8348</td><td>2.7639</td></tr>
<tr><td>18</td><td>3.0161</td><td>2.999</td><td>2.9831</td><td>2.9683</td><td>2.9546</td><td>2.9418</td><td>2.9298</td><td>2.9185</td><td>2.8354</td><td>2.7493</td><td>2.6779</td></tr>
<tr><td>19</td><td>2.9421</td><td>2.9249</td><td>2.9089</td><td>2.8942</td><td>2.8804</td><td>2.8675</td><td>2.8555</td><td>2.8442</td><td>2.7608</td><td>2.6742</td><td>2.6023</td></tr>
<tr><td>20</td><td>2.8766</td><td>2.8594</td><td>2.8434</td><td>2.8286</td><td>2.8148</td><td>2.8019</td><td>2.7898</td><td>2.7785</td><td>2.6947</td><td>2.6077</td><td>2.5353</td></tr>
<tr><td>21</td><td>2.8183</td><td>2.801</td><td>2.785</td><td>2.7702</td><td>2.7563</td><td>2.7434</td><td>2.7313</td><td>2.72</td><td>2.6359</td><td>2.5484</td><td>2.4755</td></tr>
<tr><td>22</td><td>2.7661</td><td>2.7488</td><td>2.7328</td><td>2.7179</td><td>2.704</td><td>2.691</td><td>2.6789</td><td>2.6675</td><td>2.5831</td><td>2.4951</td><td>2.4218</td></tr>
<tr><td>23</td><td>2.7191</td><td>2.7017</td><td>2.6857</td><td>2.6707</td><td>2.6568</td><td>2.6438</td><td>2.6316</td><td>2.6202</td><td>2.5355</td><td>2.4471</td><td>2.3732</td></tr>
<tr><td>24</td><td>2.6764</td><td>2.6591</td><td>2.643</td><td>2.628</td><td>2.614</td><td>2.601</td><td>2.5888</td><td>2.5773</td><td>2.4923</td><td>2.4035</td><td>2.3291</td></tr>
<tr><td>25</td><td>2.6377</td><td>2.6203</td><td>2.6041</td><td>2.5891</td><td>2.5751</td><td>2.562</td><td>2.5498</td><td>2.5383</td><td>2.453</td><td>2.3637</td><td>2.2888</td></tr>
<tr><td>26</td><td>2.6022</td><td>2.5848</td><td>2.5686</td><td>2.5535</td><td>2.5395</td><td>2.5264</td><td>2.5142</td><td>2.5026</td><td>2.417</td><td>2.3273</td><td>2.2519</td></tr>
<tr><td>27</td><td>2.5697</td><td>2.5522</td><td>2.536</td><td>2.5209</td><td>2.5069</td><td>2.4937</td><td>2.4814</td><td>2.4699</td><td>2.384</td><td>2.2938</td><td>2.218</td></tr>
<tr><td>28</td><td>2.5398</td><td>2.5223</td><td>2.506</td><td>2.4909</td><td>2.4768</td><td>2.4636</td><td>2.4513</td><td>2.4397</td><td>2.3535</td><td>2.2629</td><td>2.1867</td></tr>
<tr><td>29</td><td>2.5121</td><td>2.4946</td><td>2.4783</td><td>2.4631</td><td>2.449</td><td>2.4358</td><td>2.4234</td><td>2.4118</td><td>2.3253</td><td>2.2344</td><td>2.1577</td></tr>
<tr><td>30</td><td>2.4865</td><td>2.4689</td><td>2.4526</td><td>2.4374</td><td>2.4233</td><td>2.41</td><td>2.3976</td><td>2.386</td><td>2.2992</td><td>2.2079</td><td>2.1307</td></tr>
<tr><td>40</td><td>2.3059</td><td>2.288</td><td>2.2714</td><td>2.2559</td><td>2.2415</td><td>2.228</td><td>2.2153</td><td>2.2034</td><td>2.1142</td><td>2.0194</td><td>1.9383</td></tr>
<tr><td>60</td><td>2.1336</td><td>2.1154</td><td>2.0984</td><td>2.0825</td><td>2.0677</td><td>2.0538</td><td>2.0408</td><td>2.0285</td><td>1.936</td><td>1.8363</td><td>1.7493</td></tr>
<tr><td>100</td><td>2.0012</td><td>1.9826</td><td>1.9651</td><td>1.9489</td><td>1.9337</td><td>1.9194</td><td>1.9059</td><td>1.8933</td><td>1.7972</td><td>1.6918</td><td>1.5977</td></tr>
</tbody>
</table>

Denominator degrees of freedom

Appendix J

Binomial Distribution

Probability of x or fewer occurrences in a sample of size n

Binomial distribution

n	x	0.01	0.02	0.03	0.04	0.05	0.06	0.07	0.08	0.09	0.10	0.15	0.20	0.25	0.30	0.35	0.40	0.45	0.50
2	0	0.980	0.960	0.941	0.922	0.903	0.884	0.865	0.846	0.828	0.810	0.723	0.640	0.563	0.490	0.423	0.360	0.303	0.250
2	1	1.000	1.000	0.999	0.998	0.998	0.996	0.995	0.994	0.992	0.990	0.978	0.960	0.938	0.910	0.878	0.840	0.798	0.750
3	0	0.970	0.941	0.913	0.885	0.857	0.831	0.804	0.779	0.754	0.729	0.614	0.512	0.422	0.343	0.275	0.216	0.166	0.125
3	1	1.000	0.999	0.997	0.995	0.993	0.990	0.986	0.982	0.977	0.972	0.939	0.896	0.844	0.784	0.718	0.648	0.575	0.500
3	2	1.000	1.000	1.000	1.000	1.000	1.000	1.000	0.999	0.999	0.999	0.997	0.992	0.984	0.973	0.957	0.936	0.909	0.875
4	0	0.961	0.922	0.885	0.849	0.815	0.781	0.748	0.716	0.686	0.656	0.522	0.410	0.316	0.240	0.179	0.130	0.092	0.063
4	1	0.999	0.998	0.995	0.991	0.986	0.980	0.973	0.966	0.957	0.948	0.890	0.819	0.738	0.652	0.563	0.475	0.391	0.313
4	2	1.000	1.000	1.000	1.000	1.000	0.999	0.999	0.998	0.997	0.996	0.988	0.973	0.949	0.916	0.874	0.821	0.759	0.688
4	3	1.000	1.000	1.000	1.000	1.000	1.000	1.000	1.000	1.000	1.000	0.999	0.998	0.996	0.992	0.985	0.974	0.959	0.938
5	0	0.951	0.904	0.859	0.815	0.774	0.734	0.696	0.659	0.624	0.590	0.444	0.328	0.237	0.168	0.116	0.078	0.050	0.031
5	1	0.999	0.996	0.992	0.985	0.977	0.968	0.958	0.946	0.933	0.919	0.835	0.737	0.633	0.528	0.428	0.337	0.256	0.188
5	2	1.000	1.000	1.000	0.999	0.999	0.998	0.997	0.995	0.994	0.991	0.973	0.942	0.896	0.837	0.765	0.683	0.593	0.500
5	3	1.000	1.000	1.000	1.000	1.000	1.000	1.000	1.000	1.000	1.000	0.998	0.993	0.984	0.969	0.946	0.913	0.869	0.813
5	4	1.000	1.000	1.000	1.000	1.000	1.000	1.000	1.000	1.000	1.000	1.000	1.000	0.999	0.998	0.995	0.990	0.982	0.969
6	0	0.941	0.886	0.833	0.783	0.735	0.690	0.647	0.606	0.568	0.531	0.377	0.262	0.178	0.118	0.075	0.047	0.028	0.016
6	1	0.999	0.994	0.988	0.978	0.967	0.954	0.939	0.923	0.905	0.886	0.776	0.655	0.534	0.420	0.319	0.233	0.164	0.109
6	2	1.000	1.000	0.999	0.999	0.998	0.996	0.994	0.991	0.988	0.984	0.953	0.901	0.831	0.744	0.647	0.544	0.442	0.344
6	3	1.000	1.000	1.000	1.000	1.000	1.000	1.000	0.999	0.999	0.999	0.994	0.983	0.962	0.930	0.883	0.821	0.745	0.656
6	4	1.000	1.000	1.000	1.000	1.000	1.000	1.000	1.000	1.000	1.000	1.000	0.998	0.995	0.989	0.978	0.959	0.931	0.891
6	5	1.000	1.000	1.000	1.000	1.000	1.000	1.000	1.000	1.000	1.000	1.000	1.000	1.000	0.999	0.998	0.996	0.992	0.984
7	0	0.932	0.868	0.808	0.751	0.698	0.648	0.602	0.558	0.517	0.478	0.321	0.210	0.133	0.082	0.049	0.028	0.015	0.008
7	1	0.998	0.992	0.983	0.971	0.956	0.938	0.919	0.897	0.875	0.850	0.717	0.577	0.445	0.329	0.234	0.159	0.102	0.063
7	2	1.000	1.000	0.999	0.998	0.996	0.994	0.990	0.986	0.981	0.974	0.926	0.852	0.756	0.647	0.532	0.420	0.316	0.227
7	3	1.000	1.000	1.000	1.000	1.000	1.000	0.999	0.999	0.998	0.997	0.988	0.967	0.929	0.874	0.800	0.710	0.608	0.500
7	4	1.000	1.000	1.000	1.000	1.000	1.000	1.000	1.000	1.000	1.000	0.999	0.995	0.987	0.971	0.944	0.904	0.847	0.773
7	5	1.000	1.000	1.000	1.000	1.000	1.000	1.000	1.000	1.000	1.000	1.000	1.000	0.999	0.996	0.991	0.981	0.964	0.938
7	6	1.000	1.000	1.000	1.000	1.000	1.000	1.000	1.000	1.000	1.000	1.000	1.000	1.000	1.000	0.999	0.998	0.996	0.992

Continued

Binomial distribution *(continued)*

n	x	0.01	0.02	0.03	0.04	0.05	0.06	0.07	0.08	0.09	0.10	0.15	0.20	0.25	0.30	0.35	0.40	0.45	0.50
8	0	0.923	0.851	0.784	0.721	0.663	0.610	0.560	0.513	0.470	0.430	0.272	0.168	0.100	0.058	0.032	0.017	0.008	0.004
8	1	0.997	0.990	0.978	0.962	0.943	0.921	0.897	0.870	0.842	0.813	0.657	0.503	0.367	0.255	0.169	0.106	0.063	0.035
8	2	1.000	1.000	0.999	0.997	0.994	0.990	0.985	0.979	0.971	0.962	0.895	0.797	0.679	0.552	0.428	0.315	0.220	0.145
8	3	1.000	1.000	1.000	1.000	1.000	0.999	0.999	0.998	0.997	0.995	0.979	0.944	0.886	0.806	0.706	0.594	0.477	0.363
8	4	1.000	1.000	1.000	1.000	1.000	1.000	1.000	1.000	1.000	1.000	0.997	0.990	0.973	0.942	0.894	0.826	0.740	0.637
8	5	1.000	1.000	1.000	1.000	1.000	1.000	1.000	1.000	1.000	1.000	1.000	0.999	0.996	0.989	0.975	0.950	0.912	0.855
8	6	1.000	1.000	1.000	1.000	1.000	1.000	1.000	1.000	1.000	1.000	1.000	1.000	1.000	0.999	0.996	0.991	0.982	0.965
8	7	1.000	1.000	1.000	1.000	1.000	1.000	1.000	1.000	1.000	1.000	1.000	1.000	1.000	1.000	1.000	0.999	0.998	0.996
9	0	0.914	0.834	0.760	0.693	0.630	0.573	0.520	0.472	0.428	0.387	0.232	0.134	0.075	0.040	0.021	0.010	0.005	0.002
9	1	0.997	0.987	0.972	0.952	0.929	0.902	0.873	0.842	0.809	0.775	0.599	0.436	0.300	0.196	0.121	0.071	0.039	0.020
9	2	1.000	0.999	0.998	0.996	0.992	0.986	0.979	0.970	0.960	0.947	0.859	0.738	0.601	0.463	0.337	0.232	0.150	0.090
9	3	1.000	1.000	1.000	1.000	0.999	0.999	0.998	0.996	0.994	0.992	0.966	0.914	0.834	0.730	0.609	0.483	0.361	0.254
9	4	1.000	1.000	1.000	1.000	1.000	1.000	1.000	1.000	0.999	0.999	0.994	0.980	0.951	0.901	0.828	0.733	0.621	0.500
9	5	1.000	1.000	1.000	1.000	1.000	1.000	1.000	1.000	1.000	1.000	0.999	0.997	0.990	0.975	0.946	0.901	0.834	0.746
9	6	1.000	1.000	1.000	1.000	1.000	1.000	1.000	1.000	1.000	1.000	1.000	1.000	0.999	0.996	0.989	0.975	0.950	0.910
9	7	1.000	1.000	1.000	1.000	1.000	1.000	1.000	1.000	1.000	1.000	1.000	1.000	1.000	0.999	0.996	0.991	0.980
9	8	1.000	1.000	1.000	1.000	1.000	1.000	1.000	1.000	1.000	1.000	1.000	1.000	1.000	1.000	1.000	0.999	0.998
10	0	0.904	0.817	0.737	0.665	0.599	0.539	0.484	0.434	0.389	0.349	0.197	0.107	0.056	0.028	0.013	0.006	0.003	0.001
10	1	0.996	0.984	0.965	0.942	0.914	0.882	0.848	0.812	0.775	0.736	0.544	0.376	0.244	0.149	0.086	0.046	0.023	0.011
10	2	1.000	0.999	0.997	0.994	0.988	0.981	0.972	0.960	0.946	0.930	0.820	0.678	0.526	0.383	0.262	0.167	0.100	0.055
10	3	1.000	1.000	1.000	1.000	0.999	0.998	0.996	0.994	0.991	0.987	0.950	0.879	0.776	0.650	0.514	0.382	0.266	0.172
10	4	1.000	1.000	1.000	1.000	1.000	1.000	1.000	0.999	0.999	0.998	0.990	0.967	0.922	0.850	0.751	0.633	0.504	0.377
10	5	1.000	1.000	1.000	1.000	1.000	1.000	1.000	1.000	1.000	1.000	0.999	0.994	0.980	0.953	0.905	0.834	0.738	0.623

Appendix K
Chi-Square Distribution

Chi-square distribution

df	$\chi^2_{0.995}$	$\chi^2_{0.99}$	$\chi^2_{0.975}$	$\chi^2_{0.95}$	$\chi^2_{0.90}$	$\chi^2_{0.10}$	$\chi^2_{0.05}$	$\chi^2_{0.025}$	$\chi^2_{0.01}$	$\chi^2_{0.005}$
1	0.000	0.000	0.001	0.004	0.016	2.706	3.841	5.024	6.635	7.879
2	0.010	0.020	0.051	0.103	0.211	4.605	5.991	7.378	9.210	10.597
3	0.072	0.115	0.216	0.352	0.584	6.251	7.815	9.348	11.345	12.838
4	0.207	0.297	0.484	0.711	1.064	7.779	9.488	11.143	13.277	14.860
5	0.412	0.554	0.831	1.145	1.610	9.236	11.070	12.832	15.086	16.750
6	0.676	0.872	1.237	1.635	2.204	10.645	12.592	14.449	16.812	18.548
7	0.989	1.239	1.690	2.167	2.833	12.017	14.067	16.013	18.475	20.278
8	1.344	1.647	2.180	2.733	3.490	13.362	15.507	17.535	20.090	21.955
9	1.735	2.088	2.700	3.325	4.168	14.684	16.919	19.023	21.666	23.589
10	2.156	2.558	3.247	3.940	4.865	15.987	18.307	20.483	23.209	25.188
11	2.603	3.053	3.816	4.575	5.578	17.275	19.675	21.920	24.725	26.757
12	3.074	3.571	4.404	5.226	6.304	18.549	21.026	23.337	26.217	28.300
13	3.565	4.107	5.009	5.892	7.041	19.812	22.362	24.736	27.688	29.819
14	4.075	4.660	5.629	6.571	7.790	21.064	23.685	26.119	29.141	31.319
15	4.601	5.229	6.262	7.261	8.547	22.307	24.996	27.488	30.578	32.801
16	5.142	5.812	6.908	7.962	9.312	23.542	26.296	28.845	32.000	34.267
17	5.697	6.408	7.564	8.672	10.085	24.769	27.587	30.191	33.409	35.718
18	6.265	7.015	8.231	9.390	10.865	25.989	28.869	31.526	34.805	37.156
19	6.844	7.633	8.907	10.117	11.651	27.204	30.144	32.852	36.191	38.582
20	7.434	8.260	9.591	10.851	12.443	28.412	31.410	34.170	37.566	39.997
21	8.034	8.897	10.283	11.591	13.240	29.615	32.671	35.479	38.932	41.401
22	8.643	9.542	10.982	12.338	14.041	30.813	33.924	36.781	40.289	42.796
23	9.260	10.196	11.689	13.091	14.848	32.007	35.172	38.076	41.638	44.181
24	9.886	10.856	12.401	13.848	15.659	33.196	36.415	39.364	42.980	45.558
25	10.520	11.524	13.120	14.611	16.473	34.382	37.652	40.646	44.314	46.928
26	11.160	12.198	13.844	15.379	17.292	35.563	38.885	41.923	45.642	48.290
27	11.808	12.878	14.573	16.151	18.114	36.741	40.113	43.195	46.963	49.645
28	12.461	13.565	15.308	16.928	18.939	37.916	41.337	44.461	48.278	50.994

Continued

Chi-square distribution *(continued)*

df	$\chi^2_{0.995}$	$\chi^2_{0.99}$	$\chi^2_{0.975}$	$\chi^2_{0.95}$	$\chi^2_{0.90}$	$\chi^2_{0.10}$	$\chi^2_{0.05}$	$\chi^2_{0.025}$	$\chi^2_{0.01}$	$\chi^2_{0.005}$
29	13.121	14.256	16.047	17.708	19.768	39.087	42.557	45.722	49.588	52.335
30	13.787	14.953	16.791	18.493	20.599	40.256	43.773	46.979	50.892	53.672
31	14.458	15.655	17.539	19.281	21.434	41.422	44.985	48.232	52.191	55.002
32	15.134	16.362	18.291	20.072	22.271	42.585	46.194	49.480	53.486	56.328
33	15.815	17.073	19.047	20.867	23.110	43.745	47.400	50.725	54.775	57.648
34	16.501	17.789	19.806	21.664	23.952	44.903	48.602	51.966	56.061	58.964
35	17.192	18.509	20.569	22.465	24.797	46.059	49.802	53.203	57.342	60.275
40	20.707	22.164	24.433	26.509	29.051	51.805	55.758	59.342	63.691	66.766
45	24.311	25.901	28.366	30.612	33.350	57.505	61.656	65.410	69.957	73.166
50	27.991	29.707	32.357	34.764	37.689	63.167	67.505	71.420	76.154	79.490
55	31.735	33.571	36.398	38.958	42.060	68.796	73.311	77.380	82.292	85.749
60	35.534	37.485	40.482	43.188	46.459	74.397	79.082	83.298	88.379	91.952
65	39.383	41.444	44.603	47.450	50.883	79.973	84.821	89.177	94.422	98.105
70	43.275	45.442	48.758	51.739	55.329	85.527	90.531	95.023	100.425	104.215
75	47.206	49.475	52.942	56.054	59.795	91.061	96.217	100.839	106.393	110.285
80	51.172	53.540	57.153	60.391	64.278	96.578	101.879	106.629	112.329	116.321
85	55.170	57.634	61.389	64.749	68.777	102.079	107.522	112.393	118.236	122.324
90	59.196	61.754	65.647	69.126	73.291	107.565	113.145	118.136	124.116	128.299
95	63.250	65.898	69.925	73.520	77.818	113.038	118.752	123.858	129.973	134.247
100	67.328	70.065	74.222	77.929	82.358	118.498	124.342	129.561	135.807	140.170

Appendix L

Exponential Distribution

Exponential distribution

X	Area to left of X	Area to right of X
0	0.00000	1.00000
0.1	0.09516	0.90484
0.2	0.18127	0.81873
0.3	0.25918	0.74082
0.4	0.32968	0.67032
0.5	0.39347	0.60653
0.6	0.45119	0.54881
0.7	0.50341	0.49659
0.8	0.55067	0.44933
0.9	0.59343	0.40657
1	0.63212	0.36788
1.1	0.66713	0.33287
1.2	0.69881	0.30119
1.3	0.72747	0.27253
1.4	0.75340	0.24660
1.5	0.77687	0.22313
1.6	0.79810	0.20190
1.7	0.81732	0.18268
1.8	0.83470	0.16530
1.9	0.85043	0.14957
2	0.86466	0.13534
2.1	0.87754	0.12246
2.2	0.88920	0.11080
2.3	0.89974	0.10026
2.4	0.90928	0.09072
2.5	0.91792	0.08208
2.6	0.92573	0.07427

Continued

Exponential distribution *(continued)*

X	Area to left of X	Area to right of X
2.7	0.93279	0.06721
2.8	0.93919	0.06081
2.9	0.94498	0.05502
3	0.95021	0.04979
3.1	0.95495	0.04505
3.2	0.95924	0.04076
3.3	0.96312	0.03688
3.4	0.96663	0.03337
3.5	0.96980	0.03020
3.6	0.97268	0.02732
3.7	0.97528	0.02472
3.8	0.97763	0.02237
3.9	0.97976	0.02024
4	0.98168	0.01832
4.1	0.98343	0.01657
4.2	0.98500	0.01500
4.3	0.98643	0.01357
4.4	0.98772	0.01228
4.5	0.98889	0.01111
4.6	0.98995	0.01005
4.7	0.99090	0.00910
4.8	0.99177	0.00823
4.9	0.99255	0.00745
5	0.99326	0.00674
5.1	0.99390	0.00610
5.2	0.99448	0.00552
5.3	0.99501	0.00499
5.4	0.99548	0.00452
5.5	0.99591	0.00409
5.6	0.99630	0.00370
5.7	0.99665	0.00335
5.8	0.99697	0.00303
5.9	0.99726	0.00274
6	0.99752	0.00248

Appendix M
Poisson Distribution

Probability of x or fewer occurrences of an event

Poisson distribution

$x\downarrow\ n\rightarrow$	0	1	2	3	4	5	6	7	8	9	10	11	12	13	14	15	16	17
0.005	0.995	1.000	1.000	1.000	1.000	1.000	1.000	1.000	1.000	1.000	1.000	1.000	1.000	1.000	1.000	1.000	1.000	1.000
0.01	0.990	1.000	1.000	1.000	1.000	1.000	1.000	1.000	1.000	1.000	1.000	1.000	1.000	1.000	1.000	1.000	1.000	1.000
0.02	0.980	1.000	1.000	1.000	1.000	1.000	1.000	1.000	1.000	1.000	1.000	1.000	1.000	1.000	1.000	1.000	1.000	1.000
0.03	0.970	1.000	1.000	1.000	1.000	1.000	1.000	1.000	1.000	1.000	1.000	1.000	1.000	1.000	1.000	1.000	1.000	1.000
0.04	0.961	0.999	1.000	1.000	1.000	1.000	1.000	1.000	1.000	1.000	1.000	1.000	1.000	1.000	1.000	1.000	1.000	1.000
0.05	0.951	0.999	1.000	1.000	1.000	1.000	1.000	1.000	1.000	1.000	1.000	1.000	1.000	1.000	1.000	1.000	1.000	1.000
0.06	0.942	0.998	1.000	1.000	1.000	1.000	1.000	1.000	1.000	1.000	1.000	1.000	1.000	1.000	1.000	1.000	1.000	1.000
0.07	0.932	0.998	1.000	1.000	1.000	1.000	1.000	1.000	1.000	1.000	1.000	1.000	1.000	1.000	1.000	1.000	1.000	1.000
0.08	0.923	0.997	1.000	1.000	1.000	1.000	1.000	1.000	1.000	1.000	1.000	1.000	1.000	1.000	1.000	1.000	1.000	1.000
0.09	0.914	0.996	1.000	1.000	1.000	1.000	1.000	1.000	1.000	1.000	1.000	1.000	1.000	1.000	1.000	1.000	1.000	1.000
0.1	0.905	0.995	1.000	1.000	1.000	1.000	1.000	1.000	1.000	1.000	1.000	1.000	1.000	1.000	1.000	1.000	1.000	1.000
0.15	0.861	0.990	0.999	1.000	1.000	1.000	1.000	1.000	1.000	1.000	1.000	1.000	1.000	1.000	1.000	1.000	1.000	1.000
0.2	0.819	0.982	0.999	1.000	1.000	1.000	1.000	1.000	1.000	1.000	1.000	1.000	1.000	1.000	1.000	1.000	1.000	1.000
0.25	0.779	0.974	0.998	1.000	1.000	1.000	1.000	1.000	1.000	1.000	1.000	1.000	1.000	1.000	1.000	1.000	1.000	1.000
0.3	0.741	0.963	0.996	1.000	1.000	1.000	1.000	1.000	1.000	1.000	1.000	1.000	1.000	1.000	1.000	1.000	1.000	1.000
0.35	0.705	0.951	0.994	1.000	1.000	1.000	1.000	1.000	1.000	1.000	1.000	1.000	1.000	1.000	1.000	1.000	1.000	1.000
0.4	0.670	0.938	0.992	0.999	1.000	1.000	1.000	1.000	1.000	1.000	1.000	1.000	1.000	1.000	1.000	1.000	1.000	1.000
0.5	0.607	0.910	0.986	0.998	1.000	1.000	1.000	1.000	1.000	1.000	1.000	1.000	1.000	1.000	1.000	1.000	1.000	1.000
0.6	0.549	0.878	0.977	0.997	1.000	1.000	1.000	1.000	1.000	1.000	1.000	1.000	1.000	1.000	1.000	1.000	1.000	1.000
0.7	0.497	0.844	0.966	0.994	0.999	1.000	1.000	1.000	1.000	1.000	1.000	1.000	1.000	1.000	1.000	1.000	1.000	1.000
0.8	0.449	0.809	0.953	0.991	0.999	1.000	1.000	1.000	1.000	1.000	1.000	1.000	1.000	1.000	1.000	1.000	1.000	1.000
0.9	0.407	0.772	0.937	0.987	0.998	1.000	1.000	1.000	1.000	1.000	1.000	1.000	1.000	1.000	1.000	1.000	1.000	1.000
1	0.368	0.736	0.920	0.981	0.996	0.999	1.000	1.000	1.000	1.000	1.000	1.000	1.000	1.000	1.000	1.000	1.000	1.000
1.2	0.301	0.663	0.879	0.966	0.992	0.998	1.000	1.000	1.000	1.000	1.000	1.000	1.000	1.000	1.000	1.000	1.000	1.000
1.4	0.247	0.592	0.833	0.946	0.986	0.997	0.999	1.000	1.000	1.000	1.000	1.000	1.000	1.000	1.000	1.000	1.000	1.000
1.6	0.202	0.525	0.783	0.921	0.976	0.994	0.999	1.000	1.000	1.000	1.000	1.000	1.000	1.000	1.000	1.000	1.000	1.000
1.8	0.165	0.463	0.731	0.891	0.964	0.990	0.997	0.999	1.000	1.000	1.000	1.000	1.000	1.000	1.000	1.000	1.000	1.000
2	0.135	0.406	0.677	0.857	0.947	0.983	0.995	0.999	1.000	1.000	1.000	1.000	1.000	1.000	1.000	1.000	1.000	1.000

Continued

Poisson distribution *(continued)*

$x \downarrow n \rightarrow$	0	1	2	3	4	5	6	7	8	9	10	11	12	13	14	15	16	17
2.2	0.111	0.355	0.623	0.819	0.928	0.975	0.993	0.998	1.000	1.000	1.000	1.000	1.000	1.000	1.000	1.000	1.000	1.000
2.4	0.091	0.308	0.570	0.779	0.904	0.964	0.988	0.997	0.999	1.000	1.000	1.000	1.000	1.000	1.000	1.000	1.000	1.000
2.6	0.074	0.267	0.518	0.736	0.877	0.951	0.983	0.995	0.999	1.000	1.000	1.000	1.000	1.000	1.000	1.000	1.000	1.000
2.8	0.061	0.231	0.469	0.692	0.848	0.935	0.976	0.992	0.998	0.999	1.000	1.000	1.000	1.000	1.000	1.000	1.000	1.000
3	0.050	0.199	0.423	0.647	0.815	0.916	0.966	0.988	0.996	0.999	1.000	1.000	1.000	1.000	1.000	1.000	1.000	1.000
3.2	0.041	0.171	0.380	0.603	0.781	0.895	0.955	0.983	0.994	0.998	1.000	1.000	1.000	1.000	1.000	1.000	1.000	1.000
3.4	0.033	0.147	0.340	0.558	0.744	0.871	0.942	0.977	0.992	0.997	0.999	1.000	1.000	1.000	1.000	1.000	1.000	1.000
3.6	0.027	0.126	0.303	0.515	0.706	0.844	0.927	0.969	0.988	0.996	0.999	1.000	1.000	1.000	1.000	1.000	1.000	1.000
3.8	0.022	0.107	0.269	0.473	0.668	0.816	0.909	0.960	0.984	0.994	0.998	0.999	1.000	1.000	1.000	1.000	1.000	1.000
4	0.018	0.092	0.238	0.433	0.629	0.785	0.889	0.949	0.979	0.992	0.997	0.999	1.000	1.000	1.000	1.000	1.000	1.000
4.5	0.011	0.061	0.174	0.342	0.532	0.703	0.831	0.913	0.960	0.983	0.993	0.998	0.999	1.000	1.000	1.000	1.000	1.000
5	0.007	0.040	0.125	0.265	0.440	0.616	0.762	0.867	0.932	0.968	0.986	0.995	0.998	0.999	1.000	1.000	1.000	1.000
5.5	0.004	0.027	0.088	0.202	0.358	0.529	0.686	0.809	0.894	0.946	0.975	0.989	0.996	0.998	0.999	1.000	1.000	1.000
6	0.002	0.017	0.062	0.151	0.285	0.446	0.606	0.744	0.847	0.916	0.957	0.980	0.991	0.996	0.999	0.999	1.000	1.000
6.5	0.002	0.011	0.043	0.112	0.224	0.369	0.527	0.673	0.792	0.877	0.933	0.966	0.984	0.993	0.997	0.999	1.000	1.000
7	0.001	0.007	0.030	0.082	0.173	0.301	0.450	0.599	0.729	0.830	0.901	0.947	0.973	0.987	0.994	0.998	0.999	1.000
7.5	0.001	0.005	0.020	0.059	0.132	0.241	0.378	0.525	0.662	0.776	0.862	0.921	0.957	0.978	0.990	0.995	0.998	0.999
8	0.000	0.003	0.014	0.042	0.100	0.191	0.313	0.453	0.593	0.717	0.816	0.888	0.936	0.966	0.983	0.992	0.996	0.998
8.5	0.000	0.002	0.009	0.030	0.074	0.150	0.256	0.386	0.523	0.653	0.763	0.849	0.909	0.949	0.973	0.986	0.993	0.997
9	0.000	0.001	0.006	0.021	0.055	0.116	0.207	0.324	0.456	0.587	0.706	0.803	0.876	0.926	0.959	0.978	0.989	0.995
9.5	0.000	0.001	0.004	0.015	0.040	0.089	0.165	0.269	0.392	0.522	0.645	0.752	0.836	0.898	0.940	0.967	0.982	0.991
10	0.000	0.000	0.003	0.010	0.029	0.067	0.130	0.220	0.333	0.458	0.583	0.697	0.792	0.864	0.917	0.951	0.973	0.986
10.5	0.000	0.000	0.002	0.007	0.021	0.050	0.102	0.179	0.279	0.397	0.521	0.639	0.742	0.825	0.888	0.932	0.960	0.978

Appendix N
Median Ranks

Median ranks

n	1	2	3	4	5	6	7	8	9	10	11	12
1	0.500	0.292	0.206	0.159	0.130	0.109	0.095	0.083	0.074	0.067	0.061	0.056
2		0.708	0.500	0.386	0.315	0.266	0.230	0.202	0.181	0.163	0.149	0.137
3			0.794	0.614	0.500	0.422	0.365	0.321	0.287	0.260	0.237	0.218
4				0.841	0.685	0.578	0.500	0.440	0.394	0.356	0.325	0.298
5					0.870	0.734	0.635	0.560	0.500	0.452	0.412	0.379
6						0.891	0.770	0.679	0.606	0.548	0.500	0.460
7							0.905	0.798	0.713	0.644	0.588	0.540
8								0.917	0.819	0.740	0.675	0.621
9									0.926	0.837	0.763	0.702
10										0.933	0.851	0.782
11											0.939	0.863
12												0.944

n	13	14	15	16	17	18	19	20	21	22	23	24
1	0.052	0.049	0.045	0.043	0.040	0.038	0.036	0.034	0.033	0.031	0.030	0.029
2	0.127	0.118	0.110	0.104	0.098	0.092	0.088	0.083	0.079	0.076	0.073	0.070
3	0.201	0.188	0.175	0.165	0.155	0.147	0.139	0.132	0.126	0.121	0.115	0.111
4	0.276	0.257	0.240	0.226	0.213	0.201	0.191	0.181	0.173	0.165	0.158	0.152
5	0.351	0.326	0.305	0.287	0.270	0.255	0.242	0.230	0.220	0.210	0.201	0.193
6	0.425	0.396	0.370	0.348	0.328	0.310	0.294	0.279	0.266	0.254	0.244	0.234
7	0.500	0.465	0.435	0.409	0.385	0.364	0.345	0.328	0.313	0.299	0.286	0.275
8	0.575	0.535	0.500	0.470	0.443	0.418	0.397	0.377	0.360	0.344	0.329	0.316
9	0.649	0.604	0.565	0.530	0.500	0.473	0.448	0.426	0.407	0.388	0.372	0.357
10	0.724	0.674	0.630	0.591	0.557	0.527	0.500	0.475	0.453	0.433	0.415	0.398
11	0.799	0.743	0.695	0.652	0.615	0.582	0.552	0.525	0.500	0.478	0.457	0.439
12	0.873	0.813	0.760	0.713	0.672	0.636	0.603	0.574	0.547	0.522	0.500	0.480

Continued

Median ranks *(continued)*

n	13	14	15	16	17	18	19	20	21	22	23	24
13	0.948	0.882	0.825	0.774	0.730	0.690	0.655	0.623	0.593	0.567	0.543	0.520
14		0.951	0.890	0.835	0.787	0.745	0.706	0.672	0.640	0.612	0.585	0.561
15			0.955	0.896	0.845	0.799	0.758	0.721	0.687	0.656	0.628	0.602
16				0.957	0.902	0.853	0.809	0.770	0.734	0.701	0.671	0.643
17					0.960	0.908	0.861	0.819	0.780	0.746	0.714	0.684
18						0.962	0.912	0.868	0.827	0.790	0.756	0.725
19							0.964	0.917	0.874	0.835	0.799	0.766
20								0.966	0.921	0.879	0.842	0.807
21									0.967	0.924	0.885	0.848
22										0.969	0.927	0.889
23											0.970	0.930
24												0.971

Appendix O
Normal Scores

Normal scores

n =	4	5	6	7	8	9	10	11	12	13	14	15	16	17
1	-1.05	-1.18	-1.28	-1.36	-1.43	-1.50	-1.55	-1.59	-1.64	-1.68	-1.71	-1.74	-1.77	-1.80
2	-0.30	-0.50	-0.64	-0.76	-0.85	-0.93	-1.00	-1.06	-1.11	-1.16	-1.20	-1.24	-1.28	-1.32
3	0.30	0.00	-0.20	-0.35	-0.47	-0.57	-0.65	-0.73	-0.79	-0.85	-0.90	-0.94	-0.99	-1.03
4	1.05	0.50	0.20	0.00	-0.15	-0.27	-0.37	-0.46	-0.53	-0.60	-0.66	-0.71	-0.76	-0.80
5		1.18	0.64	0.35	0.15	0.00	-0.12	-0.22	-0.31	-0.39	-0.45	-0.51	-0.57	-0.62
6			1.28	0.76	0.47	0.27	0.12	0.00	-0.10	-0.19	-0.27	-0.33	-0.39	-0.45
7				1.36	0.85	0.57	0.37	0.22	0.10	0.00	-0.09	-0.16	-0.23	-0.29
8					1.43	0.93	0.65	0.46	0.31	0.19	0.09	0.00	-0.08	-0.15
9						1.50	1.00	0.73	0.53	0.39	0.27	0.16	0.08	0.00
10							1.55	1.06	0.79	0.60	0.45	0.33	0.23	0.15
11								1.59	1.11	0.85	0.66	0.51	0.39	0.29
12									1.64	1.16	0.90	0.71	0.57	0.45
13										1.68	1.20	0.94	0.76	0.62
14											1.71	1.24	0.99	0.80
15												1.74	1.28	1.03
16													1.77	1.32
17														1.80
18														
19														
20														
21														
22														
23														
24														
25														
26														
27														
28														
29														
30														

Continued

Normal scores *(continued)*

$n =$	18	19	20	21	22	23	24	25	26	27	28	29	30
1	-1.82	-1.85	-1.87	-1.89	-1.91	-1.93	-1.95	-1.97	-1.98	-2.00	-2.01	-2.03	-2.04
2	-1.35	-1.38	-1.40	-1.43	-1.45	-1.48	-1.50	-1.52	-1.54	-1.56	-1.58	-1.59	-1.61
3	-1.06	-1.10	-1.13	-1.16	-1.18	-1.21	-1.24	-1.26	-1.28	-1.30	-1.32	-1.34	-1.36
4	-0.84	-0.88	-0.92	-0.95	-0.98	-1.01	-1.04	-1.06	-1.09	-1.11	-1.13	-1.15	-1.17
5	-0.66	-0.70	-0.74	-0.78	-0.81	-0.84	-0.87	-0.90	-0.93	-0.95	-0.98	-1.00	-1.02
6	-0.50	-0.54	-0.59	-0.63	-0.66	-0.70	-0.73	-0.76	-0.79	-0.82	-0.84	-0.87	-0.89
7	-0.35	-0.40	-0.45	-0.49	-0.53	-0.57	-0.60	-0.63	-0.66	-0.69	-0.72	-0.75	-0.77
8	-0.21	-0.26	-0.31	-0.36	-0.40	-0.44	-0.48	-0.52	-0.55	-0.58	-0.61	-0.64	-0.67
9	-0.07	-0.13	-0.19	-0.24	-0.28	-0.33	-0.37	-0.41	-0.44	-0.48	-0.51	-0.54	-0.57
10	0.07	0.00	-0.06	-0.12	-0.17	-0.22	-0.26	-0.30	-0.34	-0.38	-0.41	-0.44	-0.47
11	0.21	0.13	0.06	0.00	-0.06	-0.11	-0.15	-0.20	-0.24	-0.28	-0.31	-0.35	-0.38
12	0.35	0.26	0.19	0.12	0.06	0.00	-0.05	-0.10	-0.14	-0.18	-0.22	-0.26	-0.29
13	0.50	0.40	0.31	0.24	0.17	0.11	0.05	0.00	-0.05	-0.09	-0.13	-0.17	-0.21
14	0.66	0.54	0.45	0.36	0.28	0.22	0.15	0.10	0.05	0.00	-0.04	-0.09	-0.12
15	0.84	0.70	0.59	0.49	0.40	0.33	0.26	0.20	0.14	0.09	0.04	0.00	-0.04
16	1.06	0.88	0.74	0.63	0.53	0.44	0.37	0.30	0.24	0.18	0.13	0.09	0.04
17	1.35	1.10	0.92	0.78	0.66	0.57	0.48	0.41	0.34	0.28	0.22	0.17	0.12
18	1.82	1.38	1.13	0.95	0.81	0.70	0.60	0.52	0.44	0.38	0.31	0.26	0.21
19		1.85	1.40	1.16	0.98	0.84	0.73	0.63	0.55	0.48	0.41	0.35	0.29
20			1.87	1.43	1.18	1.01	0.87	0.76	0.66	0.58	0.51	0.44	0.38
21				1.89	1.45	1.21	1.04	0.90	0.79	0.69	0.61	0.54	0.47
22					1.91	1.48	1.24	1.06	0.93	0.82	0.72	0.64	0.57
23						1.93	1.50	1.26	1.09	0.95	0.84	0.75	0.67
24							1.95	1.52	1.28	1.11	0.98	0.87	0.77
25								1.97	1.54	1.30	1.13	1.00	0.89
26									1.98	1.56	1.32	1.15	1.02
27										2.00	1.58	1.34	1.17
28											2.01	1.59	1.36
29												2.03	1.61
30													2.04

Appendix P
Values of t Distribution

Values of t distribution

df	$t_{0.10}$	$t_{0.05}$	$t_{0.025}$	$t_{0.01}$	$t_{0.005}$	df
1	3.078	6.314	12.706	31.821	63.656	1
2	1.886	2.920	4.303	6.965	9.925	2
3	1.638	2.353	3.182	4.541	5.841	3
4	1.533	2.132	2.776	3.747	4.604	4
5	1.476	2.015	2.571	3.365	4.032	5
6	1.440	1.943	2.447	3.143	3.707	6
7	1.415	1.895	2.365	2.998	3.499	7
8	1.397	1.860	2.306	2.896	3.355	8
9	1.383	1.833	2.262	2.821	3.250	9
10	1.372	1.812	2.228	2.764	3.169	10
11	1.363	1.796	2.201	2.718	3.106	11
12	1.356	1.782	2.179	2.681	3.055	12
13	1.350	1.771	2.160	2.650	3.012	13
14	1.345	1.761	2.145	2.624	2.977	14
15	1.341	1.753	2.131	2.602	2.947	15
16	1.337	1.746	2.120	2.583	2.921	16
17	1.333	1.740	2.110	2.567	2.898	17
18	1.330	1.734	2.101	2.552	2.878	18
19	1.328	1.729	2.093	2.539	2.861	19
20	1.325	1.725	2.086	2.528	2.845	20
21	1.323	1.721	2.080	2.518	2.831	21
22	1.321	1.717	2.074	2.508	2.819	22
23	1.319	1.714	2.069	2.500	2.807	23
24	1.318	1.711	2.064	2.492	2.797	24
25	1.316	1.708	2.060	2.485	2.787	25
26	1.315	1.706	2.056	2.479	2.779	26
27	1.314	1.703	2.052	2.473	2.771	27
28	1.313	1.701	2.048	2.467	2.763	28

Continued

Values of *t* distribution *(continued)*

df	$t_{0.10}$	$t_{0.05}$	$t_{0.025}$	$t_{0.01}$	$t_{0.005}$	df
29	1.311	1.699	2.045	2.462	2.756	29
30	1.310	1.697	2.042	2.457	2.750	30
31	1.309	1.696	2.040	2.453	2.744	31
32	1.309	1.694	2.037	2.449	2.738	32
33	1.308	1.692	2.035	2.445	2.733	33
34	1.307	1.691	2.032	2.441	2.728	34
35	1.306	1.690	2.030	2.438	2.724	35
40	1.303	1.684	2.021	2.423	2.704	40
45	1.301	1.679	2.014	2.412	2.690	45
50	1.299	1.676	2.009	2.403	2.678	50
55	1.297	1.673	2.004	2.396	2.668	55
60	1.296	1.671	2.000	2.390	2.660	60
70	1.294	1.667	1.994	2.381	2.648	70
80	1.292	1.664	1.990	2.374	2.639	80
90	1.291	1.662	1.987	2.368	2.632	90
100	1.290	1.660	1.984	2.364	2.626	100
200	1.286	1.653	1.972	2.345	2.601	200
400	1.284	1.649	1.966	2.336	2.588	400
600	1.283	1.647	1.964	2.333	2.584	600
800	1.283	1.647	1.963	2.331	2.582	800
999	1.282	1.646	1.962	2.330	2.581	999

Appendix Q

Selected National and International Quality System Standards

American National Standards Institute*

1430 Broadway
New York, NY 10018

ANSI/ASQ Z1.4-2003 Sampling Procedures and Tables for Inspection by Attributes

ANSI/ASQ Z1.9-2003 Sampling Procedures and Tables for Inspection by Variables for Percent Nonconforming

ANSI/ASQC C1-1996 (ANSI Z1.8-1971) Specifications of General Requirements for a Quality Program

ANSI/ASQC D1160-1995 Formal Design Review

ANSI/ISO/ASQ E14001-2004 Environmental management systems—Requirements with guidance for use

ANSI/ISO/ASQ Q9000-2005 Quality management systems—Fundamentals and vocabulary

ANSI/ISO/ASQ Q9001-2008 Quality management systems—Requirements

ANSI/ISO/ASQ Q9004-2000 Quality management systems—Guidelines for performance improvements

ANSI/ISO/ASQ Q10002-2004 Quality management—Customer satisfaction—Guidelines for complaints handling in organizations

ANSI/ISO/ASQ Q10005-2005 Quality management—Guidelines for quality plans

ANSI/ISO/ASQ Q10006-2003 Quality management—Guidelines for quality management in projects

ANSI/ISO/ASQ Q10007-2003 Quality management systems—Guidelines for configuration management

ANSI/ISO/ASQ QE19011S-2008 Guidelines for management systems auditing—U.S. version with supplemental guidance added

---

* Copies of these standards can be ordered from American Society for Quality (ASQ), PO Box 3005, Milwaukee, WI 53201-3005, or may be downloaded from www.e-standards.asq.org.

ANSI/ISO/ASQC Q9000-1-1994 Quality management and quality assurance standards—Guidelines for selection and use

ANSI/ISO/ASQC Q9001-1994 Quality systems—Model for quality assurance in design, development, production, installation, and servicing

ANSI/ISO/ASQC Q9002-1994: Quality systems—Model for quality assurance in production, installation, and servicing

ANSI/ISO/ASQC Q9003-1994: Quality systems—Model for quality assurance in final inspection and test

North Atlantic Treaty Organization
Autoroute De Zaventem
1110 NATO (Brussels), Belgium

AQAP-1: NATO Requirements for an Industrial Quality Control System

AQAP-2: Guide for the Evaluation of a Contractor's Quality Control System for Compliance with AQAP-1

AQAP-4: NATO Inspection Systems Requirements for Industry

AQAP-5: Guide for the Evaluation of a Contractor's Inspection System for Compliance with AQAP-4

AQAP-7: Guide for the Evaluation of a Contractor's Measurement and Calibration System for Compliance with AQAP-6

IEC Guide 102 (1996-03): Specifications Structure for Quality

British Standards Institution
101 Pentonville Road
London N19ND, England

BSI HDBK 22-1981: Quality Assurance (Contains 15 Publications)

Canadian Standards Association (CSA)
178 Rexdale Boulevard
Rexdale, Ontario
Canada M9W IR3

CAN3 Z299-1—CSA: Quality Assurance Program—Category 1

CAN3 Z299-2—CSA: Quality Assurance Program—Category 2

CAN3 Z299-3—CSA: Quality Assurance Program—Category 3

International Organization for Standardization (ISO)*

1, rue de Varembé, Case postale 56
CH-1211 Geneva 20, Switzerland

ISO 9000-1-1994: Quality management and quality assurance standards—Part 1: Guidelines for selection and use

ISO 9000-2-1997: Quality management and quality assurance standards—Part 2: Generic guidelines for the application of ISO 9001, ISO 9002, and ISO 9003

ISO 9000-3-1997: Quality management and quality assurance standards—Part 3: Guidelines for the application of ISO 9001:1994 to the development, supply, installation, and maintenance of computer software

ISO 9000-4-1993: Quality management and quality assurance standards—Part 4: Guide to dependability programme management

ISO 10019-2005: Guidelines for the selection of quality management system consultants and use of their services

ISO 13485-2003: Medical devices: Quality management systems—Requirements for regulatory purposes

ISO/TR 10013-2001: Guidelines for quality management system documentation

ISO/TR 13352-1997: Guidelines for interpretation of ISO 9000 series for application within the iron ore industry

The Department of Defense (DOD)

The Pentagon
Washington, DC 20301-1155

MIL-HDBK-50: Evaluation of a Contractor's Quality Program

MIL-Q-9858A: Quality Program Requirements

MIL-STD-1521B: Technical Reviews and Audits of System, Equipment, and Computer Software

MIL-STD-1535A: Supplier Quality Assurance Quality Requirements

MIL-STD-2164: Failure Reporting, Analysis, and Corrective Action Systems

MIL-T-50301: Quality Control System Requirements for Technical Data

---

* Copies of these standards can be ordered from American Society for Quality (ASQ), PO Box 3005, Milwaukee, WI 53201-3005, or may be downloaded from www.e-standards.asq.org.

Glossary

acceptable quality level (AQL)—The maximum percentage or proportion of variant units in a lot or batch that, for purposes of acceptance sampling, can be considered satisfactory as a process average.

acceptance sampling—Sampling inspection in which decisions are made to accept or not accept a product or service; also, the methodology that deals with procedures by which decisions to accept or not accept are based on the results of the inspection of samples.

accuracy—A qualitative term that describes the closeness of alignment between an observed value and an accepted reference value.

action plan—The detailed plan to implement the actions needed to achieve strategic goals and objectives.

activity—An action of some type that requires a time duration for accomplishment.

activity network diagram (AND) (arrow diagram)—A management and planning tool used to develop the best possible schedule and appropriate controls to accomplish the schedule; the critical path method (CPM) and the program evaluation review technique (PERT) make use of arrow diagrams.

advanced product quality planning (APQP) and control plan—APQP is a comprehensive quality planning and control system specifying protocols for product and process design and development, validation, assessment, and corrective action.

advanced quality planning (AQP)—A comprehensive system of applying quality disciplines during a product or process development effort; sometimes also called *advanced product quality planning* (APQP).

alternative hypothesis—In statistical hypothesis testing, this is the hypothesis that the null hypothesis is tested against. The hypothesis test is conducted under the assumption that the null hypothesis is true. If evidence is found against the null hypothesis, the alternative hypothesis is accepted.

analysis of variance (ANOVA)—A partitioning of total variability into components due to factors or other sources of variation. The sources of variation as well as their corresponding sums of squares and degrees of freedom are usually given in an *analysis of variance table.*

analytical study—A study that uses theory and a model in order to predict future outcomes or to lead to a change in outcomes.

assignable cause—A factor that contributes to variation and that is feasible to detect and identify.

assumptions—Conditions that must be true in order for a statistical procedure to be valid.

attributes data—Data that are categorized for analysis or evaluation. (Attributes data may involve measurements as long as the measurements are used only to place a given piece of data in a category for further analysis or evaluation. Contrast with *variables data.*)

auditee—The individual or organization being audited.

availability—A measure of the degree to which an item is in the operable and committable state at the start of the mission when the mission is called for at an unknown (random) time.

average outgoing quality (AOQ)—The expected quality of outgoing product following the use of an acceptance sampling plan for a given value of incoming product quality.

average outgoing quality limit (AOQL)—For a given acceptance sampling plan, the maximum AOQ over all possible levels of incoming quality.

average run length (ARL)—In process monitoring and statistical process control, the average number of time periods or samples that elapse until the process signals out-of-control or produces an out-of-control signal.

average sample number (ASN)—The average number of sample units per lot used for making decisions (acceptance or nonacceptance).

B

benchmark—An organization, part of an organization, or measurement that serves as a reference point or point of comparison.

benefit–cost analysis—A collection of the dollar value of benefits derived from an initiative, divided by the associated costs incurred.

bias—A quantitative term representing the systematic difference between results or measurements obtained and the true quantity of interest. In measurement system analysis, bias describes the difference between the average of measurements made on the same unit and its reference or master value.

Bernoulli trials—A set of n independent trials that will result in one of two possible outcomes, usually defined as "success" and "failure." The probability of a success is constant from trial to trial.

binomial distribution—A discrete distribution describing the number of successes in a set or series of n Bernoulli trials.

bivariate distribution—A joint distribution of two random variables. The joint distribution of two normally distributed random variables is the *bivariate normal distribution*.

block diagram—A diagram that describes the operation, interrelationships, and interdependencies of components in a system. Boxes, or blocks (hence the name), represent the components; connecting lines between the blocks represent interfaces. There are two types of block diagrams: a *functional block diagram*, which shows a system's subsystems and lower-level products, their interrelationships, and interfaces with other systems, and a *reliability block diagram*, which is similar to the functional block diagram except that it is modified to emphasize those aspects influencing reliability.

box plot—A graphical method for displaying characteristics of a set of data. The box represents the interquartile range (middle 50 percent of the data). The whiskers extend from each end of the box to some specified bounds. Also known as the *box-and-whisker plot*.

brainstorming—A problem-solving tool that teams use to generate as many ideas as possible related to a particular subject. Team members begin by offering all their ideas; the ideas are not discussed or reviewed until after the brainstorming session.

C

calibration—The comparison of a measurement instrument or system of unverified accuracy to a measurement instrument or system of known accuracy to detect any variation from the true value.

categorical variable—A variable whose possible outcomes are categories that have no numerical significance. The data are counts that can be classified into different categories.

causal factor—A variable that when changed or manipulated in some manner serves to influence a given effect or result.

cause-and-effect diagram—A graphical aid used to organize and identify possible causes of a problem or effect. Also known as a *fishbone diagram* or *Ishikawa diagram*.

chance cause variation—Variation due to chance causes. Also known as *common cause* or *random* variation.

change agent—The person who takes the lead in transforming a company into a quality organization by providing guidance during the planning phase, facilitating implementation, and supporting those who pioneer the changes.

characteristic—A property that helps to differentiate between items of a given sample or population.

client—A person or organization requesting an audit.

confidence coefficient—Associated with confidence intervals, the confidence coefficient represents the probability that the given interval of values will contain the true parameter of interest. Also known as the *confidence level* or *level of confidence.*

confidence interval—An interval of values (L, U) that is believed to contain the true parameter value of interest with a certain probability, where L and U depend only on the sample observations. The probability level refers only to the interval constructed and its properties and not the unknown parameter being estimated. The interpretation of a 99 percent confidence interval would be that if the estimation procedure is repeated over and over again, then 99 percent of all the constructed intervals would contain the true parameter of interest.

conflict resolution—A process for resolving disagreements in a manner acceptable to all parties.

consensus—Finding a proposal acceptable enough that all team members can support the decision and no member opposes it.

consumer's risk (β)—For a sampling plan, refers to the probability of acceptance of a lot the quality of which has a designated numerical value representing a level that is seldom desirable. Usually the value will be the *lot tolerance percent defective* (LTPD). Also known as the *beta risk* and probability of a type II error.

contingency table—A table of observations resulting from the classification of observations into two or more categories simultaneously.

continuous variable—A variable whose possible values form an interval set of numbers such that between each two values in the set another member of the set occurs.

control chart—A chart used to monitor a quality characteristic of interest. A control chart generally consists of three horizontal lines, one representing the mean or target level and two representing an upper limit and lower limit (although there are many instances when only an upper limit or only a lower limit are of interest). The limits are statistically determined. A process being monitored is considered out of control when points plot beyond the control limits.

control plan—A document that may include the characteristics for quality of a product or service, measurements, and methods of control.

coordinate measuring machine (CMM)—Coordinate measuring machines (CMM) can most easily be defined as physical representations of a three-dimensional rectilinear coordinate system. Coordinate measuring machines now represent a significant fraction of the measuring equipment used for defining the geometry of different-shaped workpieces.

corrective action—Action taken to eliminate the root cause(s) and symptom(s) of an existing deviation or nonconformity to prevent recurrence.

correlation—A general term describing the degree of interdependence between two or more variables.

correlation coefficient—A measure of the linear relationship between two random variables. The correlation coefficient is dimensionless and can take on any value between –1 and 1, inclusive.

Crawford slip method—A method of gathering and presenting anonymous data from a group by using various voting schemes.

critical defect—A defect that judgment and experience indicate is likely to result in hazardous or unsafe conditions for the individuals using, maintaining, or depending on the product; or a defect that judgment and experience indicate is likely to prevent performance of the unit.

critical path—The sequence of tasks that takes the longest time and determines a project's completion date.

critical path method (CPM)—An activity-oriented project management technique that uses arrow-diagramming techniques to demonstrate both the time and cost required to complete a project. It provides one time estimate—normal time.

critical region—In hypothesis testing, it is the values of the test statistic that will lead to rejection of the null hypothesis.

critical value—In hypothesis testing, it is the value (or values) to which the value of the test statistic is compared to determine if the null hypothesis can be rejected. The critical value is directly related to the significance level of the test.

criticality—An indication of the consequences that are expected to result from a failure.

cross-functional team—A group consisting of members from more than one department that is organized to accomplish a project.

cumulative distribution function (cdf)—Used to describe a probability distribution for a random variable. For a random variable X, the cumulative distribution function would be given by $P(X \leq x)$ where x is some real value.

cycle time—Refers to the time that it takes to complete a process from beginning to end.

D

defect—A departure of a quality characteristic from its intended level or state that occurs with a severity sufficient to cause an associated product or service not to satisfy intended normal or reasonably foreseeable usage requirements.

density function—See *probability density function.*

dependent events—Two events A and B are dependent if the probability of one event occurring is affected by the occurrence of the other event.

deployment—To spread around. Used in strategic planning to describe the process of cascading plans throughout the organization.

descriptive statistics—Techniques for displaying and summarizing data. Examples include histograms, run charts, mean, and standard deviation.

design of experiments (DOE), designed experiment—The arrangement in which an experimental program is to be conducted and the selection of the levels of the factors or factor combinations to be included in the experiment.

design review—Documented, comprehensive, and systematic examination of a design to evaluate its capability to fulfill the requirements for quality.

detection—The likelihood of detecting a failure once it has occurred. Detection is evaluated based on a 10-point scale. At the lowest end of the scale (1) it is assumed that a design control will detect a failure with certainty. At the highest end of the scale (10) it is assumed that a design control will not detect a failure if a failure occurs.

discrete variable—A variable whose possible values form a finite or at most countably infinite set.

distribution function—See *cumulative distribution function.*

DMAIC—An acronym denoting a sequence used in the methodology most often associated with Six Sigma: define, measure, analyze, improve, control.

E

empowerment—A condition whereby employees have the authority to make decisions and take action in their work areas, within stated bounds, without prior approval.

entity—Item that can be individually described and considered.

error—1. Error in measurement is the difference between the estimated value and the true value of a measured quantity. 2. A fault resulting from defective judgment, deficient knowledge, or carelessness. It is not to be confused with measurement error, which is the difference between a computed or measured value and the true or theoretical value.

error-proofing—See *foolproofing.*

estimate—A numerical value for a population parameter based on information collected from a sample. Also known as a *point estimate*.

estimator—A statistic used as an estimate for a parameter. Also known as a *point estimator*.

expected value—The mean of a random variable.

external failure costs—Costs associated with defects found during or after delivery of the product or service.

F

F **distribution**—A probability distribution of the ratio of two independent chi-square random variables divided by their respective degrees of freedom.

facilitator—An individual who is responsible for creating favorable conditions that will enable a team to reach its purpose or achieve its goals by bringing together the necessary tools, information, and resources to get the job done.

factor—An assignable cause that may affect the responses (test results) and of which different versions (levels) are included in the experiment.

factorial design—In experimental design, a type of design where all possible combinations of factor levels are examined.

failure—The termination, due to one or more defects, of the ability of an item, product, or service to perform its required function when called on to do so. A failure may be partial, complete, or intermittent.

failure mode and effects analysis (FMEA)—A procedure in which each potential failure mode in every sub-item of an item is analyzed to determine its effect on other sub-items and on the required function of the item.

filters—Relative to human-to-human communication, those perceptions (based on culture, language, demographics, experience, and so on) that affect how a message is transmitted by the sender and how a message is interpreted by the receiver.

fishbone diagram—See *cause-and-effect diagram*.

fixed effect—In analysis of variance, an effect is fixed if the factor levels included in the test or experiment are the only levels of interest. That is, the levels of the factor included in the experiment are the only ones to which the results of testing will apply.

flowchart—A graphical representation of the steps in a process. Flowcharts are drawn to better understand processes. The flowchart is one of the seven tools of quality.

foolproofing—A process of making a product or process immune to foolish errors on the part of the user or operator. Synonymous with *error-proofing*.

fraction nonconforming—In quality control, the proportion of the total number of units under study that are nonconforming. Also known as *fraction defective.*

fractional factorial design—In experimental design, a design consisting of only a subset or fraction of all possible combinations of a factorial design.

G

gage repeatability and reproducibility (GR&R)—Measures the capability of a gage to determine if it is suitable for use in its intended application. Repeatability represents the gage variability when it is used to measure the same unit with the same setup or operator. Reproducibility refers to the variability arising from different setups or operators.

Gantt chart—A type of bar chart used in process/project planning and control to display planned work and finished work in relation to time. Also called a *milestone chart.*

gatekeeping—The role of an individual (often a facilitator) in a group meeting in helping ensure effective interpersonal interactions (for example, to make sure someone's ideas are not ignored due to the team moving on to the next topic too quickly).

gauging—Gauging is a procedure that determines product conformance with specifications with the aid of measuring instruments such as calipers, micrometers, templates, and other mechanical, optical, and electronic devices.

Gaussian distribution—Another name for the *normal distribution,* often attributed to Karl Gauss.

goal—A statement of general intent, aim, or desire; it is the point toward which the organization (or individual) directs its efforts; goals are often nonquantitative.

H

hierarchical relationship—A set of relationships that can be ordered or arranged from general to specific.

histogram—A graphical display of observations from a sample where the class frequencies are represented by areas of rectangles over the interval for each class.

hold point—A point, defined in an appropriate document, beyond which an activity must not proceed without the approval of a designated organization or authority.

hypothesis testing—A method for testing a statement about a population using sample data. The statement to be tested may also concern a distributional form of a quality characteristic of interest.

I

independent events—Two events A and B are said to be independent if the outcome of one event has no affect on the outcome of the other event. If two events are independent, then the probability that they both occur is the product of the probabilities of their individual occurrence. That is, $P(A \cap B) = P(A)P(B)$.

inferential statistics—Techniques for reaching conclusions about a population based on analysis of data from a sample.

information system—Technology-based system used to support operations, aid day-to-day decision making, and support strategic analysis (other names often used include *management information system, decision system, information technology* (IT), *data processing*).

inspection—The process of measuring, examining, testing, gauging, or otherwise comparing a unit with the applicable requirements.

interaction—A term used to represent the phenomenon where two or more variables do not function independently of one another.

internal failure costs—Costs associated with defects found before the product or service is delivered.

intervention—An action taken by a leader or a facilitator to support the effective functioning of a team or work group.

Ishikawa diagram—See *cause-and-effect diagram.*

J

joint distribution—A probability distribution representing two or more variables that are involved in a random experiment. Also known as joint probability distribution.

K

kaizen blitz/event—An intense, short-time-frame, team approach to employing the concepts and techniques of continuous improvement (for example, to reduce cycle time or increase throughput).

L

leader—An individual recognized by others as the person to lead an effort. One can not be a "leader" without one or more "followers." The term is often used interchangeably with "manager." A "leader" may or may not hold an officially designated management-type position.

leadership—An essential part of a quality improvement effort. Organization leaders must establish a vision, communicate that vision to those in the organization, and provide the tools, knowledge, and motivation necessary to accomplish the vision.

least squares estimation—In regression analysis, a method for estimating parameters by minimizing the sum of the squared differences between the actual or observed responses and the values predicted by the fitted model.

level of significance (α)—A stated or fixed probability of wrongly rejecting a true null hypothesis that the practitioner is willing to accept. It is the probability of committing a type I error.

levels—In experimental design, the chosen values of a factor of interest to be varied in an experiment.

lot tolerance percent defective (LTPD)—LTPD, expressed in percent defective, is the poorest quality in an individual lot that should be accepted.

M

main effect—The effect on a response due to a change in a factor or variable independent of all other factors or variables in the system.

maintainability—The measure of the ability of an item to be retained or restored to a specified condition when maintenance is performed by personnel having specified skill levels using prescribed procedures and resources at each prescribed level of maintenance and repair.

major defect—A defect that will interfere with normal or reasonable foreseeable use, but will not cause a risk of damage or injury.

material control—A broad collection of tools for managing the items and lots in a production process.

materials review board—A quality control committee or team, usually employed in manufacturing or other materials-processing installations, that has the responsibility and authority to deal with items or materials that do not conform to fitness-for-use specifications.

mean—A measure of central tendency. For random variables, it is also the expected value. For a sample of data of size n, it is the sum of the observations divided by n.

mean squares—In analysis of variance, mean squares are estimates of variances. In general, they are found by dividing the sum of squares by the appropriate degrees of freedom.

mean time between failures (MTBF)—A basic measure of reliability for repairable items: the mean number of life units during which all parts of an item perform within their specified limits during a particular measurement interval under stated conditions.

mean time to failure (MTTF)—A basic measure of system reliability for nonrepairable items: the total number of life units for an item divided by the total number of failures within that population during a particular measurement interval under stated conditions.

mean time to repair (MTTR)—A basic measure of maintainability: the sum of corrective maintenance times at any specific level of repair divided by the total number of failures within an item repaired at that level during a particular interval under stated conditions.

measurement—1. The process of evaluating a property or characteristic of an object and describing it with a numerical or nominal value. 2. A series of manipulations of physical objects or systems according to a defined protocol that results in a number.

measurement process—Repeated application of a test method using a measuring system.

measuring system—In general, the elements of a measuring system include the instrumentation, calibration standards, environmental influences, human operator limitations, and features of the workpiece or object being measured.

median—A measure of central tendency that divides an ordered data set in half; 50 percent of the data lie at or below this value and 50 percent of the data lie above this value.

milestone—A specific time when a critical event is to occur; a symbol placed on a milestone chart to locate the point when a critical event is to occur.

milestone chart—Another name for a Gantt chart.

minor defect—A defect that may cause difficulty in assembly or use of a product but will not prevent the product from being properly used nor pose any hazard to users.

mistake—Similar to an error but with the implication that it could be prevented by better training or attention.

mode—The value in a data set that occurs most often. There can be more than one mode for a sample.

multi-voting—A decision-making tool that enables a group to sort through a long list of ideas to identify priorities.

mutually exclusive events—Events that do not have outcomes in common or that do not occur jointly.

Myers-Briggs Type Indicator—A method and instrument for assessing personality type based on Carl Jung's theory of personality preferences.

N

nominal group technique—A technique similar to brainstorming, used by teams to generate and make a selection from ideas on a particular subject. Team members are asked to silently come up with as many ideas as possible, writing them down. Each member is then asked to share one idea, which is recorded. After all the ideas are recorded, they are discussed and prioritized by the group.

nonconformity—A departure of a quality characteristic from its intended level or state that occurs with a severity sufficient to cause an associated product or service not to meet a specification requirement.

null hypothesis—In hypothesis testing, a statement about a population parameter or distributional form of a quality characteristic that is to be tested. It is often the statement of no difference.

O

objective—A quantitative statement of future expectations and an indication of when the expectations should be achieved; it flows from goal(s) and clarifies what people must accomplish.

objective evidence—Verifiable qualitative or quantitative observations, information, records, or statements of fact pertaining to the quality of an item or service or to the existence and implementation of a quality system element.

observation—The process of determining the presence or absence of attributes or making measurements of a variable. Also, the result of the process of determining the presence or absence of attributes or making a measurement of a variable.

observational study—Analysis of data collected from a process without imposing changes on the process.

occurrence—The likelihood of a failure occurring. Occurrence is evaluated based on a 10-point scale. At the lowest end of the scale (1) it is assumed that the probability of a failure is unlikely. At the highest end of the scale (10) it is assumed that the probability of a failure is nearly inevitable.

operating characteristic (OC) curve—For a sampling plan, the OC curve indicates the probability of accepting a lot based on the sample size to be taken and the fraction defective in the batch.

organization—Company, corporation, firm, enterprise, or institution, or part thereof, whether incorporated or not, public or private, that has its own functions and administration.

outlier—One or more observations that deviate significantly from the majority of the sample from which they came.

P

p value—The probability of getting a value of the test statistic as extreme or more extreme than that observed if the null hypothesis is true. The p value is the actual or observed significance level for a test.

parameter—A constant or coefficient that describes some characteristic of a population.

Pareto diagram—A graphical tool used to rank causes of problems from most significant to least significant.

payback period—The number of years it will take the results of a project or capital investment to recover the investment from net cash flows.

poka-yoke—A term that means to mistake-proof a process by building safeguards into the system that avoid or immediately find errors. The term comes from the Japanese terms *poka*, which means "error," and *yokeru*, which means "to avoid."

policy—A high-level overall plan embracing the general goals and acceptable practices of a group.

population—The totality of items or units of material under consideration.

power—In statistical inference, it is the probability of rejecting a false null hypothesis.

precision—The closeness of agreement between randomly selected individual measurements or test results.

probability—A measure assigned to events in a sample space. It takes on values between zero and one inclusive and provides a measure of the likelihood that the event will occur.

probability density function (pdf)—A function that describes the probability distribution of a continuous random variable.

probability mass function (pmf)—A function that describes the probability distribution of a discrete random variable.

process—An activity or group of activities that takes an input, adds value to it, and provides an output to an internal or external customer; a planned and repetitive sequence of steps by which a defined product or service is delivered.

process capability—The ability or capability of a process to meet its intended purpose. It is a measure of how well the process produces outcomes that meet specifications.

process improvement team (PIT)—A natural work group or cross-functional team whose responsibility is to achieve needed improvements in existing processes. The life span of the team is based on the completion of the team purpose and specific tasks.

process mapping—The flowcharting of a work process in detail, including key measurements.

producer's risk (α)—For a sampling plan, refers to the probability of not accepting a lot the quality of which has a designated numerical value representing a level that is generally desirable. Usually the designated value will be the acceptable quality level. Also called *alpha risk* or probability of a type I error.

product identification—A means of marking parts with a label, etching, engraving, ink, or other means so that different part numbers and other key attributes can be identified.

program evaluation and review technique (PERT)—An event-oriented project management planning and measurement technique that utilizes an arrow diagram or road map to identify all major project events and demonstrates the amount of time (critical path) needed to complete a project. It provides three time estimates: optimistic, most likely, and pessimistic.

project lifecycle—A typical project lifecycle consists of five sequential phases in project management: concept, planning, design, implementation, and evaluation.

project management—The entire process of managing activities and events involved throughout a project's lifecycle.

project plan—All the documents that comprise the details of why the project is to be initiated, what the project is to accomplish, when and where it is to be implemented, who will have responsibility, how implementation will be carried out, how much it will cost, what resources are required, and how the project's progress and results will be measured.

Q

qualitative variable—A variable whose possible outcomes are nonnumeric or categorical.

quality assurance—All the planned or systematic actions necessary to provide adequate confidence that a product or service will satisfy given needs.

quality audit—A systematic, independent examination and review to determine whether quality activities and related results comply with planned arrangements and whether these arrangements are implemented effectively and are suitable to achieve the objectives.

quality audit observation—Statement of fact made during a quality audit and substantiated by objective evidence.

quality auditor—Person qualified to perform quality audits.

quality control—The operational techniques and the activities that sustain a quality of product or service that will satisfy given needs; also, the use of such techniques and activities.

quality council—Sometimes referred to as a "quality steering committee." The group driving the quality improvement effort and usually having oversight responsibility for the implementation and maintenance of the quality management system; it is operated in parallel with the normal operation of the business.

quality function deployment (QFD)—A structured method in which customer requirements are translated into appropriate technical requirements for each stage of product development and production. The QFD process is often referred to as listening to the voice of the customer.

quality improvement—Actions taken throughout an organization to increase the effectiveness and efficiency of activities and processes in order to provide added benefits to both the organization and its customers.

quality management—The totality of functions involved in organizing and leading the effort to determine and achieve quality.

quality manual—A document stating the quality policy and describing the quality system of an organization.

quality planning—The activity of establishing quality objectives and quality requirements.

quality policy—Top management's formally stated intentions and direction for the organization pertaining to quality.

quality surveillance—Continual monitoring and verification of the status of an entity and analysis of records to ensure that specified requirements are being fulfilled.

quality system—The organizational structure, procedures, processes, and resources needed to implement quality management.

quantitative variable—A variable whose outcomes are numeric—continuous or discrete.

R

random effect—In analysis of variance an effect is random if the factor levels included in the test or experiment are randomly selected from a larger population of possible levels. The results of the test conducted would then apply to the entire population of factor levels and not just those included in the experiment.

random error—Error that occurs as a result of natural variation in a process or system. It is variation that occurs when taking repeated measurements on the same unit or item under identical conditions. Also referred to as *experimental error*.

random experiment—An experiment that has more than one possible outcome.

random sampling—The process of selecting units for a sample in such a manner that all combinations of units under consideration have an equal or ascertainable chance of being selected as the sample.

random variable—A function that associates a real number to each outcome in an experiment.

range—The difference between the largest and smallest value or observation in a data set. It provides a measure of dispersion in a set of data.

rational subgrouping—A method for collecting data that will allow for minimizing the chance of variability due to assignable causes while maximizing the chance of variability due to chance or natural causes. A fundamental and nontrivial concept in statistical process control.

readability—Readability is the ease of reading the instrument scale when a dimension is being measured.

record—A document or electronic medium that furnishes objective evidence of activities performed or results achieved.

regression analysis—Statistical techniques for determining and modeling the relationship between a dependent variable and one or more independent variables. The response variable is also referred to as a *response* and the independent variables are also referred to as *regressor* or *predictor* variables.

regressor variable—In regression analysis it is the independent variable. Also known as the *predictor* variable.

reinforcement—The process of providing positive consequences when an individual is applying the correct knowledge and skills to the job. It has been described as "catching people doing things right and recognizing their behavior." Caution: less than desired behavior can also be reinforced unintentionally.

rejection region—In significance testing, the values of the test statistic that will lead to rejection of the null hypothesis. Sometimes referred to as the *critical region*.

reliability—The probability that an item can perform its intended function for a specified interval under stated conditions.

repeatability—How close the measurements of an instrument are to each other if such measurements are repeated on a part under the same measuring conditions.

replication—The repetition of the set of all the treatment combinations to be compared in an experiment. Each of the repetitions is called a replicate.

reproducibility—Reproducibility is a measure of the degree of agreement between two single test results made on the same object in two different, randomly selected measuring locations or laboratories.

residual—The difference between the actual or observed response and the predicted response for the variable of interest.

residual analysis—An examination of the residuals used to determine the adequacy of a fitted model. It is used to check the validity of assumptions made in model fitting.

resource requirements matrix—A tool to relate the resources required to the project tasks requiring them (used to indicate types of individuals needed, material needed, subcontractors, and so on).

response variable—The variable that shows the observed results of an experimental treatment. It is the dependent variable in regression analysis.

return on investment (ROI)—An umbrella term for a variety of ratios measuring an organization's business performance, calculated by dividing some measure of return by a measure of investment and then multiplying by 100 to provide a percentage. In its most basic form, ROI indicates what remains from all money taken in after all expenses are paid.

robust designs—Products or processes that continue to perform as intended in spite of manufacturing variation and extreme environmental conditions during use.

robustness—The condition of a product or process design that remains relatively stable with a minimum of variation even though factors that influence operations or usage, such as environment and wear, are constantly changing.

S

sample—A group of units, portions of material, or observations taken from a larger collection of units, quantity of material, or observations that serve to provide information that may be used as a basis for making a decision concerning the larger quantity.

sample integrity—Samples are maintained in a unique manner to avoid corruption or confusion with others.

sample space—The set of all possible outcomes of a random process or random experiment.

sample standard deviation—A measure of dispersion for a set of observations. It is the positive square root of the sample variance.

sample variance—A measure of dispersion for a set of observations. It provides a measure of the variability in a sample of data.

sampling distribution—The probability distribution of a statistic calculated from a random sample of a given size.

scatter diagram—A two-dimensional plot of data resulting from two random variables (bivariate data). The scatter diagram is a tool that can reveal associations between two variables. Also known as a *scatter plot*.

scribe—The member of a team assigned the responsibility for recording minutes of meetings.

self-directed work team (SDWT)—A team that requires little supervision and manages itself and the day-to-day work it does; self-directed teams are responsible for whole work processes and schedules, with each individual performing multiple tasks.

sensitivity—Sensitivity can be defined as the least perceptible change in dimension detected by the measuring instrument and shown by the indicator.

severity—An indicator of the severity of a failure should a failure occur. Severity can be evaluated based on a 10-point scale. At the lowest end of the scale (1) it is assumed that a failure will have no noticeable effect. At the highest end of the scale (10) it is assumed that a failure will impact safe operation or violate compliance with regulatory mandate.

Six Sigma approach—A quality philosophy; a collection of techniques and tools for use in reducing variation; a program of improvement that focuses on strong leadership tools and an emphasis on bottom-line financial results.

special causes—Causes of variation that arise because of special circumstances. They are not an inherent part of a process. Special causes are also referred to as *assignable causes*.

sponsor—A member of management who oversees, supports, and implements the efforts of a team or initiative.

stable process—A process for which no special causes of variation are present.

stages of team growth—The four development stages through which groups typically progress: forming, storming, norming, and performing. Knowledge of the stages helps team members accept the normal problems that occur on the path from forming a group to becoming a team.

stakeholders—People, departments, and organizations that have an investment or interest in the success or actions taken by the organization.

standard—A statement, specification, or quantity of material against which measured outputs from a process may be judged as acceptable or unacceptable.

standard deviation—A measure of dispersion or spread. It is equal to the positive square root of the variance.

standard error—The standard deviation of the sampling distribution of a statistic. In general, it is the standard deviation of any estimator of a parameter.

standard normal random variable—A random variable that is normally distributed with mean zero and variance one.

statement of work (SOW)—A description of the actual work to be accomplished. It is derived from the work breakdown structure and, when combined with the project specifications, becomes the basis for the contractual agreement on the project (also referred to as scope of work).

statistic—A quantity calculated from a sample of observations, most often to form an estimate of some population parameter.

statistical control—A process is considered to be in a state of statistical control if no special causes are present.

statistical process control (SPC)—The application of statistical techniques to control a process.

stem-and-leaf plot—A graphical display using the actual observations. The "stem" consists of the leading digit(s) of the observation and the leaf consists of the next digit of the observation.

steering committee—A group responsible for overall selection of continuous improvement projects.

strategic planning—A process to set an organization's long-range goals and identify the actions needed to reach the goals.

substitute quality characteristic—A producer's view/expression of what constitutes quality in a product or service.

subsystem—A combination of sets, groups, and so on, that performs an operational function within a system and its major subdivision of the system.

supply chain—The series of processes and/or organizations that are involved in producing and delivering a product to the final user.

surface metrology—Surface metrology may be broadly defined as the measurement of the difference between what a surface actually is and what it is intended to be. It may involve other terms such as *surface roughness* and *surface finish.*

SWOT analysis—An assessment of an organization's key strengths, weaknesses, opportunities, and threats. It considers factors such as the organization's industry, competitive position, functional areas, and management.

system—A composite of equipment, skills, and techniques capable of performing or supporting an operational role, or both. A complete system includes all equipment, related facilities, material, software, services, and personnel required for its operation and support to the degree that it can be considered self-sufficient in its intended operating environment.

systematic error—Error that remains the same over repeated measurements taken under assumed identical conditions.

T

t **distribution**—The distribution of the ratio of two independent random variables. The random variable in the numerator is a standard normal random variable. The random variable in the denominator is the square root of a chi-square random variable divided by its degrees of freedom. Also known as *Student's t distribution.*

takt time—Time needed to produce a product in order to meet customer demand.

team—A set of two or more people who are equally accountable for the accomplishment of a purpose and specific performance goals; it is also defined as a small number of people with complementary skills who are committed to a common purpose.

team building—The process of transforming a group of people into a team and developing the team to achieve its purpose.

test statistic—A statistic used to test a given statistical hypothesis. It is a quantity calculated from a sample of data.

testing—A means of determining the capability of an item to meet specified requirements by subjecting the item to a set of physical, chemical, environmental, or operating actions and conditions.

timekeeper—A member of a team who monitors progress against a predefined schedule during meetings.

tolerance interval—A statistical interval that contains a stated percentage of a population with a specified level of confidence.

total sum of squares—The sum of the squared differences between each observation in a data set and the overall mean of the data set.

traceability—The ability to trace the history, application, or location of an item or activity and like items or activities by means of recorded identification.

traceability system—A formal set of procedures, usually implemented in a computerized database, that allows the manufacturer of a unit to trace it and its components back to the source.

treatment—A combination of the levels of each of the factors assigned to an experimental unit.

true quality characteristic—A customer's view/expression of what constitutes quality in a product or service.

t-test—A significance test that involves the t distribution.

type I error—The incorrect decision that a process is unacceptable when, in fact, perfect information would reveal that it is located within the zone of acceptable processes.

type II error—The incorrect decision that a process is acceptable when, in fact, perfect information would reveal that it is located within the zone of rejectable processes.

U

unbiased estimator—An estimator whose expected value is equal to the parameter for which it is an estimator.

uniform distribution—A distribution whose values are equally distributed over an interval. Each possible outcome is assigned equal probability. The uniform distribution is defined for both continuous and discrete random variables.

V

value—The net difference between customer-perceived benefits and burdens, sometimes expressed as a ratio of benefits to burdens or a ratio of worth to cost.

variables data—Data resulting from the measurement of a parameter or a variable. The resulting measurements may be recorded on a continuous scale. (Contrast with *attributes data*.)

variance—A measure of dispersion. For a set of data, it is the sum of the squared differences between the individual observations and the mean of the observations. In general, it is the expected value of the squared difference between a random variable and its mean.

variance components—In analysis of variance with random effects present, these are the variances associated with the random effects.

W

work breakdown structure (WBS)—A project management technique by which a project is divided into tasks, subtasks, and units of work to be performed.

work group—A group composed of people from one functional area who work together on a daily basis and whose goal is to manage and improve the processes of their function.

References

Aft, L. 1988. *Quality Improvement Using Statistical Process Control.* New York: Harcourt-Brace-Jovanovich.

Agresti, A. 1988. "A Model for Agreement between Ratings on an Ordinal Scale." *Biometrics* 44: 539–48.

———. 1992. "Modeling Patterns of Agreement and Disagreement." *Statistical Methods in Medical Research* 1: 201–18.

Agresti, A., and B. Coull. 1998. "Approximate Is Better Than Exact for Interval Estimation of Binomial Proportions." *The American Statistician* 52: 119–26.

Agresti, A., and J. B. Lang. 1993. "Quasi-Symmetric Latent Class Models, with Application to Rater Agreement." *Biometrics* 49: 131–39.

Aickin, M. 1990. "Maximum Likelihood Estimation of Agreement in the Constant Predictive Model, and Its Relation to Cohen's Kappa." *Biometrics* 46: 293–302.

Akao, Y., Ed. 1990. *Quality Function Deployment.* Portland, OR: Productivity Press.

American Society for Quality. 1978. *ANSI/ASQC A3-1978 Quality Systems Terminology.* Milwaukee: American Society for Quality.

American Society for Testing and Materials. 1977. *ASTM Standards on Precision and Accuracy for Various Applications.* 1st ed. Philadelphia: ASTM.

ANSI B89.6.2-1974. 1974. *Temperature and Humidity Environment for Dimensional Measurement.* New York: ASME.

ANSI Y14.5M-1982. 1983. *Dimensioning and Tolerancing.* New York: ASME.

ANSI/ASME B46.1-1095. 1986. *Surface Texture—Surface Roughness, Waviness, and Lay.* New York: ASME.

ANSI/ASME B89.1.12M-1985. Methods for Performance Evaluation of Coordinate Measuring Machines. 1985. New York: ASME.

ANSI/ASME B89.3.1-1972. R 1979. Measurement of Out-of-Roundness. 1979. New York: ASME.

ANSI/ASQ Z1.4-2003, Sampling Procedures and Tables for Inspection by Attributes. 2003. Milwaukee: American Society for Quality.

ASQ Statistics Division. 2004. *Glossary and Tables for Statistical Quality Control.* 4th ed. Milwaukee: ASQ Quality Press.

ASQC Statistics Division. 1996. *Glossary and Tables for Statistical Quality Control.* 3rd ed. Milwaukee: ASQC Quality Press.

ASQ's Product Safety and Liability Prevention Interest Group. 1981. *Product Recall Planning Guide.* Milwaukee: ASQC Quality Press.

Automotive Industry Action Group. 1995. *Measurement System Analysis Reference Manual.* Detroit, MI: AIAG.

———. 2001. *Potential Failure Modes and Effects Analysis.* 3rd ed. Detroit, MI: AIAG.

Badiru, A. B., and P. S. Pulat. 1995. *Comprehensive Project Management.* Englewood Cliffs, NJ: Prentice Hall.

Banerjee, M., M. Capozzoli, L. McSweeney, and D. Sinha. 1999. "Beyond Kappa: A Review of Interrater Agreement Measures." *The Canadian Journal of Statistics* 27: 3–23.

Barlow, R. E., J. B. Fussell, and N. D. Singpurwalla. 1975. *Reliability and Fault Tree Analysis.* Philadelphia: SIAM.

Barnard, G. A. 1959. "Control Charts and Stochastic Processes." *Journal of the Royal Statistical Society B* 21: 239–71.

Barnes, R. M. 1980. *Motion and Time Study Design and Measurement of Work.* 7th ed. New York: John Wiley & Sons.

Barrentine, L. 2003. *Concepts for R&R Studies.* Milwaukee: ASQ Quality Press.

Bartko, J. J., and W. T. Carpenter. 1976. "On the Methods and Theory of Reliability." *Journal of Nervous and Mental Disease* 163: 307–17.

Belanger, B. C. 1980. *Measurement of Quality Control and the Use of NBS Measurement Assistance Program.* NBS Special Publication 620-A. Washington, D.C.: U.S. Department of Commerce.

————. 1984. *Measurement Assurance Program—Part I: General Introduction.* NBS Special Publication 676-I. Washington, D.C.: U.S. Department of Commerce.

Besterfield, D. H. 1999. *Total Quality Management.* 2nd ed. Englewood Cliffs, NJ: Prentice Hall.

————. 2001. *Quality Control.* 6th ed. Englewood Cliffs, NJ: Prentice Hall.

Bisgaard, S. 1990. "Quality Engineering and Taguchi Methods: A Perspective." Technical Report No. 40. Madison, WI: Center for Quality and Productivity Improvement, University of Wisconsin.

Bloch, D. A., and H. C. Kraemer. 1989. "2 × 2 Kappa Coefficients: Measures of Agreement or Association." *Biometrics* 45: 269–87.

Bond, T. P. 1983. "Basics of an MRB." *Quality* (November): 48.

Borror, C. M., D. C. Montgomery, and G. C. Runger. 1997. "Confidence Intervals for Variance Components from Gauge Capability Studies." *Quality and Reliability Engineering International* 13: 361–69.

————. 1999. "Robustness of the EWMA Control Chart to Nonnormality." *Journal of Quality Technology* 31: 309–16.

Bosch, J. A. 1984. *66 Centuries of Measurement.* Dayton, Ohio: Sheffield Measurement Division.

Bosch, J. A., Ed. 1995. *Coordinate Measuring Machines and Systems.* New York: Marcel Dekker.

Bothe, D. 2001. "Back to Basics: Use Check Sheets to Identify the Causes of Downtime." *Quality Progress* 34, no. 4: 136.

Box, G. E. P. 1988. "Signal-to-Noise Ratios, Performance Criteria, and Transformations" (with discussion). *Technometrics* 30: 1–41.

————. 1989. "When Murphy Speaks—Listen." *ASQ Quality Progress* (October): 79–84.

Box, G. E. P., S. Bisgaard, and C. Fung. 1988. "An Explanation and Critique of Taguchi's Contributions to Quality Engineering." *Quality and Reliability Engineering International* 4: 123–31.

Box, G. E. P., W. Hunter, and J. S. Hunter. 2005. *Statistics for Experimenters: Design, Innovation, and Discovery.* 2nd ed. Hoboken, NJ: John Wiley & Sons.

Boyles, R. A. 2001. "Gauge Capability for Pass-Fail Inspection." *Technometrics* 43: 223–29.

Brassard, M. 1989. *The Memory Jogger Plus+.* Methuen, MA: Goal/QPC Press.

Brassard, M., and D. Ritter. 1994. *Memory Jogger II.* 1st ed. Methuen, MA: GOAL/QPC Press.

Breyfogle, F. W. 1999. *Implementing Six Sigma: Smarter Solutions Using Six Sigma.* New York: John Wiley & Sons.

————. 1999. *Implementing Six Sigma: Smarter Solutions Using Statistical Methods.* New York: John Wiley & Sons.

Breyfogle, F. W., J. Cupello, and B. Meadows. 2000. *Managing Six Sigma: A Practical Guide to Understanding, Assessing, and Implementing the Strategy That Yields Bottom-Line Success.* New York: John Wiley & Sons.

Britz, G. C., and D. W. Emerling. 2000. *Improving Performance Through Statistical Thinking.* Milwaukee: ASQ Quality Press.

Burdick, R. K., E. Allen, and G. Larsen. 2002. "Comparing Variability of Two Measurement Processes Using R&R Studies." *Journal of Quality Technology* 34: 97–105.

Burdick, R. K., C. M. Borror, and D. C. Montgomery. 2003. "A Review of Methods for Measurement Systems Capability Analysis." *Journal of Quality Technology* 35: 342–54.

———. 2005. *Design and Analysis of Gauge R&R Studies: Making Decisions with Confidence Intervals in Random and Mixed ANOVA Models.* Philadelphia: ASA-SIAM Series on Statistics and Applied Probability.

Burdick, R. K., and G. Larsen. 1997. "Confidence Intervals on Measures of Variability in Gauge R&R Studies." *Journal of Quality Technology* 29: 261–73.

Burnett, R. E. 2005. *Technical Communication.* 6th ed. Boston: Wadsworth/ITP.

Burr, W. 1976. *Statistical Quality Control Methods.* New York: Marcel Dekker.

Busch, T. 1966. *Fundamentals of Dimensional Metrology.* Albany, NY: Delmar.

Busch, T., R. Harlow, and R. Thompson. 1998. *Fundamentals of Dimensional Metrology.* 3rd ed. Albany, NY: Delmar.

Camp, R. C. 1989. "Benchmarking: The Search for Industry Best Practices That Lead to Superior Performance." *ASQ Quality Progress* (January–May).

———. 1995. *Business Process Benchmarking.* Milwaukee: ASQC Quality Press.

Caplan, F. 1980. *The Quality System.* Radnor, PA: Chilton Book Company.

Chase, G. W. 1993. *Implementing TQM in a Construction Company.* Washington, D.C.: Associated General Contractors of America.

Cianfrani, C. A., J. J. Tsiakals, and J. E. West. 2002. *The ASQ ISO 9000:2000 Handbook.* Milwaukee: ASQ Quality Press.

Cicchetti, D. V., and A. R. Feinstein. 1990. "High Agreement but Low Kappa: II. Resolving the Paradoxes." *Journal of Clinical Epidemiology* 43: 551–58.

Cohen, J. 1960. "Coefficient of Agreement for Nominal Scales." *Educational and Psychological Measurement* 20: 37–46.

Cole, R. E. 1994. "Reengineering the Corporation: A Review Essay." *Quality Management Journal* (July): 77–85.

Collins, J. C., and J. I. Porras. 1997. *Built to Last: Successful Habits of Visionary Companies.* New York: Harper Business.

Conger, A. J. 1980. "Integration and Generalization of Kappas for Multiple Raters." *Psychological Bulletin* 88: 322–28.

Croarkin, C. 1985. *Measurement Assurance Program—Part II: Development and Implementation.* NBS Special Publication 676-II. Washington, D.C.: U.S. Department of Commerce.

Crosby, P. B. 1979. *Quality Is Free.* New York: McGraw-Hill.

Crowder, S. V. 1989. "Design of Exponentially Weighted Moving Average Schemes." *Journal of Quality Technology* 21: 155–62.

Darmody, W. J. 1967. "Elements of a Generalized Measuring System." In *Handbook of Industrial Metrology.* Englewood Cliffs, NJ: Prentice-Hall (ASTME).

Day, R. G. 1993. *Quality Function Deployment: Linking a Company with Its Customers.* Milwaukee: ASQC Quality Press.

de Mast, J., and W. N. van Wieringen. 2004. "Measurement System Analysis for Bounded Ordinal Data." *Quality and Reliability Engineering International* 20: 383–95.

———. 2007. "Measurement System Analysis for Categorical Measurements: Agreement and Kappa-Type Indices." *Journal of Quality Technology* 39: 191–202.

DeBono, E. 1992. *Serious Creativity: Using the Power of Lateral Thinking to Create New Ideas.* New York: HarperCollins.

Dedhia, N. S. 2004. "ISO 9001:2000 Standard: Inspection Requirements." In *Annual Quality Congress Proceedings* 58: 17-17. Milwaukee: American Society for Quality.

Deming, W. E. 1982. *Quality, Productivity, and Competitive Position.* Cambridge, MA: M.I.T. Center for Advanced Engineering Study.

———. 1986. *Out of the Crisis.* Cambridge, MA: M.I.T. Center for Advanced Engineering Study.

Devore, J. 2007. *Probability and Statistics for Engineering and the Sciences.* 7th ed. Pacific Grove, CA: Duxbury Press.

Dhillon, B. S. 1986. *Human Reliability with Human Factors.* Oxford, New York: Pergamon.

Dhillon, B. S., and C. Singh. 1981. *Engineering Reliability: New Techniques and Applications.* New York: John Wiley & Sons.

Dolezal, K. K., R. K. Burdick, and N. J. Birch. 1998. "Analysis of a Two-Factor R&R Study with Fixed Operators." *Journal of Quality Technology* 30: 163–70.

Dorris, A. L., and B. L. Foote. 1978. "Inspection Errors and Statistical Quality Control: A Survey." *AIIE Transactions* 10, no. 2: 184–92.

Dovich, R. 1992. "Acceptance Sampling." In *Quality Engineering Handbook.* Ed. T. Pyzdek and R. Berger. Milwaukee: ASQC Quality Press; New York: Marcel Dekker.

Drews, W. E. 1978. "How to Measure Roundness." *Tooling and Production* (June).

Duncan, A. J. 1986. *Quality Control and Industrial Statistics.* 5th ed. Homewood, IL: Richard D. Irwin.

Ebeling, C. E. 2005. *Introduction to Reliability and Maintainability Engineering.* New York: McGraw-Hill.

Eckes, G. 2000. *The Six Sigma Revolution.* New York: John Wiley & Sons.

Elsayed, E. A. 1996. *Reliability Engineering.* Reading, PA: Addison Wesley.

———. 2000. "Perspectives and Challenges for Research in Quality and Reliability Engineering." *International Journal of Production Research* 38, no. 9: 1953–76.

Elshennawy, A. K., I. Ham, and P. H. Cohen. 1988. "Evaluating the Performance of Coordinate Measuring Machines." *ASQ Quality Progress* (January): 59–65.

Engel, J., and B. deVries. 1997. "Evaluating a Well-Known Criterion for Measurement Precision." *Journal of Quality Technology* 29: 469–76.

Farago, F. T. 1982. *Handbook of Dimensional Measurement.* 2nd ed. New York: Industrial Press.

Feigenbaum, A. V. 1983. *Total Quality Control.* New York: McGraw-Hill.

———. 1991. *Total Quality Control.* 3rd ed. New York: McGraw-Hill.

Feinsten, A. R., and D. V. Cicchetti. 1990. "High Agreement but Low Kappa: I. The Problem of Two Paradoxes." *Journal of Clinical Epidemiology* 43: 543–49.

Fisher, D. C. 1993. *The Simplified Baldrige Award Organizational Assessment.* New York: Lincoln-Bradley.

Fisher, R. A. 1925. *Statistical Methods for Research Workers.* London: Oliver and Boyd.

Fleiss, J. L. 1965. "Estimating the Accuracy of Dichotomous Judgments." *Psychometrika* 30: 469–79.

———. 1971. "Measuring Nominal Scale Agreement among Many Raters." *Psychological Bulletin* 76: 378–82.

Foster, S. T. 1998. "The Ups and Downs of Customer-Driven Quality." *ASQ Quality Progress* (October): 67–72.

Freedman, D., and P. Diaconis. 1981. "On the Histogram As a Density Estimator: L_2 Theory." *Zeit. Wahr. ver. Geb.* 57: 453–76.

Gale, B. T., with R. C. Wood. 1994. *Managing Customer Value: Creating Quality and Service That Customers Can See.* New York: The Free Press.

Gaylor, J. F. W., and C. R. Shotbolt. 1964. *Metrology for Engineers*. London: Cassell & Company.

Gee, G., P. McGrath, and M. Izadi. 1996. "A Team Approach to Kaizen." *Journal of Industrial Technology* (Fall): 45–48.

Gillette, B., R. Johnson, E. Polashek, J. Thornburg, and C. White. 1993. *The Art of Working Together: A Guide to Effective Collaboration*. Ames, IA: C. I. White and Associates.

Goldratt, E. M. 1997. *Critical Chain*. Great Barrington, MA: The North River Press.

Gryna, F. M. 1988a. "Manufacturing Planning." In *Juran's Quality Handbook*. 4th ed. New York: McGraw-Hill.

———. 1988b. "Training for Quality." In *Juran's Quality Control Handbook*. 4th ed. New York: McGraw-Hill.

———. 2001. *Quality Planning and Analysis: From Product Development Through Use*. 4th ed. New York: McGraw-Hill.

Gryna, F. M., R. C. H. Chua, and J. A. Defeo. 2007. *Juran's Quality Planning and Analysis for Enterprise Quality*. 5th ed. New York: McGraw-Hill.

Hallock, M. L., S. J. Alper, and B. Karsh. 2006. "A Macroergonomic Work System Analysis of the Diagnostic Testing Process in an Outpatient Health Care Facility for Process Improvement and Patient Safety." *Ergonomics* 49, no. 5–6: 544–66.

Hahn, G., N. Doganaksoy, and C. Stanard. 2001. "Statistical Tools for Six Sigma." *Quality Progress* (September): 78–82.

Hammer, M., and J. Champy. 1993. *Reengineering the Corporation: A Manifesto for Business Revolution*. New York: HarperCollins.

Harris, D. H., and F. B. Chaney. 1969. *Human Factors in Quality Assurance*. New York: John Wiley & Sons.

Harry, M. 1992. "The Nature of Six Sigma Quality." Technical report, Government Electronics Group. Scottsdale, AZ: Motorola.

Hawkins, D., and D. H. Olwell. 1998. *Cumulative Sum Charts and Charting for Quality Improvement*. New York: Springer-Verlag.

Hill, H. M., and D. J. McClaskey. 1980. "Developing Awareness of Quality Responsibilities." *ASQC Technical Conference Transactions*. Milwaukee: ASQC Quality Press.

Hines, W., and D. Montgomery. 1990. *Probability and Statistics in Engineering and Management Science*. 3rd ed. New York: John Wiley & Sons.

Hoerl, R. 2001. "Six Sigma Black Belts: What Do They Need to Know?" (with discussion) *Journal of Quality Technology* 33: 391–435.

Hoerl, R., and R. D. Snee. 2002. *Statistical Thinking: Improving Business Performance*. Pacific Grove, CA: Duxbury.

Houf, R., and D. Berman. 1988. "Statistical Analysis of Power Module Thermal Test Equipment Performance." *IEEE Transactions on Components, Hybrids, and Manufacturing Technology* 22: 516–20.

Hogg, R. V., and E. A. Tanis. 1997. *Probability and Statistical Inference*. Englewood Cliffs, NJ: Prentice Hall.

Hughes, T. A. 1995. *Measurement and Control Basics*. 2nd ed. Research Triangle Park, NC: Instrument Society of America.

Hunter, J. S. 1985. "Statistical Design Applied to Product Design." *Journal of Quality Technology* 17: 210–21.

Imai, M. 1986. *Kaizen*. New York: McGraw-Hill.

Ishikawa, K. 1985. *What Is Total Quality Control? The Japanese Way*. Englewood Cliffs, NJ: Prentice Hall.

Jardine, A. K. S., and J. A. Buzacott. 1983. "Equipment Reliability and Maintenance." *European Journal of Operational Research* 19: 285–96.

Jensen, C. R. 2002. "Variance Component Calculations: Common Methods and Misapplications in the Semiconductor Industry." *Quality Engineering* 14: 645–57.

Johnson, R. H., and R. T. Webber. 1985. *Buying Quality: How Purchasing, Quality Control, and Suppliers Work Together.* New York: Franklin Watts.

Jones, J., and J. Hayes. 1999. "A Comparison of Electronic Reliability Prediction Models." *IEEE Transactions on Reliability* 48, no. 2: 127–34.

Juran, J. M. 1988. *Juran's Quality Handbook.* 4th ed. New York: McGraw-Hill.

———. 1989. *Juran on Leadership for Quality.* New York: Free Press.

Juran, J. M., and A. Godfrey. 1999. *Juran's Quality Handbook.* 5th ed. New York: McGraw Hill.

Juran, J. M., and F. N. Gryna Jr. 1980. *Quality Planning and Analysis.* New York: McGraw-Hill.

Kanter, R. 2000. *ISO 9000 Answer Book.* New York: John Wiley & Sons.

Kececioglue, D. 1991. *Reliability Engineering Handbook,* Vols. 1 and 2. Upper Saddle River, NJ: Prentice-Hall.

Kerns, D. T., and D. T. Nadler. 1992. *Prophets in the Dark: How Xerox Reinvented Itself and Beat Back the Japanese.* New York: Harper Business.

King, B. 1987. *Better Designs in Half the Time.* Methuen, MA: GOAL/QPC Press.

Kirkpatrick, D. L. 1998. *Evaluating Training Programs: The Four Levels.* San Francisco: Berrett-Koehler.

———. 2006. *Evaluating Training Programs: The Four Levels.* 3rd ed. San Francisco: Berrett-Koehler.

Knowles, G. J., J. Antony, and G. Vickers. 2000. "A Practical Methodology for Analyzing and Improving the Measurement System." *Quality Assurance* no. 8: 59–75.

Knowles, M. S. 1996. "Adult Learning." In *The ASTD Training and Development Handbook.* 4th ed. New York: McGraw-Hill.

Kolarik, W. J. 1995. *Creating Quality: Concepts, Systems, Strategies, and Tools.* New York: McGraw-Hill.

———. 1999. *Creating Quality: Process Design for Results.* New York: McGraw-Hill.

Konz, S., G. Peterson, and A. Joshi. 1981. "Reducing Inspection Errors." *Quality Progress* no. 7: 24–26.

Kotz, S., and C. Lovelace. 1998. *Process Capability Indices in Theory and Practice.* London: Arnold Press.

Laford, R. J. 1986. *Ship-to-Stock: An Alternative to Incoming Inspection.* Milwaukee: ASQC Quality Press.

Langdon, D. J. 1994. "A New Language of Work." *Quality Digest* (October): 44–48.

Larsen, G. A. 2002. "Measurement System Analysis—The Usual Metrics Can Be Noninformative." *Quality Engineering* 15: 293–98.

Ledolter, J., and C. Burrill. 1999. *Statistical Quality Control: Strategies and Tools for Continual Improvement.* New Jersey: John Wiley & Sons.

Ledolter, J., and A. Swersey. 1997. "An Evaluation of Pre-Control." *Journal of Quality Technology* 29: 163–71.

———. 2007. *Testing 1-2-3: Experimental Design with Applications in Marketing and Service Operations.* Los Angeles: Stanford University Press.

Lee, H., and H. Awbi. "Effect of Internal Partitioning on Room Air Quality with Mixing Ventilation—Statistical Analysis" *Renewable Energy* 29: 1721–32.

Leemis, L. M. 1995. *Reliability: Probabilistic Models and Statistical Methods.* Englewood Cliffs, NJ: Prentice-Hall.

Lipton, G. M. 1998. "Product Traceability: A Guide for Locating Recalled Manufactured Goods." *52nd Annual Quality Congress Proceedings.* Milwaukee: American Society for Quality.

Long, C. S., and F. M. Gryna. 1999. *Preferred Practices in Developing a Quality Information System.* Report No. 907. Tampa, FL: College of Business.

Lucas, J., and M. Sacucci. 1990. "Exponentially Weighted Moving Average Control Schemes: Properties and Enhancements." *Technometrics* 32: 1–29.

Luceño, A. 1996. "A Process Capability Ratio with Reliable Confidence Intervals." *Communication in Statistics—Simulation and Computation* 25: 235–46.

Machinability Data Center. 1980. *Machining Data Handbook.* Cincinnati, OH: TechSolve.

Mack, D. A. 1980. "Instrument Calibration." Workshop conference on the management of laboratory instruments, Cairo, Egypt, November 7–11, 1976. (Conference proceedings collected in Huston, N. E. *Management Systems for Laboratory Instrument Services.* Research Triangle Park, NC: Instrument Society of America.)

Mader, D. P., J. Prins, and R. E. Lampe. 1999. "The Economic Impact of Measurement Error." *Quality Engineering* 15: 293–98.

Majeske, K. D. 2002. "Evaluating Measurement Systems and Manufacturing Processes Using Three Quality Measures." *Quality Engineering* 15, no. 2: 243–51.

Makino, T. 1984. "Mean Hazard Rate and Its Application to the Normal Approximation of the Weibull Distribution." *Naval Research Logistics Quarterly* 31: 1–8.

Mallette, P. 1993. "Improving Through Creativity." *Quality Digest* (May): 81–85.

Manos, T. 2006. "Value Stream Mapping—An Introduction." *Quality Progress* (June): 64–69.

Marsh, W. A. 2004. "Opinion Item: Cancelled U.S. Military Specifications." *IEEE Transactions on Reliability* 53: 1–2.

McCaslin, J. A., and G. F. Gruska. 1976. "Analysis of Attribute Gage Systems." *ASQC Technical Conference Transactions* 30: 392–99.

McKenzie, R. M. 1958. "On the Accuracy of Inspectors." *Ergonomics* 1: 258–72.

McNish, A. 1967. "The Nature of Measurement." In *Handbook of Industrial Metrology.* Englewood Cliffs, NJ: Prentice Hall.

Megaw, E. D. 1979. "Factors Affecting Visual Inspection Accuracy." *Applied Ergonomics* 10: 27–32.

MIL-STD-1629A Procedures for Performing a Failure Mode, Effects, and Criticality Analysis. 1980. Washington D.C.: Department of Defense.

MIL-STD-45662 Calibration System Requirements. 1980. Washington, D.C.: Department of Defense.

Mizuno, S., Ed. 1988. *Management for Quality Improvement.* Portland, OR: Productivity Press.

Montgomery, D. C. 2009a. *Design and Analysis of Experiments.* 7th ed. New Jersey: John Wiley & Sons.

———. 2009b. *Introduction to Statistical Quality Control.* 6th ed. New Jersey: John Wiley & Sons.

Montgomery, D. C., C. Jennings, and M. Kulahci. 2008. *Introduction to Time Series Analysis and Forecasting.* New York: John Wiley & Sons.

Montgomery, D. C., and G. C. Runger. 1993a. "Gauge Capability and Designed Experiments. Part I: Basic Methods." *Quality Engineering* 6, no. 1: 115–35.

———. 1993b. "Gauge Capability Analysis and Designed Experiments. Part II: Experimental Design Models and Variance Component Estimation." *Quality Engineering* 6, no. 2: 289–305.

———. 2006. *Applied Statistics and Probability for Engineers.* 4th ed. New Jersey: John Wiley & Sons.

Montgomery, D. C., G. C. Runger, and N. F. Hubele. 2006. *Engineering Statistics.* 4th ed. New Jersey: John Wiley & Sons.

Myers, R. H., and Montgomery, D. C. 2002. *Response Surface Methodology.* 2nd ed. New York: John Wiley & Sons.

Nadler, G., and S. Hibino. 1994. *Breakthrough Thinking.* 2nd ed. Rocklin, CA: Prima Publishing.

Nair, V. N., Ed. 1992. "Taguchi's Parameter Design: A Panel Discussion." *Technometrics* 34: 127–61.

National Institute for Standards and Technology (NIST). 1981. Special Publication 304A. Washington, D.C.: U.S. Department of Commerce.

Novack, J. L. 1995. *The ISO 9000 Quality Manual Developer.* Englewood Cliffs, NJ: Prentice Hall.

O'Connor, P. D. T. 1995. *Practical Reliability Engineering.* 3rd ed. New York: John Wiley & Sons.

Page, E. S. 1961. "Cumulative Sum Control Charts." *Technometrics* 3: 1–9.

Palady, P. 1997. *Failure Modes and Effects Analysis: Practical Applications.* Ann Arbor, MI: Library of Congress.

Park, C. S. 2007. *Contemporary Engineering Economics.* 4th ed. New Jersey: Prentice Hall.

Park, K. S. 1987. *Human Reliability—Analysis, Prediction, and Prevention of Human Errors.* Amsterdam: Elsevier.

Parsowith, B. S. 1995. *Fundamentals of Quality Auditing.* Milwaukee: ASQC Quality Press.

Paxton, K. 1996. "Corrective Action in the Real World." *ASQC Quality Progress* 29, no. 5 (May): 184.

Pearlson, K. E., and C. S. Saunders. 2004. *Managing and Using Information Systems: A Strategic Approach.* New York: John Wiley & Sons.

Perry, B. 1998 . "Seeing Your Customers in a Whole New Light." *Journal for Quality and Participation* 21, no. 6: 38–43.

Pignatiello, J. J., Jr., and J. S. Ramberg. 1992. "Top Ten Triumphs and Tragedies of Genichi Taguchi." *Quality Engineering* 4: 211–25.

Pyzdek, T. 2001. *The Six Sigma Handbook.* New York: McGraw-Hill.

Rashed, A. F., and A. M. Hamouda. 1974. *Technology for Real Quality.* Alexandria, Egypt: Egyptian University House.

Raz, T. 1986. "A Survey of Models for Allocating Inspection Effort in Multistage Production Systems." *Journal of Quality Technology* 18, no. 4: 239–47.

———. 1992. "Inspection." In *Quality Engineering Handbook.* Ed. T. Pyzdek and R. Berger. Milwaukee: ASQC Quality Press; New York: Marcel Dekker.

Reason, R. E. 1960. *The Measurement of Surface Texture.* London: CleaverHume Press.

Reiling, J. G., B. L. Knuizen, and M. Stoecklein. 2003. "FMEA—The Cure for Medical Errors." *ASQ Quality Progress* 36, no. 8 (August): 67–71.

Rice, G. O. 1980. "Measurement Systems and the Standards Laboratory." Workshop conference on the management of laboratory instruments, Cairo, Egypt, November 7–11, 1976. (Conference proceedings collected in Huston, N.E. *Management Systems for Laboratory Instrument Services.* Research Triangle Park, NC: Instrument Society of America.)

———. 1986. "Metrology." In *Quality Management Handbook.* Eds. L. Walsh, R. Wurster, and R. J. Kimber. Milwaukee: ASQC Quality Press; New York: Marcel Dekker.

Roberts, S. W. 1959. "Control Chart Tests Based on Geometric Moving Averages." *Technometrics* 1: 97–102.

Robinson, J. 1997. "Integrate Quality Cost Concepts into Teams' Problem-Solving Efforts." *ASQ Quality Progress* 30, no. 3 (March): 25.

Rodriquez, R. N. 1992. "Recent Developments in Process Capability Analysis." *Journal of Quality Technology* 24: 176–87.

Rother, M., and J. Shook. 1999. *Learning to See.* Brookline, MA: The Lean Enterprise Institute.

Saaty, T. 1982. *Decision Making for Leaders.* Belmont, CA: Lifetime Learning Publications.

Salegna, G., and F. Fazel. 2000. "Obstacles to Implementing Quality." *ASQ Quality Progress* (July): 53–57.

Schlickman, J. J. 1998. *ISO 9000 Quality Management System Design.* Milwaukee: ASQ Quality Press.

Schmidt, W. H., and J. P. Finnigan. 1992. *The Race without a Finish Line.* San Francisco: Jossey-Bass.

Scholtes, P. R. 1992. *The Team Handbook: How to Use Teams to Improve Quality.* Madison, WI: Joiner Associates.

Scott, D. 1979. "On Optimal and Data-Based Histograms." *Biometrika* 66: 605–10.

Senge, P. 1990. *The Fifth Discipline: The Art and Practice of the Learning Organization.* New York: Doubleday/Current.

Shewhart, W. A. 1980. *Economic Control of Quality Manufactured Product.* Milwaukee: ASQC Quality Press.

Shingo, S. 1986. *Zero Quality Control: Source Inspection and the Poka-Yoke System.* Portland, OR: Productivity Press.

Simpson, J. A. 1981. "Foundations of Metrology." *Journal of Research of the National Bureau of Standards* 86, no. 3 (May/June): 36–42.

Snee, R. D. 2000. "Six Sigma Improves Both Statistical Training and Processes." *ASQ Quality Progress* (October): 68–72.

Snee, R. D., and R. W. Hoerl. 2007a. *Leading Six Sigma: A Step-by-Step Guide Based on Experience with GE and Other Six Sigma Companies.* New Jersey: Prentice Hall.

———. 2007b. *Six Sigma beyond the Factory Floor: Deployment Strategies for Financial Services, Health Care, and the Rest of the Real Economy.* New Jersey: Prentice Hall.

Spragg, R. C. 1976. "Advanced System for the Measurement of Errors of Form." SME Paper No. IQ 76-807.

Stamatis, D. 2003. *Failure Mode and Effect Analysis: FMEA Theory to Execution.* 2nd ed. Milwaukee: ASQ Quality Press.

Steiner, S. H., and R. J. MacKay. 2005. *Statistical Engineering: An Algorithm for Reducing Variation in Manufacturing Processes.* Milwaukee: ASQ Quality Press.

Stevenson, W. 2000. "Supercharging Your Pareto Analysis." *ASQ Quality Progress* (October): 51–55.

Stolovitch, H. D., and E. J. Keeps, Eds. 1992. *The Handbook of Human Performance Technology.* San Francisco: Jossey-Bass.

Sturges, H. A. 1926. "The Choice of a Class Interval." *Journal of the American Statistical Association* 21: 65–66.

Sullivan, L. P. 1986. "Quality Function Deployment." *ASQC Quality Progress* (June): 39–50.

Sumithra, B., and S. Bhattacharya. 2008. "Toasting of Corn Flakes: Product Characteristics As a Function of Processing Conditions." *Journal of Food Engineering* 88: 419–28.

Sweet, A. L., S. Tjokrodjojo, and P. Wijaya. 2005. "An Investigation of the Measurements Systems Analysis 'Analytic Method' for Attribute Gages." *Quality Engineering* 17: 219–26.

Swift, J. 1995. *Introduction to Modern Statistical Quality Control and Management.* Del Ray Beach, FL: St. Lucie Press.

Taguchi, G. 1986. *Introduction to Quality Engineering: Designing Quality into Products and Processes.* White Plains, NY: Kraus International; UNIPUB (Asian Productivity Organization).

Tague, N. 2005. *The Quality Toolbox.* 2nd ed. Milwaukee: ASQ Quality Press.

Taylor, C. 1998a. "A Systematic Approach to Quality Improvement: The Interactions between the Technical, Human, and Quality Systems." *Total Quality Management* 9, no. 1 (February): 79.

————. 1998b. "A Preventive versus Corrective Action: The Horse, the Barn, and the Apple." *ASQ Quality Progress* 31, no. 3 (March): 66.

Tobias, P. A., and D. C. Trindade. 1995. *Applied Reliability.* 2nd ed. New York: Chapman and Hall.

Tricker, R. 2000. *CE Conformity Marking and New Approach Directives.* Boston: Butterworth-Heinemann.

Uebersax, J. S. 1988. "Validity Inferences from Interobserver Agreement." *Psychological Bulletin* 104: 405–16.

Uebersax, J. S., and W. M. Grove. 1990. "Latent Class Analysis of Diagnostic Agreement." *Statistical Methods* 9: 559–72.

U.S. Department of Defense. 1980. *Procedures for Performing a Failure Mode, Effects, and Criticality Analysis.* Washington, D.C.: General Accounting Office Technical Library.

van Wieringen, W. N., and E. R. van Heuvel. 2005. "A Comparison of Methods for the Evaluation of Binary Measurement Systems." *Quality Engineering* 17: 495–507.

VanGundy, A. B. 1984. *Managing Group Creativity.* New York: American Management Association.

Vardeman, S. B., and E. S. VanValkenburg. 1999. "Two-Way Random-Effects Analyses and Gauge R&R Sudies." *Technometrics* 41: 202–11.

Vendor-Vendee Technical Committee. 1977. *How to Conduct a Supplier Survey.* Milwaukee: ASQC Quality Press.

Vining, G. G., and S. Kowalski. 2006. *Statistical Methods for Engineers.* 2nd ed. Pacific Grove, CA: Brooks-Cole.

Vogt, T. L. 1980. *Optimizing Calibration Recall Intervals and Algorithms.* NIST Publication NBS-GCR-80-283.

Wald, A. 1973. *Sequential Analysis.* New York: Dover.

Watson, G. H. 1993. *Strategic Benchmarking.* New York: John Wiley & Sons.

Weiss, N. A. 2004. *Introductory Statistics.* 7th ed. New York: Addison-Wesley.

Westcott, R. T. 2003. *Stepping Up to ISO 9004:2000.* Chico, CA: Paton Press.

————. 2006. *The Certified Manager of Quality/Organizational Excellence Handbook.* Milwaukee: ASQ Quality Press.

Wheeler, D. J. 2004. *The Six Sigma Practitioner's Guide to Data Analysis.* Knoxville, TN: SPC Press.

Wheeler, D. J., and R. W. Lyday. 1989. *Evaluating the Measurement Process.* 2nd ed. Knoxville, TN: SPC Press.

Woodall, W. H., and C. M. Borror. 2008. "Some Relationships between Gage R&R Criteria." *Quality and Reliability Engineering International* 24: 99–104.

Woodall, W. H., and M. Adams. 1993. "The Statistical Design of CUSUM Charts." *Quality Engineering* 5: 559–70.

Wunchell, W. 1996. *Inspection and Measurement in Manufacturing.* Dearborn, MI: Society of Manufacturing Engineers.

Yang, K., and B. S. El Haik. 2003. *Design for Six Sigma: A Roadmap for Product Development.* New York: McGraw-Hill.

Zipin, R. B. 1971. "Dimensional Measurements and Standards in Manufacturing." *Bendix Technical Journal* 1, no. 4: 15–19.

Index

A

acceptable quality limit (AQL), 198
    under ANSI/ASQ Z1.4-2003, 210
    under ANSI/ASQ Z1.9-2003, 216
acceptance number, 200–203
acceptance sampling, 74, 193–226
    by attributes, 198
    purposes of, 193–94
accuracy, in measurement, 252, 257–58
action plan, 22
active listening, 61–62
activity network diagram (AND), 29, 304–8
ADDIE model, of quality training, 117, 119
adult learners, and quality training, 121
affinity diagrams, 290–92
alternative hypothesis (H_a), 431
American Society for Quality (ASQ), 3
    Certified Quality Engineer (CQE) Body of
        Knowledge (Appendix A), 576–84
    Code of Ethics for Professional Conduct,
        41–44
American Society for Quality Control
    (ASQC), 3
analysis of experiments, 534–74, 542
analysis of variance (ANOVA), 459–69
    approach to DOE, 558–60
    general notation and methods, 460–61
    in linear regression, 481–82
    for one-factor experiments, in DOE, 543
    one-way, 459–60
    table, 466–69
    table, for DOE, 546–47
analysis of variance method, of GR&R study,
    260–61, 265–66, 270
analytical hierarchy process (AHP), 303–4
analytical studies, 381
AND gate, 176, 296
angle measurements, 231
angular measuring devices, 232–33
ANSI/ASQ Z1.4-2003 standard, 198, 210–11,
    213–214, 215
ANSI/ASQ Z1.9-2003 standard, 216–17
ANSI/ASQC Z1.4-1993 standard, 198, 210

ANSI/ISO/ASQ QE 19011S-2004 standard,
    five purposes of quality audits under,
    101
appraisal costs, 108
Aristotle, 60–61
arrow diagram, 304–8
assignable causes, of variation, 492
attribute data, 360
attribute gage R&R studies, 270–71
attributes control charts, 503–12
    control limit formulas (Appendix B), 585
attributes data
    measurement of, 124–25
    short-run SPC for, 524–26
audit
    planning and implementation, 102–3
    quality, 100–104
    reporting and follow-up, 103–4
    versus survey and sampling inspection,
        73–74
autocorrelation, in time-series analysis,
    489–90
automatic gauging, 362
Automotive Industry Action Group (AIAG),
    rules for statistical control, 520
availability, and maintainability, 150–51
average outgoing quality (AOQ), 199, 200
    for double and multiple sampling plans,
        208
average outgoing quality limit (AOQL), 199,
    200
    for double and multiple sampling plans,
        208
average quality protection, versus lot-by-lot
    sampling, 195
average run length (ARL), 521
average sample number (ASN), 208–10

B

balanced scorecard, 20
base units, definitions of, 247–49
batch control, 224–25